ORGANIZATIONAL BEHAVIOR

READINGS, CASES AND EXERCISES

JOE KELLY
Concordia University

J. BRUCE PRINCE
Concordia University

Prentice-Hall Canada Inc. Scarborough, Ontario

Canadian Cataloguing in Publication Data

Kelly, Joe
  Organizational behavior

Includes bibliographical references.
ISBN 0-13-640723-4

1. Organizational behavior. 2. Organizational behavior – Case studies. I. Prince, J. Bruce, 1950-   II. Title.

HD58.7.K44 1987   658.4   C88-093064-0

© 1988 Prentice-Hall Canada Inc., Scarborough, Ontario

ALL RIGHTS RESERVED

No part of this book may be reproduced in any form without permission in writing from the publisher.

Prentice-Hall, Inc., Englewood Cliffs, New Jersey
Prentice-Hall International, Inc., London
Prentice-Hall of Australia, Pty., Ltd., Sydney
Prentice-Hall of India Pvt., Ltd., New Delhi
Prentice-Hall of Japan, Inc., Tokyo
Prentice-Hall of Southeast Asia (Pte.) Ltd., Singapore
Editora Prentice-Hall do Brasil Ltda., Rio de Janeiro
Prentice-Hall Hispanoamericana, S.A., Mexico

ISBN 0-13-640723-4

Production Editors: Cynthia Rathwell, Katherine Mototsune
Designer: Joanne Jordan
Production Coordinator: Matt Lumsdon
Typesetting: Q Composition Inc.

1 2 3 4 5 AP 92 91 90 89 88

Printed and bound in Canada by The Alger Press Limited.

Table of Contents

Preface vii
Introduction 2

PART ONE
INTRODUCTION 11

I A FRAMEWORK FOR ORGANIZATIONAL BEHAVIOR 13

Readings:

Michael L. Tushman and David A. Nadler, "Organizing for Innovation" 14

Daniel J. Isenberg, "How Senior Managers Think" 29

Cases:

"PNB University Bank" David A. Nadler, Michael L. Tushman and Nina G. Hatvany 40

"What's Gone Wrong with the Reichmanns?" David Olive 43

Exercises:

"A Survey of Values" Joe Kelly 55

"In-basket Exercise: The Montréal Pump and Valve Company" R.E. Dutton, J. Bruce Prince, and Luke Novelli 58

II EXECUTIVE BEHAVIOR 71

Readings:

Arthur Elliot Castle, "MacGregor" 72

Steven Kerr, Kenneth D. Hill, and Laurie Broedling, "The First-Line Supervisor: Phasing Out or Here to Stay?" 75

Cases:

Learning to Manage the Hard Way" Susan Regan 92

"A Week in the Life of a Head of Computer Services" Alan I. Phillips 94

Exercises:

"Problems for Managers and Lovers" Joe Kelly 97

"Studying Executive Behavior by Video" Joe Kelly 99

PART TWO
THE INDIVIDUAL 103

III PERCEPTION, PERSONALITY AND FEEDBACK 105

Readings:

Herbert A. Simon, "Making Management Decisions: The Role of Intuition and Emotion" 106

Edgar H. Schein, "Improving Face-to-face Relationships" 116

Cases:

"The Authoritarian Personality and the Autocratic Executive" Joe Kelly 126

"Lee Iacocca versus Henry Ford II"
Joe Kelly 128

Exercises:

"Giving Effective Feedback"
J. Bruce Prince 131

"The Zen Man: Giving and Receiving Feedback" Joe Kelly 134

"The Cushwell-West Meeting Exercise" J. Bruce Prince and Luke Novelli 137

IV MOTIVATING INDIVIDUALS 143

Readings:

Steven Kerr, "On the Folly of Rewarding A, While Hoping for B" 144

W. Clay Hamner, "How to Ruin Motivation with Pay" 155

Donald B. Fedor and Gerald R. Ferris, "Integrating OB Mod with Cognitive Approaches to Motivation" 165

Cases:

"Hausser Food Products Company" David A. Nadler, Michael L. Tushman, and Nina G. Hatvany 178

"The Bellefonte Rubber Works Case" Edward L. Christensen 186

Exercises:

"Motivating Managers at Montréal Pump and Valve Company" Luke Novelli and J. Bruce Prince 195

"Expectancy Theory: A Case Exercise Approach" Robert J. Oppenheimer 196

"Identifying Rewards" Joe Kelly 198

V SOCIALIZATION AND CAREER PROCESSES IN ORGANIZATIONS 199

Readings:

Edgar H. Schein, "Socialization and Learning to Work" 200

V.V. Baba, "Employee-Organizational Linkages: The Role of Organizational Commitment" 206

Thomas J. DeLong, "Career Orientations and How They Influence Career Decisions" 212

Cases:

"Career Crisis for Mary Menard: Manager or Consultant?" Katrina Easton 219

"Roland Martineau" V.V. Baba 224

Exercises:

"Preparing a Career Plan" Joe Kelly 229

"How an Executive Takes Over" Joe Kelly 230

"Career Orientations Inventory" Thomas J. DeLong 232

PART THREE GROUPS 239

VI MANAGING GROUPS 241

Readings:

Joe Kelly, "Surviving and Thriving in Top Management Meetings" 242

Jan Enqvist, "Goodbye to Group Assembly" 247

Daniel C. Feldman, "The Development and Enforcement of Group Norms" 250

Cases:

"The Case of the Changing Cage" C.E. Richard and H.F. Dubyns 259

"Perfect Pizzeria" Lee Neely and James G. Hunt 263

Exercises:

"Finding Out Who's Who in the Group" Joe Kelly 266

"A Training Problem" Joe Kelly 267

"The Subarctic Survival Situation" J. Clayton Lafferty 269

VII LEADERSHIP AND CREATIVITY 277

Readings:

Noel M. Tichy and David O. Ulrich, "The Leadership Challenge – A Call for the Transformational Leader" 278

Joe Kelly, "The Corporate Theater of Action" 288

Robert E. Kaplan, "Creativity in the Everyday Business of Managing" 296

Cases:

"Rothmans on a Slow Burn" Cathryn Motherwell 303

"Leadership Succession Baker Inc." A.B. Ibrahim 309

Exercises:

"My Best Boss" Joe Kelly 313

"Operating Problems" Joe Kelly 313

VIII CONFLICT MANAGEMENT AND POWER 315

Readings:

Leonard Greenhalgh, "Managing Conflict" 316

Joe Kelly, "Make Conflict Work for You" 322

Cases:

"R. Bruce Gates: The Pow-Wow Vice-President of Canadian International Computers" Joe Kelly 335

"Alex and Donald: A Power Struggle" Carole Groleau 340

Exercises:

"A Conflict Drama" Joe Kelly 345

"Conflict at Montréal Pump and Valve Company" Luke Novelli and J. Bruce Prince 347

PART FOUR
BEHAVIOR OF INDIVIDUALS AND GROUPS IN ORGANIZATIONS 349

IX HUMAN RESOURCE MANAGEMENT 351

Readings:

Edgar H. Schein, "Increasing Organizational Effectiveness through Better Human Resource Planning and Development" 352

Nina Hatvany and Vladmir Pucik, "An Integrated Management System: Lessons from the Japanese Experience" 366

Muhammad Jamal, "Do Moonlighters Really Hurt the Organization?" 378

Cases:

"Québec National Brokerage" J. Bruce Prince 386

"Communication Problems at Deco Furniture Co." A.B. Ibrahim 388

"Change in the Bell System" Zane E. Barnes 391

Exercises:

"Salary Negotiation at the Montréal Pump and Valve Company" Philip Menard 395

"Managing Careers: You're the Consultant" J. Bruce Prince 399

X ORGANIZATIONAL CULTURE 403

Readings:

Edgar H. Schein, "Coming to a New Awareness of Organizational Culture" 404

John C. Papageorgiou, "Decision Making in the Year 2000" 417

Cases:

"Steven Jobs: An Innovator Who Failed as a Manager" Nick Brown 425

"Baxter Industries Ltd." Peter E. Pitsiladis 428

Exercise:

"Characteristics of Corporate Culture" Joe Kelly 435

XI MANAGEMENT OF ORGANIZATIONS 439

Readings:

A.B. Ibrahim & J. Kelly, "Leadership Style at the Policy Level" 440

Jay R. Galbraith, "Organization Design: an Information Processing View" 446

Cases:

"Strategic Planning at ALFA Electronics Inc." A.B. Ibrahim 455

"Chemco International Inc." B.J. Austin 457

Exercises:

"Setting up a Firm: A Consultancy Problem" Joe Kelly 463

" 'Airships' The Total Organization Exercise" J.R. Goodwin 463

PREFACE

This book is intended as a source of primary material in organizational behavior for the student of management and was written to aid in learning the principles of the discipline. But the intention is to make this learning vibrant and exciting. The underlying theme of this book is that organizational behaviour is not only a set of theories, but it is also an optic, a perspective, a process for looking at events, a way of life – indeed a method of solving problems in life, in business.

To achieve these purposes, the book brings together a selection of articles, cases, and exercises that bear directly on the process by which managers achieve effective performances. The selected readings are meant to do a variety of things. Some are classical articles in the literature; most supply additional information on specific theoretical concepts; others give fuller accounts of particular concepts; a few contain illustrative material which reveals an alternative point of view; some earn their place by being useful for case discussion or problem-solving sessions.

The cases included in this book take various forms. Some are set in Canada, some in the U.S., and one in Britain. In form, some are illustrative, others are descriptive, several are narratives; but most focus on a general management problem. These cases are intended to give the student experience in defining a problem, integrating the facts of the case, formulating the criteria of the solution, developing alternatives, and selecting and implementing a solution. Of course, management problems are complex. Vital information is often lacking or unreliable and problems are difficult to structure. As well there are usually many feasible solutions to such problems. The cases in this book are meant to start the student on the road – to show them how to do the job expected of them in management. These cases will introduce them to the exciting world of managers and provide them with illustrations of how the various theories work or might have worked in real life.

The exercises that have been chosen will enable students to give new conceptual input which will allow them to draw on their own experiences and insights and to share their ideas with others. Hopefully, such a method of group-learning will be active and enjoyable. If these same groups continue throughout the course, the students should also develop some insight into the principles of group dynamics.

ACKNOWLEDGEMENTS

Many persons have been a great help in the development of this book. We would like to thank V.V. Baba, the Chairman of the Management Department at Concordia University, and our colleagues in the department, particularly Jack Goodwin, Bakr Ibrahim, Muhammad Jamal, and Peter Pitsiladis for their guidance and support. We would also like to thank the Dean of the Faculty of Commerce and Administration, Steven H. Appelbaum, for the opportunity, resources and time to research and write this book and we would like to thank CASS – the Commerce Academic Support Staff – for their support and help. Finally, thanks are due to Barrie Gibbs, Simon Fraser University, and Anne Stewart, Northern Alberta Institute of Technology, for their comments on early drafts of the manuscript.

ORGANIZATIONAL BEHAVIOR
READINGS, CASES AND EXERCISES

INTRODUCTION

The contemporary person lives and works in organizations. If the 19th century was the age of the individual, then the 20th century is essentially concerned with the emergence of organizations. The modern person is only too aware of the ambivalent sensation of living and working in organizations; of being organized and organizing. Organizational behavior is concerned with life in an organized world. It is the study of the behavior and attitudes of the individuals in an organizational setting; the organization's effect on people's perceptions, feelings, and actions; and the effect of people on the organization, particularly focussing upon how behavior affects the achievement of the organization's purposes.

A MODEL OF ORGANIZATIONAL BEHAVIOR

The model on which this book is based consists of four elements: inputs, system, outputs, and methods of study.

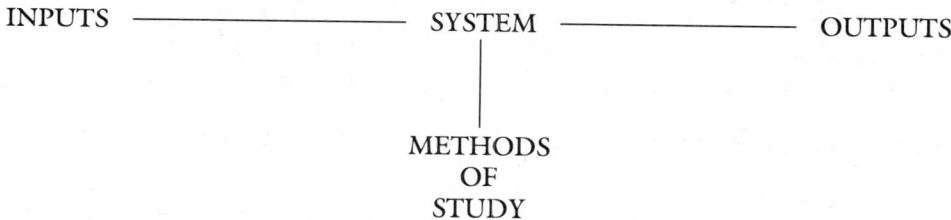

Inputs refer to the environment, the resources of the organization, and its history. The system contains three interdependent levels: the individual, the group, and the organizational context of groups and individuals. Outputs refer to task achievements (productivity and performance) and human outcomes (job satisfaction and commitment). But our subject is not the study of the organization in a vacuum; it is the study of the organization and its members in a social environment.

To pursue these matters further necessitates knowing something of the nature and structure of organizational behavior. As an organization develops, individuals are assigned tasks and required to join formal work groups. The formal or upfront organization consists of jobs, sections, departments, and committees as well as rules and procedures for getting work accomplished.

But every formal organization also creates an informal one. Cliques and cabals inevitably emerge to challenge and mock official authority as well as make up for shortcomings in the formal organization. Such formal and informal groups fall within

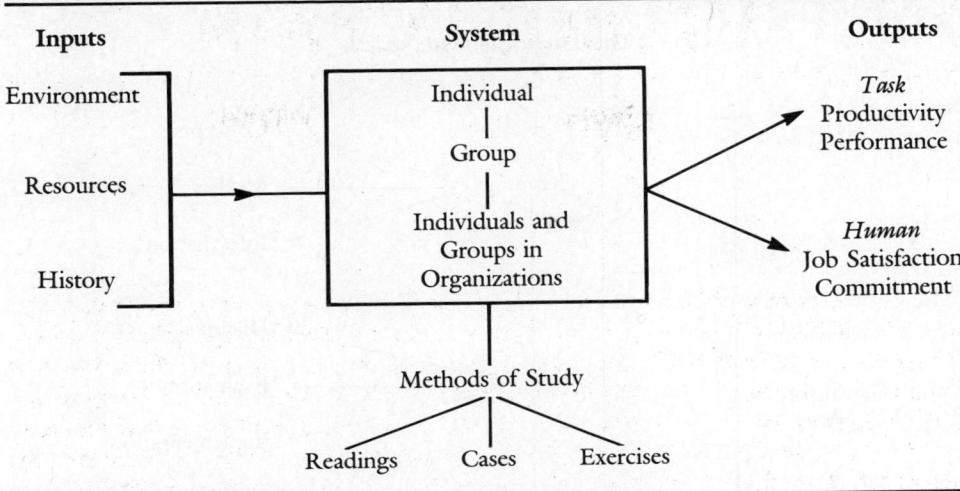

the domain of organizational behavior (OB). Thus, the OB plot begins to thicken. To follow, one must know something about not only individual psychology, but also group dynamics. To complete one's understanding of OB, however, it is necessary to push beyond the individual and group levels to get to the organization.

The organization's systems and its ways of operating, the tasks it requires of members, and the values and culture it embodies, present the social context for groups and individuals. This has a tremendous impact on people's productivity and sense of fulfillment, and is, in turn, impacted by their reactions and perceptions.

METHODS OF STUDYING ORGANIZATIONAL BEHAVIOR

To get the best from this book, it is necessary to recognize that the study of organizational behavior can do three things: impart information and concepts, foster analytical skills, and teach the tactics of managerial action. To address these three elements of the discipline, we have included readings, cases, and exercises.

Noted management theorist Theodore Leavitt once observed that "Management consists of the rational assessment of a situation and the systematic selection of goals and purposes (what is to be done?); the systematic development of strategies to achieve these goals; the marshalling of the required resources; the rational design, organization, direction, and control of the activities required to attain the selected purpose; and, finally, the motivating and rewarding of people to do the work." The objective of our book is to help the reader to discover the nature of this process and teach its practice and principles. Education in organizational behavior requires not only the acquisition of knowledge (the Readings) but also the exercise of judgment in diagnosing problems, choosing strategies and implementing solutions (the Cases). These activities demand a large element of behavioral skill and judgment which is necessary to make leadership decisions (the Exercises).

The Three Elements of OB

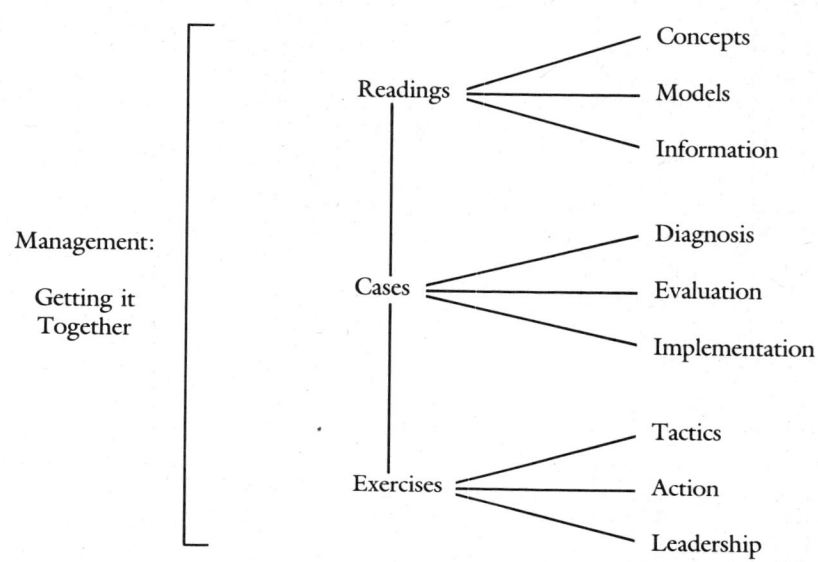

THE PRIMARY PURPOSE

The primary purpose of the book is to prepare students through readings, cases, and exercises to assume general management responsibilities. This means providing an educational environment in which students can develop the characteristics of an effective manager. This book helps create that environment through:

1. Readings which provide a generalist perspective and, in particular, teach one to grasp and understand the behavior of individuals and groups.
2. Cases which provide the opportunity to acquire analytical, creative, and integrative skills. These require the ability to pathfind, to formulate alternatives and to implement solutions.
3. Exercises which help to develop:
    a. entrepreneurial skills which enable the student to see and recognize opportunities and to know how to exploit them.
    b. behavioral skills and fluency in basic behavioral subjects such as personality, motivation, career development, group dynamics, leadership, and conflict management.
    c. integrity and personal business ethics consistent with being a rational, prudent manager.

d. professional maturity in the ability to operate in the competitive environment of North America.

THE READINGS: CONCEPTS AND MODELS FOR MANAGING

Effective management requires a good map. Maps help us navigate unfamiliar territory, avoid traps and dead-ends, and arrive at our destinations in an expedient fashion. For managers, the terrain they must navigate includes characteristics of individuals (e.g., their personality, motives, and ways of behaving), group dynamics (e.g., norms, conflict, power, and leadership), and the organizational context of groups and individuals (e.g., the human resource management approaches, culture, and the structural design of the organization). The map they use consists of concepts, models, and theories. These help managers understand, predict, and control the myriad individual, group, and organizational forces encountered in contemporary organizations. The key features of this map are presented in the chart in the figure on page 6 which juxtaposes reading titles with the topics they address.

THE MANAGER AND CASE ANALYSIS

The calibre of management is probably the most important single factor influencing not only the affluence of our society but also the very quality of our lives. The critical shortage in our society is not capital, but executive talent. What is a manager?

A manager is a person who undertakes important discretionary and directive work — work that requires creativity. To do such work effectively requires a range of skills that can be acquired best by understanding the process of critical analysis. The capacity to recognize problems, to mobilize resources, to separate the non-essential, and to take action after a careful review of relevant data is a complex ability which schools of business seek to develop. Analyzing cases is a proven technique for developing this capacity.

Stages of Analysis
The process of analyzing cases, be they actual problems a manager is confronting or written descriptions of situations a student must decipher, involves moving through the sequence of the three stages presented in the figure on page 8.

Diagnosis
The first step in the case solving process is to list the problems requiring solution, usually grouping them according to either importance or similarity. Once selected, the problem must be analyzed in terms of its causes, constraints, and the factors affecting it. A model must then be constructed so that the verbal definition of the problem is translated into a framework that relates the factors of the problem to measures of effectiveness. A model is a substitute representation of reality which, by simplifying details, helps managers think about problems in a systematic way. Once the model has been developed, experimentation and validation insure the model corresponds to reality. At this point, criteria which specify key outcomes which an effective solution should achieve must be defined.

THE READINGS: CONCEPTS AND MODELS FOR MANAGING

CHAPTER	TITLE	TOPIC
ONE	"Organization for Innovation"—Tushman and Nadler	Innovation, Analytical Framework, Informal Organization
	"How Senior Managers Think"—Isenberg	Executive Thinking, Problem Solving Intuition, Time Management
TWO	"MacGregor"—Carlisle	What Managers Do, Communications Models
	"The First Line Supervisor: Phasing Out or Here to Stay?"—Kerr, Hill, and Broedling	The First-level Supervisor's Role Participation
THREE	"Making Management Decisions: The Role of Intuition and Emotion"—Simon	Intuition, Split Brains, Decisions, Problem Solving
	"Improving Face-to-Face Relationships"—Schein	Self-insight, Communication, Negotiation
FOUR	"On the Folly of Rewarding A while Hoping for B"—Kerr	Rewards, Criteria, Behavior-Modification
	"How to Ruin Motivation with Pay"—Hamner	Merit, Performance Rating, Money, Ethics
	"Integrating OB Mod with Cognitive Approaches to Motivation"—Fedor and Ferris	OB Mod, Motivation Theory, Goal Setting, Work Design
FIVE	"Socialization and Learning to Work"—Schein	Coping with Work, Dealing with Boss, Identity Development
	"Employee-Organizational Linkages: The Role of Organizational Commitment"—Baba	Commitment, Work Contract, Management

SIX	"Surviving and Thriving in Top Management Meetings"—Kelly	Group Dynamics, Meetings, Drama, Style
	"Goodbye to Group Assembly"—Enquist	Group Norms, Autonomous Work Team Stress
	"The Development and Enforcement of Group Norms"—Feldman	Group Norms and Enforcements, Reinforcements, Supervision
SEVEN	"The Leadership Challenge — A Call for the Transformational Leader"—Tichy and Ulrich	Iacocca, Organizational Change, Transformational Leaders
	"The Corporate Theatre of Action"—Kelly	Conflict, Drama, Leadership, Body Language
	"Creativity in the Everyday Business of Managing"—Kaplan	Creativity, Leadership, Problem Solving
EIGHT	"Managing Conflict?"—Greenhalgh	Diagnostic Model, Management Skills
	"Make Conflict Work for You"—Kelly	Conflict, Power, Conflict Roles, Managing Conflict
NINE	"Increasing Organizational Effectiveness through Human Resource Planning/Development"—Schein	Human Resource Development, Job Design, Selection
	"An Integrated Management System: Lessons from the Japanese Experience"—Hatvany and Pucik	Japanese Management, Human Resources Management
	"Do Moonlighters Really Hurt the Organization?"—Jamal	Work Ethic, Job Satisfaction, Motivation, Moonlighting
TEN	"Coming to a New Awareness of Organizational Culture"—Schein	Culture, Values, Assumptions
	"Making it in this Year 2000"—Papageorgiou	Future, Computers, Production Information Culture
ELEVEN	"Leadership at the Policy Level"—Ibrahim and Kelly	Types of Leaders, Human Resources
	"Organization Design and Information Processing"—Galbraith	Organizational Design, Matrix Management

8 Organizational Behavior

Procedure For Solving The Cases

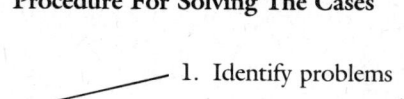
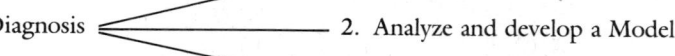

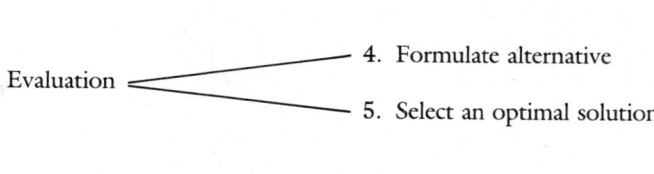

Diagnosis
1. Identify problems
2. Analyze and develop a Model
3. Develop criteria

Evaluation
4. Formulate alternative
5. Select an optimal solution

Implementation
6. Sell decision
7. Prepare a plan
8. Plan to assess effectiveness

Evaluation

After the problem has been identified and defined, alternative solutions must be generated. The model and criteria developed in the diagnosis guide the selection of the best alternative. The best solution meets the optimal level of acceptability articulated in the criteria.

Implementation

Once an optimal solution is selected, implementation issues must be confronted. Initially, the manager must sell the optimal decision to key constituencies. These are people or groups whose cooperation and support are required. They may be higher level managers, peers in other departments, lower level subordinates, or people outside of the organization. Also, the details of the action plan must be specified; key sequences of actions and time tables for accomplishment must be specified. Finally a plan for assessing the effectiveness of the solution must be specified. This allows managers to sense when key elements of the solution are not working. Without an evaluation plan, managers are less likely to be able to take quick action and fix small problems which every solution is likely to encounter.

THE EXERCISES

While many disciplines provide education for business and management in general, the Organizational Behavior exercises perform a vital, integrating and professionalizing role: An attempt is made to unify the knowledge and skill in areas such as individual psychology and group dynamics by focusing on their inter-relations and

Introduction 9

connections with the underlying disciplines, and to the operation of the business organization as a whole. The pedagogical strategy behind exercises is to develop a coherent frame of reference through which students are able to visualize the problems of managerial action in the context of the overall organization. As a logical extension of this, students are able to visualize problems of the organization in the broader context of society. The objective is to develop a well-balanced manager with a clear conception of self and the environment. To achieve this objective the book sets out in all its exercises to cultivate certain cognitive and behavioral qualities, to create a particular climate of socialization, and to develop an OB philosophy. In terms of cognitive and behavioral qualities, the aim is to develop:

  a. *behavioral efficacy:* the ability to take assertive action, influence others and create enthusiasm and commitment.
  b. *verbal fluency:* the ability to express one's findings and conclusions.
  c. *model building:* the development of the capacity to identify problems requiring the ability to select, collate data, and fit them into an appropriate model.
  d. *general analytical bite:* the ability to tease out the critical factors of a situation and ascertain the relations among them.

The exercises also seek to create an environment or climate that will help students to develop an effective managerial and leadership style. In today's society, an increasing number of people want to play a larger part in influencing how decisions are made in business. The humanistic trend or general OB philosophy is reflected in the exercises. In short, the exercises create a center of learning where creative people come together to do productive things.

EXERCISE TRACK BASED ON IN-BASKET EXERCISES: MONTRÉAL PUMP AND VALVE COMPANY

Exercise	Title	Chapter
1	In-basket Exercise: Montréal Pump and Valve Company	1
2	The Cushwell-West Meeting	3
3	Motivating Managers at Montréal Pump and Valve Company	4
4	Conflict at Montréal Pump and Valve Company	8
5	Salary Negotiation at the Montréal Pump and Valve Company	9

One particular exercise is an in-basket exercise which puts students in the role of a new plant manager. This exercise exposes students to the multitude of conflicting demands and issues which practising managers face. Additional exercises in later sections build on the initial experience at Montréal Pump and Valve Company and emphasize issues related to the topic area of each chapter. This sequence of exercises provides an integrative function that is often absent in exercises. They are identified below.

GETTING IT TOGETHER

This book, through its readings, cases, and exercises contributes to developing the abilities of analysis, literacy, and behavioral effectiveness. These are all key managerial competencies in the competitive world of North American business enterprise. The combination of material in this book addresses a rather stinging criticism of business school curriculi. Critics have argued that business schools narrowly focus on analysis, but do not develop the ability to identify the right problems to begin with or enhance students' cognitive and behavioral competencies to sell and implement the solutions they derive from their analysis. It is much easier to decompose a problem into its parts than to find the correct problem or generate support for and commitment to a plan of action. Yet each of these are needed. Paraphrasing the famous aphorism by Peter Drucker, business schools have been good at doing things right, but they have not necessarily been good at the right thing. In Drucker's terms, people coming out of business schools tend to be efficient rather than effective.

In other words, business students have been trained to exercise judgment in quantitative terms and there has been less emphasis on dealing with those critical, elusive, qualitative issues which all practising managers must resolve. To further compound this felony, many of the cases taught in business schools deal with large organizations in a bureaucratic mode rather than with small companies in the entrepreneurial mode in which an increasing number of jobs are available. Additionally, business students have been criticized as being risk adverse. As such they are unwilling or unable to take their chance in a business setting. Organizational behavior and management courses must play the key role in correcting this problem.

This book tries to develop people who have acquired useful concepts from the readings, nurtured analytical skills from the cases, and learned to behave effectively in interpersonal settings and communicate their ideas in the exercises; but just as importantly, it addresses individuals who have had their creative juices set flowing and who have some sense of entrepreneurship. In other words, what business is looking for are graduates who are not only analytical, literate, assertive, and numerate, but people who also have retained a sense of creativity and entrepreneurship. In short, business is looking for people who can act as managers.

PART ONE
INTRODUCTION

I
A FRAMEWORK FOR ORGANIZATIONAL BEHAVIOR

READINGS

ORGANIZING FOR INNOVATION*

Michael Tushman
David Nadler

In today's business environment, there is no executive task more vital and demanding than the sustained management of innovation and change. It sometimes seems that every aspect of business is in a state of flux – technology, government regulation, global competition. These rapid changes in the marketplace make it increasingly difficult, and essential, for business to think in terms of the future, to constantly anticipate tomorrow's definition of value – the right mix of quality, service, product characteristics, and price. To compete in this ever-changing environment, companies must create new products, services, and processes; to dominate, they must adopt innovation as a way of corporate life.

Sustained innovation is both important and tremendously difficult. Consider these brief examples:

- For more than 30 years General Radio dominated the market for electronic-test-equipment. While new competitors took advantage of computers, systems technology, and innovative approaches to working with customers, General Radio remained committed to the technologies and marketing practices that it knew best. During the 1960s, market share and profits declined. It took a complete transformation of the organization, driven by mostly new managers, to bring about product, market, and production innovations.
- Technicon Corporation created the automated clinical diagnostic instrument industry. Technicon initially prospered by successfully producing a number of product innovations based on their expertise in hydraulics technologies. While Technicon led with product innovation, other firms entered the market leading with process innovation (i.e., cost and quality) and with a broadened view of the clinical market. Technicon's response to the external threat was increased reliance on its old winning formula. Market share and relative performance declined. It was not until Technicon was acquired by Revlon that the organization was able to successfully develop product, process and market innovation.
- Biogen is known world-wide as an organization doing excellent basic research in genetic engineering. While science flourishes at Biogen, marketing and product development have been ignored. Nobel laureate Walter Gilbert no longer runs Biogen. A new management team has been brought in to create the conditions for enhanced product, market and process innovation.

The common theme is obvious: In all three cases, once highly innovative organizations became trapped by their own success. These examples are not unique. In one industry after another, the same factors that create a successful innovative company often plant the seeds of complacency and failure as competitive conditions change.

Nevertheless, many exceptional firms have

---

* © 1986 by the Regents of the University of California. Reprinted from the *California Management Review*, Vol. 28, No. 3 by permission of The Regents.

demonstrated that sustained innovation, though difficult, is certainly attainable. Large corporations (such as IBM, 3M, Citicorp, American Airlines, GE, Merck, and Philip Morris) as well as smaller firms (such as Rolm, Wang, Charles River Breeding Labs, Federal Express, and Dunkin' Donuts) have been highly innovative over long periods. They have simultaneously managed the dual challenges of innovating for the markets of both the present and the future.

What are the organizational factors which enhance innovation? The most innovative organizations are highly effective learning systems. Organizations that can be self-critical – and can learn to keep improving on today's work while aggressively preparing for tomorrow's – will be more successful than those organizations that evolve towards greater stability and complacency. Sustained innovation, somewhat paradoxically, requires both stability and change: stability permits scale economies and incremental learning, while change and experimentation are necessary for advances in products, processes, and technologies.

TYPES OF INNOVATION

Innovation is the creation of any product, service, or process which is new to a business unit. While innovation is often associated with major product or process advances (e.g., xerography, transistors, float-glass), the vast majority of successful innovations are based on the cumulative effect of incremental change in products and processes, or in the creative combination of existing techniques, ideas, or methods. Innovation is not just R&D; just as important are marketing, sales, and production. Effective innovation requires the synthesis of market needs with technological possibility and manufacturing capabilities.

At the most basic level, there are two kinds of innovation: *product innovation*, or changes in the product a company makes or the service it provides; and *process innovation*, a change in the way a product is made or the service provided. Within each of these two categories, there are three degrees of innovation – incremental, synthetic, and discontinuous (see Figure 1). Some illustrations help clarify these differences.

Figure 1
Types of Innovation

	Product	Process	
Incremental	Incremental Product Change	Learning by Doing	Small
Synthetic	Dominant Designs DC-3, Boeing 707, IBM 360	Major Process Improvements	↑ ↓
Discontinuous	Vacuum Tubes → Transistor Piston → Jet Steam → Diesel Locomotives	Individual Wafer → Planar Process Continuous Grinding and Polishing → Float Glass	Substantial Learning Requirements

Product Innovation

Most product innovations are *incremental* changes. They provide added features, new versions or extensions to an otherwise standard product line. Obviously, such innovations occur all the time, and large numbers of incremental innovations related to customer requirements can add up to a significant competitive advantage.

A second type of product innovation, *synthetic*, involves the combination of existing ideas or technologies in creative ways to create significantly new products. For example, the DC-3 incorporated existing airplane innovations which, together, resulted in a single airplane which combined speed, efficiency, and size. Similarly, the 707 and 747 and Merrill Lynch's Cash Management Account were important synthetic product innovations which dominated their respective industries. These product innovations didn't require any new technology. Rather, each represented a creative combination of existing technology which, when linked with marketing and production skill, resulted in a product which set the standard in its product class – until the next major product innovation came along.

The third category, *discontinuous* product innovations, involve the development or application of significant new technologies or ideas. Examples include the shift from piston airplanes to jets, the change from steam to diesel locomotives, or the move from core to semiconductor memory. These major innovations required new skills, processes, and systems throughout the organization. Each required wholesale changes in those firms moving from old to new product technologies.

As innovation moves from incremental to discontinuous, there are higher risks and greater uncertainty. It becomes increasingly important for organizations to function as effective learning systems, benefiting from both failure and success.

Process Innovation

Process innovations change the way products and services are made or delivered. Process innovation may be invisible to the user except through changes in the cost or quality of the product.

As in product innovation, most process innovations are *incremental* improvements which result in lowered costs, higher quality, or both. Learning curve efficiencies and learning-by-doing produce small process innovations that incrementally improve upon existing production processes.

Synthetic process innovations involve sharp increases in size, volume, or capacity of well-known production processes. For example, the rotary kiln in cement manufacturing or Owens' process in glassware production were significant innovations, but they were basically larger, faster, and more efficient versions of well-known existing processes.

Discontinuous process innovations are totally new ways of producing products or services. For example, the float-glass process in glass manufacturing, planar processes in semiconductors, and the use of robots in auto plants are fundamentally different ways of making established products. Major process innovations reduce costs and increase the quality of the product or service, but they require new skills, new ways of organizing, and, frequently, new ways of managing. As with product innovation, the greater the degree of process change, the greater the uncertainty and the greater the required organizational learning.

The Strategic Role of Product and Process Innovation

Both product an process innovation are important, yet their relative importance changes over time. Studies in multiple industries find predictable patterns in the amount and degree of innovation over the product life-cycle (see Figure 2). In the introductory stage, there is a substantial amount of product innovation as several forms of the same product compete for dominance. For example, during the early stages of the automobile industry, at least four automobile types (internal combustion, battery, wood, and steam-powered) competed for the relatively small market. This period of product competition leads to the emergence of a dominant design, representing industry standardization in the product's basic configuration and characteristics. For example, the DC-3, IBM 360, Smith Model 5 typewriter, the Fordson tractor, VHS design in video cassette recorders, all represent dominant designs which shaped the evolution of their respective product classes for years.

In the next stage, major product variation gives way to competition based on price, quality, and segmentation – in other words, process innovation rather than product innovation. Thus, major process innovation, combined with incremental product innovation, allows firms to enhance the product and open the market to a more diverse customer base. In the mid-1970s, for example, personal computers were sold mainly to customers with substantial computer expertise; standardization of the Apple and IBM PC's permitted the development of customized software and services for small businesses, homes, and schools.

During the mature stage of a product life-cycle, this pattern of incremental product and major process innovation continues until the product and its associated production processes are so intertwined that only incremental product and process innovation are possible. This period can be very profitable, since small changes in the product or processes can lead to significantly decreased costs or higher quality. The mature phase of product life-cycle, with its emphasis on incremental innovation, lasts until some external shock such as deregulation, technological change, or foreign competition triggers a new wave of major product innovation. For example, Ford's Model T was enormously profitable until fully-enclosed cars were made possible by advances in

Figure 2
Types of Innovation Over Product Life Cycle

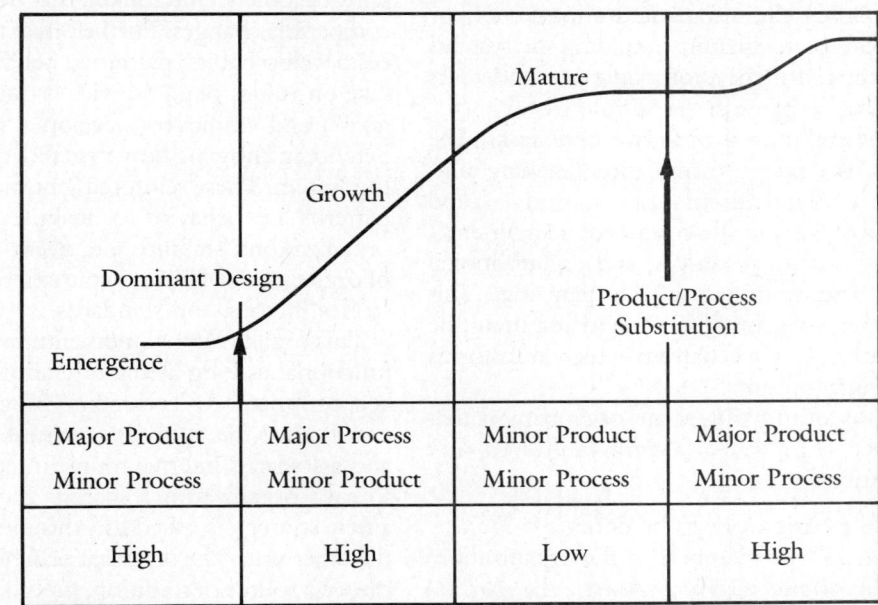

steel. Thus, product innovation initiated by General Motors forced Ford to reinitiate major product and, in turn, major process innovations.

Consequently, innovation is a complex and uncertain endeavor which shifts over time and requires the close collaboration of R&D, marketing, sales, and production. Effective organizations create conditions that allow today's work to be done well while simultaneously generating tomorrow's innovations. The challenge is to optimize today's work while producing the uncertainty and chaos so essential to tomorrow's innovation. Only those organizations which can manage stability and, at the same time, nurture the capacity to experiment and learn will be able to master both product and process innovation. Those organizations that get stuck in a single mode of operation will be incapable of producing different kinds of innovation as product lifecycles evolve.

ORGANIZING FOR TODAY'S WORK

This formula for innovation — managing for today while building the infrastructure for tomorrow — involves a basic dilemma: building the systems and processes for the short run often undercuts the innovative process.

The general manager has two basic tasks. The first task is strategy formulation; making fundamental decisions about markets, products, and competitive basis in the context of a larger environment, a set of resources, and organizational history. The second task is organizing. This involves creating, building, and maintaining the organization — a mechanism which transforms strategy into output.

One way of thinking about organizing is that there are four major components to any organization:

- *Task*: the basic work to be done
- *Individuals*: the members of the organization
- *Organizational Arrangements*: the formal structures and processes created to get individuals to perform tasks
- *Informal Organization*: the unwritten, constantly evolving arrangements — including "culture" — which define how things get done.

In the short to medium term, organizational effectiveness is greatest when two conditions are met. First, the four components are designed and managed so that they are congruent; in other words, they fit well together. Second, the pattern of congruence of the four components matches the basic requirements of the strategy.[1] (See Figure 3.)

When strategy fits environmental conditions, congruence is associated with organizational effectiveness. Since organizations are never totally congruent, part of management's job is to initiate incremental changes to fine-tune the organization more. Incremental change is relatively easy to implement and builds increasing consistency among strategy, structure, people, and processes. Increasing congruence, however, can be a double-edged sword. As organizations grow and become more successful, they develop internal pressures for stability. Organizational structures and systems become so interlinked that they allow only compatible changes. Further, over time, employees develop habits; patterned behaviors begin to take on values (e.g., "service is our number one goal") and employees develop a sense of competence in knowing how to get work done within the system. These reinforcing norms, values, and patterns of behavior contribute to increased organizational stability and, over time, to a sense of organizational history epitomized by common stories, heroes, and standards.

This organizational momentum is profoundly functional as long as the organization's strategy is appropriate. At Technicon, Biogen, and General Radio, the culture, structure and systems, and associated internal momentum were critical to each organization's success. However, when a new strategy is called for, this momentum cuts the other way. The organizational history — which can be a source of tradition, precedent, and pride — can also be an obstacle to alert problem solving and organizational learning. When faced with an

Figure 3
A Congruence Model of Organizational Behavior

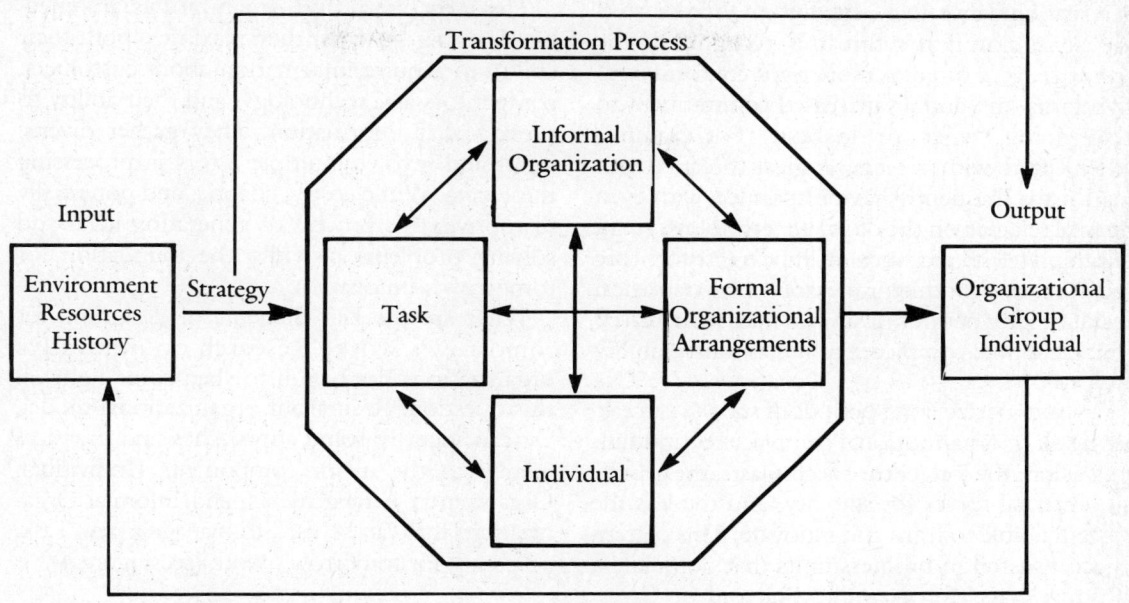

Input	Transformation Process		Output
Environment: • Markets • Competition • Government • Suppliers Resources: • Capital • Plant • Technology • People • Intangible History: • Key Decisions • Norms & Values Strategy: • Mission • Supporting Strategies • Goals & Objectives	Informal Organization: • Management Practices • Interpersonal Relationships • Informal Working Arrangements Task: • Knowledge & Skill Requirements • Uncertainty • Inherent Rewards • Basic Work To Be Done	Formal Organizational Arrangements: • Organization Structure • Job Design • Methods & Practices • Standards & Measurements • Physical Environment • Human Resource Management Systems • Reward Systems Individual: • Knowledge & Skills • Needs & Preferences • Reward Expectancies	Organizational: • Goal Attainment • Resource Utilization • Adaptability Group/Unit: • Productivity • Collaboration • Quality of Communication Individual: • Task Performance • Membership Behavior • Affective Responses

Source: Nadler and Tushman, 1979.

environmental threat, highly inertial organizations either may not register the threat due to organizational complacency and/or stunted external vigilance (e.g., the automobile or steel industries) or if the threat is recognized, the response, very often, is more rigid conformity to the status quo and an increased commitment to keep doing "what we do best." For example, when faced with a technological threat, dominant firms frequently have responded with even greater reliance on the obsolete technology (e.g., telegraph/telephone; vacuum tube/transistor; core memory/semiconductor memory). A paradoxical result of long periods of success may be increased organizational complacency and a stunted ability to learn.

To summarize, long periods of success can easily result in organizational complacency and tunnel vision: the longer the success lasts, the greater the internal forces for stability, and the less the system is able to learn and innovate. This pattern is accentuated in business units that dominate a product class (for example, Polaroid or Caterpillar), in historically regulated organizations (AT&T, GTE, or financial service firms), or in organizations that have been traditionally shielded from competition (universities, not-for-profit organizations, and government agencies).

ORGANIZING FOR TOMORROW'S WORK

Successful organizations innovate for today as well as for tomorrow. Managing this duality is an immensely difficult task. Each company described in our previous examples was a once-innovative firm which had become trapped by its own success. Put in the context of our organizational model, congruence and internal consistency, taken to extremes, diminished learning and discouraged major innovation. But firms such as 3M, Lilly, IBM, and Citibank manage to produce for the short run while keeping close to customers, competitors, technologies, and internal competence. This sensitivity to external opportunities and internal possibilities provides the stimulus for organizational learning and sustained innovation.

The most innovative organizations are effective learning systems; they maximize both their ability to acquire information about customers, competitors and technology, and their ability to process that information. They gather diverse input and involve multiple actors in processing these data. While costly, chaotic, and potentially disruptive, this process of generating ideas and solving problems provides the foundation for tomorrow's innovation.

What are the key elements of designing for tomorrow's work? Research on innovative organizations has begun to shed some light on this question.[2] Using our organizational model, we can identify some approaches and practices related to the major components (Individual, Organization Arrangements, and Informal Organization) that can be used to manage a new Task, preparing for tomorrow's work (see Figure 4).

Individuals

Because innovation requires multiple disciplines and in-depth expertise, management's challenge is to hire, train, and develop a set of individuals with diverse skills and abilities, and the capacity to innovate. But in-depth and diverse expertise is not sufficient. Because organizational learning and innovation is a group and intergroup phenomenon, individual contributors rarely produce the creative ideas or solutions required for complex or discontinuous innovation. Thus, strong individual specialization must be bolstered by skills in problem solving, communication, conflict resolution, and team building. Those skills which broaden an individual's ability to communicate with other professionals and to appreciate multiple perspectives can be developed in the organization through recruitment, training, and socialization practices. For example, IBM managers must spend 40 hours per year on managerial education. This program, which

Figure 4
Critical Factors in Managing Innovation

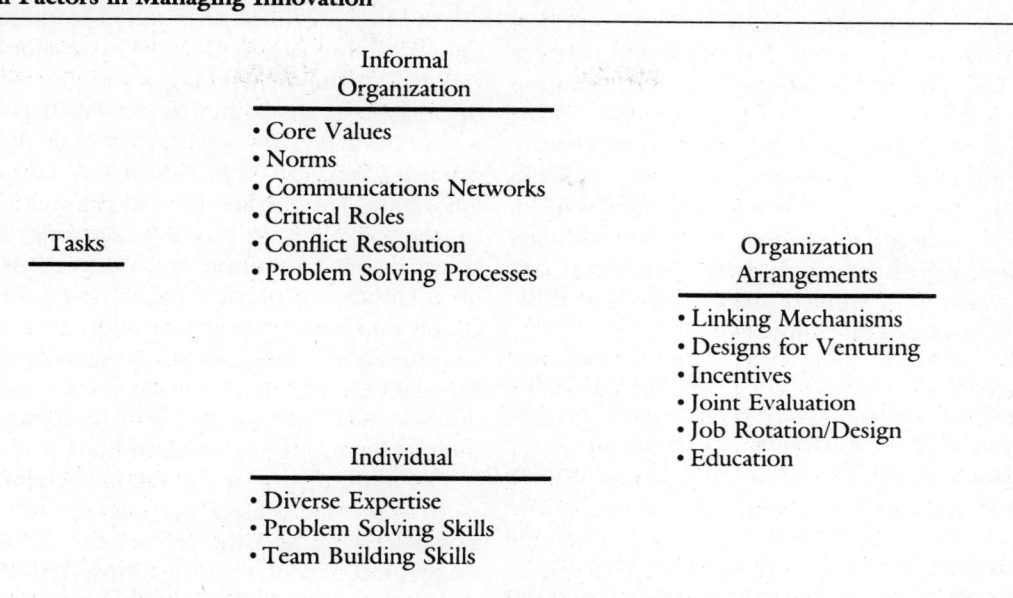

```
                        Informal
                        Organization
                        ─────────────
                        • Core Values
                        • Norms
                        • Communications Networks
                        • Critical Roles
        Tasks           • Conflict Resolution           Organization
        ─────           • Problem Solving Processes     Arrangements
                                                        ────────────
                                                        • Linking Mechanisms
                                                        • Designs for Venturing
                                                        • Incentives
                                                        • Joint Evaluation
                                                        • Job Rotation/Design
                        Individual                      • Education
                        ──────────
                        • Diverse Expertise
                        • Problem Solving Skills
                        • Team Building Skills
```

gathers individuals from different disciplines and/or divisions for up to three weeks, continually reinforces the importance of communication, collaboration, and problem solving.

The general manager has to build a top team to help provide direction, energy and enthusiasm for the organization. These are the role models who create the conditions for learning and innovation throughout the organization. This senior team needs skills and abilities which match environmental demands; it requires individuals who are respected for their disciplinary competence, and who are well-linked to external sources of information and expertise. This senior team not only manages for today, but is alert to external opportunities and threats. As competitive conditions change, so too must composition of the executive team.

Group problem-solving skills are particularly important if the senior team is to take advantage of its collective expertise to develop and communicate its vision of organizational objectives and core values. This executive team needs to develop internal processes that work against both the complacency so common in dominant organizations and the "group-think" (i.e., stunted problem solving) that often accompanies crisis conditions. The tasks of the general manager are to build a top team that has the required functional expertise and to develop the group's problem-solving processes so that it can effectively manage both today's work and tomorrow's innovation.

Formal Organizational Arrangements
Formal organizational arrangements provide structures, systems, and procedures which direct and motivate behavior. Consequently, these arrangements exert an important influence on organizational learning and innovation. Formal organizational arrangements include these key elements:

Formal Linking Mechanisms The choice of basic organization form (e.g., product, market, functional, geographic) focuses resources on critical strategic contingencies. No single organization form is inherently more conducive to innovation than the next: each can either stimulate or retard innovation. Whatever the basic form chosen, organizations must develop formal internal linking mechanisms, which are important vehicles for creativity and innovation. These links — bridges connecting disparate functions — encourage collaboration and problem solving throughout the organization. For example:

- *Teams, committees, or task forces* bring together individuals from diverse areas to work on common opportunities or problems. At Lilly Research, for example, where the laboratory was organized by disciplines, research teams organized by therapeutic area pooled the expertise of scientists and managers from different disciplines. At Xerox, an innovation board brought a diverse group of marketing, production, and R&D executives together to evaluate and provide early funding for corporate ventures.

- *Project managers* play a formal linking role which brings a general management perspective deep in the organization. A project manager works to achieve integration and coordination for new product and/or process development.

- *Formal meetings* provide a regularly scheduled setting for individuals from different areas to share information and trade ideas. These meetings also have the added benefit of building informal relationships which further facilitate cross-organization problem solving and collaboration. For example, NCR has "show and tell" meetings in which R&D, marketing, and manufacturing individuals unveil their latest ideas. At Union Carbide's product fairs, the various divisions present new products and ideas to each other. At Tetra-Pak, cross-functional teams regularly visit customers and then return to generate new product/process ideas.

Organization Designs for Venturing and Entrepreneurship Linking mechanisms are most effective when the nature of required learning and innovation is relatively small. When major innovation is required, working across the existing organizational structure may not be effective. A series of organization forms, all outside the core organization, can stimulate major corporate innovation. These major innovation forms include venture capital, joint ventures, licensing, acquisition, internal venturing, and independent business units. Some of these forms are much more closely tied to the core organization than others; venture capital, for example, is the most distant form of venturing in that it only provides a window on new technologies and markets, while internal venturing builds on in-house expertise.

The more dissimilar the required technology or markets, the greater the required organizational learning and the greater the use of the more independent venture forms. When both required technology and markets are unfamiliar, the most appropriate vehicles might be licensing, joint ventures, or venture capital. On the other hand, when organizations want to take advantage of internal expertise yet still produce major innovation, corporate venturing or independent business units may be most effective.

Independent business units or corporate venture units are separated from the core organization. These units are small and made up of individuals from all important disciplines and functions. These teams tend to be self-selected, and operate as independent ventures. Their business plans may be evaluated by a board of directors made up of corporate executives who have some interest in the venture; they act as venture capitalists, providing funding and overall review. The venture teams are not evaluated by traditional corporate yardsticks (e.g., profit, ROA), but rather on the basis of criteria more relevant to ventures — growth in sales or market share, for example. Similarly, the enterpreneur's compensation is pegged to performance against long-term targets and may involve stock or paper ownership in the new venture. The basic idea is to

- informality in problem solving
- disciplinary and organizational effectiveness
- high performance standards for short and long run
- an emphasis on human resources and the importance of individual growth and development.

As these examples suggest, core values in highly innovative firms emphasize the duality so important to the innovation process. Also, core values in innovative firms are broad enough to be meaningful across a diverse organization. Thus IBM's trilogy of service, individuals, and excellence is broad enough to fit a highly decentralized organization, yet is also pointed enough to guide and focus behavior. Though any organization can publicly espouse a set of core values, most innovative organizations have effectively infused their value system throughout the company.

Norms While core values (for example, service or excellence) have no clear behavioral referents, norms do; they elaborate and specify the meaning of core values in a particular firm. Norms are expected behaviors: if they are violated, the individual or group is informally censured. For example, norms help specify dress codes, language, work standards and hours, decision-making processes, boss-subordinate relations, inter-unit communication, conflict resolution processes, and the degree of risk taking and playfulness in the organization.

In general, highly innovative organizations have norms that stress informality in behavior, dress, and boss-subordinate relations; high work standards and individual/group performance expectations; flexibility in decision making, problem solving, and conflict resolution patterns; and strong informal linkages within and outside the organization. This informality, high work standard, and exposure to multiple sources of information facilitate collaboration, learning, and innovation. Less innovative firms, on the other hand, have norms which emphasize formality, standardization, and operating "by the book."

Rewarding Risk Highly innovative organizations deftly manage the subtleties of reward and punishment. Paradoxically, they provide highly visible rewards for success but often downplay the punishment for failure. This approach may seem contradictory, but many companies have made it work. In essence, they made decisions regarding promotions, job assignments, and careers with an eye toward strengthening the informal system's support for innovation and risk taking.

The cornerstone of this approach is that those who perform well – and in particular, the successful innovators – receive rapid promotion or successively more challenging assignments. It becomes clear to others in the organization that outstanding performance is the surest path to success.

On the other extreme, there is little tolerance for those whose performance falls short of the organization's standards. Those who perform poorly are encouraged to leave and, if necessary, are forced out.

We have just described a highly performance-oriented organization culture which is not particularly unique. But some very innovative organizations take the added step of creating conditions that tolerate failure – and sometimes even support it. They apply this approach to employees with an established record of performance, when their failure is the result of risk taking or experimentation, rather than incompetence or dereliction.

This attitude emboldens potential innovators: they see the likely prospect of tangible rewards for success and relatively few risks for trying something new and failing. As the belief spreads throughout the organization, the entire environment becomes increasingly innovative. An organization that has worked hard to nurture this culture is Citibank – one of the nation's most innovative corporations – where many senior executives have tried new things and "failed." Failure often results in assignment to the "penalty box," or a job with less responsibility. But after spending time in a "penalty box" assignment, people can return to a position comparable to – or even more responsible – than their "pre-failure" job.

Innovation occurs when organizations function as effective learning systems, and learning comes through experimentation and failure. Truly innovative organizations are those in which people can take risks, reap the rewards of success, and survive constructive failures.

Communication Networks Informal communication networks are vital to innovation. For new products and processes, direct feedback and problem solving is much more effective than formal bureaucratic procedures. The most innovative organizations have diverse informal communication networks; people know who to call. And the calls generally solve problems, if the participants share a common set of core values and language. These informal networks are important both within the organization as well as between the organization and customers, vendors, suppliers, and external professional sources. Direct contact is an effective way of keeping close to customers, competitors, and technology.

Critical Roles Several informal roles are critical in the innovation process:

- *Idea generators* are those key individuals who creatively link diverse ideas. These individuals see new approaches to linking technologies to markets, products with new processes, etc. Without idea generators, organizations have very few breakthroughs.
- *Champions or internal entrepreneurs* take creative ideas (which they may or may not have generated) and bring the ideas to life. These individuals have the aggressiveness, energy, and risk-taking personalities to actively champion their causes. Without internal entrepreneurs, organizations may have many ideas but few tangible innovations.
- *Gatekeepers or boundary spanners* link their more local colleagues to external information sources. They acquire, translate, and distribute external information within the organization or steer their colleagues to the right sources. Without gatekeepers, organizations are deaf to outside sources of information so vital to innovation.
- *Sponsors, coaches, or mentors* are senior managers who provide informal support, access to resources, and protection as new products or ventures emerge. Without sponsors and mentors, new products and processes get smothered by organizational constraints.

Each of these roles is critical; if any fails to emerge informally, innovation suffers. Formalizing these roles seems to make them disappear. While these roles cannot be formalized, they can be diagnosed, developed, and nurtured. Management can develop each role through job rotation and design, formal and informal rewards, educational programs, and personal encouragement.

Conflict Resolution and Problem-Solving Practices Innovation is an inherently disruptive phenomenon; it creates conflict among various parts of the organization, each with its own perceptions and priorities. For innovation to succeed, the informal organization must value conflict and provide constructive ways to resolve it. IBM's contention management system engenders such conflict, while relying on its deeply embedded norms and values to deal with it at low levels in the organization. At Pharmacia, a shared problem-solving framework is used to diagnose the causes of conflict and to adjudicate it in ways that benefit the company.

Clearly the informal organization is critical to innovation. Informal processes can encourage risk-taking, experimentation, and learning. Management must shape different informal processes in different parts of the organization (e.g., R&D vs. production), while providing informal linkages between these areas.[3] In the most innovative organizations, the informal organization allows individuals to be creative and learn, and promotes creative problem solving both within and outside the organization. While formal organization arrangements are relatively more important in high-volume, low-innovative settings, the informal organization is more important for tasks that require learning and innovation; the greater the required learning, the greater the importance of the informal organization.

Executive Leadership and Innovation

Beyond making choices concerning strategy, structure, individuals, and the informal organization, leaders also face the crucial, personal task of infusing their organizations with a set of values and a sense of enthusiasm that will support innovative behavior. Without a clearly committed executive team which consistently emphasizes the importance of innovation, organizations inevitably become slaves of the status quo. At the first, middle, and senior managerial levels, the management team must send a clear and consistent set of messages about the importance of short-term management and long-term innovation.

Several aspects of executive leadership behavior can help (or hinder) innovation:

- The executive team can develop and communicate a clear image of the organization's strategy and core values and the role of innovation in meeting the organization's strategy. If objectives are unclear and the role of innovation ambiguous, individuals and groups will focus on the status quo. The executive team must clearly and consistently articulate the importance of innovation and reinforce the necessary behavior.
- The executive team can be a role model for subordinates. Executive behavior, actions, and statements send important messages to subordinates about the importance of learning and innovation. Inconsistent signals about the importance of innovation confuse subordinates; if faced with ambiguity, they will stick to the safest course, the status quo. For example, though the CEO of a large advertising agency talked a lot about creativity and innovation, his actions spoke eloquently about the importance of safe, non-controversial ad campaigns. Innovation and creativity floundered. On the other hand, Jack Welch's obsession with innovation at GE sends clear messages about the importance of new product and process innovation.
- The executive team can use formal and informal rewards to reinforce innovation. Innovative individuals and groups must receive recognition, attention and support as well as formal rewards from the executive team. If mediocrity is rewarded, or if everyone is equally rewarded by the executive team, then excellence will disappear. The management team must use all the formal and informal rewards at its disposal to consistently reinforce behavior consistent with strategy and core values.
- Organizational history has an important impact on today's innovation. Key crises, events, prior executives, organizational myths, and heroes all shape and constrain current behavior. Highly stable organizations may have no tradition or precedent that fosters innovation. For example, both AT&T and General Radio had proud 75-year histories which glorified the role of engineers and minimized the relevance of marketing. For these organizations to be innovative in the 1980s, management must create new heroes, new visions, and new histories.

Executive leadership can seize upon innovative aspects of an organization's history and build new stories, myths, and heroes consistent with current competitive conditions. For example, management's challenge at Xerox is to take advantage of a proud history of innovation while trying to build a new tradition that emphasizes quality and technology transfer.

- The senior executive (that is, CEO, general manager, functional manager, etc.) cannot manage the organization alone. As stated earlier, senior executives must build executive teams with appropriate technical, social, and conceptual skills to accomplish diverse tasks. As the required innovation changes, so too must the nature of the executive team. Executive succession and promotion are powerful tools in innovation management. At General Radio, as noted earlier, the move to marketing and process innovation was driven by a new management team made up of both old-line General Radio engineers and new executives skilled in marketing and manufacturing.

The senior executive must also develop effective problem-solving processes in the top team. The team must be alert to external opportunities and threats, and possess the internal dynamics to deal effectively with uncertainty. Once the decisions are made, the executive team must implement these decisions with a single voice. Publicized dissension within the top team can bury innovation in organizational politics.

- Managing innovation requires visionary executives who provide clear direction for their organizations and infuse that direction with energy and value. Observation and research indicate that such executives frequently display three types of behavior: first, they work actively on *envisioning* or articulating a credible yet exciting vision of the future. Second, they personally work on *energizing* the organization by demonstrating their own excitement, optimism, and enthusiasm. Third, they put effort into *enabling* required behaviors by providing resources, rewarding desired behaviors, building supportive organizational structures and processes, and by building an effective senior team.

SUMMARY

Organizations cannot stand still. In ever more global markets, effective performance depends more and more on the successful management of innovation. Organizations can gain competitive advantage only by managing effectively for today while simultaneously creating innovation for tomorrow. But, as we have seen, success often breeds stagnation; in dominant companies, the challenge is to rekindle the innovative spirit that led to past success.

The challenge for executives is to build congruent organizations both for today's work and tomorrow's innovation. Organizations need to have sufficient internal diversity in strategies, structures, people, and processes to facilitate different kinds of innovation and to enhance organization learning.

There is perhaps no more pressing managerial problem than the sustained management of innovation. There is nothing mysterious about innovation: it doesn't just happen. Rather, it is the calculated outcome of strategic management and visionary leadership that provide the people, structures, values, and learning opportunities to make it an organizational way of life.

References

1. For an in-depth discussion of this congruence approach to organizational effectiveness, see D.A. Nadler and M.L. Tushman (1980) "A Congruence Model for Diagnosing Organizational Behavior." *Organizational Dynamics*.

2. See, W.A. Abernathy (1979) *The Productivity Dilemma*. Baltimore: Johns Hopkins Press; T. Allen (1983) *Managing the Flow of Technology*. Cambridge, MA: MIT Press; R.M. Kanter (1984) *The Change Masters*. New York: Simon and Schuster; P.R. Lawrence and D. Dyer (1983) *Renewing American Industry*. New York: The Free Press; D.A. Nadler and M.L. Tushman (1986) *Strategic Organization Design*. Homewood, IL: Scott, Foresman; M.L. Tushman and W. Moore (1982) *Readings in the Management of Innovation*. Marshfield, MA: Pitman Publishing.

3. For a detailed discussion of shaping informal processes, see Nadler and Tushman (1986) *op. cit.*

HOW SENIOR MANAGERS THINK*

Daniel J. Isenberg

"It is not enough to have a good mind. The main thing is to use it well."
René Descartes

Jim LeBlanc phoned Steve Baum, who formerly worked in his division, to ask about the CEO's new corporate task force on quality control that wanted to meet with Jim. Jim, the head of the industrial equipment division of Tanner Corporation, thought that Steve, now director of technology, could help him figure out why the task force wanted to meet with him in two weeks.

"It's because you're doing so damn well down there, boss!" Steve replied.

"Gee, thanks. By the way, Steve, what's the agenda for Singer's staff meeting for next week?" (Singer was the president and Jim's boss.)

"Well, we're going to talk about the reorganization and look at the overhead reduction figures for each division. Then Singer's going to report on last week's executive committee meeting and his trip to Japan."

"How did it go?"

"His telex from Osaka sounded enthusiastic, but he just got in last night and I haven't seen him yet."

"Well," said Jim, "I guess we'll just have to see, but if you hear something, call me right away because if Osaka comes through I'm going to have to hustle to get ready, and you know how Bernie hates to shake it. Now, about the task force . . ."

In the space of three minutes, Jim LeBlanc got a lot done. In addition to collecting critical information about a task force that the CEO, with unusual fanfare, had personally commissioned one month ago, he also began to plan his approach to the upcoming staff meeting. He decided *not* to try to get a presentation by his marketing people on opportunities in the Far East on the agenda. Sensing that Singer *was* optimistic about the Osaka trip, Jim decided that he should get his people ready for the possibility that the deal would materialize, which meant pulling engineers off another project for a while.

What were the thinking processes that allowed Jim to get so much done so pointedly and so rapidly? What was going on in his mind during his conversation with Steve? How, given the incomplete and uncertain information that Steve gave him, did Jim conclude that the Japan deal was imminent?

For the past two years I have studied the thought processes used by more than a dozen very senior managers while on the job. The managers that I studied ranged in age from their lower 40s to their upper 50s, in managerial experience from 10 to 30 years, and in current job tenure from 4 months to 10 years. Their companies ranged from $1 billion divisions in *Fortune* "100" companies to $10 million entrepreneurial companies just beginning to take hold in the marketplace. Company products included low- and high-technology goods, and markets ranged from rapidly expanding to precipitately deteriorating. All but two of the executives were

---

* Reprinted by permission of *Harvard Business Review* "How Senior Managers Think" by Daniel Isenberg (November/December 1984). Copyright © 1984 by the President and Fellows of Harvard College; all rights reserved.

Author's note: Among the many people who have helped my research I want to single out Paul Lawrence and John Kotter. I also extend thanks to the corporate managers who have given freely of their time and ideas. Miriam Schustack made very helpful comments on a previous version of this article.

Research methodology: In studying these dozen executives, I conducted intensive interviews, observed them on the job, read documents, talked with their colleagues and, in some cases, subordinates, and engaged them in various exercises in which they recounted their thoughts as they did their work. I also reported my observations and inferences back to the managers to get feedback. I spent anywhere from 1 to 25 days studying each manager (the mode was two and a half days in field interviews and observation).

responsible for the overall performance of their business units. As all had been frequently promoted throughout their careers and were considered excellent performers across the board, they were a representative sample of today's successful business executives.

Two findings about how senior managers do *not* think stand out from the study. First, it is hard to pinpoint if or when they actually make decisions about major business or organizational issues on their own. And second, they seldom think in ways that one might simplistically view as "rational," i.e., they rarely systematically formulate goals, assess their worth, evaluate the probabilities of alternative ways of reaching them, and choose the path that maximizes expected return. Rather, managers frequently bypass rigorous, analytical planning altogether, particularly when they face difficult, novel, or extremely entangled problems. When they do use analysis for a prolonged time, it is always in conjunction with intuition.

Let me make myself clear. Obviously, decisions *do* get made in organizations and these *are* frequently justified by data and logic. In particular, when viewed retrospectively over a long time period, effective executives often appear quite rational. Yet when studying their concurrent thinking processes, being "rational" does not best describe what the manager presiding over the decision-making process thinks about nor *how* he or she thinks.

I have a fourfold purpose in this article. First, I want to present a more accurate and empirically grounded description of what goes on inside the minds of senior managers. Second, I hope to offer a more accurate description of managerial thinking that should help provide a beginning language for talking about these elusive mental phenomena. Third, I hope that this language will also help to relieve some managers of the inconsistency between their view of how they are "supposed to" think and the thinking processes that, through experience, they have learned are actually quite effective. Fourth, I want to take advantage of successful senior managers' experiences to explore the managerial implications of their thinking processes.

WHAT SENIOR MANAGERS THINK ABOUT

Senior managers tend to think about two kinds of problems: how to create effective organizational processes and how to deal with one or two overriding concerns, or very general goals. These two domains of thought underlie the two critical activities that John P. Kotter found general managers engaged in: developing and maintaining an extensive interpersonal network, and formulating an agenda.[1]

A focus on process

The primary focus of on-line managerial thinking is on organizational and interpersonal processes. By "process" I mean the ways managers bring people and groups together to handle problems and take action. Whether proposing a change in the executive compensation structure, establishing priorities for a diverse group of business units, consolidating redundant operations, or preparing for plant closings, a senior executive's conscious thoughts are foremost among the processes for accomplishing a change or implementing a decision: "Who are the key players here, and how can I get their support? Whom should I talk to first? Should I start by getting the production group's input? What kind of signal will that send to the marketing people? I can't afford to lose their commitment in the upcoming discussions on our market strategy."

During the first months of his tenure, one area general manager I studied asked all of his business unit management teams to evaluate their own units. Subsequently, the area manager and his staff spent a day or more with each team discussing the whole area, each business unit within it, and how the two interrelated. Although he was concerned with the substance of the business-unit priorities, uppermost in his mind was a series of process concerns: How could the review process help managers be increasingly committed to their goals? How could the process help managers to become increasingly aware of the interdependencies among business units? How did his business unit managers use their people in reviewing their business units? How much management depth existed in the units?

In addition to thinking about organizational processes, successful senior managers think a lot about interpersonal processes and the people they come in contact with. They try to understand the strengths and weaknesses of others, the relationships that are important to *them*, what *their* agendas and priorities are.

For example, the CEO of a small high-technology company spent over an hour with his personnel director, a woman he rated as having performed excellently so far and whom he saw as having great potential although still inexperienced. At the time of the discussion, the CEO was considering adopting a new top-management structure under which the personnel director would report to another staff member rather than directly to him.

The CEO explained the proposed change to the personnel director, pointing out that it was not definite and that he was soliciting her reactions. Managers' "maps" of people provide them with guides to action. In this case, because of his sense of the personnel director's needs, the CEO slowed the reorganizing process so that the people who reported to him could deal with the various issues that arose.

The CEO elaborately described to me his awareness of the personnel director's concern at being new and at being a woman, and her desire to be in direct contact with him. He also understood her worry that if she reported to someone lower than him, people would perceive that the new personnel function was not very important and she would lose power.

The overriding concern

The stereotypical senior executive pays a great deal of attention to the strategy of the business, carefully formulates goals, lays out quantified and clear objectives, and sets about to achieve these objectives in the most efficient way. Whereas senior executives certainly attend to specific strategies and objectives some of the time, in their day-to-day reality specific objectives lurk in the background, not in the forefront of their thoughts.

Approximately two-thirds of the senior managers I studied were preoccupied with a very limited number of quite general issues, each of which subsumed a large number of specific issues. This preoccupation persisted for anywhere from a month to several years and, when in effect, dominated the manager's attention and provided coherence to many of his or her chaotic and disorganized activities.

The general manager of one large division of an automotive company, for example, used the word "discipline" over a dozen times in the course of a two-hour interview. For him, this concept embodied his deep concern for creating order and predictability in a division that, in his view, had become too loose before he took it over. His concern for discipline appeared in a number of diverse actions — strongly discouraging his subordinates' fire-fighting mentality, criticizing their poor preparation for corporate reviews, introducing rigorous strategic planning, encouraging time management, putting out a yearly calendar with divisional and corporate meetings printed on it, publishing agendas for many of these meetings up to a year in advance, and, by keeping recent reports in the top drawer of his desk, forcing himself to review frequently the division's activities and performance.

Regardless of its substance, the overriding concern weaves its way in and out of all the manager's daily activities, at times achieving the dimensions of an all-consuming passion.

After his first 100 days in office, an area general manager described his experience turning around a subsidiary in these words:

"The personal cost of achieving our top priorities has been huge. I dropped all outside activities. Now I have a feeling of just having emerged, like a chap who's been taken by a surf wave and rolled. Suddenly he comes up and can look at daylight again. It has been like a single-minded rage or madness. At the end of the 100 days, somehow I have awakened. It was overwhelming."

Of course senior managers do think about the content of their businesses, particularly during crises and periodic business reviews. But this thinking is always in close conjunction with thinking about the process for getting *others* to think about the business. In other words, even very senior managers devote most of their attention to the tactics of implementation rather than the formulation of strategy.

HOW SENIOR MANAGERS THINK

In making their day-by-day and minute-by-minute tactical maneuvers, senior executives tend to rely on several general thought processes such as using intuition; managing a network of interrelated problems; dealing with ambiguity, inconsistency, novelty, and surprise; and integrating action into the process of thinking.

Using intuition

Generations of writers on the art of management have recognized that practicing managers rely heavily on intuition.[2] In general, however, people have a poor grasp of what intuition is. Some see it as the opposite of rationality, others use it as an excuse for capriciousness, and currently some view it as the exclusive property of a particular side of the brain.

Senior managers use intuition in at least five distinct ways. First, they intuitively sense when a problem exists. The chief financial officer of a leading technical products company, for example, forecast a difficult year ahead for the company and, based on a vague gut feel that something was wrong, decided to analyze one business group. "The data on the group were inconsistent and unfocused," he said after doing the analysis. "I had the sense that they were talking about a future that just was not going to happen, and I turned out to be right."

Second, managers rely on intuition to perform well-learned behavior patterns rapidly. Early on, managerial action needs to be thought through carefully. Once the manager is "fluent" at performance, however, and the behavior is programmed, executives can execute programs without conscious effort. In the words of one general manager:

"It was very instinctive, almost like you have been drilled in close combat for years and now the big battle is on, and you really don't have time to think. It's as if your arms, your feet, and your body just move instinctively. You have a preoccupation with working capital, a preoccupation with capital expenditure, a preoccupation with people, and one with productivity, and all this goes so fast that you don't even know whether it's completely rational, or it's part rational, part intuitive."

Intuition here refers to the smooth automatic performance of learned behavior sequences. This intuition is not arbitrary or irrational, but is based on years of painstaking practice and hands-on experience that build skills. After a while a manager can perform a sequence of actions in a seamless fabric of action and reaction without being aware of the effort.

A third function of intuition is to synthesize isolated bits of data and experience into an integrated picture, often in an "aha!" experience. In the words of one manager: "Synergy is always nonrational because it takes you beyond the mere sum of the parts. It is a nonrational, nonlogical thinking perspective."

Fourth, some managers use intuition as a check (a belt-and-suspenders approach) on the results of more rational analysis. Most senior executives are familiar with the formal decision analysis models and tools, and those that occasionally use such systematic methods for reaching decisions are leery of solutions that these methods suggest that run counter to their sense of the correct course of action.

Conversely, if managers completely trusted intuition, they'd have little need for rigorous and systematic analysis. In practice, executives work on an issue until they find a match between their "gut" and their "head." One manager explained to me, "Intuition leads me to seek out holes in the data. But I discount casual empiricism and don't act on it."

Fifth, managers can use intuition to bypass in-depth analysis and move rapidly to come up with a plausible solution. Used in this way, intuition is an almost instantaneous cognitive process in which a manager recognizes familiar patterns. In much the same way that people can immediately recognize faces that were familiar years ago, administrators have a repertoire of familiar problematic situations matched with the necessary responses. As one manager explained:

"My gut feel points me in a given direction. When I arrive there, then I can begin to sort out the issues. I do not do a deep analysis at first. I suppose the intuition comes from scar tissue, getting burned enough times. For example, while discussing the European budget with someone, suddenly I got the answer: it was hard for us to get the transfer prices. It rang a bell, then I ran some quick checks."

By now it should be clear that intuition is not the opposite of rationality, nor is it a random process of guessing. Rather, it is based on extensive experience both in analysis and problem solving and in implementation, and to the extent that the lessons of experience are logical and well-founded, then so is the intuition. Further, managers often combine gut feel with systematic analysis, quantified data, and thoughtfulness.

It should also be clear the executives use intuition during *all* phases of the problem-solving process: problem finding, problem defining, generating and choosing a solution, and implementing the solution. In fact, senior managers often ignore the implied linear progression of the rational decision-making model and jump opportunistically from phase to phase, allowing implementation concerns to affect the problem definition and perhaps even to limit the range of solutions generated.

Problem management

Managers at all levels work at understanding and solving the problems that arise in their jobs. One distinctive characteristic of top managers is that their thinking deals not with isolated and discrete items but with portfolios of problems, issues, and opportunities in which (1) many problems exist simultaneously, (2) these problems compete for some part of his or her immediate concern, and (3) the issues are interrelated.

The cognitive tasks in problem management are to find and define good problems, to "map" these into a network, and to manage their dynamically shifting priorities. For lack of a better term, I call this the process of problem management.

Defining the problem After learning of a state health organization threat to exclude one of their major products from the list of drugs for which the state would reimburse buyers, top executives in a pharmaceutical company struggled to find a proper response. After some time, the managers discovered that the real problem was not the alleged drug abuse the availability of the drug on the street caused. Rather, the problem was budgetary: the health services department had to drastically reduce its budget and was doing so by trimming its list of reimbursable drugs. Once they redefined the problem, the pharmaceutical executives not only could work on a better, more real problem, but also had a chance to solve it — which they did.[3]

In another case, a division general manager discovered that, without his knowledge but with the approval of the division controller, one of his vice presidents had drawn a questionable personal loan from the company. The division manager told me how he defined the problem: "I could spend my time formulating rules to guide managers. But the real fundamental issue here was that I needed to expect and demand that my managers manage their resources effectively." Although he recognized the ethical components involved, he chose to define the problem as concerned with asset management rather than cheating. Because asset management was an issue the division frequently discussed, the manager felt that it was more legitimate and efficacious to define the problem in this way.

Making a network of problems By forming problem categories, executives can see how individual problems interrelate. For instance, a bank CEO had a "network" of at least nineteen related problems and issues that he was concerned about. Among these were: establishing credibility in international banking, strengthening the bank's role in corporate banking, increasing the range of financial services and products, being prepared to defensively introduce new products in response to competitors' innovations, developing systems to give product cost information, reducing operational costs, standardizing branch architecture, and utilizing space efficiently.

The bank CEO classified these problems in terms of broad issue categories. He found that many were related to the issue of expanding and broadening the bank's competence beyond consumer banking in which it was already firmly established. A second overarching issue was standardization of the bank's many branches with regard to architecture, physical layout, accounting systems, and so on.

Having an interrelated network of problems allows a manager to seize opportunities more flexibly and to use progress on one problem to achieve progress on another, related issue. The bank CEO likened himself to a frog on a lily pad waiting for the fly – the problem or issue – to buzz by. Having a mental network of problems helped him to realize the opportunities as they occurred.

Choosing which problem to work on Although managers often decide to work on the problem that seems to offer the best opportunities for attack, determining which problems they ought to tackle can be hard. As one manager commented:

"I have to sort through so many issues at once. There are ten times too many. I use a number of defense mechanisms to deal with this overload – I use delaying actions, I deny the existence of problems, or I put problems in a mental queue of sorts. This is an uncomfortable process for me. My office and responsibility say I need to deal with all of these issues, so I create smoke or offer some grand theory as my only way to keep my own sanity. One of the frustrations is that I don't want to tell my people that their number one problems have lower priorities than they think they should get."

In my observations, how managers define and rank problems is heavily influenced by how easy the problems are to solve. Very shortly after perceiving that a problem exists, managers run a quick feasibility check to see if it is solvable. Only if they find it is solvable will they then invest further energy to understand its various ramifications and causes. In other words, managers tend not to think very much about a problem unless they sense that it is solvable. Contrary to some management doctrines, this finding suggests that a general concept of what is a possible solution often precedes and guides the process of conceptualizing a problem.

Thus, the two stages of problem analysis and problem solving are tightly linked and occur reiteratively rather than sequentially. By going back and forth between these two cognitive processes, managers define the array of problems facing them in terms that already incorporate key features of solutions and that thus make it easier for them to take action.

One outcome of this process is that managers have an organized mental map of all the problems and issues facing them. The map is neither static nor permanent; rather, managers continually test, correct, and revise it. In the words of one CEO, the executive "takes advantage of the best cartography at his command, but knows that that is not enough. He knows that along the way he will find things that change his maps or alter his perceptions of the terrain. He trains himself the best he can in the detective skills. He is endlessly sending out patrols to learn greater detail, overflying targets to get some sense of the general battlefield."

Tolerating ambiguity The senior managers that I observed showed an ability to tolerate and even thrive on high degrees of ambiguity and apparent inconsistency. As one top executive said:

"I think ambiguity can be destroying, but it can be very helpful to an operation. Ambiguities come from the things you can't spell out exactly. They yield a certain freedom you need as a chief executive officer not to be nailed down on everything. Also, certain people thrive on ambiguity, so I leave certain things ambiguous. The fact is we tie ourselves too much to linear plans, to clear time scales. I like to fuzz up time scales completely."

Because demands on a manager become both stronger and more divergent as responsibility increases, the need to tolerate apparent ambiguity and inconsistency also increases. For example, the top manager has to deal with stakeholders who may have adversarial roles. By responding positively to one set of demands, the manager automatically will create other conflicting sets of demands.

The reason I have called the inconsistency "apparent" is that senior managers tend to have ways of thinking that make issues seem less inconsistent. For example, the president of a leading high-technology company was considering whether to exercise or forgo an option to lease land on which to build expensive warehouse space for one of the divisions at the same time as the division was laying off workers for the first time in history. "To spend a half million dollars on keeping the land and building warehouse space while the plant is laying off people looks terrible and makes no sense," he said, "but if next year is a good year, we'll need to be in a position to make the product."

Perceiving and understanding novelty The managers I observed dealt frequently with novel situations that were unexpected and, in many cases, were impossible to plan for in advance. For example, one division general manager found himself with the task of selling his division, which was still developing a marketable product. In response to its shareholders, the corporation had shifted its strategy and thus decided to divest the fledgling division. How should the general manager look for buyers? If buyers were not forthcoming, would the corporation retain a stake to reduce the risk to potential new partners? How should he manage his people in the process of selling? Should he himself look for a new position or commit himself to a new owner? These were some of the unique questions the division head faced while selling his own division, and there was no industry experience to give him clear answers.

In general, the human mind is conservative. Long after an assumption is outmoded, people tend to apply it to novel situations. One way in which some of the senior managers I studied counteract this conservative bent is by paying attention to their feelings of *surprise* when a particular fact does not fit their prior understanding, and then by highlighting rather than denying the novelty. Although surprise made them feel uncomfortable, it made them take the cause seriously and inquire into it – "What is behind the personal loan by my vice president of sales that appears on the books? How extensive a problem is it?" "Why did the management committee of the corporation spend over an hour of its valuable time discussing a problem three levels down in my division?" "Now that we've shown the health services department beyond a reasonable doubt that this drug is not involved in drug abuse, why don't they reinstate it on the list?"

Rather than deny, downplay, or ignore disconfirmation, successful senior managers often treat it as friendly and in a way cherish the discomfort surprise creates. As a result, these managers often perceive novel situations early on and in a frame of mind relatively undistorted by hidebound notions.

WHAT TO DO ABOUT THINKING

Having looked at the inner workings of the managerial mind, what insights can we derive from our observations? Literally hundreds of laboratory and field studies demonstrate that the human mind is imperfectly rational, and dozens of additional articles, offering arguments based on every field of study from psychology to economics, explain why.[4] The evidence that we should curtail our impractical and overly ambitious expectations of managerial rationality is compelling.

Yet abandoning the rational ideal leaves us with two glaring problems. First, whether managers think in a linear and systematic fashion or not, companies still need to strive toward rational action in the attainment of corporate goals, particularly in their use of resources. Second, we still need to spell out what kinds of thinking processes are attainable and helpful to senior managers.

Program rationality into the organization
Of course, rationality is desirable and should be manifest in the functioning of the company. One alternative to the vain task of trying to rationalize managers is to increase the rationality of organizational systems and processes. Although organizational behavior is never completely rational, managers can design and program processes and systems that will approach rationality in resource allocation and employment.

Decision support systems are one source of organizational rationality. These generally computerized routines perform many functions ranging from providing a broad and quantitative data base, to presenting that data base in easily understandable form, to modeling the impact of decisions on various financial and other criteria, to mimicking expert judgment such as in the diagnosis and repair of malfunctioning equipment or in oil field exploration.

Another rational process that many businesses employ is strategic planning. Nonrational or partly rational managers can devise, implement, and use a plan that systematically assesses a company's strengths and weaknesses, logically extrapolates a set of its competencies, proposes a quantitative assessment of environmental constraints and resources, and performs all these tasks in a time-sequenced, linear fashion.

Of course, companies have used rational systems for information gathering, strategic planning, budgeting, human resource planning, environmental scanning, and so forth for a long time. But I see these systems not only as useful but also as a necessary complement to a manager's apparent inability to be very systematic or rational in thought.

But is it possible for imperfectly rational managers to design even more perfectly rational systems? The answer is a qualified yes. There is evidence, for example, that with help people can design systems that are better than they are themselves at making judgments.[5] Creating organizational systems to improve on their own behavior is not new to managers. In order to still hear the beautiful sirens yet prevent himself being seduced by the music and throwing himself into the sea, Ulysses ordered his men to block their own ears with wax, bind him to the mast, and to tighten his bindings if he ordered them to let him go. Although Ulysses begged his sailors to release him, they obeyed his original orders and Ulysses succeeded in both hearing the sirens and surviving their perilous allure.[6]

Programming rationality into the organizational functioning is important for another reason: rational systems free senior executives to tackle the ambiguous, ill-defined tasks that the human mind is uniquely capable of addressing. Many senior managers today face problems – developing new products for embryonic markets, creating new forms of manufacturing operations, conceiving of innovative human resource systems – that are new to them and new to their companies and that they can deal with only extemporaneously and with a nonprogrammable artistic sense. In fact, it may even seem paradoxical that managers need to create rational systems in order to creatively and incrementally tackle the nonrecurrent problems that defy systematic approaches.

Hone intellectual skills
In the literature on managerial behavior there is disagreement as to how much or how often senior managers engage in thoughtful reflection. Many executives that I studied do make time for in-depth thinking, sometimes while they are alone,

Career paths also play an important role: individuals who spend an entire career in a single functional or product area will be more narrowly focused and less innovative than their colleagues with broader career experiences. Employees with experience in multiple areas and functions will have a more balanced view of the organization's strengths and weaknesses and a broader set of contacts from whom they can learn. Similarly, within many R&D organizations, scientists and engineers have the opportunity of pursuing either managerial or technical career tracks. Such dual ladders, when effectively implemented, can encourage innovation and specialization along both tracks.

Though an organizational structure that discourages job diversity can inhibit innovation, it is also true that a human resource system that produces too many promotions, and too quickly, can have the same effect. Firms that lead employees to expect a promotion every two years only encourage short time frames. Innovation and change take time; individuals must expect to stay in jobs long enough to influence both short- and long-term performance indicators. Thus, career-planning systems must find the right balance between the complacency bred by narrow career mobility, and the short-run mentality of job-hopping.

Education Education programs are also an influential tool in effecting innovation. Education and training programs expose managers from different areas of a firm to the other disciplines and functions in the organization, to the nature and importance of innovation and change, and to skills in communication, problem solving, and conflict resolution. IBM, Control Data, GTE, and Pepsico all have programs in managing innovation that involve cross-sections of the corporations in joint work on innovation-related problems.

Quite apart from their substance, these educational programs provide a relaxed setting in which individuals meet and get to know a range of different individuals from throughout the organization. These informal contacts provide a valuable informal infrastructure which nurtures both individual and organizational learning and innovation. IBM's three-week innovation program, for example, provides substantial content on innovation and change; but, even more importantly, it provides an opportunity for 50 managers from around the corporation to become much better acquainted with each other and their respective areas. IBM is not alone; the most innovative firms invest substantially in the training and education of their managers.

Informal Organization

Innovation is disruptive and complex work which requires close collaboration between actors who are usually quite separate. A competent set of individuals and the correct formal organization are not enough to deal with the complexities and uncertainties inherent in innovative work. The informal organization must bolster and complement the formal system. While formal organization arrangements facilitate corporate learning and innovation, individual creativity springs from a healthy informal organization. Several dimensions of the informal organization are particularly important in managing innovation.

Core Values Core values provide the basic normative foundation of a business unit. Core values are beliefs about what is good or bad, right or wrong in a particular firm. For example, IBM core values are the importance of individuals, service, and excellence; Tandem's are quality, personal excellence, and teamwork. A clear set of core values helps focus and motivate behavior. The most innovative firms have clear core values that provide focus in a sea of diversity, and a common objective on which disparate professionals and divisions can agree.

Some examples of core values that facilitate innovation:

- developing technology that meets users' needs
- individual autonomy and organizational identification
- risk taking and tolerance of failure

build in risk/return relationships that are similar to those encountered by outside entrepreneurs.

Corporate ventures are vehicles to marshall dedicated resources for major new products and/or process development. These entrepreneurial units can move rapidly and get quick feedback from the market. Corporate venturing and independent business units are important vehicles for organizational learning. These high-risk/high-return organizational experiments may fail nine times out of ten. Yet, they are relatively low-cost ventures and, when they fail, provide new information about technologies and markets. Further, these successes can be highly profitable and strategically important for the firm in the long run (e.g., IBM's PC business or Dupont's Nylon venture in the 1930s). Those ventures that succeed are either folded into existing divisions (e.g., IBM's PC independent business unit) or set up as distinct divisions. IBM, 3M, Dupont, Tektronix, and Control Data, among others, have had considerable success with venture units.

Incentives Incentives and rewards have a major impact on individual and group behavior. Organizations get what they reward. If organizations only measure and reward short-term performance, or if everyone is rewarded equally, then innovation suffers. To encourage innovation, organizations must base rewards on actual performance and make innovation an important dimension of individual and group performance. Bonuses, stock options, salaries, and promotions can be linked to innovation and new product/process development. For example, at Biogen, as long as scientists are evaluated solely on the quality of their pure science and marketing people strictly on the basis of sales, the firm will never enjoy sustained innovation and collaboration from these critical groups.

Management can bolster formal incentives with special recognition and rewards for particularly innovative employees. For example, the Watson awards at IBM or innovation prizes at H-P and 3M provide special status to innovative individuals and teams. At Intel, highly innovative teams may go to trade shows where their products are introduced. Formal and informal rewards are an important managerial lever to stimulate innovation. Innovative individuals and groups can clearly see the benefits of innovation; non-innovators can just as easily see the consequences of clinging to the status quo.

Joint Evaluation, Staffing, and Appraisal As innovation necessarily involves individuals from different disciplines and departments, management can use joint problem-solving teams to maximize ownership and coupling between areas. Together, such teams can develop priorities, direction, and emphasis on new products and processes. These teams can then sell their innovations to their more local colleagues and greatly improve internal technology or product transfer. Further, these problem-solving teams can evaluate their successes and failures. Such joint evaluation helps the organizations learn and reduces finger-pointing and the "not-invented-here" syndrome which together reduce learning and innovation. The most innovative organizations create these joint problem-solving teams early in the product development cycle; thus, problem solving comes to be perceived as part of the normal process, rather than a bureaucratic intrusion. For example, at Pharmacia, joint problem solving and evaluation have been institutionalized throughout the corporation and are given much credit for this firm's extraordinary innovation record.

Job Design, Job Rotation, and Careers Innovation depends on motivated employees who are willing to experiment and be creative. The design of jobs, job rotation, and career paths all have important effects on the creativity of managers and their employees. Jobs with substantial autonomy, variety, and individual involvement offer intrinsic motivation to perform well. Jobs with low involvement and autonomy cannot capture an employee's enthusiasm; motivation comes only from extrinsic factors (e.g., pay). Larger jobs involve more of the individual and create greater internal drive for learning innovation.

sometimes with their peers or subordinates, and sometimes in active experimentation.

Furthermore, most senior managers I studied constantly maintain and sharpen their intellectual abilities in order to better analyze their current or past experiences. Rigorous thinking is a way of life for them, not a task they try to avoid or to expedite superficially.

These senior managers read books outside their fields, engage in enthusiastic discussions of political and economic affairs, attend academic lectures and management seminars, and tackle brain teasers such as word problems, chess, and crossword puzzles. One company president I studied is a regular theatergoer who can discuss Shakespearean and contemporary plays at great length, while another often immerses himself in classical music and allows ideas about difficult work-related issues to float around in his consciousness. These activities are valuable not only for their content but also for the thinking processes that they establish, develop, and refine. Whether managers indulge in such "blue sky" irrelevant activities at work or outside, they are developing critical mental resources that they can then apply to problems that arise in their jobs.

Think while doing

One of the implications of the intuitive nature of executive action is that "thinking" is inseparable from acting. Since managers often "know" what is right before they can analyze and explain it, they frequently act first and think later. Thinking is inextricably tied to action in what I call thinking/acting cycles, in which managers develop thoughts about their companies and organizations not by analyzing a problematic situation and then acting, but by thinking and acting in close concert. Many of the managers I studied were quite facile at using thinking to inform action and vice versa.

Given the great uncertainty of many of the management or business issues that they face, senior managers often instigate a course of action simply to learn more about an issue: "We bought that company because we wanted to learn about that business." They then use the results of the action to develop a more complete understanding of the issue. What may appear as action for action's sake is really the result of an intuitive understanding that analysis is only possible in the light of experience gained while attempting to solve the problem. Analysis is not a passive process by a dynamic, interactive series of activity and reflection.

One implication of acting/thinking cycles is that action is often part of defining the problem, not just of implementing the solution. Frequently, once they had begun to perceive the symptoms, but before they could articulate a problem, the managers I studied talked to a few people to collect more information and confirm what they already knew. The act of collecting more data more often than not changed the nature of the problem, in part because subordinates then realized that the problem was serious enough to warrant the boss's attention. Managers also often acted in the absence of clearly specified goals, allowing these to emerge from the process of clarifying the nature of the problem.

Yet how often do managers push their subordinates to spell out *their* goals clearly and specify *their* objectives? A creative subordinate will always be able to present a plausible and achievable goal when pressed, but in the early stages of a tough problem it is more helpful for managers to provide a receptive forum in which their people can play around with an issue, "noodle" it through, and experiment. Sometimes it will be necessary for managers to allow subordinates to act in the absence of goals to achieve a clearer comprehension of what is going on, and even at times to *discover* rather than achieve the organization's true goals.

Manage time by managing problems

All managers would like to accomplish more in less time. One of the implications of the process of mapping problems and issues is that when a manager addresses any particular problem, he or she calls a number of related problems or issues to mind at the same time. One by-product is that a manager can attain economies of effort.

For example, when working on a problem of poor product quality, a division manager might see a connection between poor quality and an inadequate production control system and tackle both problems together. To address the issues, she could form a cross-functional task force involving her marketing manager, who understands customers' tolerance for defects. (One reason for bringing him in might be to prepare him for promotion in two or three years.) She might intend the task force to reduce interdepartmental conflicts as well as prepare a report that she could present to corporate headquarters.

Managers can facilitate the process of creating a problem network in many ways. They can ask their staff to list short- and long-term issues that they think need to be addressed, consolidate these lists, and spend some time together mapping the interrelationships. Or they can ask themselves how an issue fits into other nonproblematic aspects of the company or business unit. How does product quality relate to marketing strategy? To capital expenditure guidelines? To the company's R&D center with a budget surplus? To the new performance appraisal system? To the company's recent efforts in affirmative action? To their own career plans? Managers should never deal with problems in isolation. They should always ask themselves what additional related issues they should be aware of while dealing with the problem at hand.[7]

Some suggestions

A number of suggestions on how managers can improve their thinking emerge from my study of senior managers' thought processes:

Bolster intuition with rational thinking. Recognize that good intuition requires hard work, study, periods of concentrated thought, and rehearsal.

Offset tendencies to be rational by stressing the importance of values and preferences, of using imagination, and of acting with an incomplete picture of the situation.

Develop skills at mapping an unfamiliar territory by, for example, generalizing from facts and testing generalities by collecting more data.

Pay attention to the simple rules of thumb — heuristics — that you have developed over the years. These can help you bypass many levels of painstaking analysis.

Don't be afraid to act in the absence of complete understanding, but then cherish the feelings of surprise that you will necessarily experience.

Spend time understanding what the problem or issue is.

Look for the connections among the many diverse problems and issues facing you to see their underlying relationships with each other. By working on one problem you can make progress on others.

Finally, recognize that your abilities to think are critical assets that you need to manage and develop in the same way that you manage other business assets.

References

1. John P. Kotter (1982) *The General Managers*. New York: The Free Press.
2. See, for example, Chester I. Barnard (1938) *The Functions of the Executive*. Cambridge, MA: Harvard University Press. Also, Henry Mintzberg (1976) "Planning on the Left Side and Managing on the Right." *Harvard Business Review*, July-August, p. 49.
3. See my study (1980) "Drugs and Drama: The Effects of Two Dramatic Events in a Pharmaceutical Company on Managers' Cognitions." Working Paper #83-55. Boston: Harvard Business School.
4. Some of Herbert A. Simon's classic work on bounded rationality and "satisficing" is collected in (1979) *Models of Thought*. New Haven: Yale University Press. More recently, Amos Tversky, Daniel Kahneman, and other

psychologists have described the mechanisms producing imperfect judgment and nonrational choice. See, for example, Daniel Kahneman, Paul Slovic and Amos Tversky, ed., (1982) *Judgement Under Uncertainty: Heuristics and Biases*. Cambridge, UK: Cambridge University Press.

5. Louis R. Goldberg (1970) "Man vs. Model of Man: A Rationale, Plus some Evidence for a Method of Improving on Clinical Inferences." *Psychological Bulletin*, 73, p. 422.

6. John Elster (1979) *Ulysses and the Sirens: Studies in Rationality and Irrationality*. Cambridge, MA: Cambridge University Press.

7. For an interesting application of these ideas to a different leadership setting, see my chapter "Some Hows and Whats of Managerial Thinking: Implications for Future Army Leaders" in (1984) *Military Leadership on the Future Battlefield*. New York: Pergamon Press.

CASES

PNB UNIVERSITY BRANCH*

David A. Nadler
Michael L. Tushman
Nina G. Hatvany

People's National Bank (PNB) is the lead bank of a moderate-sized bank holding company located in the capital of a large midwestern state. As the major bank in the company, PNB accounts for $600 million of the company's $2 billion in assets. At the core of PNB is its branch marketing system. Unlike many East Coast banks, branch banking accounts for a large percentage of PNB's income, and many of the top managers of the bank have come up through the branch system.

The senior vice-president for branch operations, John B. Green, directly supervises the operations of twenty-one branch banks. Approximately ten more branches are planned for the next three years. Each branch is headed by a branch manager, who runs the branch with a relatively high degree of freedom. A typical branch includes a group of tellers, directed by a teller supervisor, and a "desk" staff of financial consultants, loan officers, and some clerical personnel. Some of the larger branches have assistant managers who may supervise either operations or the loan activity. Although the actual work is extremely standardized (procedures for opening accounts, processing loans, and so on), branch managers are free to manage the branch as they desire, and different branches have greatly varying structures, procedures, and atmospheres.

Each branch is a profit center within the larger bank. Branch revenue is figured by adding income from loan volume to a figure representing income derived from the funds the branch has brought in (based on deposit figures). From the revenue figure actual branch expenses, building expenses, and allocated overhead are subtracted to yield a monthly branch profit figure. Each year, the branch manager and John B.

---

* From David A. Nadler, Michael L. Tushman, and Nina G. Hatvany, *Managing Organizations*: Readings and Cases, pp. 477–479. Copyright © 1982 by David A. Nadler, Michael L. Tushman, and Nina G. Hatvany. Reprinted by permission of Little, Brown and Company. Permission granted on above terms by Little, Brown, and Company (Inc.).

Green develop a profit plan for the coming year, and managers are paid a sizeable bonus depending upon the performance of their branch against the profit plan.

A CHANGE AT THE UNIVERSITY BRANCH

On the first Friday in April 1988, the manager of the University Branch of PNB informed John B. Green that he would be leaving the bank at the end of the following week to join the ministry of God. Faced with an unanticipated managerial vacancy in a large and critical branch, Green met with his staff and decided to appoint Gary Herline, an up-and-coming young man in the commercial lending department, as manager of the University Branch. Herline was notified on Wednesday and was told to report to the University Branch on the following Monday to take up his duties as branch manager.

HERLINE'S BACKGROUND

Herline had been with the bank for a few years when he received notice of his appointment as branch manager. After receiving his MBA from a well-known business school in 1983, he accepted an offer from PNB rather than those of the large New York banks because he felt that there would be greater opportunities to move up in the organization quickly at PNB. He started out his first year in the bank's training program and was rotated through a wide variety of assignments, including a brief assignment as a financial consultant at a branch. During this period, Gary learned that he had been identified by management as a "hot prospect" and that his performance was being watched closely. After training he spent two years in the trust department and had worked in the commercial lending department for a year when he heard about his move to the University Branch.

INFORMATION ABOUT UNIVERSITY

Having heard about his move late on Wednesday, Gary spent most of Thursday and Friday talking to some of his contacts within the bank about the University Branch. At the same time he tried to conclude his work in commercial lending. The University Branch, one of the largest in the system, had been a problem branch for some time. There was quite a bit of turnover among the employees and the managerial staff. Located adjacent to the state university campus, it served a different market than almost any other branch in the system. By Friday afternoon, Gary had listed the important things he had learned about the branch (see Exhibit 1). As he prepared to start at University on Monday morning, he asked himself the following questions:

"From what I know about the branch, what are the critical issues I am going to have to deal with during the next six months at University Branch?"

"When I get to the branch on Monday, what are the first things I should do – what should my first day be like?"

Exhibit 1
Herline's Summary of Important Information About University Branch

It's a large branch; eight desk people, eighteen tellers, fairly good physical plant, high volume. Loan volume has been very poor during the past three years, but there has been an increase over the past two or three months. Some people feel that this reflects an absence of any management and that the loans are not "good" ones (that delinquency will go up in the coming months).

The staff is very young, particularly the tellers. All except two of the tellers are women and many have B.A. degrees; some have Master's degrees.

Branch has the largest number of accounts and highest volume of transactions of any branch in the system; however, many accounts are very small, and many transactions are for small amounts of money (checks for 50¢ to $5.00).

There is no official assistant manager, but one of the loan officers seems to function as an assistant manager. He is resented by the tellers, however, and seems to get into disagreements with the teller supervisor, who has been at the branch for seventeen years.

The desk staff seems to be of uneven quality. Some are excellent, but there is some deadwood also.

Turnover among tellers is very high. It has run at about 75 percent per year for the last five years. Recently the tellers submitted an informal group grievance to the manager complaining about working hours and low pay.

Competition for the university area business is keen. The other two major commercial banks in town have branches on the same blocks as PNB. Both branches are newer and better laid out than the PNB branch. Also, several savings and loan offices are close by.

Some of the key commercial accounts in the University Branch area have been taken away by agressive loan officers and branch managers of other nearby PNB branches as well as by competing banks.

For the last year, the branch has consistently failed to meet the profit plan and has even shown losses in several months.

QUESTIONS

1. What are the critical issues facing the new branch manager? Why are these issues critical?
2. How should he begin his first day? What are some key objectives he should accomplish during his first week?
3. Gary Herline's boss John Green probably has some specific expectations about the branch's future performance and Herline's strategies. How might these be discovered? If you were Herline, what expectations would you want Green to have? How would you influence Green on these matters?

WHAT'S GONE WRONG WITH THE REICHMANNS?*

David Olive

For 30 years, the Reichmann brothers have always been right. Not just about business, but *morally* right. As astute contrarians, the Toronto family seemed to have no equals. By always guessing right on their steadily larger and riskier land deals, the Reichmanns were able in a single generation to amass the world's largest real estate empire. But staggering financial success – the Reichmanns' wealth is surpassed only by a few of the world's royal families – was only the half of it. The Reichmann mystique, if it can be called that, derives mostly from their reputation for being nice guys who finish first. Who are unfailingly polite, no matter the stakes. Whose word is as good as a 3,000-word contract. Who never get anyone mad.

But that was yesterday. Two monstrous acquisitions – of oil producer Gulf Canada Ltd. last year [1985] and distillery giant Hiram Walker Resources Ltd. this spring – have put Olympia & York Developments Ltd., the principal holding company of Albert, Paul and Ralph Reichmann, into a strait-jacket of debt and a woeful reliance on depressed commodities businesses. What more, Gulf, Walker and Abitibi-Price Inc. (acquired in 1981) are all cash-hungry companies. In paying top dollar for Gulf and Walker, which cost the Reichmanns a total of about $6 billion, and then making those companies pay for the cost of their own acquisition, the family has probably blundered. Its strategy could deprive these firms of the capital they need to flourish. That's not the worst of it. Today's poor business conditions may prove temporary. But lasting damage has been done to O&Y's homey image. Where once the Reichmanns were oddities in the vainglorious real estate trade – humble men yet possessed of daring vision; street-smart but also unfailingly honest – their motives now seem rather common. In stepping from their private, almost cloistered world into the public eye, they endured a megadose of bad publicity. In fact, their past two deals were so clumsily executed the Reichmanns managed to get almost *everybody* mad at them. "The negative reaction has disturbed me greatly," says Paul Reichmann, 55, who is senior executive vice-president of the privately held O&Y. "If I'd known all this would happen, I would rather not have gone ahead with it."

By inviting Petro-Canada into their Gulf deal as purchaser of Gulf's western Canadian refineries and gas stations, the Reichmanns attracted the scorn of Tory ideologues, who want state-owned Petrocan to shrink, not grow. Liberal Leader John Turner was so incensed at the Reichmanns he put aside his party's desire to Canadianize the oil patch in order to blast them, saying that the $500 million tax break that was a key to the Gulf deal "raises extraordinary matters of ministerial responsibility, concentration of economic power, and the appearance of fairness." Then the Walker deal

---

* From *The Globe and Mail, Report on Business Magazine*, December 1986. Reprinted by permission of the publisher.

turned into a cross-Atlantic tug-of-war between the Reichmanns and a British conglomerate, and even the strongly nationalist Canadian Auto Workers turned on the Reichmanns: it lobbied furiously in Ottawa on the foreigners' behalf while loudly proclaiming that the Reichmanns were out to dismember the company's liquor business and lay off thousands of its workers. Even now, after the dust has settled, there are widespread misgivings about the Reichmanns. "It was hypocritical of the Reichmanns to raise the issue of patriotism to justify their huge tax break on the Gulf deal," says Stephen Jarislowsky, a prominent Montréal investment manager. "These patriots have made most of their fortune in New York. Now the Canadian Government thinks it's fine if the taxpayers help them make a fortune here, too."

Why did the Reichmanns put themselves through this agony? One compelling reason is that they've simply got too much cash. Their huge portfolio of buildings produces a Niagara of rental riches (about $500 million a year) that demands to be re-invested. But the real estate market is not a deep or safe enough reservoir. Most cities aren't growing fast enough to absorb the average O&Y project, which can be the size of a small city. O&Y's World Financial Center, now nearing completion in Manhattan, is the world's largest commercial office space development. When it opens next year, the landmark complex will account for 3% of all New York office space and house more than 25,000 workers.

But there's a much more important reason. The Reichmanns know that real estate is a lousy foundation on which to build a lasting industrial empire. It takes an almost magical skill to succeed at land development, whose boom-bust rhythms have reduced most of the greatest real estate fortunes to rubble after the people who built them passed from the scene. Sometimes they turn to dust *inside* of one generation. A case in point is the late great U.S. developer William Zeckendorf, who built Montréal's landmark Place Ville Marie just before his real estate empire crumbled. The founders of O&Y have absorbed that lesson: One of their earliest Toronto office developments was built on land they bought from an ailing Zeckendorf firm at a fire-sale price. The Reichmanns – whose family name, derived from the German, means "man of wealth" or "man of empire" – want their children to inherit a durable legacy, something that can survive without their genius. "Succession is the whole point of these manoeuvres," says Andrew Sarlos, a sometime renegade among Toronto money managers, and one of the Reichmanns' few intimates on Bay Street. "The Reichmanns have an immense wealth, the bulk of which is not professionally managed but is handled by the brothers themselves. That wealth has to be institutionalized, because the Reichmanns can't count on the next generation to have their special, entrepreneurial skill."

And so the Reichmann brothers, now in their mid-to-late 50s, have scrambled to shift the family's assets out of the volatile real estate sector and into something relatively goof-proof, such as a publicly traded conglomerate along the lines of Canadian Pacific. Most conglomerates can't match the profits of an astutely managed real estate portfolio. But CP has been around almost since Confederation, which is more than can be said of any large real estate developer.

As a key part of the transition, the Reichmanns have recruited a battery of high-powered professional managers, most of them plucked from the public sector. Foremost among these is Marshall (Mickey) Cohen, a former "superbureaucrat" who was deputy minister in three portfolios (finance, energy and industry) during his 15 years in Ottawa. He's also an old colleague: In 1965, long before he headed for Ottawa, Cohen was a partner with the Reichmanns in one of their real estate developments. Under the tutelage of Cohen and the other new hired hands, those among the 14 Reichmann children who choose to join the firm are expected to flourish. So far, only Albert's son Philip, 31, and Ralph's son Steven, 28, have joined the family firm. But already, Paul Reichmann declares himself pleased with the grand plan's progress. "We've basically achieved the transformation," he says. "We've created a solid, lasting base for the future."

Considering the high casualty rate among family firms whose founders can't let go, you couldn't ask for a more sensible strategy. But that base is not as solid as it could be, which raises the question of why the grand plan has been so badly implemented. Why pick Gulf and Walker? Why not something cheaper? Something with a lower profile?

The answer is that the Reichmanns acted out of habit. Those who think they have taken on too much debt, and find distasteful the apparent tax dodges inherent in every O&Y deal, forget that in real estate – the family's basic business – debt and taxes are the basic tools of the trade. The development game wouldn't exist if the players couldn't tolerate debt levels that would make executives in other industries dizzy. What makes the leverage tolerable is a tax regime that has always rewarded ambitious developers with generous depreciation allowances – so generous, in fact, that most developers pay little or no tax year after year. One must add to that the Reichmanns' patience, their abiding faith in commodities (such as oil and trees) and their enduring fear of inflation – all characteristics that are a product of their heritage.

Albert, Paul and Ralph Reichmann are the three youngest of five sons and a daughter born to Samuel and Renée Reichmann. Samuel, a strict Orthodox Jew who in his native Hungary had a large poultry business that exported eggs throughout Europe, fled to Vienna out of fear that the Russian Revolution would spread. Then he fled Vienna, where Albert, Paul and Ralph were born, after the Nazi invasion in 1938, and during the next two chaotic years stationed his family in Paris. A consequence of this nomadic existence is that the brothers each speak seven languages (English, French, German, Italian, Spanish, Hungarian and Hebrew). During this time they were inspired by the heroism of their mother, who stole behind enemy lines to give Spanish passports to Jews in Hungary. In Morocco, the family's last stop before Canada, Paul resisted the lure of the family business and became a social worker, setting up Talmudic study centres in Casablanca. But Paul, who today is chief strategist of O&Y, ultimately joined his father's merchant banking operation in Tangier and, like his brothers, learned the complexities of money and commodities trading. Beginning in 1954, the five brothers headed one by one to Canada. While the eldest sons, Edward and Louis, have since left Canada – for Israel and New York, respectively – the remaining boys and their mother have an unshakable affection for their adopted homeland. "We've been very happy and successful in Canada," Paul says.

From their father, who died in 1975, Albert, Paul and Ralph inherited an austere, no-nonsense style. In contrast to the flamboyant high-rollers who dominate the U.S.

Exhibit 1 WHAT THE REICHMANNS OWN

COMPANY	NATURE OF BUSINESS
Olympia & York Developments Ltd., *Toronto*	land developer
Trizec Corp. Ltd., *Calgary* (37%)	land developer
Cadillac Fairview Corp. Ltd., *Toronto* (26%)	land developer
O & Y Construction, *Toronto*	general contractor
Olympia Floor & Wall Tile Co., *Toronto*	building supplies
OlympiaNet, *Toronto*	electronic office networks
Block Brothers Industries Ltd., *Vancouver*	real estate broker
NRS National Real Estate Service, *Vancouver*	real estate broker
Gulf Canada Resources, *Calgary* (80%)*	oil and gas
Home Oil Co. Ltd., *Calgary* (34%)*	oil and gas
Consolidated Brinco Ltd., *Calgary* (16.5%)	oil, metals, asbestos
Interprovincial Pipe Line Ltd., *Toronto* (41%)*	oil pipeline
Consumers' Gas Co. Ltd., *Toronto* (80%)*	gas utility
Abitibi-Price Inc., *Toronto* (93%)*	forest products
Hiram Walker-Gooderham & Worts Ltd., *Toronto* (49%)	distiller
Trilon Financial Corp., *Toronto* (13%)	financial services

*Indirect interest

real estate scene, the Reichmann brothers dress conservatively (narrow-lapelled charcoal suits, white shirts and thin black ties), never curse, and shun company jets and limousines. In an industry notorious for cutting costs and scruples, the Reichmanns are renowned for erecting quality buildings on time (or faster) and on budget; when there have been cost over-runs, O&Y has absorbed them.

Samuel also instilled in his sons an instinct for seizing opportunities – no matter how daunting – and pursuing them in the faith that time will make even the riskiest bet pay off. The brothers started out in Canada in 1956 with a Toronto tile-supply business that operated out of 4,000 square feet of rented space. It employed $2^{1}/_{2}$ people, a salesman, a shipper and a part-time bookkeeper. Today that tile firm is one of North America's largest, with annual sales in the hundreds of millions of dollars; and the real estate operation it spawned controls an astounding 50 million square feet of prime office space in buildings dotted across the width and breadth of the continent. That's an amount roughly equal to all the office space in downtown Toronto.

The Reichmanns are used to the long haul. It took them four years – longer than they expected – to fully lease their 72-storey First Canadian Place in Toronto, which is Canada's tallest office building. Several years passed before rental prices quadrupled at the 10 Manhattan office towers they bought in the late 1970s, a deal that now makes them look like the sharpest operators since the Dutch bought Manhattan from the Indians for $24. And they had to endure a lingering loss on their investment in Abitibi before they emerged as winners in the newsprint game. The Gulf bid was more ambitious, and risky, than any of those ventures. But their own patience and Gulf's undeniable allure overpowered any reservations the Reichmanns might have had about making their first multibillion-dollar investment.

O&Y's diversification had begun in the late 1970s. With almost indiscriminate haste, the Reichmanns snapped up minority stakes in about a dozen, mostly resource, companies. By 1983, they were determined to buy something big: Their first deep plunge, Abitibi, was on the mend, and they had cash on their hands. Finally they settled on Gulf, the Canadian arm of Pittsburgh-based Gulf Oil Corp. They thought oil had hit bottom, and that Gulf was the perfect company on which to ride the upturn.

Like Abitibi, which is the world's largest newsprint maker, Gulf was big and classy. It was one of the four U.S.-owned multinationals that had long dominated the Canadian oil patch. And while it was the smallest of the four in sales, Gulf ranked second in return on equity because of its outsized commitment to exploration. Even better, it was for sale. Gulf represented the first opportunity to repatriate a major integrated oil company, and the Reichmanns' nationalist sentiments were roused. "We could easily have found something in the U.S. that produced more cash flow for the same purchase price," says Paul Reichmann. "But it was the wish of my brothers and our family to stay in Canada. We felt that O&Y Enterprises, being based in Canada, should have a major stake in the Canadian economy. Besides, we were encouraged in this by the Government, in fact, by several past governments."

Indeed, Prime Minister Brian Mulroney's Government, like the Liberal regime that preceded it, was all for Canadianization. But the Reichmanns' hope of winning friends in Ottawa faded when they made clear how they intended to finance the deal. O&Y was one of the few Canadian suitors with the resources to attempt a takeover this big, but even the Reichmanns couldn't digest Gulf without a lot of help. That much was clear when, in 1983, they rejected the price Gulf Oil was asking for its Canadian subsidiary.

Still, the Reichmanns persisted. When Gulf Oil was swallowed up by Chevron Corp. of San Francisco in 1984, Ottawa set the scene for another O&Y run at Gulf by demanding that Chevron at least temporarily put Gulf Canada on the block and make it available to Canadian bidders. Chevron's asking price was also steep, but this time Paul Reichmann wouldn't be deterred. In the spring of 1985, Reichmann unveiled probably the most complicated takeover proposal ever seen in Canada. First, Reichmann prevailed on no fewer than three partners – Petro-Canada, Ultramar Canada and Norcen Energy Resources – to take Gulf's marginally profitable refineries and gas stations off his hands, leaving O&Y with only Gulf's lucrative oil fields in Western Canada and its bounty of promising frontier exploration ventures. To bring O&Y's costs down still more, Reichmann sought Revenue Canada's approval of a pre-sale adjustment to Gulf's balance sheet that would restate the oil firm's assets at a much higher value. This would result in a $500 million or so tax break when those assets were depreciated after the takeover. Finally, Reichmann wanted Gulf, once in O&Y's possession, to buy O&Y's 93% interest in Abitibi for a startling $1.2 billion, or twice what the Reichmanns had paid for the paper company. In this way, Gulf would help pay for its own acquisition. All in all, it was a brilliantly choreographed plan, a $2.8-billion takeover in which the Reichmann's actual out-of-pocket expenses would be no more than a few hundred million dollars.

To Paul Reichmann's chagrin, however, many of the players missed or ignored their cues. In Ottawa, the Tories ran hot and cold on the idea of Petrocan's participation in the deal, approving it, then vetoing it, then approving it again. Similarly, Ottawa mandarins and their political bosses wavered before approving the tax break; their procrastination ensured that opposition MPs and indignant editorial writers got their licks in, and Paul Reichmann began to look painfully naive for having misjudged the incendiary nature of his legitimate but unprecedentedly huge Gulf tax break.

Much worse, though, he also miscalculated the direction that oil prices were heading. Sensing a parallel with real estate and paper, which had each responded nicely to his faith in them, Reichmann figured oil was about to break out of its steady, five-year decline. Instead, in the first three months of this year, oil prices crashed. By March, oil had lost two-thirds of its 1985 value, and was selling for $9 (U.S.) a barrel. Loaded with debt and orphaned from its network of gas stations (which continued to produce cash but had been sold off by the Reichmanns), Gulf suddenly looked more like a cripple than a cash cow.

If the Gulf deal was a bad one, it quickly begat another. The Reichmanns urgently needed a new source of cash to make up for the sudden shortfall at Gulf, and they settled on a known quantity – Walker. The Reichmanns had owned about 10% of the distiller's shares since 1981. And, according to their necessarily hasty assessment, Walker met their investment criteria. It generated a lot of cash, was not wholly a resources play, and was expected to submit meekly to the Reichmanns' entreaties. Unfortunately, only after O&Y launched its bid did the Reichmanns discover that Walker didn't fit this description.

Walker's profits were booming when the Reichmanns began plotting their takeover of the firm late last year. But that performance – a jump in profits of 30% to $319 million – belied imminent problems. Still famous as a distillery, Walker in fact got much of its revenue from its resource divisions, Home Oil Co. Ltd. and Consumers Gas Co. Ltd. And like Gulf, Home was devastated by the sudden oil crash. As for the indestructible earnings power the Reichmanns saw in distilling, they seemed unaware that the booze business has gone into serious decline. Liquor sales in North America have fallen for five years in a row; even Walker's flagship Canadian Club has been slipping steadily. The drunk-driving scare, weight-watching consumers and steadily mounting excise taxes have conspired against liquor. And Walker is not the industry's most aggressive marketer. Rival Gabor Jellinek, president of Joseph E. Seagram & Sons Inc., says, "Walker hasn't been a significant marketing force for years." Thus misery has been piled atop misery: Because of depressed liquor sales and lower oil prices, Walker's profits in the first nine months of 1986 have tumbled 40% to $160 million. So much for bailing out Gulf.

The ultimate irony, however, is that Walker management spent $35 million of the company's money trying to fight off the Reichmanns. "From my own experience trying to buy heavily into Walker in the late 1970s," says Andrew Sarlos, "I knew how protectionist the Walker board was. What the Reichmanns failed to understand is the self-destructive mentality of a management group that doesn't own the company." Walker's bosses expected a Reichmann victory would put them out on the street. Paul Reichmann attempted to ease their fears by bidding only for enough stock to boost O&Y's interest to 49%. But the Walker board, which had only months earlier watched the Reichmanns dismember Gulf and sell much of it to the four winds, was not reassured. "We knew the Reichmanns' game, they're asset buyers," says William Fatt, 35, who was vice-president and treasurer of Walker at the time. "Which meant Walker was finished as an independent company. We accepted that, but we were damned well going to hold out for the highest price."

Meanwhile, Paul Reichmann unwittingly did his best to reinforce Walker's fears. Word got out that he had entertained proposals from at least six prospective buyers of Walker's distillery, among them Seagram chief executive Edgar Bronfman. Reichmann says he only wanted to get a free appraisal of the distillery, but the tight-knit distilling industry took it as a signal that Walker's venerable booze business was indeed on the block and figured the prize would probably go to the mighty Seagram. Reichmann should have stomped all over this rumor but his natural reticence – and probably a desire to keep his options open about possibly selling parts of the distillery – kept his true intentions a mystery. And that spooked Walker. Admits O&Y Enterprises chief Mickey Cohen: "We didn't understand that relations between Seagram and Walker are like the Hatfields and the McCoys. That was ignorance on our part." Thus the Reichmanns, who abhor hostile takeovers, found themselves engaged in what would become the largest hostile takeover in Canadian history.

Using tactics more common to the U.S. takeover scene than to Canada's, Walker's board equipped its top eight executives with golden parachutes that guaranteed them three years' salary if they were laid off. Then the Walker directors drew up plans to scuttle the ship. If Paul Reichmann planned to dismember their firm, they would do it first. They decided they should be the ones to sell off the distillery, which last year accounted for 40% of Walker's profits. The buyer they found was British beverage conglomerate Allied-Lyons PLC, which makes Tetley teas, Baskin-Robbins ice cream and Harvey's sherries. The plan was for Walker management to use the proceeds of that sale to bid against the Reichmanns for the remainder of the company.

At a critical moment in the takeover, only minutes before the Walker board was about to approve that manoeuvre, Paul and Albert Reichmann attempted to intervene. In a hushed, hurried consultation with Walker CEO Albert (Bud) Downing and outside director Allen Lambert in a corridor outside the boardroom, the Reichmanns tried to make peace. They said they were preparing a sweeter offer for Walker shares, but somehow the message didn't get through. Downing and Lambert went back into the meeting, and proceeded with their plan. In the aftermath of that tense confrontation, the O&Y side cited everything from anti-Semitism to the Seagram factor as explanations of why Walker continued to resist the Reichmanns. But William Fatt has a less sinister explanation. He insists all Walker cared about was price, and Downing and Lambert did not return to the fateful board meeting with a better one. "Paul is exceptionally bright," says Fatt, "but when he's thinking hard he talks very softly and his accent becomes harder to make out. Meanwhile, Bud is hard of hearing, and Lambert is 75 years old. If the Reichmanns made a better offer, my guess is that it simply wasn't heard."

The Reichmanns probably should have pulled out then. But despite their stated aversion to hostile takeovers they were tenacious, as always, in pursuit of their prey. The result? The Reichmanns made three more bids, and what started off as a friendly $1.2-billion offer for 49% of Walker ended up as a $3.3-billion purchase of the entire company. Even then, the prized distillery appeared to have been irrevocably sold. Allied-Lyons pressed its claim by filing a breathtaking $9-billion lawsuit when the Reichmanns, once in control of Walker, threatened to renege on the deal Walker's previous management had made. After several months of haggling, the Reichmanns and Allied-Lyons finally reached a saw-off in September: Allied-Lyons would keep 51% control of Hiram Walker-Gooderham & Worts Ltd., the distillery, and O&Y would become a passive 49% investor. The Reichmanns made the best of a bad situation, again reducing their own costs by selling off Walker's Home Oil subsidiary for $1.1 billion. But in sum, the exercise was a failure since the whole point was to get complete control of the distillery. O&Y ended up only with access to 49% of the distillery's cash flow and mere observer status on its board.

The Gulf and Walker episodes raise serious questions about the vaunted management team the Reichmanns have assembled. There's no question these senior advisers – many of them plucked from City Hall in Toronto and New York – are invaluable in winning zoning approval for the often elephantine O&Y real estate projects, and then in bagging prestigious tenants to fill them. And without a doubt Mickey Cohen is a prize recruit: he has helped shape some of the most important federal policies of the past two decades, including the Anti-Inflation Board and the National Energy Program. But Cohen, who during his Ottawa days was unpopular with resentful MPs less powerful than himself, makes an easy target whenever the Reichmanns find themselves dealing with federal politicians, as happened with Gulf and Walker. Now those old enemies lie in wait for his mistakes, and Cohen made one when he seemed to suggest in a *Globe and Mail* interview last year that Brian Mulroney had personally endorsed the huge Gulf tax break. Before he had a chance to clarify this ill-advised comment, John Turner was using the interview as ammunition in attacks on the Reichmanns and Mulroney – someone the Reichmanns can hardly afford to cause trouble for.

Bringing former bureaucrats on board was intended to strengthen O&Y, not expose its weaknesses. But the hired help has not helped. They didn't guess, for instance, that Walker in its hour of crisis would turn to a kindred spirit – namely, Allied-Lyons, which for decades has distributed Walker products in Britain. There have been other mistakes, such as O&Y's bid for the huge Times Square redevelopment in New York: O&Y lost out on that one by dealing with a public-interest group that did not, as the O&Y team had believed, have City Hall's backing. And, while the Reichmanns' own integrity is not questioned, some people who've dealt with O&Y lately don't care much for their lieutenants. "O&Y's lawyers and some of the top non-family officers are pretty unpleasant to deal with," says William Fatt, who quit Walker after O&Y got control, and was quickly hired on at Morgan Bank of Canada. "They insulted me in the worst way possible before I left. In large meetings with all the staff present, they called me a conspirator and a stonewaller. Then they asked me to stay on. I said no thanks, I don't need this."

Indeed, there are a number of inconsistencies between the Reichmann image and reality. For instance, while O&Y accommodates the concerns of civic planners more than most developers, there is, after all, a steel hand inside its velvet glove. In 1980, O&Y angered city officials by evicting the prestigious Whitney Museum from one of its newly acquired Manhattan office towers. And the company is now threatening to knock down the former Toronto Stock Exchange, which it took over in 1983, unless zoning officials bow to its demands that it be permitted to erect a skyscraper on top of the historic building.

As well, some good intentions have gone by the boards. For instance, Paul Reichmann vowed that Gulf was intended to be debt-free. But the holding company into which Gulf was rolled, O&Y Enterprises, turns out to have $3.8 billion in debt. And the Reichmanns' stated goal of creating jobs for Canadians is on hold. In August, they shut down Gulf's uneconomic operations in the Beaufort, laying off 750 workers.

Still, you don't create an empire overnight without getting your hands dirty, and the Reichmanns have only proved they are not an exception. What is disturbing is that O&Y's fortunes are still riding mostly on the genius of Paul and Albert, 57 (Ralph, 53, heads the family tile business). The Reichmanns can hardly be expected to hand over the reins to their children this early; none has yet emerged as a potential leader. But the brothers haven't given much power to their professional recruits, either.

Paul Reichmann insists authority has been passed down to the ranks. "We are still hands-on, and we make the important decisions," Paul says. "But we've changed the structure so that we are out of day-to-day affairs, and managers carry on according to their capabilities and convictions." In reality, however, O&Y is still run much like a law firm. In place of the usual corporate hierarchy, executives are co-equals who cannot overrule each other, and will argue among themselves until Paul and Albert intervene. And the demands on Paul and Albert's time are tremendous. O&Y real estate executives in New York have been frustrated when trying to get information out of Toronto world headquarters, which for several months, according to a standing joke, was "enGulfed." During his frequent visits to New York, Paul spends most of his time holed up in a suite at the Waldorf Towers because whenever he appears in O&Y's offices he is immediately besieged by anxious minions.

When they are on the scene, they are welcome. "The Reichmanns command a lot of loyalty because they are great people to work with," says Estelle Nopolsky-Davis, national architectural sales manager at Olympia Floor and Wall Tile. "No matter how busy things get, they are always gentle and caring." Toronto architect Boris Zerafa says, "I'm always amazed that for people as busy and successful as they are, the Reichmanns find time to comment on every hall, lobby, ceiling and other detail. They haven't lost that touch. One senses it's because they're at the pinnacle of success that they have the confidence to be humble."

But that trademark humility is taking on a steely edge. These days, Paul Reichmann sometimes sounds more angry than hurt over his unfavorable reviews. "I can't keep 750 people with no work to do on Gulf's payroll, even if this becomes an issue," he says. "And while it is a pity so many people misunderstand the things we're trying to do, this will not stop us from doing them. If a businessman – or a scientist or an artist – has that attitude, he simply vegetates."

Far from vegetating, the Reichmanns are as ambitious as ever. Yet Paul denies that he's becoming addicted to takeovers. "We are still dedicated to real estate," he says. "We are constantly looking for real estate sites, and definitely not always on the lookout for takeovers." There likely *will* be more takeovers; it's just that, as Cohen says, "The Walker deal was an urgent thing. Now we can be more leisurely and contemplative about future acquisitions." O&Y's next target, Cadillac Fairview Corp. Ltd., is a prime example. The Reichmanns have been sizing up the giant Toronto developer since 1984, when they astutely snapped up about one-fifth of its shares on the stock market at a bargain price. Now that the controlling interest in Cadillac is up for grabs (the Montreal branch of the Bronfman family put its 51% stake on the auction block in August), the Reichmanns cannot lose. O&Y can choose to either sell its shares along with the Bronfmans – and as a result pocket a handsome capital gain – or use its sizable head start to buy control of Cadillac itself.

O&Y appears to have enough to digest already, without still more acquisitions. But O&Y has remarkable resources. Most estimates place the Reichmanns' assets at more than $20 billion, which puts O&Y in the same league as Canadian Pacific or Bell Canada Enterprises. O&Y's bulging property portfolio will produce still higher levels of rental income in the next few years, and most of the O&Y Enterprises divisions are performing well. Abitibi, for instance, turned a higher profit than any other forest products company last year. And 13%-owned Trilon Financial Corp., which the Reichmanns co-founded with Edward and Peter Bronfman in 1982, is one of the continent's most profitable financial conglomerates (it controls Royal Trustco and London Life).

Oil, of course, is the Reichmanns' biggest headache. But if, as many experts predict, oil reserves world-wide continue to dwindle, the Middle East will soon be in a position to hold the West to ransom again. If that happens, Gulf's awesome reserves in the Beaufort and in Hibernia off the Newfoundland coast – the two largest oil discoveries in recent Canadian history – will make the Reichmanns look like heroes again.

What the Reichmanns are attempting to create, in fact, is a perpetual, unstoppable money machine. In order to buy Abitibi and Gulf, the Reichmanns had to borrow against their real estate mother lode. That was easy enough to do since, like squares on a giant Monopoly board, the O&Y properties can be mortgaged and unmortgaged whenever the Reichmanns need cash. But future financial needs – such as the $5 billion or so it will take to bring Gulf's Beaufort and Hibernia reserves into production – will probably be handled by selling shares of O&Y Enterprises and each of its subsidiaries. That means the public, not the Reichmanns, will finance O&Y's next stage of growth. "We want to give Canadians an opportunity to invest in all these companies," says Cohen. Altruism? Well, sort of. "The idea is that we get to have our cake and eat it too." But the real beauty of this money machine is in the mutual back-scratching. When O&Y Developments wants to raise money for a new project, O&Y Enterprises could act as guarantor of the financing; with O&Y Enterprises' blue-chip backing, the development subsidiary would have no trouble obtaining cut-rate financing for its new real estate projects. And those projects, in turn, would eventually produce still more rental income for the Reichmanns to plow back into O&Y Enterprises.

Still, there is no escape from the nagging question of succession. The Reichmann children will inherit an astonishing legacy. But as global deal makers, they will be playing on a much bigger and tougher field than the one on which their fathers won so many victories. The Reichmanns have simply run out of opportunities in Canada. "We've done so much in Canada that we'd prefer now to buy in the U.S.," says Paul Reichmann. However, as they face the rigors of the global marketplace, the next generation must cope with their family's odd ambivalence.

The Reichmanns already are wedded to the real world. Every month, some of the best-known companies in North America – Merrill Lynch & Co., American Express Co. and the publishers of *The Wall Street Journal*, to name a few – make out a rent cheque to them. Every day, thousands of tipplers raise a snifter of Courvoisier in an unwitting salute to the family's ubiquity.

But the Reichmann children live their private lives apart from that world. They have been steeped in the spiritual traditions of their elders, and have stuck close to home, a quiet, upper-middle-class neighborhood in Toronto. And their elders, who have been known to employ bodyguards, are protective of them. "I've lost my privacy," says Paul Reichmann. "I don't want them to lose theirs."

"It must be said that the Reichmann children are a more appealing group than the second generation of most billionaire families," says Cohen. "They don't have dollar bills falling out of their pockets. They're sombre, serious kids who aren't running around in big cars collecting speeding tickets. I think they have fun, but they are different." Heirs to their parents' reserve and introspection, they may be destined to struggle even more awkwardly with directing a work force that is 40,000 strong, and growing. "When they leave the office at night, it's not only that the public doesn't see the Reichmanns," says Cohen. "*I* don't see them – not at parties, movies or the theatre. They are wrapped in a small, tight world of family and a few friends, strangers in a strange land who don't often venture into the secular world."

For all the recent troubles he has seen, Paul Reichmann doesn't show the strain. There are other interests, outside of business, that mean more to him. "Business is not the purpose of life," he says. "I never want to be subservient to my wealth, to have it running my life instead of the other way around. The things I'm proudest of are things I do outside business." Reichmann refuses to elaborate but his reference is to the religious studies and charitable works to which he has been drawn all his life. His mother has always devoted herself to those pursuits. And while Paul stayed with the business, he has hardly deserted the faith. "Some people lose themselves in

TV or a squash game after a hard day at work," says an O&Y executive. "The Reichmanns do that by reading the Torah. It's their release."

Paul abided by his father's wishes, and helped propel the business to heights Samuel couldn't have dreamed of, but he kept a pact with himself. "The most intense part of my life was long ago," he says, "in the eight years before I turned 25. In those years, my most formative, I worked day and night on my scripture studies and in social education, setting up schools. If I have succeeded since then, I think it is because I vowed to challenge the belief that, when you hunger for something, you have to compromise. I was not going to be enslaved by the popular image of the entrepreneur who is consumed with his success." Reichmann believes he has kept his pact. "To the extent that our business accomplishments do matter," says Paul, "I am proud our family has been at the forefront of major undertakings, such as the largest development projects in the world, and yet has adhered to principles and has not compromised."

Still, there has been a break with past practice. Says Andrew Sarlos: "If the Reichmanns' reputation has suffered, it is because in the last year and a half they have been buying assets rather than building them. The Reichmanns are Canada's most important entrepreneurs because they have beautified cities and created wealth. To restore that image, they must divert their energies away from acquiring things back to creating. With their money, they have the power to increase employment, finance technological advances, lead Canada to energy self-sufficiency . . . it's almost endless."

The Reichmanns do have an urge to build, and "to be seen to be doing the right thing," Paul Reichmann says. "I'm not running for elected office, but of course it matters what people think." External criticism is very painful because, even when O&Y is praised, Reichmann wonders if he is guilty of temporal excess. To reconcile this internal conflict between secular and spiritual urges, Reichmann cites the great 12th-century Spanish rabbi, Maimonides. "Maimonides preferred that his students pursue the intellectual rather than the material, but some of his students asked him, 'Who then shall develop the material world?' And Maimonides said, 'Don't worry, there are enough crazies out there who will take care of that.'" Reichmann pauses and grins broadly. "I'm probably one of the crazies."

Another Spanish-born philosopher, George Santayana, may provide an instructive corollary. "Fanaticism," he said, "consists of redoubling your efforts when you have forgotten your aim." If not fanatical, the Reichmanns lately have been frantic, and largely to no avail. They are said to be worth about $6 billion, free and clear of debt. It boggles the mind. Not the money, but what a family with unswerving morals *and* street-smarts might do with it.

QUESTIONS

1. Describe how the Reichmanns made their fortune.
2. How did they conceptualize business?
3. What are the weaknesses of their current thinking about their business?
4. How can their executives help?
5. Apply Isenberg's ideas developed in "How Senior Managers Think" to the Reichmanns' business problems.

EXERCISES

A SURVEY OF VALUES

In order for young managers to be successful, they must understand the traits which their superiors prize most highly and the values which motivate the actions of modern executives. The following exercise reviews the findings of the Posner and Schmidt research into managerial values. The review is followed by questions which encourage you to become conscious of important organizational values.

It is a characteristic of management that it requires its practitioners to choose from multiple and possibly conflicting courses of action if the objectives of the firm are to be realized. Under such conditions more than purely rational analysis is required; the manager must draw upon his own experiences and biases – his values – to guide him. It is only logical therefore that the actions of the corporation are predicated to a large extent by these values.

Posner and Schmidt have polled 6,000 managers with the express intent of pinpointing those values most widespread among them. Participants were given a "menu" of seven commonly recognized organizational objectives and asked to indicate their importance. Gender, education, salary, and age of each respondent were also recorded and correlated with the survey data.

The results show a marked preference for "effectiveness" as the single most important goal, although just what constitutes "effectiveness" is, as the authors admit, open to subjective interpretation (this faddish choice of language is the study's most obvious flaw). High productivity, leadership, high morale, reputation, and efficiency were all of secondary, but by no means minor, importance. Ranked in the third echelon of importance were profit maximization, organizational growth and stability. Profit maximization, note the authors, was the only goal exhibiting any variance in importance: predictably, executives showed the strongest concern for it, although none ranked it highly. Perhaps the most significant finding of all was the consistency of the rankings; a result that prompts Posner and Schmidt to speculate on the existence of a managerial "psyche."

The questions of loyalty and responsibility were also probed by the authors' study. Asked to indicate the importance of various groups having an interest in the corporation's affairs, most executives nominate the customers as the most important. Supervisors, on the other hand, clearly favored "myself"; the second most popular selection of both middle managers and executives. This consistent (and defiantly selfish) choice elicits the following comment from the authors: "Perhaps it is more than just stylish to pay attention to one's self interests; it may be a realistic part of the managerial orientation." Equally noteworthy is the preference for "general public" over "stockholders." This contradicts the common supposition that North American managers are first and foremost answerable to the corporation's owners. In fact, it is evidence of the effect of widespread dilution of ownership of many American corporations.

Personal qualities are also a frequent subject of value judgments on the part of managers. Survey respondents, when queried on the most desirable traits in their peers answered, "integrity," "cooperation" and "competency." Integrity was also the most valued characteristic of both superiors and subordinates, with "leadership" and "determination" the second choices, respectively. That integrity and competence should be so consistently and highly valued comes as no surprise to the authors, who point out that both are essential to "doing a good job"; managers of all ranks and gender abhor a laggard it seems. Again it is not the results per se but their consistency that surprises. The 24% that favored integrity was invariant with respect to both rank and gender — indication once again of a distinctive cast of mind.

As might be expected, Posner and Schmidt's survey revealed that personal values become more closely aligned with those of the corporation the longer a manager has been a part of it. Survey data reveals that only 20% of executives ever felt any need to compromise their own beliefs in favour of the corporation, whereas the figures for middle management and supervisors were 27% and 41%, respectively. Once again, however, the authors' phraseology gives way to ambiguity, for in the very next question (is pressure to conform to organizational standards relatively weak or strong?) there were no discernible differences in response between the three levels of management. The only evident correlation was with gender: 77% of women felt a strong pressure to conform versus 60% of men. The results are likely an outcome of the fact that women are still very much a minority in management; as such the pressure for conformity will inevitably be higher.

In an effort to reproduce and update the results of a survey conducted twenty years ago by Raymond Baumhart, a portion of Posner and Schmidt's study is devoted to the pressures that induce managers to make unethical decisions. By and large, Baumhart's findings were confirmed: the single most important influence on managerial ethics was the behavior of superiors. Both male and female managers displayed a marked tendency to model their own conduct on that of their superiors. When finding themselves in an ethical dilemma, managers of all levels chose, in the main, to consult colleagues, their spouses, or their superiors. The latter choice declines in popularity as the manager ascends in the ranks; it is replaced (apparently) by self-reliance. Again the influence of superiors is noteworthy. The combined popularity of peers and superiors as a source of reference suggests the mechanism by which corporate values evolve and are maintained.

The authors are reluctant to draw any more than tentative conclusions from their results. The relative unimportance of stockholders and profit maximization, and the regard given to customers are at odds with the picture of North American managers given by the popular press. There is little evidence of the disdain for customers implied by the authors of *In Search of Excellence*, for example.

Despite the influence of the "me decade" and the self-indulgence of the sixties, managers are under just as much pressure to align their values with those of the organization as they were twenty years ago, and therefore the seeds of ethical conflict are ever present. It is no coincidence then that integrity is the most highly prized trait of colleagues and subordinates alike. Managers are still heavily reliant on a social group for ethical judgement and value reinforcement, whether that group be the corporation itself or some subset thereof. Ethics are a matter for relative judgement, not absolute.

References

Barry Z. Posner and Warren H. Schmidt (Spring 1984) "Values and the American Manager: An Update." *California Management Review*, Volume XXVI, Number 3, pp. 202–216.

QUESTIONS

Defining Your Values and Your Organization's Values

1. For your organization rank these objectives (1 to 8).
   - Productivity
   - Quality
   - Morale
   - Reputation
   - Profit Maximization
   - Growth
   - Stability
   - Effectiveness

2. Rank these constituencies for your organization (1 to 6).
   - Management
   - Customers
   - Stockholders
   - General Public
   - Workers
   - Supervisors

3. Underline the two most desirable traits for managers in your organization.
   - Leadership
   - Determination
   - Competency
   - Cooperation
   - Integrity

4. Define the pressure to conform.

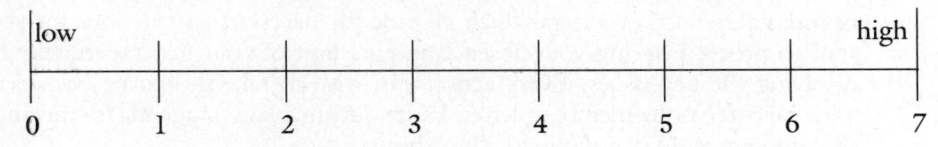

   ```
   low                                                                high
   |----+----+----+----+----+----+----|
   0    1    2    3    4    5    6    7
   ```

5. Does your job require you to act unethically?

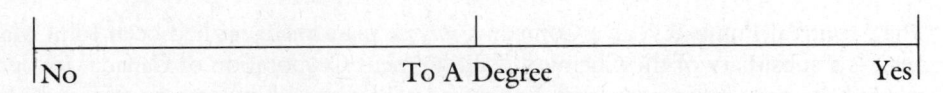

   ```
   |--------------------|--------------------|
   No                 To A Degree           Yes
   ```

6. Check your answers against the Posner and Schmidt survey.

IN-BASKET EXERCISE: THE MONTRÉAL PUMP AND VALVE COMPANY*

R.E. Dutton
J. Bruce Prince
Luke Novelli

Effective management requires a number of skills. Being able to size up a new situation, determine subordinates' skills and abilities as well as their relationships with one another, and identify key organizational problems is certainly a key managerial skill. This exercise puts you in the role of a new plant manager who must do all of these things with very limited information. It tests your managerial savvy and sets the stage for a number of additional exercises throughout the text.

INSTRUCTIONS

After setting aside an uninterrupted period of time, analyze the in-basket material (the background material and items 1 through 12 that follow) and complete one of the options below. The three options are:

A. Draw an organizational chart, identify three to four top priority issues which need to be resolved and be prepared to discuss and defend your points. (Time required: one and a half hours)

B. Do option A, and also develop a specific action strategy for resolving the priority issues. (Time required: two hours)

C. Do option A and B, plus take notes about the issues or questions which *each* piece of correspondence suggests. Also, prepare (1) a written summary of your action strategy and the priority issues which need to be resolved, and (2) drafts of internal memos or letters which provide the necessary instructions for your staff to proceed during your absence and are part of your general strategy for resolving the key issues. Every action you wish to take should be backed up with a written note, memo, or letter. Write out any plans or agenda for meetings or conferences. (Time required: three hours)

BACKGROUND INFORMATION

The Montréal Pump & Valve Company, whose plant manager had been John Manners, is a subsidiary of the Chemical & Equipment Corporation of Canada. Its operations have been quite successful. Beginning with a capital investment of slightly less

---

* Adapted by J. Bruce Prince and Luke Novelli from "The Tampa Pump & Valve Company" exercise by R.E. Dutton. Reprinted by permission of R.E. Dutton.

than $750,000 shortly after the end of World War II, its capital investment today is in excess of $65,000,000. The Montréal Pump & Valve Company possesses a newly constructed office building and a manufacturing and assembly plant. There are two sales outlets – one in Montréal and one in Toronto.

The company, excluding top management, is currently staffed with 60 engineers and 32 technicians. Approximately 1000 persons are employed in the production department, working two 40-hour shifts a week.

Joan O'Malley is the general superintendent in charge of production. All valve and pump assemblies, as well as components that are not purchased, are manufactured and assembled in the production department according to job and design specifications. These are either shipped to various sites and locations according to orders, or they are stored in the company's two warehouses in Toronto and Montréal. Centralized production and planning enables the company to maintain rigid production and quality controls over all units that become a part of completed products. In addition, carefully planned production and shipping schedules reduce the amount of time that completed units must be stored at receiving stations. Thus, shipping costs are reduced and the company is better able to insure that contracted completion dates are met.

The research and development division, currently under the direction of Tom Everts, has grown from two engineers to its present size of 30 engineers and 12 technicians and draftsmen. Partly because of the plant manager's intense interest in this division, 10 percent of the company's profits are allocated to research and development. The research staff recently developed a less expensive and longer lasting rust inhibitor than that previously manufactured. New rotary arc-welding units for the plant have also been developed, as has a new method for testing the strength and quality of welded unions. Also, the division was responsible for the design of expansion joints which are formed and assembled in the company's plant, ready for immediate installation at construction sites.

In addition to being the controller, Bill Marshall is general counsel for the plant. A staff of two attorneys and three legal assistants report directly to him, as does the chief accountant and his staff. The accounting department employs approximately 15 people.

The industrial and employee relations department, under A.C. Cushwell, has a staff of approximately fifteen people. Moreover, a total of 82 employees are employed in the marketing department, which is headed by James Barber.

On April 12, John Manners suffered a severe heart attack and died. It had been noticed that he appeared tired and overworked recently. At this time, Richard (or Rachel) West was transferred from the Ottawa Pump and Valve Plant, which is a slightly smaller subsidiary of the Chemical & Equipment Corporation of Canada, to fill the position.

Today is Sunday, April 14, 1988. West has just come into the office for the first time, at 6:45 p.m. and must leave in time to catch the 10:00 p.m. plane for Caracas, Venezuela, for an important meeting. West will not be back until next Monday, April 23. Pearl Powell, who was secretary to John Manners before he died, will be continuing as West's secretary.

The accompanying materials (Items 1-12) were left in Manner's in-basket by Pearl Powell. You are to assume the role of Richard or Rachel West and go through the entire packet of materials. The day is Sunday, April 14, and the time is 6:45 p.m. You cannot call on anyone for assistance. The telephone switchboard is not operating. You must work with the materials at hand. You will be out of the office from 9:45 tonight until Monday, April 23.

Remember you are not to exceed the time period indicated in the option you have been assigned. Also, remember that you cannot contact anyone by phone or alter your trip plans in any way. You must be out of town until Monday, April 23.

CORRESPONDENCE ITEMS

Item 1A

```
                                          April 13, 1988

     Office Memorandum

     TO:        R. West

     FR:        Pearl Powell

     Subject:   SAM Presentation (see Attached)

     Mr./Ms. West:

          Just a note to let you know that Mr. Manners
     did nothing toward developing the program scheduled
     April 25, except to send the title to Mr. Johnson
     via phone.  The title was announced to the members
     some time ago.  I don't think Mr. Manners discussed
     the matter with any of the department heads.

                            Pearl
```

Item 1B

```
         THE SOCIETY FOR THE ADVANCEMENT OF MANAGEMENT
                        Hull Chapter
                        P.O. Box 9106
                        Hull, Quebec

                                      April 4, 1988

     Mr. John Manners
     Plant Manager
     Montréal Pump & Valve Company
     Montréal, Quebec   H3G 1M8

     Dear John:

          This is a reminder that we are counting on
     you and on the Montréal Pump & Valve Company to
     provide us with the three-hour evening program for
     our meeting April 25.

          I know you and your representatives will
     provide a stimulating and worthwhile program.  The
     title of the program you are to present, "The
     Image of Today's Executive," sounds very interest-
     ing and already the dinner and program is a "sell-
     out."  Therefore, you can look forward to a full
     house on the night of your presentation.

          Could you prepare a brief outline of the
     program and text of any speeches that will be
     presented indicating who will present them.  In
     this way we can go ahead with the programs and
     press releases.

          We are all looking forward to seeing you
     then.

                              Best regards,

                              Paul

                              Paul Johnson, Secretary
                              Hull Chapter
                              Society for the
                              Advancement of Management


     PJ:am
```

Item 2

<u>P E R S O N A L</u>

April 10, 1988

<u>OFFICE MEMORANDUM</u>

TO: John Manners

FROM: A.C. Cushwell, Industrial and Employee Relations

SUBJECT: Frank Batt

    I have heard through the grapevine and "unimpeachable" sources that Frank Batt has been looking around and has had an outside job offer on which he is going to give a firm answer next week. I don't think anyone else knows this yet. I just happened to run across it. I understand that he has been offered more money than we can offer him now based on present wage and salary policy. As you know, Batt has only been with the company a short time and is already making somewhat more than others at his rank. This presents a problem which needs to be ironed out. I am afraid I mentioned the possibility of just such a situation as this when you instituted the plan last November. Perhaps we need to reconsider some of the aspects of your plan before we make offers to June graduates.

    I know that you and Everts feel that Frank is one of the most valuable men in research and development, and I thought I would let you know about this for what ever action you want to take.

                                    A.C. Cushwell

Item 3

April 7, 1988

OFFICE MEMORANDUM

TO: John Manners

FROM: A.C. Cushwell, Industrial and Employee Relations

SUBJECT: Testing Program

You recently suggested that we institute a testing program for hiring secretarial and clerical personnel. The following are some suggested tests and other criteria that we might want to consider. Do you have any further suggestions for types of tests or other hiring procedures which we might want to look into before we finalize a program?

  (1) Clerical Personnel:

   (a) Whitney General Clerical Survey (includes measures on spelling, arithmetic, alphabetizing, and general aptitude).

   (b) Mann-Watson Typing Test.

   (c) Age to 40.

  (2) Secretarial Personnel:

   (a) Whitney General Clerical Survey

   (b) Mann-Watson Typing Test

   (c) Collins Shorthand Skill Inventory (via recording).

   (d) High School Diploma.

   (e) Age to 40.

A.C. Cushwell

Item 4

April 10, 1988

OFFICE MEMORANDUM

TO: John Manners

FROM: Bill Marshall

SUBJECT: Termination of Robert Roberts, Employee #6897

This is a summary of my reasons for terminating Robert Roberts. As you know, Mr. Roberts was employed as a legal assistant on March 4, 1986. For almost two years he has been working for us on a full-time basis while attending law school at night. He has continually been a source of irritation to those who have been working closely with him. The problem in general has been one of overstepping his authority. He has frequently been involved in controversies with the legal staff over problems with which we felt he was not adequately prepared to deal nor which were any of his concern since they did not involve his own work assignments. In general, he did an adequate job on the work he was assigned but many of the staff felt that he was not putting forth a full effort because he seemed to have a lot of free time which he spent in the coffee bar or in conversations with others in the department. The incident that caused his termination took place about three days before his termination. He was told to contact a party concerning a pending contract. All he was to do was to secure the necessary signatures from the other party. The attorney handling the contract for our company in the particular case was George Slavin. Mr. Roberts, instead of simply securing signatures, evidently discussed the contract with the outside party, recommending changes, and in general so disrupted proceedings that now the whole contract is in question. After the customer contacted George, George immediately discussed the occurrence with me, and we felt that the incident was serious enough to warrant dismissal.

Bill

Item 5

```
                              April 6, 1988

OFFICE MEMORANDUM

TO:      John Manners

FROM:    James Barber

SUBJECT: Sales Promotion of Rust Inhibitor

     As you know, we are moving into our campaign
to push the new rust inhibitor.  I would like to
have your permission to set up a contest among our
sales representatives with a trip to Hawaii for
the sales representative who sells the highest
dollar volume in the next six-month period.  I
want to make the prize good enough to tempt the
sales force.

                              Jim
```

Item 6

```
                              April 11, 1988

OFFICE MEMORANDUM

TO:      John Manners

FROM:    A.C. Cushwell

SUBJECT: Employment of John Jones, Engineer

     I would like to bring you up to date on my
feelings concerning the engineer, John Jones, whom
Everts wishes to employ.  Everts is from Calgary,
and I don't think that he fully understands the
morale problems we would have if we hired a black
engineer who would have supervision over several
white assistants.  I realize that we are going to
have to protect our interests in government
contracts, but I think we can find a better way to
do so than starting at this level.  I would
suggest that you talk with Everts about this
problem and the possible complications that could
arise.

                              A.C. Cushwell
```

Item 7

> April 9, 1988
>
> OFFICE MEMORANDUM
>
> TO: John Manners
>
> FROM: Bill Marshall
>
> SUBJECT: Annual Budget Requests
>
>   We are late in turning in our budget proposal to the Chemical and Equipment Company of Canada for the next fiscal year since the report from R & D is still not in. All other department heads have turned in sound budgets which, if approved, should greatly facilitate the cutting of costs next year. Can you do something to speed up action?
>
>   Bill Marshall

Item 8

> April 6, 1988
>
> OFFICE MEMORANDUM
>
> TO: John Manners
>
> FROM: Bill Marshall
>
> SUBJECT: Coffee Breaks
>
>   This morning I timed a number of people who took 40 minutes standing in line and drinking their coffee. These people were mainly from the production and research departments. I am able to control this in my department, and I feel you should see that this matter is taken care of by the heads of the other departments. I estimate that the waste amounts to 125,000 man hours (approximately $500.00) a year.
>
>   Bill

Item 9

April 9, 1988

OFFICE MEMORANDUM

TO: John Manners

FROM: Tom Everts

SUBJECT: Allocations for Research

This department has been successful in developing an efficient method for extracting certain basic compounds from slag and other similar by-products that are currently classified as waste by a large number of chemical plants within this area.

It is my recommendation that this company take every step necessary to develop this extraction method commercially. I have brought this matter to Bill Marshall's attention on two separate occasions, requesting that the necessary funds be allocated to fully develop this program. I have been advised by him both times that the funds could not possibly be made available within the next fiscal year. He has also indicated that we should de-emphasize research in the chemical area, since this is an unnecessary duplication of functions with the Ottawa and Calgary plants.

It is my opinion that this company should capitalize on its advantageous position now, before our competitors are able to perfect a similar method.

The above is for your consideration and recommendation.

Tom Everts

cc: Mr. O.J. Thompson, Vice-President
Research & Development

Item 10

```
          AMERICAN FEDERATION OF FOUNDRY WORKERS
                        Local 801
                    Montréal, Quebec

                                              April 6, 1988

Mr. John Manners, Manager
Montréal Pump & Valve Company
Montréal, Quebec H3G 1M8

Dear Sir:

     On several recent occasions, I have noticed
that you and your staff have employed your company
newspaper as a vehicle for undermining the present
union administration.

     In addition, a series of supervisory bulle-
tins have been circulated that were designed to
cause supervisory personnel to influence the
thinking of union members in the forthcoming union
election.  I am also well aware of your "support"
for Jessie Sims and others, who have been more
than sympathetic towards company management.

     As you know, such behavior as I have
described is in direct violation of labor-
management legislation, as well as being a
violation of Article 21 of our contract with your
company.  I am sure that you are also aware of the
negative impact the filing of a charge of unfair
management practices could have on future
elections and negotiations.

     I trust such action will not become necessary
and that you will take steps to prevent any further
discrimination against this administration.

                              Sincerely yours,

                              R.L. Loper

                              R.L. Loper, President
                              A.F.F.W., Local 801

RLL:jg

cc:  A.C. Cushwell
```

Item 11

April 10, 1988

OFFICE MEMORANDUM

TO: John Manners

FROM: Joan O'Malley

SUBJECT: Quality Control

    The marketing department has put pressure on us to increase production for the next two months so that promised deliveries can be made. At the present time we cannot increase production without some risk in terms of quality. The problem is that marketing does not check with us before committing us to specific delivery dates. This problem has come up before, but nothing has been done. Could I meet with you in the near future to discuss this situation?

                              Joan

Item 12

```
OFFICE MEMORANDUM

TO:      John Manners

FROM:    Joan O'Malley

SUBJECT: Pay rate for maintenance men who worked
         on the Canadian National Day of Mourning.

    It was necessary for me to bring in seven
maintenance men last Monday in spite of your
order that we would observe the National Day of
Mourning due to the sudden death of Prime Minister
Harris.

    The question has arisen as to whether these
men should be paid straight time for the work or
double time, which is customary for work during
holidays. I also had 40 people on vacation during
this period. Ordinarily, when a legal holiday
falls during their vacation they are given an
extra day. Since this was an unusual situation I
am not sure how to handle it and would like your
recommendation.

                         Joan
```

II
EXECUTIVE BEHAVIOR

READINGS

MACGREGOR*
Arthur Elliot Carlisle

No question about it – some managers are better organized then others, but how often have you run into a really well organized manager – I mean *really* well organized?

MacGregor, who at the time was manager of one of the largest refineries in the country, was the last of more than 100 managers I interviewed in the course of the study. Although the interview had been scheduled in advance, the exact time had been left open; I was to call MacGregor at his office early in the week that I would be in the vicinity and set up a specific date and time.

Here's how that phone call went: The switchboard operator answered with the name of the refinery. When I asked for MacGregor's office, a male voice almost instantly said, "Hello." I then asked for MacGregor, whereupon the voice responded, "This is he." I should have recognized at once that this was no ordinary manager; he answered his own phone instantly, as though he had been waiting for it to ring. To my question about when it would be convenient for me to come see him, he replied, "Anytime." I said, "Would today be all right?" His response was, "Today, tomorrow, or Wednesday, would be O.K.; or you could come Thursday, except don't come between 10:00 a.m. and noon; or you could come Friday or next week – anytime." I replied feebly, "I just want to fit in with your plans." Then he said, "You are just not getting the message; it makes no difference to me when you come. I have nothing on the books except to play golf and see you. Come in anytime – I don't have to be notified in advance, so I'll be seeing you one of these days," and he then hung up. I was dumbfounded. Here was a highly placed executive with apparently nothing to do except play golf and talk to visitors.

I took MacGregor at his word and drove over immediately to see him without any further announcement of my visit.

MACGREGOR'S MODUS OPERANDI

"Do you hold regular meetings with your subordinates?" I asked.

"Yes, I do," he replied.

"How often?" I asked.

"Once a week, on Thursdays, between 10:00 a.m. and noon; that's why I couldn't see you then," was his response.

"What sorts of things do you discuss?" I queried, following my interview guide.

"My subordinates tell me about the decisions they've made during the past week," he explained.

"Then you believe in participative decision making," I commented.

"No – as a matter of fact, I don't," said MacGregor.

"Then why hold the meetings?" I asked. "Why not just tell your people about the operating decisions you've made and let them know how to carry them out?"

---

* Reprinted, by permission of the publisher, from "MacGregor," Arthur Elliot Carlisle, ORGANIZATIONAL DYNAMICS, Summer 1976, pp. 50–55, © 1976 American Management Association, New York. All rights reserved.

"Oh, I don't make their decisions for them and I just don't believe in participating in the decisions they should be making, either; we hold the weekly meeting so that I can keep informed on what they're doing and how. The meeting also gives me a chance to appraise their technical and managerial abilities," he explained. "I used to make all the operating decisions myself; but I quit doing that a few years ago when I discovered my golf game was going to hell because I didn't have enough time to practise. Now that I've quit making other people's decisions, my game is back where it should be."

"You don't make operating decisions any more?" I asked in astonishment.

"No," he replied. Sensing my incredulity, he added, "Obviously you don't believe me. Why not ask one of my subordinates? Which one do you want to talk to?"

SUBORDINATES' VIEWS OF MACGREGOR

I walked over to Johnson's unit and found him to be in his early thirties. After a couple of minutes of casual conversation, I discovered that MacGregor and all eight of his subordinates were chemical engineers. Johnson said, "I suppose MacGregor gave you that bit about his not making decisions, didn't he? That man is a gas."

"It isn't true though, is it? He does make decisions, doesn't he?" I asked.

"No, he doesn't; everything he told you is true. He simply decided not to get involved in decisions that his subordinates are being paid to make. So he stopped making them, and they tell me he plays a lot of golf in the time he saves," said Johnson.

Then I asked Johnson whether he tried to get MacGregor to make a decision and his response was:

"Only once. I had been on the job for only about a week when I ran into an operating problem I couldn't solve, so I phoned MacGregor. He answered the phone with that sleepy 'Hello' of his. I told him who I was and that I had a problem. His response was instantaneous: 'Good, that's what you're being paid to do, solve problems,' and then he hung up. I was dumbfounded. I didn't really know any of the people I was working with, so because I didn't think I had any other alternative, I called him back, got the same sleepy 'Hello,' and again identified myself. He replied sharply, 'I thought I told you that you were paid to solve problems. Do you think that I should do your job as well as my own?' When I insisted on seeing him about my problem, he answered, 'I don't know how you expect me to help you. You have a technical problem and I don't go into the refinery any more; I used to, but my shirts kept getting dirty from the visits and my wife doesn't like washing all the grime out of them, so I pretty much stick in my office. Ask one of the older men. They're all in touch with what goes on out there.'

"I didn't know which one to consult, so I insisted again on seeing him. He finally agreed – grudgingly – to see me right away, so I went over to his office and there he was in his characteristic looking-out-the-window posture. When I sat down, he started the dirty-shirt routine – but when he saw that I was determined to involve him in my problems, he sat down on the sofa in front of his coffee table and, pen in hand, prepared to write on a pad of paper. He asked me to state precisely what the problem was and he wrote down exactly what I said. Then he asked what the conditions for its solution were. I replied that I didn't know what he meant by that question. His response was, 'If you don't know what conditions have to be satisfied for a solution to be reached, how do you know when you've solved the problem?' I told him I'd never thought of approaching a problem that way and he replied, 'Then you'd better start. I'll work through this one with you *this* time, but don't expect me to do your problem solving for you because that's *your* job, not mine.'

"I stumbled through the conditions that would have to be satisfied by the solution. Then he asked me what alternative approaches I could think of. I gave him the first one I could think of – let's call it X – and he wrote it down and asked me what would happen if I did X. I replied with my answer – let's call it A. Then he asked me how A compared with the conditions I had established for the solution of the problem. I replied that it did not meet them. MacGregor told me that I'd have to think of another. I came up with Y, which I said would yield result B, and this still fell short of the solution conditions. After more prodding from MacGregor, I came up with Z, which I said would have C as a result; although this clearly came a lot closer to the conditions I had established for the solution than any of the others I'd suggested, it still did not satisfy all of them. MacGregor then asked me if I could combine any of the approaches I'd suggested. I replied I could do X and Z and then saw that the resultant A plus C would indeed satisfy all the solution conditions I had set up previously. When I thanked MacGregor, he replied, 'What for? Get the hell out of my office; you could have done that bit of problem solving perfectly well without wasting my time. Next time you really can't solve a problem on your own, ask the Thursday man and tell me about it at the Thursday meeting.'"

I asked Johnson about Mr. MacGregor's reference to the Thursday man.

"He's the guy who runs the Thursday meeting when MacGregor is away from the plant. I'm the Thursday man now. My predecessor left here about two months ago."

"Where did he go? Did he quit the company?" I asked.

"God, no. He got a refinery of his own."

HEAD-OFFICE ASSESSMENT OF MACGREGOR

By the time I had finished with Johnson and Peterson, it was time for lunch. I decided I'd go downtown and stop in at the head office to try to find out their assessment of MacGregor and his operation. I visited the operations chief for the corporation. I had wanted to thank him for his willingness to go along with my study, anyway. When I told him I had met MacGregor, his immediate response was, "Isn't he a gas?" I muttered something about having heard that comment before and asked him about the efficiency of MacGregor's operation in comparison with that of other refineries in the corporation. His response was instantaneous, "Oh, MacGregor has by far the most efficient producing unit."

"Is that because he has the newest equipment?" I asked.

"No. As a matter of fact he has the oldest in the corporation. His was the first refinery we built."

"Does MacGregor have a lot of turnover among his subordinates?"

"A great deal," he replied.

Thinking I had found a chink in the MacGregor armor, I asked, "What happens to them; can't they take his system?"

"On the contrary," said the operations chief. "Most of them go on to assignments as refinery managers. After all, under MacGregor's method of supervision, they are used to working on their own."

PERSPECTIVE ON MACGREGOR'S USE OF TIME

... In his informational role, MacGregor monitored the output of the management information system he had devised, but he did so after the same information had been reviewed by his subordinates. The dissemination function was partly achieved by the management information system and partly through the joint review of managerial decisions conducted at the Thursday morning meetings. As spokesman for his unit, he was easily accessible to individuals inside and outside the corporation.

What sets MacGregor apart from other managers is that he had consciously thought out his role as an upper-level administrator. He did not blindly adopt the methods of his predecessor;

neither did he merely adapt the *modus operandi* he had previously found reasonably successful to the greater demands of running a larger unit. Rather, MacGregor reflected on what the key responsibilities of the executive in charge of a large operating facility really are and concluded that they involve being well informed on changes occurring in the environment that might have an impact on his operation and determining how best to adjust operations to benefit from these changes. At the same time, MacGregor recognized that profitable operations must be carried out in the here-and-now and that a supply of qualified subordinates must be developed for the future.

THE FIRST-LINE SUPERVISOR: PHASING OUT OR HERE TO STAY?*

Steven Kerr
Kenneth D. Hill
Laurie Broedling

*There's going to be a vacancy
Above you later on,
Some day you'll find the foreman
Or the superintendent gone.
And are you growing big enough
When this shall be the case
To quit the post you're holding now
To step into his place?*[1]

Peter Drucker (1983) has recently noted that "no job is going to change more in the next decade than that of the first-line supervisor. And few people in the work force are less prepared for the changes and less likely to welcome them."[2] In fact, the first-line supervisory position has generally been acknowledged to be problematic by researchers, trainers, and managers. Although this awareness is not new, a number of changes in the organizational environment are lending particular credence to Drucker's position. These changes include: the increasing education level of the work force, with concomitant increases in level of expectations about work outcomes; computer automation of the workplace and the resultant impact on job design and employment; growing governmental intervention in the workplace; and other influences such as union and staff involvement with first-line supervision. These changes, though gradual, have been building to the point at which the position may become impossibly complex and yet impotent.

The purpose of this paper is to examine the historical development of the first-line supervisory position, its status today, and societal trends that will dramatically alter its future characteristics. A secondary purpose is to help rekindle an interest in the first-line supervisor as distinct from middle and upper management positions.

FIRST-LINE SUPERVISION: HISTORY

Although specific first-line supervisory activities necessarily have varied with the industry, technology, size of the organization, experience of the work force and numerous other characteristics, a number of activities and functions traditionally have been part of most first-line supervisory jobs. These typically have included:

---

* From *Academy of Management Review*, 1986, Volume 11, Number 1, 103–117. Reprinted by permission of the publisher and authors.

1. Planning and scheduling; documentation of records and reports
2. Carrying out "human relations" counseling
3. Coordination and control; organizing work
4. Maintaining external relations
5. Managing performance-reward contingencies
6. Maintaining quality and efficiency
7. Maintaining safety and cleanliness
8. Maintaining machinery and equipment
9. Selecting employees
10. Training employees
11. Stimulating suggestions
12. Maintaining union-management relations

In this context, the definition of the supervisory position presented in the Taft-Hartley Act [Section 2(11)] is even more revealing:

> The term "supervisor" means any individual having authority, in the interest of the employer, to hire, transfer, suspend, lay off, recall, promote, discharge, assign, reward, or discipline other employees, or responsibility to direct them, or to adjust their grievances, or effectively to recommend such action if in connection with the foregoing the exercise of such authority is not of a merely routine or clerical nature, but requires the use of independent judgment.[3]

In the early days of the industrial age the foreman, as the position was commonly called, typically acted as a wholly independent contractor to a manufacturing plant owner. The foreman hired a crew, instructed them in the performance of their tasks, supervised their efforts, and paid them their wages if he was satisfied or dismissed them if he was not. No one – neither the government, the union, nor the inhabitants of the organization to whom he contracted his services – told the foreman how to do his job.

The traditional independence of the first-line supervisor has been eroded by the following six events:

1. Frederick Taylor (1911),[4] as part of his concept of scientific management, popularized the notion of a "functional foremanship," whereby the planning of activities was to be distinct from carrying them out, and workers would report to any number of foremen, depending on which aspects of the task were involved. Although functional foremanship was never widely adopted in Taylor's original form, Taylor's writings, along with those of Fayol, Mooney, Urwick, and other classical management theorists, limited the scope and discretion of the foreman's role by transferring many of the foreman's responsibilities to upper management. Organizations began to assume responsibility for selecting and training workers, and foremen as well as workers came increasingly under organizational control, with the foreman playing the role of a "man in the middle" between labor and management.

2. As workers united to form unions to negotiate wages and improve working conditions, union representatives and higher level management took over much of what was previously within the worker-foreman relationship. Whereas Taylor had helped to narrow the foreman's scope of responsibility and to simplify the technical aspects of his work, the growth of unionism further complicated matters by introducing a new power structure with which the foreman had to cope. As Sasser and Leonard (1980) pointed out:

> It has become increasingly difficult to hire or fire without union involvement. Hiring often has to come from the union list; firing has to follow a strict interpretation of the contract, often requiring a number of warnings. Layoffs are normally by seniority, not according to productivity. Disciplinary action was formally taken away from the prerogative of the first-lien supervisor's judgment.[5]

Sasser and Leonard also observed that the union has further eroded the first-line supervisor's prestige by winning wage increases, job security, and better working conditions for its members.

3. Incredible growth of organizational staff has sharply eroded the first-line supervisor's authority. Personnel staffs have gradually assumed much of the responsibility for hiring and training, and industrial engineers have become responsible for managing the technology-worker

interface. These changes, by their very nature, have increased the distance between supervisors and higher management, adding to supervisors' role and status conflicts. Argyris presented an interesting illustration of why this is so:

> Let us assume that a finance man discovers an error in a particular foreman's department. How is this error reported? . . . The finance man cannot take the "shortest" route between the foreman and himself. For one reason, it may be a violation of policy for staff personnel to go directly to line personnel. Even more important (from a human point of view), the finance man achieves his success when *his* boss knows he is finding errors.[6]

In the same vein, Patten has pointed out:

> Because the variety of materials available today makes it a complicated matter to make changes in production methods, the production or manufacturing engineering department sets the rules in this area. Correspondingly, with the foreman's subordinates restricted to making standard parts in standard ways, it has seemed logical to establish a group of inspectors or quality control personnel (reporting elsewhere) to decide whether the foreman's subordinates have done so. Underlying all these matters is the serious business of cost control – which, too, is directed by staff people.[7]

4. The rapidly increasing rate of technological change also has taken its toll on the first-line supervisor. In blue-collar areas, *Business Week* reported that computer-based technology is beginning to take control and monitoring of production flow and quality out of the foreman's hands.[8] In white-collar areas, first-line supervisors are beginning to experience great difficulties in adjusting to the "office of the future." It is becoming all but impossible for foremen to understand fully all the complex equipment and processes for which they are responsible.

5. The increasingly active role of government has, according to Cummings (1975),[9] stripped away much of the first-line supervisor's authority but has increased his or her responsibilities to conform to imposed regulations. The influence of government on first-line supervisors takes many forms, including labor laws, OSHA initiatives, and formal reporting and informational requirements. Possibly the government's emphasis on affirmative action has had the most impact. Affirmative action has increased the heterogeneity of the work force, but decreased the first-line supervisor's ability to maintain work group effectiveness, work roles, and bases of authority (Hammer, 1979).[10] It is ironic, according to Hammer, that the effects of affirmative action with respect to the personnel division are constantly studied, but its effects on the shop floor receive so little attention. Hammer pointed out that supervisors often have little influence over who is hired and that "shop floor supervisors report a noticeable lack of support from both personnel staffs and their own superiors when complaints are lodged against women and minority workers" (1979, p. 386).[11]

6. The changing demographics of the American work force also have affected the foreman's job. *Business Week* (1983, p. 74) noted that more and more younger workers come on the job with computer literacy and with a better understanding of electronics than their supervisors.[12] The increasing education level of the American work force has resulted in higher expectations of workers regarding the quality of their work life. Workers' interest in leisure activities has risen, and their tolerance for authority has diminished (Zierden, 1980).[13] These changes have resulted in further stresses and role strains for first-line supervisors.

The level of sophistication of the foreman's subordinates has risen along with their level of education. By way of contrast, consider Shrank's (1982) reminder that the fences around many industrial plants at the turn of the century were intended not to keep outsiders away, but to keep workers in![14] Workers were often farmhands, seduced or coerced by foremen to work in the labor-short industrial plants. Because the supply of labor was so important to the foreman's success, he spent considerable time pursuing footloose laborers in taverns or pulling them from their beds and herding them back to the plant.

Not only has the foreman lost whatever edge in formal education he or she once enjoyed, but the heterogeneity of the work force has also increased sharply. As a result of "the graying of America," as well as the many recent challenges to mandatory retirement policies, the age spread of American workers has widened. Women and minorities also are an increasing portion of the work force. This means that, in general, the first-line supervisor has a greater variety of subordinates to deal with and satisfy.

FIRST-LINE SUPERVISION: TODAY

It should come as little surprise that these historical events have created serious problems for most first-line supervisors. Among these problems are: role and status conflicts; peer relations among supervisors; and relationships with superiors.

Role and Status Conflicts

Many authors have described the ways that most organizations create and operate the position of first-line supervisor. It is interesting to note how little these descriptions have changed over the years. As an example, the first of the two quotations below was written in 1945, the second more than a quarter of a century later. Descriptions from the 1980s are no different.

> Nowhere in the industrial structure more than at the foreman level is there so great a discrepancy between what a position ought to be and what a position is. . . . Separated from management and separated from his men, dependent and insecure in his relation to his superiors and uncertain in his relations to his men, asked to give cooperation but in turn receiving none, expected to be friendly but provided with tools which only allow him to be "fair" – in this situation of social deprivation our modern foreman is asked to deliver the goods (Roethlisberger, 1945).[15]

> To become a foreman the skilled workman gives up a great deal and gains comparatively little. He gives up his seniority – that is, his investment of time on the job. He gives up his circle of friends, his long-established union protection. . . . He loses the active utilization and practice of his trade. He works a great deal harder . . . but he seldom receives overtime compensation . . . . (Occasionally, his subordinates earn more than he does, through overtime.) (Dale, 1971).[16]

Patten (1968) has pointed out that the first-line supervisory position today is usually salaried, but is responsible for supervising hourly employees.[17] The position is managerial, but is responsible for supervising nonmanagerial workers. To a considerable extent, the inherent conflicts and tensions associated with the position, even today, are evident from Patten's description.

In an early study that has been informally replicated many times, Wray (1949) found that first-line supervisors at two plants did not enter into meaningful decision making, but merely implemented decisions made by others.[18] Most first-line supervisors are screened from both managerial communications networks and meaningful decision making. For example, often they are not informed about the disposition of grievances beyond the first stage. Sometimes union stewards know the results of organizational decisions before the supervisor does.

Another important difference between treatment of first-line supervisors and other levels of management is that some supervisors are not even awarded "permanent" salaried employee status. Patten (1968) pointed out that in many firms there is considerable movement of foremen between the salaried and hourly personnel roles.[19] Patten added that under such circumstances the foreman "is treated like a hired hand, dispensed with when not needed. It becomes exceedingly difficult for such a person to identify permanently with management" (1968, p. 166).[20] Moreover, the Taft-Hartley Act effectively precludes them from organizing.

Still another difference in treatment becomes obvious when perks and status symbols are considered. First-line supervisors often lack access to reserved parking and management cafeterias, and they may be denied secretarial and clerical assistance. Even their organizational title, the ultimate status symbol, is seldom selected with an eye toward maximizing subordinate respect. Several authors have recommended changing their title, for example to "production supervisor" (Patten, 1968)[21] or "shop manager" (Dale, 1971).[22] Smiley and Westbrook (1975) suggested removing one or two layers of management above the first-line supervisor, leaving each unit supervisor responsible for a discrete production unit — complete, integrated, and accountable for manpower, quality, quantity, costs, and other factors of production.[23] In their ideal system the unit supervisor would be under general rather than close supervision. Consistent with these recommendations is Tombari's (1980) suggestion that the status of first-line supervisors be improved by authorizing them to administer the organization's labor-management relations.[24]

Peer Relations Among Supervisors

Most first-line supervisors spend little time interacting with their peers — in particular, with their fellow supervisors. For example, Latham, Fay, and Saari (1979) found in one study that first-line supervisors were observed to interact 38 times with bosses and subordinates, and only 3 times with their peers.[25] Jasinski (1956), in a thought-provoking study, found that the most successful foremen spent the least time with their own subordinates.[26] Specifically, 54 percent of effective supervisors' interaction time was spent outside their work group. However, it is impossible from this study to say whether this pattern of interaction is primarily the cause, or the result, of effective group performance.

Data on how much time first-line supervisors spend with peers differ sharply. Guest (1956) reported that foremen spent 7 percent of their time with other foremen and 30 percent of their time with people outside the work unit.[27] Consistent with Jasinski (1956), Guest noted that foremen who were rated better in performance had more time in contact with people outside their unit than did foremen who were rated lower in performance. As to the nature of first-line supervisory peer interactions, little is known. In Jasinski's study, nearly 75 percent of contacts with other foremen were with the foreman contiguously situated along the product line.[28] Foremen spoke to one another primarily about product quality (35.8 percent of the interaction incidents), work progress, and personnel administration. As has been pointed out many times, organizations seldom show much concern, in either task design or supervisory training programs, for the importance of lateral relationships, even though several studies have identified the importance of good lateral relationships to effective foremanship.

First-Line Supervisor Relationships with Superiors

Another area of importance to the effectiveness of first-line supervisors is their relationship with their superiors. Pelz (1952), in a study of 8,000 nonsupervisory employees, found that their supervisors' "influence within the department" was the critical factor in the subordinates' job satisfaction. Influence was described as how much weight the supervisor swings in obtaining needed resources on time, getting the best work, and obtaining favors for employees.[29] Similar findings were reported by Pelz (1952), who found that supervisory influence was the moderating factor in the relationship between subordinate satisfaction and first-line supervisor behavior.[30]

Literature on first-line supervision has almost no information on how to improve the supervisor's influence with higher management. No training program in which "influence with superiors" was a topic of discussion has been described. Although his relationship is cited as critical to supervisory effectiveness, first-line supervisors apparently are left to their own devices in managing it.

Correlates and Consequences of Supervisory Behavior

In addition to problems which surfaced because of the changing nature of the first-line supervisors' job, writers and researchers have identified a number of correlates and consequences that various leadership behaviors have on subordinate criteria. Most of these criteria are subjective (satisfaction, morale, cohesion, etc.). Only a handful of researchers have obtained hard, objective data (Cleven & Fiedler, 1956; Fleishman & Harris, 1962; Yukl & Kanuk, 1979) such as sales, profits, grievance rates and turnover.[31] Table 1 summarizes those studies which found that specific behaviors do lead to improved performance of subordinates and ratings of the first-line supervisor or both by their superiors. It should be noted that many variables did not correlate systematically with the attitudes and performance of subordinates. Among these are such demographics as age and experience (Child, 1980)[32] and education and length of service (Westerlund & Stromberg, 1965).[33] Studies that failed to find significant relationships between leader variables and criteria are excluded from Table 1.

Also omitted from Table 1 are studies of leadership above the first-line supervisory level. A particularly difficult question for the present authors to resolve was: To what extent can research findings from middle and upper management studies safely be extrapolated to the first-line supervisor position? Among others, Bass (1981) has underscored how different first-line supervisors' activities are from those of other managers.[34] Both the methods of communication and the amount of personal contact with subordinates vary sharply between first-level and middle-level managers. In addition, first-line supervisors traditionally have been concerned with internal matters, rather narrowly defined; higher management typically focuses on broader external issues. Mahoney, Jerdee, and Carroll (1965) have shown how time spent supervising others shrinks as one moves up the hierarchical ladder, but time spent planning expands.[35] Bass (1981) reported that first-line supervisors tend to be engaged in activities that produce results within two weeks; upper-level managers are involved with activities of much longer time frames.[36] From these and other studies it is concluded that it is risky to draw conclusions from the general management literature to the first-line supervisory position.

A number of variables were consistently related to subordinate attitudes and performance only after contingency variables were taken into account. For example, Patchen (1962) found that "encouraging efficiency" was positively related to improved group performance norms only when a foreman was seen as willing to "go to bat" for subordinates. When a foreman was not so viewed, "encouraging efficiency" had a negative relationship with performance norms.[37]

Little research exists on the topic of why leaders tend to select different leadership styles. Some theorists attribute choice of style primarily to relatively stable personality attributes; others consider situational factors to be of paramount importance. One convergent finding is that the desires and expectations of higher management appear to play a large part in determining low-level supervisors' leadership styles. For example, Fleishman (1951, 1953) found that the less foremen perceived that their bosses desired "consideration," the higher were the grievance rates in the groups these foremen supervised.[38] Fleishman et al. (1955) found that training was less a conditioner of subsequent leader behavior than were the cues from higher management.[39] In other words, first-line supervisors tend to do as their managers do. Finally, Pfeffer and Salancik (1975) found that the expectations of superiors were the most important determinants of first-line supervisors' work/task behaviors – though *subordinate expectations were the most important determinants* of supervisors' social or nontask behaviors.[40]

Table 1 also shows that considerate, egalitarian leadership can have a positive impact upon subordinate absence, lateness, grievances, and turnover – although it does not consistently improve productivity (Kerr, Schriesheim, Murphy, & Stogdill, 1974).[41] However, the general literature on leadership reveals, and the specific literature on first-line supervision confirms, the subtle interplays between considerate, egalitarian

Table 1
First-Line Supervisor Behaviors Associated with Improved Subordinate Attitudes and Performance

Supervisor behavior	Dependent variable	Citation
1. Accepts criticism and suggestions	Respondent ratings of effective foreman behavior	Kay, 1959
2. Lets subordinates know what (s)he thinks of their work	Boss' ratings of first-line supervisor's performance	Mann & Dent, 1954
3. Displays flexibility	Boss' ratings of first-line supervisor's performance	Child, 1980
4. Goes to bat for subordinates, recommends promotions	Boss' ratings of first-line supervisor's performance	Mann & Dent, 1954
5. Emphasizes production, gives direction, plans operations	Profit, outsider ratings, subordinate descriptions of ideal foremanship, boss' ratings of first-line supervisor's performance	Kay, 1959; Colyer, 1951; Yukl & Kanuk, 1979
6. Follows instructions, company policies, chain of command	Respondent ratings of effective first-line supervisor's behavior	Kay, 1959
7. Keeps boss informed	Boss' ratings of first-line supervisor's performance	Child, 1980
8. Gives praise verbally to subordinates and in reports to bosses	Boss' and respondent ratings of first-line supervisor's performance	Mann & Dent, 1954; Kay, 1959
9. Develops subordinates, trains subordinates for better jobs	Boss' and respondent ratings of first-line supervisor's performance	Mann & Dent, 1954; Kay, 1959
10. Uses rewards and punishments	Profit, sales, outsider ratings, boss' ratings of first-line supervisor's performance	Patchen, 1962; Yukl & Kanuk, 1979
11. Displays competence in human relations	Subordinate satisfaction with the supervisor	Mann & Hoffman, 1960
12. Creates a climate whereby subordinates feel free to discuss problems with the leader	Productivity, absenteeism, boss' ratings of first-line supervisor's performance	Mann & Baumgartel, 1953; Kahn & Katz, 1953; Mann & Dent, 1954

Table 1 continued

Supervisor behavior	Dependent variable	Citation
13. Displays technical knowledge of task	Subordinates' descriptions of ideal foremanship	Colyer, 1951; Turner, 1954; Sasser & Leonard, 1980
14. Displays consideration and egalitarianism, uses tact and diplomacy, uses general supervision	Grievances, turnover, boss' and respondent ratings of first-line supervisor's performance attitudes toward supervisor	Mann & Dent, 1954; Kay, 1959; Fleishman & Harris, 1962; Parker, 1963
15. Identifies with higher management	Boss' ratings of effective foremanship	Balma, Maloney, & Lawshe, 1958[a]
16. Holds different perceptions of most and least preferred co-worker	Objective measure of group performance	Cleven & Fiedler, 1956[a]

Note This table shows only those studies that found significant relationships between predictors and criteria. Numerous studies exist to show that the supervisor behaviors described in the table often fail to relate to criteria statistically.
[a]These studies investigate the effects of leader perceptions rather than behaviors.

leadership and many other variables. For example, Parker (1963) found that consideration toward subordinates by first-line supervisors improved attitudes toward supervision, but was unrelated to group performance.[42] Fleishman and Harris (1962) showed that, if leader consideration was low, high levels of subordinate grievances and turnover would result irrespective of the foreman's level of initiating structure; on the other hand, highly considerate foremen could initiate considerable structure without accompanying gains in grievances and turnover.[43] Cummins (1971)[44] and Lahat-Mandelbaum and Kipnis (1973)[45] reported similar findings using such criteria as quality, productivity, and satisfaction.

A related question concerns how much "social mixing" by a hierarchical superior is appropriate. Most first-line supervisors were once employed at the level of those they are now supervising. Some first-line supervisors were actually members of the particular peer group they are now responsible for, and had enjoyed the company of these people as friends and equals. Therefore, it is important for first-line supervisors to prevent subordinate perceptions of politics, favoritism, and diluted authority (Colyer, 1951)[46] by creating social differentiation from erstwhile colleagues (Karp, 1981).[47]

FIRST-LINE SUPERVISION: THE FUTURE

In addition to the difficulties inherent in the first-line supervisory position, a number of predicted future trends seem to have ominous implications for the supervisor's autonomy and influence. Perhaps the four most important of these are: (a) heightened emphasis on various participative management techniques; (b) increased use of self-managed, autonomous work groups; (c) increasing application of computer-driven automation and information management in the workplace; and (d) continued growth in the size and importance of specialized staff units.

Emphasis on Participative Management

Spurred by Japan's successes, American managers have shown increasing willingness to experiment with participative philosophies and techniques. One implication of this is that first-line supervisors are increasingly invited to share leadership and decision maing with their subordinates.

Although many leadership theorists recommend participation as an effective strategy, at least in certain situations (Vroom & Yetton, 1973),[48] and though instances of successful participation in mass-production industries have been reported, participative leadership nevertheless tends to be particularly problematic in this setting. Patten (1968)[49] pointed out the difficulties of pulling people away from machine-paced operations to attend meetings or have discussions. Union contracts can also be encumbering, especially when they limit a foreman's discretion in relating to workers. Another potential impediment was described by Patten:

> By having their work fractionalized . . . most hourly workers . . . have a minimum of contact with one another. There is no reason for them to work interdependently. As a consequence, the foreman in many respects deals with an aggregate of men or women working independently of one another, rather than with an integrated team working together and assisting one another (1968).[50]

As a result, group-based participation is less likely to be effective. Other factors peculiar to first-line supervision, such as span of control, make one-on-one styles of participative leadership difficult to apply. For example, Woodward (1958) found that the median span of control for first-line supervisors was between 11 and 20 subordinates in continuous process firms, between 21 and 30 in unit production firms, and between 41 and 50 in mass-production industries. Given such large spans of control, it is hardly surprising to learn, as did Parker (1963),[51] that larger groups tend to be led by first-line supervisors who are higher in initiating structure than they are in participation.

Overall, it is one thing for leadership theorists to recommend participative, egalitarian, and other heavily labor-intensive leadership styles, but quite another for most first-line supervisors to find the time, the means, the shared goals, and the interdependence necessary to use such styles effectively.

Use of Autonomous Work Groups

Although participative leadership is the least autocratic of the leadership styles catalogued by Vroom and Yetton (1973),[52] leaders who employ this style are involved in their subordinates' decision making process from start to finish. Through participation in the generation and evaluation of alternatives, leaders retain the power to prevent consideration of alternatives they deem unacceptable. By requiring subordinate unanimity for the group's solution to be adopted (as do Vroom and Yetton), leaders often must make the eventual decision. Leaders employing this style also retain the power to set time limits for group discussion, thus limiting and even eliminating evaluation of alternatives that the group might otherwise find attractive.

Some researchers have taken the concept of subordinate participation a great deal further by asking: How important is the presence of a supervisor to a work group's performance? Could a work group function as well, or even better, if organized to be autonomous, that is, self-governing? Self-governing means that the group makes its own decisions and the supervisor holds it accountable only for results, not for method. In any case, there is a supervisor to whom the group reports. Bass and Shackleton referred to the idea of autonomous work groups as constituting "direct participation," because of its underlying concern "with the actual day-to-day content of a worker's job. Its aim is to increase autonomy and decision-making discretion as much as possible. Workers often take responsibility for their own inspections and process control and may be self-managing from receipt of orders to inspection dispatch" (1979).[53]

The limited evidence concerning the productivity of autonomous work groups suggests that they can be effective (Cummings, Malloy, & Glen, 1977).[54] Data pertaining to how first-line supervisors take to the idea of autonomous work groups, although even more limited, suggest that supervisors view the concept with some reservations. Walton and Schlesinger (1979) found that first-line supervisors felt that they were unrewarded for good group performance (because higher management attributed favorable results to the system), but blamed for poor performance.[55] The authors stated that problems tended to stem from inaccurate expectations of results, inadequate selection of supervisors, inadequate supervisory training in participative management techniques, failing to link supervisory evaluation and reward to team development, and the absence of plans to utilize freed supervisory time. Walton and Schlesinger's comments were primarily directed at participative management, but seem equally applicable to autonomous work groups.

How important are autonomous work groups likely to be in the future? Bass and Shackleton (1979) noted that they are already popular in a number of European countries, much more so than in the United States.[56] Consistent with this is O'Toole's observation that "in general, American workers appear to be oversupervised. At the Honda car plant, the ratio of supervisor/inspectors to production workers is 1:200. In some U.S. car plants, the ratio is 1:10" (1981).[57] A safe prediction, therefore, is that these groups will become more important in the United States by the 1990s.

In the presence of autonomous work groups, what remains for the first-line supervisor to do? According to Cummings (1978),[58] the two remaining key supervisory responsibilities are: developing group members and helping the group to maintain its boundaries. These responsibilities, Cummings pointed out, are not traditionally assigned to first-line supervisors and, therefore, maybe uncomfortable for many supervisors.

Computer-Driven Automation and Information Management

The trend for computers to change the face of

the workplace will accelerate as the advantages of using the new technologies become increasingly apparent. These new technologies will affect everyone's job, but their greatest impact to date has been on workers whose work is labor-intensive, requires relatively little discretion and judgment, and tends to be closely supervised – in short, the kind of work managed by the first-line supervisor.

First, computers or robots will entirely take over certain functions currently performed manually. Therefore, the amount and sophistication of equipment for which the average supervisor is responsible will probably increase. Second, many workers will perform their activities directly through computers, most often using a video display tube (VDT). These computers will be able to record and store large amounts of detailed information on workers' activities and production output. In both offices and factories, computerized information systems will make it possible for upper management to obtain information about individual workers, missed target dates, and many other matters without going to the first-line supervisor. Supervisors will still be responsible for monitoring the equipment, monitoring various system functions, and (of course!) explaining variances between planned and actual production. Many activities the first-line supervisor is responsible for will be performed out of the supervisor's sight – in some cases, at the employee's residence.

Thurley and Wirdenius (1973) identified four kinds of automation situations based on two variables: type of decision and type of technology.[59] Taken together a two-by-two matrix can be identified, as shown in Figure 1.

According to Thurley and Wirdenius:

> Popular attention has focused on Situation I, where supervision might be seen as likely to be reduced to monitoring results and carrying out routine procedures. In all the other situations, however, supervisors might play a much more active and responsible role. In Situation II, process supervisors can contribute to the development program by assisting with plant experiments and observing effects ... In Situation III, supervisors may well have to carry out precise recording of data in order to feed it back to the computer. Crises and unexpected events cannot be avoided, and new skills are required. . . . It is increasingly recognized that the computerization of planning in construction projects, for example, may increase the responsibilities of supervisors and not diminish them.
>
> Situation IV is obviously an unprogrammed area and hence it is necessary only to assert that supervisory experience . . . may be an essential component of such teams, in order to avoid the otherwise inevitable gaps between theoretical reasoning and actual performance (1973).[60]

Mann and Hoffman's (1960) work is consistent with Thurley and Wirdenius' description of Situation I. They compared the differences between operating a newly automated electric power plant and an older, mechanized plant, and found that automation decreased the number of foremen, but increased the influence of those who remained. Human relations competence, as opposed to technical competence, was found to be key in both the old and the new plants.[61]

Situation I also is consistent with earlier work by Atchison (1970), who reported that specializing and narrowing job scope impairs first-line supervisory influence.[62] In the future, computers will be able to take over these specialized and narrow supervisory functions. Situation II is consistent with Jasinski's (1956) prediction that changes in technology, particularly assembly line or process technology, require horizontal (peer to peer) and diagonal (supervisor to nonsubordinate) interactions.[63]

In Situations II, III, and IV, supervisory interactions with external staff will be necessary to aid in system analysis, to obtain maintenance and repair services, and to secure resources for the work to proceed. Boundary spanning must increase as a result of automation.

Growth of Specialized Staff

Clash of wills between specialized staff and first-line supervisors is hardly a recent phenomenon.

For example, Dalton stated that tension typically was produced because "as methods refiners and technique formulators, the staffs are really specialists in change and reorganization" whereas "line people see changes as interfering with production" (1959).[64] From his own classic study, Dalton found that "foremen are likely to regard most staff projects as manipulative devices. They cooperate with production workers and general foremen to defeat . . . staff people."[65]

Though this friction has probably always existed, it is likely to be exacerbated by future events. The first-line supervisory position will continue to evolve in response to a multitude of pressures, including changes in management policies, union influence, governmental intervention, and technological innovations. These societal forces will cause organizations to employ more and more staff experts. Management consultants increasingly will be asked to advise on new philosophies and techniques; industrial relations and EEO experts increasingly will be invited to comment on labor relations and legal changes; automation experts and MIS specialists in greater and greater numbers will be added to corporate staffs to implement the new technologies; and a wide variety of futurists and "environmental scanners" will be asked to read the tea leaves concerning likely market forces, legislation, and changes in demographics and societal values.

Figure 1
Four types of automation

	Programmed Decisions Necessary	Nonprogrammed Decisions
Process Technology	Situation I Stable automated system – electric power plants, flour mills, breweries, etc.	Situation II Planned development of automated systems – oil refineries, steel, chemical, and paper plants
Unit (tailor-made) Technology	Situation III Computer controlled projects (planning and administration) – construction, large capital projects, ships, aircraft, space technology	Situation IV Computers used to service R and D teams in developing models. Simulation of problems and system key activity

Note: From Thurley and Wirdenius, 1973 (p. 207).

All of this means that first-line supervisors probably will spend more and more of their time with people outside their immediate work unit, and will require training in boundary spanning, and in nonhierarchical interactions and modes of influence. All of this also means that the authority and discretion of the position will be further reduced, as supervisors are required to implement programs created by others, in highly specified formats.

Combined Impact

Table 2 predicts the direction of impact of the four societal forces discussed on the activities of first-line supervisors. The amount of time supervisors will spend performing the 12 traditional activities described earlier will decrease for 6, increase for 2, and remain essentially unchanged for 4 activities.

What can be concluded from this analysis? First-line supervisors will interact with more and more people outside the work group. Within the work group, supervisors will perform more counseling, nurturing, and group facilitation. Naisbitt (1982) noted that as technology makes further and further encroachments into people's lives, they tend to compensate by participating in more personal interactive activites – what Naisbitt labels "high-tech/high-touch" phenomena.[66] It follows that, as technology makes its presence felt in organizations, there will be an increasing need for nurturant behavior by supervisors.

All four forces – worker participation, autonomous work groups, MIS/automation, and staff involvement – feed on and support one another. The increase in strength and number of specialized staffs will stimulate worker participation, autonomy, and application of new technologies. As worker participation increases, so will the need for staff assistance and computer monitoring of work force outputs and processes. Finally, as technological advances become more accessible, there will be greater need for both staff assistance and worker involvement in implementing and operating the new technologies.

CONCLUSIONS

The title of this paper asks whether the first-line supervisory position is "phasing out or here to stay." The authors propose that the position is here to stay. It is true that in some cases technological advances will render the supervisory position redundant, but in most future scenarios – generally corresponding to Situations II, III, and IV in Thurley and Wirdenius' (1973) conceptualization, shown in Figure 1 – the position will remain essential to the successful operation of future systems.[67]

In one important respect, however, the present authors are begging the question. That is, though the position will probably remain important, there will be far fewer first-line supservisors employed in organizations than today, and its future functions and activities will so poorly resemble those traditionally assigned to the position that the title "first-line supervisor" is probably inappropriate. As shown in Table 2, supervisors will perform fewer activites in the future than they do now, and those activities they do perform will center around (a) external representation and (b) internal human relations.

One positive aspect of this evolution is that future occupants may experience fewer of the role and status conflicts that have so plagued the position throughout its history. On the other hand, these changes probably will require organizations to refine their selection techniques for new supervisors and their training methods for incumbents. Tomorrow's first-line supervisors will have to be more technically proficient, as well as more highly skilled in human relations than their predecessors. Also, such individuals probably will expect compensation levels that match these increased skill levels. This will help to position the first-line supervisor closer to the ranks of lower level management and further from their subordinates.

Even after careful selection and training, the job of the future first-line supervisor will not be easy. Occupants will inherit the legacy of a position fraught with conflict created by differing

Table 2
Impact of Predicted Forces of First-Line Supervisory Activities

Activity	Impact on First-line supervisors' time				
	Workers' participation	Autonomous work group	MIS[a], automation	Staff involvement	Net impact
1. Work planning and scheduling, documentation of records and reports	0	−	−	−	−
2. Carrying out "human relations;" counseling, nurturing	+	0	+	−	+
3. Coordination and control, organizing subordinate work	−	−	−	−	−
4. Maintaining external relations; boundary spanning	+	+	+	+	+
5. Managing performance-reward contingencies	+	[b]	−	0	0
6. Maintaining quality and efficiency	−	−	+	−	−
7. Maintaining safety and cleanliness	−	−	0	0	−
8. Maintaining machinery and equipment	−	−	+	0	−
9. Selection of employees	+	+	−	−	0
10. Training of employees	+	−	−	−	0
11. Stimulating suggestions	+	+	0	0	0
12. Maintaining union-management relations	0	0	−	−	−

Note + = increase in first-line supervisory (FLS) time required. 0 = no predictable change in FLS time required. − = Reduction in FLs time required.
[a]MIS = Management information system.
[b]Change in orientation from individual to group based system.

demands from workers, staff, and upper management. This conflict is not easily resolved; it is the result of gradual changes in organizational power relationships over time. Though supervisory retraining and role restructuring can significantly improve the supervisor's lot, it is likely that the supervisor of the future will still be labeled as "the man or woman in the middle" – caught between the often-conflicting expectations of upper management and the work force. Allowing the supervisor's position to take its natural course will not resolve these problems. As Willens (1984) has pointed out in quoting an ancient Chinese proverb, "If we do not change our direction, we are likely to end up where we are headed."[68] What will resolve these problems is for organizational leaders to begin to address systematically the areas of concern noted here.

References

1. E. Guess (1955) "Ready for Promotion?" in Chinoy, ed., *Automobile Workers and the American Dream*. Boston: Beacon Press. p. 43.
2. P.F. Drucker (1983, June 7) "Twilight of the First-Line Supervision?" *The Wall Street Journal*. p. 28.
3. Taft-Hartley Act, United States Statutes at Large. Volume 61, p. 136. P.L. 80–120, Sect. 2(11), (1947).
4. F.W. Taylor (1911) *The Principles of Scientific Managment*. New York: Harper.
5. W.E. Sasser and F.S. Leonard (1980) "Let First-Level Supervisors Do Their Job." p. 116. *Harvard Business Review*, 58(2), pp. 113–121.
6. C. Argyris (1953) "Human Problems with Budgets." p. 104. *Harvard Business Review*, 31(1), pp. 97–110.
7. T. Patten (1968) *The Foreman: Forgotten Man of Management*. New York: American Management Association, pp. 34–35.
8. "The Old Foreman is on the Way Out, and the New One Will Be More Important." (1983, April 25), p. 74. *Business Week*, pp. 74–75.
9. P. Cummings (1975) "Occupation: Supervisor." *Personal Journal*, 54, pp. 448–450.
10. T.H. Hammer (1979) "Affirmative Action Programs: Have We Forgotten the First-Line Supervisor?" *Personnel Journal*, 58, pp. 384–389.
11. *Ibid.*, p. 386.
12. "The Old Foreman is on the Way Out, and the New One Will Be More Important." (1983, April 25), p. 74. *Business Week*. pp. 74–75.
13. W.E. Zierden (1980) "Needed: Top Management Attention to the Role of the First-Line Supervisor." *S.A.M. Advanced Management Journal*, 45(3), pp. 18–25.
14. R. Shrank. (1982, January) "Productivity at the Point of Production." Unpublished working paper, University of Southern California School of Business Administration Seminar.
15. F.J. Roethlisberger (1945) "The Foreman: Master and Victim of Double Talk." pp. 284, 293. *Harvard Business Review*, (23)3, 283–298.
16. L.A. Dale (1971) "The Foreman as Manager." p. 62. *Personnel*, 48(4), pp. 61–64.
17. T. Patten (1968) *op. cit.*
18. D.E. Wray (1949) "Marginal Men of Industry: The Foremen." *American Journal of Sociology*, 55, pp. 298–301.
19. T. Patten (1968) *op. cit.*
20. *Ibid.*, p. 166.
21. *Ibid.*
22. L.A. Dale. *op. cit.*
23. L.M. Smiley and P.R. Westbrook (1975) "The First-Line Supervisory Problem Redefined." *Personnel Journal*, 54, pp. 620–623, 638.
24. H.A. Tombari (1980) "Determinants of Equity of Rewards for Supervisors." *Public Personnel Management*, 9(1), pp. 25–30.
25. G.P. Latham, C.H. Fay and L.M. Saari (1979) "The Development of Behavioral Observation Scales for Appraising the Performance of Foremen." *Personnel Psychology*, 32(2), pp. 299–311.

26. F.J. Jasinski (1956) "Foreman Relationships Outside the Work Group." *Personnel*, 33(2), pp. 130–136.
27. R. Guest (1956) "Of Time and the Foreman." *Personnel*, 32(6), pp. 478–486.
28. F. Jasinski, *op. cit.*
29. D. Pelz (1952) "Influence: A Key to Effective Leadership in the First Line Supervisor." *Personnel*, 29(3), pp. 209–217.
30. *Ibid.*
31. See W.A. Cleven and F.E. Fiedler (1956) "Interpersonal Perceptions of Open Hearth Foremen and Steel Production." *Journal of Applied Psychology*, 40, pp. 312–314; E.A. Fleishman and E.F. Harris (1962) "Patterns of Leadership Behavior Related to Employee Grievances and Turnover." *Personnel Psychology*, 15(1), 43–56; G.A. Yukl and L. Kanuk (1979) "Leadership Behavior and Effectiveness of Beauty Salon Managers." *Personnel Psychology*, 32(4), pp. 663–675.
32. J. Child (1980) "Factors Associated with the Managerial Rating of Supervisory Performance." *Journal of Management Studies*, 17, pp. 275–302.
33. G. Westerlund and L. Stromberg (1965) "Measurement and Approval of the Performance of Foremen." *British Journal of Industrial Relations*, 3, pp. 345–362.
34. B.M. Bass (1981) *Stogdill's Handbook of Leadership*. New York: The Free Press.
35. T.A. Mahoney, T.H. Jerdee and S.I. Carroll (1965) "The Job(s) of Management." *Industrial Relations*, 4, pp. 97–110.
36. B.M. Bass. *op. cit.*
37. M. Patchen (1962) "Supervisory Methods and Group Performance Norms." *Administrative Science Quarterly*, 6, pp. 275–294.
38. E.A. Fleishman (1951) *The Relationship Between Leadership Climate and Supervisory Behavior*. Unpublished doctoral dissertation. Ohio State University, Columbus, Ohio. Also see E.A. Fleishman (1953) "The Description of Supervisory Behavior." *Journal of Applied Psychology*, 37, pp. 1–6.
39. E.A. Fleishman, E.F. Harris and H.E. Burtt (1955) *Leadership and Supervision in Industry*. Research monograph number 33. Columbus, OH: Ohio State University, Bureau of Education Research.
40. J. Pfeffer and G.R. Salancik (1975) "Determinants of Supervisory Behavior: A Role Set Analysis." *Human Relations*, 28, pp. 139–153.
41. S. Kerr, C.A. Schriesheim, C. Murphy and R.M. Stogdill (1974) "Toward a Contingency Theory of Leadership Based on the Consideration and Initiating Structure Literature." *Organizational Behavior and Human Performance*, 12, pp. 62–82.
42. T.C. Parker (1963) "Relationships Among Measures of Supervisory Behavior, Group Behavior, and Situational Characteristics." *Personnel Psychology*, 16(4), pp. 319–334.
43. E.A. Fleishman and E.F. Harris, *op. cit.*
44. R.C. Cummins (1971) "Relationship of Initiating Structure and Job Performances as Moderated by Consideration." *Journal of Applied Psychology*, 55, pp. 489–490.
45. B. Lahat-Mandelbaum and D. Kipnis (1973) "Leader Behavior Dimensions Related to Students' Evaluation of Teaching Effectiveness." *Journal of Applied Psychology*, 58, pp. 250–253.
46. D. Coyler (1951) "The Good Foreman – As His Men See Him." *Personnel* 28(2), pp. 140–147.
47. H.B. Karp (1981) "Executive Development for First-Line Supervisors." *Training/HRD*, 18(8), pp. 95–98.
48. V.H. Vroom and P.W. Yetton (1973) *Leadership and Decision Making*. Pittsburgh: Pittsburgh Press.
49. T. Patten. *op. cit.*
50. T. Patten. *op. cit.* p. 51.
51. T.C. Parker. *op. cit.*
52. V.H. Vroom and P.W. Yetton. *op. cit.*
53. B.M. Bass and V.J. Shackleton (1979) "Industrial Democracy and Participative Management: A Case for Synthesis." p. 394. *Academy of Management Review*, 4, pp. 393–414.

54. T.G. Cummings, E.S. Malloy and R. Glen (1977) "A Methodological Critique of Fifty-Eight Selected Work Experiments." *Human Relations*, 30, pp. 675–708.
55. R.E. Walton and L.A. Schlesinger (1979) "Do Supervisors Thrive in Participative Work Systems?" *Organizational Dynamics*, 7(3), pp. 25–38.
56. B.M. Bass and V.J. Shackleton. *op. cit.*
57. J. O'Toole (1981) *Making America Work*. New York: Continuum Press, p. 61.
58. T.G. Cummings (1978) "Self-Regulating Work Groups: A Socio-technical Synthesis." *Academy of Management Review*, 3, pp. 625–634.
59. K. Thurley and H. Wirdenius (1973) *Supervision: A Reappraisal*. London: Heinemann.
60. *Ibid.*, p. 207.
61. F.C. Mann and K.R. Hoffman (1960) *Automation and the Worker*. New York: Holt.
62. T.J. Atchison (1970) "The Fragmentation of Authority." *Personnel*, 47(4), pp. 8–14.
63. F.J. Jasinski. *op. cit.*
64. M. Dalton (1959) *Men Who Manage*. New York: Wiley, p. 75.
65. *Ibid.*, p. 100.
66. J. Naisbitt (1982) *Megatrends*. New York: Warner.
67. K. Thurley and H. Wirdenius. *op. cit.*
68. H. Wilens (1984) *The Trimtab Factor*. New York: Morrow, p. 8.

Additional Readings

Balma, M.J., Maloney, J.C. and Lawshe, C.H. (1958) "The Role of the Foreman in Modern Industry; II. Foremen Identification with Management, Work Group Productivity and Employee Attitudes Towards Foremen." *Personnel Psychology*, 11(3), pp. 367–368.

Kahn, R.L. and Katz, D. (1953) "Leadership in Relation to Productivity and Morale," in Cartwrit and Zander, eds., *Group Dynamics*. Evanston, IL: Row Peterson.

Kay, B. (1959) "Key Factors in Effective Foreman Behavior." *Personnel*, 36(1), pp. 25–31.

Mann, F.C. and Baumgartel, H. (1953) *The Supervisor's Concern with Cost in an Electric Power Company* Ann Arbor, MI: University of Michigan, Survey Research Center.

Turner, A.N. (1954) "Foreman – Key to Worker Morale." *Harvard Business Review*, 32(1), pp. 76–86.

CASES

LEARNING TO MANAGE THE HARD WAY*

Susan Regan

On Friday afternoon, Mandy burst into tears. She realized as she sat weeping behind the stacks of envelopes and pin-hole paper that it was very unprofessional and unmanagerial, and probably right at the top of the Harvard Business School list of things women managers were never supposed to do, but she just could not help it.

The time was 4:45 and the office was scheduled to close for the weekend in another fifteen minutes. In ten minutes, Dr. Smithman from the Management Department would arrive to pick up his survey questionnaires, cover letter, and five hundred addressed envelopes from the Word Processing Center and Mandy would have to tell him that they were not ready. Coming as it did after an unnerving and hectic month, this crisis was Mandy's breaking point. She blew her nose hard and wiped the tears away. Resting her head on her hands she began to think over the events of the last few weeks that had led up to this catastrophe.

Six months ago, Mandy had been a department secretary in the Faculty of Commerce. She was bored and utterly frustrated in that position. With a good Arts degree she felt she was capable of doing so much more than the position demanded (basically non-stop typing and telephone answering from nine to five), and that was why she had applied to Human Resources to be the coordinator of the yet-to-be-implemented word processing center.

She was so delighted that she was given an interview for the position that she made a rash decision. She told Dean Abbott that she was willing to take on the responsibilities of the position without accepting a raise in pay, as long as her salary would be re-evaluated after a period of six months, based on the success of the word processing center.

Dean Abbott agreed to hire her, but made it clear that he had "serious reservations." First, he stated that he had serious reservations about hiring a twenty-three-year-old

---

* Reprinted by permission of the author.

girl to do the job. He had envisioned a "motherly, grey-haired" person for the job. Second, he believed her academic background had limited value in terms of the position (and Mandy had to agree – a BA in English Literature didn't seem the best qualification for the job). Third, he himself was not entirely in favor of the administration's imposed changes. He was quite happy with the departmental secretary who had handled his typing work successfully for the last 22 years.

He hinted that the word processing center was bound to fail, no matter who took the position. He pointed out that this was an experiment on the part of the administration – and that if results were not impressive, the center would probably be shut down. Just before he rose to signify that the interview was over, he said, "Of course you realize that, should you fail in this new position, your old position will no longer be available.

Mandy realized she was taking a gamble but since she feared that the lack of opportunities for advancement in her secretarial position would trap her forever in a dead-end job, she felt it was a gamble worth taking.

She enjoyed the next few months: researching word processing in the library, meeting with the university's planning committee and physical plant people, ordering supplies and furniture, visiting equipment vendors – and finally watching the workmen actually assemble the new offices from the floor up. She interviewed what seemed to be hundreds of people for the five positions Dean Abbott had granted her, and was ultimately satisfied with her choices. The university print shop delivered the forms she had designed, the photocopying machines arrived first, then the word processing machines. One month ago, the center had opened for business. It was a very exciting time, and for the first time Mandy found personal fulfillment in seeing her plans become reality on the job.

Yet now she had collapsed in a heap all over the paperwork. Something had gone very wrong – despite all the planning she had done and the care and devotion she had lavished on the center. Why, she had been in the office from 7:30 in the morning, sometimes until 11:00 at night. She had not taken one single lunch hour since the center opened a month ago. She typed like crazy to get jobs done. She ran the word processor when the operators were at lunch or on breaks. She stapled the photocopies together so the clerk would not have to do it. Some days she even ran the completed jobs over to the print shop or delivered them personally to their originators.

As well as being a personal point of honor that the center run smoothly and accomplish all the work in record time, Mandy felt that Dean Abbott's eye was constantly on the department. Although during the month of operation he had never set foot in the center nor communicated at all with Mandy, she felt he was assessing the center and deciding whether to keep it open or to close it down.

She was doing a hundred times the amount of work she had done as departmental secretary, and it seemed as though the work was endless – she could not get ahead of the work, she could not even control it. All day long she was running from one menial job to another. If anyone made a comment about the center, she was unable to take it any way but personally. She felt her soul, not only her job, was on the line.

The center met or exceeded all anticipated goals for each of the first weeks of operation. There were only two minor complaints from users. Why, then, had today been such a crisis?

First one, then another, of the word processing operators had left early. The office clerk had taken a two-hour lunch, instead of the hour she was allocated. One of the word processing operators had lost a document that morning, and it contained the text of Dr. Smithman's cover letter. Mandy had spend most of the afternoon trying to re-input it and print out the 500 letters – in between interruptions and problems and questions and interpersonal conflicts.

It seemed to Mandy that the harder she worked, the harder she had to work. The support staff workers could goof off and take long lunch hours, because their work always got done. It didn't matter to them *who* did the work – even if it was their boss. Mandy had held the view that people like to work and would seek responsibility actively. She was Theory Y all the way. It went against her grain to admit she'd been wrong about people. They were a bunch of lazy slobs and she felt they'd sabotaged her best efforts to run the center efficiently.

She hated to admit it, but maybe her boss had been right when he'd said, "Young lady, you are looking for unnatural satisfactions in this job. You want your staff to love you and you want your clients to love you. Love isn't for work, it's for home. Please check your emotions at the door."

QUESTIONS

1. How is Mandy presented in this case? Why is Dean Abbott so patronizing in his approach to Mandy? Does his attitude reflect a measure of sexism?
2. Did Mandy establish a realistic contract with the Dean before she took up her duties?
3. What is wrong with Mandy's conception of her role as coordinator of the Word Processing Center? How should she sort out this problem of defining her managerial role?
4. Is Mandy's search for job satisfaction unreal? What should Mandy really expect from her job?

A WEEK IN THE LIFE OF A HEAD OF COMPUTER SERVICES*

Alan I. Phillips

MONDAY

First day of employment at the polytechnic. Start at 9:00 a.m. with interviews for my personal secretary. At least Personnel are well organized with technical competence tests but it still takes up a full morning. Yippie – make an appointment but brought

---

* From *The Times Higher Education Supplement*, September 19, 1986. Reprinted by permission.

down to earth by a 40-minute wait to get lunch in the polytechnic refectory. Yes, I know 40 minutes is so long that I should have gone elsewhere but I get mesmerized by the queue's slow progression and they have an interesting "vegetable pie" flagged as "today's special." When I get there, of course, the only pie is steak and kidney.

Really need that secretary as I spend most of the afternoon seeing one "pop-in" visitor after another. Someone resigns. I wonder if 12 vacancies are normal?

Walk home to listen to Phil Collins in the flat above mine. I've got the same tape but can't seem to get it synchronized with upstairs so just listen to his. I still sign the rental agreement for the flat to *Shades of Sade*.

TUESDAY

Something like this was just waiting for me to arrive so it could happen. Our PCAS computer system exposes an analysis error and some potential students get their confirmations late.

The academic registrar demonstrates how to control anger which is mainly directed at our administrative support division. I very much doubt if all the blame lies with them.

Try to convince a friendly but unconvinced staff that my wonderfully symmetrical departmental structure is really as radical as I obviously think it is. Find it difficult to sort out cynicism from maturity.

Dry my hands on the hot-air machine in the lavatory and a straw hat on top of it falls slowly on to me and I try to avoid grabbing it as my hands are still wet. I succeed in doing a Maradona and get it on to my head. On second thoughts, he would have used his hands. Turns out that the hat belongs to the dean of computing and information studies, who introduces himself and very generously solves all my budget problems by suggesting I spend it all on him. This was a very quick reaction – or was he planning to meet me there? I am getting a lavatory complex as the one near the director's office has a large mirror as you walk in, displaying the player at the end stall in all his finery. From what I've seen there already, this could be planned as well.

The damned TSB cash dispenser doesn't work again on the way home. I only joined this bank last month and three of the four dispensers I have tried haven't worked. I had only one failure with Lloyds in 10 years.

WEDNESDAY

After a romp around the main site looking for rooms with the polytechnic secretary, the following meeting still leaves me without a feel that the departmental budget is "mine" as I haven't fought for it at committee. A meeting with the bursar, however, explains the considerable amount of freedom I have to spend as I like within my global departmental allocation. But I quickly discover what this really means when I find I have £2,000 left to cover all areas of expenditure to the end of the year! This rapidly concentrates my mind on what word-processing machine to buy for the incoming secretary.

Must get a light switch in my room as people in the departmental office keep unwittingly switching my lights on and off as both rooms' lights are all on one switch! Doesn't half liven up meetings though, so perhaps I should leave well alone?

THURSDAY

Job adverts for 10 of my vacancies appear in the paper – not bad going to get this sorted so soon since my appointment.

Really pleased last night as got no sounds from above in my flat. The reason is that its occupant has fallen and broken his clavicle. Apart from this not being at all funny for him, my personal gain at night is my polytechnic loss of the day as he is one of my technical support staff!

Assure staff in the learning support division, who complain about my moving them into a room that only has a window into a vestibule, that it was part of my grand plan to move them out again.

Just to keep up my reputation with anyone still reading this, I have to inform you that the polytechnic has an odd habit of wedging open doors to nearly all their lavatories. Of course, these are the very doors with little pictures on them. And yes, this bit is as true as everything else written here. I did go in the wrong one and, moreover, the person I met there is the one who then served me in the refectory. This enables me to build on our new relationship to find out why there was no vegetable pie on Monday. The refectory is short-staffed and the person who updates the menu is not working. The menu dates from the last day of the summer term and was never there to queue for anyway!

Poly still a bit like a morgue as most academics are thinking: "I'm-floating-in-and-out-this-week-as-I'm-not-really-supposed-to-be-here." Glad of the respite as I'm "here-all-this-week-but-feel-as-if-I'm-floating-in-and-out."

FRIDAY

Getting my own light switch causes my room to explode with dangling wires all day.

Manage to get agreement to have a status symbol – our own departmental copier. Have to modify my grand room plan already!

Now I have a real problem of dealing with those staff in that room which only has a window into a vestibule.

Compromise by agreeing to "grow" their area out into the vestibule behind a newly constructed counter and to be persistent in addressing one of the section's complaints about unease when using a VDU.

The week hasn't turned out how I'd thought. It has been one where simple things have seemed important. I wonder if this is the onset of a Sartre nausea or a return to childhood? It seems to me that our passage through life can become the practice of the art of noticing less and less detail. A child is like a fractal adult in so far as it sees so much more detail than the adult does. Definitely the end of a fractal week.

QUESTIONS

1. Make a list of the problems which Alan I. Phillips faces in his job as head of Computer Services.
2. Categorize these problems into three categories: organizational, technical, and personal.
3. As a consultant, recommend some solutions to his problems.

EXERCISES

PROBLEMS FOR MANAGERS AND LOVERS

Modern organizations are managed by women and men and, realistically, we may expect at some time in our careers to encounter the problems generated by managerial love affairs in the organizations where we work. An exercise such as this one allows you an opportunity to review, with your colleagues in your class, the effect of these love affairs on the efficiency and morale of the organization. Moreover, you may discuss how the organization can deal with such problems.

Eliza Collins, in her article "Managers and Lovers,"[1] explores the effects of a love affair between top managers upon the organization. Although love is wonderful, the author warns that it often has serious repercussions for the lovers, co-workers, and organizational health.

In the past there were few female executives. Most managers were male, and their sexual partners were invariably of a much lower status: a manager and his secretary. These relationships were usually " . . . short term sexual sprees" with minor consequences for the organization.

Today more women are reaching top management positions. This, the author states, leads to an opportunity for people with similar education and status to develop mature love relationships. To define mature love, Ms. Collins turns to Erich Fromm's *The Art of Loving*[2] in which he states:

> In contrast to symbiotic union, mature love is union under the condition of preserving one's integrity, one's individuality. Love is an active power in man; a power which breaks through the walls, which separates man from his fellow men, which unites him with others; love makes him overcome the sense of isolation and separateness, yet it permits him to be himself, to retain his integrity . . . Because sexual desire is in the minds of most people coupled with the idea of love, they are easily misled to conclude that they love each other when they want each other physically.

As men reach the highest management levels they realize that there is more to life than work. They are usually reaching mid-life crisis and may be looking for love and acceptance from their female peers.

The organizational reaction to an "office affair" is determined by a number of factors. First, it is determined by the CEO's executive style, and the corporate morality.

Moreover, the informal communications network may be crossed by this new alliance. Ms. Collins uses an example in which the subordinate is excluded from luncheons as her peers were afraid their comments would be repeated to her lover. Additionally, subordinates may feel, rightly or wrongly, that the lover will be receiving special consideration.

The women, usually in a subordinate managerial position, are often the butt of co-workers' hostility and insecurity. The women often feel victimized by this and their lovers feel trapped and powerless. "In such predicaments, the male executives become angry that they cannot protect the women they love."

The role of the superior, usually the CEO, in this matter can be extremely difficult. The author suggests four guidelines to help the manager.

1. Treat the relationship as a conflict of interest. In this manner the focus is returned to the effect of the affair on organizational efficiency and less on personality and emotions. The boss should not allow his or her personal morality to interfere – this is a business problem and should be handled as such.
2. Advise the couple to get outside help. An outside counselor brings a fresh, professional viewpoint to the situation.
3. Persuade the couple that either the person least essential to the company, or both, have to go. From an organizational standpoint this is probably the best and, in the long run, the only solution.
4. Help the ousted executive find a new and perhaps better job. By helping to relocate the executive who is dismissed the organization can assuage its feelings of guilt and demonstrate its humanity.

Ms. Collins concludes her article by reviewing what she considers the most important issues.

1. Women executives will continue to be the prime victims in corporate love affairs.
2. Male executives will create difficulties for themselves and their partners when the women are of a subordinate rank.
3. Managers do the corporation a disservice by turning a blind eye to disruptive affairs.

References

1. Eliza Collins (September-October 1983) "Managers and Lovers." *Harvard Business Review*, pp. 142–153.
2. Erich Fromm (1956) *The Art of Loving*. New York: Harper and Row.

QUESTIONS

1. How do love affairs in the workplace affect the quality of work?
2. How do they affect others at work?
3. How can an affair be resolved?
4. Who are the victims?
5. In general, what should organization policy towards such love affairs be?

STUDYING EXECUTIVE BEHAVIOR BY VIDEO*

INSTRUCTIONS

To become successful in management it is necessary to develop skill in observing and understanding the behavior of executives with whom you work. These exercises require you to analyse the behavior of executives whom you will see on video. Exercises such as the following ones will allow you to form judgments about the behaviors of executives and to compare these judgments with those formed by other students.

The video-tape you are about to watch shows an executive in action. This exercise consists of a series of evaluation forms which you can use to evaluate the executive while viewing the videotape. Proceed as follows:

1. Before you start it would be useful to get some information about yourself. Please fill in the following background information sheets.
2. Now you are ready to start the evaluation process.
3. You will find two types of evaluation forms that you can use in rating the executives. The first type you should use while viewing the videotape. The second type is a rating summary sheet which you should use at the end of the video.

Describe yourself briefly. _____

_____

What are your major strengths, weaknesses? _____

_____

Of what achievements are you most proud? Why? _____

_____

Do you describe yourself as introvert or extrovert? _____

In the following exercise, place a check mark in the appropriate column you think describes you most. The direction toward which you check, of course, depends upon which of the two ends of the scale seem most characteristic of yourself. If you consider yourself to be neutral on the scale, or if the scale is completely irrelevant, then you should place your check mark in the middle space.

---

* This exercise can be carried out with the videos: *Fred Henderson* and *Renn Zaphiropoulos* (Xerox Corporation). These 20-minute videos are available from Xerox Learning Corporation, Harvard Business School Publications, Cambridge MA, 02163.

Part One Introduction

Example   active   ___ ___ ✓ ___ ___   passive

friendly   ___ ___ ___ ___ ___   unfriendly
insensitive   ___ ___ ___ ___ ___   sensitive
weak   ___ ___ ___ ___ ___   strong
unselfish   ___ ___ ___ ___ ___   selfish
soft   ___ ___ ___ ___ ___   hard
excitable   ___ ___ ___ ___ ___   calm
optimistic   ___ ___ ___ ___ ___   pessimistic
shy   ___ ___ ___ ___ ___   forward
prohibitive   ___ ___ ___ ___ ___   permissive
aimless   ___ ___ ___ ___ ___   motivated
cautious   ___ ___ ___ ___ ___   rash
sociable   ___ ___ ___ ___ ___   unsociable
aggressive   ___ ___ ___ ___ ___   passive
deliberate   ___ ___ ___ ___ ___   impulsive
immature   ___ ___ ___ ___ ___   mature
deep   ___ ___ ___ ___ ___   shallow
tolerant   ___ ___ ___ ___ ___   intolerant

Part I Based on the videotape. To be completed immediately after the video.

Evaluate the executive on the characteristics shown in the box below. Select the event when he showed that particular characteristic here.

Characteristic	Description of Event
Autocratic	
Democratic	
Open	
Closed	
Honest	
Credible	
Intelligent	

Part II Answer the following questions:

1. What did you like most about the executive?
2. What information in the video tape influenced you most?
3. During the video did you change your mind about the executive? If yes, why?
4. Did the executive remind you of any famous person? Yes _____ No _____
   Name that person.
5. Did the order of information in the video influence your decision? Yes _____ No _____
6. In your own words, describe the executive's appearance.
7. What are the executive's major strengths?
8. What are the executive's major weaknesses?
9. Would you describe the executive as an effective manager?
10. What favorable information (if any) influenced your decision?
11. What negative information (if any) about the executive influenced your decision?
12. Place a check mark in the appropriate column you think describes the executive most. The direction toward which you check, of course, depends upon which of the two ends of the scale seem most characteristic of the person you are judging. If you consider the person to be neutral on the scale, or if the scale is completely irrelevant, unrelated to the concept, then you should place your check mark in the middle space.

Example	active	___	___	✓	___	___	passive
	friendly	___	___	___	___	___	unfriendly
	insensitive	___	___	___	___	___	sensitive
	weak	___	___	___	___	___	strong
	unselfish	___	___	___	___	___	selfish
	soft	___	___	___	___	___	hard
	excitable	___	___	___	___	___	calm
	optimistic	___	___	___	___	___	pessimistic
	shy	___	___	___	___	___	forward
	prohibitive	___	___	___	___	___	permissive
	aimless	___	___	___	___	___	motivated
	cautious	___	___	___	___	___	rash
	sociable	___	___	___	___	___	unsociable
	aggressive	___	___	___	___	___	passive

deliberate	___	___	___	___	___	impulsive
immature	___	___	___	___	___	mature
deep	___	___	___	___	___	shallow
tolerant	___	___	___	___	___	intolerant

13. Would you describe the video you are watching as:
    _____ Realistic
    _____ Unrealistic

Part III

The Executive

1. Write a sketch of that person in about 50 words, making clear why he impressed you so.
2. How did his style affect his subordinates?
3. Define his leadership style.
4. If he had a second-in-command, can you comment on his personality and style?
5. Would you like to work for this executive? Yes _____ No _____ Give reasons for your answer.
6. Review in your mind the encounters which the executive portrayed had with his colleagues. What are the three most pressing problems which you feel this executive creates for those who have to work with him?

Part IV

Test of Imagination

Please read the following instructions carefully before going on.

Imagination and creative ability can be very useful for analyzing and understanding executive behavior. The following exercise gives you the opportunity to use your imagination by asking you to describe common situations that occur in executive life.

Instructions

Write out a brief story with the executive presented in the video as the central character. You have been shown a video tape that you can interpret and around which you can build your story.

Work Rapidly. Do not spend over five minutes on this story.

1. What is going on? Who are the executives?
2. How did this story develop? What caused it?
3. What is in the minds of the executives? What do they want?
4. What is going to happen? What action will be taken?

PART TWO
THE INDIVIDUAL

III
PERCEPTION, PERSONALITY, AND FEEDBACK

READINGS

MAKING MANAGEMENT DECISIONS: THE ROLE OF INTUITION AND EMOTION*

Herbert A. Simon

The work of a manager includes making decisions (or participating in their making), communicating them to others, and monitoring how they are carried out. Managers must know a great deal about the industry and social environment in which they work and the decision-making process itself to make decisions well. Over the past forty years, the technique of decision making has been greatly advanced by the development of a wide range of tools — in particular, the tools of operations research and management science, and the technology of expert systems.

But these advances have not applied to the entire domain of decision making. They have had their greatest impact on decision making that is well-structured, deliberative, and quantitative; they have had less impact on decision making that is loosely structured, intuitive, and qualitative; and they have had the least impact on face-to-face interactions between a manager and his or her coworkers — the give and take of everyday work.

In this article, I will discuss these two relatively neglected types of decision making: "intuitive"

---

* From the *Academy of Management Executive*, February 1987, pp. 57–64. Reprinted by permission of the publisher and author.

decision making and decision making that involves interpersonal interaction. What, if anything, do we know about how judgmental and intuitive processes work and how they can be made to work better? And why do managers often fail to do what they know they should do — even what they have decided to do? What can be done to bring action into closer accord with intention?

My article will therefore have the form of a diptych, with one half devoted to each of these topics. First, I will discuss judgmental and intuitive decision making; then I will turn to the subject of the manager's behavior and the influence of emotions on that behavior.

Sometimes the term rational (or logical) is applied to decision making that is consciously analytic, the term nonrational to decision making that is intuitive and judgmental, and the term irrational to decision making and behavior that responds to the emotions or that deviates from action chosen "rationally." We will be concerned, then, with the nonrational and the irrational components of managerial decision making and behavior. Our task, you might say, is to discover the reason that underlies unreason.

INTUITION AND JUDGMENT

As an appendix to the *Functions of the Executive* (Harvard University Press, 1938), Chester I. Barnard published an essay, based on a talk he had given in 1936 at Princeton, entitled "Mind in Everyday Affairs."[1] The central motif of that essay was a contrast between what Barnard called "logical" and "nonlogical" processes for making decisions. He speaks of "the wide divergence of opinion . . . as to what constitutes a proper intellectual basis for opinion or deliberate action." And he continues:

> By "logical processes" I mean conscious thinking which could be expressed in words or by other symbols, that is, reasoning. By "non-logical processes" I mean those not capable of being expressed in words or as reasoning, which are only made known by a judgment, decision or action.[2]

Barnard's thesis was that executives, as contrasted, say, with scientists, do not often enjoy the luxury of making their decisions on the basis of orderly rational analysis, but depend largely on intuitive or judgmental responses to decision-demanding situations.

Although Barnard did not provide a set of formal criteria for distinguishing between logical and judgmental decision making, he did provide a phenomenological characterization of the two styles that make them easily recognizable, at least in their more extreme forms. In logical decision making, goals and alternatives are made explicit, the consequences of pursuing different alternatives are calculated, and these consequences are evaluated in terms of how close they are to the goals.

In judgmental decision making, the response to the need for a decision is usually rapid, too rapid to allow for an orderly sequential analysis of the situation, and the decision maker cannot usually give a veridical account of either the process by which the decision was reached or the grounds for judging it correct. Nevertheless, decision makers may have great confidence in the correctness of their intuitive decisions and are likely to attribute their ability to make them rapidly to their experience.

Most executives probably find Barnard's account of their decision processes persuasive; it captures their own feelings of how processes work. On the other hand, some students of management, especially those whose goal is to improve management-decision processes, have felt less comfortable with it. It appears to vindicate snap judgments and to cast doubt on the relevance of management-science tools, which almost all involve deliberation and calculation in decision making.

Barnard did not regard the nonlogical processes of decision as magical in any sense. On the contrary, he felt they were grounded in knowledge and experience:

> The sources of these non-logical processes lie in physiological conditions or factors, or in the physical and social environment, mostly impressed upon us unconsciously or without conscious effort on our part. They also consist of the mass of facts, patterns, concepts, techniques, abstractions, and generally what we call formal knowledge or beliefs, which are impressed upon our minds more or less by conscious effort and study. This second source of non-logical mental processes greatly increases with directed experience, study and education.[3]

At the time I wrote *Administrative Behavior* (1941–42), I was troubled by Barnard's account of intuitive judgment largely, I think, because he left no clues as to what subconscious processes go on while judgments are being made.[4] I was wholly persuaded, however, that a theory of decision making had to give an account of both conscious and subconscious processes. I finessed the issue by assuming that both the conscious and the unconscious parts of the process were the same, that they involve drawing on factual premises and value premises, and operating on them to form conclusions that became the decisions.

Because I used logic (drawing conclusions from premises) as a central metaphor to describe the decision-making process, many readers of *Administrative Behavior* have concluded that the theory advanced there applies only to "logical" decision making, not to decisions that involve intuition and judgment. That was certainly not my intent. But now, after nearly 50 years, the ambiguity can be resolved because we have acquired a solid understanding of what the judgmental and intuitive processes are. I will take up the new evidence in a moment; but first, a word must be said about the "two brains" hypothesis, which argues that rational and intuitive processes are so different that they are carried out in different parts of the brain.

Split Brains and Forms of Thought
Physiological research on "split brains" – brains in which the corpus callosum, which connects the two hemispheres of the cerebrum, has been severed – has provided encouragement to the idea of two qualitatively different kinds of decision making – the analytical, corresponding to Barnard's "logical," and the intuitive or creative, corresponding to his "non-logical." The primary evidence behind this dichotomy is that the two hemispheres exhibit a division of labor: in right-handed people, the right hemisphere plays a special role in the recognition of visual patterns, and the left hemisphere in analytical processes and the use of language.

Other evidence in addition to the split-brain research suggests some measure of hemispheric specialization. Electrical activity in the intact brain can be measured by EEG techniques. Activity in a brain hemisphere is generally associated with partial or total suppression in the hemisphere of the alpha system, a salient brain wave with a frequency of about ten vibrations per second. When a hemisphere is inactive, the alpha rhythm in that hemisphere becomes strong. For most right-handed subjects, when the brain is engaged in a task involving recognition of visual pattern, the alpha rhythm is relatively stronger in the left than in the right hemisphere; with more analytical tasks, the alpha rhythm is relatively stronger in the right hemisphere. (See Doktor and Hamilton, 1973, and Doktor, 1975, for some experiments and a review of the evidence.)[5]

The more romantic versions of the split-brain doctrine extrapolate this evidence into the two polar forms of thought labeled above as analytical and creative. As an easy next step, evaluative nuances creep into the discussion. The opposite of "creative," after all, is "pedestrian." The analytical left hemisphere, so this story goes, carries on the humdrum, practical, everyday work of the brain, while the creative right hemisphere is responsible for those flights of imagination that produce great music, great literature, great art, great science, and great management. The evidence for this romantic extrapolation does not derive from the physiological research. As I indicated above, that research has provided evidence only for some measure of specialization between the hemispheres. It does not in any way imply that either hemisphere (especially the right hemisphere) is capable of problem solving, decision making, or discovery independent of the other. The real evidence for two different forms of thought is essentially that on which Barnard relied: the observation that, in everyday affairs, men and women often make competent judgments or reach reasonable decisions rapidly – without evidence indicating that they have engaged in systematic reasoning, and without their being able to report the thought processes that took them to their conclusion.

There is also some evidence for the very plausible hypothesis that some people, confronted with a particular problem, make more use of intuitive processes in solving it, while other people make relatively more use of analytical processes (Doktor, 1978).[6]

For our purposes, it is the differences in behavior, and not the differences in the hemispheres, that are important. Reference to the two hemispheres is a red herring that can only impede our understanding of intuitive, "non-logical" thought. The important questions for us are "What is intuition?" and "How is it accomplished?" not "In which cubic centimeters of the brain tissue does it take place?"

New Evidence on the Processes of Intuition
In the 50 years since Barnard talked about the mind in everyday affairs, we have learned a great deal about the processes human beings use to solve problems, to make decisions, and even to create works of art and science. Some of this new knowledge has been gained in the psychological laboratory; some has been gained through observation of the behavior of people who are demonstrably creative in some realm of human endeavor; and a great deal has been gained through

the use of the modern digital computer to model human thought processes and perform problem-solving and decision-making functions at expert levels.

I should like to examine this body of research, which falls under the labels of "cognitive science" and "artificial intelligence," to see what light it casts on intuitive, judgmental decision making in management. We will see that a rather detailed account can be given of the processes that underlie judgment, even though most of these processes are not within the conscious awareness of the actor using them.

THE EXPERT'S INTUITION

In recent years, the disciplines of cognitive science and artificial intelligence have devoted a great deal of attention to the nature of expert problem solving and decision making in professional-level tasks. The goal of the cognitive science research has been to gain an understanding of the differences between the behavior of experts and novices, and possibly to learn more about how novices can become experts. The goal of the artificial intelligence research has been to build computer systems that can perform professional tasks as competently as human experts can. Both lines of research have greatly deepened our understanding of expertise.[7]

Intuition in Chessplaying

One much studied class of experts is the grandmasters in the game of chess. Chess is usually believed to require a high level of intellect, and grandmasters are normally full-time professionals who have devoted many years to acquiring their mastery of the game. From a research standpoint, the advantage of the game is that the level of skill of players can be calibrated accurately from their official ratings, based on their tournament success.

From the standpoint of studying intuitive thinking, chess might seem (at least to outsiders) an unpromising research domain. Chess playing is thought to involve a highly analytical approach, with players working out systematically the consequences of moves and countermoves, so that a single move may take as much as a half hour's thought, or more. On the other hand, chess professionals can play simultaneous games, sometimes against as many as 50 opponents, and exhibit only a moderately lower level of skill than in games playing under tournament conditions. In simultaneous play, the professional takes much less than a minute, often only a few seconds, for each move. There is no time for careful analysis.

When we ask the grandmaster or master how he or she is able to find good moves under these circumstances, we get the same answer that we get from other professionals who are questioned about rapid decisions: It is done by "intuition," by applying one's professional "judgment" to the situation. A few seconds' glance at the position suggests a good move, although the player has no awareness of how the judgment was evoked.

Even under tournament conditions, good moves usually come to a player's mind after only a few seconds' consideration of the board. The remainder of the analysis time is generally spent verifying that a move appearing plausible does not have a hidden weakness. We encounter this same kind of behavior in other professional domains where intuitive judgments are usually subjected to tests of various kinds before they are actually implemented. The main exceptions are situations where the decision has to be made before a deadline or almost instantly. Of course we know that under these circumstances (as in professional chess when the allowed time is nearly exhausted), mistakes are sometimes made.

How do we account for the judgment or intuition that allows the chess grandmaster usually to find good moves in a few seconds? A good deal of the answer can be derived from an experiment that is easily repeated. First, present a grandmaster and a novice with a position from an actual, but unfamiliar, chess game (with about twenty-five pieces on the board). After five or ten seconds, remove the board and pieces and ask the subjects to reproduce it. The grandmaster will usually reconstruct the whole position correctly, and on average will place twenty-three or twenty-four pieces on their correct squares. The novice will only be able to replace, on average, about six pieces.

It might seem that we are witnessing remarkable skill in visual imagery and visual memory, but we can easily dismiss that possibility by carrying out a second experiment. The conditions are exactly the same as in the first experiment, except that now the twenty-five pieces are placed on the board at random. The novice can still replace about six pieces and the grandmaster — about six! The difference between them in the first experiment does not lie in the grandmaster's eyes or imagery, but in his knowledge, acquired by long experience, of the kinds of patterns and clusters of pieces that occur on chessboards in the course of games. For the expert, such a chess board is not an arrangement of twenty-five pieces but an arrangement of a half dozen familiar patterns, recognizable old friends. On the random board there are no such patterns, only the twenty-five individual pieces in an unfamiliar arrangement.

The grandmaster's memory holds more than a set of patterns. Associated with each pattern in his or her memory is information about the significance of that pattern — what dangers it holds, and what offensive or defensive moves it suggests. Recognizing the pattern brings to the grandmaster's mind at once moves that may be appropriate to the situation. It is this recognition that enables the professional to play very strong chess at a rapid rate. Previous learning that has stored the patterns and the information associated with them in memory makes this performance possible. This, then, is the secret of the grandmaster's intuition or judgment.

Estimates have been made, in a variety of ways, of the number of familiar patterns (which psychologists now call chunks) that the master or grandmaster must be able to recognize. These estimates fall in the neighborhood of 50,000, give or take a factor of two. Is this a large number? Perhaps not. The natural language vocabularies of college graduates have been estimated to be in the range of 50,000 to 200,000 words, nearly the same range as the chess expert's vocabularies of patterns of pieces. Moreover, when we recognize a word, we also get access to information in our memories about the meaning of the word and to other information associated with it as well. So our ability to speak and understand language has the same intuitive or judgmental flavor as the grandmaster's ability to play chess rapidly.

Intuition in Computerized Expert Systems
A growing body of evidence from artificial intelligence research indicates that expert computer systems, capable of matching human performance in some limited domain, can be built by storing in computer memory tens of thousands of *productions*. Productions are computer instructions that take the form of "if-then" pairs. The "if" is a set of conditions or patterns to be recognized; the "then" is a body of information associated with the "if" and evoked from memory whenever the pattern is recognized in the current situation.

Some of our best data about this organization of expert knowledge come from the areas of medical diagnosis. Systems like CADUCEUS and MYCIN consist of a large number of such if-then pairs, together with an inference machine of modest powers. These systems are capable of medical diagnosis at a competent clinical level within their respective limited domains. Their recognition capabilities, the if-then pairs, represent their intuitive or judgmental ability; their inferencing powers represnt their analytical ability.

Medical diagnosis is just one of a number of domains for which expert systems have been built. For many years, electric motors, generators, and transformers have been designed by expert systems developed by large electrical manufacturers. These computer programs have taken over from professional engineers many standard and relatively routine design tasks. They imitate fairly closely the rule-of-thumb procedures that human designers have used, the result of a large stock of theoretical and practical information about electrical machinery. Recognition also pays a large role in these systems. For example, examination of the customer's specifications "reminds" the program of a particular class of devices, which is then used as the basis for the design. Parameters for the design are then selected to meet the performances requirements of the device.

In chemistry, reaction paths for synthesizing organic molecules can be designed by expert systems. In these systems, the process appears relatively analytic, for it is guided by reasoning in the form of means-ends analyses, which work backward from the desired molecule, via a sequence of reactions, to available raw materials. But the reasoning scheme depends on a large store of knowledge of chemical reactions and the ability of the system to recognize rapidly that a particular substance can be obtained as the output of one or more familiar reactions. Thus, these chemical synthesis programs employ the same kind of mixture of intuition and analysis that is used in the other expert systems, and by human experts as well.

Other examples of expert systems can be cited, and all of them exhibit reasoning or analytic processes combined with processes for accessing knowledge banks with the help of recognition cues. This appears to be a universal scheme for the organization of expert systems – and of expert human problem solving as well.

Notice that there is nothing "irrational" about intuitive or judgmental reasoning based on productions. The conditions in a production constitute a set of premises. Whenever these conditions are satisfied, the production draws the appropriate conclusion – it evokes from memory information implied by these conditions or even initiates motor responses. A person learning to drive a car may notice a red light, be aware that a red light calls for a stop, and be aware that stopping requires applying the brakes. For an experienced driver, the sight of the red light simply evokes the application of brakes. How conscious the actor is of the process inversely, how automatic the response is, may differ, but there is no difference in the logic being applied.

Intuition in Management

Some direct evidence also suggests that the intuitive skills of managers depend on the same kinds of mechanisms as the intuitive skills of chessmasters or physicians. It would be surprising if it were otherwise. The experienced manager, too, has in his or her memory a large amount of knowledge, gained from training and experience and organized in terms of recognizable chunks and associated information.

Marius J. Bouwman has constructed a computer program capable of detecting company problems from an examination of accounting statements.[8] The program was modeled on detailed thinking-aloud protocols of experienced financial analysts interpreting such statements, and it captures the knowledge that enables analysts to spot problems intuitively, usually at a very rapid rate. When a comparison is made between the responses of the program and the responses of an expert human financial analyst, a close match is usually found.

In another study, R. Bhaskar gathered thinking-aloud protocols from business school students and experienced businessmen, who were all asked to analyze a business policy case.[9] The final analyses produced by the students and the businessmen were quite similar. What most sharply discriminated between the novices and the experts was the time required to identify the key features of the case. This was done very rapidly, with the usual appearances of intuition, by the experts; it was done slowly, with much conscious and explicit analysis, by the novices.

These two pieces of research are just drops of water in a large bucket that needs filling. The description, in detail, of the use of judgmental and analytical processes in expert problem solving and decision making deserves a high priority in the agenda of management research.

Can Judgment Be Improved?

From this and other research on expert problem solving and decision making, we can draw two main conclusions. *First*, experts often arrive at problem diagnoses and solutions rapidly and intuitively without being able to report how they attained the result. *Second*, this ability is best explained by postulating a recognition and retrieval process that employs a large number – generally tens of thousands or even hundreds of thousands – of chunks or patterns stored in long term memory.

When the problems to be solved are more than trivial, the recognition processes have to be organized in a coherent way and they must be supplied with reasoning capabilities that allow inferences to be drawn from the information retrieved, and numerous chunks of information to be combined. Hence intuition is not a process that operates independently of analysis; rather, the two processes are essential complementary components of effective decision-making systems. When the expert is solving a difficult problem or making a complex decision, much conscious deliberation may be involved. But each conscious step may itself constitute a considerable leap, with a whole sequence of automated productions building the bridge from the premises to the conclusions. Hence the expert appears to take giant intuitive steps in reasoning, as compared with the tiny steps of the novice.

It is doubtful that we will find two types of managers (at least, of good managers), one of whom relies almost exclusively on intuition, the other on analytic techniques. More likely, we will find a continuum of decision-making styles involving an intimate combination of the two kinds of skill. We will likely also find that the nature of the problem to be solved will be a principal determinant of the mix.

With our growing understanding of the organization of judgmental and intuitive processes, of the specific knowledge that is required to perform particular judgmental tasks, and of the cues that evoke such knowledge in situations in which it is relevant, we have a powerful new tool for improving expert judgment. We can specify the knowledge and the recognition capabilities that experts in a domain need to acquire as a basis for designing appropriate learning procedures.

We can also, in more and more situations, design expert systems capable of automating the expertise, or alternatively, of providing the human decision maker with an expert consultant. Increasingly, we will see decision aids for managers that will be highly interactive, with both knowledge and intelligence being shared between the human and the automated components of the system.

A vast research and development task of extracting and cataloging the knowledge and cues used by experts in different kinds of managerial tasks lies ahead. Much has been learned in the past few years about how to do this. More needs to be learned about how to update and improve the knowledge sources of expert systems as new knowledge becomes available.

Progress will be most rapid with expert systems that have a substantial technical component. It is no accident that the earliest expert systems were built for such tasks as designing motors, making medical diagnoses, playing chess, and finding chemical synthesis paths. In the area of management, the analysis of company financial statements is a domain where some progress has been made in constructing expert systems. The areas of corporate policy and strategy are excellent candidates for early development of such systems.

What about the aspects of executive work that involve the managing people? What help can we expect in improving this crucial component of the management tasks?

KNOWLEDGE AND BEHAVIOR

What managers know they should do – whether by analysis or intuitively – is very often different from what they actually do. A common failure of managers, which all of us have observed, is the postponement of difficult decisions. What is it that makes decisions difficult and hence tends to cause postponement? Often, the problem is that all of the alternatives have undesired consequences. When people have to choose the lesser of two evils, they do not simply behave like Bayesian statisticians, weighing the bad against the worse in the light of their respective possibilities. Instead, they avoid the decision, searching for alternatives that do not have negative outcomes. If such alternatives are not available, they are likely to continue to postpone making a choice. A choice between undesirables is a dilemma, something to be avoided or evaded.

Often, uncertainty is the source of the difficulty. Each choice may have a good outcome under one set of environmental contingencies, but a bad outcome under another. When this occurs, we also do not usually observe Bayesian behavior; the situation is again treated as a dilemma.

The bad consequences of a manager's decision are often bad for other people. Managers sometimes have to dismiss employees or, even more frequently, have to speak to them about unsatisfactory work. Dealing with such matters face to face is stressful to many, perhaps most, executives. The stress is magnified if the employee is a close associate or friend. If the unpleasant task cannot be delegated, it may be postponed.

The manager who has made a mistake (that is to say, all of us at one time or another) also finds himself or herself in a stressful situation. The matter must be dealt with sooner or later, but why not later instead of sooner? Moreover, when it is addressed, it can be approached in different ways. A manager may try to avoid blame – "It wasn't my fault!" A different way is to propose a remedy to the situation. I know of no systematic data on how often the one or the other course is taken, but most of us could probably agree that blame-avoiding behavior is far more common than problem-solving behavior after a serious error has been made.

The Consequences of Stress

What all of these decision-making situations have in common is stress, a powerful force that can divert behavior from the urgings of reason. They are examples of a much broader class of situations in which managers frequently behave in clearly nonproductive ways. Nonproductive responses are especially common when actions have to be made under time pressure. The need to allay feelings of guilt, anxiety, and embarrassment may lead to behavior that produces temporary personal comfort at the expense of bad long-run consequences of the organization.

Behavior of this kind is "intuitive" in the sense that it represents response without careful analysis and calculation. Lying, for example, is much more often the result of panic than of Machiavellian scheming. The intuition of the emotion-driven manager is very different from the intuition of the expert whom we discussed earlier. The latter's behavior is the product of learning and experience, and is largely adaptive; the former's behavior is a response to more primitive urges, and is more often than not inappropriate. We must not confuse the "nonrational" decisions of the experts – the decisions that derive from expert intuition and judgment – with the irrational decisions that stressful emotions may produce.

I have made no attempt here to produce a comprehensive taxonomy of the pathologies of organizational decision making, but simply have given some examples of the ways that stress interacts with cognition to elicit counterproductive behavior. Such responses can become so habitual for individuals or even for organizations that they represent a recognizable managerial "style."

Organizational psychologists have a great deal to say about ways of motivating workers and executives to direct their efforts toward organizational goals. They have said less about ways of molding habits so that executives can handle situations in a goal-directed manner. When it comes to handling situations, two dimensions of behavior deserve particular attention: the response to problems that arise, and the initiation of activity that looks to the future.

Responding to Problems

The response of an organization to a problem or difficulty, whether it results from a mistake or some other cause, is generally one that looks both backward and forward. It looks backward to establish responsibility for the difficulty and to diagnose it, and forward to find a course of action to deal with it.

The backward look is an essential part of the organization's reward system. The actions that have led to difficulties, and the people responsible for those actions, need to be identified. But the backward look can also be a source of serious pathologies. Anticipation of it – particularly anticipation that it will be acted on in a punitive way – is a major cause for the concealment of problems until they can no longer be hidden. It can also be highly divisive, as individuals point fingers to transfer blame to others. Such outcomes can hardly be eliminated, but an organization's internal reputation for fairness and objectivity can mitigate them. So can a practice of subordinating the blame finding to a diagnosis of causes as a first step toward remedial action.

Most important of all, however, is the forward look: the process of defining the problem and identifying course of action that may solve it. Here also the reward system is critically important. Readiness to search for problem situations and effectiveness in finding them need to be recognized and rewarded.

Perhaps the greatest influence a manager can have on the problem-solving style of the organization as a role model is making the best responses to problems. The style the manager should aim for rests on the following principles:

1. Solving the problem takes priority over looking backward to its causes. Initially, backward looks should be limited to diagnosing causes; fixing responsibility for mistakes should be postponed until a solution is being implemented.
2. The manager accepts personal responsibility for finding and proposing solutions instead of seeking to shift that responsibility either to superiors or to subordinates, although the search for solutions may, of course, be a collaborative effort involving many people.
3. The manager accepts personal responsibility for implementing action solutions, including securing the necessary authority from above if required.
4. When it is time to look backward, fixing blame may be an essential part of the process, but the primary focus of attention should be on what can be learned to prevent similar problems from arising in the future.

These principles are as obvious as the Ten Commandments and perhaps not quite as difficult to obey. Earlier, I indicated that stress might cause departures from them, but failure to respond effectively to problems probably derives more from a lack of attention and an earlier failure to cultivate the appropriate habits. The military makes much use of a procedure called "Estimate of the Situation." Its value is not that it teaches anything esoteric, but that through continual training in its use, commanders become habituated to approaching situations in orderly ways, using the checklists provided by the formal procedure.

Habits of response to problems are taught and learned both in the manager's one-on-one conversations with subordinates and in staff meetings. Is attention brought back repeatedly to defining the problems until everyone is agreed on just what the problem is? Is attention then directed toward generating possible solutions and evaluating their consequences? The least often challenged and most reliable base of managerial influence is the power to set the agenda, to focus attention. It is one of the most effective tools the manager has for training organization members to approach problems constructively by shaping their own habits of attention.

The perceptive reader will have discerned that "shaping habits of attention" is identical to "acquiring intuitions." The habit of responding to problems by looking for solutions can and must become intuitive – cued by the presence of the problem itself. A problem-solving style is a component of the set of intuitions that the manager acquires, one of the key components of effective managerial behavior.

Looking to the Future

With respect to the initiation of activity, the organizational habit we would like to instil is responsiveness to cues that signal future difficulties a well as to those that call attention to the problems of the moment. Failure to give sufficient attention to the future most often stems from two causes. The first is interruption by current problems that have more proximate deadlines and hence seem more urgent; the second is the absence of sufficient "scanning" activity that can pick up cues from the environment that long-run forces not impinging immediately on the organization have importance for it in the future.

In neither case is the need for sensitivity to the future likely to be met simply by strengthening intuitions. Rather, what is called for is deliberate and systematic allocation of organizational resources to deal with long-range problems, access for these resources to appropriate input from the environment that will attract their attention to new prospects, and protection of these planning resources from absorption in current problems, however urgent they may be. Attention to the future must be institutionalized; there is no simpler way to incorporate it into managerial "style" or habit.

It is a fallacy to contrast "analytic" and "intuitive" styles of management. Intuition and judgment – at least good judgment – are simply analyses frozen into habit and into the capacity for rapid response through recognition. Every manager needs to be able to analyze problems systematically (and with the aid of the modern arsenal of analytical tools provided by management science and operations research). Every manager needs also to be able to respond to situations rapidly, a skill that requires the cultivation of intuition and judgment over many years of experience and training. The effective manager does not have the luxury of choosing between "analytic" and "intuitive" approaches to problems. Behaving like a manager means having command of the whole range of management skills and applying them as they become appropriate.

References

1. C.I. Barnard (1938) *The Functions of the Executive*. Cambridge, MA: Harvard University Press, contains the essay on the contrast between logical and nonlogical processes as bases for decision making.
2. C.I. Barnard. *op. cit.*
3. *Ibid.*, p. 302.
4. H.A. Simon (1978) *Administrative Behavior*, 2nd ed. New York: The Free Press.
   For a review of the artificial intelligence research on expert systems, see A. Barr and E.A. Figenbaum, eds., (1982) *The Handbook of Artificial Intelligence*, Volume 2, Los Alamos, CA: William Kaufmann, pp. 77–294.
5. Two works that examine the split brain theory and forms of thought are R.H. Doktor (1978) "Problem Solving Styles of Executives and Management Scientists," in A. Charnes, W.W. Cooper and R.J. Niehaus, eds., *Management Science Approaches to Manpower Planning and Organization Design*. Amsterdam: North Holland; and R.H. Doktor and W.F. Hamilton "Cognitive Style and the Acceptance of Management Science Recommendations." *Management Science*, 19:884–893.
6. R.H. Doktor (1978) "Problem Solving Styles of Executive and Management Scientists," in A. Charnes, W.W. Cooper and R.J. Niehaus, eds., *Management Science Approaches to Manpower Planning and Organization Design*. Amsterdam: North Holland.
7. For a survey of cognitive science research on problem solving and decision making, see H.A. Simon (1979) *The Science of the Artificial*, 2nd ed., Cambridge, MA: MIT Press, Chapters 3 and 4.
8. Marius J. Bouwman (1978) *Financial Diagnosis*. Doctoral dissertation. Carnegie-Mellon University, School of Industrial Administration, Pittsburgh, Pennsylvania.
9. R. Bhaskar (1978) *Problem Solving in Semantically Rich Domains*. Doctoral dissertation. Carnegie-Mellon University, School of Industrial Administration, Pittsburgh, Pennsylvania.

IMPROVING FACE-TO-FACE RELATIONSHIPS*

Edgar H. Schein

The challenges of management in the 1980s are enormous, but they are fairly easy to identify. The great difficulties that we face lie not in deciding *what* our goals should be, but in determining *how* to achieve them. Our problems in this area are problems of *implementation: how* can we reach goals that are often perfectly clear but seemingly impossible to attain.

Several explanations of these problems readily come to mind:

- Large systems have become too complex to be understood.
- "Bureaucracy" makes it impossible to get anything done.
- Intergroup hostility paralyzes all constructive effort.
- Power politics undermine and subvert rational action.
- Irrationality and human resistance to change defeat even the wisest programs.

All of these explanations are true, but they are also incomplete. Sometimes they are used only as excuses for failure rather than as constructive analyses of our management problems. On the other hand, we have learned something about implementation in the last forty years or so, and what we have learned takes us back to one fundamental principle; societies, organizations, and families are human groups, and the face-to-face relationships among the members of these groups are a basic element of any social action. Whatever else we need in the way of systems, procedures, and mechanisms, the process of social action always starts with face-to-face relationships among people.

Face-to-face relationships can be thought of as the glue that holds organizations together, and such relationships are the links in the implementation chain. Therefore, we should take a fresh look at these relationships to see if we can articulate some of the skills which can make them more constructive, and thus enable us to move toward solving some of the pressing problems of the 1980s.

THE ELEMENTS OF FACE-TO-FACE RELATIONSHIPS

What does it take to build, maintain, improve, and, if need be, repair face-to-face relationships? I would like to discuss nine different elements, which are all closely interrelated yet distinct in important ways. These elements reflect motives and values, perceptual skills, and behavior skills:

1. *Self-Insight* – a sense of one's own identity;
2. *Cross-cultural sensitivity* – the ability to decipher other people's values;
3. *Cultural/moral humility* – the ability to see one's own values as not necessarily better or worse than another's values;
4. *A proactive problem-solving orientation* – the conviction that interpersonal and cross-cultural problems can be solved;
5. *Personal flexibility* – the ability to adopt different responses and approaches as needed by situational contingencies;
6. *Negotiation skills* – the ability to explore differences creatively, to locate some common ground, and to solve the problem;
7. *Interpersonal and cross-cultural tact* – the ability to solve problems with people without insulting them, demeaning them, or destroying their "face";

---

* Reprinted from "Improving Face-to-Face Relationships," by Edgar H. Schein, SLOAN MANAGEMENT REVIEW, Winter 1981, pp. 43–52. Copyright © 1981 by the Sloan Management Review Association. All rights reserved.

The author would like to acknowledge the Centre D'Etudes Industrielle, Geneva, Switzerland for its support in writing this paper. This paper is adapted from an address delivered to the 50th Anniversary Convocation of the Sloan Fellows Program, Cambridge, Massachusetts on October 4, 1980.

8. *Repair strategies and skills* – the ability to resurrect, to revitalize, and to rebuild damaged or broken face-to-face relationships;
9. *Patience.*

I would like to discuss each of these elements in turn, putting most of the attention on those which have been insufficiently attended to in prior analyses and on those which are especially relevant to repair strategies.

Self-Insight
One can hardly work out common goals with others if one does not know where one's own values and goals lie. Leaders and managers especially must know where they are going, and they must be able to articulate their own goals. Parents and spouses must make a valiant effort to lift to the surface what is often left implicit – their own life goals and targets – so that there can be genuine negotiation among family members in the different life stages.

Self-insight is a *competence* – the ability to see oneself accurately and to evaluate oneself fairly. Through feedback from others and through systematic self-study, we can improve our ability to see ourselves. As we increase in self-insight, we lay the foundations for self-acceptance, which is to some extent, a prerequisite for some of the other skills to be discussed.

Cross-Cultural Sensitivity
It goes without saying that we cannot offer leadership if we do not have perspective on ourselves and on others, and we cannot gain such perspective if we continue to be ethnocentric – to notice and appreciate only our own culture and values. Cross-cultural issues are not limited to the dramatic differences which can be identified in how different countries operate. Many of the most harmful cases of cultural misunderstanding occur right under our noses – with our spouses, friends, children, and subordinates – because norms, values, and behavioral codes vary widely within any country. American managers often tell tales of woe of trying to transfer people from the deep South to Manhattan, or from an urban center to a rural plant site.

A costly misunderstanding occurred in the small town where we used to spend our summers. The local wood-turning mill employed both men and women from the community, and the pay scales had developed historically around the status system in the town. A new manager who had experience in a progressive urban mill noticed that some of the skilled women operators were grossly underpaid in relation to their male counterparts. He set about to rationalize the pay structure to reflect actual skill levels. This action led to wives bringing home bigger paychecks, which neither they nor their husbands could accept in terms of the status system in the town. The dissatisfaction and turmoil that resulted from upsetting the social order was completely unanticipated by this manager.

Deciphering values, motives, aspirations, and basic assumptions across *occupational* and *social class lines* is particularly difficult. It is hard for the son of a successful middle-class businessman to understand the values and career aspirations of the son of an immigrant or an unskilled worker. It is hard for the general manager to understand the values and career aspirations of the technically oriented person and vice versa. It is hard for people in the different functional areas of a business to decipher each other's values and aspirations.[1]

Cultural Differences between Countries
When we go to countries where a different language is being spoken and where the culture is obviously different, we do wake up to the need to sharpen our deciphering skills. But even then we have a strong tendency to look for similarities and to rationalize that "people are people" and "business is business" no matter where it is conducted. My own tendency to ignore differences was brought home to me during a visit to Australia, which is superficially and historically similar to the U.S. It took me quite a while to discover that while Australians (like Americans) are achievement oriented, they also have the "tall

poppy syndrome": one must not stand out above the crowd; one must accomplish things without seeming to work too hard at them; and one must not take too much personal credit for one's accomplishments. The son of a friend of mine told us how, after waiting all day for the perfect wave, he had finally succeeded in having a brilliant ride on his surfboard. When he hit the beach, he told his watching friends – as he knew he had to – "Boy that was a *lucky* one."

I kept hearing how complacent and security oriented the Australians were even when I was dealing with what seemed to be some pretty tough, aggressive managers. What one's true motives are and what is culturally acceptable as a legitimate explanation of one's motives are, of course, not necessarily the same. In comparing America and Australia, one sees a paradoxical reversal. In Australia, people claim to be mostly security oriented, though companies admitted they had many aggressive, ambitious, power-seeking managers working for them. In the U.S., the popular image is that most people are ambitious and want to climb right to the top of the organization – though I encounter a growing number of allegedly ambitious managers who admit in private that they are not motivated to continue the "rat race," that they would like early retirement, or that they are considering another career altogether. Both public images reflect cultural norms, yet both are to some degree a misrepresentation of the actual state of affairs. The public selves we wear – the way we are supposed to present ourselves to others – is a strongly ingrained set of cultural values in its own right, and tact prevents us from puncturing the illusions which cultures teach us to project.

"Face Work"

Erving Goffman has written articulately about what he calls "face work" – the behavior of people in a social situation which is designed to help everyone maintain the self which they choose to project in that particular situation.² Selves are forever constructed, and the audience for any given performance is culturally bound to uphold as much as possible the identities which the actors claim. At the minimum, we nod and say "uh huh" when someone is talking to us, or we try to laugh politely at a joke that is not really funny, or we ignore embarrassing incidents. If our boss tells us through his actions or demeanor that he believes himself to be very competent in handling a given meeting, we rarely challenge this claim even though we may privately believe the he will totally mismanage it. The skill in this situation is our ability to compensate for his incompetence or to repair what damage may have been done. But we do not destroy his face.

The Reciprocity of Relationships

One of the most interesting features of the cultural norms of face-to-face interactions is their symmetric, reciprocal, exchange nature. We sometimes get into difficulty because we do not know how to complete an interaction. When someone in a strange country offers you an object in his house because you have admired it, are you supposed to take it and reciprocate at some future time when the visitor is in your home, or is it appropriate to refuse? The whole question of when and how to say yes or no is fraught with difficulty if we are talking across cultures or subcultures. And, as many businessmen have found out, how to interpret a yes or a no is even more difficult.

The ability to detect the subtleties of how others perceive situations and of what the values of others are requires both formal training and practical experience. Learning a new language would seem to be a prerequisite since so much of every culture is encoded into the language. Many people pride themselves on their extensive travel, even making lists of how many countries they have been in, without ever encountering or deciphering any of the cultures of those countries; they do not learn the languages and therefore miss the important nuances of what is going on. On the other hand, I have heard repeatedly from multinational companies that one of the best prescriptions for success in an overseas assignment is to take time to learn the local language.

CULTURAL/MORAL HUMILITY

Beyond self-insight and the ability to understand others, we need something which we might call cultural/moral *humility*. Can we not only sense the values of other people but, more importantly, positively appreciate them? Can we see our own culture and values only as *different*, not necessarily as *better*? Our tendency to think of things as "funny" or "odd" is a good diagnostic here. I have often been shown or told about funny things people do in other countries. An American visitor to the mainland of China found it very amusing that some Chinese farmers were so proud of owning tractors which were, in fact, useless; the tractors could not turn on the tight terraces and they did not have attachable plows to pull. The fact that a Chinese farmer did not even know the function of the pin to which the plow attaches struck the American as very funny and weird. It never occurred to him that his own utilitarian, pragmatic values might not be the only relevant ones in this situation.

A few years ago, a group of American students teased one of their German peers about his heel-clicking, head-nodding, hand-shaking formality. After some months of being teased, he stopped them one day with the statement: "When I go to work in the morning, I go to my boss's office, click my heels, bow my head, shake his hand, and then tell him the truth." The teasing stopped.

Many American managers lack cultural humility. We are more pragmatic than other people, and if we encounter people less pragmatic, we view them as odd rather than wonder about the oddity of our being so pragmatic. We don't consider our own culture as funny, odd, and in need of explanation, yet *it is our culture which is probably in a statistical sense the most different from all other cultures*. Let me give a couple of examples:

1. Our mercantile attitude – embodied in our marketing skills and our efforts to sell anything to anybody – strikes people in other parts of the world as being rather crass and superficial. I have encountered managers in other countries who have real reservations about making products which they consider to have no intrinsic value, and who have even greater reservations about using advertising skills to create markets for such products.
2. Our attitude towards efficiency – attempting to reduce all costs for the sake of higher profit margins, even if those costs are people's jobs – is clearly out of line with the value systems in some other countries. Yet we take the importance of efficiency for granted. We do not think of people as capital investments and we find it hard to comprehend systems of guaranteed lifetime employment.

My point is not to dissect the value system of the U.S. but rather to identify a strong tendency I have seen in managers all over the world (Americans and non-Americans alike) to be ethnocentric – to assume that one's own values are the best, and that one is excused from having to know what others think and value, or at least from having to take very seriously what others think and value. Such an absence of cultural humility can be a dangerous weakness when we are attempting face-to-face negotiations or problem solving. This point is important whenever we deal with people whose values are different from our own, whether these people are within our society or are from other countries.

PROACTIVE PROBLEM-SOLVING ORIENTATION

Solving face-to-face problems, especially where difficult cross-cultural understanding and humility are required, presupposes a faith that problems *can* be solved if one works at them and an assumption that active problem solving will produce positive results. Communication and understanding are difficult to achieve, but if one does not even try, then there is no possibility for achievement.

A proactive orientation is itself to some degree a cultural characteristic. When Americans take the "can do" attitude, how do we determine when we are coming on too strongly, or when we are actually intruding in private lifespace in our eagerness to establish constructive face-to-face relationships in order to solve problems. The anthropologist Edward Hall has given us many excellent examples of how conducting business in different cultural contexts must be delicately handled, lest we invade people's territory and unwittingly destroy the possibility of better relationships.[3]

What I mean by a "proactive orientation" is a *motivation* to work on problems, not necessarily a high level of overt *activity*. We must base our actual course of action on genuine cultural understanding and not simply on a desire to act. As in the case of international diplomacy, we should always be ready to negotiate. No matter how bad the situation is between management and employees in a company or industry, each party should always be ready to sit down and try again to talk face-to-face.

PERSONAL FLEXIBILITY

It does us little good to sense situations accurately if we cannot take advantage of what we perceive. I know people who can tell you exactly what is going on but who cannot alter their own behavior to adjust to what they know to be the realities. One of the reasons why experiential learning methods — such as sensitivity training or transactional analysis workshops — have been so successful is that they allow experimentation on the part of participants, thus permitting the participants to enlarge their repertory of face-to-face behavior. Role playing is perhaps the prototype of such behavioral training and is clearly a necessary component of face-to-face skill development.[4]

NEGOTIATION SKILLS

Much has been written about the process of negotiation and the skills needed to be an effective negotiator. To a considerable degree, what has been said reflects the same themes that I am focusing on here. Negotiation requires great sensitivity, humility, self-insight, motivation to solve the problem, and behavioral flexibility. Part of the sensitivity required is the ability to decipher others' values. Another part is the ability to elicit information from others and to judge the validity of that information. Face-to-face relationships are not always benign, not always comfortable, not always safe, and not always open, yet they are always crucial to problem solving. Especially in situations where there initially is conflict, we need the ability to maintain relationships so that negotiations can continue, to decipher messages when deliberate concealment is attempted, to convince and to persuade, to bluff when necessary, and to figure out what the other will do in response to our own moves.

As we know, negotiations can become so dangerous and threatening to one's face that we have to resort to neutral third parties as catalysts, go-betweens, message carriers, and the like. Often what is most needed is to explain the values and goals of each principal to the other. Principals often lack the skills to reveal themselves to each other without making themselves seem either too vulnerable or too threatening.[5]

One of my Australian manager friends speculated that a lack of verbal articulation skills seriously hampers negotiation in his country. He noticed that in many labor-management confrontations in Australia each side would blurt out bluntly, and with some pride at their own ability to be so open, exactly what their *final* demands were. When these demands proved to be incompatible, an impasse occurred. The situation then deteriorated to name calling and to seeing the other side as being stubborn and exploitative. This manager speculated that the educational system was partly responsible for this situation in that written English is heavily emphasized in school while spoken English is hardly attended to at all. He thought of Australians as being quite inarticulate, on the average, and therefore at a real disadvantage in face-to-face negotiations.

The important point is to recognize that openness is not an absolute value in face-to-face relationships. For some purposes, it is better not to reveal exactly where one stands. One of the ways that relationships become more intimate is through successive minimal self-revelations which constitute interpersonal tests of acceptance: if you accept this much of me, then perhaps I can run the risk of revealing a bit more of myself. Total openness may be safe and charming when total acceptance is guaranteed, but it can become highly dangerous when goals are not compatible, and acceptance is therefore not guaranteed at all.[6]

INTERPERSONAL AND CROSS-CULTURAL TACT

Negotiation requires great tact. The tactfulness I refer to here is the *behavioral* manifestation of the cultural humility discussed above. If we don't feel humble in the face of others' values, we will certainly offend them. On the other hand, if we feel that there is genuinely room for different values in this world, then we have the basis for showing in our speech and behavior an adequate level of respect for others.

REPAIR STRATEGIES AND SKILLS

The repair strategies and repair skills needed to fix broken or spoiled relationships, careers, lives, negotiations, and other interpersonal or intergroup situations are probably the most important yet least understood of face-to-face skills. As the world becomes more complex and more intercultural, there will be more communication breakdowns, diplomatic disasters, losses of confidence and trust, hurt feelings between individuals and groups, hostilities, wars, and other forms of social pathology and disorder. It will not help us to resign ourselves to such situations, to lament our cruel fate, or to merely explain why something happened; what *will* be helpful is our attempting to repair these situations.

The concept of "repair strategies" was brought to my attention by Jacqueline Goodnow, a cognitive social psychologist who now teaches in Australia. She has been struck by the Australian tendency to "knock" things rather than to solve problems. I often heard the phrase in Australia that "we are a nation of knockers," which means that when things go wrong there is a tendency to blame government, unions, management, multinationals, OPEC, or any other handy group rather than to figure out how to repair the situation.

The Perception of New Elements

Repair strategies presume and require not only constructive motivation but also *the ability to see new elements in the situation which one may not have noticed before*. The new elements may be in *oneself*; one may discover that one has been unfair or selfish, or lacking insight concerning one's own behavior or concerning one's true motives. In this instance repair may begin with apology.

One may also discover new things in the *other people* in the situation; *they may have changed in significant ways*. One of the most damaging things we do in our face-to-face relationships is to freeze our assumptions about ourselves and others. Our stereotype of the other person can become a straight jacket or a self-fulfilling prophecy. McGregor gave us the best example of this years ago in noting that if we assume people are lazy we will begin to treat them as if they *are* lazy, which will eventually train them to *be* lazy.[7] The energy and creativity which they might have applied to their jobs then gets channeled either into other situations or into angry attempts to defeat the organization.

We want and need predictability in our relationships, but that very need often prevents us from repairing damaged relationships. It may be psychologically easier to see the worker as lazy and hostile because we can then predict his or her behavior and can know exactly how to respond. To renegotiate the relationship, to permit some participation, or to admit that we may have been wrong in our assessment is to make ourselves psychologically vulnerable. We then enter a period in the relationship that may be less predictable.

As in the case of negotiation, we may need the help of third parties – counselors, therapists, consultants, or other helpers – to get through the period of vulnerability and instability. Often the motivation to repair is there but the skill is not – in the sense that neither party has self-insight, the capacity to hear the values or goals of the other, the articulateness to negotiate without further destruction of face, or the emotional strength or self-confidence to make concessions to reach at least a common ground of understanding.

Taking the Other's Perspective

Sociologists taught us long ago that in childhood the very process of becoming social is a process of learning to take the role of the other. We could not really understand each other at all – even though we live in the same culture and speak the same language – without the ability to put ourselves in the other person's shoes. We could not develop judgments, standards, and morals without the ability to see our own behavior from the standpoint of others, which gradually becomes abstracted into what sociologists call the "generalized other," or what we sometimes label as our "reference group." Guilt and shame, the products of one's internalized conscience, can be thought of as the accumulated empathy of a decade of growing up. As adults we have the capacity to see ourselves from others' perspectives and this capacity should help us to develop repair strategies. Why is it, then, that so often we end up in complete disagreement, convinced that the only thing the other party really wants is to gain a selfish advantage at our expense?

One factor certainly is our need to maintain our position and our pride. Having suffered an affront, a loss of face, or a loss of advantage sometime in the past, we feel the only safe thing to do is to protect ourselves from any repetition of such an unpleasant event. We may, in addition, recognize that our own interest and that of the other party are genuinely in conflict. If we are in a zero-sum game, we may not be able to afford too much sympathy for our opponent. In such an instance, a repair strategy would call for the ability to locate some superordinate goals, where goal conflict is not intrinsic, and to build a new set of interactions around such superordinate goals. Skillful diplomats, negotiators, and statesmen build their entire careers around the development of such repair strategies. They create one repair strategy after another as the people they deal with destroy one relationship after another.

Ordinary day-to-day relations within families, between managers and subordinates, and between groups in organizations are forever in danger of breaking down. We must be prepared to diagnose the situation when breakdown occurs and to have the skills to repair it, if repair is needed. Let me give two examples of what is involved.

REPAIR STRATEGIES IN MIDLIFE

Much of the research on midlife is beginning to point to the presence of two very broad phases, each lasting a decade or more.[8] In the first phase, which lasts roughly from age twenty-five to age forty, the family in a sense colludes with the primary career occupant to build a successful career. The primary career occupant, his or her spouse or partner, and the children all learn that our occupational structure requires that one go to school and then put in an intensive decade or so building up one's career (and one's organizational membership if the career is pursued within an organization). The support by the family may be silent and stoic. The children are kept out of the career builder's hair while he or she is busy. The spouse or partner – gladly or resentfully – makes sacrifices and actively develops a viable ancillary support role as homemaker and as mother and father combined.

But something else is going on during these years. The homemaker is in a terminal career and knows it; at some point the children will all be off to school, the house will have had all the attention it needs, and being the ancillary spouse may not be a full enough life. The spouse builds up expectations that at some point "it will be my turn; I have helped you to build your career and now I want something in return – something for myself." As these feelings grow and are articulated, as teenage children begin to say "Why are you working so hard? What's it all about anyway?", and as the career occupant begins to reexamine his or her career, a new phase begins. In this phase, there may be a need for repair strategies, renegotiation of the family contract, and reassessment of who wants what and how it is best achieved. People discover either that their relationships are already damaged and need to be repaired or that they *will* be damaged if no preventive maintenance is undertaken.

Cross-cultural Sensitivity within the Family
It should be noted that each family member has, in a sense, been living in a different subculture and that cross-cultural understanding and humility will therefore become very important. The career occupant will have to understand and respect the serious requirements of the spouse and the young adult children. The spouse and children will have to understand and respect the serious requirements of the world of work and organizations with which the career occupant grapples. This will tax each member's self-insight, commitment to the family, sensitivity, and perspective.

The moral humility issue is central here because the cause of a damaged relationship is often a devaluing of each other's goals and aspirations. The career occupant looks down on what may be regarded as the trivial or threatening values of the next generation; he or she cannot really appreciate why the homemaker spouse should have an issue about self-identity, the need to feel important and worthwhile in a society in which worth is defined almost exclusively by paid work and career involvement. The spouse (and most likely the children) find it easy to devalue organizational goals, to identify organizational careers with exploitation of the poor, marginal product quality, questionable business ethics, overworked people who are eventually cast off by cruel employers, and so on. If midlife family relationships are damaged by such feelings, then how can they be repaired?

The Interplay of Face-to-Face Skills
Each party in the relationship must first achieve some self-insight, some sense of one's own commitments so that defensiveness and denial can be reduced. We cannot hear others if we cannot accept ourselves. Next we need the kind of cross-cultural sensitivity I have been talking about, the relaxed, open ability to hear others' values with empathy and perspective. Once we can hear each other, we can begin to seek the common ground, the goals or aspirations around which some common activities can be designed; we can begin to renegotiate the relationships to make it possible for the desirable activities to happen. If, in hearing each other, we find a genuine lack of common ground, we can negotiate a reduced level of intimacy in the relationship yet maintain a high degree of mutual acceptance of what each cares about; this can lead to nondestructive separations, more limited interactions with children, or both.

LABOR-MANAGEMENT RELATIONS

My second example has to do with face-to-face skills and repair strategies in labor-management situations. I am struck by the degree to which these situations seem to turn into intergroup struggles – struggles among unions, managements, and government bodies or political parties. Once the conflicts have escalated to the intergroup level, it is easy to give up one's proactive problem-solving orientation and to resign oneself to the idea that the problem is essentially unsolvable. Yet when one looks at successful enterprises – those which have managed to maintain harmony between management and employees – one realizes that the key to this harmony is a high degree of mutual trust, active listening, appropriate levels of participation, and consistently constructive face-to-face communications.

An example will highlight what I mean. A plant manager told me that he had spent many years developing a constructive relationship with his employees, in spite of the fact that they belong to a strong national union which periodically calls for national strikes. One year his employees refused to strike. They were told by the national union that it would get all the suppliers of the plant to refuse to deliver, thus effectively shutting the plant down. Under these conditions, the manager and the employees got together and agreed that the employees should go out on strike, but everyone knew that it was not over local issues. The manager did not hold it against his subordinates that they had gone out on strike.

Intergroup trust, reinforced by open face-to-face communications on relevant issues, was strong enough to keep this plant functioning well even in a larger context that made periodic strikes inevitable. What we can learn from this is that constructive face-to-face relationships are necessary even though they may not be sufficient. Solving a problem at the national level will probably be useless if there continue to be destructive low-trust relationships within the enterprise.

DISENGAGING THE CRITICAL MIND

Achieving trust in a labor-management situation that has developed into a hostile intergroup conflict over a period of decades seems like a tall order. One prerequisite to working out the problem at the group level will be, as I have argued, the reestablishment of constructive face-to-face relationships. This will only be possible if both managers and workers find a way to see each other in less stereotypic ways. There is a need here to introduce in the interpersonal arena what Zen, gestalt training, encounter groups, and other training programs have emphasized – relaxing the active critical mind enough to let our eyes and ears see and hear what is really out there rather than what we expect to see and hear. Just as the person who is learning to draw must suspend what he or she knows intellectually about what things should look like, and instead, must learn to see what is really out there, so the person concerned about repairing human relationships must first see not what he or she expects or knows should be there, but what is actually there.[9]

I don't think it is accidental that Americans are so preoccupied with sensitivity training, Zen meditation, inner tennis, and, most recently, right-side brain functions.[10] What all of these programs and approaches have in common is a focus on learning how to perceive oneself, others, and the environment realistically, which apparently requires a certain relaxation of our active critical functions and a deliberate disengaging of our analytical selves. We cannot improve face-to-face relationships if we cannot perceive accurately. And accurate seeing and hearing is for many of us a lost skill that we must somehow regain. The place to begin practicing this skill is in our families and in our immediate superior-subordinate and peer relations.

If we cannot see ourselves and others in this relaxed, uncritical way, then we cannot develop perspective, humility, or tact, and we run the danger of acting on incorrect data. On the other hand, if we can really learn to see each other, and if we can combine more accurate perception with the ninth element in my list – patience – then we have some chance of improving and repairing face-to-face relationships.

"Even though you try to put people under some control, it is impossible. You cannot do it. The best way to control people is to encourage them to be mischievous. Then they will be in control in its wider sense. To give your sheep or cow a large, spacious meadow is the way to control him. So it is with people: first let them do what they want, and watch them. This is the best policy. To ignore them is not good; that is the worst policy. The second worst is trying to control them. The best one is to watch them, just to watch them, without trying to control them. The same way works for yourself as well." (S. Suzuki, *Zen Mind, Beginner's Mind*.)[11]

References

1. See P.R. Lawrence and J.W. Lorsch (1967) *Organization and Environment*. Boston: Division of Research, Harvard Business School.

2. See E. Goffman (1967) *Interaction Ritual*. Chicago: Aldine.
3. See E. Hall (1977) *Beyond Culture*. Garden City, NY: Anchor.
4. See E.H. Schein (1980)*Organizational Psychology*, 3rd ed., Englewood Cliffs, NJ: Prentice-Hall, chapters 9 and 13; T.A. Harris (1967) *I'm OK – You're OK*. New York: Avon; E. Polster and M. Polster (1973) *Gestalt Therapy Integrated* New York: Bruner/Mazel.
5. See R.E. Walton (1969) *Interpersonal Peacemaking: Confrontations and Third-Party Consultation*.Reading, MA: Addison-Wesley.
6. See W. Bennis, J. Van Maanen, E.H. Schein, and F.I. Steele (1979) *Essays in Interpersonal Dynamics*. Homewood, IL: Dorsey.
7. See D. McGregor (1960) *The Human Side of Enterprise*. New York: McGraw-Hill.
8. See F. Bartolome and P.A.L. Evans (1980) *Must Success Cost So Much?* London: Grant McIntyre.
9. See B. Edwards (1979) *Drawing on the Right Side of the Brain*. Los Angeles: J.P. Tarcher.
10. See R.E. Ornstein (1972) *The Psychology of Consciousness*. San Fransico: W.H. Freeman.
11. See S. Suzuki (1979) *Zen Mind, Beginner's Mind*. New York: Weatherhill, p. 32.

CASES

THE AUTHORITARIAN PERSONALITY AND THE AUTOCRATIC EXECUTIVE

Joe Kelly

Learning how to exercise authority and power wisely is a necessary executive skill which every business student must study and develop. Being an executive requires exercising authority and power. Exercising authority means one must act in a way that structures the other person's perception, attitudes, and behavior. Technically, this is referred to as establishing a superordinate relationship. Unfortunately, however, the first exercises of authority for the young executive can be so demanding that he or she may develop a kind of autocratic persona or mask as a means of concealing his or her initial insecurities about the use of such power.

The odd thing about the authority business, as most people know from their own experience, is that some people seem to take to it as a duck to water. One kind of individual who gets a kick out of exercising authority is the authoritarian personality. It is worth looking at the authoritarian personality in some depth because it provides insight into both his or her dynamic and our own. A good way of beginning our look at the authoritarian personality is to examine a famous piece of research by Adorno et al. (1950). He developed a measuring instrument called the F-scale which measures the tendency to Fascism. Adorno managed to document a picture of the true autocrat.

The authoritarian personality believes that the most important thing children should learn is obedience to authority. Moreover, they must be taught that introspection is bad, that businesspeople are more important than actors, that wild and dangerous things are going on out there, and that there is a dichotomy between sexual pleasure and moral goodness. Additionally, the authoritarian personality likes to make a sharp split between work and nonwork. Adorno's findings suggest that the authoritarian may equate his or her perceptions of promiscuous, lustful sexual partners with his or her images of lax, sloppy subordinates at work. In both cases, authoritarians may view hostile treatment as the proper behavior towards such individuals.

Stanley Milgram carried out a series of experiments at Yale University in the sixties investigating the topic of obedience to authority. The question for Milgram was, "If

X tells Y to hurt Z by giving Z severe electric shocks when Z makes mistakes in a test, will Y do as he is told?" What Milgram discovered was that if Y thinks he is receiving a command from a legitimate authority X, Y will obey and shock Z.

A PORTRAIT OF THE AUTHORITARIAN

By putting Adorno's and Milgram's research work together it is possible to build up a portrait of the authoritarian personality. The authoritarian scenario has the following elements. When things go bad, the people involved feel insecure and they turn to an autocratic person for direction and guidance. The autocrat is someone they turn to naturally first of all because he or she possesses conventional values. Authoritarian persons also tend to possess stereotypical images of others and usually regard superiors as omniscient, omnipotent, and omnipresent. Moreover, they are inherently cynical about others and tend to show contempt for any form of weakness. They find it very difficult to accept people of other ethnic groups who display behavior and attitudes which are outside their range of experience. In general, it is possible to say that authoritarians 1) display hostility towards members of the outgroup, 2) prefer strong leadership, and 3) have a low tolerance for ambiguity.

Research and popular psychology suggest that authoritarians are attracted to powerful and tough people. The Great Depression, a period of intense economic hardship and political tenuity, led both individuals and societies to feel insecure. Such insecurity produced authoritarian personalities on a mass scale as people sought stability. Perhaps due to the psychological influences of the crisis, the sales of machismo magazines, featuring such heroes as Superman, dramatically increased.

Interestingly, this research on authoritarianism has again come into vogue to explain the emergence of the neo-conservative forces which are in our society as a reaction to the liberalism of the 1960s. Again we are witnessing a resurgence in fundamental religion, a preoccupation with fictional characters such as those played by Sylvester Stallone, and a renewal of support for local police forces.

Understanding this phenomenon is especially important for the young student of management to assist them in coming to terms both with the authoritarian bosses they will encounter and, more particularly, with their own autocratic impulses. It is essential that students of management gain insight into the real psychic forces behind the self or ego.

In brief, what scientific research and common sense are arguing for is a re-examination of the fidelity bond in the executive relationship. Getting into the nature of this bond is a difficult process. As our review of the research shows, the authority bond is interlocked with child rearing styles, religious taboos, fantasy needs and deeply felt proprietorial needs enjoined in "husband and wife," "master and servant," and "employer and employee" relationships which are held together by a social fabric of magic, myth, and mystery.

For the executive and business student the study of the exercise of authority is not only demanded but demanding. It is demanded because executive work requires the exercise of authority. But the exercise of authority is demanding because it leaves with the author (the executive) the burden of responsibility. Taking the initiative means breaking some bond and re-establishing a new one. This is tough but necessary executive work.

QUESTIONS

1. Make a list of the characteristics of the autocratic executive.
2. How many of these characteristics do you exhibit?
3. What makes a person autocratic?
4. How does a manager exhibit autocratic behavior?
5. Is autocratic behavior useful?
6. How can autocratic behavior be modified?

LEE IACOCCA VERSUS HENRY FORD II

Joe Kelly

THE CORPORATE ZOO

As we know from ethology, or the study of animal behavior by such eminent behavioral scientists as Konrad Lorenz, Karl von Frisch and Nicolas Tinbergen, aggression, hierarchy and sexual behavior are linked. Actual physical combat leading to serious injury or death is not common among animals because of the existence of fairly stable pecking orders. To ensure that the pecking hierarchy is still in position, the lesser animal defers to the higher by presenting its hindquarters, as a symbol of both sexual availability and as a token of respect.

TOP DOG – UNDER DOG

Hierarchy imposes a necessary strain between the "top gun" and the managerial hired help who are not lesser people but only further down the totem. This situation produces a "winner takes all" syndrome in business. The problem is that the CEO Top Dogs are not only articulate, aggressive and persuasive; they also love creating "win-lose" competition among the under-dogs. All this aggressive strutting causes problems in the vertical dimension.

As Professor Chris Argyris of Harvard has noted, CEOs are not unaware of the extent of this tension but they creatively exploit it. All these dog fights are dominated by executives who like to dominate their turf or territory and who love movies like *The Godfather* and *Patton*. Although they are common, it would be naive to believe that such dog fights are easy to deal with. In fact, territorial conflict is often expressed in subtle and elusive ways that defy simple and logical explanations.

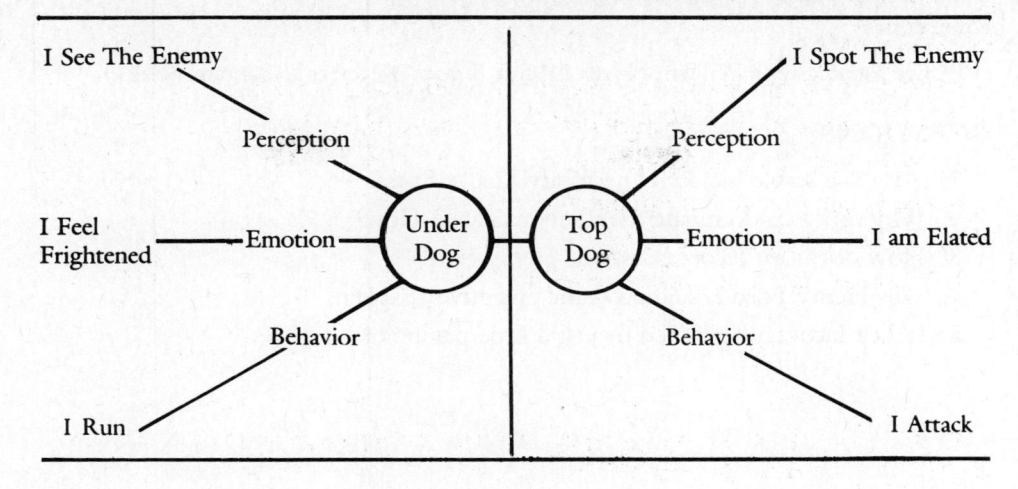

```
I See The Enemy                                               I Spot The Enemy
            \                                                 /
             \  Perception                       Perception  /
              \                                             /
I Feel         \         ┌─────┐        ┌─────┐           /    I am Elated
Frightened ——— Emotion ——│Under│        │ Top │── Emotion ———
                         │ Dog │        │ Dog │
              /          └─────┘        └─────┘           \
             /  Behavior                       Behavior    \
            /                                               \
I Run                                                          I Attack
```

Listening to Top Dog chief executives talk can be a revealing experience. As Lee Iacocca points out in his autobiography,

> Until I became president, Henry Ford had always been a pretty remote figure. But now my office was right next to his in the Glass House, and we saw quite a lot of each other, although only in meetings. The better I got to know Henry Ford, the more I worried about the company's future – and my own.
>
> The Glass House was a palace, and Henry reigned supreme. Whenever he entered the building, the word would go out: **The king has arrived.** Executives would linger in the halls, hoping to run into him. If they were lucky, Mr. Ford might notice them and say hello. At times he might even deign to speak to them.
>
> Each time Henry walked into a meeting, the atmosphere changed abruptly. He held the power of life and death over all of us. He could suddenly say "off with his head" – and he often did. Without a fair hearing, one more promising career at Ford would bite the dust.
>
> It was the superficial things that counted for Henry. He was a sucker for appearances. If a guy wore the right clothes and used the right buzz words, Henry was impressed. But without the right veneer, forget it.
>
> One day Henry ordered me to fire a certain executive who was, in his judgment, "a fag."
>
> "Don't be silly," I said. "The guy's a good pal of mine. He's married and has a kid. We have dinner together."
>
> "Get rid of him," Henry repeated. "He's a fag."
>
> "What are you talking about?" I said.
>
> "Look at him. His pants are too tight."
>
> "Henry," I said calmly, "what the hell do the guy's pants have to do with anything?"
>
> "He's queer," said Henry. "He's got an effeminate bearing. Get rid of him."
>
> In the end, I had to demote a good friend. I moved him out of the Glass House and into the boondocks, hating every minute of it. But the only alternative was to fire him.
>
> This arbitrary use of power wasn't merely a character flaw. It was something Henry actually **believed** in.

References

1. Lee Iacocca with William Novak (1984) *Iacocca*. New York: Bantam Books.

QUESTIONS

1. Why is a stable hierarchy necessary in a business?
2. Why do CEOs dominate their subordinates? How?
3. How does Lee Iacocca describe Henry Ford II?
4. Was Henry Ford II an autocratic executive? Explain.
5. Is Lee Iacocca frightened or just a little paranoid?

EXERCISES

GIVING EFFECTIVE FEEDBACK

J. Bruce Prince

Giving useful feedback is an essential skill of an effective manager. This exercise provides you with an opportunity to practise giving effective feedback during the course of three different role plays. Your instructor will organize you into groups of three. One person will take the role of the supervisor, another will take the role of the subordinate, and the third will be an observer. After determining who is going to play which role, read Incident A and conduct a brief role play. At the conclusion of the role play, the observer will provide feedback on the supervisor's performance. Once this process is complete, rotate roles and do Incident B and C in a similar fashion. At the conclusion of incident C role play and feedback process, everyone should have had a chance to play all three roles.

GUIDELINES FOR EFFECTIVE FEEDBACK

Those playing the roles of supervisor and observer should try to make their feedback as effective as possible. If the other person reacts negatively to your comments and starts defending his- or herself, then one or more of the following guidelines have probably been violated.

Generally, interpersonal feedback is most effective when:

1. It is immediate. The closer it follows performance the better.
2. It describes a specific behavior. It deals with what a person *does*, rather than what that person *is*. Another way to say this is that effective feedback is descriptive rather than evaluative.
3. It is authentic. That is, the person really means it.
4. It emphasizes the positive aspects of an individual's behavior rather than dwelling on the negative aspects of the person's performance. Negative feedback is most useful when it is given in tolerable doses.
5. It is equality oriented, not superiority oriented. Giving others the impression that you are perfect and they are somehow inferior will quickly turn them off.
6. It is flexible, not rigid. Being open to new information or different points of view encourages the other person to respond in a similar fashion.
7. It involves the other person as a participant rather than simply a target. Engaging in a two-way discussion is more effective than giving a lecture.

Observers can use the above list by checking off the qualities the person in the supervisor role has been successful in achieving. It is also useful for observers to involve the person in the subordinate role during the feedback process. Asking that person how he or she felt at such and such a point can be very helpful in elaborating on the key aspects of the supervisor's performance. This can make an observation more than simply one person's opinion and provide more of a factual basis for the discussion.

INCIDENT A

The Individuals
Jack Jones, Supervisor
Dick Johnson, Subordinate

Background Information
Dick Johnson joined Jack Jones' Contracts Department four months ago right after his graduation from the University of Toronto. His work has been average overall. However, a more detailed look at his performance indicates that some areas of his performance are quite excellent, while others are definitely in need of improvement.

In the first couple of months on the job, Dick attacked the great mass of knowledge on contracting with the government with great vigor. He could frequently be seen asking questions to Jack and his own peers about some procurement regulation or another aspect of contracting. For the last two months, however, there has been a noticeable lack of such instances. In fact, there is even a fair amount of dust accumulating on his contracting manual.

Dick's job requires both internal and external interfacing. The internal interface of his job relates to his contacts within the company such as with marketing, pricing, and most important, engineering. On numerous occasions he has pursued threads of information and gotten important facts that really made a substantial contribution to the proposal effort. One example was the XYZ proposal just yesterday. Dick found that part of the technical input was not totally responsive to the Government's proposal request. He pursued that deficiency with appropriate engineering people and as a result the proposal was significantly improved.

The external interfacing part of Dick's job requires him to contact buyers and contracting officers at various government agencies. A good relationship with these individuals is critical. Dick has been rather insensitive to this fact of life and has on numerous occasions failed to answer their telephone calls promptly or get them the information they request on a timely basis. An example of this was the ABC proposal. Soon after receiving the company's proposal the buyer called to request further price justification on purchase parts. Dick never did return the buyer's first call and was two days late in returning the buyer's second call. To top it off he was late getting the requested pricing input back to the buyer.

Jack Jones' (supervisor) Role You have just left a meeting and have run into Dick in the hall. You are both on your way back to your common work areas and you think that now is an excellent time to give Dick some feedback on his performance. You may be inventive in order to add depth to your comments; however, don't deviate too far from the facts.

Dick Johnson's (subordinate) Role Your role is to listen to what Jack has to say and respond to any questions. Be aware and keep track of your reactions to what is said. You should give these reactions when the observer provides his or her response.

Observer's Role You are to observe what is said and then at the conclusion of the role play give the participants feedback on their performance.

INCIDENT B

The Individuals
Cathy Johnson, Supervisor
Roger Rice, Subordinate

Background Information
Roger Rice has been an employee with the company for 24 years and is 57 years old. For the last five years he has been with the Reproduction department. His job is to make copies of engineering drawings. People see Roger as basically waiting for retirement. Previously in his career he was a foreman and has had considerably more complex jobs than his present one. The move which brought him to the reproduction job was requested by Roger because he was unhappy with being a foreman.

His attendance record has been quite bad, although he has not missed a day in the last four weeks which is quite the exception.

The standardized rate for Roger's job is 45 drawings per hour. Roger's usual rate was 30 per hour prior to this week. This week, at the suggestion of his supervisor, Roger has started keeping track of and plotting his output on a graph. This is the first day that Roger has been measuring his output and with not even half the day gone Roger's output has increased to 39 drawings per hour.

Cathy Johnson's (supervisor) Role You have just passed by Roger's work station and noted that he is up to 39 drawings per hour. Roger glances at you and seems to be waiting for some sort of reaction.

Roger Rice's (subordinate) Role Your role is to listen to what Cathy has to say and respond to any questions. Be aware and keep track of your reactions to what is said. You should give these reactions when the observer provides his or her response.

Observer's Role You are to observe what is said and then at the conclusion of the role play provide the participants with feedback on the role play.

INCIDENT C

The Individuals
Gary Thompson, Supervisor
Anne Arrow, Subordinate

Background Information

Anne joined Gary Thompson's Purchasing Department two years ago. Over this period of time she has slowly, but steadily, improved her general performance. Unfortunately, all too frequently Anne's procurement packages have not been in proper order. As a consequence, Gary can not approve the package and must send it back to Anne to correct the deficiencies. Over the past two months only about one-half of the procurement packages that have gone to Gary for approval have passed without needing corrections.

In an effort to speed up the improvement of Anne's performance, Gary has suggested that she keep track of the number of proposal packages that get approved without correction versus the total. She will add this information to her weekly report. Also, Anne is graphing the weekly percentages so that she can see if she is improving or not.

Two weeks have gone by since this procedure was started. After the first week, Anne's percentage of packages going out without correction was 50%, the same as her baseline average. After the first week Gary encouraged Anne to keep trying and pointed out the time savings that could be realized if the percent correct were improved. The second week has now gone by and Anne was able to improve her percentage to 65%. This is still short of her 85% goal.

Gary Thompson's (supervisor) Role Anne has recently submitted her weekly report to you. You have just concluded a discussion of planned procurement action this week. The subject has turned to the percentage of packages going out without correction.

Anne Arrow's (subordinate) Role Your role is to listen to what Gary has to say and respond to any questions. Be aware and keep track of your reactions to what is said. You should give these reactions when the observer provides his response.

Observer's Role You are to observe what is said and then at the conclusion of the role play give the participants feedback on their performance.

THE ZEN MAN – GIVING AND RECEIVING FEEDBACK

Joe Kelly

Giving and receiving feedback is integral to executive life. To develop this capacity it is necessary to know something about the values and attitudes of the rater and ratee. Remember the rating tells you something about both of these individuals.

Some guidelines for giving and receiving feedback are as follows:

1. The raters must sort out their own intentions and make sure that they intend to be helpful.

2. The ratees must (a) try not to be defensive, (b) be able to accept information, and (c) have choices.
3. The feedback must be specific, with recent examples. Additionally, it should be descriptive rather than evaluative.

MODEL 1

Top Dog : How do you think you are making out in the plant?
Under Dog : You know how it is.
Top Dog : I'm sorry. I don't.
Under Dog : What do you mean then?
Top Dog : How are you getting on with people?
Under Dog : Some O.K. Some not so O.K. It's hard to tell.
Top Dog : Would you like me to relay some feedback?
Under Dog : Sure, why not?
Top Dog : A lot of people don't like you... You're too aggressive. Pushy... too.
Under Dog : I didn't know that. I need time to think this over.

MODEL 2

Top Dog : I think it's about time you faced the facts of life. Do you want to know the score? What people think of you around here?
Zen Man : No. But I would be very glad to hear what *you* think of me.
Top Dog : What *I* think of you? You want my opinion?
Zen Man : Yes, provided it's what you believe. And hopefully you can give some "for instances."
Top Dog : Everybody around here knows you are a real SOB and what's more...
Zen Man : Hang on, old chap, for a moment. It's what you think...
Top Dog : Cut the crap. Who needs this?

MODEL 3

Zen Man One : Can I ask you a question? About me?
Zen Man Two : Go ahead.
Zen Man One : What do you think of me?
Zen Man Two : What brought this on?
Zen Man One : I'm running into a lot of static with my people getting them to use this new MBO form.
Zen Man Two : Such as?
Zen Man One : They think I'm "too results oriented," which is O.K. But what is not O.K. is they think I'm just joining the MBO thing to placate you.
Zen Man Two : They think you are too dependent, perhaps overdependent on me.

Zen Man One : More or less.
Zen Man Two : Do you feel this yourself?
Zen Man One : I do, and I resent it.
Zen Man Two : Good. You should.
Zen Man One : What do you mean?
Zen Man Two : You're getting into the organizational bind — looking for a supportive nonthreatening boss and laying it on your *subordinates*.
Zen Man One : Don't give me that old BS.
Zen Man Two : I'm giving you RS, high quality BS. Properly tested. I know. I lived off it long enough.

QUESTIONS

1. Fill in the boxes with the appropriate definitions.

EXECUTIVE	TOP DOG	UNDERDOG	ZEN MAN
VALUES			
ATTITUDE TO GIVING OR RECEIVING FEEDBACK			
TACTIC			
EVALUATION			
CONTINGENCY WHEN APPROPRIATE			

2. When and how should feedback be given?
3. Describe your experiences that correspond to models 1, 2, and 3.
4. What does model 3 tell you about counterdependency in executives?

THE CUSHWELL-WEST MEETING EXERCISE

J. Bruce Prince
Luke Novelli

Managers frequently have to get information and give feedback, direction and guidance one-on-one with subordinates. Often this involves establishing or re-building an effective relationship. These sessions can be challenging to even the most competent of managers. This exercise builds on the material presented in the in-basket exercise from the first section of this book and provides you with an opportunity to test your skills at managing a difficult one-on-one meeting.

INSTRUCTIONS

1. Prior to class, review the in-basket materials (i.e., items 1 to 12) presented in the Montréal Pump & Valve Company exercise in the first section of the book. Pay particular attention to items #2, #3, #4, #6, and #10.
2. During class the instructor will select two people (or several pairs of people) to play Cushwell and West in a role play.
3. Those not selected will participate as observers and are to read the background information presented below. Observers are to review the Observer Guidelines in preparing for their role.
4. Those playing West or Cushwell are to review the accompanying instructions for their particular role. Do not look at the instructions for the other role.
5. West should keep the meeting under 20 minutes. Both players' behavior in the role play should be consistent with the information provided in the background role instructions.
6. At the conclusion of the meeting, the instructor will debrief the participants.

Background Information for Cushwell-West Meeting

It is Monday, April 23, Richard/Rachel West's first day in the office as the new plant manager for the Montréal Pump & Valve Company. West had a meeting with all functional area managers to clarify important issues facing the company. It was a good meeting in a number of respects. However, a number of personnel and industrial relations issues were left hanging due to the abrupt departure of Allan/Alice Cushwell mid-way through the meeting. In order to address some of those issues, a 20-minute meeting has been scheduled in West's office. It is now 2:30 pm and time to start that meeting.

ALLAN/ALICE CUSHWELL ROLE INSTRUCTIONS

What a day — your new boss's first, and all hell breaks loose! You are hoping that West will manage more effectively than your previous boss, John Manners, and put you in charge of personnel matters in this company. The way West ran the first staff meeting seemed to indicate a change for the better. Unfortunately, you were called out of the meeting on an emergency before personnel and industrial relations issues were discussed.

Hopefully, West will encourage people to take initiative. You wonder if he will respect your decision to leave the meeting. Manners was so autocratic you felt you almost had to ask permission to go to the rest room. He made most of the decisions and kept a lot of the information to himself. This made it pretty tough for you to do your job. No wonder he had a heart attack. He tried to solve all of the organization's problems himself.

The situation which necessitated your leaving the meeting was a major one! The local union president, R.L. Loper herself, was waiting in your office. She was ready to call in the lawyers over some interference people in O'Malley's production operation have been giving her. Frankly, she's got a good case and you've tried to get O'Malley's people to stop trying to sway the election towards Loper's opponent. They just don't appreciate the legal aspects of union-management relations. Fortunately, you were able to calm Loper down and she is willing to give the company one last chance. The company has got to start behaving in a coordinated fashion or Loper's army of lawyers will tie everybody up in knots in an unfair labor practice law suit.

Interfering in the union election is only part of the problem. On many occasions, people are being fired without regard for proper procedure. If only they would involve you when problems first surface, you could prevent minor problems from becoming major disasters. The latest example was young Robert Roberts in Bill Marshall's operation. Roberts is probably smart enough to realize he can nail the company with a wrongful dismissal suit. If people don't follow procedures and carefully document their case the company could lose plenty. Roberts was long gone before your people were even notified. Now Personnel has to try to establish a case after the damage has been done.

Manners is largely to blame for these problems in that he encouraged people to side step Personnel. He seemed to think that the only expertise needed was keeping the paper work filed in an orderly fashion and that managers in each functional area could handle personnel matters themselves. This attitude led to what is probably the worst problem of all — inequity in the company's salary structure. It has lead to all kinds of grumbling (except by those who are overpaid) and, on more than one occasion, losing a good employee to the competition. Frank Batt, one of the most valuable men in R&D, is about 20% below his fair market value and will be the next to go if something is not done quickly. Manners didn't want to take the "trouble," as he called it, to survey firms with comparable jobs and figure out what the prevailing wage rates are for various job categories.

Chaos and confusion is the consequence of the old-fashioned attitude that many people have towards human resource management. Manners seemed to start figuring this out only recently when he finally let you develop hiring criteria for clerical and secretarial employees. It wasn't exactly your area of expertise, but fortunately you've supervised many of these employees and have an intuitive feel for the general job demands they face. Manners would never have sat still for what was really needed, namely a formal job analysis.

People in the company just don't appreciate how complicated personnel and industrial relations decisions can be. For example, the recent tendency to hire clerical and secretarial personnel who are well into middle age contributes unnecessarily to pension costs. These costs may be off in the future, but they are very real. It is better to hire younger people. They probably work harder and many leave before they've earned a pension. If people would depend on personnel more, these problems could be anticipated. Another example is Everts in R&D trying to hire a black person to supervise white employees. The same thing was tried several years ago in that area and led to the resignation of the two top technicians. A young guy like Everts just doesn't have the experience to anticipate these kinds of problems. One has to recognize the social reality of some departments. Some of these minority hiring decisions can lead to lots of problems and move us away from our affirmative action goals.

A special meeting with West is almost ready to start. This will be a good time to start to resolve the company's numerous personnel and industrial relations problems. The meeting should also be a good time to get the new plant manager's support. The priorities you have formulated for this meeting are:

1. Get West to put your department really in charge of personnel and IR issues and you in a central position to coordinate these matters. That would be a 180 degree turn from the direction Manners was steering the ship!
2. Gain West's support for your efforts to stop all union election interference activities.
3. Get West to slap Bill Marshall's hands for not following procedures or involving Personnel in the recent Robert Roberts dismissal and communicate that Personnel should be involved in all *firing* decisions.
4. Gain West's support for your position on hiring criteria for clerical and secretarial positions as well as your position on the hiring of a black supervisor in Everts' R&D area.
5. Get West to put you in charge of coming up with answers to the salary structure inequity problem.

RICHARD/RACHEL WEST ROLE INSTRUCTIONS

This is your first day in the office as Montréal Pump & Valve Company's new plant manager. The morning meeting of all functional area managers which directly report to you went pretty well. However, just when some conflicts over the R&D budget were being worked through, Cushwell received a message and then disappeared from the meeting. Later on a number of issues which were related to personnel and industrial relations came up and were left hanging since Cushwell wasn't there.

You had some doubts about Cushwell in the past and his standing has not exactly improved today. You're willing to give him the benefit of the doubt, but several memos that were in Manners' in-basket when you took over as plant manager caused some doubts about just how effective the Personnel function is being handled. The personnel specialist from the parent company, the Chemical & Equipment Corporation of Canada, didn't exactly give Cushwell a ringing endorsement. He said that he hadn't had many occasions to talk to Cushwell, but that whenever he had, Cushwell seemed uninformed and always had to say "I'll have to get back to you with that information."

The other managers were hardly supportive of his competence and seemed to be doing plenty of personnel and IR activities themselves. On more than one occasion at this morning's meeting you wanted to ask why Cushwell's people were not attending to certain matters. However, given that Cushwell was absent, you thought a private meeting would provide a better setting. Some of the key issues you want to address with Cushwell are:

1. *Selection processes* One of Cushwell's memos recommended that we should not hire clerical or secretarial personnel over 40. This is clearly age discrimination and very illegal! Production and R&D had both indicated that they were not satisfied with their track record of selecting high quality technical employees, but had people working on it. Why wasn't Cushwell working on it? That's Personnel's job! To top it off, Cushwell wrote a memo suggesting that the company should think twice about hiring a black supervisor! What is Cushwell thinking about here?

2. *Salary structure inequity* All of the other managers mentioned problems with the current salary structure. Some jobs seemed to be over-paid, while other jobs are pegged way under the rates other employers in the area are paying. Everyone agrees that the company is losing good employees and we have to start being more flexible. Where did this salary structure come from? Has anyone bothered to do a survey of other firms to figure out what they are paying people in jobs comparable to our positions? Job analysis would also be useful. Has anybody done this? Not only could it guide the development of valid selection criteria and help solve those problems, but it could help make sure that the company has internal equity in its salary structure so that higher skilled jobs will, in fact, be pegged at a higher wage level, etc.

3. *Unfair labor practices* When O'Malley, the production manager, was pressed about charges of interfering with a union election, she was particularly non-supportive of Cushwell. O'Malley seemed to be unaware that an unfair labor practices law suit could result from supervisory bulletins which encourage supervisors to influence an election. It would have been nice if Cushwell had been there to help clarify the situation. Of course, O'Malley should know better, but why isn't someone in the company educating her!

Earlier you had your secretary arrange a 2:30 pm meeting with Cushwell in your office and that time is quickly approaching. You only have about twenty minutes to spend with Cushwell before you have to meet with Everts in R&D on a pressing matter. However, it is high time to get to the bottom of the various personnel and industrial relations issues and start things moving in the right direction. Clearly Cushwell is going to be in charge of this function. The corporate people you report to have been quite firm in their belief that firing or transferring department heads very soon after taking over is out of the question. That would violate some inviolable corporate norm. So, no matter what happens, you've got to make the best of this situation, while keeping all of your direct reports in their current positions for at least six months. A lot can happen to a company in that period of time!

As you ponder these thoughts and the various choices you have, you hear Cushwell chatting with your secretary. A glance at your watch tells you it's time to get moving with this meeting. Remember that you hope to address the following issues:

1. Where did the current salary structure come from? What can we do to get rid of the inequities and develop a sound salary structure?
2. What is the basis for Cushwell's hiring criteria for clerical and secretarial positions (see item #3 in the in-basket material) and does he recognize he is suggesting age discrimination?
3. What is the basis for Cushwell's memo (item #6) which stated we should not hire a black supervisor? This seems to be racial discrimination and totally unacceptable!
4. What does Cushwell see as Personnel's role in the company? What are his priority issues?
5. Can Cushwell give me any more information on the union election interference charges? If they are true, how could he let them happen? How will he control this in the future?

OBSERVERS' GUIDELINES

1. What kind of relationship was established between the two role players? What were some key interchanges which impacted their relationship?
2. To what extent did the person in West's role get new information about the situation he or she faces as the new plant manager? What key episodes in the role play impacted the extent to which West was able to get new information?
3. To what extent did the person in Cushwell's role become defensive? What caused this reaction?
4. Was the meeting a useful problem-solving session? What factors contributed to its effectiveness? Did Cushwell and West both leave this meeting in a better position to more effectively handle their responsibilities?

IV
MOTIVATING INDIVIDUALS

READINGS

ON THE FOLLY OF REWARDING A, WHILE HOPING FOR B*

Steven Kerr

Whether dealing with monkeys, rats, or human beings, it is hardly controversial to state that most organisms seek information concerning what activities are rewarded, and then seek to do (or at least pretend to do) those things, often to the virtual exclusion of activities not rewarded. The extent to which this occurs of course will depend on the perceived attractiveness of the rewards offered, but neither operant nor expectancy theorists would quarrel with the essence of this notion.

Nevertheless, numerous examples exist of reward systems that are fouled up in that behaviors which are rewarded are those which the rewarder is trying to *discourage*, while the behavior he desires is not being rewarded at all.

In an effort to understand and explain this phenomenon, this paper presents examples for society, from organizations in general, and from profit-making firms in particular. Data from a manufacturing company and information from an insurance firm are examined to demonstrate the consequences of such reward systems for the organizations involved, and possible reasons why such reward systems continue to exist are considered.

* Reprinted with permission of the author and publisher. *Academy of Management Journal*, Volume 18, no. 4, 1975. Pp. 769–783. © 1975.

SOCIETAL EXAMPLES

Politics

Official goals are "purposely vague and general and do not indicate . . . the host of decisions that must be made among alternative ways of achieving official goals and the priority of multiple goals . . . ."[1] They usually may be relied on to offend absolutely no one, and in this sense can be considered high acceptance, low quality goals. An example might be "build better schools." Operative goals are higher in quality but lower in acceptance, since they specify where the money will come from, what alternative goals will be ignored, etc.

The American citizenry supposedly wants its candidates for public office to set forth operative goals, making their proposed programs, "perfectly clear," specifying sources and uses of funds, etc. However, since operative goals are lower in acceptance, and since aspirants to public office need acceptance (from at least 50.1 percent of the people), most politicians prefer to speak only of official goals, at least until after the election. They of course would agree to speak at the operative level if "punished" for not doing so. The electorate could do this by refusing to support candidates who do not speak at the operative level.

Instead, however, the American voter typically punishes (withholds support from) candidates who frankly discuss where the money will come from, rewards politicians who speak only of official goals, but hopes that candidates (despite the reward system) will discuss the issues operatively. It is academic whether it was moral for Nixon, for example, to refuse to discuss his 1968 "secret plan" to end the Vietnam war, his 1972 operative goals concerning the lifting of price controls, the reshuffling of his cabinet, etc. The point is that the reward system made such refusal rational.

It seems worth mentioning that no manuscript can adequately define what is "moral" and what is not. However, examination of costs and benefits, combined with knowledge of what motivates a particular individual, often will suffice to determine what for him is "rational."[2] If the reward system is so designed that it is irrational to be moral, this does not necessarily mean that immorality will result. But is this not asking for trouble?

War

If some oversimplification may be permitted, let it be assumed that the primary goal of the organization (Pentagon, Luftwaffe, or whatever) is to win. Let it be assumed further that the primary goal of most individuals on the front lines is to get home alive. Then there appears to be an important conflict in goals – personally rational behavior by those at the bottom will endanger goal attainment by those at the top.

But not necessarily! It depends on how the reward system is set up. The Vietnam war was indeed a study of disobedience and rebellion, with terms such as "fragging" (killing one's own commanding officer) and "search and evade" becoming part of the military vocabulary. The difference in subordinates' acceptance of authority between World War II and Vietnam is reported to be considerable, and veterans of the Second World War often have been quoted as being outraged at the mutinous actions of many American soldiers in Vietnam.

Consider, however, some critical differences in the reward system in use during the two conflicts. What did the GI in World War II want? To go home. And when did he get to go home? When the war was won! If he disobeyed the orders to clean out the trenches and take the hills, the war would not be won and he would not go home. Furthermore, what were his chances of attaining his goal (getting home alive) if he obeyed the orders compared to his chances if he did not? What is being suggested is that the rational soldier in World War II, *whether patriotic or not*, probably found it expedient to obey.

Consider the reward system in use in Vietnam. What did the man at the bottom want? To go home. And when did he get to go home? When his tour of duty was over! This was the case *whether or not* the war was won. Furthermore, concerning the relative chance of getting home alive by obeying orders compared to the chance if they were disobeyed, it is worth noting that a mutineer in Vietnam was far more likely to be assigned rest and rehabilitation (on the assumption that fatigue was the cause) than he was to suffer any negative consequence.

In his description of the "zone of indifference," Barnard stated that "a person can and will accept a communication as authoritative only when . . . at the time of his decision, he believes it to be compatible with his personal interests as a whole."[3] In light of the reward system used in Vietnam, would it not have been personally irrational for some orders to have been obeyed? Was not the military implementing a system which *rewarded* disobedience, while *hoping* that soldiers (despite the reward system) would obey orders?

Medicine

Theoretically, a physician can make either of two types of error, and intuitively one seems as bad as the other. A doctor can pronounce a patient sick when he is actually well, thus causing him needless anxiety and expense, curtailment of enjoyable foods and activities, and even physical danger by subjecting him to needless medication and surgery. Alternately, a doctor can label a sick person well, and thus avoid treating what may be a serious, even fatal ailment. It might be natural to conclude that physicians seek to minimize both types of error.

Such a conclusion would be wrong.[4] It is estimated that numerous Americans are presently afflicted with iatrogenic (physician *caused*) illnesses.[5] This occurs when the doctor is approached by someone complaining of a few stray symptoms. The doctor classifies and organizes these symptoms, gives them a name, and obligingly tells the patient what further symptoms may be expected. This information often acts as a self-fulfilling prophecy, with the result that from that day on the patient for all practical purposes is sick.

Why does this happen? Why are physicians so reluctant to sustain a type 2 error (pronouncing a sick person well) that they will tolerate many type 1 errors? Again, a look at the reward system is needed. The punishments for a type 2 error are real: guilt, embarrassment, and the threat of lawsuit and scandal. On the other hand, a type 1 error (labeling a well person sick) "is sometimes seen as sound clinical practice, indicating a healthy conservative approach to medicine."[6] Type 1 errors also are likely to generate increased income and a stream of steady customers who, being well in a limited physiological sense, will not embarrass the doctor by dying abruptly.

Fellow physicians and the general public therefore are really *rewarding* type 1 errors and at the same time *hoping* fervently that doctors will try not to make them.

GENERAL ORGANIZATIONAL EXAMPLES

Rehabilitation Centers and Orphanages

In terms of the prime beneficiary classification[7] organizations such as these are supposed to exist for the "public-in-contact," that is, clients. The orphanage therefore theoretically is interested in placing as many children as possible in good homes. However, often orphanages surround themselves with so many rules concerning adoption that it is nearly impossible to pry a child out of the place. Orphanages may deny adoption unless the applicants are a married couple, both of the same religion as the child, without history of emotional or vocational instability, with a specified minimum income and a private room for the child, etc.

If the primary goal is to place children in good homes, then the rules ought to constitute means toward that goal. Goal displacement results when these "means become ends-in-themselves that displace the original goals."[8]

To some extent these rules are required by law. But the influence of the reward system on the orphanage's management should not be ignored. Consider, for example, that the:

1. Number of children enrolled often is the most important determinant of the size of the allocated budget.
2. Number of children under the director's care also will affect the size of his staff.
3. Total organizational size will determine largely the director's prestige at the annual conventions, in the community, etc.

Therefore, to the extent that staff size, total budget, and personal prestige are valued by the orphanage's executive personnel, it becomes rational for them to make it difficult for children to be adopted. After all, who wants to be the director of the smallest orphanage in the state?

If the reward system errs in the opposite direction, paying off only for placements, extensive goal displacement again is likely to result. A common example of vocational rehabilitation in many states, for example, consists of placing someone in a job for which he has little interest and few qualifications, for two months or so, and then "rehabilitating" him again in another position. Such behavior is quite consistent with the prevailing reward system, which pays off for the number of individuals placed in any position for sixty days or more. Rehabilitation counselors also confess to competing with one another to place relatively skilled clients, sometimes ignoring persons with few skills who would be harder to place. Extensively disabled clients find that counselors often prefer to work with those whose disabilities are less severe.[9]

Universities

Society *hopes* that teachers will not neglect their teaching responsibilities but *rewards* them almost entirely for research and publications. This is most true at the large and prestigious universities. Clichés such as "good research and good teaching go together" notwithstanding, professors often find that they must choose between teaching and research oriented activities when allocating their time. Rewards for good teaching usually are limited to outstanding teacher awards, which are given to only a small percentage of good teachers and which usually bestow little money and fleeting prestige. Punishments for poor teaching also are rare.

Rewards for research and publications, on the other hand, and punishments for failure to accomplish these, are commonly administered by universities at which teachers are employed. Furthermore, publication oriented resumés usually will be well received at other universities, whereas teaching credentials, harder to document and quantify, are much less transferable. Consequently it is rational for university teachers to concentrate on research, even if to the detriment of teaching and at the expense of their students.

By the same token, it is rational for students to act based upon the goal displacement which has occurred within universities concerning what they are rewarded for. If it is assumed that a primary goal of a university is to transfer knowledge from teacher to student, then grades become identifiable as a means toward that goal, serving as motivational, control, and feedback devices to expedite the knowledge transfer. Instead, however, the grades themselves have become much more important for entrance to graduate school, successful employment, tuition refunds, parental respect, etc., than the knowledge or lack of knowledge they are supposed to signify.

It therefore should come as no surprise that information has surfaced in recent years concerning fraternity files for examinations, term paper writing services, organized cheating at the service academies, and the like. Such activities constitute a personally rational response to a reward system which pays off for grades rather than knowledge.

BUSINESS RELATED EXAMPLES
Ecology
Assume that the president of XYZ Corporation is confronted with the following alternatives:

1. Spend $11 million for antipollution equipment to keep from poisoning fish in the river adjacent to the plant; or
2. Do nothing, in violation of the law, and assume a one in ten chance of being caught, with a resultant $1 million fine plus the necessity of buying the equipment.

Under this not unrealistic set of choices it requires no linear program to determine that XYZ Corporation can maximize its probabilities by flouting the law. Add the fact that XYZ's president is probably being rewarded (by creditors, stockholders, and other salient parts of his task environment) according to criteria totally unrelated to the number of fish poisoned, and his probable course of action becomes clear.

Evaluation of Training
It is axiomatic that those who care about a firm's well-being should insist that the organization get fair value for its expenditures. Yet it is commonly known that firms seldom bother to evaluate a new GRID, MBO, job enrichment program, or whatever, to see if the company is getting its money's worth. Why? Certainly it is not because people have not pointed out that this situation exists; numerous practitioner oriented articles are written each year to just this point.

The individuals (whether in personnel, manpower planning, or wherever) who normally would be responsible for conducting such evaluations are the same ones often charged with introducing the change effort in the first place. Having convinced top management to spend the money, they usually are quite animated afterwards in collecting vignettes and anecdotes about how successful the program was. The last thing many desire is a formal, systematic, and revealing evaluation. Although members of top management may actually *hope* for such systematic evaluation, their reward systems continue to *reward* ignorance in this area. And if the personnel department abdicates its responsibility, who is to step into the breach? The change agent himself? Hardly! He is likely to be too busy collecting anecdotal "evidence" of his own, for use with his next client.

Miscellaneous
Many additional examples could be cited of systems which in fact are rewarding behaviors other than those supposedly desired by the rewarder. A few of these are described briefly below.

Most coaches disdain to discuss individual accomplishments, preferring to speak of teamwork, proper attitude, and a one-for-all spirit. Usually, however, rewards are distributed according to individual performance. The college basketball player who feeds his teammates instead of shooting will not compile impressive scoring statistics and is less likely to be drafted by the pros. The ballplayer who hits to right field to advance the runners will win neither the batting nor home run titles, and will be offered smaller raises. It therefore is rational for players to think of themselves first, and the team second.

In business organizations where rewards are dispensed for unit performance or for individual goals achieved, without regard for overall effectiveness, similar attitudes often are observed. Under most Management by Objectives (MBO) systems, goals in areas where quantification is difficult often go unspecified. The organization therefore often is in a position where it *hopes* for employee effort in the areas of team building, interpersonal relations, creativity, etc., but it formally *rewards* none of these. In cases where promotions and raises are formally tied to MBO, the system itself contains a paradox in that it "asks employees to set challenging, risky goals, only to face smaller paychecks and possibly damaged careers if these goals are not accomplished."[10]

It is *hoped* that administrators will pay attention to long run costs and opportunities and will institute programs which will bear fruit later on. However, many organizational reward systems pay off for short run sales and earnings only. Under such circumstances it is personally rational for officials to sacrifice long term growth and profit (by selling off equipment and property, or by stifling research and development) for short term advantages. This probably is most pertinent in the public sector, with the result that many public officials are unwilling to implement programs which will now show benefits by election time.

As a final, clear-cut example of a fouled-up reward system, consider the cost-plus contract or its next of kin, the allocation of next year's budget as a direct function of this year's expenditures. It probably is conceivable that those who award such budgets and contracts really hope for economy and prudence in spending. It is obvious, however, that adopting the proverb "to him who spends shall more be given," rewards not economy, but spending itself.

TWO COMPANIES' EXPERIENCES
A Manufacturing Organization
A midwest manufacturer of industrial goods had been troubled for some time by aspects of its organizational climate it believed dysfunctional. For research purposes, interviews were conducted with many employees and a questionnaire was administered on a companywide basis, including plants and offices in several American and Canadian locations. The company strongly encouraged employee participation in the survey, and made available time and space during the workday for completion of the instrument. All employees in attendance during the day of the survey completed the questionnaire. All instruments were collected directly by the researcher, who personally administered each session. Since no one employed by the firm handled the questionnaires, and since respondent names were not asked for, it seems likely that the pledge of anonymity given was believed.

A modified version of the Expect Approval scale (7) was included as part of the questionnaire. The instrument asked respondents to indicate the degree of approval or disapproval they could expect if they performed each of the described actions. A seven point Likert scale was used, with one indicating that the action would probably bring strong disapproval and seven signifying likely strong approval.

Although normative data for this scale from studies of other organizations are unavailable, it is possible to examine fruitfully the data obtained from this survey in several ways. First, it may be worth noting that the questionnaire data corresponded closely to information gathered through interviews. Furthermore, as can be seen from the results summarized in Table 1, sizable differences between various work units, and between employees at different job levels within the same work unit, were obtained. This suggests that response bias effects (social desirability in particular loomed as a potential concern) are not likely to be severe.

Most importantly, comparisons between scores obtained on the Expect Approval scale and a statement of problems which were the reason for the survey revealed that the same behaviors which managers in each division thought dysfunctional were those which lower level employees claimed were rewarded. As compared to job levels 1 to 8 in Division B (see Table 1), those in Division A claimed a much higher acceptance by management of "conforming" activities. Between 31 and 37 percent of Division A employees at levels 1-8 stated that going along with the majority, agreeing with the boss, and staying on everyone's good side brought approval; only once (level

Table 1
Summary of Two Divisions' Data Relevant to Conforming and Risk-Avoidance Behaviors (Extent to Which Subjects Expect Approval)

				Percentage of Workers Responding		
Dimension	Item	Division and Sample	Total Responses	1, 2, or 3 Disapproval	4	5, 6, or 7 Approval
Risk Avoidance	Making a risky decision based on the best information available at the time, but which turns out wrong.	A, levels 1–4 (lowest)	127	61	25	14
		A, levels 5–8	172	46	31	23
		A, levels 9 and above	17	41	30	30
		B, levels 1–4, (lowest)	31	58	26	16
		B, levels 5–8	19	42	42	16
		B, levels 9 and above	10	50	20	30
	Setting extremely high and challenging standards and goals, and then narrowly failing to make them.	A, levels 1–4	122	47	28	25
		A, levels, 5–8	168	33	26	41
		A, levels 9+	17	24	6	70
		B, levels 1–4	31	48	23	29
		B, levels 5–8	18	17	33	50
		B, levels 9+	10	30	0	70

Table 1 continued

Dimension	Item	Division and Sample	Total Responses	Percentage of Workers Responding		
				1, 2, or 3 Disapproval	4	5, 6, or 7 Approval
	Setting goals which are extremely easy to make and then making them.	A, levels 1–4	124	35	30	35
		A, levels 5–8	171	47	27	26
		A, levels 9+	17	70	24	6
		B, levels 1–4	31	58	26	16
		B, levels 5–8	19	63	16	21
		B, levels 9+	10	80	0	20
Conformity	Being a "yes man" and always agreeing with the boss.	A, levels 1–4	126	46	17	37
		A, levels 5–8	180	54	14	31
		A, levels 9+	17	88	12	0
		B, levels 1–4	32	53	28	19
		B, levels 5–8	19	68	21	11
		B, levels 9+	10	80	10	10
	Always going along with the majority.	A, levels, 1–4	125	40	25	35
		A, levels 5–8	173	47	21	32
		A, levels 9+	17	70	12	18
		B, levels 1–4	31	61	23	16
		B, levels 5–8	19	68	11	21
		B, levels 9+	10	80	10	10
	Being careful to stay on the good side of everyone, so that everyone agrees that you are a great guy.	A, levels 1–4	124	45	18	37
		A, levels 5–8	173	45	22	33
		A, levels 9+	17	64	6	30
		B, levels 1–4	31	54	23	23
		B, levels 5–8	19	73	11	16
		B, levels 9+	10	80	10	10

5-8 responses to one of the three items) did a majority suggest that such actions would generate disapproval.

Furthermore, responses from Division A workers at levels 1-4 indicate that behaviors geared toward risk avoidance were as likely to be rewarded as to be punished. Only at job levels 9 and above was it apparent that the reward system was positively reinforcing behaviors desired by top management. Overall, the same "tendencies toward conservatism and apple-polishing at the lower levels" which divisional management had complained about during the interviews were those claimed by subordinates to be the most rational course of action in light of the existing reward system. Management apparently was not getting the behaviors it was *hoping* for, but it certainly was getting the behaviors it was perceived by subordinates to be *rewarding*.

An Insurance Firm

The Group Health Claims Division of a large eastern insurance company provides another rich illustration of a reward system which reinforces behaviors not desired by top management.

Attempting to measure and reward accuracy in paying surgical claims, the firm systematically keeps track of the number of returned checks and letters of complaint received from policyholders. However, underpayments are likely to provoke cries of outrage from the insured, while overpayments often are accepted in courteous silence. Since it often is impossible to tell from the physician's statement which of two surgical procedures, with different allowable benefits, was performed, and since writing for clarifications will interfere with other standards used by the firm concerning "percentage of claims paid within two days of receipt," the new hire in more than one claim section is soon acquainted with the informal norm: "When in doubt, pay it out!"

The situation would be even worse were it not for the fact that other features of the firm's reward system tend to neutralize those described. For example, annual "merit" increases are given to all employees, on one of the following three amounts:

1. If the worker is "outstanding" (select category, into which no more than two employees per section may be placed): 5 percent
2. If the worker is "above average" (normally all workers not "outstanding" are so rated): 4 percent
3. If the worker commits gross acts of negligence and irresponsibility for which he might be discharged in many other companies: 3 percent.

Now, since (a) the difference between the 5 percent theoretically attainable through hard work and the 4 percent attainable merely by living until the review date is small and (b) since insurance firms seldom dispense much of a salary increase in cash (rather, the worker's insurance benefits increase, causing him to be further overinsured), many employees are rather indifferent to the possibility of obtaining the extra one percent reward and therefore tend to ignore the norm concerning indiscriminate payments.

However, most employees are not indifferent to the rule which states that, should absences or latenesses total three or more in any six-month period, the entire 4 or 5 percent due at the next "merit" review must be forfeited. In this sense the firm may be described as *hoping* for performance, while *rewarding* attendance. What it gets, of course, is attendance. (If the absence-lateness rule appears to the reader to be stringent, it really is not. The company counts "times" rather than "days" absent, and a ten-day absence therefore counts the same as one lasting two days. A worker in danger of accumulating a third absence within six months merely has to remain ill [away from work] during his second absence until his first absence is more than six months old. The limiting factor is that at some point his salary ceases, and his sickness benefits take over. This usually is sufficient to get the younger workers to return, but for those with 20 or more years' service, the company provide sickness benefits of 90 percent of normal salary, tax-free! Therefore . . . .)

CAUSES

Extremely diverse instances of systems which reward behavior A although the rewarder apparently hopes for behavior B have been given. These are useful to illustrate the breadth and magnitude of the phenomenon, but the diversity increases the difficulty of determining commonalities and establishing causes. However, four general factors may be pertinent to an explanation of why fouled up reward systems seem to be so prevalent.

Fascination with an "Objective" Criterion

It has been mentioned elsewhere that:

> Most "objective" measures of productivity are objective only in that their subjective elements are a) determined in advance, rather than coming into play at the time of the formal evaluation and b) well concealed on the rating instrument itself. Thus industrial firms seeking to devise objective rating systems first decide, in an arbitrary manner, what dimensions are to be rated, . . . usually including some items having little to do with organizational effectiveness while excluding others that do. Only then does Personnel Division churn out official-looking documents on which all dimensions chosen to be rated are assigned point values, categories, or whatever.[11]

Nonetheless, many individuals seek to establish simple, quantifiable standards against which to measure and reward performance. Such efforts may be successful in highly predictable areas within an organization, but are likely to cause goal displacement when applied anywhere else. Overconcern with attendance and lateness in the insurance firm and with number of people placed in the vocational rehabilitation division may have been largely responsible for the problems described in those organizations.

Overemphasis on Highly Visible Behaviors

Difficulties often stem from the fact that some parts of the task are highly visible while other parts are not. For example, publications are easier to demonstrate than teaching, and scoring baskets and hitting home runs are more readily observable than feeding teammates and advancing base runners. Similarly, the adverse consequences of pronouncing a sick person well are more visible than those sustained by labeling a well person sick. Team-building and creativity are other examples of behaviors which may not be rewarded simply because they are hard to observe.

Hypocrisy

In some of the instances described the rewarder may have been getting the desired behavior, notwithstanding claims that the behavior was not desired. This may be true, for example, of management's attitude toward apple-polishing in the manufacturing firm (a behavior which subordinates felt was rewarded, despite management's avowed dislike of the practice). This also may explain politicians' unwillingness to revise the penalties for disobedience of ecology laws, and the failure of top management to devise reward systems which would cause systematic evaluation of training and development programs.

Emphasis on Morality or Equity Rather than Efficiency

Sometimes consideration of other factors prevents the establishment of a system which rewards behaviors desired by the rewarder. The felt obligation of many Americans to vote for one candidate or another, for example, may impair their ability to withhold support from politicians who refuse to discuss the issues. Similarly, the concern for spreading the risks and costs of wartime military service may outweigh the advantage to be obtained by committing personnel to combat until the war is over.

It should be noted that only with respect to the first two causes are reward systems really paying off for other than desired behaviors. In the case of the third and fourth causes the system *is* rewarding behaviors desired by the rewarder, and the systems are fouled up only from the standpoints of those who believe the rewarder's public statements (cause 3), or those who seek to maximize efficiency rather than other outcomes (cause 4).

CONCLUSIONS

Modern organization theory requires a recognition that the members of organizations and society possess divergent goals and motives. It therefore is unlikely that managers and their subordinates will seek the same outcomes. Three possible remedies for this potential problem are suggested.

Selection

It is theoretically possible for organizations to employ only those individuals whose goals and motives are wholly consonant with those of management. In such cases the same behaviors judged by subordinates to be rational would be perceived by management as desirable. State-of-the-art reviews of selection techniques, however, provide scant grounds for hope that such an approach would be successful (for example, see 12).

Training

Another theoretical alternative is for the organization to admit those employees whose goals are not consonant with those of management and then, through training, socialization, or whatever, alter employee goals to make them consonant. However, research on the effectiveness of such training programs, though limited, provides further grounds for pessimism (for example, see 3).

Altering the Reward System

What would have been the result if:

1. Nixon had been assured by his advisors that he could not win reelection except by discussing the issues in detail?
2. Physicians' conduct was subjected to regular examination by review boards for type 1 errors (calling healthy people ill) and to penalties (fines, censure, etc.) for errors of either type?
3. The President of XYZ Corporation had to choose between (a) spending $11 million dollars for antipollution equipment, and (b) incurring a fifty-fifty chance of going to jail for five years?

Managers who complain that their workers are not motivated might do well to consider the possibility that they have installed reward systems which are paying off for behaviors other than those they are seeking. This, in part, is what happened in Vietnam, and this is what regularly frustrates societal efforts to bring about honest politicians, civic-minded managers, etc. This certainly is what happened in both the manufacturing and the insurance companies.

A first step for such managers might be to find out what behaviors currently are being rewarded. Perhaps an instrument similar to that used in the manufacturing firm could be useful for this purpose. Chances are excellent that these managers will be surprised by what they find — that their firms are not rewarding what they assume they are. In fact, such undesirable behavior by organizational members as they have observed may be explained largely by the reward systems in use.

This is not to say that all organizational behavior is determined by formal rewards and punishments. Certainly it is true that in the absence of formal reinforcement some soldiers will be patriotic, some presidents will be ecology minded, and some orphanage directors will care about children. The point, however, is that in such cases the rewarded is not *causing* the behaviors desired but is only a fortunate bystander. For an organization to *act* upon its members, the formal reward system should positively reinforce desired behaviors, not constitute an obstacle to be overcome.

It might be wise to underscore the obvious fact that there is nothing really new in what has been said. In both theory and practice these matters have been mentioned before. Thus in many states Good Samaritan laws have been installed to protect doctors who stop to assist a stricken motorist. In states without such laws it is commonplace for doctors to refuse to stop, for fear of involvement in a subsequent lawsuit. In college basketball additional penalties have been instituted against players who foul their opponents deliberately. It has long been argued by Milton Friedman and others that penalties should be altered so as to make it irrational to disobey the ecology laws, and so on.

By altering the reward system the organization escapes the necessity of selecting only desirable people or of trying to alter undesirable ones. In Skinnerian terms,[12] "As for responsibility and goodness — as commonly defined — no one . . . would want or need them. They refer to a man's behaving well despite the absence of positive reinforcement that is obviously sufficient to explain it. Where such reinforcement exists, 'no one needs goodness.'"

References

1. C. Perrow (1969) "The Analysis of Goals in Complex Organizations" in A. Etzioni, ed., *Readings on Modern Organizations*. Englewood Cliffs, NJ: Prentice-Hall, p. 66.
2. H.A. Simon (1957) *Administrative Behavior*. New York: The Free Press. In Simon's terms, a decision is "subjectively rational" if it maximizes an individual's valued outcomes so far as his or her knowledge permits. A decision is "personally rational" if it is oriented toward the individual's goals.
3. C.I. Barnard (1964) *The Functions of the Executive*. Cambridge, MA: Harvard University Press, p. 165.
4. L.H. Garland "Studies of the Accuracy of Diagnostic Procedures" (1959) American *Journal of Roentgenological, Radium Therapy Nuclear Medicine*, Volume 82, 25–38. In this study of 14,867 films for signs of tuberculosis, 1,216 positive readings turned out to be clinically negative; on 24 negative readings proved clinically active, a ratio of 50 to 1.
5. T.J. Scheff (1965) "Decision Rules, Types of Error, and Their Consequences in Medical Diagnosis," in F. Massarik and P. Ratoosh, eds., *Mathematical Explorations in Behavioral Science*. Homewood, IL: Irwin.
6. *Ibid*., p. 69.
7. P.M. Blau and W. Richard Scott (1962) *Formal Organizations*. San Francisco: Chandler.
8. *Ibid*., p. 229.
9. Personal interviews conducted during 1972–1973.
10. S. Kerr (1973) "Some Modification in MBO as an OD Strategy," *Academy of Management Proceedings*, pp. 39–42.
11. S. Kerr (1973) "What Price Objectivity?" *American Sociologist*, Volume 8, pp. 92–93.
12. G.E. Swanson (1972) "Review Symposium: Beyond Freedom and Dignity," *American Journal of Sociology*, Volume 78, pp. 702–705.

Additional Readings

Fiedler, F.E. (1972) "Predicting the Effects of Leadership Training and Experience from the Contingency Model," *Journal of Applied Psychology*, Volume 56, pp. 114–119.

Litwin, G.H. and R.A. Stringer, Jr. (1968) *Motivation and Organizational Climate*. Cambridge, MA: Harvard University Press.

Webster, E. (1964) *Decision Making in the Employment Interview*. Montreal: Industrial Relations Center, McGill University.

HOW TO RUIN MOTIVATION WITH PAY*

W. Clay Hamner

MERIT PAY – SHOULD IT BE USED?

Most behavioral scientists believe in the "law of effect," which states simply that behavior which appears to lead to a positive consequence tends to be repeated. This principle is also followed by most large organizations which have a merit pay system for their management team. Merit pay or "pay for performance" is so widely accepted by compensation managers and academic researchers that criticizing it seems foolhardy.

Despite the soundness of the principle of the law of effect on which merit pay is based, academic researchers have criticized the merit system as being detrimental to motivation rather than enhancing motivation as designed. These criticisms generally fall into one of two categories. The first group of researchers criticize the failure of the merit plan to increase the motivation of the work force because of mismanagement or lack of understanding of the merit program by managers. The second group of researchers criticize the use of merit pay because it utilizes externally mediated rewards rather than focusing on a system where individuals can be motivated by the job itself. This second criticism centers on the proposition that employees who enjoy their job (i.e., are intrinsically motivated) will lose interest in the job when a merit pay plan is introduced because they soon believe they are doing the job for the money and not because they enjoy their job. Therefore, for the first group of researchers, the recommendation is that compensation managers need to examine ways to improve the introduction of merit plans, while the second group of researchers, albeit fewer in number, would recommend that compensation managers need to deemphasize the merit pay plan system and concentrate on improving other aspects of the job.

The purpose of this presentation will be to examine the research behind both of these positions and then present recommendations which, it is hoped, will enable the compensation manager to utilize a "pay performance" plan as a method of improving the quality and quantity of job performance. Let's begin the discussion by examining possible reasons why merit pay systems fail.

REASONS WHY MERIT PAY SYSTEMS FAIL

As noted earlier, one group of researchers has concluded that the failure of merit pay plans is due not to a weakness in the law of effect, but to a weakness in its implementation by compensation managers and the line managers involved in the merit increase recommendations. For example, after reviewing pay research from General Electric and other companies, H. H. Meyer (1975) concluded that despite the apparent soundness of the simple principle on which merit pay is based, experience tells us that it does not work with such elegant simplicity. Instead, managers typically seemed to be inclined to make relatively small discriminations in salary treatment among individuals in the same job regardless of perceived differences in performance. As a matter of fact, Meyer notes, when discriminations are made, they are likely to be based on factors other than performance – such as length of service, future potential, or perceived need for "catch up," where one employee's pay seems low in relation to others in the group.[1]

Michael Beer (Beer & Gery, 1972), Director of Organizational Development at Corning Glass, explains why the implementation of the merit system has lost its effectiveness when he states that pay systems evolve over time and adminis-

---

* Reprinted by permission of the publisher, from *COMPENSATION REVIEW*, Third Quarter 1975 © 1975 American Management Association, New York. All rights reserved.

trative considerations and tradition often override the more important considerations of behavioral outcomes in determining the shape of the system and its administration.[2] Therefore, both of these researchers seem to say that it is not the merit pay theory that is defective. Rather, the history of the actual implementation of the theory is at fault. Let us look at the shortcomings – noted in the literature – that may cause low motivation to result from a merit pay program.

Pay is Not Perceived As Being Related to Job Performance
Edward E. Lawler, III, a leading researcher on pay and performance, has noted that one of the major reasons managers are unhappy with their wage system is that they do not perceive the relationship between how hard they work (productivity) and how much they earn. Lawler (1966), in a survey of 600 middle and lower level managers, found virtually no relationship between their pay and their rated performance.[3] Of the managers studied, those who were most highly motivated to perform their jobs effectively were characterized by two attitudes: (1) they said that their pay was important to them and (2) they felt that good job performance would lead to higher pay for them.

There are several reasons why managers do not perceive their pay as being related to performance even when the company claims to have a merit pay plan. First, many rewards (e.g., stock options) are *deferred payments*, and the time horizon is so long that the employee loses sight of its relationship to performance. Second, the *goals* of the organization on which performance appraisals are based are either unclear, unrealistic, or unrelated to pay. W.H. Mobley (1974) found only 36 percent of the managers surveyed from a company using an MBO program saw goal attainment as having considerable bearing on their merit increase, while 83 percent of their bosses claim that they used the goal attainments to determine their pay increase recommendations.[4] Third, the *secrecy* of the annual merit increases may lead managers to conclude that their recommended pay increase has no bearing on their past year's performance. R.L. Opsahl and M.D. Dunnette (1966) claimed that secrecy is due in part to a fear by salary administrators that they would have a difficult time mustering convincing arguments in favor of many of their practices.[5] E.E. Lawler (1971) summarized his extensive research on secrecy of pay by stating that managers did not have an accurate picture of what other managers were earning. There was a general tendency for the managers to overstate the pay of managers at their own level (thereby reducing their own pay, relatively speaking), and at one level below them (again reducing their own pay, relatively speaking), while they tended to under-estimate the pay of managers one level above them (thus reducing the value of future promotions).[6]

Performance Ratings Are Seen As Biased
While many managers working under a merit program believe that the program is a good one, they are dissatisfied with the evaluation of their performance given them by their immediate superior. A merit plan is based on the assumption that managers can make objective (valid) distinctions between good and poor performance. Unfortunately, most evaluations of performance are subjective in nature, and consist of a "summary score" from a general (and sometimes dated) performance evaluation form. As H. H. Meyer (1975) notes, the supervisor's key role in determining pay creates a problem in that it reminds the employee very clearly that he or she is dependent on the supervisor for rewards. Therefore, the merit plan should, whenever possible, be based on objective measures (e.g., group sales, cost reduction per unit, goal attainment, etc.) rather than subjective measures (e.g., cooperation, attitude, future potential, etc.).[7]

As an aside, it should be noted that in the area of fair employment of minorities, both the courts (e.g., see *Rowe v. General Motors Corporation*, 1972) and the new EEOC (1974) guidelines recognize the potential of bias in subjective performance appraisals, and organizations must begin examining the validity of their performance ratings to see if they are, in fact, job related. My recent research has shown that, even when objective measures of job performance are clearly spelled out, supervisors have a tendency to rate blacks differently than whites and females differently than males even though their performance levels are identical (e.g., see Scott & Hamner, 1975; Hamner, Kim, Baird, & Bigoness, 1974).[8] E.E. Lawler, III, feels that the complaints of managers and employees about the subjective nature of their performance evaluations may be a sign of a system of poor leadership. Lawler (1971) notes that many plans seem to fail not because they are mechanically defective, but because they are ineffectively introduced, there is a lack of trust between superiors and subordinates, or the quality of the supervisor is too low. He adds that no plan can succeed in the face of low trust and poor supervision, no matter how well-constructed it may be.[9] L.W. Gruenfield and P. Weissenberg (1966) reported support for this theory of poor leadership espoused by Lawler when they found that good managers are much more amenable than poor managers to the idea of basing pay on performance.[10]

Rewards Are Not Viewed As Rewards

A third problem in administering a merit increase deals with management's inability to communicate accurately to the employee the information that they are trying to communicate through the pay raise. There is no doubt that the pay raise is more than money; it tells the employee "You're loved a lot," "You're only average," "You're not appreciated around here," "You'd better get busy," etc. Often management believes it is communicating a positive message to the employee, but the message being received by the employee is negative. This may have a detrimental effect on his or her future potential. Opsahl and Dunnette (1966) warn us that the relation between performing certain desired behaviors and attainment of the pay-incentive must be explicitly specified.[11]

The reasons that the reward message may not be seen as a reward include the following: (1) Conflicting reward schedules may be operating. (2) A problem of inequity among employees is perceived to exist. (3) The merit increase is threatening to the self-esteem of the employee. All three of these problems center on the fact that the pay increases are generally kept secret – thus causing the employees to draw erroneous conclusions – or on the fact that there is little or no communication in the form of coaching and counselling coming from the supervisor during the year, or following the performance appraisal. Instead, the employee is "expected to know" what the supervisor thinks about his or her performance. As Beer and Gery (1972) stated, the more frequent the formal and informal reviews of performance and the more the individual is told about reasons for an increase, the greater his preference for a merit increase and the lower his preference for a seniority system.[12]

Conflicting reward schedules Such schedules come about because of a defect in the merit plan itself. For example, individual rewards (e.g., the best manager will get a free trip to Hawaii) are set up in such a way that cooperation with other managers is discouraged, or perhaps a cost-reduction program is introduced at the expense of production, and one department (sales) suffers while another department (manufacturing) benefits in the short run. As Kenneth F. Foster, Manager of Composition at Xerox, has noted (see *Harvard Business Review*, July-August 1974),[13] pay plans must be constantly changing because of general business conditions, shifts in management philosophy, competitive pressures, participant feedback, and modification in the structure and objectives of the organization. Nevertheless, these changes should be designed in such a way that the negative side effect of reduced cooperation does not result. For this reason, many companies are using a company-wide merit plan (e.g., the Scanlon Plan; see Frost, Wakeley, & Ruh, 1974)[14] where there is a financial incentive to everyone in the organization based on the performance of the total organization.

Inequity Inequity in pay can come about for one of two reasons. First, the employee perceives the merit increase to be unfair relative to his own past year's performance. That is, he is dissatisfied with the performance evaluation, or else feels the performance evaluation is fair, but believes his supervisor failed to reward him in a manner consistent with his rating. A much more common problem is that while the employee may agree with the dollar amount of his pay, he perceives that others who are performing at levels below him are receiving as large an increase as he, or else those who are performing at his same level are receiving higher raises. For example, an employee who was rated as above average receives an 8 percent pay increase. He perceives this to be low since he believes that the average increase was 9 percent, when in fact it was $6^1/_2$ percent. In order to avoid the feeling of inequity, which will contribute to dissatisfaction with pay and possible lower job performance, Lawler (1973) recommends that managers tell their employees how the salary raises were derived (e.g., 50 percent based on cost of living and 50 percent on merit) and tell them the range and mean of raises given in the organization for people at their job level.[15] Lawler (1965) advocated the abandonment of secrecy policies: "There is no reason why organizations cannot make salaries public information."[16]

Threat to self-esteem H.H. Meyer, in an excellent paper, argues that the problem with merit pay plans may be more than a problem of equity. Drawing on his previous research (Meyer, Kay, & French, 1965), he concluded that 90 percent of the managers at General Electric rated themselves as above average.[17] Bassett and Meyer (1968)[18] and Beer and Gery (1972)[19] found similar results. Meyer concludes that the inconsistency in the information of the merit raise with the employee's evaluation of his or her performance will be a threat to the manager's *self-esteem*, and the manager may cope with this threat by either denying the importance of hard work or disparaging the source. Meyer concludes:

The fact that almost everyone thinks he is an above average performer probably causes most of our problems with merit pay plans. Since the salary increases most people get do not reflect superior performance (as determined by interpersonal comparisons, or as defined in the guide book for the pay plan), the effects of the actual pay increases on motivation are likely to be more negative than positive. The majority of the people feel discriminated against because, obviously, management does not recognize their true worth (1975).[20]

Managers of Merit Increases Are More Concerned with Satisfaction with Pay than Job Performance

Most studies which survey managers' satisfaction with their pay have shown high levels of dissatisfaction. Porter (1961) found that 80 percent of the managers surveyed from companies throughout the United States reported dissatisfaction with their pay.[21] These same findings have been reported in surveys at General Electric (Penner, 1967)[22] and a cross-section of managers from many companies (Lawler, 1965).[23] Beer (Beer & Gery, 1972)[24] points out that too often dissatisfaction with pay is assumed to mean dissatisfaction with amount. However, his research suggests that a change to a merit system with no increase in amount paid out by the company will increase satisfaction if the reasons for the increases are explained.

Opsahl and Dunnette (1966)[25] noted that while there is a great deal of research on satisfaction with pay, there is less solid research in the area of the relationship between pay and job performance than any other field. Because of this failure to deal with the role of pay, Lawler (1966) notes that many managers have come to the erroneous conclusion that the experts in "human relations" have shown that pay is a relatively unimportant incentive.[26]

In fact, Cherrington, Reitz, and Scott (1971) found that the magnitude of the relationship between satisfaction and performance depends primarily upon the performance-reinforcer contingencies that have been arranged (i.e., people who were appropriately reinforced were satisfied with their pay, while those people who were dissatisfied with their pay were those who were inappropriately rewarded).[27] Likewise, Hamner and Foster (1974) found that the best performers working under a contingent (piece rate) pay plan were more satisfied than the poorer performers, but that there was no relationship between satisfaction and performance for those paid under a noncontingent (across the board) pay plan.[28]

Managers need to be concerned with two questions. First, *is the merit raise being based on performance?* Numerous studies (e.g., see Lee, 1969; Belcher, 1974)[29] show that pay is not closely related to performance in many organizations that claim to have merit ranges. Typically, these studies show that pay is much more closely related to job level and seniority than performance. In fact, Belcher (1974) reports that low, zero, and even negative correlations between pay and supervisory ratings of performance occur even among managers where the correlation would be expected to be high.

Second, *who is doing the complaining?* Donald Finn, Compensation Manager at J.C. Penney, says we are often "hung up" as managers about the satisfaction of employees with our pay recommendations. He says:

> So who is complaining and why? If low producers are low earners, the pay plan is working – but there will be complaints. If a company wants an incentive plan in which rewards are commensurate with risk, it must be willing to accept a relatively broad range of earnings and corresponding degrees of manager satisfaction.[30]

Beer agrees with Finn when he says:

> A merit system can probably be utilized effectively by management in motivating employees. This concept has been in disfavor lately, but our findings indicate that more might be done with money in motivating people, particularly those who are work and achievement oriented in the first place.

While a merit system would seem to be less need satisfying to the security-oriented individual and, therefore, potentially less motivating, there is probably a net gain in installing a merit system. Those who are high in achievement-oriented needs will be stimulated by such a system to greater heights of performance, while those high in security-oriented needs will become more dissatisfied and it is hoped, will leave.[31]

Trust and Openness about Merit Increases Is Low

A merit system will not be accepted and may not have the intended motivational effects if managers do not actively administer a performance appraisal system, practice good human relations, explain the reasons for the increases and ensure that employees are not forgotten when eligibility dates come and go. The organization must provide an open climate with respect to pay, and an environment where work and effort are valued.[32]

The Xerox Corporation has recognized the problem of trust and openness and states a philosophy that "If pay and satisfaction is to be high, pay rates must vary according to job demands in such a way that each perceived increment in a job demand factor will lead to increased pay."[33] This same document at Xerox notes that organizations expect extremely high levels of trust on the part of their employees, in that:

(a) Only 72% of 184 employing organizations had a written statement of the firm's basic compensation policy covering such matters as paying competitive salaries, timing of wage and salary increases, and how raises are determined.

(b) Only 51% of these same organizations communicate their general compensation policies directly to all employees, while 21% communicate the policy only to managers.

(c) Contrarily, 69% of the firms do not provide their employees with wage and salary schedules or progression plans that apply to their own categories, thus indicating a low trust level toward employees.

(d) Over 50% of the firms do not tell their employees where this information is available.

(e) In only 48% of the firms do managers have access to salary schedules applying to their own level in the organization, and in only 18% of the companies do managers have knowledge of the salaries of other managers at their own level or higher levels.[34]

Some Organizations View Money As the Primary Motivator, Ignoring the Importance of the Job Itself

The first five shortcomings deal with the criticism of researchers that the failure of the merit plan is due to poor implementation, and not due to a weakness in the theory of the "law of effect." However, the sixth shortcoming under discussion now centers on the second criticism that employees who have intrinsically interesting jobs will lose interest in the job when a merit pay plan is introduced. An intrinsically motivating job can be defined as one that is interesting and creative enough that certain pleasures or rewards are derived from completing the task itself. Until recently, most theories dealing with worker motivation (e.g., Porter & Lawler, 1968)[35] have assumed that the effects of intrinsic and extrinsic reinforcement (e.g., merit pay) are additive; i.e., a worker will be more motivated to complete a task which combined both kinds of rewards than a task where only one kind of reward is present.

Deci (1971, 1972a, b),[36] among others (Likert, 1967; Vroom & Deci, 1970),[37] criticizes behavioral scientists who advocate a system of employee motivation that utilizes externally mediated rewards, i.e., rewards such as money administered by someone other than the employee. In so doing, according to Deci, management is attempting to control the employee's behavior so he or she will do as told. The limitations of this method of worker motivation, for Deci, is that it only satisfies a person's "lower order" needs (Maslow, 1943)[38] and does not take into account "higher order" needs for self-esteem and self-actualization.

Deci (1972,a) recommends that we should move away from a method of external control, and toward a system where individuals can be motivated by the job itself. He says that this approach will allow managers to focus on higher-order needs where the rewards are mediated by the recipient (intrinsically motivated). To motivate employees intrinsically, tasks should be designed which are interesting, creative, and resourceful, and workers should have some say in decisions which concern them "so they will feel like causal agents in the activities which they engage in."[39]

Deci (1972,b) has introduced evidence which reportedly shows that a person's intrinsic motivation to perform an activity decreases when he or she receives contingent monetary payment for performing an interesting task. Deci (1972,b) concludes from these findings that:

> Interpreting these results in relation to theories of work motivation, it seems clear that the effects of intrinsic motivation and extrinsic motivation are not additive. While extrinsic rewards such as money can certainly motivate behavior, they appear to be doing so at the expense of intrinsic motivation; as a result, contingent payment systems do not appear to be compatible with participative management systems.[40]

Deci brings out an important point: Managers should not use pay to offset a boring or negative task. However, like Herzberg before him, his results don't appear to completely support his conclusion about the effect of money as a motivator. Research by both Hamner and Foster (1974)[41] and Calder and Staw (1975)[42] has shown that the effect of intrinsic and extrinsic monetary rewards is additive and that even Deci's results themselves, on close examination, support this more traditional argument. In addition, I am not sure that merit pay plans are incompatible with a participative management system. The noted psychologist B.F. Skinner offers advice to managers on both of these last two arguments.

Skinner (1973) recommends that the organization should design feedback and incentive systems in such a way that the dual objective of getting things done and making work enjoyable are met. He says:

It is important to remember that an incentive system isn't the only factor to take into account. How pleasant work conditions are, how easy or awkward a job is, how good or bad tools are – many things of that sort make an enormous difference in what a worker will do for what he receives. One problem of the production-line worker is that he seldom sees any of the ultimate consequences of his work. He puts on left front wheels day in and day out and he may never see the finished car. . . .[43]

Skinner also suggested that people be involved in the design of the contingencies of reinforcements (in this case, merit pay plans) under which they live. This way the rewards come from the behavior of the worker in the environment, and not the supervisor. Both Kenneth F. Foster at Xerox and Joe W. Rogers, Chairman of the Board of Waffle House, agree. Foster, commenting on the McDonald pay plan, said, "McDonald's management is to be commended for recognizing a number of important incentive reward axioms. Foremost, the reward system must be meaningful to the recipient. They must also see it as equitable and its financial outcomes and rewards as within their power to control."[44] Rogers agreed, saying, "In the restaurant industry, a bonus system must be self-monitoring and deal only with the facts. All areas of judgment by a friendly or unfriendly superior should be absent in a bonus system. . . . let people participate in the design of the new pay. Credibility with the participants is much more critical."[45]

Deci's recommendation that jobs be designed so that they are interesting, creative, and resourceful should be wholeheartedly supported by proponents of a merit pay plan. Skinner (1969) warns managers that too much dependency on force and a poorly designed monetary reward system may actually reduce performance, while designing the task so that it is automatically reinforcing can have positive effects on performance. He says:

> The behavior of an employee is important to the employer, who gains when the employee works industriously and carefully. How is he to be induced to do so? The standard answer was once physical force: men worked to avoid punishment or death. The by-products were troublesome however, and economics is perhaps the first field in which an explicit change was made to positive reinforcement. Most men now work, as we say, "for money."
>
> Money is not a natural reinforcer; it must be conditioned as such. Delayed reinforcement, as in a weekly wage, raises a special problem. No one works on Monday morning because he is reinforced by a paycheck on Friday afternoon. The employee who is paid by the week works during the week to avoid losing the standard of living which depends on a weekly system. Rate of work is determined by the supervisor and special aversive contingencies maintain quality. The pattern is therefore still aversive. It has often been pointed out that the attitude of the production-line worker toward his work differs conspicuously from that of the craftsman, who is envied by workers and industrial managers alike. One explanation is that the craftsman is reinforced by more than monetary consequences, but another important difference is that when a craftsman spends a week completing a given set object, each of the parts produced during the week is likely to be automatically reinforcing because of its place in the completed object.[46]

RECOMMENDATIONS FOR OVERCOMING FAILURES IN MERIT PAY SYSTEM

In the discussion of the shortcomings of merit pay plans, my suggestions for overcoming these deficiencies have been implied or suggested. Let us briefly review and outline several of these suggestions as a point of departure for our discussion.

1. *Openness and trust should be stressed by the compensation manager.* As a minimum, employees should know the formula for devising the merit increases and should be told the range and mean of the pay increases for people at their job level. This alone should reduce some of the feeling of low self-esteem and inequity present in many organizations today.
2. *Supervisors should be trained in rating and feed-*

back techniques. Compensation managers should help personnel design and carry out training programs which emphasize the necessity of having consistency between performance ratings, other forms of feedback, and pay increases. In addition, managers should be trained to emphasize objective rather than subjective areas of job performance. Skinner (1973) sees one of the greatest weaknesses in the motivation of workers through reinforcement principles as due to poor training of managers. He says that what must be accomplished, and what he believes is currently lacking, is an effective training program for managers. "In the not too distant future, a new breed of industrial managers may be able to apply the principles of operant conditioning effectively."[47]

3. *Components of the annual pay increase should be clearly and openly specified*. Compensation managers need to allocate a certain percentage for a cost-of-living increase (not to cover the total cost of living, however) and a percentage for merit. The percentage for merit should be an average and not a maximum, and the manager should be able to distribute this percentage in any way he or she deems appropriate. In other words, it should not be an either-or situation where the worker either gets the full amount of the merit increase or none at all. Any pay increase due to an adjustment for past inequities and pay increases due to promotions should come out of the payroll increase first, but should not be included in the stated average pay increase. Frequently, if the organization can afford a 10 percent increase in wages and benefits, it might take 2 percent of wages and benefits to use for the adjustments mentioned above, and then allocate an 8 percent average increase to cost of living (e.g., 4 percent) and merit (e.g., 4 percent). Therefore, the range of pay increases would be from 4 percent to 12 percent – not including adjustments – where the average for the department would be 8 percent. Along these same lines, I feel it is important to give the increases in percentages and not dollar amounts since managers have a tendency to "cheat" long-term good performers (i.e., high pay managers) when a dollar amount is used.

4. *Each organization should tailor its pay plan to the needs of the organization and individuals therein – with participation a key factor in the merit pay plan design*. One of the reasons the Scanlon plan has been so successful is that it combines participation with the company's ability to afford a merit increase. Workers understand how they get the increase they do and why it is the amount it is. In addition each company using a Scanlon approach has a unique pay plan designed especially for that organization by the members of the organization.

5. *Don't overlook other rewards*. Compensation managers should work with other staff people in the organization to improve the climate of the organization, the task design, and other forms of feedback to ensure that an employee has as much chance of success as possible.

ETHICAL IMPLICATIONS: EXCHANGE, NOT CONTROL

No discussion of effective uses of merit pay plans would be complete without a discussion of the compensation manager's ethical responsibilities in using pay as a motivator. There is no doubt that poorly designed reward structures can interfere with the development of spontaneity and creativity. Reinforcement systems which are deceptive and manipulative are an insult to everyone's integrity. The employee should be a willing party to an attempt to influence, with both parties benefiting from the relationship.

Nord (1974), referring to a well designed incentive plan, says:

> I would add that to the degree that such approaches increase the effectiveness of man's exchanges with his environment, the potential for expanding freedom seems undeniable. To me these outcomes seem highly humanistic, although, for some reason this approach is labeled anti-

humanistic and approaches which appear to have less potential and human advancement are labeled humanistic.[48]

I concur with Nord, and think the ethical responsibility of compensation managers is clear. The first step in the ethical use of monetary control in organizations is the understanding by managers of the determination of behavior (see Hamner, 1974). Since reinforcement is the single most important concept in the learning process, managers must learn how to design effective reinforcement programs that will encourage productive and creative employees. This presentation has attempted to outline the knowledge and research available for this endeavor.

References

1. H.H. Meyer (1975) "The Pay for Performance Dilemma." *Organizational Dynamics*, Volume 3, Number 3, pp. 39–50.
2. M. Beer and G.J. Gery (1972) "Individual and Organizational Correlates of Pay System Preferences" in H.L. Tosi, R. House and M.D. Dunnette, eds., *Managerial Motivation and Compensation*. East Lansing, MI: Michigan State University Press.
3. E.E. Lawler (1966) "The Mythology of Management Compensation." *California Management Review*, Volume 9, pp. 11–22.
4. W.H. Mobley (June 1974) "The Linkage Between MBO and Merit Compensation." *Personnel Journal*, pp. 423–427.
5. R.L. Opsahl and M.D. Dunnette (1966) "The Role of Financial Compensation in Industrial Motivations." *Psychological Bulletin*, Volume 66, pp. 94–118.
6. E.E. Lawler (1971) *Pay and Organizational Effectiveness*. New York: McGraw-Hill.
7. H.H. Meyer, *op. cit.*
8. W.E. Scott and W.C. Hamner (1975) "The Influence of Variations in Performance Profiles on the Performance Evaluation Process: An Examination of the Validity of the Criteria." *Organizational Behavior and Human Performance*, Volume 14, pp. 360–370. W.C. Hamner, J. Kim, L. Baird and W. Bigtoness (1974) "Race and Sex as Determinants of Ratings by Potential Employees in a Simulated Work Sampling Task." *Journal of Applied Psychology*, Volume 59, pp. 705–711.
9. E.E. Lawler (1971) *op. cit.*
10. L.W. Gruenfeld and P. Weissenberg (1966) "Supervisory Characteristics and Attitudes Toward Performance Appraisals." *Personnel Psychology*, pp. 143–152.
11. R.L. Opsahl and M.D. Dunnette, *op. cit.*
12. M. Beer and G.J. Gery, *op. cit.*
13. *Harvard Business Review*, (July-August, 1974).
14. C.F. Frost, J.H. Wakeley and R.H. Ruh (1974) *The Scanlon Plan for Organization Development: Identity, Participation and Equity*. East Lansing, MI: Michigan State University Press.
15. E.E. Lawler (1973) *Motivation in Work Organization*. Monterey, CA: Brooks/Cole.
16. E.E. Lawler (1965) "Managers' Perceptions of Their Subordinates' Pay and Their Superiors' Pay." *Personnel Psychology*, Volume 18, pp. 413–422.
17. H.H. Meyer. *op. cit.*
18. G.L. Basset and H.H. Meyer (1968) "Performance Appraised Based on Self-Review." *Personnel Psychology*, Volume 21, pp. 421–430.
19. M. Beer and G.J. Gery. *op. cit.*
20. H.H. Meyer, *op. cit.*, p. 13.
21. L.W. Porter (1961) "A Study of Perceived Need Satisfactions in Bottom and Middle Management Jobs." *Journal of Applied Psychology*, Volume 45, pp. 1–10.
22. D.D. Penner (1967) "A Study of the Causes and Consequences of Salary Satisfaction." General Electric Company: *Behavioral Research Service Report*, 1967.
23. E.E. Lawler (1965) *op. cit.*
24. M. Beer and G.J. Gery, *op. cit.*
25. R.L. Opsahl and M.D. Dunnette. *op. cit.*
26. E.E. Lawler (1966) *op. cit.*
27. D.L. Cherrington, J.J. Reitz and W.E. Scott (1971) "Effects of Reward and Contingent

Reinforcement on Satisfaction and Task Performance." *Journal of Applied Psychology*, Volume 55, pp. 521–536.
28. W.C. Hamner and L.W. Foster (1974) "Are Intrinsic and Extrinsic Awards Additive? A Test of Deci's Cognitive Evaluation Theory." Paper presented to the National Academy of Management, Seattle.
29. D.W. Belcher (1974) *Compensation Administration*. Englewood Cliffs, NJ: Prentice-Hall. S.M. Lee (1969) *Salary Equity: Its Determination, Analysis and Correlates*. Unpublished doctoral dissertation, University of Georgia.
30. *Harvard Business Review* (July-August, 1974), p. 8.
31. M. Beer and G.J. Gery. *op. cit.*
32. *Ibid.*
33. *Xerox Compensation Planning Model* (June, 1972). Rochester, NY: Xerox Corporation.
34. *Ibid.*, pp. 68–69.
35. L.W. Porter and E.E. Lawler (1968) *Managerial Attitudes and Performance*. Homewood, IL: Irwin-Dorsey.
36. Deci, E.L. (1971) "Effects of Externally Mediated Rewards on Intrinsic Motivation. *Journal of Personality and Social Psychology*, Volume 18, pp. 105–115. Deci, E.L. (1972b) "The Effects of Contingent and Noncontingent Rewards and Controls on Intrinsic Motivation." *Organizational Behavior and Human Peformance*, Volume 8, pp. 217–229.
37. V.H. Vroom and E.L. Deci (1970) "An Overview of Work Motivation" in V.H. Vroom and E.L. Deci, eds., Management and Motivation. Baltimore, MD: Penguin Press.
38. A.H. Maslow (1943) "A Theory of Human Motivation." *Psychological Review*. Volume 50, pp. 370–396.
39. E.L. Deci (August 1972a) "Work: Who Does Not Like It and Why?" *Psychology Today*, Volume 92, pp. 57–58.
40. E.L. Deci (1972b) *op. cit.*
41. W.C. Hamner and L.W. Foster (1974) *op. cit.*
42. B.J. Calder and B.M. Straw (1975) "The Interaction of Intrinsic and Extrinsic Motivation: Some Methodological Notes." *Journal of Personality and Social Psychology*, Volume 31, pp. 599–605.
43. B.F. Skinner (Winter 1973) "Conversations with B.F. Skinner," p. 49. *Organizational Dynamics*, pp. 31–40.
44. "Case of Big Mac's Pay Plans" (July-August 1974), p. 5. *Harvard Business Review*, pp. 1–8.
45. *Ibid.*, p. 6.
46. B.F. Skinner (1969) *Contingencies of Reinforcement*. New York: Appleton-Century-Crofts.
47. B.F. Skinner (1973) *op. cit.*
48. W.R. Nord (1974) Some issues in the application of operant conditioning to the management of organizations. Paper presented to the National Academy of Management, Seattle.

Additional Readings

Blood, M.R. (August, 1974) "Applied Behavioral Analysis from an Organizational Perspective." Paper presented at the 82nd Annual Convention of the American Psychological Association, New Orleans.

Drucker, P.F. (1973) "Beyond the Stick and Carrot: Hysteria Over the Work Ethic." *Psychology Today, 87*, pp. 89–93.

"Employee Survey Finds Most Like Their Work." (March 18, 1974) *Equinews*. Volume III, Number 6.

Equal Employment Opportunity Commission Guidelines (Rev. ed.) (1974) Washington, D.C.: U.S. Government Printing Office.

Likert, R. (1967) *New Patterns of Management* (2nd ed.) New York: McGraw-Hill.

Meyer, H.H., Kay, E. and French, J.R.P. (January-February 1965) "Split Roles in Performance Appraisals." *Harvard Business Review*.

INTEGRATING OB MOD WITH COGNITIVE APPROACHES TO MOTIVATION*

Donald B. Fedor
Gerald R. Ferris

In efforts to explain behavior in organizations, behavioral scientists traditionally have conceptualized motivational processes and phenomena in either cognitive or behaviorist frameworks. While such attempts to maintain the differentiation of perspectives are regarded as advancing our understanding of behavioral outcomes, it appears that a related purpose is to set off the more widely accepted cognitive theories from the less popular behaviorist approaches. Such differentiation, regardless of intent, has served to deprive us of a potentially richer understanding of motivation and organizational behavior. Particularly for the practitioner who attempts to translate organization theories into useful prescriptions, confusion abounds. With this in mind, our purpose with this paper is to take an eclectic approach, providing specific suggestions for blending the divergent perspectives that offer prescriptive methods for maximizing worker motivation. Our focus is on bringing this blending of perspectives to bear on the legitimization and utility of what has come to be known as organizational behavior modification (OB Mod), in an attempt to address the controversy that has recently emerged in this area (Grey 1979; Locke, 1977, 1979; Parmerlee & Schwenk, 1979).[1]

---

* From the *Academy of Management Review*, 1981, Volume 6, Number 1, pp. 115–125. Reprinted by permission of the authors and publisher.

Author's note: We wish to thank Michael K. Moch, Kendrith M. Rowland, and Jeffrey J. Sucec for their comments on earlier drafts of this paper.

UNDERLYING ASSUMPTIONS

The principal cognitive motivation theories in the organization literature are need-satisfaction models (Maslow, 1965),[2] expectancy/valence theory (Vroom, 1964),[3] and goal-setting theory (Locke, 1968).[4] Clearly, the cognitive component, focusing on rational behavior, is the common thread linking all three theories. Needs have been equated with the concept of "drive," a purely behavioral, non-cognitive notion in the experimental psychology literature (e.g., Hull, 1943);[5] the organizational literature extends the need concept to cognitive elements such as self-actualization. The notion that individuals exhibit needs for growth and development traditionally has enjoyed considerable acceptance by practitioners, presumably owing to the intuitive appeal and face validity of the arguments.

The assumption that individuals are composed of complex internal mechanisms that determine their behavior is perpetuated in the expectancy/valence theory of motivation (Vroom, 1964).[6] This theory and subsequent elaborations (e.g., Porter & Lawler, 1968)[7] assume that individuals formulate subjective probability estimates of the extent to which a given level of effort leads to work performance (expectancies), and the extent to which a given performance level leads to certain valued outcomes (instrumentalities). Presumably, the greater the certainty in these two links, the stronger the predictability of work motivation or effort expected.

The work-design literature (e.g., Hackman & Oldham, 1980)[8] perhaps represents a blend of the need-satisfaction and expectancy/valence theories of motivation. The approach is explicit in specifying that work itself should be designed to maximize the rewarding properties and facilitate the psychological growth of the individual.

The other work-motivation theory reflecting a cognitive orientation is the goal-setting formulation (Locke, 1968).[9] Sharing the idea, with expectancy/valence theory, that behavior is intentional or purposive (Tolman, 1932),[10] this theory makes the assumption that motivation and performance are functions of goal accomplishment. While sharing certain ideas, goal setting differs from expectancy/valence theory in contextual prediction. That is, motivation is believed to be highest, in the expectancy/valence framework, when effort-to-performance and performance-to-outcome links are well defined and certain, leading to more informed subjective probability estimates structuring behavior. Alternatively, in the goal-setting framework, motivation is believed to be highest when the goals set are difficult. The inconsistency between prediction using expectancy/valence and goal-setting theories is evident. Goals perceived as difficult would be translated into low effort-to-performance probabilities, which would result in lower motivation according to expectancy/valence theory.

The alternative perspective concerning motivation in work organizations is behavioristic in nature, and is exemplified by OB Mod. OB Mod is based on the assumption that individual behavior is a function of its consequences (e.g., Luthans & Kreitner, 1975).[11] By definition, the antecedents of behavior are found in the environment, not embodied in an internal state, such as personality or mind. This view differs from the cognitive one of individuals actively seeking their destiny through independent, self-determined action, and instead represents a view of behavior as a function of past and present reinforcement contingencies. This view, of course, has its roots in principles of operant conditioning, which has existed in the experimental literature for quite some time [Skinner, 1953].[12] Much of the present antagonism toward the application of operant conditioning principles to explaining behavior in organizations derives from reactions against the issues of determinism and control, perhaps first exemplified in a popular novel on behavioral control in society (Skinner, 1948).[13] This also has resulted in charges of manipulative control and Machiavellianism, which have contributed to the less-than-favorable image of OB Mod, since many are reluctant to accept the belief that behavior is determined totally by the environment.

To date, no truly eclectic approach has emerged to functionally integrate aspects of OB Mod with the cognitive orientation of widely espoused management philosophies. Thus the practitioner has been dependent on intuitive guidance to make implementation choices.

Nord (1969)[14] took the first step toward merging these different orientations by examining the frameworks of behaviorism and Theory X and Y assumptions detailed by McGregor (1960).[15] He believed that "the importance of environmental factors in determining behavior is the crucial and dominant similarity between Skinner and McGregor."[16] In this integrative attempt, Nord demonstrated, theoretically, not only the strong congruence between these supposedly competing approaches, but also the manner in which concepts of reinforcement contingency contribute to organizational effectiveness, even under the guise of a more cognitive framework. Additionally, he noted that factors of the job can be analyzed as reinforcers, whether they are considered to be intrinsic or extrinsic.

Luthans and Kreitner (1975)[17] took the next step by demonstrating how an understanding of OB Mod techniques can facilitate the design of job enrichment, management-by-objectives programs, and organizational development interventions. These authors argue that job enrichment could profit by contingently enriching the worker's task, based on performance. Therefore, the more enriching job components would serve as naturally occurring rewards for good performance. This would be expected to eliminate the problems of reinforcing poor performance (i.e., enriching the job of the below-standards worker) or changing the job against the worker's will. Management-by-objectives is also a popular management technique that should profit from OB Mod principles. Luthans and Kreitner propose that many management-by-objectives programs are failing because employees are not adequately reinforced for achieving performance objectives. Finally, they believe that OB Mod can legitimately play a role in organizational development interventions, because theoretically these programs are intended to facilitate or stimulate reward processes in organizations. The techniques employed typically focus on interpersonal relationships while disregarding environmental factors. Although their suggestions are appealing, there has been a virtual absence of empirical investigations directed toward testing these ideas.

Proceeding further in reducing the distance between these divergent orientations necessitates identifying specific opportunities where framework boundaries have created an absence of *concrete* data. Overlapping studies must be used to assess the relative merits of the different management approaches. The attempts to integrate and differentiate these motivational schemes to date have focused on paradigm or rightful domain implications (Grey, 1979; Locke, 1979; Parmerlee & Schwenk, 1979).[18] This confrontation over primarily theoretical issues is not serving the development of a motivational system that will contribute to individual and organizational effectiveness. We hope to cast this conflict in a somewhat different light, proposing new areas of investigation that will benefit the practitioner.

We will borrow from the eclectic approach recommended by Peters (1960),[19] who argued that no single theory of motivation could explain all behavior. In essence, he proposed combining portions of a number of contributing approaches to account for all relevant factors within a construct as complex as human motivation. This advice seems particularly appropriate in that management must be concerned with both worker performance and satisfaction, neither of which has been reduced to a simple cause-effect relationship. According to some theory and research, performance and satisfaction are dependent on different variables (e.g., Lawler, 1973).[20] Even within the performance area, both cognitive and behavioral aspects appear relevant. Campbell and Stanley (1966)[21] claimed that when competent researchers are strongly split over an issue, both sides are likely to be examining a different but valid portion of the complete answer.

Perhaps one of the most notable and effective attempts at integrating the cognitive and behavioral perspectives with respect to motivation is social learning theory (Bandura, 1977).[22] Social learning theory purportedly overemphasizes neither internal forces nor environmental factors in explaining behavior. Rather, individual functioning is seen as a continuous interaction among cognitive, behavioral, and environmental factors. Social learning theory has received attention primarily in experimental and clinical settings, but recently a concerted attempt has been made to apply it directly to explaining behavior in organizations (Davis & Luthans, 1980).[23] This effort focuses attention on observable behavior in "organization member-behavior-environment interaction."[24]

Additionally, principles of social learning theory have been incorporated in training and development techniques. Goldstein and Sorcher (1974)[25] incorporated the principles of social learning in their behavior modeling program for supervisors, intended to instill functional work-related behaviors. Extending this idea, it has been demonstrated that social learning theory can explain the development of supervisory styles (Weiss, 1977) and the adoption of work values in organizations (Weiss, 1978). Most recently, Latham and Saari (1979)[26] applied principles of the theory in another training program for supervisors through behavior modeling.

An extensive review of OB Mod applications in business organizations revealed that research of this sort has assumed a narrow and perhaps defensive position, owing perhaps to its somewhat controversial nature. Integration of this area with others must be preceded by systematic research that begins to address some of the questions regarding the behavioral perspective. A principal question of our paper is whether the results of field studies using OB Mod methods in work organizations are providing the necessary data for effective application and integration. We have identified a number of artificial boundaries being perpetuated in research designs that are counter-productive to the potential contributions of OB Mod.

Field studies in business organizations have taken a very myopic view of the factors considered as dependent variables. Most of the current OB Mod research is conducted and interpreted as if it were an isolated discipline (Petrock & Gamboa, 1976).[27] Advocates of OB Mod seek to demonstrate that the method works as predicted. Luthans and Kreitner (1975)[28] argue that changing research environments does not alter rules for behavior control. Support for the operant approach in organizational settings has been provided by several studies (At Emery Air Freight, 1973; McCarthy, 1978; Nord, 1970; Pedalino & Gamboa, 1974; Runnion, Watson & McWhorten, 1978).[29] However, despite the semblance of success, the research being conducted is not adequately addressing fundamental issues that will continue to plague OB Mod regardless of the level of sophistication in either statistical analysis or the environmental control of variables. Previous analyses of field studies by Kazdin (1973) and Andrasik (1979) are primarily concerned with whether behavior change can be attributed to the intervention as it is designed and reported.[30] Although some commentary is valuable, this alone will not earn OB Mod a place of respect. A broadening of the research scope, as discussed later, must address the multifaceted criticisms raised by cognitively oriented behavioral scientists such as Fry (1974), Argyris (1971), and Hackman (1979).[31] Before detailing the areas for future investigation, we will discuss the potential benefits and costs of utilizing OB Mod.

POTENTIAL BENEFITS AND COSTS OF OB MOD

OB Mod is behavior- or performance-oriented. Unlike the case with need- and expectancy-based theories, managers focus on performance-related behaviors of workers, not on underlying psychological states as a means of achieving performance goals. Thus, the manager is not forced into the position of playing the role of clinician. Management based on worker needs or expectancies necessitates a considerable degree of subjective evaluation and, perhaps, periodic professional assessment. With OB Mod however, it is incumbent upon management to determine and communicate specific performance objectives and definitive plans of action. The reduction in management's flexibility and room for arbitrary action could be cause for resisting the use of such a system. Despite this requirement, Cummings and Molloy (1977) in their discussions of OB Mod conclude that "one of its major contributions . . . is to show how qualitative aspects of performance can be quantified."[32]

Luthans and Kreitner (1975)[33] emphasize that managers using OB Mod do not directly manage the individual. Instead, an environment is created that reinforces desired behavior. The implication is that the operant approach turns control of supervision over to workers, since supervisory behavior is directly contingent on subordinate actions. In the typical OB Mod intervention utilizing positive verbal reinforcement, the manager is trained to wait for the appropriate response from the worker. So while the worker's reinforcement is contingent on his own behavior, the manager's behavior becomes directly dependent on it. Interestingly, this appears to be a refinement of what naturally occurs between subordinates and their superiors. There is some empirical support in the leadership literature for the claim that subordinate performance causes leader behavior (e.g., Barrows, 1976; Lowin & Craig, 1968).[34] An additional perspective on this issue is presented by Luthans and Davis (1979).[35] They discuss how the individual can use structuring of the environment and planning of consequences to enhance behavioral self-control.

In conjunction with a performance orientation, OB Mod strongly de-emphasizes the use of punishment in organizational settings. Laboratory research results support the belief that desirable behavior should be reinforced and that undesirable behavior should be allowed to extinguish through the withholding of reinforcement. Lack of punishment in work settings can be important for employee relations and the general working climate. One reason is that the worker may associate the punishment with the supervision instead of the punished act. An additional cost of punishment is increased employee stress, which can result in retaliation or withdrawal from work (Gupta & Beehr, 1979).[36] It may be worthwhile to consider the predominance of punitive control in light of the current pervasiveness of worker alienation (Walton, 1980).[37]

Reese (1966)[38] believes that punishment may be the dominant method of behavior control because of its innate capacity to immediately halt undesired behavior. Presumably, an immediate halt would convey to management a feeling of greater accomplishment and control. However, punishment does not ensure or even direct proper performance, as OB Mod purports to do. The benefit of using punishment is that its effects require less diligence and patience than operant techniques. So while positive reinforcement can be viewed as beneficial to human relations and employee training, it does appear to necessitate additional time and effort that must be absorbed by management during the initial conditioning phases.

It should be noted that management is expected to fully analyze the tasks assigned to its workers. The implementation of an OB Mod program is typically preceded by a "performance audit." Management cannot justifiably base recommendations for performance improvement intervention solely on work-group attitude. In our own experience in supervisor training, we have observed that different behavioral components become aggregated along with the inferences concerning individual attitudes. The charge against the worker then is escalated from mere poor performance to an assumed personality flaw as well. Typically there is little attempt to separate the components of performance, to zero-in on those aspects in need of improvement. The supervisor's reaction to the worker will then be based on the image held of that individual as a poor worker, troublemaker, and so forth, virtually ignoring observable behaviors in many cases. In contrast, the performance audit provides a systematic framework within which to make such behavioral determinations. It sets a base line that can be compared to the objective the organization has established. In some cases, the audit identifies unforeseen discrepancies (At Emery Air Freight, 1973).[39]

OB Mod's measurement bias reflects its behaviorist heritage. It is a scientifically based theory that allows managers and supervisors to accurately assess program progress. Changes in quantifiable variables are recorded and used instead of attitudinal measures. The inclusion of psychological states currently confounds the motivation issue for practitioners. Therefore, the ability of management to generate and analyze its own data, after appropriate training, adjusts the intervention to the practitioner's level of sophistication. As Nord (1969) states, "the Skinnerian approach leads to rational planning in order to control outcomes previously viewed as spontaneous consequences. This approach could expand the area of planning and rational action in administration."[40]

Most applications of behavior modification in work organizations include positive verbal feedback or objective feedback as a reinforcer to effect performance changes. The belief that feedback is a major factor in the OB Mod intervention is not at all unusual. Feedback is a core dimension of contemporary measures of job characteristics (Hackman & Oldham, 1975; Sims, Szilagyi, & Keller, 1976)[41] and is consistent with performance appraisal systems objectives to let workers know where they stand (Haynes, 1980),[42] and with the philosophy implicit in the quality of working life movements. OB Mod takes a substantially different approach by formalizing both the types and the timing of reinforcement, regardless of whether the focus is on feedback, pay, or other valued rewards. Although the question of whether rewards must be immediately contingent on behavior/performance will likely remain a debatable issue for some time, OB Mod utilizes a schedule of reinforcement stressing timing as an issue in the development of a supportive environment that will elicit and reinforce desired behavior. Such a prescriptive strategy may offend practitioners and theorists who emphasize individual needs and differences, but it does ensure that the worker will be provided with feedback concerning correct behavior. This is essential for practical application where the prescription "more feedback" is found lacking in specificity.

OB Mod interventions often begin with a great deal of verbal reinforcement and then gradually lessen the frequency of this external feedback. The expectation is that the direct performance feedback from the task will naturally take over the reinforcer role. So, over the course of an OB Mod program, there is a shift in emphasis from supervision to aspects of the job itself. For individuals beginning a new job, the OB Mod prescription is consistent with results presented by Katz (1978).[43] He found that during the initial stages of an individual's job, task feedback is strongly desired. Following the usual OB Mod schedule of reinforcement, early frequent feedback tapers off to later permit greater autonomy.

In summary, OB Mod provides a definitive framework from which to implement and test an intervention by taking into account the types and timing of reinforcement that supports or punishes job behaviors. It is obvious that we have a positive view of OB Mod; we believe that this approach has an orientation and associated techniques that are useful and complementary to popular motivation schemes. The next step is to begin collecting organizational data that will test the fit between OB Mod and other orientations. This necessitates expanding the parameters considered appropriate by behaviorist researchers. The following topics represent a partial list of issues OB Mod researchers need to consider more directly.

THE ROLE OF PARTICIPATION

Participation in decision making has become a popular issue during this decade, owing largely to its convergence with individual growth, job involvement, and job enrichment. OB Mod, on the other hand, has been viewed typically as a top-down approach that is applied to the employee with virtually no concern for individual development (Hackman, 1979).[44] In theory, these orientations are in clear opposition. The role of participation in operant conditioning can be viewed in a number of ways. Since people presumably react to their environment based on reinforcement history, feelings of involvement and individual growth could be considered irrelevant. Participation might be perceived as a confounding factor in the intervention if it causes changes in the experimental design or in the reinforcers. Conversely, getting the participants to assist in developing the OB Mod program, such as determining the proper reinforcers, designating the "best" behaviors to accomplish the stated objectives, and discovering the reinforcers utilized by the informal organization could eliminate some of the problems. The feeling of involvement itself may be an effective reinforcer.

Komaki, Waddell, and Pearce (1977)[45] were forced to use a participative approach in order to secure the cooperation of the participants in conducting their experiment. Although this was mentioned, it was not cited as a relevant factor in interpreting the reported success of the experiment. Nord (1970)[46] suggests using worker ideas about the type of program and rewards as valuable input with which to modify and refine the OB Mod project. In this way, the positive verbal reinforcement is seen as a way to enhance communication between managers and workers.

In each of these cases, as in most OB Mod interventions, there is a conspicuous attempt to account for those factors that cannot be controlled directly. It is interesting that researchers concerned with the generalizability of their experimental designs feel justified in ignoring the facilitative function of a cognitive factor as potentially persuasive as participation. Unfortunately, no research reviewed to date has compared the efficacy of OB Mod interventions for groups with and without participant involvement. A comparative research design would address the question of the extent to which these theoretically divergent orientations are, in fact, complementary.

OB MOD AND GOAL SETTING

We believe that OB Mod and goal setting are complementary techniques originating from divergent perspectives. Both orientations focus on goal attainment, but traditionally have selected different factors for experimentation. For this reason, the distinction between OB Mod and goal setting can be blurred in an applied setting. As previously noted, the objective of most OB Mod interventions is to have the standards and feedback from the task eventually take over the reinforcement role (At Emery Air Freight, 1973).[47] The individual presumably is performing at a higher level, owing to greater goal difficulty (Locke, 1968).[48] Many of the goal-setting investigations have been concerned with the effect of incentives on performance and the extent to which they affect performance through goal level (Locke, 1968; Pritchard & Curtis, 1973; Terborg, 1976).[49] The overlap of these two orientations is apparent, but it is virtually always ignored. None of the organization-based OB Mod studies we reviewed discussed differential target levels of performance. The relevant factors for behaviorists doing field research seem to be the following: to determine the correct or desirable behavior, to select the appropriate reinforcement(s) and the schedule of application, and to test the level of goal attainment within an appropriate experimental design. Our argument is that OB Mod and goal setting focus on different aspects of the same issue. The information concerning differential goal setting should be tested in conjunction with OB Mod.

We find it interesting that the goal-setting literature (e.g., Latham & Yukl, 1975, 1976)[50] has focused on the relationship between assigned goals and those set participatively. Operant conditioning techniques traditionally have relied on unilaterally set target behaviors and standards of performance. This adds further support to the belief that OB Mod ignores individual perceptions and expectations. The gain or loss caused by assigning objectives also has not been explored adequately to date.

WORKER AND MANAGER RESPONSES TO BEHAVIOR MODIFICATION

OB Mod has been criticized severely for being dehumanizing and ignoring individual cognitive processes (e.g., Fry, 1974).[51] Even though findings from current research do not support the belief that satisfaction is consistently related to productivity (Locke, 1976),[52] worker responses to their jobs can have an impact on labor relations, absenteeism, tardiness, and turnover — areas of particular concern to management. Typically, OB Mod field experiments measure the effects of an intervention on, for example, absenteeism, with the issue of morale addressed only briefly in the conclusion. Cummings and Molloy (1977)[53] cite the lack of attitudinal references in their review of OB Mod research. Only Adams (1975)[54] has examined the relationship between positive reinforcement and attitudes about product quality. His results, however, were inconclusive.

A related issue has to do with management's reaction to workers when positive verbal reinforcement is used as part of an OB Mod program. Adams noted that one supervisor adopted a less autocratic style of management as a result of the forced interaction with subordinates. Nord (1970)[55] suggested using the increased level of supervisory response as a method for involving the individual in the job. In addition, the negative sanctions used by management (i.e., punishment) are greatly reduced, because managers are forced to relate to their subordinates on a positive basis. Presumably, this experience should precipitate some attitudinal change in managers, but such potential benefits have not been evaluated to date. So, although the application of operant conditioning techniques is less Machiavellian than the underlying theory might suggest, research has not shown any sustained interest in dispelling this negative image. Regardless of the behaviorist bias against attitudinal measures, the worker's response to any intervention is an important factor for managers. Therefore, assessing these attitudes should be equally relevant to the research and should be incorporated in future OB Mod designs.

OB MOD AND WORK DESIGN

When viewing work design within a systems framework, one must account for the worker, the work itself, and the work context (pay, coworkers, supervision, etc.). Corresponding to the above factors and their interaction, a number of salient issues arise for practitioners interested in a pragmatic approach to work design. These issues can be classified under three headings: individual differences, locus of control, and tradeoffs between different design alternatives.

Traditional work design theorists deal with both individual differences and the work context by measuring growth-need strength (GNS) and satisfaction with specific contextual variables (see Hackman & Oldman (1980) for a review).[56] Essentially, if the focal individual has a sufficient level of GNS and demonstrates satisfaction with the job context, then the work design process is intended to create an enriching task (Oldham, Hackman & Pearce, 1976).[57] This entails designing the task to provide such things as increased skill variety, autonomy, and feedback. The implication is that the locus of control should reside with the individual worker. Factors typically of concern in traditional work design research are those intrinsic to the task. These factors occur through the process of performing the task, and are therefore mediated by the worker and not by other organizational agents or mechanisms external to the individual. This orientation suggests that work design fits neatly into a managerial framework where the worker is granted greater latitude within which to function. Deci's (1975)[58] research on internal motivation indicates that for tasks which are intrinsically enriched, extrinsic variables, which supposedly alter the locus of control from internal to external, cause a decrease in internal motivation. As a result, at the managerial end of the job spectrum, where tasks exhibit more design flexibility, the traditional job design method seems appropriate and possible to implement.

OB Mod again poses a divergent orientation. Individual differences are literally ignored and the notion of determining individual satisfaction with compensation and work context, as advocated by Oldham, Hackman, and Pearce (1976)[59] and equity theory research (Adams, 1965),[60] does not fit its behaviorist framework. The reinforcers, in an OB Mod intervention, generally are mediated externally – despite Nord's (1969)[61] argument that, owing to the contingent nature of the reinforcement, the individual retains ultimate control. For tasks that cannot be sufficiently enriched, OB Mod offers an attractive alternative. This may be one reason why this motivational technique has been predominantly applied to blue-collar positions. Presumably it is better to provide external feedback when the task itself does not than to simply ignore the deficiency.

From the above approaches to work design, it is easy to conceptualize a number of potential alternatives available to the organization designer when tasks fall somewhere between the extremes of "impossible" and "easily enriched." For example, an organization could expend its resources to redesign a task, building in greater skill variety, or use the same resources to provide the job holder with a greater variety of reinforcers external to the task. Cummings and Molloy (1977)[62] identify such alternatives as the choice within the organization. In situations where different action levels represent realistic alternatives, the incongruity between these orientations becomes extremely confusing. Despite Nord's (1969)[63] belief that reinforcers are the common denominators, there are different costs and benefits to these available choices. Perceptual differences may not directly affect motivation or performance, but these factors could be important to other organizational elements, such as the climate and the attractiveness of the organization.

An additional consideration is that jobs are sometimes designed or redesigned to correct for anticipated problems in worker motivation or satisfaction. Management may desire to act before predicted behavioral changes take place. Therefore, the responses workers have to different job components are sometimes used as behavioral predictors. For example, if the research suggesting that absenteeism is not an effective indicator of future turnover is correct, there may be no behavioral antecedents to identify a worker's propensity to leave the organization. In other words, if "behavioral units" of job tenure cannot be identified, then it may not be possible to determine the efficacy of current reinforcement until it fails to produce the desired results. In this case, valued employees could be lost before the necessity for a design change would be realized. So despite the inexact and unstable nature of internal states (Salancik & Pfeffer, 1977),[64] assessing worker attitudes may, in some instances, be the only available indicator of future difficulties.

The focal problem here is a paucity of comparative studies between behaviorist and non-behaviorist methods. Apparently, only Cummings and Molloy (1977)[65] have reviewed and compared different orientations within the framework of the quality of working life and productivity to determine the different action levers relied on and the types of outcomes achieves in research interventions. More detailed studies are necessary to determine the immediate outcomes and the more indirect implications of selecting different approaches. To date, there are no available data on whether the choice of an intervention should be influenced by the individual(s) being targeted, the type of task, or the climate of the organization. Work design theorists sensitive to the locus-of-control issue presumably would argue that substituting OB Mod techniques for intrinsic components will never be a satisfying tradeoff for the worker. Nord (1969), Luthans and Kreitner (1975),[66] and others would likely counter with the argument that if reinforcement is designed properly, there should be no qualitative differences. At this point consultants and practitioners must rely on their own intuition in the absence of concrete evidence.

COMPLEXITY AND CREATIVITY

As previously noted, most of the jobs used to generate test data for OB Mod could be classified as blue-collar positions. The environment is usually stable and the worker's function can be dissected into reinforceable behavioral events. Two related issues emerge from these factors, concerning complexity and creativity. One question is: How is OB Mod adapted to *complex managerial positions* that do not have clearly defined tasks? In spite of the case cited by Luthans and Kreitner (1975)[67] suggesting that complex behaviors, such as initiative, can be effectively reinforced, OB Mod may, in fact, be more applicable to lower-level organizational positions. From anecdotal accounts such as those presented by Kerr (1975),[68] it is evident that we must not merely reinforce the components of the job that are quantifiable. If the entire job is not reinforced, employee responses will center on activities that consistently gain positive feedback. The remaining functions of the job will be allowed to extinguish along with the inappropriate behaviors.

To our knowledge, no comparative studies exist demonstrating the efficiency of OB Mod in relation to other motivational techniques. Andrasik confirms this conclusion in stating that "none of the [interventions reviewed] consisted of comparisons with alternative, non-behavioral approaches."[69] In the absence of quantifiable data, how is the manager in charge of the OB Mod intervention to deal with qualitative information? Needless to say, behavioral researchers must begin to report and analyze interventions involving all levels of the organizational hierarchy.

The more important question, however, deals with *creativity*. If the individual's job is broken down into behavioral units, will this not drastically reduce worker flexibility in making behavioral (qualitative) adjustments? The incentive to search for more efficient work patterns would be greatly decreased unless reinforcement for creativity were built into the program. Unfortunately, this idea was not tested in any of the experiments reviewed. This potential problem coincides with the discussion concerning participation. Involving employees in project design and maintenance may circumvent the problems of selecting the most effective behavior, determining appropriate reinforcement for creative activities, or encouraging feedback with which to change ineffective or inappropriate elements of the OB Mod program. However, with no evidence available at present, such a hypothesis awaits empirical examination.

CONCLUSION

OB Mod is a behavior- or performance-oriented management technique. Quantitative output data are used to design a reinforcing environment for appropriate work behavior. This offers management a straightforward method for analyzing the effect of supervision and other reinforcers, such as pay, on worker conduct. As a perspective divergent from more intuitively appealing and generally accepted cognitive motivation theories, OB Mod has been cast as a separate discipline and forced to justify its existence and defend its viability. Possibly because of this ostracism, OB Mod proponents have narrowed their research focus to charting behavioral changes while ignoring implications of their interventions, such as the participants' attitudinal responses resulting from the intervention.

We have sought to illuminate the differences between the two orientations on the issue of employee motivation. Our emphasis has been on suggesting further research that may necessitate a reconceptualization of the purpose of OB Mod assessments in business organizations. Instead of escalating this conflict over paradigm definition and justification as others have done (e.g., Parmerlee & Schwenk, 1979),[70] we have tried to take a pragmatic view of the linkages between these now competing perspectives.

We hope this paper will encourage the functional incorporation of effective motivational techniques, whether currently labeled cognitive or behaviorist. The current state of the art is generating considerable confusion for those interested in applying social science research findings to real problems of creating work environments that are motivating and satisfying.

References

1. J.L. Grey (1979) "The Myths of the Myths about Behavior Modification in Organizations: A Reply to Locke's Criticism of Behavior Modification." *Academy of Management Review*, 4, pp. 121–129. E.A. Locke (1977) "The Myths of Behavior Modification in Organizations." *Academy of Management Review*, 2, pp. 543–553. E.A. Locke (1979) "The Myths of the Myths about Behavior Mod in Organizations." *Academy of Management Review*, 1, 131–136. M. Parmerlee and C. Schwenk (1979) "Radical Behaviorism in Organizations: Misconceptions in the Locke-Grey Debate." *Academy of Management Review*, 4, pp. 601–607.

2. A.H. Maslow (1965) *Eupsychian Management*. Homewood, IL: Irwin-Dorsey.

3. V.H. Vroom (1964) *Work and Motivation*. New York: Wiley.

4. E.A. Locke (1968) "Toward a Theory of Task Motivation and Incentives." *Organizational Behavior and Human Performance*, 3, pp. 157–189.

5. C.L. Hull (1943) *Principles of Behavior*. New York: Appleton-Century-Crofts.

6. V.H. Vroom (1964) *op. cit.*

7. L.W. Porter and E.E. Lawler (1968) *Managerial Attitudes and Performance*. Homewood, IL: Irwin-Dorsey.

8. J.R. Hackman and G.R. Oldham (1975) "Development of the Job Diagnostic Survey." *Journal of Applied Psychology*, 60, pp. 159–170.

9. E.A. Locke (1968) *op. cit.*
10. E.C. Tolman (1932) *Purposive Behavior in Animals and Men*. New York: Century.
11. F. Luthans and T.R.V. Davis (Summer, 1979) "Behavioral Self-Management: The Missing Link in Managerial Effectiveness." *Organizational Dynamics*, pp. 42–60.
12. B.F. Skinner (1953) *Science and Human Behavior*. New York: The Free Press.
13. B.F. Skinner (1948) *Walden Two*. New York: MacMillan.
14. W.R. Nord (1969) "Beyond the Teaching Machine: The Neglected Area of Operant Conditioning in the Theory and Practice of Management." *Organizational Behavior and Human Performance*, 5, pp. 375–401.
15. D. McGregor (1960) *The Human Side of Enterprise*. New York: McGraw-Hill.
16. *Ibid.*, p. 377.
17. F. Luthans and R. Kreitner (1975) *Organizational Behavior Modification*. Glenview, IL: Scott, Foresman.
18. J.L. Grey (1979) *op. cit.*, E.A. Locke (1979) *op. cit.* and M. Parmerlee and C. Schwenk (1979) *op. cit.*
19. R.S. Peters (1960) *The Concept of Motivation*. New York: Humanities Press.
20. E.E. Lawler (1973) *Motivation in Work Organizations*. Monterey, CA: Brooks/Cole.
21. P.T. Campbell and J.C. Stanley (1966) *Experimental and Quasi-Experimental Designs for Research*. Chicago: Rand McNally.
22. A. Bandura (1977) *Social Learning Theory*. Englewood Cliffs, NJ: Prentice-Hall.
23. T.R.V. Davis and F. Luthans (1980) "A Social Learning Approach to Organizational Behavior." *Academy of Management Review*, 5, pp. 281–290.
24. *Ibid.*, p. 287.
25. A.P. Goldstein and M. Sorcher (1974) *Changing Supervisor Behavior*. New York: Pergamon.
26. G.P. Latham and L.M. Saari (1979) "Application of Social Learning Theory to Training Supervisors Through Behavioral Modelling." *Journal of Applied Psychology*, 64, pp. 239–246.
27. F. Petrock and V.V. Gamboa (1976) "Expectancy Theory and Operant Conditioning: A Conceptual Comparison" in W.R. Nord, ed., *Concepts and Controversy in Organizational Behavior*, (2nd ed.). Santa Monica, CA: Goodyear.
28. F. Luthans and R. Kreitner (1975) *op. cit.*
29. "At Emery Air Freight: Positive Reinforcement Boosts Performance" (1973) *Organizational Dynamics*, 1, pp. 41–50. M. McCarthy (1978) "Decreasing the Incidence of 'High Bobbins' in a Textile Spinning Department Through Group Feedback Procedure." *Journal of Organizational Behavior Management*, 1, pp. 150–154. Nord (1970) *op. cit.* E. Pedalino and V.V. Gamboa (1974) "Behavior Modification and Absenteeism: Intervention in One Industrial Setting." *Journal of Applied Psychology*, 59, pp. 694–698. A. Runnion, J.O. Watson and J. McWhorten (1978) "Energy Savings in Interstate Transportation Through Feedback and Reinforcement." *Journal of Organizational Behavior Management*, 1, pp. 180–191.
30. A.E. Kazdin (1973) "Methodological and Assessment Considerations in Evaluating Reinforcement Programs in Applied Settings." *Journal of Applied Behavioral Analysis*, 6, pp. 517–521. F. Andrasik (1979) "Organizational Behavior Modification in Business Settings: A Methodological Content Review." *Journal of Organizational Behavior Management*, 2, pp. 85–103.
31. F.L. Fry (1974) "Operant Conditioning in Organizational Settings: Of Mice or Men?" *Personnel*, 51, pp. 17–24.
32. T.C. Cummings and E.S. Molloy (1977) *Improving Productivity and the Quality of Work Life*. New York: Praeger.
33. F. Luthans and R. Kreitner (1975) *op. cit.*
34. J.C. Barrows (1976) "Worker Performance and Task Complexity as Causal Determinants of Leader-Behavior Style and Flexibility." *Journal of Applied Psychology*, 61, p. 443. A. Lowin and J.R. Craig (1968) "The

34. (cont.) Influence of Level of Performance on Managerial Style: An Experimental Object-Lesson in the Ambiguity of Correlational Data." *Organizational Behavior and Human Performance*, 3, pp. 449–458.

35. F. Luthans and T.R.V. Davis (1979) "Job Stress and Employee Behaviors." *Organizational Behavior and Human Performance*, 23, pp. 373–387.

36. Gupta and Beehr, 1979.

37. R.E. Walton (1980) "How to Counter Alienation in the Plant," in K.M. Rowland, M. London, G.R. Ferris, and J.L. Sherman, eds., *Current Issues in Personnel Management*. Boston: Allyn and Bacon.

38. E.P. Reese (1966) *The Analysis of Operant Behavior*. Dubuque, IA: William C. Brown.

39. "At Emery Air Freight: Positive Reinforcement Boosts Performance." (1973) *Organizational Dynamics*, 1, pp. 41–50.

40. W.R. Nord (1969) *op. cit.*, p. 401.

41. J.R. Hackman and G.R. Oldham (1976) *op. cit.* H.P. Sims, R.T. Szilagyi and R.T. Keller (1976) "The Measurement of Job Characteristics." *Academy of Management Journal*, 19, pp. 195–224.

42. M.G. Haynes (1980) "Developing an Appraisal Program," in K.M. Rowland, M. London, G.R. Ferris and J.L. Sherman, eds., *Current Issues in Personnal Management*. Boston: Allyn and Bacon.

43. R. Katz (1978) "Job Longevity as a Situational Factor in Job Satisfaction." *Administrative Science Quarterly*, 28, pp. 204–222.

44. J.R. Hackman and G.R. Oldham (1975) *op. cit.*

45. J. Komaki, W.M. Waddell and G.M. Pearce (1977) "The Applied Behavior Analysis Approach and Individual Employee: Improving Performance in Two Small Businesses." *Organizational Behavior and Human Performance*, 19, pp. 337–352.

46. W.R. Nord (1970) *op. cit.*

47. "At Emery Air Freight: Positive Reinforcement Boosts Performance" (1973) *Organizational Dynamics*, 1, 41–50.

48. E.A. Locke (1968) *op. cit.*

49. E.A. Locke (1968) *op. cit.* R.D. Pritchard and M.J. Curtis (1973) "The Influence of Goal Setting and Financial Incentive on Task Performance." *Organizational Behavior and Human Performance*, 10, pp. 175–183. J.R. Terborg (1976) "The Motivational Components of Goal-Setting." *Journal of Applied Psychology*, 61, pp. 613–621.

50. G.P. Latham and G.A. Yukl (1975) "Assigned versus Participative Goal Setting with Educated and Uneducated Woods Workers." *Journal of Applied Psychology*, 60, pp. 299–302. G.P. Latham and G.A. Yukl (1976) "Effects of Assigned and Participative Goal Setting on Performance and Job Satisfaction." *Journal of Applied Psychology*, 51, pp. 166–171.

51. F.L. Fry (1974) "The Nature and Causes of Job Satisfaction," in M.D. Dunnette, ed., *Handbook of Industrial and Organizational Psychology*. Chicago: Rand McNally.

52. E.A. Locke (1976) "The Nature and Causes of Job Satisfaction," in M.D. Dunnette, eds., *Handbook of Industrial and Organizational Psychology*. Chicago: Rand McNally.

53. T.C. Cummings and E.S. Molloy (1977) *op. cit.*

54. E.E. Adams (1975) "Behavior Modification in Quality Control." *Academy of Management Journal*, 18, pp. 662–679.

55. W.R. Nord (1970) *op. cit.*

56. J.R. Hackman and G.R. Oldham (1980) *Work Redesign*. Reading, MA: Addison-Wesley.

57. G.R. Oldham, J.R. Hackman and J.L. Pearce (1980) "Conditions Under Which Employees Respond Positively to Enriched Work." *Journal of Applied Psychology*, 61, pp. 395–403.

58. E.L. Deci (1975) *Intrinsic Motivation*. New York: Plenum.

59. G.R. Oldham, J.R. Hackman and J.L. Pearce (1976) *op. cit.*

60. J.S. Adams (1965) "Inequity in Social Exchange," in L. Berkowitz, ed., *Advances*

61. W.R. Nord (1969) *op. cit.*
62. T.C. Cummings and E.S. Molloy (1977) *op. cit.*
63. W.R. Nord (1969) *op. cit.*
64. G.R. Salanick and J. Pfeffer (1977) "An Examination of the Need-Satisfaction Model of Job Attitudes." *Administrative Science Quarterly*, 22, pp. 427–456.
65. T.C. Cummings and E.S. Molloy (1977) *op. cit.*
66. W.R. Nord (1969) *op. cit.* F. Luthans and R. Kreitner (1975) *op. cit.*
67. F. Luthans and R. Kreitner (1975) *op. cit.*
68. S. Kerr (1975) "On the Folly of Rewarding A, While Hoping For B." *Academy of Management Journal*, 18, pp. 769–783.
69. F. Andrasik (1979) *op. cit.*, p. 99.
70. M. Parmelee and C. Schwenk (1979) *op. cit.*

(reference 60 continued:) in *Experimental Social Psychology*. New York: Academic Press.

CASES

HAUSSER FOOD PRODUCTS COMPANY*

David A. Nadler
Michael L. Tushman
Nina G. Hatvany

Brenda Cooper, the southeastern regional sales manager for the Hausser Food Products Company (HFP), expressed her concern to a researcher from a well-known eastern business school:

> I think during the past year I've begun to make some progress here, but the situation is a lot more difficult than I thought when I first arrived. Our current methods of selling products just are not adequate, and the people in the field don't seem interested in coming up with new ideas or approaches to selling.

BACKGROUND

Hausser Food Products Company is a leading producer and marketer of baby foods in the United States. The company manufactures and markets a whole line of foods for the baby market including strained meats, vegetables, fruits, and combination dishes. The product line includes foods that are completely strained, for infants, as well as foods that are partially strained or chopped, for children six months and older. HFP has traditionally been the leader in this field. The company has no other major product lines. Its products are known for their high quality and the Hausser name is well known to most consumers.

HFP owns its production and warehousing facilities. Its well-developed distribution network provides direct delivery of products to the warehouses and stores of most

---

* From David A. Nadler, Michael L. Tushman, and Nina G. Hatvany, *Managing Organizations: Readings and Cases*, pp. 483–488. Copyright ©1982 by David A. Nadler, Michael L. Tushman and Nina G. Hatvany. Reprinted by permission of Little, Brown and Company. Permission granted on above terms by Little, Brown and Company (Inc.).

major food chains. The smallest segment of its market is composed of a limited number of institutions for children, which purchase HFP products in bulk.

HFP has a long history in the baby food business. Traditionally the market leader, it has over the years maintained a market share of approximately 60 percent. During the 1960s the firm experienced rapid expansion and growth. The number of different types of baby food products increased tremendously to keep up with increasing demand for more foods and a greater variety of products. During the period from the middle 1960s through the mid 1970s, growth in sales approached 15 percent compounded yearly.

During the past few years, HFP has faced a greatly changing market for infant foods. The sudden decrease in the birth rate brought about major changes in the infant food business, and projections of sales had to be altered drastically. In addition, the new concern about food additives, including flavorings, dyes, and preservatives, also had its impact on the baby food market. Many consumer advocates argued that it would be safer for parents to make their own baby foods than to purchase the commercially prepared products such as those manufactured by HFP. Finally, competition in the baby food market also increased. Private names competed on the basis of price against the nationally advertised brand names.

These changing conditions have been viewed with great alarm by the top management of HFP. The drop in growth of sales (to 3 percent in the most recent year) was accompanied by an even greater drop in earnings as management found itself with unused plant and warehouse capacity. Management is currently concerned with looking for new ways of stimulating demand for HFP products as well as the longer-range problem of finding new complementary products to develop and market.

THE MARKETING ORGANIZATION

In 1986 a researcher from a major business school became involved in studying the marketing organization of HFP as part of a larger-scale research project. His inquiries led him to look closely at the sales department and to investigate some of the problems that were being experienced there.

The marketing function at HFP is directed by a vice-president for marketing who reports directly to the president of HFP (see a partial organizational chart in Exhibit 1). The vice-president for marketing has five functional directors reporting to him. Each of these directors is responsible for one of the major areas of marketing activity, including market research, market planning, sales promotion, advertising, and sales. The sales department, which has been the focus of much recent concern, is headed by the director of sales, who directs selling activities for the entire United States. The country is broken up into seven regions, each of which has a regional sales manager. Regions are further broken up into districts (each of which may include a range of area from several states to part of a city, depending upon the particular location). The district manager heads up the HFP "sales team" for each district. It is this sales team that has the ultimate job of selling HFP products to customers, offering promotions, maintaining contact with the customers, assuring adequate shelf space, and so on.

Exhibit 1
Partial Chart of Formal Organization Structure of Hausser Food Products

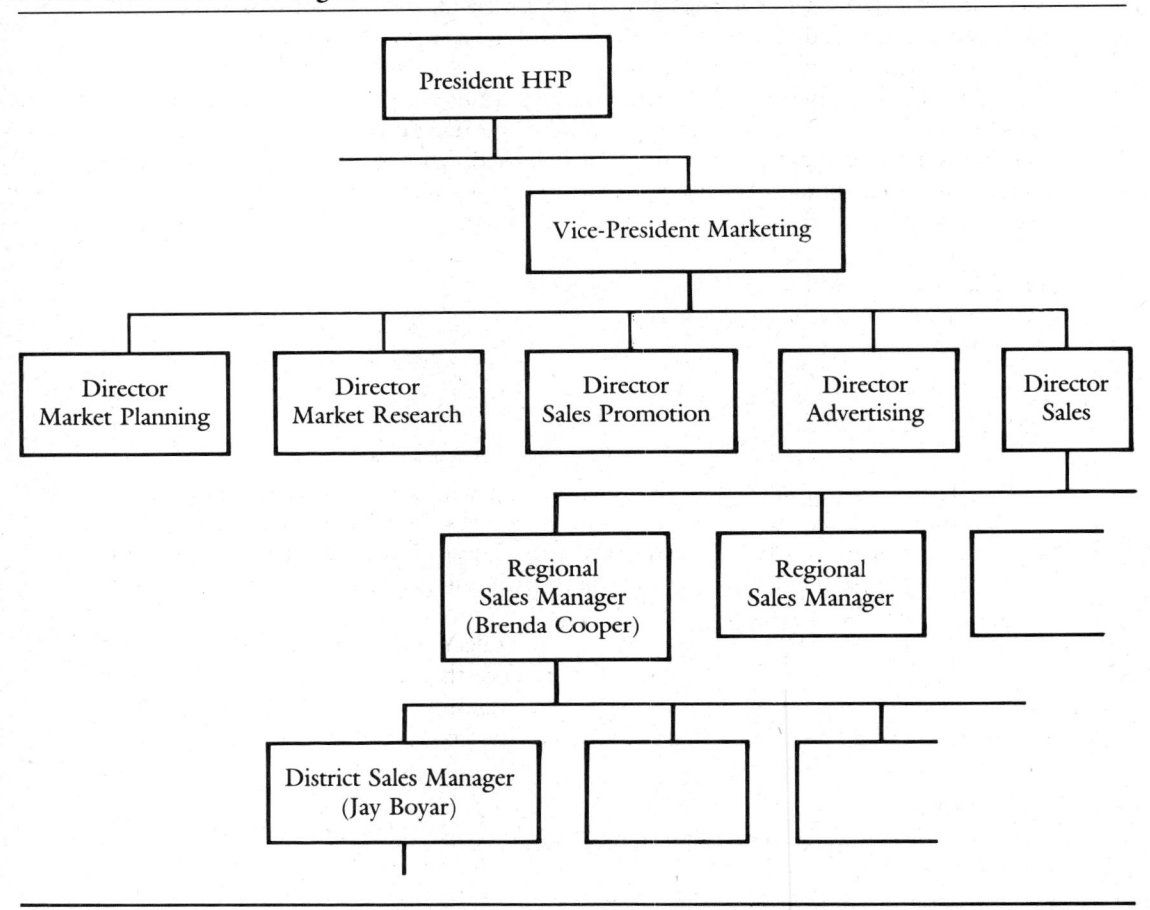

```
                          President HFP
                               │
                      Vice-President Marketing
                               │
    ┌──────────┬───────────┬───┴────────┬──────────────┐
 Director   Director     Director     Director      Director
 Market     Market       Sales        Advertising   Sales
 Planning   Research     Promotion                     │
                                           ┌───────────┼───────────┐
                                       Regional    Regional
                                       Sales Manager   Sales Manager
                                       (Brenda Cooper)
                                           │
                                  ┌────────┼────────┐
                             District Sales Manager
                                  (Jay Boyar)
```

A key element in the marketing organization is the regional sales manager. This has been an entry position to HFP for many bright, aggressive, and well-trained young people who subsequently have risen to high-level jobs within the company. The current president of the company, the vice-president for marketing, and three of the five marketing directors all began their careers at HFP as regional sales managers.

Brenda Cooper, the southeast regional sales manager, is fairly typical of the kind of person who is placed in that position. Brenda entered an MBA program immediately following graduation from one of the best women's colleges in the country. Majoring in marketing, she did extremely well in business school and graduated near the top of her class. Upon graduation she received many job offers and took a position as an assistant product manager in a large nonfood consumer products company. During four years at that firm she performed extremely well both in the management of existing products and in the launching of new products. By the end of her fourth year, however, she was becoming restless, and seeing no opportunities for quick advancement, decided to accept an offer to become a regional sales manager at HFP. The salary was attractive, plus she would receive a potentially large bonus based on the profit performance of the entire company. Brenda was also attracted by the possibility of advancement within the company. She had heard that many of the senior staff had started as regional managers. At the end of her first year Brenda is still very concerned about doing well in her job; in particular she is adjusting to her role as manager with six district managers reporting to her.

THE SALES PLAN

Much of the activity of the regional managers centers around the yearly sales plan. The sales plan is essentially a budget that includes projections of sales, expenses, and profit. It serves as the basic yardstick against which the performance of regional managers is measured.

Each year the sales plan is developed through the following multistage process:

1. The director of market planning comes up with a projection of sales for the coming year. At the same time, the director of sales asks regional managers for their projections of sales for the next year. These projections are usually extrapolations of the previous year's figures with adjustments for major changes in the market year (if any).
2. The two directors (market planning and sales) and their staffs go through a negotiation process to resolve the difference that usually exists between their two projections (market planning always tending to be higher). Out of these negotiations emerges the sales plan for the coming year. This plan includes budgeted expenditures for promotions, advertising, expenses, and the like, as well as projected sales volume and profit.
3. The sales director allocates portions of the sales plan to regional managers, who are responsible for "meeting plan" within their own regions. Regional managers in turn allocate parts of the plan to each of their district sales managers and teams.
4. The district managers receive the plan in the form of sales targets and expense budgets for the coming year. The district manager typically receives a relatively low base salary combined with a relatively large yearly bonus, which is based entirely on the performance, as measured against the sales plan, of the sales team. At the end of the year, the district manager is also given a pool of bonus dollars, also based on team performance against plan, to be distributed to the individual salespeople. Salespeople also receive relatively low base salaries and look to their yearly bonuses as a major source of income.

THE PROBLEM OF THE REGIONAL SALES MANAGERS

As part of his investigation, the researcher visited Brenda Cooper in her Atlanta office. After describing the operations of her region, Brenda began to talk about some of the problems she was facing:

We in HFP are currently wrestling with the problem of a very mature product line. Top management has begun to see the critical need to diversify, in other words to hedge our bets with some other lines of products which are not dependent upon a steadily increasing birth rate. They have been talking about some interesting and exciting things, but any new product is still a few years away from being introduced. . . . In the meantime, it is the job of us out here in the field to come up with new ideas to help keep up sales of our existing product line. I think there must be better ways of selling our product, and I am sure that there are new things that we can do to get much more performance out of the line than we are seeing now. The problem is that the best ideas usually come in from the field, from the salesmen themselves, and we really have had very little from our sales teams. They seem content to continue to let the products sell themselves and just keep the shelves stocked, as they have for years. I just don't get any new ideas or approaches from my sales teams.

Brenda and the researcher then spent some time going over the figures for sales in her region, and in particular the sales performance of the different regions. As they were going over the figures, Brenda noted:

Look here at Jay Boyar and his group in Florida. This is a prime example of the kind of problem I am facing. While we have been facing decreasing growth in sales, and actual drop off of sales some places, Jay's group consistently comes in at 10 percent above the sales plan. I've been down there and met with them and I've talked with Jay numerous times, but I can't figure out how they do it. They must be doing something that could be used in other places; but every time I ask how they do it, I get very vague answers like, "Well, we work very hard down here," or "We work together as a group; that's how we are able to do well." I'm sure it must be more than that, but I can't seem to get them to open up.

A VISIT TO THE FLORIDA SALES TEAM

Intrigued with the Florida figures, the researcher arranged an extended visit (during January and February) with the Florida sales team. The researcher was given a letter of introduction from the vice-president for marketing. This letter explained that he was collecting background information for a major research project that would help the company, that any information collected would be confidential, and that the sales team should provide him with any assistance that he needed.

At first Jay Boyar and his group made no attempt to hide their suspicion of the researcher. Slowly, however, as the researcher spent numerous days in the field, riding around the Florida roads with each of the salespeople, they began to trust him and open up about how they felt about their jobs and the company. (See Exhibit 2 for a listing of the staff of the Florida sales team.)

David Berz, the unofficial assistant team manager, talked at length about why he liked his job:

What I really like is the freedom. I'm really my own boss most of the time. I don't have to be sitting in an office for the whole day, with some supervisor hanging over my shoulder and looking at all my work. I get to be outside, here in the car, doing what I like to be doing – being out in the world, talking to people, and making the sale.

Exhibit 2
Listing of Staff of Florida Sales Team

Name	Position	Age	Years w/HFP	Education
Jay Boyar	District sales manager	52	30	high school
David Berz	Salesman (assistant manager)	50	30	high school
Neil Portnow	Salesman	56	36	high school
Alby Siegel	Salesman	49	18	½ year college
Mike Wolly	Salesman	35	12	2 years college
John Cassis	Salesman	28	4	B.A.
Fred Hopengarten	Salesman	30	3	B.A.

Neil Portnow, who had been with the company longer than any of the other team members, commented on the group:

> This is really a great bunch of guys to work with. I've been with a couple of different groups, but this is the best. I've been together with Dave and Jay for about fifteen years now, and I wouldn't trade it for anything. Jay is really one of us; he knows that we know how to do our jobs, and he doesn't try to put a lot of controls on us. We go about doing the job the way we know is best, and that is OK with Jay.
>
> The guys are also good because they help you out. When I was sick last year, they all pitched in to cover my territory so that we could make our plan plus 10 percent without reporting my illness to the company. They can also be hard on someone who doesn't realize how things work here. A few years back, when one of the young guys, Fred, came with us, he was all fired up. He was gonna sell baby food to half the mothers in Florida, personally! He didn't realize that you have to take your time and not waste your effort for the company. The other guys gave him a little bit of a hard time at first – he found his orders getting lost and shipments being changed – but when he finally came to his senses, they treated him great and showed him the ropes.

Following up on the references to the company, the researcher asked Neil to talk more about HFP as a place to work:

> It's all pretty simple; the company is out to screw the salesperson. Up in Atlanta and New York, all they are concerned about is the numbers; meet the plan, no matter what. The worst thing is if you work hard, meet the plan, and then keep going so you can earn some decent money. Then they go and change the plan next year. They increase the sales quota so that you have to work harder just to earn the same money! It just doesn't pay to bust your ass. . . .
>
> The people in Atlanta also want all kinds of paperwork; sales reports, call reports, all kinds of reports. If you filled out all of the things that they want you to fill out, you'd spend all your time doing paperwork and no time out selling, looking for new accounts, making cold calls, or any of the things that a salesman really is supposed to do if he's gonna keep on top of his area.

As he talked with the other salesmen, the researcher found general agreement with Neil's views on the company. Alby Siegel added:

The biggest joke they got going is the suggestion plan. They want us to come up with new ideas about how the company should make more money. The joke of it is, if you come up with an idea that, for instance, makes the company a couple of hundred thousand in profit across the country, they are generous enough to give you $500. That's the top figure; $500 for your idea. That amount of money is an insult. . . .

One thing you have to remember is that in one way or another, we're all in this for the money. Despite what they say, it's not the greatest life being out on the road all of the time, staying in motels, fighting the competition. But it's worth it because I can earn more money doing this job than anything else I could do. I can live better than most professional men with all their college degrees. . . . Jay is pretty good about the money thing, too. He makes sure that we get our bonus, year in and year out, and he keeps the people in Atlanta from taking our bonus checks away from us. He's not management – he's one of us. You can really tell it during the team meetings. Once every two months we all meet in Tampa and spend a day going over the accounts and talking about ideas for selling. We spend the whole day in this hotel room, working, and then we go out and spend the whole night on the town, usually drinking. Jay is one of us . . . many is the night that I've helped carry him back to the hotel.

After about four weeks with the team, the researcher got a chance to participate in one of the bimonthly team meetings. During lunch, Jay came over to him and began to talk:

Listen, I need to talk over something with you before we start the afternoon meeting. We trust you so we're going to let you in on our little discovery. You may have noticed that we aren't doing so badly, and you're right. The reason is a little finding made by Alby about three years ago. He was out in one of the stores and he noticed that a lot of people buying our products were not mothers of young children, but old people! We started looking around, and we began to notice that a lot of older people were buying HFP jars. We talked with some of them, and it turns out that they like out stuff, particularly those people who have all kinds of teeth problems.

Since then we've developed a very lucrative trade with a number of old folks' homes, and we've been able to sell to them through some of the supermarkets that are located in areas where there is a larger older population. It's a great new piece of the market; it takes the pressure off of us to make plan, and we don't even have to push it very hard to keep making plan and about 10 percent.

We've also been pretty successful in keeping Atlanta from finding out. If they knew, they'd up our plan, leaving us no time to sell, no time to develop new customers, no time to make cold calls, or anything. This way we use this new area as a little cushion, and it helps us to stay on top of our territory. I had to tell you because we'll be talking about the old people this afternoon. The boys seem to think you are OK, so I'm trusting you with it. I hope I'm not making a mistake telling you this.

BACK IN ATLANTA

Soon after the Tampa meeting, the researcher left the Florida sales team and headed back for New York. On the way back he stopped off for a final brief visit with Brenda Cooper. He found her even more concerned about her problems:

I'm getting all kinds of pressure from New York to jack up my sales in the region. They are pushing me to increase plan for the next year. I really am beginning to feel that my job is on the line on this one. If I can't come up with something that is good in the coming year, the future for me at HFP looks bleak.

At the same time I'm getting flak from my district managers. They all say that they're running flat out as is and they can't squeeze any more sales out of the district than they already are. Even Jay Boyar is complaining that he may not make plan if we have another increase next year. At the same time, he always seems to pull out his 10 percent extra by the end of the year. I wonder what they're really doing down there.

QUESTIONS

1. If you were Jay Boyar (the Sales Manager of the Florida District), would you do what he has done? Specifically, would you keep the group's marketing secret from your boss, Brenda Cooper? Why?

2. What are the key factors in the case which explain why the Florida Team is withholding their discovery? Use motivation theory to explain their behaviour.

3. If you were the researcher, what advice would you give Brenda Cooper? Remember that this advice should be given without violating the promise of confidentiality given by the marketing vice-president. What specific changes in company procedures would you recommend?

THE BELLEFONTE RUBBER WORKS CASE*

Edward L. Christensen

Works manager Bill Dalton looked pensively at the heavy raindrops as they beat against the glass sections of the window in his corner office at the Bellefonte Rubber plant. It suddenly occurred to Bill that in his four years as manager at the plant, he had never before allowed himself the luxury of watching the raindrops splash against the plant windows. He had been too busy with internal plant problems.

He thought to himself: "When it rains, it really pours at Bellefonte." Then he turned his back on the July cloudburst and looked at the letter of resignation on his desk. It was signed by Jack Fletcher, one of the day foremen. Jack had worked at the plant seven years – the last four years as a foreman of the Belt Department. Because of his apparent progress, Jack was promoted to a day foreman about a year ago on Bill's recommendation. Jack seemed to appreciate the prestige of his new position and the straight day shift, even though he was on call at the plant 24 hours a day if trouble developed in the Belt Department. However, Jack's attitude had changed considerably in the last few months. Jack's problems on the floor had become more serious as well as more frequent.

The first sign of serious trouble in the Belt Department after Jack became day foreman developed in the weeks preceding December 31, 1962. The inventory at the end of the year showed a terrific shortage in the Belt Department where Jack assumed a consistent profit was being made. Jack became very antagonistic toward the Accounting Department head whose records showed that the materials and labor input in the Belt Department, when balanced against the value of the Belt Department's output, left a shortage of over $45,000 for 1962.

Jack refused to believe that the Accounting Department's monthly book inventory of work in progress gave a true picture of his operation. (See Exhibit 1). Even though he was no statistician, Jack could see where the materials drawn and the labor cost had deviated from the desired norm. He had tightened down on his crew's use of rubber and fabric drawn for belt making after July; and, as a result, the department approached the norm or a full accounting of the raw materials requisitioned in August and September. The chart did indicate this all right. He also had checked carefully the direct and indirect labor time card reports of his men during the same period. The chart reflected a favorable trend toward the desired norm during August and September. Then, after September, the amount of materials actually accounted for in belts produced dropped off, and the labor time going into the belts increased even though the actual belt footage produced did not increase.

It was the first week in January, 1963, that Bill Dalton had a long talk with Jack about the need for operating the Belt Department as if it were a separate business in

---

* Reprinted with permission of the author, Edward L. Christensen, Brigham Young University.

Exhibit 1
Average Monthly Materials, Labor and Overhead Outlays At Bellefonte Rubber Works

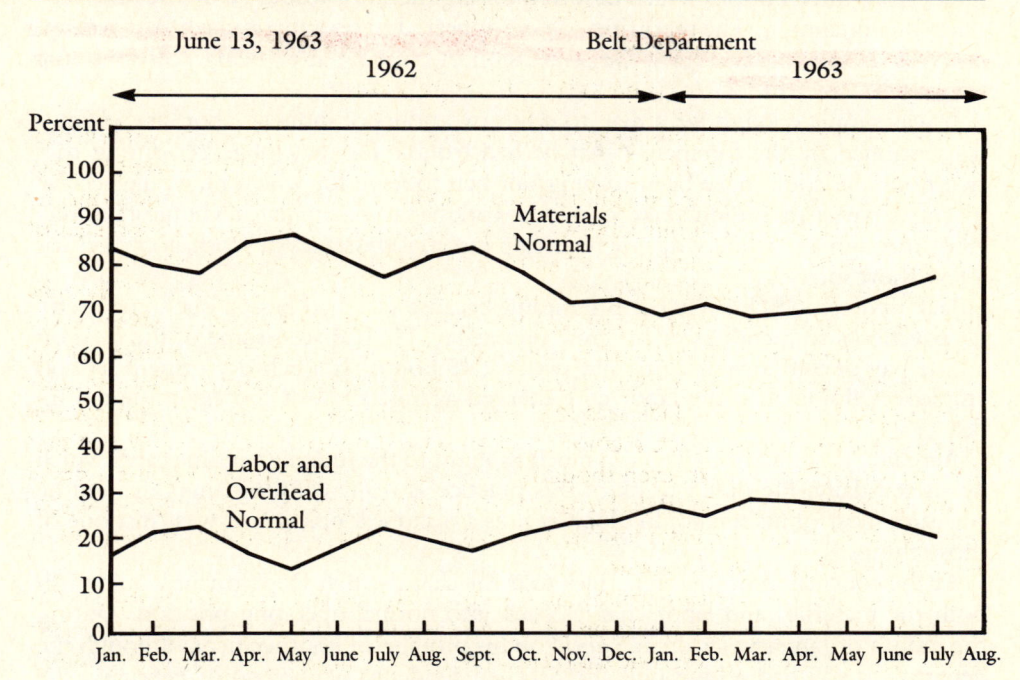

June 13, 1963   Belt Department

← 1962 →   ← 1963 →

Percent

(Materials Normal — upper line ranging approximately 70–85%)

(Labor and Overhead Normal — lower line ranging approximately 15–28%)

Jan. Feb. Mar. Apr. May June July Aug. Sept. Oct. Nov. Dec. Jan. Feb. Mar. Apr. May June July Aug.

Percentage Relationship, Materials to Labor and Overhead
Work in Process Book Inventory By Month

---

downtown Bellefonte. Bill pointed out the difficulty of staying in business very long with raw materials being drawn for work in process only to have large amounts ending up as waste in the city dump. Didn't Jack think a foreman ought to hold his crew responsible for unusual and increasing material wastage?

Perhaps a bigger drain on the profit anticipated in the Belt Department was because of the way Jack was failing to control the time reported by his crew. Bill had insisted there was no point in arguing with the Accounting Department about the reliability of its reports on the belt operation. Jack was told that if he approved unreliable, inaccurate information on the time cards, he was likely to get back an unreliable, inaccurate summary of the month's operation. It was clear enough to Jack what Bill was trying to tell him.

Jack's men were paid a base rate plus an incentive for so many items produced above a minimum set by a time-and-motion study. Time spent on directly producing belts was charged and paid as "direct labor." In case of a breakdown or other direct work stoppage, the men would go to work cleaning up, getting supplies, or doing other maintenance chores. Time spent in such "nonproductive" work was charged and paid as "indirect labor."

The record of so much direct or indirect labor time was submitted to the foreman at the end of the shift by each man. The foreman, who supposedly was aware of any direct labor interruptions which occurred during the shift, would verify the time card claim by initialing it. The reporting of time appeared to operate on the honor system, especially if the foreman gave the impression of blinking at or being oblivious to a "doctored" time card.

It was simple enough for a man to claim two hours of indirect labor, and claim – if questioned by the foreman – that he had trouble for that long. Yet during that two hours he could have been turning out belt footage for which he would receive incentive pay, also. It didn't take long for a workman to accumulate an hour of indirect labor through an ordinary day by reporting material shortages or work stoppages for a few short intervals.

Jack understood clearly what Bill meant, because Jack had passed out some pretty fat paychecks to members of his crew on payday. He had seen some of the men on a base pay of $40 a week come out with a $45 bonus! If a belt department had 60 employees doing this, the labor cost charged against the belt footage mounted up fast.

Actually, Jack had not given too much thought to the fudging on time cards which he signed daily. He didn't think of this practice as really cheating anybody, and he was sure most of his men didn't look at it as a dishonest practice. It was "just one of those things."

At the conclusion of their talk, Jack told Bill that the Belt Department would push both the materials and labor charges back into normal operating position. During the month of January, Jack made good on his promise of improvement, although the department still had a long pull ahead. Then suddenly, at the end of February, the Belt Department made its poorest production record in 14 months.

Bill, who had been anxiously watching this plant trouble spot, manuevered Jack into his office for a chat. The foreman half anticipated what was coming. In fact, he didn't wait for Bill to ask him about his family or about Jack's plans for a trip to Pittsburgh to see his son, who was a freshman at Carnegie Tech. Jack came right to the point of issue by saying: "I know what's on your mind, Bill; but before you start boring into me about competition and profits, I want to tell you something."

"Good enough, Jack," Bill agreed, "Why don't you tell me what's on your mind?"

A deep sigh escaped Jack as he settled down in his chair and wondered momentarily where he should begin. "Have you ever seriously considered the pressures that I face every day out on that floor?" Jack began. Bill nodded understandingly and Jack, feeling encouraged, continued. "You know, I'm the fall guy for everything that goes wrong in the Belt Department. Not one man in my crew is faced with taking initiative to improve our operation. Not one of them will make the most trivial decision. I guess the union won't let them. Brother, when I was working on the line years ago – before the union came along – we felt responsible. Where is the pressure today? On the worker? Oh no! Right on the back of the foreman whose hands are tied more often than they are free to clean house out there.

"At our foremen's training sessions on Wednesdays, Bill, you have stressed the importance of the service departments (See Exhibit 2) to production. Without doubt

Exhibit 2
Plant Organization at Bellefonte Rubber Works

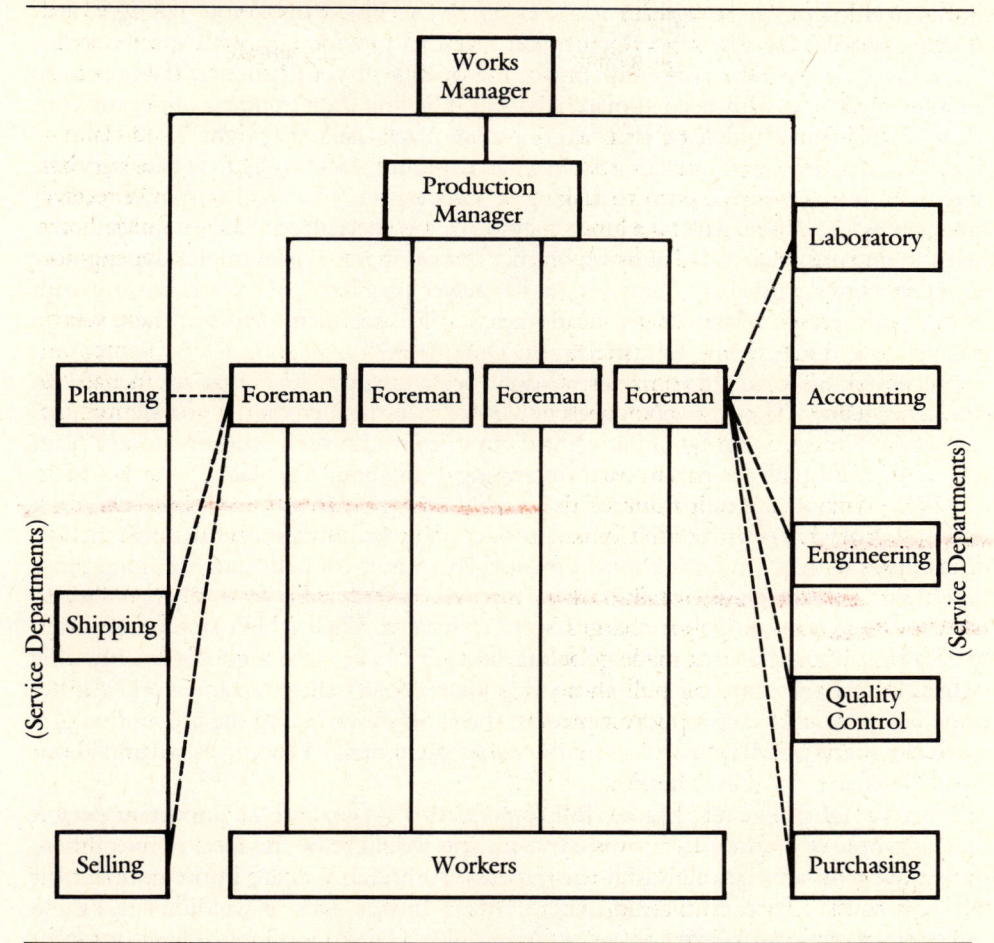

```
                        Works
                       Manager
                          |
                      Production
                       Manager
                          |
      ┌────────┬──────────┼──────────┬────────┐
   Foreman  Foreman    Foreman    Foreman

Planning                                        Laboratory

Shipping                                        Accounting

                                                Engineering

                                                Quality
                                                Control

Selling              Workers                    Purchasing

(Service Departments)              (Service Departments)
```

you are right or you wouldn't keep them on the payroll. But they never have produced a single foot of belt that ever went out of this plant. Am I right?"

Bill nodded in partial agreement. "Yes, in a way. But, I think you will agree that if, for example, the Planning Department failed to provide you with specifications; if the Laboratory didn't test and control the quality of your product; if Purchasing didn't supply you with needed materials; and if Selling didn't find an outlet for your belts – you just wouldn't be able to go it alone, Jack. Isn't that right?"

"Well, yes, in a way; but that isn't what I meant," Jack replied. "These services, like Accounting which is always making reports on our costs and output, are never under pressure. Their work – I guess they work – is specialized. Every contact I have with them turns out to be pressure on me, not on them. For example, the engineer is much better paid than I am; yet he has fewer problems. He works mostly with things, not people. If he has any headaches, I fail to see them. Most of these service people have quiet, clean, unhurried jobs. Don't they?"

Bill shook his head. "Sometimes we don't see all the pressures that are focused on the other fellow. They do wear different clothes than the men on the production line. However, I'm sure you wouldn't want them to try to do their work in a noisy place or on a greasy table. What are you suggesting I do about this, Jack?"

"Well, I'm not suggesting anything. I'm only saying that a foreman has the toughest job in this plant. From the time I get a production order until I meet the time schedule that comes with it I'm on the spot. I must keep a variety of belts moving along those lines. I'm responsible for costs, waste, supplies, quality control, stoppages, breakdowns, maintenance. You name it; I seem to have it. Then I can't step on anyone's toes. I'm supposed to maintain discipline, and yet I have to be a good guy. My time schedule stay the same even though some joker doesn't show up for work. All the time I have quality control, the inspector, the shop steward, and the accounting guy with the sharp pencil on my back. How about my morale? Who gives a damn about Jack Fletcher or how he feels?"

"You're right in general, Jack," Bill responded, "But you are an important person in this whole operation. If this were not so, you wouldn't be the focal point of these pressures. You are the catalyst in this process. Although you are in the middle of it all, you have to keep everything under control. In fact, Jack, if we didn't feel these pressures in this competitive industry, we wouldn't be around long. These pressures aren't mean, or vindictive, or intended by anyone. They are a sign we are sensitive to potential trouble, and we ought to recognize them for what they are worth in our productive efforts."

Jack looked thoughtfully out of the window for a moment. Then he ventured: "You make this sound better than I feel about it. I don't know what a catalyst is, unless he is a guy with a thick skin and a thick head. Now you take last week. My paycheck was $437.50 for the month. I put in about ten hours a day, five days a week, not to mention three Saturdays, for that check. When I handed out the checks to the crew that works for me, I noticed that about a dozen of the men made something over $500. A foreman must have a thick skull all right to stay here after every shift for an hour or two signing time cards, checking other things, and helping the next foreman get under way. I can't leave the minute the whistles blows like the hourly men do. In fact, if they have serious trouble in the Belt Department on the next shift,

I might be called out here in the middle of the night, just because I'm day foreman. Do you think this setup is fair to a foreman, Bill?"

Bill shifted uneasily in his chair. He knew this was a tough one to explain. "I can honestly say I think you are worth more to this operation than one of those men who got a bigger paycheck than you did last month. But I also believe that your envelope didn't contain something you get in addition — something which goes only to a man in your position. If you should become sick, Jack, as you were two years ago, we carry you on the payroll, and we are glad to do it. We are not able to do that for your crew. If you need an afternoon off to take your family to Lewistown or your wife to a doctor, you need only suggest this to me. Moreover, you have been recognized by your men as a leader. I know they have confidence in you. People in Bellefonte respect you because of your position here at the plant. This prestige means something to your family, believe me. I might ask you, Jack, how many of those twelve who had a larger paycheck than you, fully earned it? We can't account for their excess time in the inventory. I'm not so sure many of them were entitled to a larger check than you received."

Jack sat studying his safety helmet for a brief time. Then he stood up. "Thanks anyway, Bill," he said. "If it's all right with you, I'll give this thing another try. I better get back on the floor."

"Thanks for the chat, Jack. I know you can put the Belt Department back in the black, if anyone can," Bill said as he opened the door and gave Jack a parting pat on the back.

Bill had been pleased to observe that, during June and July, the Belt Department made obvious improvement in its operation. (See Exhibit 1.) Jack was apparently getting on top of all those pressures that had laid him low a couple of months ago. Then, out of the clear blue sky comes Jack's letter of resignation. The letter was brief:

Dear Bill,
This thing isn't getting any better. It may be even worse. I guess I want out. Can you use me in the Maintenance Department where they were short-handed this week?
Jack

Here was a chance to move someone else into the position of day foreman in the Belt Department. Bill wasn't certain whom he could confidently move into that position. He wasn't at all sure he wanted to let Jack step down, although he knew Jack was having a struggle. But this could be said about nearly every one of the other ten foremen at Bellefonte Rubber Works.

Bill felt he understood the situation faced by his foremen — especially the day foreman on the lead-off shift. He had followed a policy of placing the night-shift foremen on the day shift. This gave them some experience with the larger crews, the ringing telephones, and the full impact of contacts with the service departments as well as customers. After two weeks of this, the foremen were usually happy to get back on the night shifts. There was a good reason for Bill's paying the day foreman a little more money each month, which he did.

No one knew better than Bill that good foremen were scarce. A good foreman had to be many things. He had to be a diplomat, a disciplinarian, a counselor, an instructor, an example to his men, an engineer, a repairman, a lawyer, an inspector, a judge, a manager, a psychologist. While wearing all these hats, he had better arrange to be making a profit in his department. Bill just didn't keep this kind of man on reserve. In fact, if a foreman possessed a fair capability in these desirable areas, he was usually promoted to a higher position in management.

As Bill mentally scanned his roster of eleven foremen and those he considered potential foremen, he was not inspired. Yet, he could argue with anyone that these eleven foremen compared favorably with those in any other plant in his company. Still, each of his foremen had specific weaknesses and certain strengths. At the moment he could think of three men who had indicated an interest in becoming day foremen at the Bellefonte plant. They were Sam Craven, Chuck Weatherby, and George Maitland.

Sam Craven had been a foreman twenty years ago for Sharon Rubber Products in Sharon, Pennsylvania. Although he had been fairly young at the time, Sam had established himself at the Sharon plant as a foreman who made things move. His crews turned out items on schedule or else. He didn't spare himself, and he developed a reputation for not sparing his men. One of Bill's older friends told him that he had worked for Sam at Sharon. This friend confirmed the fact that Sam had an enviable work record for output, but he had no friends among his crew. Bill was reminded, too, that Sam worked in a place where the plant was not unionized.

When Sam came to see Bill about possible openings at the Bellefonte plant, the former had expressed an interest in working as a foreman. This meeting had taken place last December. Sam had recently been retired from the U.S. Army as a master sergeant. According to his discharge, Sam had entered the Army soon after leaving his job as foreman at Sharon Rubber Products. The earlier part of his Army career had been spent in the infantry. The last twelve years Sam had been attached to a number of different finance-disbursing units.

Chuck Weatherby had been working for the past eleven years at the Bellefonte Rubber Works. During the last six years he had been a foreman on the night shift. Bill felt that Chuck leaned rather heavily on the day foreman whenever a problem of any consequence came along in his department. Moreover, he had only 35 men on his shift, whereas the Belt Department typically had over 75 men on a day crew.

The men on Chuck's shift seemed to like him all right. At times Bill felt he had to practically force Chuck to use the tools and techniques available to a foreman. During the years, Chuck had attended all the training sessions that had been sponsored for the plant foremen on Wednesday afternoons. It was debatable how effective these sessions had been in upgrading his performance.

Bill recalled that it was on Chuck's shift that a costly mistake had been made on a large ore conveyor belt. The specifications had called for a belt 48″ wide, 3/4″ thick, 1,000′ long, six plys of cotton-nylon fabric, and a heavy rubber compound all around. The belt, which had to be out in three weeks, was contracted for $14,000. By mistake, Chuck had started the belt through with five, instead of six, plys of fabric. By the time the error was picked up, valuable time had been lost and an enormous waste had occurred. Chuck had blamed the error on "scheduling in" the custom order when his shift had a four-week backlog of other belts.

About two months ago, Chuck had mentioned that he was interested in the day shift and asked Bill to keep him in mind. Chuck said he could use the money that went with handling the larger crew on the day shift.

The third person who had expressed an interest in becoming a day foreman was a college graduate by the name of George Maitland. George, who was married and about 25 years of age, had majored in psychology at Pennsylvania State University. He had worked at the Bellefonte plant for the past three years. In fact, it was the only job he had even held other than parttime summer work in a grocery chain store.

The foremen under whom George had worked were unanimous in classifying him as a very reliable and effective employee. However, this opinion was qualified in each instance by some reference to the fact that George was good in spite of his college education.

George had taken an interest in problems of the foremen. Occasionally, he had asked them questions about their work. Some of the foremen answered his questions; others let him feel he was getting a bit too "nosey." George did appear to show a great deal of insight into the forces that constantly impinged upon the individual foreman. They didn't know, however, that George was taking courses in foreman training in an extension program at Penn State.

Bill knew that George was taking classes in production control, labor law, and human relations. One of the professors at Penn State had mentioned the fact to Bill during a Rotary luncheon some time ago. Later Bill had asked George about his evening courses and his plans for the future. It was during the ensuing conversation that George expressed a desire to get into management – the sooner the better. George had some ready answers, too, for plant problems that had bothered Bill and his foremen for a long time. It was clear, this young man didn't lack confidence.

Could it be that Jack Fletcher, whose resignation Bill held in his hand, would want to reconsider? Bill looked again at the promising record of the last two months. Then his eyes settled upon the dismal record of the preceding months. Whatever he did, Bill would have to act promptly. He needed a day foreman to manage the Belt Department, the basic producing unit at Bellefonte Rubber Works.

QUESTIONS

1. Why does Jack want to transfer out of the day foreman position?
2. Why do the belt department workers hand in incorrect or "doctored" time cards? Why doesn't Jack check these cards more closely and take action to insure that only accurate cards are submitted?
3. What motivation theories explain the problems Jack and Bill are facing?
4. What should Bill (the Works Manager) do with Jack's request for a transfer? What should he say to Jack?

EXERCISES

MOTIVATING MANAGERS AT MONTRÉAL PUMP & VALVE COMPANY

Luke Novelli
J. Bruce Prince

Diagnosing subordinates' motivational problems is something that every manager eventually confronts. This exercise provides an opportunity to use various theories of motivation to diagnose the motivation of a subordinate first introduced in the in-basket exercise in the first section of this book.

EXERCISE

You discovered in memo #2 in the in-basket material provided in the first section of this book that Frank Batt was considering leaving Montréal Pump & Valve for a higher paying job. Use the various pieces of information provided below to analyze Frank's motivation.

1. Frank recently attended a career development workshop during which he completed several self-assessment instruments. The information he obtained is presented below.

    Motives
    Need for Achievement – High
    Need for Power – Low
    Need for Affiliation – Moderate

    Needs
    Existence – Low
    Relatedness – Moderate
    Growth – High

Expectancies, Instrumentalities and Valence
Effort will lead to high performance = 1.00
High performance will lead to outcome = .25
Outcome valence is five (on a 1–10 scale)

2. You have also discovered that at the last project planning meeting, Frank was informed by his supervisor, "What I'm looking for from you is maximum work effort on your behalf. I expect you to be in the upper-half of the work group as far as productivity goes when we next review your progress in six months."

3. In conversation with friends, Frank has commented:

    a. "I was really excited when I first came to work here. But it turns out that the projects I've worked on are not as interesting as the stuff we did in my last year in school. I was hoping I'd get a chance to work on the cutting edge of my field."

    b. "I've been shifted from project to project as various deadlines come and go. Just when I get my teeth into a project, it seems I'm moved to another one. It keeps things interesting, but I hardly ever get to see how my work turns out in the overall project."

    c. "I've just found out what some of my friends from college are earning. It's no wonder they have money to spend on entertainment and their apartments. I can handle things now, because I want to learn as much as I can, but I don't want to get too far behind them financially."

QUESTIONS

Given the additional information provided above, use what you know about various motivation theories to answer the following questions.

1. Why Frank might be looking for another job?
2. What could be done to entice Frank to stay at MP&V?

EXPECTANCY THEORY: A CASE EXERCISE APPROACH*

Robert J. Oppenheimer

The purpose of this exercise is to clarify and operationalize the Expectancy Theory of Motivation.

---

* "Expectancy Theory: A Case Exercise Approach" is used by permission of the author.

Step 1
Read the following case.

CASE

You have been asked to interview Harry and find out how he feels about his job and a few aspects relating to it. The following is the dialogue that resulted.

Interviewer: Hi, Harry. I have been asked to talk to you about your job. Do you mind if I ask you a few questions?

Harry: No, not at all.

Interviewer: Thanks, Harry. What are the things that you would anticipate getting satisfaction from as a result of your job?

Harry: What do you mean?

Interviewer: Well, what is important to you with regard to your job here?

Harry: I guess most important is job security. As a matter of fact, I can't think of anything that is more important to me. I think getting a raise would be nice, and a promotion would be even better.

Interviewer: Anything else that you think would be nice to get, or for that matter, that you would want to avoid?

Harry: I certainly would not want my buddies to make fun of me. We're pretty friendly, and this is really important to me.

Interviewer: Anything else?

Harry: No, not really. That seems to be it.

Interviewer: How satisfied do you think you would be with each of these?

Harry: What do you mean?

Interviewer: Well, assume that something that you would really like has a value of $+1.0$ and something you would really not like, that is you would want to avoid, has a value of -1.0, and something you are indifferent about has a value of 0.

Harry: O.K. Getting a raise would have a value of .5; a promotion is more important, so I'd say .7; and having my buddies make fun of me, .9.

Interviewer: But I thought you didn't want your buddies to make fun of you.

Harry: I don't.

Interviewer: But, you gave it a value of .9.

Harry: Oh, I guess it should be $-.9$.

Interviewer: O.K. I just want to be sure I understand what you're saying. Harry, what do you think the chances are of these things happening?

Harry: That depends.

Interviewer: On what?

Harry: On whether my performance is high or just acceptable.

Interviewer: What if it is high?

Harry: I figure I stand about a 50-50 chance of getting a raise and/or promotion, but I also think that there is a 90% chance that my buddies will make fun of me.

Interviewer: What about job security?

Harry: I am certain my job here is secure, whether my performance is high or just acceptable. I can't remember the last guy, who was doing his job, and got fired. But if my performance is just acceptable, my chances of a raise or promotion are about 10%. However, then the guys will not make fun of me. That I am certain about.

Interviewer: What is the likelihood of your performance level being high?

Harry: That depends. If I work very hard and put out a high degree of effort, I'd say that my chances of my performance being high is about 90%. But if I put out a low level of effort, you know – if I just take it easy, then I figure that the chances of my doing an acceptable job is about 80%.

Interviewer: Well, which would you do: put out a low level, or a high level, of effort?

Harry: With all the questions you asked me, you should be able to tell me.

Interviewer: You may be right!

Harry: Yeah? That's nice. Hey, if you don't have any other questions, I'd like to join the guys for coffee.

Interviewer: O.K. Thanks for your time.

Harry: You're welcome.

Step 2

Calculate the motivational force for Harry to engage in: (a) a low effort, and (b) a high effort. Figures 1 and 2 may be utilized to help make these determinations.

According to the Expectancy Theory Model:
Motivation (or Effort) = f (E→P) $\Sigma[(P\to 0)V]$

FIGURE 1

Probability
(Low Effort → Acceptable Performance)x:

Probabilities	**Valences**
Acceptable Performance → Secure Job	x
Acceptable Performance → A Raise	x
Acceptable Performance → A Promotion	x
Acceptable Performance → Buddies Making Fun of Him	x

FIGURE 2

Probability
(High Effort → High Performance)x:

Probabilities	**Valences**
High Performance → Secure Job	x
High Performance → A Raise	x
High Performance → A Promotion	x
High Performance → Buddies Making Fun of Him	x

Step 3
According to Expectancy Theory, will Harry engage in a low or a high degree of effort? Why?

IDENTIFYING REWARDS

Positive reinforcement involves "giving a reward." This can range from providing something physical (money) or non-physical (a simple "thank-you"). It can be quite dependent on the supervisor (giving a raise) or quite independent of the supervisor (an interesting or enjoyable task in which the reward comes from doing the task). Since behavior (a person's performance) that is followed by something positive (a reward or positive enforcer) tends to be repeated, it makes sense for supervisors to arrange to have their subordinates' desirable or effective performance followed by something rewarding. This will increase in the frequency of desirable performances and make the subordinate (as well as the supervisor) more effective. The greater the number and variety of rewards the supervisor is aware of, the more likely he or she will be able to come up with rewards that are (1) desirable to the employee and (2) available to the supervisor for use.

THE TASK

Your instructor will organize you into groups. Your group's task is to develop the longest possible list of rewards that employees find desirable. Some rewards you come up with may not be readily available to you due to organizational constraints. Do not be too concerned about this, the idea is to come up with the longest possible list of *potentially* available rewards. Someone in your group needs to write down the rewards your group comes up with. Your list will be shared and compared with the lists of other groups at the completion of this exercise. In creating your list try to organize them into different categories.

Time:
Each group has 15 minutes to come up with their list of rewards.

V
SOCIALIZATION AND CAREER PROCESSES IN ORGANIZATIONS

READINGS

SOCIALIZATION AND LEARNING TO WORK*

Edgar H. Schein

The most salient feature of entry into one's first major job is what Hughes (1958) aptly called "reality shock."[1] It occurs in different forms in most major occupations because no matter how carefully the work world has been explained in school and no matter how much part-time or apprenticeship work one has had, the reality of one's first full commitment is shocking because for the first time one confronts the gap between one's expectations and dreams on the one hand and what it is really like to work and be in an organization on the other hand.

The major developmental tasks of this period all derive from various aspects of the gap between expectations and realities and can be illustrated best by various comments of a panel of Sloan School alumni who graduated in 1961, 1962, and 1963 when they were reinterviewed after 9–12 months at work (Schein, 1964, 1968).[2] The focus is on the tasks of a group entering business and industry.

TASKS OF THE SOCIALIZATION STAGE

Task I: Accepting the Reality of the Human Organization

"All the problems I encounter boil down to communication and human relations...." (consumer goods company)

"I thought I could sell people with logic and was amazed at the hidden agendas people have, irrational objections; really bright people will come up with stupid excuses... they have their own little empires to worry about." (aerospace company)

"The number of unproductive people there are in corporations is simply astounding." (chemical company)

For many new employees, particularly those who entered in staff or managerial roles (as opposed to hourly work), reality shock consisted of the discovery, among other things, that other people in the organization were a roadblock to what they wanted to get done. Others in the organization did not seem as smart as they should be, seemed illogical or irrational, or seemed lazy, unproductive, or unmotivated.

As I listened to the group members discuss their first year at work, I had the feeling that at an emotional level many of them did not want to have to learn to deal with other people; they simply wanted them to go away. I got the impression that those few graduates who accepted the human organization, with all its foibles, as a reality soon learned to apply their analytical abilities and high intelligence to getting their jobs done within it, but that those who resisted this reality at an emotional level used up their energy in denial and complaint rather than in problem solving. The "selling," and "compromising," and "politicking" necessary to get their ideas accepted were seen as "selling out" to some lower value

---

* Schein, E.H. (1978) *Career Dynamics: Matching Individual and Organizational Needs.* (Chapter 8, pp. 94–111.) Addison-Wesley: Reading, MA. Used by permission of the publisher.

system. The same person who would view a complex technical problem as a great challenge found the human problem illegitimate and unworthy of his efforts. The unlearning of this attitude may be one of the key processes in becoming an effective supervisor and manager. At the time I interviewed the alumni, most of them were still in a state of shock and had not begun to reexamine or unlearn this attitude, however.

Task 2: Dealing with Resistance to Change

"You can't get agreement on a diagnosis, and then you get resistance to change . . . you are told 'stick around for 30 years and if it is still a problem, we'll look into it.'" (public utility)

Closely related to the first area is the shock of discovering that good solutions to problems are not automatically accepted. Recalcitrant and illogical people, formal and informal procedures, organizational politics, and plain disorganization all conspire to keep the new employee from implementing his or her prepared solution to things. Almost every alumnus interviewed in the study in one way or another stated that he was shocked by the degree to which his "good ideas" were undermined, sidetracked, sabotaged, or just plain ignored.

A typical first job was an assignment to look into some procedure being used by the organization, analyze it, and make recommendations for improvement. The new hire would do the analysis, find some flaws based on his education and newly acquired skills, recommend changes, and then discover that his recommendations were not implemented for one reason or another. Most of the alumni felt well-prepared technically to analyze problems, but completely unprepared to deal with resistance to change or the necessity to "sell" ideas and solutions (Avery, 1960).[3] The degree to which people learn how to cope with resistance to change may well determine their future career path — whether they end up in more technical staff work, managerial work, or out of the organization altogether.

Task 3: Learning How to Work: Coping with too Much or too Little Organization and too Much or too Little Job Definition.

"They let me go, and I'm going, but I don't know where." (aerospace company)

"I got no guidance from my own boss; had to define my own job." (computer manfuacturing company)

"Adjusting to routine, keeping time, filling out forms." (chemical company)

The quotes above highlight the frustration of not knowing what to do and how to contribute. Many of the graduates recognized that learning to live with ambiguity was something important which they would need in their future assignments, but that made it no less shocking or frustrating to encounter initially. Similarly, many were happy to have as much freedom to define their own work as they were given, yet were shocked at the degree to which the organization seemed to be abdicating its responsibilities of defining the job.

This area is especially shocking to the new employee, because in school things are typically well organized, highly structured, and rational. Problems are clearly defined and either have a solution, or, in case discussions, everyone at least knows that there is no solution. The failure to be guided in the first job was often seen by the alumni as incompetence on the part of the boss or as evidence of disorganization and inefficiency, leading to disillusionment with the organization in general. In school the students had learned that organizations should be efficient and effective in the pursuit of profit. Once in an organization, however, the new hires learned that things moved more slowly and much less efficiently than they had imagined and not always in ways that were profit-oriented.

Some of the graduates found themselves having to not only define their own jobs, but also help their bosses define theirs; others felt such a tight rein on them that they did not feel free to make any mistakes. In either case, the new hires felt prevented from learning anything about their own capacities; in the former case they usually got no feedback, and in the latter case they got so much guidance that they were hardly acting on their own at all.

A number of graduates were satisfied with the amount of automony they enjoyed, but still had problems obtaining adequate feedback on their own performance. What fed the dissatisfaction in all these cases, of course, was the underlying expectation that they *should* learn something on their first jobs and that their supervisors *should* feel responsible for teaching them. It is not surprising that this expectation would be held by a group so recently out of school. The important ultimate learning for them may be how to obtain valid feedback in a situation in which it is not automatically forthcoming from others — i.e., *how to become a good judge of one's own performance*. In this sense all of the alumni expressed a degree of dependency on the organization which might be unrealistic; by ignoring this need in new employees, on the other hand, the organization may be missing an important opportunity to train them.

In summary, carving out one's own job is an essential aspect of the more general task of learning *how* to work — how to define problems, look for relevant information, overcome resistance to change, and be able to judge one's own performance validly.

Task 4: Dealing with the Boss and Deciphering the Reward System – Learning How to Get Ahead

"You are evaluated silently without being given any feedback for the first six months, then suddenly terminated if you are unacceptable." (manufacturing company)

"Make your boss look good, sell as hard as possible, use any available levers, and be an effective communicator." (chemical company)

"It's a dilemma, should you make the boss look good and go up the ladder with him or work on your own visibility?" (oil company)

As the comments above indicate, one of the major problems of this stage is deciphering the boss and the reward system. There is first the immediate problem of how to get along with the boss – he or she may be overcontrolling or undercontrolling, too absent or too present, too incompetent or too competent. No one in the first job was entirely satisfied with the boss, because the very fact of having a boss was inherently uncomfortable after the autonomy of student life. The new employee was likely to experience a conflict between needs for dependence and needs for independence. In the early part of the career new employees are still learners; hence a certain amount of dependence is desirable and appropriate. On the other hand, in order to succeed, new employees must display an ability to function on their own, to take initiative, to define problems accurately by themselves, and even to evaluate their own performance to some degree. So the ability to handle the conflict between dependence and independence is one of the major accomplishments of the early career.

Beyond learning how to relate to the boss is the problem of how to decipher the reward system — what is really expected of one, what is really rewarded, how much one can trust the official formal statements. As the quotes above indicate, different graduates saw very different kinds of things as important to getting ahead, covering almost the entire spectrum of possible alternatives from pure ability and performance to pure politics and "image control." One reason for the ambiguity is that managerial careers are themselves highly variable, and it is possible to succeed in organizations in different ways. Another reason is that new employees must evaluate the accuracy and relevance of much of the information offered by older employees or supervisors, because the situation may have changed.

The early part of the career is a kind of mutual testing and exploration period; it is not clear at this point what mix of talent, personality, motivation, and values will lead to high long-range performance. It is as if the organization is saying, "Let's take in some high-talent people and watch them for a while before we attempt to match up specific people with specific career paths." At the same time, the individual is facing from his or her perspective a similar question: "Let's see what this organization has to offer me in the way of options and types of work, before I decide where to put my commitment."

Given this mutual-exploration process, it is not surprising that criteria for advancement are very ambiguous at this early stage. Indeed, from the point of view of the organization, either too much or too little concern with how to get ahead could be viewed as inappropriate at this stage; the new employee should be learning how to perform well in the new culture, not be overconcerned about "promotion." On the other hand, complacency also raises concern because it might reflect lack of long-run motivation. As we will see later, the learning of complacency is one of the dangerous negative outcomes of this period.

Task 5: Locating One's Place in the Organization and Developing an Identity

"What is your appropriate reference group? To whom do you owe allegiance or loyalty? What is the relevant domain or empire?" (manufacturing company)

"I'm the man without a home, changing departments every three months because of this training program; first I identified with the trainee group, then had split loyalties between them and departments." (consumer goods company)

Entering a new organization involves a process of gaining acceptance from both the hierarchy (the boss) and the peer group. For those new employees who have a clear assignment in a well-defined group, the only problem is how to match their own needs and talents with the requirements of the group. However, for many new employees there is a prior problem — locating an appropriate peer group and deciding with which of several groups to align oneself. This problem arises because of the common practice of bringing management trainees into the organization through rotational types of training programs or in vaguely defined administrative, staff, or consultant roles which permit them to roam freely in the organization and to define their own jobs to a considerable degree. They may be given the task of examining procedures in a given department and then selecting on their own some area where they see a problem. Or they may be hired into a staff group that does analytical studies for various line groups, confronting the new members with the potential conflict of loyalty to either the staff department or the line group for which the project is being done. Some of the graduates went into administrative groups in R&D organizations and found themselves in conflict between helping the technical person get his or her job done even if administrative procedures had to be subverted, or, conversely, upholding the administrative procedures even if that meant slowing down technical progress on a project. If a new employee was identified as on a "fast track," he or she had the dilemma of whether or not to identify with the department in which the current rotational assignment was located. Some alumni expressed this as a problem of status — placing themselves in the pecking order could not be done without deciding which reference group to use, partly because it was not clear which group had how much status. An important part of the learning process during this stage, then, is to decipher the status system and to build one's own membership and sense of identity accordingly.

Summary

The various tasks described above interrelate and can be seen as an effort on the part of the new member to form what has been called by sociologists of work "a perspective" toward the organization and one's role in it. The major problem in developing this perspective, as Van Maanen (1975)[4] has pointed out, is to locate oneself in time and space — to get a sense of one's own progress, likely future, and relationship to the hierarchy and to the peer group. The perspective one forms is what gives meaning to one's work and one's career; it is the subjective inner learning which accompanies one's external work life and which influences one's future behavior in the organization. For this reason, the particular perspective one learns during the socialization stage has important consequences for the future career.

NEGATIVE OUTCOMES AND WHAT TO DO ABOUT THEM

The Organizational Perspective

... Once the person has decided on a job and reports for work, the initiative shifts to the organization and the boss. The organization has now made an investment to be protected and developed. The major negative outcomes for the organization, then, are that the person: (1) quits before he or she has made a contribution (given the organization a return on its investment); (2) becomes complacent and demotivated so that the organization never obtains a contribution in line with the person's potential; and/or (3) does not quit when he or she should and becomes "dead wood" at an early age. Turnover is a relatively visible cost, easy to measure. The learning of complacency and failing to quit are potentially more dangerous because they may be invisible, and their true consequences may not surface until the employee is well embedded in the organization.

The solution to this set of potential problems is to: (1) *give the new hire some challenging work as soon as possible*, and (2) *ensure that the new employee gets feedback on whatever he or she does*. This strategy does not necessarily mean full-time, high-challenge, high-risk work. But some *mix* of training and "real" working seems essential, and valid feedback is crucial if the new employee is to learn anything.

The organization must discover lack of competence, if it exists, *early* in the career. One of the real dangers of periods of prolonged training and "safe" assignments is that the organization never tests the new employee, so that neither the employee nor the organization obtains accurate information on the person's capabilities. In other words, it is in the best interests of *both* the organization and the new employee to become involved in some amount of challenging real work as soon as possible, so that if a real mismatch exists between what the organization needs and what the individual can provide in the way of talent, it can be identified early enough before either has invested too much in the mismatched relationship.

Another possible negative outcome for the organization is that the new employee learns norms and values which are out of line with those that will be needed later in the career. It is not uncommon for organizations to have different values at different hierarchical levels. For example, top management may value creativity and initiative in higher levels of the organization, but its own managerial practices may have created a climate for middle management and below which teaches conformity and complacency. The employee's first supervisor and first peer group are the representatives of the organizational culture and will shape the employee's view of the total organization and how to get along within it. In order to avoid the possibility that the wrong things will be learned, it is essential that higher levels of management diagnose and assess the culture which is operating at the bottom of the organization and explicitly monitor the early induction and socialization process. For example, in one company that relies heavily on engineering there has been a conscious tradition to have every design engineer follow his or her project through into production and the marketplace. As the company has grown and as the products have become more complex and dependent on many engineering groups, the engineer has had to become more of a specialist, working on similar aspects of many different products. But a new engineer coming into the organization might be socialized very differently, depending on whether he or she was assigned to a project run by (1) an "old-line" engineer who still believes in seeing each product through to the marketplace and who encouraged the new engineer to become broad in outlook, or (2) a "new" supervisor who believes that the way to succeed in engineering is to become highly competent as a specialist in some specific aspect of product design. Both kinds of socialization are simultaneously going on in this company, probably without higher management's clear awareness that this is happening.

The implication is that the first supervisors of new employees must be chosen carefully in terms of several criteria. (1) Will they feel secure enough so that the destructive behavior of giving too hard or too easy work is minimized; i.e., can they deal realistically with the new employee without their own feelings and needs distorting the relationship? (2) Will they be innovative enough to find the right mix of learning tasks and meaningful, challenging tasks to permit the new employee to experience realistic self-tests? (3) Will they be able to make a valid assessment of how the new employee is doing and give valid feedback on performance? (4) Will they transmit the right kinds of values and norms to the new employees in terms of the long-run contribution that is expected of them?

The Individual Perspective

The worst outcome from the point of view of the individual is that the needs for a self-test are still not met after some period of time in a job. Work that is too difficult or too easy, meaningless, or purely "practice" or exercise (what trainees call "mickey-mouse") leads to this negative outcome. One reason why many companies have abandoned lengthy, full-time training programs in favor of early assignments to challenging jobs is that so many high-potential employees were demotivated and quit if they were kept for too long in a training program. If the company does not have the insight to deal with this problem what can the individual do to help himself or herself?

Probably the most important thing one can do is to learn that one must be *both* dependent and independent, *both* a learner and a self-starter. The early part of the career revolves around the *balance* between: (1) learning and responding to the demands of others, and (2) identifying and acting on opportunities to take the initiative and develop challenging activities of one's own (Dalton, Thompson, and Price, 1977).[5] One must avoid the trap of trying to get along at either extreme . . . .

The more insight one has into the dynamics of entering a new organization, the less likely one is to become a victim of some of the traps outlined above. New employees should talk to one another, their bosses, and others in the organization to get perspective on what is happening to them, not simply draw their own conclusions silently. If they do not check out what they are perceiving and learning, they cannot correct for biases which may emanate from a particular boss or a particular group or may result from fortuitous events. As one insightful panelist put it, "I am pretty frustrated right now, but am not sure that my experience up to now is representative. I figure I'll give it one more year before drawing final conclusions about this company and deciding whether to move or not."

The Institutional Perspective

The process of socialization and learning to work occurs pretty much within the boundaries of an organization or occupation and is relatively little influenced by outside forces. However, from the point of view of society and its educational system, it is highly desirable that human resources be used optimally. The more that educational and research institutions can study the process of organizational socialization and the more they can educate both new employees and those already in positions of power to understand the dynamics of the early career, the better the chances of reducing costly mismatches. The prime effort probably must come from the educational institutions to teach their graduates how to manage the early part of the career by recognizing clearly what their own needs are and how best to protect themselves from socializing experiences which may be destructive. One example of efforts in this direction is the growing number of courses in business schools directed toward career counseling, organizational diagnosis, self-analysis of career aspirations, etc. If new hires have a clear insight into the process of socialization, they will be in a better position to negotiate realistically with their employing organizations as the career unfolds . . . .

References

1. E.C. Hughes (1958) *Men and Their Work.* Glencoe, IL: The Free Press.
2. E.H. Schein (1964) "How to Break in the College Graduate." *Harvard Business Review,* 42, pp. 68–76. E.H. Schein (1968) "Organizational Socialization and the Profession of Management." *Industrial Management Review* (M.I.T.), 9, pp. 1–15.
3. R. Avery (1960) "Enculturation in Industrial Research." *IRE Transactions on Engineering Management,* 7, pp. 20–24.
4. J. Van Maanen (1973) "Observations on the Making of Policemen" *Human Organization,* 4, pp. 407–418.
5. G.W. Dalton, P.H. Thompson, and R. Price (Summer, 1977) "Career Stages: A Model of Professional Careers in Organizations." *Organizational Dynamics,* pp. 19–42.

EMPLOYEE-ORGANIZATIONAL LINKAGES: THE ROLE OF ORGANIZATIONAL COMMITMENT*

V.V. Baba

Individuals and organizations have a symbiotic relationship with each other in all modern societies. Though the mechanisms by which such ties are maintained might vary from society to society, it is difficult to deny their existence or importance. These mechanisms play a large role in explaining how an individual joins an organization, maintains attachment, or as in some cases, severs ties with the organization. An understanding of this process of joining, maintaining or severing connections with one's employing organization is of considerable importance to individuals, organizations, and societies.

This paper attempts to explore the nature of these ties that bind individuals to organizations as it will help us understand the quality and nature of our employment in various organizations. Specifically, we are interested in exploring how people form these linkages with their employing organizations, what the antecedents and consequences of these linkages are and how they develop over time. It stands to reason that there are certain personal factors, job related factors, and factors pertaining to the employing organization, which might influence the quality of an employee's attachment to the organization as revealed by the individual's commitment to the organization, satisfaction with the job, and involvement in work. These indicators of quality in turn influence the nature of an individual's attachment. Absence behavior, turnover, effort, performance, individual well-being, service above and beyond

---

* "Employee – Organizational Linkages: The Role of Organizational Commitment" by V.V. Baba is used by permission of the author.

Acknowledgement: Preparation of this article was supported by a grant from Formation de chercheurs et d'action concertée (FAC - 86EQ2650) of the Government of Quebec to the author.

the call of duty are some outcomes which determine whether the individual is fully connected to the organization or not. They indicate the nature of an individual's attachment to the organization. What is suggested here is that there are some possible predictors of this attachment which pertain to an individual's background, role in the organization, and work experiences, as well as to some specific features of the organization to which the individual belongs. Thus a three stage model linking the individual to the organization, as shown below, is proposed.

Personal, Job, and Organizational Factors → Quality of Attachment → Nature of Attachment

Research dealing with the notion of organizational attachment tends to be supportive of the above model (Mowday, Porter, & Steers, 1982)[1]. Though the notion of attachment to the organization encompasses concepts such as organizational commitment, job involvement, and job satisfaction, this article will mainly concentrate on organizational commitment because of its key role in explaining major outcomes of attachment such as turnover, absenteeism, extra role behavior, performance, etc.

Organizational commitment refers to a strong desire to remain a member of the employing organization, willingness to exert high levels of effort on behalf of the organization, and a definite belief in and acceptance of the values and goals of the organization (Mowday, Steers, & Porter, 1979).[2]

This definition suggests a relationship between the employee and the organization where the worker is willing to contribute in a proactive way to the welfare of the organization be it through greater effort on the job, talking up the organization to friends, or seeking out ways to improve its image in the community. Exchange theory provides the theoretical framework for understanding this phenomenon according to which commitment is seen as the outcome of the exchange relationship between the individual and the organization. The theory suggests that as the exchange becomes more favorable to the individual, his or her commitment to the organization increases. Subsequent developments include the notion of sidebets and time (Becker, 1960)[3] as well as behavioral commitment (Salancik, 1977).[4]

According to Becker (1960),[5] the more an individual invests his or her time, energy, skill and other personal assets including his or her sense of identity, the more he or she has at stake in leaving the organization. Therefore, it is natural to expect greater intensity of commitment on the part of the individual toward the organization as the links between the individual and the organization become stronger and broad-based. The employee, by making a sidebet, links interests that were originally extraneous to his or her employment, with a consistent line of activity connected with his or her employment. These sidebets could be economic, such as a nonvested pension plan, social, such as friendship networks, and personal, such as uniqueness of job training, spouse's employment, or children's schooling. The individual, by involving other interests that were originally unrelated to the employing organization, has increased the cost of severance and as a result is likely to view other alternatives as being unattractive. This notion is also supported by research on cognitive dissonance theory.

The other stream of research on commitment is oriented toward strengthening an individual's commitment to the organization by focusing on the employee's behavior at work. According to Salancik (1977),[6] there are three characteristics that bind an individual to a course of action and hence commit him or her to certain behaviors. They are visibility, irrevocability, and volition. By publicizing an employee's agreement to pursue certain goals, the organization invariably increases the individual's commitment to those goals. The employee, all of a sudden, finds himself or herself honor-bound to engage in activities that he or she could have easily gotten out of, had it not been publicized. Organizations often try to increase an employee's commitment by publicizing the individual's identification with the organization through the media. The notion of irrevocability is somewhat akin to the notion of sidebets discussed earlier. The more irreversible an action is, the more committing it becomes (Salancik, 1977).[7] Signing a contract of employment with clauses which make breaking the contract unattractive tends to increase one's commitment to the organization even if it is, at first, merely a way of reducing cognitive dissonance. The next factor is volition where a course of action is chosen out of free will. Such actions include involvement in organizational activities and come out of a sense of personal responsibility. An individual becomes committed to a sales target or a production quota because he or she chose it out of his or her own volition.

It is important to realize here that the sidebet notion of commitment and the behavioral model of commitment are neither mutually exclusive nor contradictory. The notion of sidebets can be easily expanded to include acts that result from visible and irreversible behavior that are engaged in on a volitional basis. Similarly, sidebets can also include psychological factors, such as an individual's sense of identity, in addition to economic, geographic, and job related factors. The behavior manifested in making a sidebet is likely to influence the employee's attitude in the direction of that behavior. Thus we can see the connections between the two theoretical frameworks. Now, using the sidebet theory of commitment, we can propose that a person choosing a career in an organization tends to settle down as more and more of his or her extraneous interests are linked to the organization. Thus these sidebets become the antecedents of the individual's commitment to the organization. The committed individual, by virtue of both the favorable attitudes toward the organization that typify commitment as well as those binding acts which are visible, irreversible, and volitional tends to engage in behaviors that are beneficial to the organization. These behaviors include high performance, increased attendance, reduced turnover intention, extra role behavior, to mention a few. This observation justifies the model presented earlier. The discussion will now focus on the antecedents and consequences of organizational commitment. As mentioned earlier, the antecedents which incorporate different sidebets that the individual makes during the course of his or her employment can include personal, job, and organizational factors. This conceptualization is supported in the literature (Steers, 1977).[8]

PERSONAL FACTORS

It is conceivable that certain personal factors such as age, gender, education, tenure, values, and personality might influence the degree to which one is committed to his or her employing organization. As one advances in age, he or she might accrue investments with the organization leading to greater commitment. This notion is also supported in the empirical literature (Baba & Jamal, 1979).[9]

Theories of differential sex role socialization tend to suggest that females are less likely to make important sidebets in the organization compared to their male counterparts due to the ambivalence they might experience *vis-à-vis* their role in society. Thus gender influences the sidebets people make in the organization and therefore their commitment (Mowday, Steers, & Porter, 1979).[10]

As for education, the more educated often can get a placement in a variety of organizations according to their expectations. Therefore, instead of looking around for an appropriate niche in one organization, these individuals are ready to move to other organizations. They make few investments in their organizations and as a result tend not to increase their commitment (Morris & Sherman, 1981).[11]

Years of uninterrupted service in the organization encourages people to invest a variety of sidebets in the organization thereby increasing their commitment (Angle & Perry, 1981).[12] Similarly, work values and work ethic of the North American variety prescribe that we must be committed to the idea of working and develop commitments toward the organization which provides that work (Buchanan, 1974).[13]

Since the concept of commitment as defined earlier is tied to the notions of career advancement, value congruence, and willingness to exert effort, it is conceivable that those who believe they could control their life outcomes tend to use the organization as a vehicle for such outcomes. Thus, people with an internal locus of control might assume responsibility for their actions and when rewarded for such actions, develop an enhanced sense of commitment toward the organization (Salancik, 1977).[14] Thus, personality factors such as locus of control also influence organizational commitment.

JOB FACTORS

The job-related factors that might influence the development of organizational commitment include job scope, role ambiguity, role conflict, role overload, participation in decision making, and leader behavior. Since commitment refers to the relative strength of an individual's identification with and involvement in a particular organization, the factors which facilitate such identification and involvement tend to influence the development of commitment. If the job an employee is engaged in offers scope and challenge and the employee is excited by it, it stands to reason that such a job contributes to the development of organizational commitment. Similarly, a job situation that is clearly defined and described with expectations that match the individual's capabilities, opportunities to participate in decisions that are important to the individual, and an enlightened supervision, is likely to evoke certain positive feelings toward the organization that offers such a job (Bateman & Strasser, 1984., Morris & Sherman, 1981., Mowday, Porter, & Steers, 1982).[15]

ORGANIZATIONAL FACTORS

Among organizational factors, size, social involvement in the organization, and equity perceptions appear to have some theoretical relevance to organizational commitment. People working for large organizations seem to derive a sense of power in the community because of the organization's impact on the community. This feeling contributes toward enhancing their commitment to the organization. However, research has also shown that smaller subunits within an organization facilitate greater social interaction among members which these members value (Porter, Lawler, & Hackman, 1975).[16] If they find such an atmosphere in their employing organization, it is likely they develop commitment toward it. The argument is similar for the role of social involvement in the organization in building organizational commitment (Buchanan, 1974).[17] Further, organizational policies regarding pay, benefits, and other forms of rewards and compensation influence employees' perceptions of equity and fair treatment. Such perceptions of equity facilitate the process of making sidebets with an attendant increase in commitment.

OUTCOMES OF COMMITMENT

Since commitment calls for an acceptance of the organization's goals and values, exertion of effort to accomplish those goals, and a strong sense of membership, it can be readily seen that committed employees tend to put in greater effort on the job and perform better (Mowday, Steers, & Porter, 1979).[18] They also absent themselves from work less and are less likely to leave the organization (Angle & Perry, 1981).[19] Therefore, an organization that has a highly committed work force tends to be high in organizational effectiveness.

It is important at this point to realize that organizational commitment can be passive or active. With passive commitment, loyalty aspects and value congruence play a dominant role in developing commitment toward the organization though behavioral consequences such as high effort and performance do not necessarily result. Individuals who are passively committed are quite effective in a public relations role such as talking up the organization, and participating in its image-building efforts, yet, they may not see high levels of performance as role relevant (Steers, 1977).[20] On the other hand, active commitment displays an attitude toward the organization that readily translates into behavioral intention and actual behavior. People who exhibit this aspect of commitment are stressing that part of the definition of commitment which refers to exerting high levels of effort on behalf of the organization and working toward higher performance goals. Though employees with either passive or active commitment toward their organization differ in their orientation toward effort and performance, they behave in a very similar fashion with regard to absenteeism and turnover.

Another factor that might influence the way antecendents and consequences of commitment are linked is the notion of organizational independence (Kerr, House, & Wigdor, 1971).[21] When an individual possesses knowledge and skills that are readily marketable to other organizations, it is conceivable that it affects the process by which he or she develops commitment toward the organization. This is likely to be different for the individual whose knowledge and skills are unique to the employing organization and who may not be able to find employment elsewhere. The latter is dependent on the employing organization while the former is not.

For example, the organizationally independent employees could leave the organization if they are not satisfied with what the organization offers in return for their efforts. As a result, they will be inclined to choose sidebets that are varied and portable. They also tend to demonstrate their commitment to the organization in the active mode referred to earlier. On the other hand, the organizationally dependent employees, in an attempt to reduce the dissonance created by this dependency, may make fewer sidebets in the organization, and as a consequence, exhibit commitment in a more passive way. Thus, the notion of organizational independence has implications for the manner in which employee-organizational linkages get established (Baba & Knoop, 1981).[22]

MANAGEMENT AND ORGANIZATIONAL COMMITMENT

The conceptual importance of organizational commitment lies in its potential to address many questions that have engaged the attention of management scholars and practitioners alike. Commitment, as discussed, leads to concrete manifestations of behavioral outcomes such as performance, absence, turnover, etc., which have both theoretical and practical significance to management. In addition, commitment is shown to be linked to a variety of personal, job, and organizational factors which have implications to work and organization design, as well as human resource management. Thus, organizational commitment plays a central role in understanding and managing organizational behavior.

From a practical point of view, without strong linkages between employees and organizations, the quality of societal output would suffer. Further, the costs of turnover and absenteeism could be considerably reduced if there were a better understanding, and active management of the process by which employee-organizational linkages are established and maintained. We believe that commitment is a major factor in bringing about innovative and other forms of extra-role behavior especially when the payoffs sought are either insufficient or uncertain (Salancik, 1977).[23] Therefore, building organizational commitment through focused training programs and incentive schemes is an important step in the socialization of employees and is likely to pave the way for an effective organization. Organizational commitment is indeed the crucial knot in the ties that bind individuals to organizations.

References

1. R.T. Mowday, L.W. Porter, and R.M. Steers (1982) *Employee-Organizational Linkages: The Psychology of Commitment, Absenteeism, and Turnover*. New York: Academic Press.
2. R.T. Mowday, R.M. Steers, and L.W. Porter (1979) "The Measurement of Organizational Commitment." Journal of *Vocational Behavior*, 14, pp. 224–247.
3. H.S. Becker (1960) "Notes on the Concept of Commitment: The Socialization of Managers in Work Organizations." *American Journal of Sociology*, 66, pp. 32–40.
4. G.R. Salancik (1977) "Antecedents and Outcomes of Organizational Commitment." *Administrative Science Quarterly*, 22, pp. 46–56.
5. H.S. Becker (1960) *op. cit.*
6. G.R. Salancik (1977) *op. cit.*
7. G.R. Salancik (1977) *op. cit.*
8. R.M. Steers (1977) "Antecedents and Outcomes of Organizational Commitment." *Administrative Science Quarterly*, 22, pp. 46–56.
9. V.V. Baba and M. Jamal (1979) "On Becker's Theory of Commitment: An Empirical Verification among Blue Collar Workers." *Relations Indusutrielles*, 34, pp. 123–139.
10. R.T. Mowday, R.M. Steers, and L.W. Porter (1979) *op. cit.*
11. J.H. Morris and J.D. Sherman (1981) "Generalizability of an Organizational Commitment Model." *Academy of Management Journal*, 24, pp. 512–526.
12. H. Angle and J. Perry (1981) "An Empirical Assessment of Organizational Commitment and Organizational Effectiveness." *Administrative Science Quarterly*, 26, pp. 1–14.
13. B. Buchanan (1974) "Building Organizational Commitment: The Socialization of Managers in Work Organizations." *Administrative Science Quarterly*, 19, pp. 533–546.
14. G.R. Salancik (1977) *op. cit.*
15. T.S. Bateman and S. Strasser (1984) "A Longitudinal Analysis of Organizational Commitment." *Academy of Management Journal*, 27, 95–112. J.H. Morris and J.D. Sherman (1981) *op. cit.* R.T. Mowday, L.W. Porter and R.M. Steers (1982) *op. cit.*
16. L.W. Porter, E.E. Lawler, and J.R. Hackman (1975) *Behavior in Organizations*. Toronto: McGraw-Hill.
17. B. Buchanan (1974) *op. cit.*
18. R.T. Mowday, R.M. Steers, and L.W. Porter (1979) *op. cit.*
19. H. Angle and J. Perry (1981) *op. cit.*
20. R.M. Steers (1977) *op. cit.*
21. S. Kerr, R.J. House, and L.A. Wigdor (1971) "Some Moderating Effects of Organizational Independence." Proceedings of the *Eastern Academy of Management Journal*, 24, pp. 512–526.
22. V.V. Baba and R. Knoop (1981) "If I Can Leave the Organization, Why Do I Stay: A Study of Commitment and Independence Among Canadian Managers." *Proceedings of the Midwest Academy of Management*, Chicago, IL.
23. G.R. Salancik (1977) *op. cit.*

CAREER ORIENTATIONS AND HOW THEY INFLUENCE CAREER DECISIONS*

Thomas J. DeLong

Now that I have been working for 15 years and have changed jobs twice, it is clear to me that I become less interested each day with moving up the organization ladder. All I want to do is design new products. I wish I could get this message over to my supervisor.

A 40-year-old engineer

The aforementioned quote represents one of many central drives or orientations which direct the decision making of individuals in the work place. More and more individuals are realizing that as they collect information about themselves, they are virtually driven to meet a particular inner drive or need. These inner drives become more evident the more one works and the more one realizes what his or her strengths and weaknesses are. Before understanding what your scores mean it is critical to have a working knowledge of what each score represents, and what is meant by a career orientation.

THE CAREER ANCHOR MODEL

In 1975 Edgar H. Schein of the Massachusetts Institute of Technology (MIT) introduced the concept of career anchors. Later, in his book *Career Dynamics: Matching Individual and Organizational Needs* (Addison-Wesley, 1978), he emphasized the need to create a model that would describe an individual's career experiences. Since its development, the career anchor model has drawn considerable attention from researchers and industrial organizations. Since 1978, for example, this investigator has, through an iterative process with Schein, attempted to validate and refine the definition of Schein's career anchor model. This validation process used a questionnaire to pinpoint and measure specific career anchors. Schein used in-depth interviews to collect his original data on self-perceived talents, but the questionnaire uses a Career Orientations Inventory to measure values, attitudes, and career needs rather than self-perceived talents.

DEFINING THE CAREER ANCHOR

The career anchor is, by definition, a combination of one's self-perceived needs, values, and talents. It is a self-concept and does not necessarily include the individual's actual needs, drives, or talents as they might surface through some other process — for example, through interviews or career assessment centers. The career anchor concept is powerful because self-perceptions guide and constrain a person's future career decisions no matter how accurate, or inaccurate, those self-perceptions are.

As employees' careers evolve, they gradually form a career anchor that begins to stabilize and guide their careers. Schein suggests that as people move through their careers, they gradually develop a clearer self-concept in terms of the following:

1. *Their abilities and talents*: What they are good at and what they are not good at.
2. *Their motives and needs*: What they ultimately seek in their careers (for example, good income, security, interesting work).
3. *Their values*: What kind of company, work environment, product, or service they want to be associated with.

As people gain more information about themselves in relation to their values, needs and self-perceived talents, an occupational self-concept emerges. Often, the collection of information from one's working environment is not pleasant because the information is different from what was

---

* © 1987 Thomas J. DeLong & Associates. All Rights Reserved. Reprinted with permission.

expected. For example, if a person has always wanted to work for a large organization yet finds the reality of the organization to be too restrictive, then problems may arise. The real workplace is where a person's anchor actually manifests itself. That is why the first three to five years are so crucial to one's career plans. Only through actual work experience can one collect the information that is necessary to determine one's actual career anchor. Therefore, it may be healthy for people to change careers or vocations in order to find an appropriate match between an organization and their own needs, values, and self-perceived talents.

In Schein's initial longitudinal study, completed in 1974, clear patterns emerged in the responses of those he interviewed: Although the actual job histories of the 44 alumni of the Alfred P. Sloan School of Management included in that study differed, the consistency in the reasons given for their career decisions was great.

The following five career anchors or central areas that guide people's career decisions emerged from that study:

Anchor 1: Security People whose anchor is security tie their careers to a particular organization. In his recent works, Schein emphasizes that for some people security and stability become the all-consuming elements of any career decision. The implications: People who are security-oriented will accept, to a greater degree than the other career-anchor types, the organization's definition of their careers. Such a person is concerned with long-term stability and benefits.

Our research indicates that at least two types of people seek out security-oriented careers. The organization man as defined by William H. Whyte typifies one type of person who is security-oriented; those who want to remain in the organization must socialize themselves to its values and norms. The other security orientation has roots in a particular geographical location. Frequently, geographically oriented people will move from company to company to ensure tht they can remain permanently in a geographic area. Many security-oriented people also have a great need to spend considerable time with their families. Often, these people will sacrifice advancement for opportunity to work a set number of hours with little overtime.

Once an individual recognizes that his or her career anchor is security, he or she may feel forced to take a defensive posture – primarily because security tends to carry a negative connotation in our culture and society. This may stem from attitudes of managerially oriented people who frequently judge harshly those individuals who make career decisions different from theirs and who choose not to climb the organization's hierarchy.

Anchor 2: Technical/functional competence Technical/functional people are motivated by the challenge of the actual work they do (for example, financial analysis, marketing, systems analysis, corporate planning). Their anchor is the technical field, functional area, or content of their work – not the managerial process itself. The self-image of this group is tied to feelings of competence in their particular area.

There is a tendency in organizations to move those with specific expertise up the hierarchy so that they can influence others. However, such experts may find the process of supervising to be frustrating at best.

Another facet of technically/functionally-oriented individuals is the idea that the longer they remain in a specific area of expertise, the more their self-image becomes linked with their ability to function well in this area. These people want to be recognized by their talents. However, many organizations find it difficult to provide enough challenge for this particular type of person. Thus, the technically oriented person may switch jobs frequently, searching for the right mix between job challenge and personal recognition.

Anchor 3: Managerial competence The fundamental basis of the managerial competence anchor is competence in the complex activities that compose the idea of management. Managerial competence-oriented people perceive that their competencies lie in the ability to analyze problems and to remain emotionally stable and interpersonally competent. Their career experiences enable them to develop the self-image that they possess the skills and values necessary to rise to general management levels. It is the opportunity to lead others that interests these people. They want to advance quickly up the organizational hierarchy. The possibility of making large sums of money while influencing others is important to the managerially-oriented person. Schein suggests that those who wish to function effectively as managers must have these three abilities:

1. *Analytical competence*: the ability to identify, analyze, and solve problems in situations of incomplete information and uncertainty.
2. *Interpersonal and intergroup competence*: the ability to influence, supervise, lead, manipulate, and control people at all organizational levels to help them achieve organizational goals.
3. *Emotional competence*: the capacity to be stimulated by emotional and interpersonal issues and crises rather than be exhausted or debilitated by them; the capacity to bear high levels of responsibility without becoming paralyzed; and the ability to exercise power and make difficult decisions without guilt or shame.

The general manager uses these three abilities to influence the organization. Such a person is also energized by the processes involved in making decisions that influence others.

Anchor 4: Creativity Creativity-anchored people need to create something on their own. For example, creating is the fundamental need of the entrepreneur. Creativity-oriented individuals seek new ventures and try their hand at new kinds of projects. Such people are also generally very central and very visible when they work on projects.

Some people want to create a new business or organization around a product or service in which they have a great investment. Entrepreneurs have a great need to show others that they have accomplished something for which they can take primary credit. Such people may spend the early years of their careers within an organization; then, typically, they break out on their own.

Of the people we have studied, fewest fit this description. It is also rather obvious that creativity-oriented people may have problems operating within the large organization, unless they are given great freedom.

Anchor 5: Autonomy The autonomy anchor encompasses those who have found organizational life too restrictive. They are primarily concerned about their own sense of freedom and autonomy. Autonomy-oriented individuals seek work situations in which they will be maximally free of constraint to pursue their professional or technical/functional competence. However, many organizations and job descriptions provide many degrees of freedom within the organization itself. Also, the general management function consists of various tasks that allow a person to work within the organization's structure while retaining the autonomy necessary to meet individual needs.

Other career anchors may exist and through lengthy discussions among faculty members at both MIT and Purdue, I developed a list of plausible, but perhaps less common, career anchors. Three such career concepts are:

1. *Identity* Identity-oriented people are guided throughout their careers by the status and prestige of belonging to certain companies or organizations. They want to be identified with a powerful or prestigious employer.
2. *Service* Service-oriented people are concerned with helping others and seeing the change their efforts made. They want to use their interpersonal skills in the service of others.

3. *Variety* Variety-oriented people desire a large number of different types of challenges. Thus they seek careers that provide a maximum variety of assignments and work projects.

OTHER CAREER ORIENTATIONS

Along with the five career anchors already discussed, the three orientations (service, identity, variety) clearly factored out as separate and distinct career orientations. These three career orientations are described in greater detail below.

Service As we used various samples in our research, it became clear that some individuals valued and made career decisions because they wanted to be of service to someone or something.

Many educators verbalize their need to serve other people in a helping fashion. When asked what anchor they were least willing to give up, many educators said "service." Interestingly, few MBAs expressed a concern for serving as a driving force in career decision making.

It is also obvious that not all those categorized as having jobs in a helping profession are security oriented. A clinical psychologist may value assisting others; however, he or she may also find the autonomy that is part of being on a faculty, having a private practice, and so forth, to be more central to the career decision-making process. Another psychologist may also value having a particular expertise in his or her field – for example, using behavior modification or using hypnosis to treat weight loss. Thus, within a particular job, title, or job classification, all the anchors may coexist.

Variety Throughout their interviews some people mentioned that they need variety in their work. A sense of urgency to change jobs frequently or tasks within a particular job was an implicit need. In the research that focused on MBA alumni, a number of graduates believed they selected general management because they would be allowed to do many things.

When he was originally trying to determine whether other career anchors existed, the investigator assumed there would be little difference between autonomy and variety. However, further investigation suggested that many people saw autonomy and variety very differently. Autonomy suggests more the need for an individual to be his or her own boss, while variety focuses more on the need for an individual to have an array of work responsibilities.

A number of school teachers were emphatic that variety was their central career self-image. One veteran teacher explained, "To be able to teach four different subjects throughout the day, plus to work different jobs during the summer vacation – I just couldn't ask for a better job. I also get bored working with the same people over and over again. These kids are all different and so energetic. The combination of kids, subject matter, and time away from school makes this a great deal for me."

Identity A few individuals expressed a need to be identified with a large or prestigious organization. The central drive seemed to be status. Although identity may also be a concept under the rubric of management, a few people believed that identity played the central role in shaping their occupational self-concept. One manager stated, "The organization for which I work is known throughout the world. People are impressed when I tell them who I work for. I will never leave this organization for anything."

Other career orientations may surface as research continues on the career anchor concept. For example, Brooklyn Derr suggests another anchor, the "warrior." This career concept is a combination of technical competence and autonomy. An example of the "warrior" is the fighter pilot who thrives on putting his life on the line. Others suggest that power and influence may be an anchor worthy of further investigation. However, needs for variety, identity, service, power, and influence may also be encompassed by other anchors, especially the managerial anchor.

MORE ON SECURITY

It seemed logical that identity (identifying with an organization or employer) and security (concern for geographical location, benefits, and long-term stability) would factor together because of an underlying assumption in both variables of an acceptance of organizational norms. However, all of the factor analyses run depicted a strong separation in the definition of the career anchor, security. In the original factor analysis, statements that defined security in relation to long-term stability factored under one specific factor. The correlation coefficients of the next factor correlated with the security statements that focused on geographical location as a dimension of security. The more we identified this difference, the more people in interviews also stated that they see security from these two perspectives.

Security as a career value seemed to play a major role in the career decision-making processes of many educators, who realized their need either to remain in a particular geographical location or to retain long-term benefits.

When I first studied the MBAs in 1979, it looked as though there was a rather obvious dichotomy – security on one end of the continuum and autonomy on the other. However, in separating security by definition into two components, it is possible for someone to value both autonomy and security.

The more we study the career concept of security, the more our research suggests how differently people see and define security. Clearly, geographical location and stability are two important terms in the definition of security as an anchor.

Finally, the more I discuss the concept of security the more it becomes obvious that security can have a negative connotation for some individuals. There is a feeling that if one is security oriented then the individual might lack initiative or risk-taking skills. This is not necessarily the case. Rather, the individual is simply more interested in the long term implications of financial security or living in a particular geographical location.

LIFESTYLE CHOICES

Although the questionnaire does not identify what we call a "lifestyle" orientation, there is some evidence that such a drive exists. As we interview individuals about their careers, more and more discuss finding a balance in life which not only focuses on work but family and leisure. One manager stated, "I see myself making lifestyle decisions, not career decisions. I guess I want to be more of a juggler where I have a number of balls in the air at once. My life would not feel complete if I focused too much on one particular area."

As the demographics change in our society and there are fewer employees for more jobs, organizations will have to adapt and become more attractive for those individuals who are guided by the process of balancing many dimensions of their lives. This phenomenon will increase as more workers want very different things out of work.

COMPARING YOURSELF WITH OTHERS

The Career Orientations Inventory cannot tell anyone what they should do with their career. It is not a test of intelligence or aptitude. It simply allows the respondent to understand more about his or her career decision-making process.

To assist those who score the questionnaire themselves ranges are provided below for the eight career orientations. These scores have been created from thousands of students who have responded to the questionnaire.

Technical/functional competence A score of 40 or above would indicate a high interest in a particular functional or technical area, i.e. financial analysis, marketing, systems analysis, computer work, etc. A low score on this career orientation does *not* indicate incompetence in a particular field. A low score (30 or below) would indicate the respondent simply values other career orientations more.

Managerial Competence The fundamental basis for

the "managerial competence" orientation is to be competent in the complex activities that comprise the idea of "management." "Managerial competence"-oriented individuals will perceive that their competencies lie in the ability to analyze problems, remain emotionally stable, and interpersonally competent. Their career experiences would enable them to develop the self-image that they had the skills and values necessary to rise to general management levels. A high score in this dimension (over 40) does *not* necessarily mean the respondent is a competent leader, but that this person values the process of managing. Likewise, a low score (below 25) does not mean the respondent is a poor manager.

Autonomy The "autonomy" orientation encompasses those who have found organizational life to be restrictive, irrational, and/or intrusive into their lives. They are primarily concerned about their own sense of freedom and autonomy. "Autonomy"-oriented individuals are seeking work situations in which they will be maximally free of constraints to pursue their professional or technical/functional competence. A score of 45 would indicate high interest and values in relation to autonomy. A low score would be considered 25 or less.

Security Individuals with security as their orientation have tied their careers to a particular organization. The implications are that individuals who are "security" oriented will accept, to a greater degree than other career orientation types, an organizational definition of their careers. The "security"-oriented individual would focus on entering organizations which provide long-run stability, good benefits, and basic job security. A high score would be considered 40 or above and a low security-oriented person would have a score of 20 or less.

Another central theme of the individual who has security as a central career orientation is the interest in a specific geographical location. Individuals who are security oriented typically would not move from a certain geographical location unless the organizational rewards would merit a move. The security concept should not be seen as a negative concept but rather a value within a person. A high score would be 45 or higher while a low score would be 25 or lower.

Service Individuals who are "service" oriented are concerned with seeing people change because of their efforts. They want to use their interpersonal and helping skills in the service of others or in support of an important cause. An individual who has a low service orientation may find helping professions frustrating. Likewise, a high service orientation may indicate a person's need to be involved with others, e.g., in counseling, teaching, or social work. A score of 40 or higher would be high and a score of 25 or lower would be indicative of those who value service less than other career orientations.

Identity Individuals who are guided throughout their careers by the status and prestige of belonging to certain companies or organizations are "identity" oriented. They want to be identified with a powerful or prestigious employer. Certain individuals value working for organizations which have high visibility and a particular reputation either locally or nationally. Forty and higher as a score is a high score while 28 or lower is considered significantly low.

Variety Individuals who desire an endless number of different jobs or challenges are "variety" oriented. They want careers which provide maximum variety of assignments and work projects. A low score in the variety dimension may suggest that a person may be bored easily in certain types of jobs. A score of 45 or higher is considered a high score while 25 or lower indicates little interest in variety.

Creativity "Creative"-oriented individuals have a need to create something on their own. "Creating" is the fundamental need operating, for example, in the entrepreneur. Individuals with a creative orientation keep getting into new ventures and trying their hand in new kinds of projects. They also want to be central and visible while working on projects. A score of 35 or higher would be considered high while 20 or less would be considered low.

FINAL NOTE

One of the reasons for administering this questionnaire to you is to give you more insight into your own career decision-making process. Some people may feel frustrated in a particular job and not know why they are feeling stress or tension. The results of this instrument may only illuminate the fact that you do not value or need to manage, yet you may be spending the major portion of your work time as a manager. This lack of "fit" between organizational needs and your personal needs may be one reason for job dissatisfaction. Similarly, if you need a great deal of variety in your job and your present job allows you that variety, you may to be experiencing a great deal of satisfaction in your career. Finally, if you have more information about yourself in relation to why you make the career decisions you do, you will be able to make more satisfying career decisions in the future.

CASES

CAREER CRISIS FOR MARY MENARD: MANAGER OR CONSULTANT?*

Katrina Easton

Mary Menard is the head of the Data Administration department at Reliable Insurance Company. She has just returned from a two-week holiday, and has discovered that while she was away, her staff had been pressured into taking an action which was against the mandate of her department. She was not sure how to handle the situation.

Mary had started work at Reliable in 1975 in a clerical position immediately after finishing high school. Although she enjoyed working, her job was not very demanding, and she often approached her supervisor with requests for more work and more responsibility.

In 1977, company began a trainee program for systems analysts in order to "grow" their own analysts with knowledge of the insurance business. Mary was asked if she would like to take part in the program. She wrote the required aptitude test and passed it with flying colours. After six months of intensive training, she joined the data processing department as an analyst trainee and progressed quickly.

She loved the work. She read avidly in the field, subscribing to trade magazines and buying books at her own expense. She worked long hours and then often spent the rest of the evening reading.

She rose quickly to the position of Systems Analyst and then senior Systems Analyst. She continued to thrive on the work, but did not always get along with her colleagues. They considered her a workaholic. She considered them not dedicated enough and often bemoaned their lack of knowledge of new trends in the industry. In 1982, Mary was promoted to Supervisor of the pensions products team.

---

* "Career Crisis for Mary Menard: Manager or Consultant?" by Katrina Easton is used by permission of the author.

COMPANY BACKGROUND

Reliable Insurance Company is a medium-sized insurance company with its head office in Ottawa, Ontario. As of January 1, 1987 it had 2.3 billion dollars in assets and its premium income for 1986 was 1.3 million dollars. The company has branches in Ontario, Quebec, Halifax, and Vancouver, and is planning to open an office in Winnipeg next year.

Reliable specializes in individual life insurance and annuity products and prides itself on the variety and innovativeness of its products. It sells both individual and group plans and is hoping to enter the health insurance market in the next two years. The company is trying to increase its market share of financial products such as RRSP's and RRIF's. Occasionally it is the first company to introduce a new product to the insurance market, and it is always prepared to match whatever its main competitors are selling.

DESCRIPTION OF THE INFORMATION SYSTEMS DEPARTMENT(S)

A Data Processing department was set up in 1970, and at that time consisted of two programmers and two analysts and a supervisor. By 1984 the department had grown into four teams of four programmers and five analysts, with at least one senior analyst per team. A supervisor manages each team and the supervisors report to the department head. Each team is responsible for the computer systems for a particular area of the company (life insurance products, pension products, other financial products, human resources systems).

In 1984, Mary, with the support of the Information Systems VP, convinced upper management that Reliable should be developing corporate data bases and should set up a Data Administration department. The executive committee agreed to give her a mandate to create this department, with some reluctance. Although they were very knowledgeable in their own fields, most of them were unaware of the latest trends in data processing, and they were concerned with the increased costs with no visible benefits for several years.

With insurance companies being able to compete more and more on an even footing with banks and other financial institutions, their ability to react quickly to what was happening in the market place was extremely important. Also, the government was in the habit of passing legislation with which insurance companies were expected to comply on very short notice.

Mary and Ed, the Information Systems VP, were convinced that by going to a corporate data base format, Reliable would increase its ability to respond quickly to its information systems needs. At that time, each product that the company was selling had its own computer system and set of files that contained the customer information, financial information, etc., for that product.

With a corporate data base approach, all the data of the company would be organized by subject into "subject" data bases. For example, the customer basic information for all products would be stored in one place. Therefore, a client's basic information (name, address, date of birth, etc.) would be stored in one place only regardless of how many products he or she bought from the company. Then if, for example, a client moved, and informed Reliable of the address change, the address would only have to be changed in one place. And the customer would not be required to supply all of his or her policy numbers for all of his or her Reliable products. This is just a small but significant example of the advantages of using corporate data bases. There were other technological advantages to this type of data organization, and other insurance companies were moving in this direction.

Subject data bases would reduce duplication and decrease the effort required to create a new computer system whenever the company put a new product on the market. It would simplify the development of new systems because, for example, once the programs to store basic client information had been developed, all other systems could use these same programs.

Eventually, they would have to convert all existing systems to use the corporate data bases, but Mary and Ed did not consider this a major draw-back as most systems had to be rewritten every five to ten years anyway.

Mary and Ed both knew the change would be painful in the short term. The biggest problems encountered by other companies who changed to this type of organization were political, not technical. At the moment, everyone thought they "owned" their systems, and were very proprietory about the data in them. Mary's department would be administering all data and this would surely cause resentment.

In the long run, this approach should improve Reliable's customer relations and shorten the time required to develop a computer system to support new products or enhancements to existing products.

Mary proceeded to form her department by hiring two people – one from DP and the other from another department in the company. Later in 1984, she hired two more people as trainees. Although the jobs were posted in the company, Mary was not pleased with any of the applicants from Reliable, most of whom were from DP, and eventually hired two Concordia graduates.

For the first year and a half, Mary and her staff were mainly involved in education and learning about the various computer systems used by the company. Mary had to decide on a plan of attack for the conversion of existing systems, and look at new systems being developed. Although it was an enormous job just to learn about all the current systems, it appeared to some people that her department was not doing much because they did not see any results.

In mid-1986, Mary began meeting with the Data Processing department head and the supervisors about how their two departments would interact. In order for Mary's department to meet its goals, it was absolutely essential that the two departments co-operate. They agreed that Mary's department would be involved on all new systems development.

Although in public everyone was very supportive and positive about the new approach, Mary heard through the grapevine that some people in DP resented her rise in the company.

Mary had a particular problem with the Data Processing department head. Although he publicly expressed complete agreement with the new direction being taken by their departments, she knew he belittled her and her department in private. She felt he resented losing complete control over the development of computer systems. She was also half his age and now on equal footing with him in the organization chart. (See Exhibits 1 and 2)

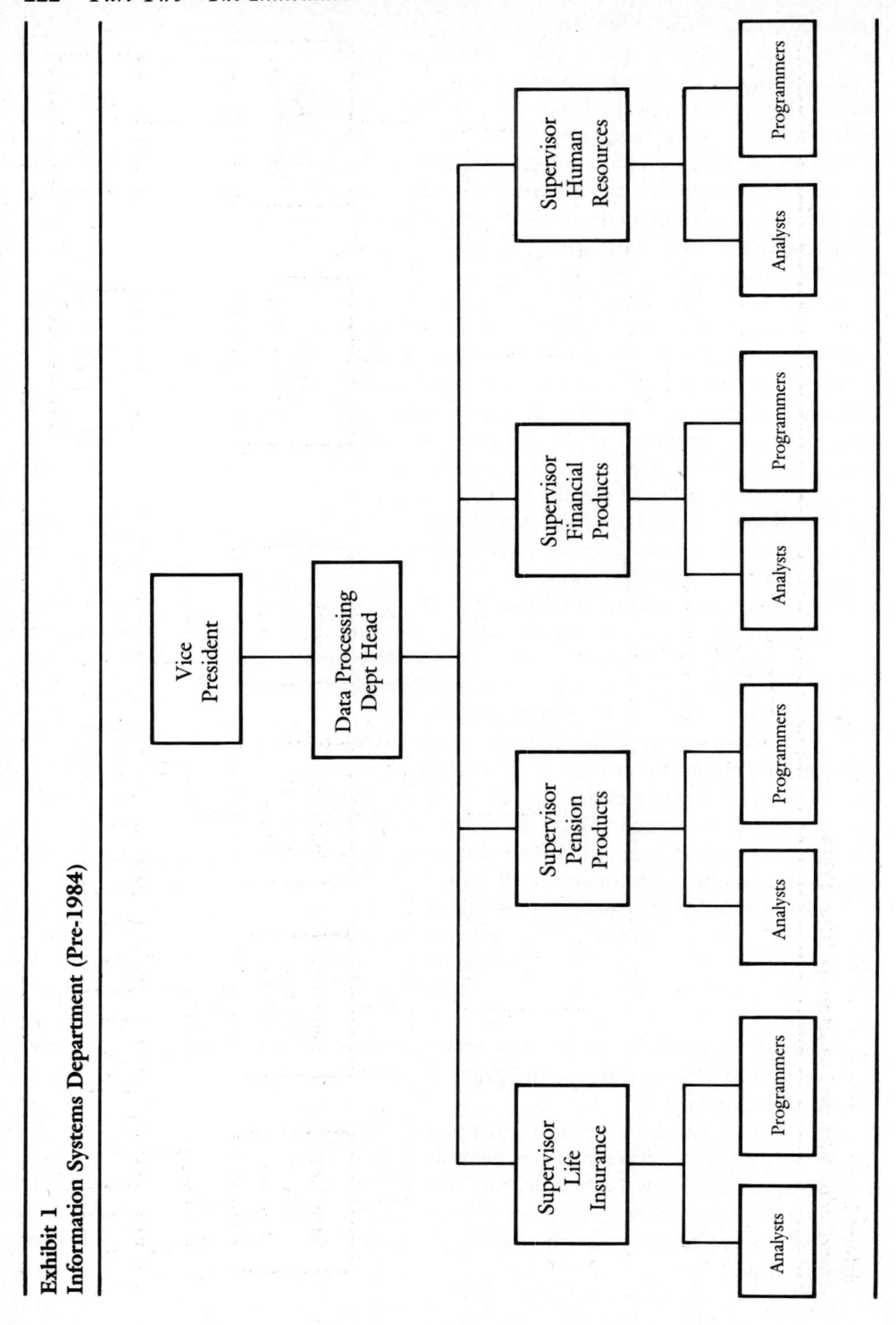

Exhibit 1
Information Systems Department (Pre-1984)

```
                    Vice
                  President
                     |
               Data Processing
                  Dept Head
                     |
   ┌─────────────────┼─────────────────┬─────────────────┐
Supervisor       Supervisor        Supervisor       Supervisor
   Life            Pension          Financial          Human
Insurance         Products          Products         Resources
   |                 |                 |                 |
┌──┴──┐          ┌──┴──┐          ┌──┴──┐           ┌──┴──┐
Analysts Programmers  Analysts Programmers  Analysts Programmers  Analysts Programmers
```

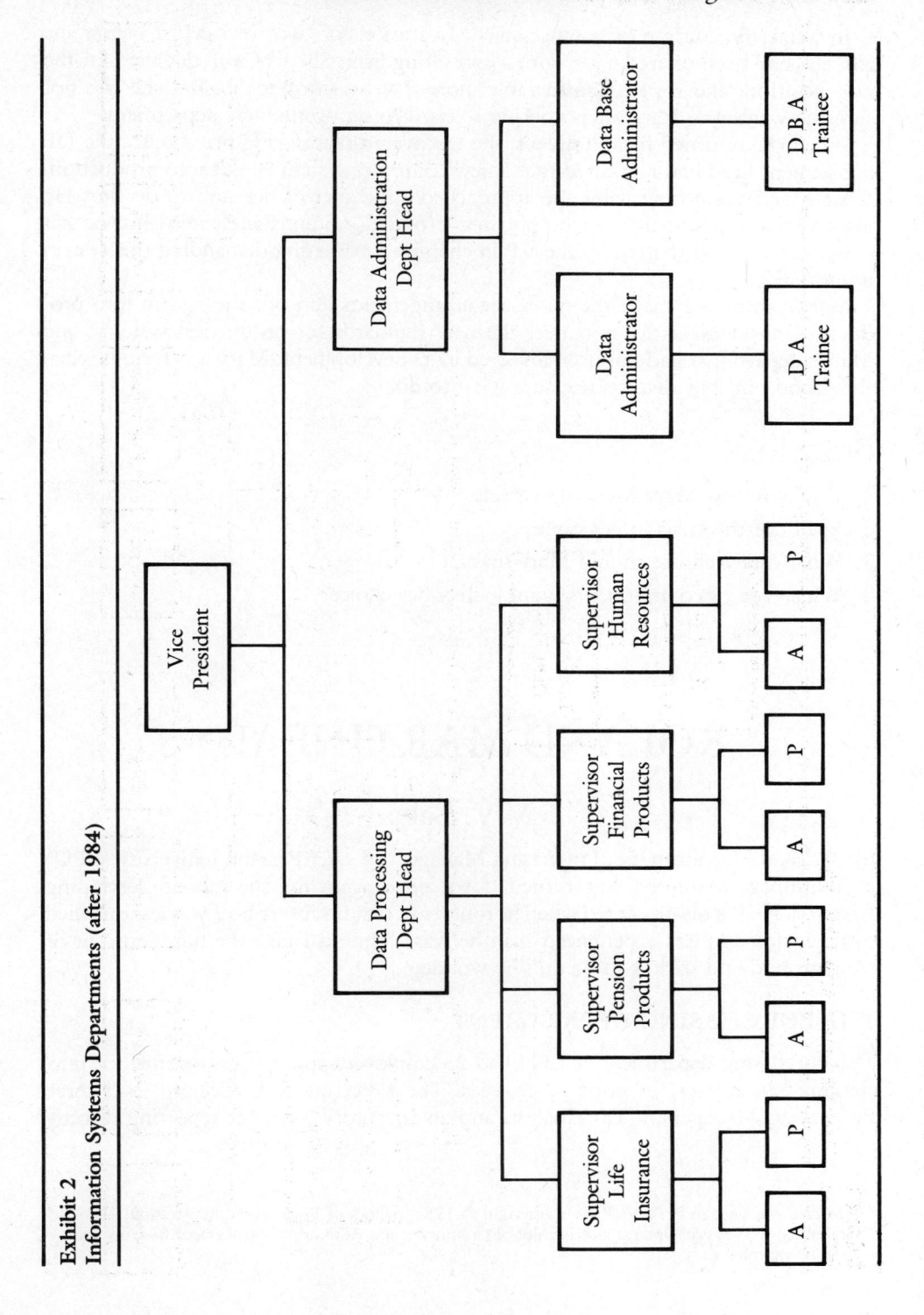

Exhibit 2
Information Systems Departments (after 1984)

```
                                    Vice President
                                    /            \
                       Data Processing          Data Administration
                         Dept Head                 Dept Head
                       /    |    |    \            /          \
              Supervisor  Supv.  Supv.  Supv.   Data            Data Base
              Life        Pension Financial Human Administrator  Administrator
              Insurance   Products Products Resources   |              |
                /  \      /  \    /  \     /  \       DA             DBA
               A    P    A    P  A    P   A    P    Trainee         Trainee
```

In February, Mary took a much needed vacation for two weeks. Just before she left, she had been offered a job with a consulting firm. She was well-qualified for the new position, and it paid considerably more that her current job. But she was not sure she wanted to leave after working so hard to set up the new department.

When she returned from holidays, she discovered that during her absence the DP department head had requested that a new computer system be put into production. Since Mary was not available, he approached a member of her staff to do this. He insisted that the system must be put into production immediately and showed her employee a memo written by the VP in charge of marketing demanding this system immediately.

Mary's employee made the necessary arrangements and put the system into production, although it did not meet the new standards for production systems, and Mary's department had not been involved in its development. Mary was furious when she found out, but she was not sure what to do.

QUESTIONS

1. Briefly review Mary Menard's career.
2. Spell out the crisis in her career.
3. What career choice should Mary make?
4. What type of commitments would affect her choice?

ROLAND MARTINEAU*

V.V. Baba

Mr. Roland Martineau, 58, Purchasing Manager at Lester Pearson University (LPU) in Winnipeg, Manitoba was turned down once again for the job of Purchasing Director. He felt disappointed when he found out that his future boss was less qualified than himself and less experienced than he was. "Should I take the hint and quit or hang around and stick-it-to-them?" he wondered.

THE PURCHASING DEPARTMENT

The Purchasing department at LPU had 23 employees and was responsible for purchasing $30 million of goods each year. The Director, Eric McCord, had three Purchasing Managers, a Tax Analyst, and an Inventory Manager reporting directly

---

* This case was written by V.V. Baba. Copyright © 1984, School of Business Administration, The University of Western Ontario and Faculty of Commerce and Administration, Concordia University. Used by permission.

to him in addition to his own support staff. (See Exhibit 1 for the organization chart of the Purchasing department). Mr. Martineau was responsible for the purchase of business equipment including computers, business forms, printing material, athletic supplies, etc., and supervised purchases of approximately $8 million a year.

THE PURCHASING MANAGER

The job of the Purchasing Manager at LPU involved dealing with a high level of uncertainty. Often, one had to make purchase decisions without really knowing whether the money had been allocated or not. Furthermore, the manager had to deal with two different clientele, one internal and the other external. This called for considerable tact and diplomacy. In addition, there was little staff support through systematic information management. Often, decisions had to be made with virtually no relevant information on past trends or practices.

A job in purchasing in and of itself could not be considered a profession. In order to be recognized as a professional, one had to obtain professional qualification in materials management. This might involve some training in engineering as well as business administration. In the 1950s, all one needed was a high school diploma in order to become a Buyer. After a few years experience, one could easily become a manager. In the 1980s, however, to become a Buyer, one has to have community college or university education with specialization in a particular area.

ROLAND MARTINEAU

Mr. Martineau had a high school education and ten years of purchasing experience when he joined LPU as a Buyer in 1964. He moved up the ranks and became a Purchasing Manager in less than ten years. During this period he had acquired an RIA diploma and, more recently, a diploma in professional purchasing.

Mr. Martineau considers himself as being honest with himself, willing to speak his mind and "tell it like it is." He was individualistic and had no use for the various groups and associations on campus. For example, he was neither a member of the Staff Association nor the Professional Managers Association at LPU. These associations were negotiating bodies within the university system much like the faculty association.

CAREER PLANNING AT LPU

While an academic career path was clearly defined at LPU with well articulated expectations in terms of performance and seniority, no such thing existed for university service departments. As in most universities, the service departments did not rank high compared to the academic departments in the "class hierarchy." In addition, the Personnel department did not coordinate the personnel activities of other service departments nor advise people regarding opportunities available within the university system.

Similarly, within the Purchasing department, there was no well defined career planning and development. A Buyer, for example, in spite of superior performance,

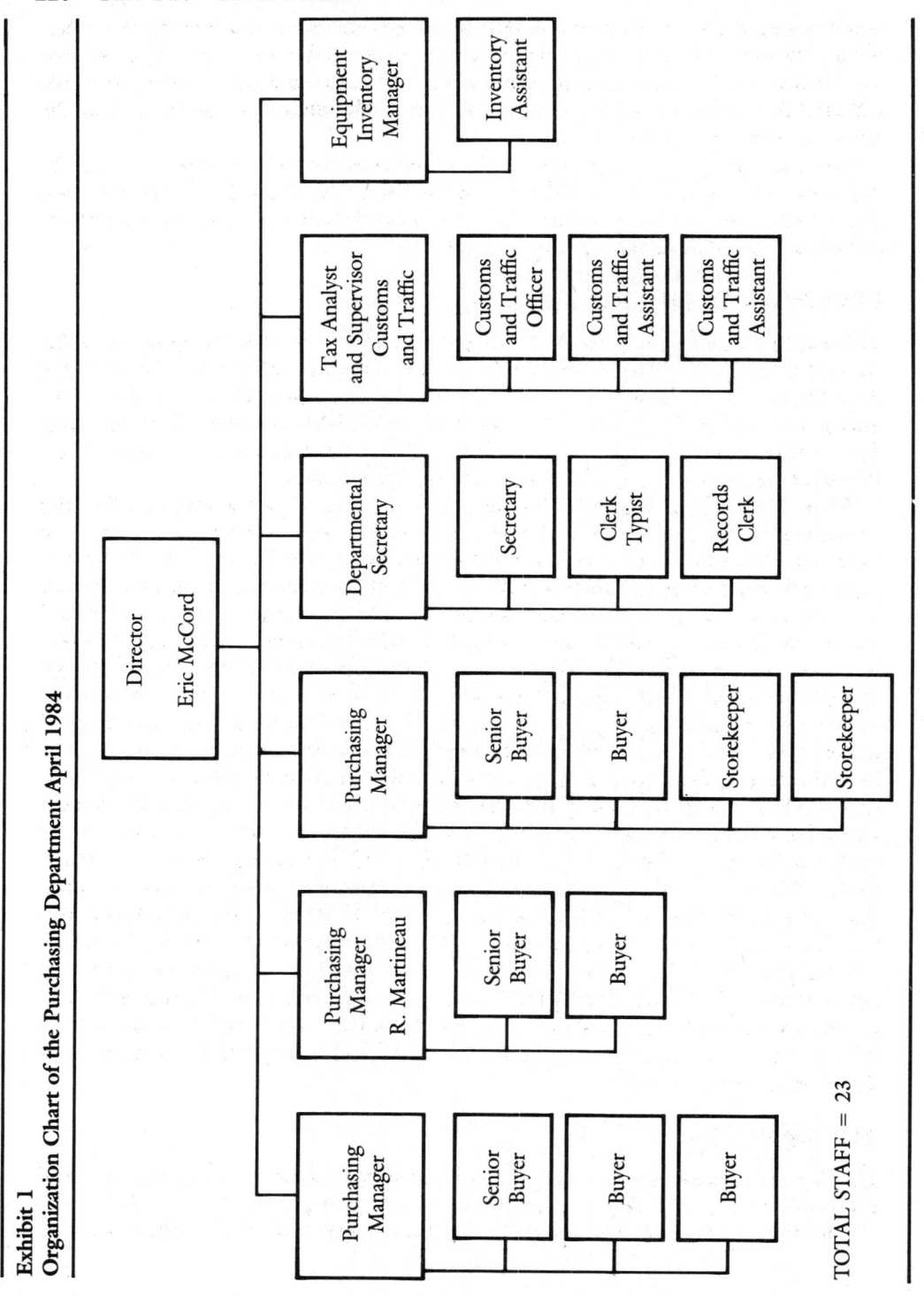

Exhibit 1
Organization Chart of the Purchasing Department April 1984

```
                          Director
                         Eric McCord
    ┌──────────┬──────────┬──────────┬──────────┬──────────┐
 Purchasing  Purchasing Purchasing Departmental  Tax Analyst  Equipment
  Manager     Manager    Manager    Secretary   and Supervisor Inventory
            R. Martineau                        Customs       Manager
                                                and Traffic
    │          │          │          │              │            │
  Senior    Senior     Senior     Secretary     Customs      Inventory
  Buyer     Buyer      Buyer                    and Traffic  Assistant
    │          │          │          │          Officer
  Buyer     Buyer      Buyer      Clerk            │
    │                              Typist       Customs
  Buyer                             │           and Traffic
                                  Records       Assistant
                                   Clerk          │
                        Storekeeper            Customs
                            │                  and Traffic
                        Storekeeper            Assistant
```

TOTAL STAFF = 23

226 Part Two The Individual

could not hold even reasonable expectations of upward movement within the department. Though individual performance would be assessed every year, one could not say whether it led systematically to promotion as a manager or director. Salary increases reflected the performance component to an extent, although this was the only mechanism by which merit was recognized.

No clear policy existed for promotions. However, recently, it appeared that the university administration favored promotions from within. People in most service departments were ignorant of procedures or policy though mention was made occasionally of the existence of a policy manual.

PROCEDURES FOR PROMOTION

The usual procedure for choosing a Purchasing Director involved forming an *ad hoc* committee which consisted of two academic deans, a nominee from an administrative department, the Director of Physical Plant and the Director of Personnel. This committee was usually chosen by the Vice-President of Administration. Potential candidates were interviewed by the committee and one was recommended to the Vice-President, Administration, who then made the appointment.

When Martineau first applied for the job of director of purchasing in 1976, the committee turned him down, and appointed someone from outside. This came as a shock to Martineau as he was expecting to be chosen for the job. The committee suggested that the person they had hired was a good manager, though he did not have the same length of experience as Martineau. Martineau felt this was unfair and attributed this setback to the fact that the Executive Assistant to the Vice-President, who was on the committee, did not particularly appreciate his frankness. Though Martineau considered quitting at this point, he decided to stay on and wait until the job became available again. After four years, when the Purchasing Director resigned under questionable circumstances, Martineau felt that his chances for the top job looked even brighter, especially because he had additional qualifications through part-time studies as a professional purchaser. Martineau was surprised when the former Executive Assistant to the Vice-President of Administration, who was retired at the time, was brought back and given the role of interim Purchasing Director. Furthermore, when the selection committee was formed, Martineau found out, to his dismay, that the interim director was one of the members. However, Martineau still hoped that his qualifications and experience would carry some weight and land him the coveted promotion, though he felt that the inclusion of the interim Director in the committee was not entirely proper. By this time, Martineau had learned that these committee decisions were heavily influenced by the more vocal members of the committee, who were not entirely above playing politics in persuading the committee to decide in a particular way.

THE DECISION

The day the decision was to be announced, the interim Director of Purchasing called Martineau in and told him that he was not successful in getting the job. Martineau's disappointment turned to anger when he learned that one of his colleagues, Eric

McCord, who was less qualified than himself and who had less experience, landed the job.

Martineau wondered whether the university administration was trying to give him a message. "I work hard, I'm qualified, I have experience, what more do they want? Why wouldn't they tell me earlier if they didn't like me?" He felt cheated. At 58, the prospect of starting on a new career was not very appealing to Martineau.

QUESTIONS

1. Why is there no career planning in a university service department such as at LPU?
2. Why is it difficult to prepare a career plan for purchasing people in a university setting?
3. Briefly summarize Roland Martineau's career. Why did he not get the job of Purchasing Director?
4. What should Roland Martineau do now?

EXERCISES

PREPARING A CAREER PLAN

Joe Kelly

Most people spend time thinking about their careers. Very few people, on the other hand, think their careers through and write out career goals. Keep in mind that a career is a sequence of positions occupied by a person during the course of a lifetime. Written career plans have a number of advantages of unwritten plans:

1. They are defined as specific.
2. They are easier to analyze and update.
3. They help to identify challenges and crises.

After graduating with a B.Comm. with a specialization in management, you have just received an appointment in the Personnel department at the head office of Air Canada. You are scheduled to have a meeting with the Personnel Director tomorrow and have been asked to develop a career plan for yourself. You know the Personnel Director is keen on new people in the company beginning their career by working in the Ticketing Office as a sales clerk for one month followed by periods of work in other departments. You are not too keen in following this particular plan because you wish to follow-up on a project in the training of airline flight attendants which you initiated while at university. You are debating in your mind which is the best approach to employ in your meeting with the Personnel Director.

QUESTIONS

1. Prepare a career plan for yourself.
2. What information do you need from Air Canada?
3. Flag possible problems and crises.

HOW AN EXECUTIVE TAKES OVER

Many comments have been made with respect to the best way to take over a new department or group. It is important that you develop more than just an intuitive feel for what is going on. The following exercise is based on John Gabarro's study of managerial transitions and is intended to widen the experience of business students and to help them when that key promotion comes along. In this exercise, you should think of an organization you are familiar with (perhaps one in which you are currently involved or one you have been part of in the past).

John Gabarro's study of managerial transitions is the result of close observation of fourteen management successions over three years. He describes the process as a sequence of five predictable stages with varying durations, each distinguished by characteristic patterns of activity. The first stage, "taking hold," is typically an intense effort to adjust to new surroundings, as the manager assumes the reins of command. Organizational changes made tend to be corrective rather than fundamental; the manager is intent on acclimatizing himself or herself to the organization and vice versa.

The immersion period that follows is, by contrast, placid. The manager has mastered the rudiments of his or her function and is engaged on understanding the subtleties of the organization and his or her role in it. With most of the more pressing issues in hand, fundamental questions of personnel deployment and organizational design are considered, and a strategic plan of attack formulated. The combined duration of both phases is 13 to 18 months (the duration of both is highly variable).

The third stage Gabarro labels "reshaping." It is during this period that the incumbent manager is likely to exercise his most important influence on the organization, as he implements the strategic plans conceived during the immersion phase. It is at this point that incoming managers leave their stamp on the organization's culture. Learning (from the manager's point of view) does not cease altogether but is largely confined to monitoring the changes underway.

The consolidation phase is, as the name implies, devoted to consolidating the gains made in the reshaping phase; results of changes are examined and adjustments made accordingly. Loose ends are tidied up and unanticipated complications dealt with.

The final phase and denouement is "refinement," and as the name suggests it is marked by minor adjustments; the manager's function has become largely routine. If the manager has successfully negotiated the five previous phases, then he can be said to be firmly in control.

Gabarro's researchers have pinpointed several factors that determine the success of newly promoted managers. The first, unsurprisingly, is prior experience within the same functional area; managers showed a marked tendency to make their first moves in areas that fell within their own expertise. Specific experience in the same industry is also important. Industry insiders are more confident of the ground on which they tread and are therefore quicker, as a rule, to implement change.

A second factor is the manager's ability to maintain a cordial atmosphere with his lieutenants. Naturally, a poor working relationship with subordinates will detract from the manager's capability but it is noteworthy that subordinates should play so important a role. Similarly, the manager's relationship with his superiors is a determinant of success, particularly during the early phases of the transition. Gabarro notes a high correlation between failed successions and discord among managers and their superiors (control and delegation were frequently cited as sore points).

Gabarro's findings are yet another nail in the coffin for the truly general manager: "the all-purpose general manager who can parachute into any situation and succeed is a myth. Experience and special competencies do matter." The latter-day practice of "face-tracking" promising executives is also cast in an unfavorable light; clearly the duration of a successful changeover is longer than is generally supposed.

The corporation is therefore presented with a dilemma: it must widen the experience of likely leaders, (which is only accomplished through greater responsibility and authority, i.e., promotion) but promotions are more likely to be successful for those with relevant experience. The solution, suggests Gabarro, is to ensure that likely candidates for high office are given new assignments that encompass their previous field of expertise—assignments of sufficient duration to allow all of the phases of transition.

REFERENCES

1. J.J. Gabarro (May-June 1985) "When a New Manager Takes Charge." *Harvard Business Review*, pp. 110–123.

QUESTIONS

1. Complete the TAKE OVER form.

STAGE	DESCRIPTION	PROBLEMS
Taking Hold		
Immersion Period		
Reshaping		
Consolidation		
Refinement		

232 Part Two The Individual

2. Think of a time when you were taking over some unit of organization (a section or department in a company, a university club, a sports team, a small business). Compare your experiences with others in your group.
3. What does it take to take over?
4. How would you go about taking over next time?
5. What are the group dynamics of "take over"?

CAREER ORIENTATIONS INVENTORY

Thomas J. DeLong

The main reason for administering this questionnaire to you is to give you more insights into your own career decision-making process. Some people may feel frustrated in a particular job and not know why they feel stress or tension. The results of this instrument may illustrate that you do not value or need to manage, yet you are spending the major portion of your work time as a manager. This lack of "fit" between organizational needs and your personal needs may be one reason for your current job dissatisfaction. Similarly, if you need a great deal of variety in your job and your present job allows you that variety, you may be experiencing a great deal of satisfaction in your career. Finally, if you have more information about yourself in relation to why you make the career decisions you do, you will be able to make more satisfying career decisions in the future.

THE INVENTORY

Think back to your recent years in your career. By what kinds of criteria have you made decisions about job moves, company moves, whether or not to accept new assignments, and other career decisions. Think also about the kinds of criteria which are important to you as you think about future career decisions you will be making.

The items below are designed to help you identify what kind of criteria you have used in the past and which may be important to you in the future.

For each criterion, circle a number which best describes how important that criterion has been and continues to be in your career decisions.

---

* Developed by Thomas J. DeLong and Edgar H. Schein. Used with the permission of Thomas J. DeLong & Associates. All Rights Reserved. Reprinted with permission of Thomas J. DeLong.

If you feel that your present or future criteria are different from past ones, answer in terms of the present or future. We want to understand how you look at these criteria now and how they will influence future career decisions, even though some of them are worded in terms of the past.

There are no right or wrong answers, except in terms of their importance to you. So be honest with yourself.

HOW IMPORTANT IS EACH ONE OF THE FOLLOWING STATEMENTS FOR YOU?

	Of No Importance				Centrally Important	
1. To build my career around some specific functional or technical area of expertise is . . .	1	2	3	4	5	6
2. The process of supervising, influencing, leading and controlling people at all levels is . . .	1	2	3	4	5	6
3. The chance to pursue my own lifestyle and not to be constrained by the rules of an organization is . . .	1	2	3	4	5	6
4. An organization which will provide security through guaranteed work, benefits, a good retirement program, etc., is . . .	1	2	3	4	5	6
5. The use of my interpersonal and helping skills in the service of others is . . .	1	2	3	4	5	6
6. Being identified with and gaining status from my occupation is . . .	1	2	3	4	5	6
7. An endless variety of challenges in my career is . . .	1	2	3	4	5	6
8. To be able to create or build something that is entirely my own product or idea is . . .	1	2	3	4	5	6
9. Remaining in my specialized area as opposed to being promoted out of my area of expertise is . . .	1	2	3	4	5	6
10. To be in a position of leadership and influence is . . .	1	2	3	4	5	6
11. A career which is free from organizational restrictions is . . .	1	2	3	4	5	6
12. An organization which will give me long term stability is . . .	1	2	3	4	5	6
13. The process of seeing others change because of my effort is . . .	1	2	3	4	5	6

		Of No Importance					Centrally Important
14.	To be recognized by my title and status is . . .	1	2	3	4	5	6
15.	A career which provides a maximum variety of types of assignments and work projects is . . .	1	2	3	4	5	6
16.	The use of my skills in building a new business enterprise is . . .	1	2	3	4	5	6
17.	Remaining in my area of expertise rather than being promoted into general management is . . .	1	2	3	4	5	6
18.	To rise to a position of general management is . . .	1	2	3	4	5	6
19.	A career which permits a maximum of freedom and autonomy to choose my own work, hours, etc., is . . .	1	2	3	4	5	6
20.	Remaining in one geographical area rather than being prompted into moving because of a promotion is . . .	1	2	3	4	5	6
21.	Being able to use my skills and talents in the service of an important cause is . . .	1	2	3	4	5	6
22.	Being identified with a powerful or prestigious employer or organization is . . .	1	2	3	4	5	6

HOW TRUE IS EACH ONE OF THE FOLLOWING STATEMENTS FOR YOU?

		Not At All True					Completely True
23.	The excitement of participating in many areas of work has been the underlying motivation behind my career.	1	2	3	4	5	6
24.	I have been motivated throughout my career by the number of ideas or products which I have been directly involved in creating.	1	2	3	4	5	6
25.	I will accept a management position only if it is in my area of expertise.	1	2	3	4	5	6
26.	I would like to reach a level of responsibility in an organization where my decisions really make a difference.	1	2	3	4	5	6

	Not At All True				Completely True	
27. During my career I have been mainly concerned with my own sense of freedom and autonomy.	1	2	3	4	5	6
28. It is important for me to remain in my present geographical location rather than move because of a promotion or new job assignment.	1	2	3	4	5	6
29. I have always sought a career in which I could be of service to others.	1	2	3	4	5	6
30. I like to be identified with a particular organization and the prestige that accompanies that organization.	1	2	3	4	5	6
31. An endless variety of challenges is what I really want from my career.	1	2	3	4	5	6
32. To invent something on my own or create a new idea are important elements of my career.	1	2	3	4	5	6
33. I would leave my company rather than be promoted out of my area of expertise or interest.	1	2	3	4	5	6
34. I want to achieve a position which gives me the opportunity to combine analytical competence with supervision of people.	1	2	3	4	5	6
35. I do not want to be constrained by either an organization or the business world.	1	2	3	4	5	6
36. I prefer to work for an organization which provides tenure (life-time employment).	1	2	3	4	5	6
37. I want a career in which I can be committed and devoted to an important cause.	1	2	3	4	5	6
38. I want others to identify me by my organization and my job title.	1	2	3	4	5	6
39. I have been motivated throughout my career by using my talents in a variety of different areas of work.	1	2	3	4	5	6
40. I have always wanted to start and build up a business of my own.	1	2	3	4	5	6
41. I prefer to work for an organization which will permit me to remain in one geographical area.	1	2	3	4	5	6

SCORING OF CAREER ORIENTATIONS

Under each of the orientation headings transfer your answers to the items indicated. Then add the total score for the column and divide by the number of items in that column to get your average for that orientation.

T/F*	MGR	AUT	SEC-1	SEC-2	SER	ID	VAR	CRET
1___	2___	3___	4___		5___	6___	7___	8___
9___	10___	11___	12___		13___	14___	15___	16___
17___	18___	19___		20___	21___	22___	23___	24___
25___	26___	27___		28___	29___	30___	31___	32___
33___	34___	35___	36___		37___	38___	39___	40___
				41___				

_____ _____ _____ _____ _____ _____ _____ _____ _____ TOTAL

÷5   ÷5   ÷5   ÷3   ÷3   ÷5   ÷5   ÷5   ÷5

_____ _____ _____ _____ _____ _____ _____ _____ _____ AVERAGE

* Abbreviation Guide:
T/F = Technical/functional competence anchor.
MGR = Managerial competence anchor.
AUT = Autonomy anchor.
SEC-1 = Security anchor (future stability).
SEC-2 = Security anchor (geographic area stability).
SER = Service anchor.
ID = Identity anchor.
VAR = Variety anchor.
CRET = Creativity anchor.

GENERAL DESCRIPTION OF CAREER ORIENTATIONS

Note: In analyzing your scores it is important for you to understand that no scores whether low or high should have negative connotations. The questionnaire you responded to measures values and needs, not competency levels.

Technical/Functional Competence Technical/functional people are motivated by the challenge of the actual work they do, e.g., financial analysis, marketing, systems analysis, or corporate planning. Their career orientation is the technical field, functional area, or content of their work, not the managerial process itself. The self-image of individuals in the technical/functional competence group are tied up with their feelings of competence in the particular area they are in. A low score on this career orientation does not indicate incompetence in a particular field. A low score would indicate that the respondent values other career orientations more than technical competence.

Managerial Competence The fundamental basis for the "managerial competence" anchor is to be competent in the complex activities that comprise the idea of "management". "Managerial competence"-oriented individuals will perceive that their competencies lie in the ability to analyze problems, remain emotionally stable, and interpersonally competent. Their career experiences would enable them to develop the self-image that they had the skills and values necessary to rise to general management levels. A high score in this dimension does not necessarily mean the respondent is a competent leader but that the person enjoys the process of managing. Likewise, a low score does not mean the respondent is a poor manager.

Autonomy The "autonomy" orientation encompasses those who have found organizational life to be restrictive, irrational, and/or intrusive into their lives. They are primarily concerned about their own sense of freedom and autonomy. "Autonomy" oriented individuals are seeking work situations in which they will be maximally free of constraints to pursue their professional or technical/functional competence.

Security (stability) Individuals with security as their orientation have tied their careers to a particular organization. The implications are that individuals who are "security" oriented will accept, to a greater degree than the other career orientation types, an organizational definition of their careers. The "security" oriented individual will focus around entering organizations which provide long-run stability, good benefits, and basic job security.

Security (geographic) Another central theme of the individual who has security as a central career orientation is the interest in a specific geographical location. Individuals who are security oriented typically would not move from a certain geographical location unless the organizational rewards would merit a move. The security concept should not be seen as a negative concept but rather a value within a person.

Service Individuals who are "service" oriented are concerned with seeing people change because of their efforts. They want to use their interpersonal and helping skills in the service of others. An individual who has a low service orientation may find helping professions frustrating. Likewise, a high service orientation may indicate a person's need to be involved with others, e.g., in counseling, teaching, or social work.

Identity Individuals who are guided throughout their careers by the status and prestige of belonging to certain companies or organizations are "identity" oriented. They want to be identified with a powerful or prestigous employer. Certain individuals value working for organizations which have high visibility and a particular reputation either locally or nationally.

Variety Individuals who desire an endless number of different jobs or challenges are "variety" oriented. They want careers which provide a maximum variety of assignments and work projects. A low score in variety may suggest that a person may be bored easily in certain types of jobs.

Creativity "Creative"-oriented individuals have a need to create something on their own. "Creating" is the fundamental need operating, for example, in the entrepreneur. "Creative"-oriented individuals keep getting into new ventures and trying their hand in new kinds of projects. They are also very central and visible while working on projects.

PART THREE
GROUPS

VI
MANAGING GROUPS

READINGS

SURVIVING AND THRIVING IN TOP MANAGEMENT MEETINGS*

Joe Kelly

If you want to be a chief executive officer, you have to act like one – especially in executive committee meetings. These are the meetings in which you will probably be coolly appraised by reigning members of the management group who are deciding whether to let you in. They will be watching vigilantly to see whether you are going to become a member of the inner circle or just another vice-president of human resources.

Surviving in this environment requires a fairly cool understanding of what makes a top management meeting different from a middle management meeting. When middle managers get together, they usually analyze computer printouts, drawings, and other materials in an earnest search for feasible options to sell to the next level up. Differences of technical opinion may arise and tempers may soar, but nearly all involved are anxious to find and support an optimum solution.

On the other hand, video studies reveal that a top management meeting is more likely to be an adversarial proceeding – not necessarily an open clash of wills, but a group of opposing viewpoints in a struggle to achieve dominance. Such a meeting will usually be conducted in a courteous, formal, almost legalistic atmosphere, but it's nevertheless a game of getting the upper hand. If you want to survive in this paradoxical environment, you must learn how the players interrelate, what roles they play, and what weapons they consider acceptable.

WHAT HAPPENS IN MEETINGS – AND WHY

Sometimes the camera catches participants off camera as they are milling around waiting to begin the meeting. The scene is reminiscent of a platoon of infantry trying to organize itself before heading for the front. Everybody is nervous but trying to be genial; nobody really knows what is happening. The first minute of the meeting is everything; the video shows conclusively that more things happen in that first minute than any person can rationally absorb. To see this, you need only advance the video one frame at a time and watch carefully.

Researchers in one project, who studied a meeting in a large, international telecommunications company, observed several striking things after a number of careful viewings of their video. The meeting consisted of four executives in a data-processing group; the two leaders were assistant vice-presidents, one from Montréal and the other from Toronto. As the meeting was about to begin, the assistant vice-president from Montréal asked. "Are any of you people going to the operations research meeting at lunchtime?" As it turned out, nobody was going except the assistant vice-president from Montréal. He

---

* Reprinted, by permission of the publisher, from PERSONNEL, June 1987, © 1987 American Management Association, New York. All rights reserved.

then said, "Okay, that's fine, but I want to get there on time, so I'll give a signal 15 minutes before the lecture starts." Thus he began the meeting by structuring the time frame to show that his time was important.

Sitting to the left of the assistant vice-president from Montréal was his colleague from Toronto. The Montréal assistant vice-president next asked one of his staff to make a presentation on a technical computer subject. As his staffer began, the Montréal man leaned forward so that he blocked the line of vision between the assistant vice-president from Toronto and the speaker, thus "protecting" the speaker, in a sense, until he had picked up momentum and was off to a good start. Once the speaker was in stride, the Montréal assistant vice-president put his feet on the desk and pushed his chair back from the table so that he was behind his colleague from Toronto, who then seemed at the outset of the meeting to be cast in an adversarial relationship.

One explanation for such behavior is that the nonlinear part of a manager's brain is involved in the process of running meetings. The process apparently involves a kind of nonverbal communication; it requires an executive to have a sense of where his body should be and how he should respond to a particular situation. In such cases, the right hemisphere of the brain – the hemisphere responsible for intuitive spatial relations and creative thinking required in many artistic pursuits – is supplementing the usual analytical skills that an executive brings to a meeting. Managers are apparently able to balance the functions of both hemispheres in order to achieve what they want. All this interaction seems to reflect the ideas expressed by George A. Miller in his book *Spontaneous Apprentices: Children and Language* when he speaks of the "left hand of subjective accidents, odd metaphors, wild guesses, happy hunches, and chance permutation of ideas that come from who knows where."[1] Managers are apparently very skillful in utilizing this right side of the brain – in other words, in developing this intuitive skill in non-linear logic. Much of this skill is revealed in their unconscious ability to make a spontaneous physical intervention in a meeting.

ROLE-PLAYING IN MEETINGS

What these videos reveal, then, is that sophisticated role-playing is a major part of the drama of managerial life. Playing a role is like playing a hand in poker; things are happening at a number of different levels. Since roles, rules, and relations are socially ordained, behavior conforms to probabilities and perceptions. "Play it as it lays" and "Play it by ear" are expressions that describe the subtle double-dealing of role-playing.

A video may show a chief executive using psychological gamesmanship to throw a scare into opponents even though his aboveboard behavior is impeccable. For many managers, a meeting is psychological warfare waged at nerve-wracking intensity. Sometimes these psychological games are elevated to the level of a debate. These managerial debates have a certain entertainment value; moreover, they can sometimes help clarify a political situation. The ultimate aim of the exercise is to make the opponent appear ridiculous. Because executives are frequently quite skilled in debating techniques, they will often give a real display of verbal pyrotechnics.

The aim of the debating game is not necessarily to be right; rather, one must sound convincing and denigrate one's opponent as coolly and elegantly as possible. Body language and facial expressions are tremendously important in this context; smiling subtly while your opponent delivers his main point can often be as telling as coming up with an objective rejoinder. The need, above all else, is to give a good performance.

In trying to find a suitable role model for developing this performance, one can examine the Brian Mulroney, John Turner, and Ed Broadbent debates of 1984. Broadbent scored points against his opponents by adopting a certain openness that made the others look less than forthcoming by comparison. The truly effective executive debater has an uncanny knack for improvising effects and verbal ploys that make his opponent look gauche.

Perhaps the most important thing to keep in mind about executive encounters is that the format can shift very quickly. There is no guarantee that an orders-giving session will not degenerate into a debate in which logic and loyalty give way to a mere display of wit.

MEETINGS AS DRAMA

Running a meeting is an exciting activity, but from a scientific point of view it consists of long, boring lists of things to do. When you consider the manager who actually has to run the meeting, you soon realize the need for myth, magic, and meaning. Producing and directing meetings become the art of transforming inputs into outputs with the addition of value. This "two plus two equals five" aspect of meetings demands a certain *savoir-faire* that owes more to theater than it does to science.

This new approach to meetings assumes an imaginative integration of structure (the cast of characters) and values (myth, magic, and meaning). If the meeting is seen from this perspective, it is transformed into a powerful theatrical experience.

All groups work through three phases: clarification ("What is it?"), evaluation ("How do we feel about it?"), and decision ("What are we going to do about it?"). To work through this process, the group selects two individuals: the task specialist (who "zeroes in on the problem") and the human relations specialist (who offers "first-aid" to help alleviate group tension).

The executive who has studied group dynamics might find nothing particularly new in all this. Nevertheless, executive meetings have undergone a dramatic change in tone and content. Naked conflict has begun to emerge, conflict so common and visible that executives have been forced to find both a rationale and a ritual to contain it.

The executive as entertainer can learn much from the playwright about how to figure out the scenario, interpret the script, and enter and exit on cue. He must grasp the meaning of the phrase, "We will entertain this motion" — that is, "We will fool around with it, pummel it, and see generally what it is made of." Like a good chess player, the successful top manager is a sportsman in a meeting. He never squirms while he is losing, never crows when he is winning. Like the chess player, he merely concentrates on trying to outwit and outpsych his opponent.

However, this entire process cannot work unless the right kind of values is involved. The conflict between democratic values and task-oriented values can create dilemmas at executive meetings. The members of the meeting must state what is on their minds; at the same time, they must be ready to bow to the emerging consensus. The task-oriented values are espoused by the chairman, who makes his members realize that they must finish the agenda on schedule. Putting these values together can cause a lot of tension, especially when the public agenda is to develop a policy for promotion based on merit, while the hidden agenda is to try to chastise the "Young Turks" or sink the "Old Guard."

THE DEEPER STRUCTURES OF EXECUTIVE MEETINGS

In one video, which depicts the behavior of a typical day in the life of an executive, the day begins with a meeting between the executive and his immediate employees, a meeting devoted essentially to the executive's reading of a speech he plans to give that evening at a local hotel. During this meeting, the executive, whom we'll call Bill Andrews (not his real name), is going to read his speech to his team so they can check it for "emphasis and content." On the surface of things, nothing particularly important seems to be happening.

But is this really the case? Just as the meeting is about to begin, Bill Andrews interrupts himself to make some administrative arrangements, set schedules, and so on. Andrews is getting his business done — all in a democratic setting. In fact, many of the most important moves seem to happen almost parenthetically; things are happening in the "white spaces" between the printed formal behavior.

One possible analysis of this behavior is that the meeting is essentially a tribal assembly in which the attending managers are reassured that they are "on the team." This line of argument follows the idea of an executive meeting proposed by Anthony Jay in his article, "How to Run a Meeting."[2] In this article Jay sees one of the meeting's functions as the reestablishing of tribal commitment – a kind of giving and receiving homage that is a necessary part of executive life.

DRAMA AND TRAUMA: REIGNING AND REINING

While referring a matter to a committee can dilute authority, diffuse responsibility, and delay decisions, meetings do fulfill a deep human need. According to Anthony Jay, human resources executives should be familiar with the functions that make a meeting superior to more recent communication devices:

- A meeting provides a simple definition of the team, the group, or the unit. Those present belong to it; those absent do not.
- A meeting is the place where the group revises, updates, and adds to what it knows as a group. An enormous amount of material can be left unsaid that would have to be made explicit to an outsider.
- A meeting helps every individual understand both the collective aim of the group and the way in which every individual's work contributes to the group's success.
- A meeting creates a commitment in all present. Once something has been decided, even if you originally argued against it, your membership in the group creates an obligation to accept the decision.
- A meeting is very often the only occasion on which the team or group actually exists and works as a group.
- A meeting is a status arena. People are and should be concerned with their status relative to the other members in a group.
- To do all these things means drama, catharsis, therapy, and trauma – all of which are revealed on video.[3]

The whole process can be quite subtle. For example, how does a CEO get advice? Some have a "Kitchen Cabinet," but more chief executives work with a formal committee that somehow facilitates the CEO's actions without preempting his or her authority. The CEO reigns; his top management committee "reins." If these committees are handled properly, good things can happen. In their article "How CEOs Use Top Management Committees", Richard F. Vancil and Charles H. Green point out that:

> Formal committees also help to bind senior officers into a corporate management team. Most top executives work toward this end – in part by arranging social activities and corporate retreats in addition to holding regular meetings. The meetings themselves create, over time, a large base of shared experiences. As committee members work together, discussion becomes more efficient, a common database evolves, a shared jargon develops, and biases become clear. Managers who have been through many wars together can handle a heavy agenda because they need not waste a lot of time trying to understand each other. In times of crisis, a well-organized top management team can mobilize corporate resources quickly.[4]

Most CEO's use high-level committees for drama and trauma that create a calendar-driven series of events; this keeps those who report to them off balance but productive. Top management committees have a "continual agenda" that keeps executives under review. Such committees become expert in diagnosing ill-defined issues.

CREATING AN IMAGE OF ACTION

We have seen that the drama of these meetings gives expression to subtle and elusive forces that defy logical explanation. A meeting, when properly exercised, always induces an imaginative response that participants find startling, vivid, and exciting. The essential ingredient of any meeting is drama linked to conflict. This conflict may take several forms: an enemy to be defeated, a contract to be signed, a production quota to be beaten, and so forth. Whatever the issue, the people in the meeting must face choices and make decisions – in other words, they must take action. Getting involved in a meeting means getting a slice of this action. The action may involve negotiation, hiring or firing people, or simply providing verbal support. Such action will need more than just "a good line"; it will require strong verbal communication that helps to resolve the conflict. Ineffective managers may be good at "shooting a line," but they cannot follow through with action. For effective managers, talk by itself is not enough; the talk must advance the action.

When viewed from a dramatic perspective, the chairman's function is to induce an imaginative response, and the other actors in turn receive not an answer to a question but an experience. The art of meeting management allows the chairman to develop a complex and captivating ambience. Such an ambience is not easily defined; nevertheless, it helps him get the action he wants. This executive style creates an image of action, of force, of probabilities controlled. The image sets the scene, fixing the action and determining the choice of the other actors.

THE POWER OF NONVERBAL COMMUNICATION

How can you tell whether an executive you have just met will be hostile or friendly? Studies reveal that the answer lies not only in spoken words but also in the vocal tones, facial expressions, and body postures that emerge during the initial conversation. The nonverbal element is a message that apparently carries more weight than the actual words.

The ways people look at each other reveal more than most people realize. The right amount of eye contact can determine who is going to be the dominant person in an exchange; for example, a committee member has a way of signaling an intent to claim the floor. People can instantly assert their position in the pecking hierarchy by the exchange of a single glance. One must be able to see the other person's eyes to know when he or she intends to start or stop; without this kind of feedback, it is difficult to synchronize the conversation. Furthermore, studies show that:

- People move into positions in which they can see better in order to dominate the conversation.
- Women executives make more use of visual feedback than men.
- Executives in general make more eye contact when listening.
- Eye contact promotes good relations only when it is associated with a friendly facial expression.
- Executives tend to look away when talking, especially when exceeding their "allotted time."
- Different ethnic groups use eye expressions in different ways.
- In meetings, members direct more comments to people seated opposite them than to people seated adjacent to them; when a strong leader is present, however, members direct their comments to adjacent individuals rather than to opposite ones.

Posture is also important; a person can establish dominance by throwing his or her head back and speaking in a loud voice. On the other hand, people who put their hands behind their backs while being addressed may be seen as taking a subordinate role.

THE "HOLY IDIOT" DEFENSE

A surprising number of executive meetings are either left unchaired or are chaired by a relatively junior manager (the second-in-command or an organization development specialist). These junior managers' formats seem to give top management more space to play around with. In one exercise, the OD person in charge tried to protect his "top dog" boss by ruling a vice-president out of order. Quick as a flash, the two parties he was trying to separate allied themselves against the

OD man. Strangely enough, however, the OD man seemed to relish his emergent role and promptly told a joke on himself; furthermore, everybody seemed to appreciate his capacity for self-vilification. The OD man, caught in a double bind, simply moved from the role of scapegoat into the role of "holy idiot," thereby achieving an important rapprochement.

Scientific analysis of the events in an executive meeting reveal clearly that a large proportion of conflict is expressed in these get-togethers. A good manager will use humor to reduce the tension.

Time after time, videos show that humor, especially irony, is particularly important. The non-linear logic of the right brain must be brought into play. Executives, even good ones, often fail simply because they have lost their sense of the ridiculous.

CONCLUSION

To win or even to survive in meetings at the top, managers may have to use a more sophisticated game strategy. To develop such a strategy, they can follow debates, observe the techniques of motion picture and television actors, and examine their own and others' meeting behavior. Above all, to participate effectively in executive meetings, managers must understand their own style, recognize the "script," figure out the roles, watch the action, and keep up with the pace. In short, to avoid trauma, they should join in the drama.

References

1. G.A. Miller (1977) *Spontaneous Apprentices: Children and Language*. Seabury Press.
2. A. Jay (March–April 1976) "How to Run a Meeting." *Harvard Business Review*.
3. *Ibid.*, pp. 43–57.
4. R.F. Vancil and C.H. Green (January–February 1984) "How CEOs Use Top Management Committees." *Harvard Business Review*, p. 66.

GOODBYE TO GROUP ASSEMBLY*

Jan Enqvist

Group assembly, the production method that used to egg on the weaker workers to produce on a par with their stronger colleagues, has come to an end. Now everybody can work at his own pace – or her, since most of these workers are women. Robots or automats do the monotonous and heavy jobs. Manual final assembly exists only for light parts on the engine blocks, which come – vertically adjustable, turnable and tiltable – on loop-controlled assembly carts.

The new method of production, which also provides for easy shifting between some 40 engine models, was introduced at Saab-Scania's engine plant at Södertölie during the summer vacation period of 1983. It will, hopefully, mark the end of stress and muscular pain in female assembly workers.

The new production line – which cost about SEK 20 million ($2.5 million) – is now in full swing. But there are of course no sure signs yet that it too will not cause load injuries. During the 12 years that the old system – the once much-lauded group assembly system – was in operation, it took one or two years for load injuries to develop in new employees. The only thing that can be said with absolute certainty today is that the new plant is probably better!

---

* From *Arbetsmiljö: Working Environment*, 1984. Published by the Swedish Work Environment Association. Reprinted by permission of the publisher.

"It will take a couple of years before we know if the assembly workers will escape load injuries," says Inga Lundblad, industrial physician at Saab-Scania.

It is the final assembly of small parts that may cause trouble. The workers have to stand still a lot, and stretch to reach tools hanging on a stand that looks like a Christmas tree.

MAXIMUM PRODUCTIVITY

The old system with self-governing groups was introduced in 1971. In those days it was considered a miracle of progressive thinking. From a main conveyer, the engine blocks were brought out on seven smaller loops, each with room for four engines – and four assemblers. The workers were surrounded by stands for engine parts which formed their workplace. They worked together, organized the jobs themselves, and rotated the tasks among themselves in order to reduce monotony, increase independence and make the production as immune as possible to absences.

This system had its advantages over conventional assembly line production. The workers liked it: they stayed on the job longer, got to know each other better, had a chance to talk with each other while working and could break when they wanted. They had the option of assembling an entire engine individually or splitting up the job between themselves.

The pattern that developed was that each worker chose to assemble as many parts as she could, mostly the entire engine. The system resulted in high productivity and a low rejection percentage.

Each worker could – and should – do 11 engines per shift. After the model had been simplified, this number was increased to 14. If the worker did not manage this, she suffered no wage deduction. Instead, a discussion was started about the reasons for her failure and what could be done about it.

The system implied that if the working pace was accelerated, everybody could relax at the end of the shift, sometimes for two hours or more. This was many women's only real break in the day, since at home the kids and the household chores were waiting. Nobody was allowed to leave before the end of the shift.

Gradually, the pace was speeded up because the workers in the groups egged each other on. When a worker had finished an engine she could not push it on to the conveyer and start working on a new block until the workers in front of her had finished their engines.

WOMEN IN THE RISK ZONE

Not all women could cope with the prevailing working pace; and in the long run, even the strongest ones may not have been able to do so. The abnormally high pace resulted in the use of a lot of sick-leave. The workers complained about neck, shoulder, and arm pains. The company physiotherapists got a lot of work, particularly because the women delayed reporting problems to the company health service. They were afraid of being placed on other jobs or perhaps losing their jobs.

Transfers to new jobs and early retirements were other signs that the group assembly was not a healthy workplace.

Working in cooperation with the company health service, a team of independent researchers came in to investigate what could be done about these problems.

"Our first task was to locate the women who might be in for trouble next," said Bengt Edgren, one of the researchers. "We tried using a chart where the worker could estimate and tick off her strain. We had two control groups for comparison. One group consisted of women who had jobs similar to those of the group assemblers.

"But it didn't work out as we had expected. Self-estimation of strain was apparently not a good way of finding women in the risk zone. The assembly group women did not report any strain. They repressed their feelings of strain as a result of the competition within and between the groups. This, at least, was our hypothesis. It was supported by other evidence as well."

The other evidence Bengt Edgren had in mind

is the findings from experiments with people on exercise bikes. The cyclists are told to adjust the bike to a load that they themselves regard as requiring one-half of their strength. If, instead, the leader of the experiment makes the adjustment and sets the load at exactly the same value, the subjects feel that they have to use more than one-half of their strength. Thus, if you yourself are in control you feel less strain than if others are, even if the load is identical.

ONE-FOURTH ON SICK LEAVE

The next step in the researchers' efforts to find "risk women" was a large enquiry covering all Saab-Scania employees working in engine assembly – not only in group assembly. The purpose was to find a link between problems on the job and outside it.

"We found no positive connection at all." Bengt Edgren said. "The only thing was that those who had had assembly work before seemed to cope better than those who had not."

At the time of the interviews, over one-fourth of the group assemblers had been on sick-leave for either neck, shoulder or arm complaints for an average of nine months. Only one of the 28 other assemblers was on sick leave.

The third step was to come to grips with the high working pace which the researchers now strongly suspected to be the underlying cause of the troubles. If the pace is high even a "light" job becomes strenuous.

"The company thought it would be possible to slow down the working pace. But the union was against this and argued instead that the work was too heavy. Still, none of the individual work operations could be proved to be too heavy, though it was difficult to say anything definite about the totality."

CHEATING

Finally, the assemblers agreed to voluntarily check the working pace. During six weeks they would work at a pace that would spread the work equally over the entire working day. During the six following weeks, they would work as usual, and then again for six weeks at a controlled pace, and so on.

"And what happened? Well, everybody worked just as before! They put the control system out of operation by cheating," Bengt Edgren said.

It is apparent that the production system in combination with group psychological phenomena – competition, above all – releases powers in us that make us work faster than is healthy. And it is not possible to curb these forces by agreements to keep the working pace down.

The last step was to test the strength of the workers in different ways so as to find those who were in the risk zone, if possible. Both static and dynamic tests were used. The static tests were carried out by Prof. Asa Kihlbom of Sweden's National Board of Occupational Safety and Health.

One of the dynamic tests was to pedal an exercise bike at a certain pace – using the arms. First, the workers were to lower the load from "too high" to one that they thought felt good. Then they were to increase the load from "too low" to one that felt good. The load that "felt good" turned out to be stable and constant. The conclusion is that for every person there is a load level that is adequate for a certain job. This is in accordance with earlier findings.

SELF-COMPETING

The researchers repeated these strength tests after about a year. "Then we found the 'high risk girls'," Bengt Edgren said. "The women whose problems had become worse belonged to the weaker portion of the workforce, but they had chosen a load on the exercise bike as high as the stronger women. It is not clear if they did this because they were used to a certain pace or because they have a high level of ambition.

"Strong and lazy is the thing to be," Bengt Edgren added. "That's the way to avoid injuries due to wear. But if you are weak and ambitious you run a risk of acquiring such injuries."

All this does not prove that the pressure from

the fastest workers and the lure of a large break at the end of the day were the only factors that speeded up the working pace in the group assembly. Perhaps some workers compete with themselves? If this is so, it is a factor that has not been eliminated in the new plant.

The findings of the researchers may, however, warrant the following recommendation: assembly workers should work at their own pace.

Here's how the production goes after the reorganization of the assembly line: pre-assembled engine blocks glide on a roller-conveyer along which robots and automats do certain monotonous jobs (screw driving) and one heavy job (fly-wheel assembly). Thereafter the engines are lifted on to electrically-driven, loop-controlled carts, out of sight of the final assemblers until — by pressing a button — they order them to be brought to their workplaces.

Keeping the engines out of sight eliminates the stress factor of seeing engines waiting in line to be assembled. The engines can be turned and twisted on their carts so that each worker can choose the working position she prefers.

"But essentially it's the same job as before," says Sisko Arminen, a worker on the assembly line. "It has not become more interesting.

"Rather less interesting," she adds, "since we can no longer assemble an entire engine by ourselves. Another drawback is that we have less chance of talking, joking, and laughing with each other than we had before."

THE DEVELOPMENT AND ENFORCEMENT OF GROUP NORMS*

Daniel C. Feldman

Group norms are the informal rules that groups adopt to regulate and regularize group members' behavior. Although these norms are infrequently written down or openly discussed, they often have a powerful, and consistent, influence on group members' behavior (Hackman, 1976).[1]

Most of the theoretical work on group norms has focused on identifying the types of group norms (March, 1954)[2] or on describing their structural characteristics (Jackson, 1966).[3] Empirically, most of the focus has been on examining the impact that norms have on other social phenomena. For example, Seashore (1954)[4] and Schachter, Ellertson, McBride, and Gregory (1951)[5] use the concept of group norms to discuss group cohesiveness; Trist and Bamforth (1951)[6] and Whyte (1955a)[7] use norms to examine production restriction; Janis (1972)[8] and Longley and Pruitt (1980)[9] use norms to illuminate group decision making; and Asch (1951)[10] and Sherif (1936)[11] use norms to examine conformity.

This paper focuses on two frequently overlooked aspects of the group norms literature. First, it examines *why* group norms are enforced. Why do groups desire conformity to these informal rules? Second, it examines *how* group norms develop. Why do some norms develop in one group but not in another? Much of what is known about group norms comes from *post hoc* examination of their impact on outcome variables; much less has been written about how these norms actually develop and why they regulate behavior so strongly.

Understanding how group norms develop and why they are enforced is important for two reasons. First, group norms can play a large role in

---

* "The Development and Enforcement of Group Norms," Daniel C. Feldman (1984) *Academy of Management Review,* Vol. 9(1), pp. 47–53. Used by permission of the author and publisher.

determining whether the group will be productive or not. If the work group feels that management is supportive, groups norms will develop that facilitate – in fact, enhance – group productivity. In contrast, if the work group feels that management is antagonistic, group norms that inhibit and impair group performance are much more likely to develop. Second, managers can play a major role in setting and changing group norms. They can use their influence to set task-facilitative norms; they can monitor whether the group's norms are functional; they can explicitly address counterproductive norms with subordinates. By understanding how norms develop and why norms are enforced, managers can better diagnose the underlying tensions and problems their groups are facing, and they can help the group develop more effective behavior patterns.

WHY NORMS ARE ENFORCED

As Shaw (1981)[12] suggests, a group does not establish or enforce norms about every conceivable situation. Norms are formed and enforced only with respect to behaviors that have some significance for the group. The frequent distinction between task maintenance duties and social maintenance duties helps explain why groups bring selected behaviors under normative control.

Groups, like individuals, try to operate in such a way that they maximize their chances for task success and minimize their chances of task failure. First of all, a group will enforce norms that facilitate its very survival. It will try to protect itself from interference from groups external to the organization or harassment from groups internal to the organization. Second, the group will want to increase the predictability of group members' behaviors. Norms provide a basis for predicting the behavior of others, thus enabling group members to anticipate each other's actions and to prepare quick and appropriate responses (Shaw, 1981; Kiesler & Kiesler, 1970).[13]

In addition, groups want to ensure the satisfaction of their members and prevent as much interpersonal discomfort as possible. Thus, groups also will enforce norms that help the group avoid embarrassing interpersonal problems. Certain topics of conversation might be sanctioned, and certain types of social interaction might be openly discouraged. Moreover, norms serve an expressive function for groups (Katz & Kahn, 1978).[14] Enforcing group norms gives group members a chance to express what their central values are, and to clarify what is distinctive about the group and central to its identity (Hackman, 1976).[15]

Each of these four conditions under which group norms are most likely to be enforced is discussed in more detail below.

(1) *Norms are likely to be enforced if they facilitate group survival.* A group will enforce norms that protect it from interference or harassment by members of other groups. For instance, a group might develop a norm not to discuss its salaries with members of other groups in the organization, so that attention will not be brought to pay inequities in its favor. Groups might also have norms about not discussing internal problems with members of other units. Such discussions might boomerang at a later date if other groups use the information to develop a better competitive strategy against the group.

Enforcing group norms also makes clear what the "boundaries" of the group are. As a result of observation of deviant behavior and the consequences that ensue, other group members are reminded of the *range* of behavior that is acceptable to the group (Dentler & Erikson, 1959).[16] The norms about productivity that frequently develop among piecerate workers are illustrative here. By observing a series of incidents (a person produces 50 widgets and is praised; a person produces 60 widgets and receives sharp teasing; a person produces 70 widgets and is ostracized), group members learn the limits of the group's patience: "This far, and no further." The group is less likely to be "successful" (i.e., continue to sustain the low productivity expectations of management) if it allows its jobs to be reevaluated.

The literature on conformity and deviance is consistent with this observation. The group is more likely to reject the person who violates group norms when the deviant has not been a "good" group member previously (Hollander, 1958, 1964).[17] Individuals can generate "idiosyncrasy credits" with other group members by contributing effectively to the attainment of group goals. Individuals expend these credits when they perform poorly or dysfunctionally at work. When a group member no longer has a positive "balance" of credits to draw on when he or she deviates, the group is much more likely to reject that deviant (Hollander, 1961).[18]

Moreover, the group is more likely to reject the deviant when the group is failing in meeting its goals successfully. When the group is successful, it can afford to be charitable or tolerant towards deviant behavior. The group may disapprove, but it has some margin for error. When the group is faced with failure, the deviance is much more sharply punished. Any behavior that negatively influences the success of the group becomes much more salient and threatening to group members (Alvarez, 1968; Wiggins, Dill, & Schwartz, 1965).[19]

(2) *Norms are likely to be enforced if they simplify, or make predictable, what behavior is expected of group members.* If each member of the group had to decide individually how to behave in each interaction, much time would be lost performing routine activities. Moreover, individuals would have more trouble predicting the behaviors of others and responding correctly. Norms enable group members to anticipate each other's actions and to prepare the most appropriate response in the most timely manner (Hackman, 1976; Shaw, 1981).[20]

For instance, when attending group meetings in which proposals are presented and suggestions are requested, do the presenters really want feedback or are they simply going through the motions? Groups may develop norms that reduce this uncertainty and provide a clearer course of action: for example, make suggestions in small, informal meetings but not in large, formal meetings.

Another example comes from norms that regulate social behavior. For instance, when colleagues go out for lunch together, there can be some awkwardness about how to split the bill at the end of the meal. A group may develop a norm that gives some highly predictable or simple way of behaving: for example, split evenly, take turns picking up the tab, or pay for what each ordered.

Norms also may reinforce specific individual members' roles. A number of different roles might emerge in groups. These roles are simply expectations that are shared by group members regarding who is to carry out what types of activities under what circumstances (Bales & Slater, 1955).[21] Although groups obviously create pressure toward uniformity among members, there also is a tendency for groups to create and maintain *diversity* among members (Hackman, 1976).[22] For instance, a group might have one person whom others expect to break the tension when tempers become too hot. Another group member might be expected to keep track of what is going on in other parts of the organization. A third member might be expected to take care of the "creature" needs of the group – making the coffee, making dinner reservations, and so on. A fourth member might be expected by others to take notes, keep minutes, or maintain files.

None of these roles are *formal* duties, but they are activities that the group needs accomplished and has somehow parcelled out among members. If the role expectations are not met, some important jobs might not get done, or other group members might have to take on additional responsibilities. Moreover, such role assignments reduce individual members' ambiguities about what is expected specifically of them. It is important to note, though, that who takes what role in a group also is highly influenced by individuals' personal needs. The person with a high need for structure often wants to be in the note-taking role to control the structuring activity in the group; the person who breaks the tension might dislike conflict and uses the role to circumvent it.

(3) *Norms are likely to be enforced if they help the group avoid embarrassing interpersonal problems.* Goffman's work on "facework" gives some

insight on this point. Goffman (1955)[23] argues that each person in a group has a "face" he or she presents to other members of a group. This "face" is analogous to what one would call "self-image," the person's perceptions of himself or herself and how he or she would like to be seen by others. Groups want to insure that no one's self-image is damaged, called into question, or embarrassed. Consequently, the group will establish norms that discourage topics of conversation or situations in which face is too likely to be inadvertantly broken. For instance, groups might develop norms about not discussing romantic involvements (so that differences in moral values do not become salient) or about not getting together socially in people's homes (so that differences in taste or income do not become salient).

A good illustration of Goffman's facework occurs in the classroom. There is always palpable tension in a room when either a class is totally unprepared to discuss a case or a professor is totally unprepared to lecture or lead the discussion. One part of the awkwardness stems from the inability of the other partner in the interaction to behave as he or she is prepared to or would like to behave. The professor cannot teach if the students are not prepared, and the students cannot learn if the professors are not teaching. Another part of the awkwardness, though, stems from self-images being called into question. Although faculty are aware that not all students are serious scholars, the situation is difficult to handle if the class as a group does not even show a pretense of wanting to learn. Although students are aware that many faculty are mainly interested in research and consulting, there is a problem if the professor does not even show a pretense of caring to teach. Norms almost always develop between professor and students about what level of preparation and interest is expected by the other because both parties want to avoid awkward confrontations.

(4) *Norms are likely to be enforced if they express the central values of the group and clarify what is distinctive about the group's identity.* Norms can provide the social justification for group activities to its members (Katz & Kahn, 1978).[24] When the production group labels rate-busting deviant, it says: "We care more about maximizing group security than about individual profits." Group norms also convey what is distinctive about the group to outsiders. When an advertising agency labels unstylish clothes deviant, it says: "We think of ourselves, personally and professionally, as trend-setters, and being fashionably dressed conveys that to our clients and our public."

One of the key expressive functions of group norms is to define and legitimate the power of the group itself over individual members (Katz & Kahn, 1978).[25] When groups punish norm infraction, they reinforce in the minds of group members the authority of the group. Here, too, the literature on group deviance sheds some light on the issue at hand.

It has been noted frequently that the amount of deviance in a group is rather small (Erikson, 1966; Schur, 1965).[26] The group uses norm enforcement to show the *strength* of the group. However, if a behavior becomes so widespread that it becomes impossible to control, then the labeling of the widespread behavior as deviance becomes problematic. It simply reminds members of the *weakness* of the group. At this point, the group will redefine what is deviant more narrowly, or it will define its job as that of keeping deviance *within bounds* rather than that of obliterating it altogether. For example, though drug use is and always has been illegal, the widespread use of drugs has led to changes in law enforcement over time. A greater distinction now is made between "hard" drugs and other controlled substances; less penalty is given to those apprehended with small amounts than large amounts; greater attention is focused on capturing large scale smugglers and traffickers than the occasional user. A group, unconsciously if not consciously, learns how much behavior it is capable of labeling deviant *and* punishing effectively.

Finally, this expressive function of group norms can be seen nicely in circumstances in which there is an inconsistency between what group members *say* is the group norm and how people actually *behave*. For instance, sometimes groups will engage in a lot of rhetoric about how much independence its managers are allowed and how much it values entrepreneurial effort; yet the harder data suggest that the more conservative, deferring, or dependent managers get rewarded. Such an inconsistency can reflect conflicts among the group's expressed values. First, the group can be ambivalent about independence; the group knows it needs to encourage more entrepreneurial efforts to flourish, but such efforts create competition and threaten the status quo. Second, the inconsistency can reveal major subgroup differences. Some people may value and encourage entrepreneurial behavior, but others do not – and the latter may control the group's rewards. Third, the inconsistency can reveal a source of the group's self-consciousness, a dichotomy between what the group is really like and how it would like to be perceived. The group may realize that it is too conservative, yet be unable or too frightened to address its problem. The expressed group norm allows the group members a chance to present a "face" to each other and to outsiders that is more socially desirable than reality.

HOW GROUP NORMS DEVELOP

Norms usually develop gradually and informally as group members learn what behaviors are necessary for the group to function more effectively. However, it also is possible for the norm development process to be short-cut by a critical event in the group or by conscious group decision (Hackman, 1976).[27]

Most norms develop in one or more of the following four ways: explicit statements by supervisors or co-workers; critical events in the group's history; primacy; and carry-over behaviors from past situations.

(1) *Explicit statements by supervisors or co-workers.* Norms that facilitate group survival or task success often are set by the leader of the group or powerful members (Whyte, 1955b).[28] For instance, a group leader might explicitly set norms about not drinking at lunch because subordinates who have been drinking are more likely to have problems dealing competently with clients and top management or they are more likely to have accidents at work. The group leader might also set norms about lateness, personal phone calls, and long coffee breaks if too much productivity is lost as a result of time away from the work place.

Explicit statements by supervisors also can increase the predictability of group members' behavior. For instance, supervisors might have particular preferences for a way of analyzing problems or presenting reports. Strong norms will be set to ensure compliance with these preferences. Consequently, supervisors will have increased certainty about receiving work in the format requested, so they can plan accordingly; workers will have increased certainty about what is expected, so they will not have to outguess their boss or redo their projects.

Managers or important group members also can define the specific role expectations of individual group members. For instance, a supervisor or a co-worker might go up to a new recruit after a meeting to give the proverbial advice: "New recruits should be seen and not heard." The senior group member might be trying to prevent the new recruit from appearing brash or incompetent or from embarrassing other group members. Such interventions set specific role expectations for the new group member.

Norms that cater to supervisor preferences also are frequently established even if they are not objectively necessary to task accomplishment. For example, although organizational norms may be very democratic in terms of everybody calling each other by their first names, some managers have strong preferences about being called Mr., Ms., or Mrs. Although the form of address used in the work group does not influence group effectiveness, complying with the norm bears little cost to the group member, whereas noncompliance could cause daily friction with the supervisor. Such norms help group members avoid embarrassing interpersonal interactions with their managers.

Fourth, norms set explicitly by the supervisor frequently express the central values of the group. For instance, a dean can set very strong norms about faculty keeping office hours and being on campus daily. Such norms reaffirm to members of the academic community their teaching and service obligations, and they send signals to individuals outside the college about what is valued in faculty behavior or distinctive about the school. A dean also could set norms that allow faculty to consult or do executive development two or three days a week. Such norms, too, legitimate other types of faculty behavior and send signals to both insiders and outsiders about some central values of the college.

(2) *Critical events in the group's history.* At times there is a critical event in the group's history that established an important precedent. For instance, a group member might have discussed hiring plans with members of other units in the organization, and as a result new positions were lost or there was increased competition for good applicants. Such indiscretion can substantially hinder the survival and task success of the group; very likely the offender will be either formally censured or informally rebuked. As a result of such an incident, norms about secrecy might develop that will protect the group in similar situations in the future.

An example from Janis's *Victims of Groupthink* (1972)[29] also illustrates this point nicely. One of President Kennedy's closest advisors, Arthur Schlesinger, Jr., had serious reservations about the Bay of Pigs invasion and presented his strong objections to the Bay of Pigs plan in a memorandum to Kennedy and Secretary of State Dean Rusk. However, Schlesinger was pressured by the President's brother, Attorney General Robert Kennedy, to keep his objections to himself. Remarked Robert Kennedy to Schlesinger: "You may be right or you may be wrong, but the President has made his mind up. Don't push it any further. Now is the time for everyone to help him all they can." Such critical events led group members to silence their views and set up group norms about the bounds of disagreeing with the President.

Sometimes group norms can be set by a conscious decision of a group after a particularly good or bad experience the group has had. To illustrate, a group might have had a particularly constructive meeting and be very pleased with how much it accomplished. Several people might say, "I think the reason we got so much accomplished today is that we met really early in the morning before the rest of the staff showed up and the phone started ringing. Let's try to continue to meet at 7:30 a.m." Others might agree, and the norm is set. On the other hand, if a group notices it accomplished way too little in a meeting, it might openly discuss setting norms to cut down on ineffective behavior (e.g., having an agenda, not interrupting others while they are talking). Such norms develop to facilitate task success and to reduce uncertainty about what is expected from each individual in the group.

Critical events also can identify awkward interpersonal situations that need to be avoided in the future. For instance, a divorce between two people working in the same group might have caused a lot of acrimony and hard feeling in a unit, not only between the husband and wife but also among various other group members who got involved in the marital problems. After the unpleasant divorce, a group might develop a norm about not hiring spouses to avoid having to deal with such interpersonal problems in the future.

Finally, critical events also can give rise to norms that express the central, or distinctive, values of the group. When a peer review panel finds a physician or lawyer guilty of malpractice or malfeasance, first it establishes (or reaffirms) the rights of professionals to evaluate and criticize the professional behavior of their colleagues. Moreover, it clarifies what behaviors are inconsistent with the group's self-image or its values. When a faculty committee votes on a candidate's tenure, it, too, asserts the legitimacy of influence of senior faculty over junior faculty. In addition, it sends (hopefully) clear messages to junior faculty about its values in terms of quality of research, teaching, and service. There are important "announcement effects" of peer reviews; internal group members carefully reexamine the group's values, and outsiders draw interferences about the character of the group from such critical decisions.

(3) *Primacy.* The first behavior pattern that emerges in a group often sets group expectations. If the first group meeting is marked by very formal interaction between supervisors and subordinates, then the group often expects future meetings to be conducted in the same way. Where people sit in meetings or rooms frequently is developed through primacy. People generally continue to sit in the same seats they sat in at their first meeting. Most friendship groups of students develop their own "turf" in a lecture hall and are surprised/dismayed when an interloper takes "their" seats.

Norms that develop through primacy often do so to simplify, or make predictable, what behavior is expected of group members. There may be very little task impact from where people sit in meetings or how formal interactions are. However, norms develop about such behaviors to make life much more routine and predictable. Every time a group member enters a room, he or she does not have to "decide" where to sit or how formally to behave. Moreover, he or she also is much more certain about how other group members will behave.

(4) *Carry-over behaviors from past situations.* Many group norms in organizations emerge because individual group members bring set expectations with them from other work groups in other organizations. Lawyers expect to behave towards clients in Organization I (e.g., confidentiality, setting fees) as they behaved towards those in Organization II. Doctors expect to behave toward patients in Hospital I (e.g., "bedside manner," professional distance) as they behaved in Hospital II. Accountants expect to behave towards colleagues at Firm I (e.g., dress code, adherence to statutes) as they behaved towards those at Firm II. In fact, much of what goes on in professional schools is giving new members of the profession the same standards and norms of behavior that practitioners in the field hold.

Such carry-over of individual behaviors from past situations can increase the predictability of group members' behaviors in new settings and facilitate task accomplishment. For instance, students and professors bring with them fairly constant sets of expectations from class to class. As a result, students do not have to relearn continually their roles from class to class; they know, for instance, if they come in late to take a seat quietly at the back of the room without being told. Professors also do not have to relearn continually their roles; they know, for instance, not to mumble, scribble in small print on the blackboard, or be vague when making course assignments. In addition, presumably the most task-successful norms will be the ones carried over from organization to organization.

Moreover, such carry-over norms help avoid embarrassing interpersonal situations. Individuals are more likely to know which conversations and actions provoke annoyance, irritation, or embarrassment to their colleagues. Finally, when groups carry over norms from one organization to another, they also clarify what is distinctive about the occupational or professional role. When lawyers maintain strict rules of confidentiality, when doctors maintain a consistent professional distance with patients, when accountants present a very formal physical appearance, they all assert: "These are the standards we sustain *independent* of what we could 'get away with' in this organization. This is *our* self-concept."

SUMMARY

Norms generally are enforced only for behaviors that are viewed as important by most group members. Groups do not have the time or energy to regulate each and every action of individual members. Only those behaviors that ensure group survival, facilitate task accomplishment, contribute to group morale, or express the group's central values are likely to be brought under normative control. Norms that reflect these group needs will develop through explicit statements of supervisors, critical events in the group's history, primary, or carry-over behaviors from past situations.

Empirical research on norm development and enforcement has substantially lagged behind descriptive and theoretical work. In large part, this may be due to the methodological problems of measuring norms and getting enough data points either across time or across groups. Until such time as empirical work progresses, however, the usefulness of group norms as a predictive concept, rather than as a *post hoc* explanatory device, will be severely limited. Moreover, until it is known more concretely why norms develop and why they are strongly enforced, attempts to *change* group norms will remain haphazard and difficult to accomplish.

References

1. J.R. Hackman (1976) "Group Influences on Individuals," in M. Dunnette, ed., *Handbook of Industrial and Organizational Psychology*. Chicago: Rand McNally, pp. 1455–1525.
2. J. March (1954) "Group Norms and the Active Minority." *American Sociological Review*, 19, pp. 733–741.
3. J.A. Jackson (1966) "A Conceptual and Measurement Model for Norms and Roles." *Pacific Sociological Review*, 9, pp. 35–47.
4. S. Seashore (1954) *Group Cohesiveness in the Industrial Work Group*. Ann Arbor: Institute for Social Research, University of Michigan.
5. S. Schachter, N. Ellerston, D. McBride and D. Gregory (1951) "An Experimental Study of Cohesiveness and Productivity." *Human Relations*, 4, pp. 229–258.
6. E.L. Trist and K.W. Bamforth (1951) "Some Social and Psychological Consequences of the Longwall Method of Coal-Getting." *Human Relations*, 4, pp. 1–38.
7. W.F. Whyte (1955a) *Money and Motivation*. New York: Harper.
8. I. Janis (1972) *Victims of Groupthink: A Psychological Study of Foreign Policy Decisions and Fiascos*. New York: Houghton-Mifflin.
9. J. Longley and D.C. Pruitt (1980) "Groupthink: A Critique of Janis' Theory," in Ladd Wheeler, ed., *Review of Personality and Social Psychology*. Beverly Hills: Sage, pp. 74–93.
10. S. Asch (1951) "Effects of Group Pressure upon the Modification and Distortion of Judgement," in M.H. Guetzkow, ed., *Groups, Leadership and Men*. Pittsburgh: Carnegie, pp. 117–190.
11. M. Sherif (1936) *The Psychology of Social Norms*. New York: Harper.
12. M.E. Shaw (1981) *Group Dynamics*, 3rd ed. New York: McGraw-Hill.
13. M.E. Shaw (1981) *op. cit*. C.A. Kiesler and S.B. Kiesler (1970) *Conformity*. Reading, MA: Addison-Wesley.
14. D. Katz and R.L. Kahn (1978) *The Social Psychology of Organizations*, 2nd ed. New York: Wiley.
15. J.R. Hackman (1976) *op. cit*.
16. R.A. Dentler and K.T. Erikson (1959) "The Functions of Deviance in Groups." *Social Problems*, 7, pp. 98–107.
17. E.P. Hollander (1958) "Conformity, Status and Idiosyncrasy Credit," *Psychological Review*, 65, pp. 117–127. E.P. Hollander (1964) *Leaders, Groups, and Influence*. New York: Oxford University Press.
18. E.P. Hollander (1961) "Some Effects of Perceived Status on Responses to Innovative Behavior." *Journal of Abnormal and Social Psychology*, 63, pp. 247–250.
19. R. Alvarez (1968) "Informal Reactions to Deviance in Simulated Work Organizations: A Laboratory Experiment." *American Sociological Review*, 33, pp. 895–912. J.A. Wiggins, F. Dill and R.D. Schwartz (1965) "On Status Liability." *Sociometry*, 28, pp. 197–209.
20. J.R. Hackman (1976) *op. cit*.
21. R.F. Bales and P.E. Slater (1955) "Role Dif-

ferentiation in Small Groups," in T. Parsons, R.F. Bales, J. Olds, M. Zelditch, and P.E. Slater, eds., *Family, Socialization and Interaction Process*. Glencoe, IL: The Free Press, pp. 35–131.
22. J.R. Hackman (1976) *op. cit.*
23. E. Goffman (1955) "On Face-Work: An Analysis of Ritual Elements in Social Interaction." *Psychiatry*, 18, pp. 213–231.
24. D. Katz and R.L. Kahn (1978) *op. cit.* M.E. Shaw (1981) *op. cit.*
25. *Ibid.*
26. K.T. Erikson (1966) *Wayward Puritans*. New York: Wiley. E.M. Schur (1965) *Crimes Without Victims*. Englewood Cliffs, NJ: Prentice-Hall.
27. J.R. Hackman (1976) *op. cit.*
28. W.F. Whyte (1955b) *Street Corner Society*. Chicago: University of Chicago Press.
29. J. Janis (1972) *op. cit.*

CASE

THE CASE OF THE CHANGING CAGE*

C.E. Richard

H.F. Dubyns

PART I

The voucher-check filing unit was a work unit in the home office of the Atlantic Insurance Company. The assigned task of the unit was to file checks and vouchers written by the company as they were cashed and returned. This filing was the necessary foundation for the main function of the unit: locating any particular check for examination upon demand. There were usually eight to ten requests for specific checks from as many different departments during the day. One of the most frequent reasons checks were requested from the unit was to determine whether checks in payment of claims against the company had been cashed. Thus efficiency in the unit directly affected customer satisfaction with the company. Complaints or inquiries about payments could not be answered with the accuracy and speed conducive to client satisfaction unless the unit could supply the necessary document immediately.

Toward the end of 1952, nine workers manned this unit. There was an assistant (a position equivalent to a foreman in a factory) named Miss Dunn, five other full-time employees, and three part-time workers.

The work area of the unit was well-defined. Walls bounded the unit on three sides. The one exterior wall was pierced by light-admitting north windows. The west interior partition was blank. A door opening into a corridor pierced the south interior partition. The east side of the work area was enclosed by a steel mesh reaching from wall to wall and floor to ceiling. This open metal barrier gave rise to the customary name of the unit – "The Voucher Cage." A sliding door through this mesh gave

---

* Adapted from "Topography and Culture: The Case of the Changing Cage," by Cara E. Richards and Henry F. Dobyns. Reproduced by permission of the Society for Applied Anthropology from *Human Organization* 16(1): 16–20, 1957.

access from the unit's territory to the work area of the rest of the company's agency audit division, of which it was a part, located on the same floor.

The unit's territory was kept inviolate by locks on both doors, fastened at all times. No one not working within the cage was permitted inside unless his name appeared on a special list in the custody of Miss Dunn. The door through the steel mesh was used generally for departmental business. Messengers and runners from other departments usually came to the corridor door and pressed a buzzer for service.

The steel mesh front was reinforced by a rank of metal filing cases where checks were filed. Lined up just inside the barrier, they hid the unit's workers from the view of workers outside their territory, including the section head responsible for overall supervision of this unit according to the company's formal plan of operation.

PART II

On top of the cabinets which were backed against the steel mesh, one of the male employees in the unit neatly stacked pasteboard boxes in which checks were transported to the cage. They were later reused to hold older checks sent into storage. His intention was less getting these boxes out of the way than increasing the effective height of the sight barrier so the section head could not see into the cage "even when he stood up."

The girls stood at the door of the cage that led into the corridor and talked to the messenger boys. The workers also slipped out this door unnoticed to bring in their customary afternoon snack. Inside the cage, the workers sometimes engaged in a good-natured game of rubber band "sniping."

Workers in the cage possessed good capacity to work together consistently and workers outside the cage often expressed envy of those in it because of the "nice people" and friendly atmosphere there. The unit had no apparent difficulty keeping up with its work load.

PART III

For some time prior to 1952 the controller's department of the company had not been able to meet its own standards of efficient service to clients. Company officials felt the primary cause to be spatial. Various divisions of the controller's department were scattered over the entire twenty-two-story company building. Communication between them required phone calls, messengers, or personal visits, all costing time. The spatial separation had not seemed very important when the company's business volume was smaller prior to World War II. But business had grown tremendously since then, and spatial separation appeared increasingly inefficient.

Finally in November of 1952 company officials began to consolidate the controller's department by relocating two divisions together on one floor. One was the agency audit division, which included the voucher-check filing unit. As soon as the decision to move was made, lower-level supervisors were called in to help with planning. Line workers were not consulted, but were kept informed by the assistants of planning progress. Company officials were concerned about the problem of transporting many tons of equipment and some 200 workers from two locations to another single location without disrupting work flow. So the move was planned to occur over a single weekend, using the most efficient resources available. Assistants were kept busy planning positions for files and desks in the new location.

Desks, files, chairs, and even wastebaskets were numbered prior to the move, and relocated according to a master chart checked on the spot by the assistant. Employees were briefed as to where the new location was and which elevators they should take to reach it. The company successfully transported the paraphernalia of the voucher-check filing unit from one floor to another over one weekend. Workers in the cage quit Friday afternoon at the old stand, reported back Monday at the new.

The exterior boundaries of the new cage were still three building walls and the steel mesh, but the new cage possessed only one door – the sliding door through the steel mesh into the work area of the rest of the agency audit division. The territory of the cage had also been reduced in size. An entire bank of filing cabinets had to be left behind in the old location to be taken over by the unit moving there. The new cage was arranged so that there was no longer a row of metal filing cabinets lined up inside the steel mesh obstructing the view into the cage.

PART IV

When the workers in the cage inquired about the removal of the filing cabinets from along the steel mesh fencing, they found that Mr. Burke had insisted that these cabinets be rearranged so his view into the cage would not be obstructed by them. Miss Dunn had tried to retain the cabinets in their prior position, but her efforts had been overridden.

Mr. Burke disapproved of conversation. Since he could see workers conversing in the new cage, he "requested" Miss Dunn to put a stop to all unnecessary talk. Attempts by female clerks to talk to messenger boys brought the wrath of her superior down on Miss Dunn, who was then forced to reprimand the girls.

Mr. Burke also disapproved of an untidy work area, and any boxes of papers which were in sight were a source of annoyance to him. He did not exert supervision directly, but would "request" Miss Dunn to "do something about those boxes." In the new cage, desks had to be completely cleared at the end of the day, in contrast to the work-in-progress piles left out in the old cage. Boxes could not accumulate on top of filing cases.

The custom of afternoon snacking also ran into trouble. Lacking a corridor door, the food-bringers had to venture forth and pack back their snack tray through the work area of the rest of their section, bringing a hitherto unique custom to the attention of workers outside the cage. The latter promptly recognized the desirability of afternoon snacks and began agitation for the same privilege. This annoyed the section head, who forbade workers in the cage from continuing this custom.

PART V

Mr. Burke later made a rule which permitted one worker to leave the new cage at a set time every afternoon to bring up food for the rest. This rigidity irked cage personnel, accustomed to a snack when the mood struck, or none at all. Having made his concession to the cage force, Mr. Burke was unable to prevent workers outside the cage from doing the same thing. What had once been unique to the workers in the cage was now common practice in the section.

Although Miss Dunn never outwardly expressed anything but compliance and approval of superior directives, she exhibited definite signs of anxiety. All the cage workers reacted against Burke's increased domination. When he imposed his decisions upon the voucher check filing unit, he became "Old Grandma" to its personnel. The cage workers sneered at him and ridiculed him behind his back. Workers who formerly had obeyed company policy as a matter of course began to find reasons for loafing and obstructing work in the new cage. One of the changes that took place in the behavior of the workers had to do with their game of rubber band sniping. All knew Mr. Burke would disapprove of this game. It became highly clandestine and fraught with dangers. Yet shooting rubber bands *increased*.

Newly-arrived checks were put out of sight as soon as possible, filed or not. Workers hid unfiled checks, generally stuffing them into desk drawers or unused file drawers. Since boxes were forbidden, there were fewer unused file drawers than there had been in the old cage. So the day's work was sometimes undone when several clerks hastily shoved vouchers and checks indiscriminately into the same file drawer at the end of the day.

Before a worker in the cage filed incoming checks, she measured with her ruler the thickness in inches of each bundle she filed. At the end of each day she totaled her input and reported to Miss Dunn. All incoming checks were measured upon arrival. Thus Miss Dunn had a rough estimate of unit intake compared with file input. Theoretically she was able to tell at any time how much unfiled material she had on hand and how well the unit was keeping up with its task. Despite this running check, when the annual inventory of unfiled checks on hand in the cage was taken at the beginning of the calendar year 1953, a seriously large backlog of unfiled checks was found. To the surprise and dismay of Miss Dunn, the inventory showed the unit to be far behind schedule, filing much more slowly than before the relocation of the cage.

QUESTIONS

1. What was the performance and satisfaction level of the voucher-check filing unit prior to the various changes? What factors contributed to that performance and satisfaction level?
2. How did the various changes (relocation of the work unit and moving the filing cabinets) impact the performance, norms and satisfaction of the group? Explain the group's reaction.
3. If you were Ms. Dunn, how would you improve the situation now that the damage has been done?

PERFECT PIZZERIA*

Lee Neely
James G. Hunt

Perfect Pizzeria in Southville, in deep southern Illinois, is the second largest franchise of the chain in the United States. The headquarters is located in Phoenix, Arizona. Although the business is prospering, employee and managerial problems exist.

Each operation has one manager, an assistant manager, and from two to five night managers. The managers of each pizzeria work under an area supervisor. There are no systematic criteria for being a manager or becoming a manager trainee. The franchise has no formalized training period for the manager. No college education is required. The managers for whom the case observer worked during a four-year period were relatively young (ages 24 to 27) and only one had completed college. They came from the ranks of night managers or assistant managers, or both. The night managers were chosen for their ability to perform the duties of the regular employees. The assistant managers worked a two-hour shift during the luncheon period five days a week to gain knowledge about bookkeeping and management. Those becoming managers remained at that level unless they expressed interest in investing in the business.

The employees were mostly college students, with a few high school students performing the less challenging jobs. Since Perfect Pizzeria was located in an area with few job opportunities, it had a relatively easy task of filling its employee quotas. All the employees, with the exception of the manager, were employed part time. Consequently, they worked for less than the minimum wage.

The Perfect Pizzeria system is devised so that food and beverage costs and profits are computed according to a percentage. If the percentage of food unsold or damaged in any way is very low, the manager gets a bonus. If the percentage is high, the manager does not receive a bonus; rather, he or she receives only his or her normal salary.

There are many ways in which the percentage can fluctuate. Since the manager cannot be in the store 24 hours a day, some employees make up for their paychecks by helping themselves to the food. When a friend comes in to order a pizza, extra ingredients are put on the friend's pizza. Occasional nibbles by 18 to 20 employees throughout the day at the meal table also raise the percentage figure. An occasional bucket of sauce may be spilled or a pizza accidentally burned. Sometimes the wrong size of pizza may be made.

---

* Adapted from a case assignment prepared by Lee Neely for Professor James G. Hunt, Southern Illinois University at Carbondale. The case appears in John E. Dittrich and Robert A. Zawacki, eds., *People and Organizations: Cases in Management and Organizational Behavior*, pp. 126–128. © Business Publications, 1981. All rights reserved. Used by permission.

In the event of an employee mistake or a burned pizza by the oven operator, the expense is supposed to come from the individual. Because of peer pressure, the night manager seldom writes up a bill for the erring employee. Instead, the establishment takes the loss, and the error goes unnoticed until the end of the month when the inventory is taken. That's when the manager finds out that the percentage is high and that there will be no bonus.

In the present instance, the manager took retaliatory measures. Previously, each employee was entitled to a free pizza, salad, and all the soft drinks he or she could drink for every 6 hours of work. The manager raised this figure from 6 to 12 hours of work. However, the employees had received these 6-hour benefits for a long time. Therefore, they simply took advantage of the situation whenever the manager or the assistant was not in the building. Although the night manager theoretically had complete control of the operation in the evenings, he did not command the respect that the manager or assistant manager did. This was because he received the same pay as the regular employees, he could not reprimand other employees, and he was basically the same age or sometimes even younger than the other employees.

Thus, apathy grew within the pizzeria. There seemed to be a further separation between the manager and his workers, who started out as a closely knit group. The manager made no attempt to alleviate the problem, because he felt it would iron itself out. Either the employees that were dissatisfied would quit or they would be content to put up with the new regulations. As it turned out, there was a rash of employee dismissals. The manager had no problem in filling the vacancies with new workers, but the loss of key personnel was costly to the business.

With the large turnover, the manager found that he had to spend more time in the building, supervising and sometimes taking the place of inexperienced workers. This was in direct violation of the franchise regulation, which stated that a manager would act as a supervisor and at no time take part in the actual food preparation. Employees were now placed under strict supervision with the manager working alongside them. The operation no longer worked smoothly because of differences between the remaining experienced workers and the manager concerning the way in which a particular function should be performed.

Within a two-month period, the manager was again free to go back to his office and leave his subordinates in charge of the entire operation. During this two-month period, the percentage had returned to the previous low level, and the manager received a bonus each month. The manager felt that his problems had been resolved and that conditions would remain the same, since the new personnel had been properly trained.

It didn't take long for the new employees to become influenced by the other employees. Immediately after the manager had returned to his supervisory role, the percentage began to rise. This time the manager took a bolder step. He cut out any benefits that the employees had – no free pizzas, salads, or drinks. With the job market at an even lower ebb than usual, most employees were forced to stay. The appointment of a new area supervisor made it impossible for the manager to "work behind the counter," since the supervisor was centrally located in Southville.

The manager tried still another approach to alleviate the rising percentage problem and maintain his bonus. He placed a notice on the bulletin board, stating that if the percentage remained at a high level, a lie detector test would be given to all employees. All those found guilty of taking or purposefully wasting food or drinks would be immediately terminated. This did not have the desired effect on the employees, because they knew if they were all subjected to the test, all would be found guilty and the manager would have to dismiss all of them. This would leave him in a worse situation than ever.

Even before the following month's percentage was calculated, the manager knew it would be high. He had evidently received information from one of the night managers about the employees' feelings toward the notice. What he did not expect was that the percentage would reach an all-time high. That is the state of affairs at the present time.

QUESTIONS

1. What are the group norms of the employees of the Perfect Pizzeria?
2. How effective were the manager's efforts to control the "percentage" and lessen food and beverage costs? Why? What did you think of his plan to use a lie detector?
3. If you became the new manager of this operation, what would you do? If you became the president of this company, what are some things you would do to avoid the problems we see in this case?

EXERCISES

FINDING OUT WHO'S WHO IN THE GROUP

Joe Kelly

Executives spend a great deal of time in meetings. If you want to become skilled in leading meetings, you have to be able to identify the different roles that executives play in these. You can check your skill in this exercise by first doing the exercise on your own and then meeting with your group to compare judgments.

You are attending your first meeting, in the first week of your new job as a Systems Analyst in a company that manufactures snowmobiles. The company has pulled together a bunch of young executives to decide whether to invest in a small company which builds ATVs (all terrain vehicles) but which is trying to develop a model which can be driven legally on the roads. It's all very confusing but certain things are obvious.

The Chairman, Jack Jones, is a young mechanical engineer, an exuberant, energetic man with Robert Redford good looks that are enhanced by aviator-type glasses. His voice is raspy and his comments (most of them are instructions) are so crisp that they border on being brusque. When he speaks, the others sit up and take notice. Two of the group of seven scowl at him and never take their eyes off him.

Jack uses a lot of phrases like: "Let's get the show on the road"; "Check, check, check"; "OK, OK, OK, Okaay"; "Let's bear down on the problem" (everyone grimaces at this); "Are you out to lunch or do you have something to say?"

He coolly evaluates everything, everyone says. He seems to be writing all the time. You are wondering to yourself how he gets away with it. After all you have read about human relations management, he does seem a bit odd. He is too much of a task specialist for you to stomach.

The guy that seems to like Jack Jones best and supports him most is a very different kind of person. Tony Marcello is a very quiet-spoken, thoughtful kind of person who smiles a lot and beams out a lot of good will. You find out later that his nickname is Mr. Clean. He uses a lot of stock phrases to soften Jack's hard lines, including "What Jack is trying to say ——"; "What I like about your idea," and then goes on to build up on it; "I think Bill's point is worth developing."

It all sounds a bit like Dale Carnegie and seems to go over pretty well with the group except for the two guys who do all the scowling when Jack pushes hardest.

What puzzles you most is how a human relations specialist like Tony can work so closely with such a hard nosed, tough, hard hitting, pushy task specialist like Jack.

The guy you like most in the group is a small grizzly looking personnel type named Larry Strange who comes up with some very odd ideas. For example, when they are discussing the engine for the vehicle, he suddenly blurts out, "Does it have pistons?" Everyone looks sort of odd at him, and he follows up with, "What about a Wankel rotary engine?" The group discusses and eventually rejects the Wankel but agrees to explore further the idea of different prime movers including electrical and internal combustion (both gas and diesel). In the process of this discussion, the group agrees to use a belt transmission instead of a propeller shaft.

You notice that the group has an odd procedure attaining agreement on issues. When Jack Jones thinks the group is ready, he always turns to Brenda Raffles and says, "What do you think, Brenda? Will it fly upstairs?"

Brenda is a slight woman in her early thirties. She is a Personal Assistant to the President.

During a coffee break, which Jack allows when people start getting cranky, you overhear the two guys who do all the scowling at Jack say, "Brenda has got a terrible weakness – she is a professional staff person. She has been trained to serve her boss totally and unswervingly." Just then Tony breezes past and comments, "True, but if she says a thing is OK, it's OK."

You, yourself, take very little part in the meeting and when they ask you if you can work out a parts-price program to cost the car, you muff your lines and say, "I don't know. I'll have to take the issue under advice."

Cursing yourself for using "advice" instead of "advisement" you mumble on and end by saying, "I'll try."

When they break off for lunch, Jack, Tony, Larry, and Brenda go out together to eat, as do the two guys who did all the scowling. You go along to the company cafeteria and are joined by the other member of the group who, besides yourself, did little talking.

You ask him who was doing what to whom and he replies by asking you to put the various members into roles. He gives you the following ones to choose from: Task Specialist, Human Relations Specialist, Eccentric, Exemplar, Isolate, Observer, Leader of the Opposition.

A TRAINING PROBLEM

Joe Kelly

Managers have to learn how to operate in unstructured situations where the information about a problem is incomplete. This exercise, with the title "A Training Problem" will test your skill in operating in such a stressful environment.

The class should be divided into two groups – participants and observers. The participants are placed around a table in the center of the room and given the following problem. The observers have two tasks in this exercise. They must define roles emerging in the discussion process and specify stages in the discussion process. One group of observers should be given the task of ascertaining roles and another should be required to deal with the stages of the discussion.

You are the management of a firm employing 500 people. You have been instructed by the Managing Director to set up a supervisory training program. You are to consider the main difficulties which the scheme will have to overcome to get started and, secondly, the subjects to be included in the course. You will not appoint a chairman. You will not appoint a secretary.

ROLES EMERGING IN DISCUSSION GROUPS

1. Task Specialist (Look for the person who uses phrases such as "zeroing in on the problem," "let's bear down on the subject," "let's attack the problem," and so on.)

2. Human Relations Specialist (His style is essentially placatory – uses phrases such as "How do we feel about ——?, "This is kinda fun, kinda interesting." Generally tries to ease tension in the group.)

3. Eccentric (Look for bizarre and stochastic behavior.)

4. Scapegoat (Who is the group picking for this role? Does this person welcome it?)

5. Isolates (These people are not part of the group proper.)

6. Observers (Such figures are scientifically or intentionally detached!)

DISCUSSION PROCESS

Look for the stages of Clarification, Evaluation and Decision.

Clarification (what definitions and assumptions are made? what is the problem?)

Evaluation (How do they feel about the problem in emotional terms?)

Decisions (what did they decide to do?)

THE SUBARCTIC SURVIVAL SITUATION*

J. Clayton Lafferty

Group decision making is a fact of life for most managers. Managing group decision processes effectively and making articulate and persuasive presentations are important skills for managers. This exercise provides an opportunity to use both of these skills.

The situation described in this problem is based on actual cases in which men and women lived or died depending upon the survival decision they made. Your "life" or "death" will depend upon how well your group can share its present knowledge of a relatively unfamiliar problem, so that the group can make decisions which will lead to your survival.

THE SITUATION

It is approximately 2:30 p.m., October 5th and you have just crash-landed in a float plane on the east shore of Laura Lake in the subarctic region of the Northern Quebec-Newfoundland border. The pilot was killed in the crash, but the rest of you are uninjured. Each of you is wet up to the waist and has perspired heavily. Shortly after the crash, the plane drifted into deep water and sank with the pilot's body pinned inside.

The pilot was unable to contact anyone before the crash. However, ground sightings indicated that you are 30 miles south of your intended course and approximately 22 air miles east of Schefferville, your original destination, and the nearest known habitation. (The mining camp on Hollinger Lake was abandoned years ago when a fire destroyed the buildings.) Schefferville (population 5,000) is an iron ore mining town approximately 300 air miles north of the St. Lawrence, 450 miles east of the James Bay/Hudson Bay area, 800 miles south of the Arctic Circle, and 300 miles west of the Atlantic Coast. It is reachable only by air or rail, all roads ending a few miles from town. Your party was expected to return from northwestern Labrador to Schefferville no later than October 19th and filed a Flight Notification Form with the Department of Transportation via Schefferville radio to that effect.

The immediate area is covered with small evergreen trees (one and a half to four inches in diameter). Scattered in the area are a number of hills having rocky and barren tops. Tundra (arctic swamps) make up the valleys between the hills and consist

---

* Reprinted by permission. Copyright © 1973 by Human Synergistics, Inc. Subarctic Survival Situation is an exercise developed by J. Clayton Lafferty, Ph.D., of Human Synergistics, 39819 Plymouth Road, Plymouth, Michigan 48170, (313) 459-1030. The exercise was developed in consultation with the men and officers of the Para Rescue Specialists, 413 Transport and Rescue Squadron, Canadian Forces Base, Summerside, Prince Edward Island, Canada. Reproduction is not permitted.

only of small scrubs. Approximately 25% of the area in the region is covered by long, narrow lakes which run northwest to southeast. Innumerable streams and rivers flow into and connect the lakes.

Temperatures during October vary between 25°F and 36°F, although it will occasionally go as high as 50°F and as low as 0°F. Heavy clouds cover the sky three quarters of the time, with only one day in ten being fairly clear. Five to seven inches of snow are on the ground; however, the actual depth varies enormously because the wind sweeps the exposed areas clear and builds drifts 3' to 5' deep in other areas. The wind speed averages 13–15 miles per hour and is mostly out of the west-northwest.

You are all dressed in insulated underwear, socks, heavy wool shirts, pants, knit gloves, sheepskin jackets, knitted wool caps and heavy leather hunting boots. Collectively, your personal possessions include: $153 in bills and two half dollars, four quarters, two dimes, one nickel and three new pennies; one pocket knife (two blades and an awl which resembles an ice pick); one stub lead pencil; and an air map.

THE PROBLEM

Before the plane drifted away and sank, you were able to salvage the 15 items listed in Exhibit 1. Your task is to rank these items according to their importance to your survival, starting with "1" the most important, to "15" the least important.

You may assume:
1. the number of survivors is the same as the number on your team;
2. you are the actual people in the situation;
3. the team has agreed to stick together;
4. all items are dry and in good condition.

Step 1:
Individually, without discussing the Situation or the items with anyone else, rank each item according to how important it is to your survival.

Step 2:
After everyone has finished the individual ranking, rank order the 15 items as a team.

You will have until _____ o'clock to complete this step.

ABOUT THE EXPERTS

While the Canadian Subarctic is beautiful, this wilderness, and its weather, is notorious as a people-killer. The Para Rescue Specialists for the 413 Transport and Rescue Squadron, in the eastern Canadian Subarctic, is responsible for finding and rescuing people lost in this area, on both land and sea in all weather conditions. The Para Rescue Specialists, especially Corporal John Clark, provided invaluable help in the

Exhibit 1 List of Items

Items	Step 1 Your Individual Ranking	Step 2 The Team Ranking	Step 3 Survival Experts' Ranking	Step 4 Difference Between Steps 1 and 3	Step 5 Difference Between Steps 2 and 3
A magnetic compass					
A gallon can of maple syrup					
A sleeping bag per person (arctic type down filled with liner)					
A bottle of water purification tablets					
A 20' × 20' piece of heavy duty canvas					
13 wood matches in a metal screwtop, waterproof container					
250 ft. of 1/4 inch braided nylon rope, 50 lb. test					
An operating 4 battery flashlight					
3 pairs of snowshoes					
A fifth Bacardi rum (151 proof)					
Safety razor shaving kit with mirror					
A wind-up alarm clock					
A hand axe					
One aircraft inner tube for a 14 inch wheel (punctured)					
A book entitled, *Northern Star Navigation*					
Totals (the lower the score the better)				Individual Score Step 4	Team Score Step 5

Exhibit 1 continued
Team Performance Data

Please complete the following steps and insert the scores under your team's number	Team 1	Team 2	Team 3	Team 4	Team 5	Team 6
Step 6 Average Individual Score Add up all the individual scores (Step 4) on the team and divide by the number on the team.						
Step 7 Team Score (Step 5)						
Step 8 Gain Score The difference between the Team Score and the Average Individual Score. If the Team Score is lower than Average Individual Score, then Gain is "+". If Team Score is higher than Average Individual Score, then Gain is "−".						
Step 9 Lowest (Best) Score on the team.						
Step 10: Number of Individual Scores lower than the Team Score.						

Team Performance Data

Figures based on 2,173 participants (430) teams

Average Individual Score (Step 6)	47.7§
Average Ind. Score on Winning Teams	47.0§
Average Ind. Score on Losing Teams	50.3‡
Average Team Score (Step 7)	30.1‡
Average Winning Team Score	21.4‡
Average Losing Team Score	41.1‡
Average Gain Score (Step 8)	17.5‡
Average Gain Score on Winning Teams	25.5‡
Average Gain Score on Losing Teams	9.2‡
Average Best Score on Team (Step 9)	32.7§
Average Best Score on Winning Team	31.7§
Average Best Score on Losing Team	35.9‡
Percent of Individuals Having Scores Better Than Their Teams	10.2%
On Winning Teams	3.4%
On Losing Teams	32.0%
Percent of Teams Having Scores Better Than Their Best Individual Score	56.7%

Statistically within each group there is:
‡ a highly significant (0.01) difference between these scores.
§ no significant difference between these scores.

construction of this Situation. They hope the people experiencing the simulated situation will be better prepared should they ever find themselves in a real survival situation. The Specialists point out, however, that one of the best preparations for your survival is to see to it that the plane you fly in is equipped with an automatic emergency locator transmitter. This beacon automatically transmits a signal, which can easily be followed by rescuers, when triggered by the impact of a crash. This is becoming mandatory flight equipment in both Canada and the U.S.

J. Clayton Lafferty of Human Synergistics is concerned primarily with the response to crisis, and with ways of helping people work together more effectively. The Subarctic Survival Situation is intended to demonstrate that when people are supportive of one another and follow a rational sequence in dealing with their problems, they are able to perform beyond the sums of their individual resources; or, in other words, the whole is greater than the sum of its parts. This is the meaning of "synergy," and the philosophy of Human Synergistics, a consulting firm dedicated to tapping the wealth of resources available to individuals, groups, and organizations.

SYNERGISTIC DECISION MAKING

The algorithm (Exhibit 2) illustrates the skills and resources involved in Synergistic Decision Making, a method of utilizing the human resources available in a group. The effectiveness of a given decision is determined by the results of the decision. The results are a product of the available *resources* and the *process* by which those resources are utilized. Resources consist of all the natural and manmade materials, as well as the people's knowledge and skills. The process, by which human and material resources are utilized, is the skills people employ in obtaining results. These skills are in three primary areas: *Interpersonal Skills* (the skills of working with others cooperatively); *Rational Skills* (the skills necessary for dealing with a situation with systematic creativity); and *Task Skills* (skills necessary for implementing a specific course of action). These are described more fully in the algorithm.

In crisis situations, such as a survival situation, the task skills are often lacking. Since a crisis is a new, sudden, unexpected set of circumstances, the people involved usually have not had time to develop the task skills necessary to deal with the crisis. Consequently, in a crisis like the one simulated in this Situation, it becomes even more critical than usual that people fully utilize their Rational and Interpersonal skills. When people are able to use these skills, they produce results which go beyond the sum of their individual efforts.

The Subarctic team performance data is an indication of the synergistic effect. The average individual score and the average best score for losing teams which are significantly worse than the general average suggests that a lack of information is a prime reason for their poor performance (i.e., the relatively small average gain score). However, the average individual score and the average best score for winning team is *not* significantly different from the average of all the 430 teams who have dealt with the Situation. Therefore, winning teams do better not because they have more information on the subject but because of the more effective way their teams reached their decisions.

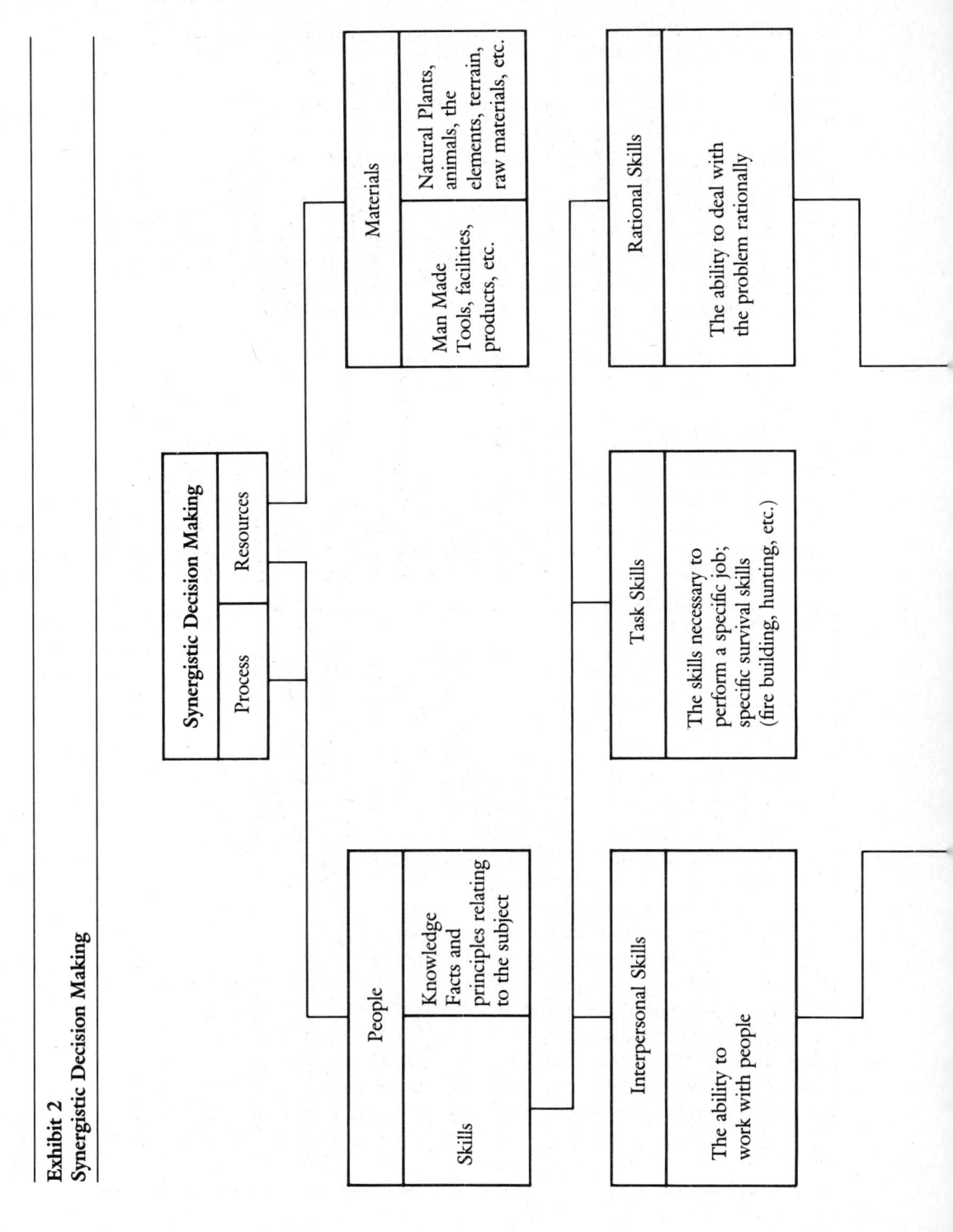

Exhibit 2
Synergistic Decision Making

```
                        ┌─────────────────────────────┐
                        │ Synergistic Decision Making │
                        ├──────────────┬──────────────┤
                        │   Process    │  Resources   │
                        └──────────────┴──────┬───────┘
                                              │
                        ┌─────────────────────┴─────────────────────┐
                        │                                           │
                    People                                       Materials
        ┌──────────────────────────┐              ┌──────────────────────────────┐
        │ Knowledge                │              │ Man Made      │ Natural      │
        │ Facts and                │              │ Tools,        │ Plants,      │
        │ principles relating      │              │ facilities,   │ animals, the │
        │ to the subject           │              │ products,     │ elements,    │
        │                          │              │ etc.          │ terrain, raw │
        │                          │              │               │ materials,   │
        │                          │              │               │ etc.         │
        └──────────────────────────┘              └──────────────────────────────┘

Skills
        ┌──────────────────┐    ┌──────────────────┐    ┌──────────────────┐
        │ Interpersonal    │    │ Task Skills      │    │ Rational Skills  │
        │ Skills           │    │                  │    │                  │
        │                  │    │ The skills       │    │                  │
        │ The ability to   │    │ necessary to     │    │ The ability to   │
        │ work with people │    │ perform a        │    │ deal with the    │
        │                  │    │ specific job;    │    │ problem          │
        │                  │    │ specific         │    │ rationally       │
        │                  │    │ survival skills  │    │                  │
        │                  │    │ (fire building,  │    │                  │
        │                  │    │ hunting, etc.)   │    │                  │
        └──────────────────┘    └──────────────────┘    └──────────────────┘
```

The Interpersonal Skills	The Rational Skills	
Active Listening/Clarifying by: Paying attention and responding to others' feelings and ideas Not interrupting Making open-ended inquiries Not judging others Summarizing and reflecting back others' ideas and feelings	Deciding on a Rational Process What issues need to be dealt with, and in what sequence, in order to arrive at a rational decision?	Developing Alternative Courses of Action What actions could possibly be taken to achieve: • the minimum outcomes? • the best outcomes?
Supporting/Building by: Accepting what others have to say Not debating, persuading, controlling or manipulating others Speaking in friendly, warm terms Creating opportunities for others to make their thoughts and feelings known Assuming others have useful ideas, information, etc.	Analyzing the Situation Survivors' mental/physical condition Materials on hand and their utilization Location Weather conditions Surrounding environment What are the teams' concerns? How serious is each?	Identify Obstacles and Adverse Consequences What would stand in the way of taking each course of action? What would be the adverse consequences of each alternative? How likely are they to occur? How serious would it be if they did?
Building on others' ideas Responding in an open, spontaneous way Encouraging divergent points of view Freely offering new ideas at appropriate times	Setting Objectives What are the minimum outcomes hoped for? What are the best outcomes that can be reasonably hoped for? What are the probable outcomes?	Deciding Which alternative is most likely to achieve: • the minimum outcomes? • the best outcomes? • the least adverse consequences?
Differing/Confronting by: Continually focusing attention on the problem solving process Questioning own and others' assumptions in a non-threatening way Dealing directly and specifically with apparent discrepancies Reflecting on how the team is doing with regard to: • progress • personal relations • time		

Suggested Readings

Barber, L. (1971) *Listening Behavior*. Englewood Cliffs, NJ: Prentice-Hall.

Gregory, C. (1967) *The Management of Intelligence: Scientific Problem Solving*. New York: McGraw-Hill.

Kepner, C. and B. Tregoe (1965) *The Rational Manager*. New York: McGraw-Hill.

Maier, N. (1952) *Principles of Human Relations*. New York: John Wiley and Sons.

Marrow, A., et al. (1967) *Management by Participation*. New York: Harper and Row.

Nesbitt, P., A. Pond, and W. Allen (1959) *The Survival Book*. New York: Funk and Wagnalls.

Nichols, R. and L. Stevens (1957) *Are You Listening?* New York: McGraw-Hill.

Prince, G. (1970) *The Practice of Creativity*. New York: Harper and Row

Whyte, W. (1950) *Is Anybody Listening?* New York: Simon and Schuster.

VII
LEADERSHIP AND CREATIVITY

READINGS

THE LEADERSHIP CHALLENGE — A CALL FOR THE TRANSFORMATIONAL LEADER*

Noel M. Tichy
David O. Ulrich

Some optimists are heralding in the age of higher productivity, a transition to a service economy, and a brighter competitive picture for U.S. corporations in world markets. We certainly would like to believe that the future will be brighter, but our temperament is more cautious. We feel that the years it took for most U.S. companies to get "fat and flabby" are not going to be reversed by a crash diet for one or two years. Whether we continue to gradually decline as a world competitive economy will largely be determined by the quality of leadership in the top echelons of our business and government organizations. Thus, it is our belief that now is the time for organizations to change their corporate lifestyles.

To revitalize organizations such as General Motors, American Telephone and Telegraph, General Electric, Honeywell, Ford, Burroughs, Chase Manhattan Bank, Citibank, U.S. Steel, Union Carbide, Texas Instruments, and Control Data — just to mention a few companies currently undergoing major transformations — a new brand of leadership is necessary. Instead of managers who continue to move organizations along historical tracks, the new leaders must transform the organizations and head them down new tracks. What is required of this kind of leader is an ability to help the organization develop a vision of what it can be, to mobilize the organization to accept and work toward achieving the new vision, and to institutionalize the changes that must last over time. Unless the creation of this breed of leaders becomes a national agenda, we are not very optimistic about the revitalization of the U.S. economy.

We call these new leaders transformational leaders, for they must create something new out of something old: out of an old vision, they must develop and communicate a new vision and get others not only to see the vision but also to commit themselves to it. Where transactional managers make only minor adjustments in the organization's mission, structure, and human resource management, transformational leaders not only make major changes in these three areas but they also evoke fundamental changes in the basic political and cultural systems of the organization. The revamping of the political and cultural systems is what most distinguishes the transformational leader from the transactional one.

Lee Iacocca: A Transformational Leader

One of the most dramatic examples of transformational leadership and organizational revitalization in the early 1980s has been the leadership of Lee Iacocca, the chairman of Chrysler Cor-

---

* Reprinted from "The Leadership Challenge" by Noel M. Tichy and David O. Ulrich, SLOAN MANAGEMENT REVIEW, Fall 1984, Volume 26, Number 1, pp. 59–68, by permission of the publisher. Copyright © by the Sloan Management Review Association. All rights reserved.

poration. He provided the leadership to transform a company from the brink of bankruptcy to profitability. He created a vision of success and mobilized large factions of key employees toward enacting that vision while simultaneously downsizing the workforce by 60,000 employees. As a result of Iacocca's leadership, by 1984 Chrysler had earned record profits, had attained high levels of employee morale, and had helped employees generate a sense of meaning in their work.

Until Lee Iacocca took over at Chrysler, the basic internal political structure had been unchanged for decades. It was clear who reaped what benefits from the organization, how the pie was to be divided, and who could exercise what power. Nonetheless, Mr. Iacocca knew that he needed to alter these political traditions, starting with a new definition of Chrysler's link to external stakeholders. Therefore, the government was given a great deal of control over Chrysler in return for the guaranteed loan that staved off bankruptcy. Modification of the political system required other adjustments, including the "trimming of fat" in the management ranks, limiting financial rewards for all employees, and receiving major concessions for the UAW. An indicator of a significant political shift was the inclusion of Douglas Frazer on the Chrysler Board of Directors as part of UAW concessions.

Equally dramatic was the change in the organization's cultural system. First, the company had to recognize its unique status as a recipient of a federal bailout. This bailout came with a stigma: thus, Mr. Iacocca's job was to change the company's cultural values from a loser's to a winner's feeling. Still, he realized that employees were not going to be winners unless they could, in cultural norms, be more efficient and innovative than their competitors. The molding and shaping of the new culture was clearly and visibly led by Mr. Iacocca, who not only used internal communication as a vehicle to signal change but also used his own personal appearance in Chrysler ads to reinforce these changes. Quickly, the internal culture was transformed to that of a lean and hungry team looking for victory. Whether Chrysler will be able to sustain this organizational phenomenon over time remains to be seen. If it does, it will provide a solid corporate example of what Burns referred to as a transforming leader.[1]

Lee Iacocca's high visibility and notoriety may be the important missing elements in management today: there seems to be a paucity of transformational leader role models at all levels of the organization.

ORGANIZATIONAL DYNAMICS OF CHANGE

Assumption One: Trigger Events Indicate Change Is Needed

Organizations do not change unless there is a trigger which indicates change is needed. This trigger can be as extreme as the Chrysler impending bankruptcy or as moderate as an abstract future-oriented fear that an organization may lose its competitiveness. For example, General Electric's trigger for change is a view that by 1990 the company will not be world competitive unless major changes occur in productivity, innovation, and marketing. Thus, Chairman Jack Welch sees his role as that of transforming GE even though it does not face imminent doom. Nonetheless, the trick for him is to activate the trigger; otherwise, complacency may prevail. Similarly, for AT&T, technological, competitive, and political forces have led it to undertake its massive transformation. For General Motors, economic factors of world competition, shifting consumer preferences, and technological change have driven it to change.

In a decade of increased information, international competition, and technological advances, triggers for change have become commonplace and very pressing. However, not all potential trigger events lead to organizational responses, and not all triggers lead to change. Nonetheless, the trigger must create a felt need in organizational leaders. Without this felt need, the "boiled frog phenomenon" is likely to occur.

Table 1
A List of Technical, Political, and Cultural System Resistances

Technical System Resistances include:

Habit and inertia. Habit and inertia cause task-related resistance to change. Individuals who have always done things one way may not be politically or culturally resistant to change, but may have trouble, for technical reasons, changing behavior patterns. Example: some office workers may have difficulty shifting from electric typewriters to word processors.

Fear of the unknown or loss of organizational predictability. Not knowing or having difficulty predicting the future creates anxiety and hence resistance in many individuals. Example: the introduction of automated office equipment has often been accompanied by such resistances.

Sunk costs. Organizations, even when realizing that there are potential payoffs from a change, are often unable to enact a change because of the sunk costs of the organizations' resources in the old way of doing things.

Political System Resistances include:

Powerful coalitions. A common threat is found in the conflict between the old guard and the new guard. One interpretation of the exit of Archie McGill, former president of the newly formed AT&T American Bell, is that the backlash of the old-guard coalition exacted its price on the leader of the new-guard coalition.

Resource limitations. In the days when the economic pie was steadily expanding and resources were much less limited, change was easier to enact as every part could gain – such was the nature of labor management agreements in the auto industry for decades. Now that the pie is shrinking decisions need to be made as to who shares a smaller set of resources. These zero-sum decisions are much more politically difficult. As more and more U.S. companies deal with productivity, downsizing, and divestiture, political resistance will be triggered.

Indictment quality of change. Perhaps the most significant resistance to change comes from leaders having to indict their own past decisions and behaviors to bring about a change. Example: Roger Smith, chairman and CEO of GM, must implicitly indict his own past behavior as a member of senior management when he suggests changes in GM's operations. Psychologically, it is very difficult for people to change when they were party to creating the problems they are trying to change. It is much easier for a leader from the outside, such as Lee Iacocca, who does not have to indict himself every time he says something is wrong with the organization.

Cultural System Resistances include:

Selective perception (cultural filters). An organization's culture may highlight certain elements of the organization, making it difficult for members to conceive of other ways of doing things. An organization's culture channels that which people perceive as possible; thus, innovation may come from outsiders or deviants who are not as channeled in their perceptions.

Security based on the past. Transition requires people to give up the old ways of doing things. There is security in the past, and one of the problems is getting people to overcome the tendency to want to return to the "good old days." Example: today, there are still significant members of the white-collar workforce at GM who are waiting for the "good old days" to return.

Lack of climate for change. Organizations often vary in their conduciveness to change. Cultures that require a great deal of conformity often lack much receptivity to change. Example: GM with its years of internally developed managers must overcome a limited climate for change.

The Boiled Frog. This phenomenon is based on a classic experiment in biology. A frog which is placed in a pan of cold water but which still has the freedom to jump out can be boiled if the temperature change is gradual, for it is not aware of the barely detectable changing heat threshold. In contrast, a frog dropped in a pot of boiling water will immediately jump out: it has a felt need to survive. In a similar vein, many organizations that are insensitive to gradually changing organizational thresholds are likely to become "boiled frogs"; they act in ignorant bliss of environmental triggers and eventually are doomed to failure. This failure, in part, is a result of the organization having no felt need to change.

Assumption Two: A Change Unleashes Mixed Feelings

A felt need for change unleashes a mix of forces, both a positive impetus for change as well as a strong negative individual and organizational resistance. These forces of resistance are generated in each of three interrelated systems – technical, political, cultural – which must be managed in the process of organizational transitions (see Table 1).[2] Individual and organizational resistance to change in these three systems must be overcome if an organization is to be revitalized.[3]

Managing technical systems refers to managing the coordination of technology, capital, information, and people in order to produce products or services desired and used in the external marketplace. Managing political systems refers to managing the allocation of organizational rewards such as money, status, power, and career opportunities and to exercising power so employees and departments perceive equity and justice. Managing cultural systems refers to managing the set of shared values and norms which guides the behavior of members of the organization.

When a needed change is perceived by the organizational leaders, the dominant group in the organization must experience a dissatisfaction with the status quo. For example, in the late 1970s John DeButts, chairman and chief executive officer of AT&T, was not satisfied with the long-term viability of AT&T as a regulated telephone monopoly in the age of computers and satellite communication systems. Likewise, when Roger Smith became CEO at General Motors in the early 1980s, he could hardly be satisfied with presiding over GM's first financial loss since the depression. In these two cases, the felt need provided the impetus for transition; yet, such impetus is not uniformly positive.

The technical, political, and cultural resistances are most evident during early stages of an organizational transformation. At GM the early 1980s were marked by tremendous uncertainty concerning many technical issues such as marketing strategy, production strategy, organization design, factory automation, and development of international management. Politically, many powerful coalitions were threatened. The UAW was forced to make wage concessions and accept staffing reductions. The white-collar workers saw their benefits being cut and witnessed major layoffs within the managerial ranks. Culturally, the once dominant managerial style no longer fit the environmental pressures for change: the "GM way" was no longer the right way.

One must be wary of these resistances to change as they can lead to organizational stagnation rather than revitalization. In fact, some managers at GM in late 1983 were waiting for "the good old days" to return. Such resistance exemplifies a dysfunctional reaction to the felt need. As indicated in Figure 1, a key to whether resistant forces will lead to little or inadequate change and hence organizational decline or revitalization lies in an organization's leadership. Defensive, transactional leadership will not rechannel the resistant forces. A case in point is International Harvester which appears to have had a defensive transactional leadership. Thus, in the early 1980s, International Harvester lacked a new vision which would inspire employees to engage in new behaviors. In contrast, Lee Iacocca has been a transformational leader at Chrysler by creating a vision, mobilizing employees, and working toward the institutionalization of Chrysler's transition.

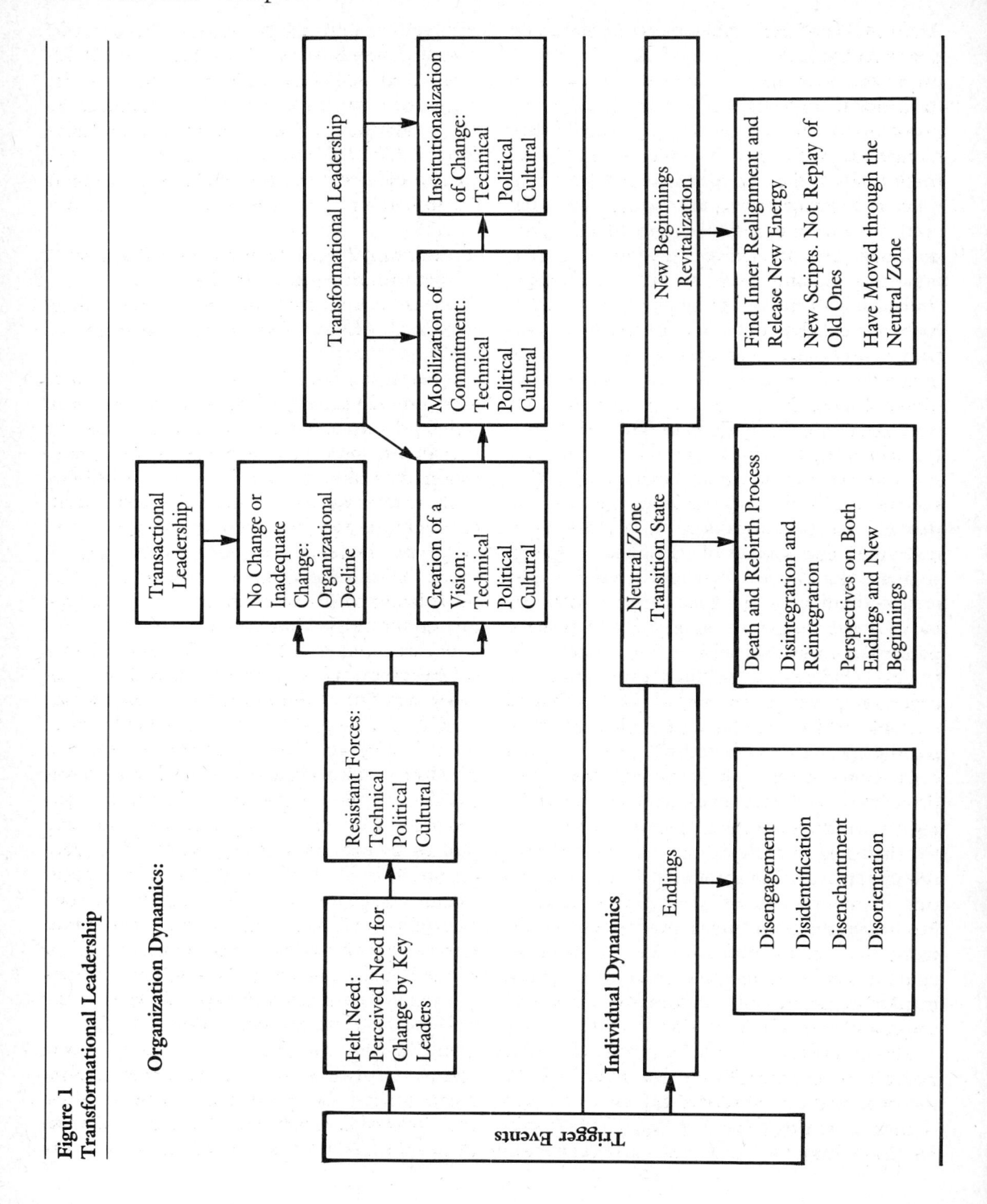

Figure 1
Transformational Leadership

Organization Dynamics:

Transactional Leadership → No Change or Inadequate Change: Organizational Decline

Felt Need: Perceived Need for Change by Key Leaders → Resistant Forces: Technical Political Cultural → No Change or Inadequate Change: Organizational Decline

Resistant Forces: Technical Political Cultural → Creation of a Vision: Technical Political Cultural

Transformational Leadership → Creation of a Vision: Technical Political Cultural → Mobilization of Commitment: Technical Political Cultural → Institutionalization of Change: Technical Political Cultural

Individual Dynamics:

Endings → Disengagement, Disidentification, Disenchantment, Disorientation

Neutral Zone Transition State → Death and Rebirth Process, Disintegration and Reintegration, Perspectives on Both Endings and New Beginnings

New Beginnings Revitalization → Find Inner Realignment and Release New Energy, New Scripts. Not Replay of Old Ones, Have Moved through the Neutral Zone

Trigger Events

Assumption Three: Quick-Fix Leadership Leads to Decline

Overcoming resistance to change requires transformational leadership, not defensive, transactional managers who are in search of the one minute quick fix. The transformational leader needs to avoid the trap of simple, quick-fix solutions to major organizational problems. Today, many versions of this quick-fix mentality abound: the book, *One Minute Manager*, has become a best seller in companies in need of basic transformation.[4] Likewise, *In Search of Excellence* has become a cookbook for change.[5] In fact, a number of CEOs have taken the eight characteristics of the "excellent" companies and are trying to blindly impose them on their organizations without first examining their appropriateness. For example, many faltering organizations try to copy such company practices as Hewlett-Packard's (HP) statement of company values. Because they read that HP has a clearly articulated statement of company values – the HP equivalent of the ten commandments – they want to create their list of ten commandments. The scenario which has been carried out in many major U.S. firms in the past year goes something like this: the CEO wants to develop the company value statement, so he organizes an off-site meeting in order to spend a couple of days developing the company XYZ corporate value statement. The session is usually quite enlightening – managers become quite thoughtful, and soul-searching takes place. At the end of the session, the group is able to the list the XYZ company's "ten commandments." The CEO is delighted that they are now well on the way to a major cultural change. He brings the ten commandments back to the corporation and calls in the staff to begin the communication program so that all company employees can learn the new cultural values. This about ends the transformational process.

The problem with the ten-commandments quick fix is that the CEOs tend to overlook the lesson Moses learned several thousand years ago – namely, getting the ten commandments written down and communicated is the easy part; getting them implemented is the challenge. How many thousands of years has it been since Moses received the ten commandments, and yet today there still seems to be an implementation challenge. Transformational leadership is different from defensive, transactional leadership. Lee Iacocca did not have to read about what others did to find a recipe for his company's success.

Assumption Four: Revitalization Requires Transformational Leadership

There are three identifiable programs of activity associated with transformational leadership.

1. Creation of a Vision The transformational leader must provide the organization with a vision of a desired future state. While this task may be shared with other key members of the organization, the vision remains the core responsibility of the transformational leader. The leader needs to integrate analytic, creative, intuitive, and deductive thinking. Each leader must create a vision which gives direction to the organization while being congruent with the leader's and the organization's philosophy and style.

For example, in the early 1980s at GM, after several years of committee work and staff analysis, a vision of the future was drafted which included a mission statement and eight objectives for the company. This statement was the first articulation of a strategic vision for General Motors since Alfred Sloan's leadership. This new vision was developed consistently with the leadership philosophy and style of Roger Smith. Many people were involved in carefully assessing opportunities and constraints for General Motors. Meticulous staff work culminated in committee discussions to evoke agreement and commitment to the mission statement. Through this process a vision was created which paved the way for the next phases of the transformation at GM.

At Chrysler, Lee Iacocca developed a vision without committee work or heavy staff involvement. Instead, he relied more on his intuitive and directive leadership, philosophy, and style. Both GM and Chrysler ended up with a new vision because of transformational leaders proactively shaping a new organization mission and vision. The long-term challenge to organizational revitalization is not "how" the visions are created but the extent to which the visions correctly respond to environmental pressures and transitions within the organization.

2. Mobilization of Commitment Here, the organization, or at least a critical mass of it, accepts the new mission and vision and makes it happen. At General Motors, Roger Smith took his top 900 executives on a five-day retreat to share and discuss the vision. The event lasted five days not because it takes that long to share a one-paragraph mission statement and eight objectives, but because the process of evolving commitment and mobilizing support requires a great deal of dialogue and exchange. It should be noted that mobilization of commitment must go well beyond five-day retreats; nevertheless, it is in this phase that transformational leaders get deeper understanding of their *followers*. Maccoby acknowledges that leaders who guide organizations through revitalization are distinct from previous leaders and gamesmen who spearheaded managers to be winners in the growth days of the 1960s and early 1970s. Today, Maccoby argues:

> The positive traits of the gamesman, enthusiasm, risk taking, meritocratic fairness, fit America in a period of unlimited economic growth, hunger for novelty, and an unquestioned career ethic. The negative traits for manipulation, seduction, and the perpetual adolescent need for adventure were always problems, causing distrust and unnecessary crises. The gamesman's daring, the willingness to innovate and take risks are still needed. Companies that rely on conservative company men in finance to run technically based organizations (for example, auto and steel) lose the competitive edge. But unless their negative traits are transformed or controlled, even gifted gamesmen become liabilities as leaders in a new economic reality. A period of limited resources and cutbacks, when the team can no longer be controlled by the promise of more, and one person's gains may be another's loss, leadership with values of caring and integrity and a vision of self-development must create the trust that no one will be penalized for cooperation and that sacrifice as well as rewards are equitable.[6]

After transformational leaders create a vision and mobilize commitment, they must determine how to institutionalize the new mission and vision.

3. Institutionalization of Change Organizations will not be revitalized unless new patterns of behavior within the organization are adopted. Transformational leaders need to transmit their vision into reality, their mission into action, their philosophy into practice. New realities, action, and practices must be shared throughout the organization. Alterations in communication, decision making, and problem-solving systems are tools through which transitions are shared so that visions become a reality. At a deeper level, institutionalization of change requires shaping and reinforcement of a new culture that fits with the revitalized organization. The human resource systems of selection, development, appraisal, and reward are major levers for institutionalizing change.

INDIVIDUAL DYNAMICS OF CHANGE

The previous section outlined requisite processes for organizational revitalization. Although organizational steps are necessary, they are not sufficient in creating and implementing change. In managing transitions, a more problematic set of forces which focuses on individual psychodynamics of change must be understood and managed. Major transitions unleash powerful conflicting forces in people. The change invokes simultaneous positive and negative personal feelings of fear and hope, anxiety and relief, pressure and stimulation, leaving the old and accepting a new direction, loss of meaning and new meaning, threat to self-esteem and new sense of value. The challenge for transformational leaders is to recognize these mixed emotions, act to help people move from negative to positive emotions, and mobilize and focus energy that is necessary for individual renewal and organizational revitalization.

Figure 1 provides a set of concepts for understanding the individual dynamics of transitions. The concepts, drawn from the work by Bridges, propose a three-phase process of individual change; first come endings, followed by neutral zones, and then new beginnings.[7] During each of these phases, an identifiable set of psychological tasks can be identified which individuals need to successfully complete in order to accept change.

THE THREE-PHASE PROCESS

Endings All individual transitions start with endings. Endings must be accepted and understood before transitions can begin. Employees who refuse to accept the fact that traditional behaviors have ended will be unable to adopt new behaviors. The first task is to disengage, which often accompanies a physical transaction. For example, when transferring from one job to another, individuals must learn to accept the new physical setting and disengage from the old position: when transferred employees continually return to visit former colleagues, this is a sign that they have inadequately disengaged. The second task is to disidentify. Individual self-identity is often tied to a job position in such a way that when a plant manager is transferred to corporate staff to work in the marketing department, he or she must disidentify with the plant and its people and with the self-esteem felt as a plant manager. At a deeper personal level, individual transactions require disenchantment. Disenchantment entails recognizing that the enchantment or positive feelings associated with past situations will not be possible to replicate in the future. Chrysler, GM, AT&T, or U.S. Steel employees who remember the "good old days" need to become disenchanted with those feelings: the present reality is different and self-worth cannot be recaptured by longing for or thinking about the past. A new enchantment centered on new circumstances needs to be built. Finally, individuals need to experience and work through disorientation which reflects the loss of familiar trappings. As mature organizations become revitalized, individuals must disengage, disidentify, disenchant, and disorient with past practices and discover in new organizations a new sense of worth or value.

To help individuals cope with endings, transformational leaders need to replace past glories with future opportunities. However, leaders must also acknowledge individual resistances and senses of loss in a transitional period while encouraging employees to face and accept failures as learning opportunities. Holding on to past accomplishments and memories without coming to grips with failure and the need to change may be why companies such as W.T. Grant, International Harvester, and Braniff were unsuccessful at revitalization. There is a sense of dying in all endings, and it does not help to treat transactions as if the past can be buried without effort. Yet, one should see the past as providing new directions.

Neutral Zone The key to individuals being able to fully change may be in the second phase which Bridges terms the neutral zone.[8] This phase can be interpreted as a seemingly unproductive "time out" when individuals feel disconnected from people and things of the past and emotionally unconnected with the present. In reality, this phase is a time of reorientation where individuals complete endings and begin new patterns of behavior. Often Western culture, especially in the U.S., avoids this experience and treats the neutral zone like a busy street, to be crossed as fast as possible and certainly not a place to contemplate and experience. However, running across the neutral zone too hurriedly does not allow the ending to occur nor the new beginning to properly start. A death and rebirth process is necessary so that organizational members can work through the disintegration and reintegration. To pass through the neutral zone requires taking the time and thought to gain perspective on both the ending – what went wrong, why it needs to be changed, and what must be overcome in both attitude and behavioral change – and the new beginning – what the new priorities are, why they are needed, and what new attitudes and behaviors will be required. It is in this phase that the most skillful transformational leadership is called upon.

A timid, bureaucratic leader who often reels in the good old days will not provide the needed support to help individuals cross through the neutral zone. On the other hand, the militaristic dictatorial leader who tries to force a "new beginning" and does not allow people to work through their own feelings and emotions may also fail to bring about change. The purported backlash toward the "brash" Archie McGill at American Bell in June 1983 may have been an example of trying to force people through the neutral zone in order to get to a new beginning. Archie McGill was known to rant and rave about the stodgy, old fashioned, and noninnovative "bell-shaped men" at AT&T. While he was trying to help and lead individuals to become innovative and marketing orientated, he may not have allowed them to accept the endings inherent in the transition. Although his enthusiasm may have been well placed he may have lacked the sensitivity to individual endings and neutral phases of transactions.

Failure to lead individuals through the neutral zone may result in aborted new beginnings. In 1983, International Harvester appeared to be stuck in the neutral zone. In order for International Harvester to make a new beginning, it must enable people to find a new identification with the future organization while accepting the end of the old organization. Such a transformation has successfully occurred at Chrysler Corporation where morale and *esprit de corps* grew with the new vision implanted by Lee Iacocca. In the end, organizational revitalization can only occur if individuals accept past failures and engage in new behaviors and attitudes.

New Beginnings After individuals accept endings by working through neutral zones, they are able to work with new enthusiasm and commitment. New beginnings are characterized by employees learning from the past rather than reveling in it, looking for new scripts rather than acting out old ones, and being positive and excited about current and future work opportunities rather than dwelling on past successes or failures. When Mr. Iacocca implemented his vision at Chrysler, many long-term employees discovered new beginnings. They saw the new Chrysler as an opportunity to succeed, and they worked with a renewed vigor.

WHAT QUALITIES DO TRANSFORMATIONAL LEADERS POSSESS?

So what does it take to transform an organization's technical, political, and cultural systems? The transformational leader must possess a deep understanding, whether it be intuitive or learned, of organizations and their place both in society at large and in the lives of individuals. The ability to build a new institution requires the kind of political dialogue our founding fathers had when Jefferson, Hamilton, Adams, and others debated issues of justice, equity, separation of powers, checks and balances, and freedom. This language may sound foreign to corporate settings but when major organization revitalization is being undertaken, all of these concepts merit some level of examination. At Chrysler, issues of equity, justice, power, and freedom underlay many of Mr. Iacocca's decisions. Thus, as a start, transformational leaders need to understand concepts of equity, power, freedom, and the dynamics of decision making. In addition to modifying systems, transformational leaders must understand and realign cultural systems.

In addition to managing political and cultural systems, transformational leaders must make difficult decisions quickly. Leaders need to know when to push and when to back off. Finally, transformational leaders are often seen as creators of their own luck. These leaders seize opportunities and know when to act so that casual observers may perceive luck as a plausible explanation for their success; whereas, in reality it is a transformational leader who knows when to jump and when not to jump. Again, Mr. Iacocca can be viewed either as a very lucky person or as the possessor of a great ability to judge when to act and when not to act.

THE SIGNIFICANCE OF CORPORATE CULTURES

Much has been written about organizational cultures in recent years.[9] We suggest that every organization has a culture, or a patterned set of activities that reflects the organization's underlying values. Cultures don't occur randomly. They occur because leaders spend time on and reward some behaviors and practices more than others. These practices become the foundation of the organization's culture. At HP, for example, Bill Hewlett and Dave Packard spent time wandering around, informally meeting with and talking to employees. Such leadership behavior set the HP cultural tone of caring about and listening to people. Similarly, Tom Watson, Sr., at IBM spent a great deal of time with customers. His practice led to a company culture of commitment to customers. Indeed, corporate cultures exist. Leaders can shape cultures by carefully monitoring where and how they spend their time and by encouraging and rewarding employees to behave in certain ways.

Culture plays two central roles in organizations. First, it provides organizational members with a way of understanding and making sense of events and symbols. Thus, when employees are confronted with certain complex problems, they "know" how to approach them the "right" way. Like the Eskimos who have a vocabulary that differentiates the five types of snow, organizations create vocabularies to describe how things are done in the organization. At IBM, it is very clear to all insiders how to form a task force and to solve problems since task forces and problem solving are a way of life in IBM's culture.

Second, culture provides meaning. It embodies a set of values which helps justify why certain behaviors are encouraged at the exclusion of other behaviors. Companies with strong cultures have been able to commit people to the organization and have them identify very personally and closely with the organization's success. Superficially, this is seen in the "hoopla" activities associated with an IBM sales meeting, a Tupperware party, or an Amway distributor meeting. Outsiders often ridicule such activities, yet they are part of the process by which some successful companies manage cultural meaning. On one level, corporate culture is analogous to rituals carried out in religious groups. The key point in assessing culture is to realize that in order to transform an organization the culture that provides meaning must be assessed and revamped. The transformational leader needs to articulate new values and norms and then to use multiple change levers ranging from role modeling, symbolic acts, creation of rituals, and revamping of human resource systems and management processes to support new cultural messages.

CONCLUSION

Based on the premise that the pressure for basic organizational change will intensify and not diminish, we strongly believe that transformational leadership, not transactional management, is required for revitalizing our organizations. Ultimately, it is up to our leaders to choose the right kind of leadership and corporate lifestyle.

References

1. J.M. Burns (1978) *Leadership*. New York: Harper and Row.
2. N.M. Tichy (1983) *Managing Strategic Change: Technical, Political and Cultural Dynamics*. New York: John Wiley and Sons.
3. *Ibid.*
4. K.H. Blanchard and S. Johnson (1982) *The One Minute Manager*. New York: Berkeley Books.
5. T.J. Peters and R.J. Waterman, Jr. (1982) *In Search of Excellence*. New York: Harper and Row.
6. M. Maccoby (1981) *The Leader*. New York: Ballantine Books.
7. W. Bridges (1980) *Making Sense of Life's Transitions*. New York: Addison-Wesley.
8. *Ibid.*

THE CORPORATE THEATER OF ACTION*

Joe Kelly

Running a company is an exciting activity. But as a scientific discipline, it is a bore, broken down into long lists of acronyms such as MBWA (managing by wandering around) and POLE (planning, organizing, leading, evaluation). The manager who has actually to keep the show on the road and meet the payroll soon realizes the need for myth, magic, and meaning. Managing and directing then become a black theatrical art, transforming inputs into outputs with value added. This "two plus two equals five" aspect of managing demands a certain *je ne sais quoi* that owes much more to theater than to management science.

The objective of this article is to come up with an explanation of management that feels right to practising managers who wonder about *In Search of Excellence*. In developing this explanation, we must examine the link between management and the theater. An increasing number of managers are realizing that executive life, when it is not a black tragedy, is often a gloriously funny comedy if seen from the right posture and perspective. Management becomes a theater of action: sometimes the theater of the absurd, sometimes a theater of cruelty. This zaniness has driven sophisticated executives to recognize the "I'm insane, you're insane" dimension of corporate life.

Dramatic new developments in video technology have given management researchers the chance to study managers when they are actually managing. What these video verities of executive behavior reveal is *style*: hard balls changing into soft balls in midflight, gestures contradicting the spoken word. And Candid Camera, please note: executives love being videoed, all day long if you like, until the last cartridge has been used up. Why? Because executives soon realize that they are or have become natural actors and all the organization is a stage.

What these videos reveal is that organizations are where the action is. Organizations are modern corporate theaters, where people go to play their roles, speak their scripts, say their pieces, and earn their bread. Executives can't wait to make their entrances, get on stage, and play their parts. Shakespeare could have had executives in mind when he wrote in *Henry V*, "I see you stand like greyhounds in the slips, straining upon the start."

STAGECRAFT, OR THE MANAGEMENT OF FICTIONS

But you can't play your part if you don't know your lines. And you can't know your lines unless you know your play. And you can't get the best out of your part unless you know where to stand on the stage, what your cues are, how to project your voice, how to hide your bad side, where the prompter is. This is exactly what the drama

---

* Reprinted from *Business Horizons* January/February 1986 No. 86112.

of executive conflict is all about – the stagecraft of the corporate theater in action.

Let us strip back for a moment the surface innocence of conventional corporate civility that allows the deceiver to deceive the deceived. "Oh, what a tangled web we weave when [in modern times] we practice to deceive." The drama of management deals with the ancient art of deception, sly sophistry, and useful manipulations that make up the infrastructure of executive life.

Let us introduce an executive play, to show how it progresses from the beginning through the middle to the end (or if you like, from exploitation, through complication, to resolution or denouement). Management frequently happens at great speed and involves the manipulation of fictions. This incident deals with a CEO firing a COO and involves a widely used routine or ritual which has to be highly structured, rehearsed, and carried out with great gusto to be effective.

THE DRAMA OF AN EXECUTIVE EXECUTION

Robert Johns, COO of New York Management Consulting Services, is sitting in his office gazing out the window. He is thinking about a friend who went through the Harvard Business School with him in the early 1960s. He's just seen a note in the *Wall Street Journal* saying that his friend has "decided to pursue private interests." He shivers involuntarily as he wonders what in fact is going on in business. Suddenly the phone rings. He is being summoned to a meeting in Chicago to attend a board meeting of his company.

Robert Johns feels pretty good about himself and the performance of the consultancy operations under his control. The only fly in the ointment is that the CEO and chairman of the board has asked him to siphon off his most effective product line and turn it over to the control of the CEO's son. Johns refused. At a previous board meeting he had tried to raise the issue.

Johns flies to Chicago. No sooner is he installed in his hotel than he receives a call from the chairman, who says that he'd like to talk to Johns before the board meeting. Johns suggests coming half an hour before the actual meeting so that any difficulties can be ironed out. The CEO tells Johns that won't be necessary; he's on his way over to the hotel right now to meet the COO. The CEO arrives. With him are the three most powerful men on the board. The following conversation ensues:

CEO: "Robert, I've got some news for you which I think you ought to have before tomorrow's meeting."
Johns: "What exactly is that?"
CEO: "We on the board have decided that we're going to dispense with your services."
Johns: "Why is that? I want an answer now."
CEO: "I want to make it clear to you that we have a legal opinion. The by-laws of the company charter do not require us to give reasons for such an action. But what I will say to you is that I feel I've no choice but to ask you to either resign or face the unnecessary embarrassment of being fired."

Executives are being fired in the U.S. at a sharply accelerating rate. When performance pauses for a moment, boards move in and fire. This helps to give the impression that the board is biting the bullet and doing something savage to sort things out.

What is the cause of all these boardroom traumata? According to Douglas Bauer, when American business began to decentralize in the 1950s and 1960s, it created a group of "fast-track" executives. These fast-track men compressed fifteen years of training and experience into five, moved all over the world, and ended up as chief executives. But when firms began to falter, these executives were the first to fall.[1]

Apparently, what happens in these top executive confrontations is an encounter of egos. For example, when Liman Hamilton was brought in as COO and president of I.T.T., he couldn't get along with Harold S. Geneen, who had built up I.T.T. in the 1960s and 1970s.

Apparently, Hamilton would go to Geneen and say, "Here's what I'd like to do."

Geneen would retort, "No, I want to do it this way."

Hamilton would go along with Geneen. But when Hamilton became the CEO and Geneen objected to his plans, Hamilton would say, "OK, I hear you. But until we take it up at the board, we're going to go ahead and do it my way."

Liman Hamilton lasted eighteen months before he was fired by Geneen.

THE STING AND THE HIT MEN

An executive can learn a great deal about the perverse process called firing (letting go, making redundant, separating, the shake-out – a variety of terms are in use) from reading the book or seeing the film *The Sting*. Even a quick glance at the chapter headings alerts the reader to the different stages of the process: the setup; the hook; the take; the shutout; the sting. Many similar cons in business are nearly as elaborate and certainly as dramatic. Most successful managers know how to do what *The Sting* shows blow by blow: how to take the other guy for all he's worth.

Dealing in deceptions and manipulations gives the whole subject a conspiratorial ring. When the theatrical is driven out, what is left is a lifeless and sterile set of structures, processes, and values.

THE POLITICAL STRUCTURE OF CONFLICT DRAMA

The structural view presupposes that conflict arises from the shape of the system, the anatomy of the organization. Conflict arises when two structures, two sets of rules, roles, and relations, cannot be fit together, cannot be easily synchronized. In the contemporary organization the rules are unclear, inchoate, and ill-defined; the roles create demarcation disputes; and the relations are confused because managers and subordinates send the wrong signals.

Why do executives play these roles? To entertain others? Yes, but only in the complete sense that an effective actor entertains: reaching out to his audience, establishing rapport, focusing their attention, stopping them from nervous diversions such as coughing and fidgeting, and passing a "message" to them. An old show biz line says, "If you're going to send a message, use Western Union." So people do not get an ordinary telegraphic message from contemporary playwrights like Edward Albee or Harold Pinter. It is a message like an artistic Rorschach inkblot – full of promise, but promises that vary with the perspective.

ENTER AND EXIT ON CUE

Executives set out to entertain in the same way as actors. Their entrances are carefully timed; they choose their dialogue with care; they exit on cue. They capture and captivate the audience. They have too much to do to send all their messages by Western Union. So they must signal, some of the time, by inkblot. All of this can't be learned from a textbook on management, and so the fledgling manager grasps every clue on how to "make like an executive." Constant practice and careful imitation, coupled with a brilliant imagination and reinforced by trips to the right movies and plays, can produce virtuoso performances.

Reciprocity is one purpose of all this role-playing. Each person must play his or her role fully if other persons are to play theirs. The executive must transmit signals that reflect the objectives he or she is shooting for. Of course, misperceptions may develop in regard to objectives and role interpretations. To get things back on track, further signaling may be required.

RECOGNIZE THE ACTORS IN THE EXECUTIVE SUITE

People who want to take a part have to recognize not only the script but also the other actors. The first problem is to separate the stars from the bit players, the principals from the supporting players, and both from the extras who are just along for the ride.

Failure to make this distinction can be fatal. In an exercise with an internationally famous energy company, the consultant made the error on day one, hour one. She mentioned that every time one participant, Eric, spoke, there was no further discussion of that topic. Eric took little or no part in the rest of the exercise – that is, until the wrap-up or debriefing on Day Three. Evaluations were moderately favorable or neutral until Eric took a hand. He accused his colleagues of being dishonest in not expressing their true assessments. Soon the participants were vying with one another to denounce the exercise. This exercise was on video, for everyone to see. The consultant had failed to recognize a principal; she had failed to pay homage to the star – to pay the price to get him on board.

KEEP TRACK OF THE PLOT

People who want to keep their place and follow the script have to keep track of the plot. The worst thing they can do is to come in once the "Big Picture," the main feature, has started. In other words, timing is extremely important to understanding the meaning of the story.

Managing the meaning is simply the exercise of power of persuasion in interpersonal relations. But basic to the drama theory of management is the belief that power must be exercised in a meaningful way to get change, to overcome organizational inertia. Legitimacy may have to be broken by non-legitimate means.

Thus far we have dealt with the structure or cast or *dramatis personae* of executive conflict. Now we must turn to the process, the plot, the scenario.

THE PROCESS: FROM OVERTURE TO DENOUEMENT

The process is essentially concerned with the sequencing of events, the plot of act, scenes, lines. The plot has its own pattern, its own momentum. A story, even a prosaic corporation operation, must have a beginning, a middle, and an end. To put the process in more dramatic terms, there must be an overture, openers, rising action, a climax, falling action, a conclusion, and then a denouement.

All these events interlock. Episode One generates Episode Two. Historical parallels abound. For example, the Allies imposed such a harsh settlement on Germany at the Treaty of Versailles in 1919 that World War II became an inevitable consequence. The German nation experienced the frustration of economic ruin; it felt itself victimized by Bolsheviks and the Allies. Germany decided to rearm. Rearmament led to its occupation of the Rhineland, Austria, Czechoslovakia, and Poland, and thus to World War II.

Let's look at a business example and see how the different episodes interlock.

Episode 1. Corporate HQ in New York discovers that a Los Angeles plant manager is shipping out defective PCs to maintain production.

Episode 2. New York decides to make an example of the case.

Episode 3. A valuable plant manager is rapped on the knuckles. A dispensable MBA is fired as an example to others.

A conflict that broke out in Episode 1 is resolved in Episode 3 only by garroting a weaker party. More typically these conflicts are not on individual issues but between cliques and cabals, who fight according to certain rules that the players grasp intuitively.

The executive guard have power, understand the drama of power, and use both power and drama. They maneuver and manipulate in order to get a job done and, in many cases, to strengthen and enhance their own position. They are in fact political actors. Their success depends on managing the vast intricacy of human relationships that make up the political universe of the executive.

MANAGING THE MEANING IS THE POWER OF PERSUADING

The basic proposition underlying such efforts is the belief that there is no management without drama, that every executive act involves an imposition of meaning, the executive's meaning. Getting action means imposing meaning on a situation.

But strangely enough, today's values often reflect a sense of meaninglessness. Combined with a post-Freudian emphasis on sickness rather than wrong-doing, this meaninglessness may have weakened the executive's sense of responsibility for his or her actions. So the contemporary corporate theater seems either eventless or full of nonevents. It is pathetic rather than tragic. Hence, the interest in the violence and conspiracy of *The Godfather* and of Watergate. Many executives believe these are not atypical case studies and in fact describe organizational actualities. They simplify life. A don whispers in the ear of his consiglieri and enemies are blown away.

THE CONSPIRACY THEORY OF ORGANIZATIONS

The conspiracy theory of organizations has captured the popular imagination. Therefore, it is not surprising that a number of contemporary movies, including *The Verdict* and *Chinatown*, have dealt explicitly with organizational intrigue. Executives find the conspiracy theory comforting because it provides a rational explanation for many bewildering corporate experiences.

Jan Kott is a Polish drama critic who lived through both the Nazi tyranny and the Stalinist occupation of Poland. He argues persuasively that the power politics, Machiavellianism, downright chicanery, low cunning, and violence of twentieth-century corporate life have their counterparts in Shakespeare's tragedies, particularly in *Macbeth*.[2]

Especially in *Macbeth*, Shakespeare provided us with what Kott calls the "Grand Mechanism." This blood-stained struggle for power with all its terrible consequences can be usefully invoked to explain corporate conspiracies.

In *Macbeth* Shakespeare provided a brilliant panoramic view of the struggle for power. It is as relevant today as it was when it was written in 1606. Most executives who have made it even a little way up the corporate ladder know the real meaning of anguish and guilt. They can recognize the feeling in:

Is this a dagger which I see before me.
The handle toward my hand?

And it is a short step to the world of the existentialist:

... or art thou but a dagger of the mind, a false creation,
Proceeding from the heat-oppressed brain?

The existential view of perception, "You describe what you see and you see what you describe," is but an echo of another Shakespearean tragic hero. In the words of Hamlet, "There is nothing either good or bad but thinking makes it so."

"Thinking makes it so" underscores the ability to move effortlessly between drama and real life.

SOME PRACTICAL ADVICE

Now comes the moment of agonizing truth. "So what?" you say. "What's the big deal? All very funny. But I'm not an actor."

And your ever obedient retainer, as always at your elbow, replies, "You may never have been on Broadway, but when you play the simpleton at those international meetings in Brussels, a deadly hush falls over the house. And then they stop their alibiing."

"You are putting me on," you modestly reply. "*You* are the one who always says just before that moment of simplicity, 'Our chairman is too much of a gentleman to ask this question, but I feel I have to.' It's not that I'm a gentleman; I just haven't done my homework."

"With all due respect, Sir," your retainer retorts, "I know you are dissembling when you peer over those half-moon specs."

All good clean fun, part of the inevitable aftermath of any executive encounter. But you may be wondering if there are any ground rules, any tactical doctrine, that can be drawn up on the drama of executive conflict.

RECOGNIZE THE DRAMA OF THE MOMENT

The show cannot begin until somebody recognizes the drama of the moment. Innocent bystanders quickly learn their parts in bank robberies and get down on the floor with their eyes shut tightly. There are only a few basic plots. Everybody knows them, but nobody can tell what they are. They work out in the movies but not always in practice.

One way to recognize the drama is to stay in touch with the contemporary theater, movies, novels, and music. Many executives answer, "I'm too busy – working." Some thirty years ago Sune Carlson established the same point in the first observational study of chief executives. In his classic *Executive Behavior*, Carlson found that CEOs were so busy working that they did not have time for cultural activities.[3] Before the show can begin, however, it is necessary to recognize the drama.

SET THE STAGE CAREFULLY

Next the stage has to be set with some care. The setting is extremely important. The Germans in 1940 brought out the famous World War I rail car from the museum at Compiegne to humiliate the French at the signing of the armistice with the Vichy government. General Douglas MacArthur staged the famous scene on the USS *Missouri* in 1945 that ended the war in the Pacific. Before he got his come-uppance, MacArthur was on the receiving end at Wake Island, being forced to receive the Commander in Chief, Harry S. Truman. Another President, Lyndon B. Johnson, received high officers while seated on "the throne." And so on.

Many of the same capers are to be witnessed in the executive suite, with the same deadly effect. Recently someone was brought on board as President of a large telecommunication company in order to trim the fat by cleaning house. He wielded the hatchet with some abandon. He established for himself a formidable reputation, and the company began to prosper again. The President required each production and functional unit head to present to the board the unit's accomplishments and the most important of its plans. The VP/Personnel, an internationally acclaimed expert in the field, made the presentation on organizational development and then asked for questions.

The President had established the procedure that he would ask the first – and, as it turned out on this occasion, the only – question: "Is that all there is?"

The distinguished Vice-President was soon working as a consultant.

HIGH PROFILE: THE IMAGE OF SUCCESS

The most important thing managers should know about the political dramas of conflict is that they are important, interesting, and ubiquitous. They must learn to love the game. That means not only developing a successful style, but also making a commitment to surefire, visible success. Loving the game means projecting the right image, giving visible success a high profile, acting with distinction and great force. Managers with a dramatic sense produce superior performance and morale.

This capacity can be developed. Basically, it is a capacity to grasp, develop, and impose meaning on relatively unstructured situations. To manage meaning effectively, a manager must take his or her part in the *structure* and *process* and have what it takes in terms of *values*.

To develop the capacity to impose meaning, it is useful to keep in mind such theatrical ideas as the script ("let's see how we are going to play this one"), the size of parts (stars, supporting cast, walk-ons), props, how to get off and on the stage. Consider the drama called *Structure the Succession*.

STRUCTURE THE SUCCESSION: A POWER PLAY

The scene is a meeting of the top management of a well-known automobile accessory company that operates along the Eastern seaboard from Maine to Florida. The CEO, who is about to retire, has called his five senior executives together, ostensibly to work on the strategic plan – but in fact to plan the succession. Two of the less senior executives are members of his family, one by marriage. The most senior VP fears that he is going to be "excluded" – amputated.

The senior executives, dressed in their cardigans, open-neck sports shirts, doubleknit stretch pants, and Adidas shoes, look like extras for a Pinter play. These ancient Laurence Oliviers and John Gielguds look like dried-up, spent forces as they shuffle about their business. They appear incompetent, incontinent, indeed insignificant. The meeting in the company motel in Vermont has been going on for two hours. Nothing much is happening. The VP/Planning runs through the upcoming five-year strategic plan.

Suddenly there is an intervention from the senior VP.

> *Senior VP:* "Look, this has gone on long enough. Let's get down to business. Let's get this problem out on the table."
>
> *CEO:* "What do you have on your mind? I didn't spend twenty years building a successful $10 billion a year business by cutting off criticism...."
>
> *Senior VP (lighting his pipe):* "It's your job to spell out the future objectives and structure of the company, so that we can solve the problem of succession."
>
> *CEO (getting really annoyed and puffing on his cigar):* "I could spend the rest of these days reading from the company policy documents on our objectives and policies."

This exchange continues acrimoniously for about thirty minutes.

> *VP/Planning:* "This discussion is getting out of hand..., it is counterproductive. Nothing good will come from attacking the CEO...."
>
> *CEO:* "No, no, no. I think..."
>
> *Senior VP (interrupting):* "Look, let's go round the room and get each person to present an idea of this structure."

The group carries on like a bunch of MBAs solving an HBS case. The blackboard is covered with organizational charts. One moment it is metaphysical; suddenly all is light.

> *Senior VP:* "So what I am proposing is that we should have a chairman's cabinet made up of the new CEO and the two more senior VPs in this room."

A few minutes later:

> *CEO:* "This has been a most useful and productive discussion. I accept your proposal, and I will accept total responsibility for its implementation."

What the CEO is showing is his genius for total delegation, picking winners (and dumping losers), and above all for "accepting total responsibility."

One of the most potent myths, almost a sacred cow of classical management, is the "acceptance of total responsibility." As priests take vows of charity and chastity, so does the manager accept complete and personal responsibility for everything that happens in his bailiwick.

When managers "accept total responsibility," their subordinates are free in turn to accept total responsibility. This kind of organizational power play is how iron commitment is established in any organization.

Only this kind of corporate "going for broke" is sufficient to mobilize the moral energies needed to get things done in the corporate world.

BODY LANGUAGE AND NONVERBAL COMMUNICATION

People communicate not only through what they say but also through the message sent by their behavior, particularly their body language. Where people sit gives a direct signal as to the role they wish to play in the meeting. Correspondingly, where the interviewer and interviewee sit relative to each other indicates whether the relationship is cooperative or competitive.

Someone can show interest in another person by pointing his or her body at that person. How we interpret these nonverbal cues tells a great deal about our personalities. For example, if you are talking with someone who leans back in his or her chair and gazes at the ceiling, you should follow suit. That way you avoid giving the appearance of a complete sycophant. On the other hand, if you persist in leaning forward and staring intently at the interviewer, all is lost.

The angle of your head, the way you place your feet, your breathing, your repetitive gestures, your tone of voice: all are dead giveaways. To be effective with people, it is necessary to establish rapport through body language. To do this effectively, it is necessary to read the other person's cues by listening carefully.

SURRENDER THE STAGE OCCASIONALLY, AND LISTEN

There is some evidence to support the proposition that the managers who are most effective are somewhat androgynous; that is to say, they have the proper mixture of masculine and feminine qualities. Michael Billington, in *The Modern Actor*, has argued that no male actor ever made more creative positive use of his feminine qualities than did Sir Laurence Olivier.[4]

This particular point was raised with Olivier in an interview:

> "Of course," replied Olivier. "A man who is entirely masculine isn't really normal, is he? I'm not saying he has to be as queer as a three-dollar bill. Ha! I mean if he hasn't a certain amount of absolute feminine in him – feminine, mind you, *not* femininity – I doubt he'd be very interesting."[5]

Executives are very much like actors. They have to have sufficient masculinity to allow them to structure the task, to define objectives, to set schedules, and to reach their goals. But they also have to have sufficient feminine qualities to be able to hear what other people are saying, to be passive at least some of the time, to be able to let their intuition work for them. And of course they have to learn to act like executives. That means imitating the superior performance of their superiors, which means being ready to surrender some autonomy – and that surrender until recently has been defined a feminine characteristic.

THE SHOW MUST GO ON

Inevitably, such demanding role-playing leaves the system somewhat unbalanced. Odd games have to be invented to dispel the anxieties generated. A great variety of games and subroutines can be observed in any workplace.

Many executives greet with hoots of derision the fact that, in the Hawthorne Studies, some workers whiled away their time shutting the windows that others had just opened.[6] In ice hockey, the player who scores a goal receives a tap on the bottom from the sticks of his teammates, presumably to show not only their congratulations but also to calm his euphoria and to remind him that he is still a member of a team.

Organizational life is suffused with games and pranks that are calculated to clean up some of the tensions and anxieties generated by the difficult work required to keep the organization operational. Psychologists have had a field day looking at the bizarre behavior of participants as they wander off and on stage, frequently upstaging others.

The metaphor of the theater is never far away. But finding a part, guessing the game, learning the lines, and making an exit remain constant problems. The scene is always shifting, and the playwrights keep changing the plot. Still, in the words of *Hamlet*, "The play's the thing." The cardinal rule remains: The show must go on.

References

1. D. Bauer (March 8, 1981) "Why Big Business is Firing the Boss." *New York Times*. Bauer is also the source for the anecdote of Hamilton and Geneen.
2. J. Kott (1964) *Shakespeare Our Contemporary*. London: Methuen.
3. S. Carlson (1951) *Executive Behaviour: A Study of the Work Load and the Working Methods of Managing Directors*. Stockholm: Stromberg.
4. M. Billington (1973) *The Modern Actor*. London: Hamilton.
5. C.W. Pepper (March 25, 1979) "Interview

with Laurence Olivier." *New York Times Magazine*, 18.
6. F.J. Roethlisberger and W.J. Dickson (1939) *Management and the Worker: An Account of a Research Program Conducted by the Western Electric Company, Hawthorne Works, Chicago*. Cambridge, MA: Harvard University Press.

CREATIVITY IN THE EVERYDAY BUSINESS OF MANAGING*

Robert E. Kaplan

Asked to list different types of creative professions, the participants in Creativity Week V mentioned writers, scientists, artists, engineers, architects, inventors, musicians, poets, psychologists, creativity specialists, and entrepreneurs. No one mentioned managers. But managers — at least the good ones — are creative all the time. They have to be to meet the confusing, fast-changing procession of demands on their intelligence, adaptability, and people-handling skill.

Creativity is evident in the *process* of management — the moment-to-moment and day-to-day flow of events in the manager's worklife. Claiming that management texts have ignored the management process, Leonard Sayles (1979) described it as:

> ... the actual day-to-day behavior and fragmented give-and-take, and the art of coping and negotiating with the unanticipated, the ambiguous, and the contradictory.
>
> First-rate managers ... seek to orchestrate ... the behavior of aggregations of personnel, some motivated, but many obtuse and recalcitrant. The nimble and complex behavior patterns of these superb managers is a delight to behold as they move to motivate, integrate, and modify the structure and personnel that surround them. Yet few texts capture the spirit of excitement and challenge [Sayles might also have said creativity] inherent in these tasks.[1]

Sayles used language that evokes images of the management process as an art form. Although often overlooked, the artistic qualities of the effective manager deserve their share of appreciation.

CREATING RHYTHMS IN THE MANAGER'S WORKDAY

Managers are busy, beseiged, harassed, in demand, and verging out of control. A manager's day is a miscellany of activities: scheduled meetings, impromptu conversations, reading, writing, making presentations, going on tours. Managers jump from one thing to another, from one person or group to another. To fashion order from this potential chaos is a creative act.

What managers create are rhythms, or alternations between giving in to the swirl of events and getting out of the swirl. Three of these rhythms are the alternation between accessibility and inaccessibility, the alternation between activity and reflection, and the alternation between work and leisure.

Rhythm: Accessibility and Inaccessibility

Interruptions pose a dilemma because, although they are the bane of the manager's existence, they are also the lifeline to fresh and necessary information. Managers can afford neither a truly open-door policy, which would rip their workdays to

---

* Reprinted from *Issues and Observations* by permission of the Center for Creative Leadership, Greensboro, North Carolina. © 1983.

shreds, nor can they afford to close themselves off entirely and miss important news while alienating the very people upon whom they themselves rely for ready accessibility and instant responsiveness.

Effective managers create an ebb and flow; they regulate their boundaries, making them more and then less permeable, admitting intrusions and then resisting or deferring them. The boundaries become more or less permeable depending on the competing pressures – the individual's need to focus on the task at hand versus the pressure to respond to people and events impinging from outside the bounds of the task at hand. Robert Townsend (1970) former president of Avis Rent-A-Car, handled incoming phone calls by having them taken by a secretary until 11:00 a.m., when he returned the calls and accepted additional calls. He used the same method in the afternoon, having calls taken for him from noon to 4:00 p.m., then answering them for the next hour. His was a highly structured way of achieving a rhythm of accessibility and inaccessibility. Other, more flexible methods can be equally effective.

Rhythm: Activity and Reflection

For managers, the time for reflection is hard to come by. Barbara Tuchman (1980), writing about working for the government, observed:

> Given schedules broken down into 15 minute appointments and staffs numbering in the hundreds and briefing memos of never less than 30 pages, policy makers never have time to *think*.[2]

For some managers, the only respite from the from the swift currents of activity comes when they are away from the office – at home, traveling between home and work, on trips. But those who manage their days creatively find havens from activity while at the office. President Nixon had a knack for this (Webber, 1982).[3] He would escape from the White House to a hide-away office across the street in the Executive Office Building where, with his yellow legal pads in front of him, he would concentrate on the larger issues.

As Warren Bennis discovered while he was president of the University of Cincinnati, routine work commonly drives out nonroutine work; only creative managers avoid having the larger issues banished by the details (Bennis, 1976).[4]

Nevertheless, the bustle of the manager's day is not entirely to blame. While sheer activity can overwhelm managers, so can it tempt them. Managers may allow themselves to be seduced by mere activity when the alternative is the anxiety-provoking challenge of reflection and creativity (Ashkenas & Schaffer, 1981).[5] Effective managers find the time to reflect despite being busy and despite the temptation to stay that way.

Alternating rhythmically between action and reflection is partly a matter of making dexterous transitions from one to the other. Managers struggle, after a long bout of activity, to face the unsettling quiet of contemplative work. But activity need not inhibit reflection afterwards, if the period of activity is short. A short burst of activity to start the day can build the momentum needed to glide into reflection later on (Webber, 1982).[6] The key is keeping activity in proportion.

Rhythm: Work and Leisure

Managers work long and hard; "brute persistence" is important to their success (Peters, 1980).[7] Even so, all work and no play can dull a manager's wits and dampen creativity. According to a board chairman:

> When I hear a man talk about how hard he works, and how he hadn't taken a vacation in 5 years, and how seldom he sees his family, I am almost certain that this man will not succeed in the creative aspects of the business, and most of the important things that have to be done are the result of creative acts.[8]

When managers proclaim proudly that they haven't taken a vacation in years, the implication is that they are highly committed to their work and uncommonly loyal to their corporation – qualities that are indeed necessary to career advancement in large organizations (Kanter, 1977).[9] But what does a single-minded devotion to the job sacrifice in the long run? Vaillant (1977)[10] studied 100 men from their college years into their 50's and found that success (in career and family) was associated with, among other things, taking interesting vacations. May (1975) called this pattern the "alternation of the marketplace and the mountain."[11]

Sticking tenaciously to the task can be counterproductive; one can't always attack problems frontally. That may be why Einstein was prompted to ask, "Why is it I get my best ideas in the morning while I'm shaving?" Perhaps because "the mind needs the relaxation of inner controls – needs to be freed in reverie or daydreaming – for the unaccustomed ideas to emerge."[12]

Creative managers achieve this rhythmic interplay between work and diversion in fashioning their workdays and their worklives. If work is fight and diversion is flight, then the diversion considered here is what John Glidewell called constructive flight – not escapism, but a renewal through involvement in other spheres of activity or inactivity.

With these three rhythms, managers attempt to exercise a modicum of creative control over forces that would control them. The rhythms constitute an order that managers with a talent for orchestrating workday and worklife create out of the disorder of their jobs.

GIVING SHAPE TO PROBLEMS

Despite the play given in the management literature to the solving of problems, managers are equally challenged to find, in the first place, the problems in need of solving. (I mean here, problems as situations to resolve *or* exploit, difficulties *or* opportunities.) "Problem finding is no less important a task than problem solving."[13] This is not to suggest that all of the items in a manager's short- and long-range docket are there because the manager sought them out. Certainly, a sizeable proportion of a manager's work comes already defined. But, to varying degrees, managers are responsible for ferreting out problems – for being attuned to the cues that indicate trouble or opportunity, and for developing a sense of what the cues mean and what action is indicated.

Finding and defining problems is a creative act with similarities to the visual arts. The manager gives form to a problem in the way a potter sees and then shapes the possibilities in a lump of clay. The difference is that managers practise their craft using an intangible medium – information.

Whether they are employed in an organization that manufactures goods or offers services, managers are more or less removed from the reality of making the product or service. Managers function in a social-informational milieu, in which reality is *constructed*. In other words, managers often decide what is real and what is not. John F. Kennedy and his cabinet interacted in such a way that they came to believe, wrongly, that an invasion of Cuba at the Bay of Pigs would meet with no significant opposition (Janis, 1972).[14] When reality has an indisputable physical basis, there is less room for argument – or construction – although social psychologists have shown that, in a certain percentage of cases, a group can lead an individual to deny the evidence of his or her senses (Asch, 1956).[15] By contrast, social reality is up for grabs. Was the meeting we just attended a productive one or a waste of time? Is morale high, medium or low in this organization? Are women and minorities treated fairly or unfairly in this organization? Does the future of this organization look rosy or bleak? To questions like these, which are the substance of the manager's job, answers are developed – reality is constructed – by a complex mental, emotional, interactive, political process; ultimately, by a creative process.

One way in which managers construct reality is by setting agendas. The notion of agenda setting as a major task of management was developed in an intensive study by Kotter (1982)[16] of 15 general managers. Kotter found that these high-level managers all entered their new positions with only a half-formed idea of what needed to be done. It was in the first 6 to 12 months on the job that these managers developed a firm sense of their short- and long-range goals and the projects that would serve as vehicles to achieve these goals.

The GM's formed their agendas through an elaborate, continuous, and incremental process in which they aggressively collected information – primarily from people, not documents, and to a large extent, from people with whom they already had relationships. In addition they sought information constantly and certainly did not limit their quest to formal planning meetings. Finally, they shaped plans using a combination of analysis and intuition. Out of this searching, sifting, and shaping came a loose and largely unwritten configuration of goals, plans, and projects (Kotter, 1982).[17] In this way the GM's created their sense of what the reality of their organization was and should be.

John DeLorean, whose recent fall from grace should not erase his earlier accomplishments, provides an example of how a GM goes about creating such an agenda (Wright, 1979).[18] Upon taking over the reins as general manager of General Motors' Chevrolet Division in 1969, DeLorean knew the division was in trouble but he didn't know why. Profits were dropping, budgets were being overspent, departments were not coordinating well. To discover the causes of the problem and to give direction to his executive strategy, DeLorean set out on a three-month personal inquiry into the Chevy situation.

What distinguished his search was its inclusiveness. By no means did he limit himself to the people in the immediate organizational vicinity. Instead he visited plants and talked to managers and employees alike; he met with Chevy dealers; he sought out disgruntled employees, even those who had left the division; he consulted with competitors and other informed individuals in and outside of the automobile industry. He neither sat in his office responding to day-to-day problems, nor did he attempt to assess the state of the organization by reading reports. He approached a variety of people and so gave shape to the sources of the division's problems and to a strategy for dealing with those problems.

The urge of managers to make sense of their complex, fast-changing world can be described as a "passion for form" (May, 1975).[19] Fundamentally, it is a worldly version of the artistic instinct that enabled Michelangelo to see and sculpt the statue of David out of Carrera marble.

CREATING SOCIAL ARRANGEMENTS

When we consider the *products* of creative endeavor, we tend to think of *things* – physical objects like industrial products or works or art, or mental objects like ideas. We don't often think of an arrangement as being the creative product itself.

But good managers regularly create social arrangements. Although organizational structure is an obvious example of social creativity, it is a semipermanent structure that becomes an object. More to the point here are the temporary arrangements of people around a task. These arrangements vary from a task force that exists for months, to a group that meets one time on an issue of common concern, to the sequence of people that a manager calls upon during the course of a day to solve a problem.

Creating relationships is a basic form of social creativity, upon which the rest of the manager's work is built. There is no alternative to the development of relationships; managers depend on a whole host of others without whom they can't perform their jobs at any level of effectiveness (Kaplan & Mazique, 1983).[20] Making up the networks of job-relevant others of the general managers Kotter (1982)[21] studied were hundreds and sometimes thousands of people in and outside of the organization.

Relationships are now bestowed upon a manager; they are developed as a product of individual roles and personalities. A good relationship exists when a manager can depend on another person for a cooperative response. The other person will tend to respond cooperatively when the manager has something to offer. In other words, relationships are based on exchange, whether of tangible or intangible commodities. Effective relationships are reciprocal.

An appreciation of the need to develop reciprocal relationships is shown by an executive who several years ago faced the challenge of introducing computers to the several divisions of his corporation. He headed a new staff function and none of the division heads reported to him. "I spent a lot of time on the opposing forces trying to build credibility – my own and my group's. It was a slam-dunk operation, not loved. I saw us as a change agent, and my approach was to teach a need, induce a need. I tried to build relationships when we weren't in a fight so that when a burning issue came up, you've got money in the bank. When fires broke out, we fought them with face-to-face meetings with our antagonists." This executive had a knack for building relationships under adversity. He gained influence with the division heads by making them aware of how the new function could meet their needs, built trust by interacting when there wasn't conflict, dealt with conflict by sitting down face to face.

Creating contact is what the manager must do to build or to call upon relationships. The episodes in which a manager and others come together can be likened to a dance. Sayles (1979) wrote vividly about how the parties to an effective interaction coordinate their movements. They simultaneously move and respond to the other's movement. As he puts it, "These verbal strokings, this mutual adaptation, appeal to the basic animal nature that calls for rhythmical give-and-take."[22]

Just as managers can synchronize their interactions, can dance together, they can also be out-of-step. Managers show a clumsiness on the dance floor of interactions when they only talk and rarely listen, when they only listen and hardly talk, when they can't hold anything but long drawn-out conversations, or when they can only converse on the run.

If contact is dance, then part of creating contact is choosing a suitable stage on which to perform the dance. A plant manager tells the story of how, when he first took over the plant, his predecessor brought him along to a meeting with the union bargaining committee. The adversarial relationship between union and management was demonstrated by the haranguing between the old plant manager and the union president from opposite ends of a long conference table. After his predecessor had left for good, the new man went to the next union-management meeting and sat down immediately beside the union president, who began as usual to shout and gesture dramatically. But, because it is difficult to yell at a person sitting next to you, the union president moderated his tone and approach, and the relationship between union and management eventually became more cooperative. Thus, by his choice of seating, the manager created a contact with his opposite number that signalled the relationship he wanted. Although his predecessor sought to usher him into the hostile tradition, the new manager saw a choice where others might have thought none existed.

Activating relationships is another dimension of creating social arrangements. With relationships at their disposal, managers get work done by mobilizing these relationships at particular times, in particular ways (some of which have to do with creating contact), around particular tasks.

If contact is dance, then activating relationships is choreography. To begin a project, managers must decide whom to bring on stage to work on which piece of the larger task, in what combinations actors are to be brought together, in what sequence these subgroups are to be convened, and what mode of contact (telephone, written communication, scheduled meeting, impromptu conversation) is to be used among the manager and the others. The manager as choreographer, however, has nothing like a set script to follow, but must improvise the arrangements as he or she goes along.

Something of the quality of the social choreography managers perform is evident in the observation by Bennis (1976):

> To function properly, the leader must have an "executive constellation" [which works] through temporary systems of assembling task forces for

a particular assignment, then reassembling others for a different task.[23]

Friend, et al. (1974) also recognize this choreographic talent:

> Knowing how to make effective use of a network is ... the mobilization of decision networks in an intelligently selective way, which depends on the capacity to understand both the structure of a problem and the structure of organizational and political relations that surround them.[24]

The choreographic art lies in activating relationships in light of the structure of the problem being attacked. Rosebeth Kanter (1982), writing from research on 165 innovative middle managers from five corporations, shows how the success of a project hinges upon the manager's ability to activate relationships.[25] To keep up the commitment of key players over the long course of a project, innovative middle managers make use of briefings, assignments, meeting (both formal and informal), team-building, praise, new structural arrangements, timely appearances by high-level supporters, and the careful management of the impressions of higher-ups (Kanter, 1982).[26] When to resort to which of these and other involvement-building mechanisms is part of the skill of activating relationships.

Thus, managers who are creative in the social sphere invent what we might call microsocial structure – small scale and often ephemeral arrangements of people – designed in such a way as to enlist the help of others in the performance of the bits and pieces of larger tasks.

THE MANAGER AS ARTIST

Managers exhibit creativity in the way they arrange and rearrange, collect and disperse information, ideas, tasks and people. Managers are forever making small departures, and sometimes radical departures, from what has been. Drawing on their talents, energies and history, they make up their responses to situations as they go along. Like the jazz musician, effective managers play variations within a larger thematic framework; they improvise in dealing with problems and people. Ineffective managers replay the same tune, use the same instrument, operate in a narrow band mentally and interpersonally. Versatility separates the effective from the ineffective manager.

But let's not romanticize creativity. It takes *energy* to create, more energy than it does to follow routines. Creative challenges also provoke anxiety. The stress takes a pure form in artists like Giacometti who suffered visibly as he painted, despairing of capturing on canvas his vision of the subject: "Maybe the canvas will become completely empty; then what will become of me? I'll die of it!"[27] Managers may not agonize as much or as obviously but they do worry about the tough issues that march steadily in their direction. Anxiety in the face of creative tasks can tempt managers to escape into the fast-paced routines of their job.

No joyride for the manager, creativity often carries with it a certain destructive element. Picasso observed that "every act of creation is first of all an act of destruction."[28] For this reason, established industries tend not to make the next technological advance. The manufacturers of manual typewriters did not invent the electric typewriter, and the manufacturers of electric typewriters did not invent the word processor. The huge capital investment in existing technology works as a disincentive to develop truly new technology (Galbraith, 1982).[29] The next technological breakthrough is, in this sense, destructive. In a small way managers destroy an old idea when they adopt a new one, reject one colleague when they choose another for a desirable assignment.

We can avoid making a fetish of creativity if we recognize the limits of creativity for creativity's sake. Executives with a talent for innovation can do more harm than good if they take over a stable, effective organization and immediately go to work revamping it. Creativity has value to the extent that it is directed to useful purposes. One participant in the Looking Glass simulation, overwhelmed by the material and feeling out of his element, adjusted to his plight by putting on a show of playing his role. Stumped by a question at one point, he excused himself from the meeting and went back to his office to consult his calendar about a time to meet the next day (there was no next day). Observing this, I admired the ingenuity but regretted this manager's response to his ignorance, which was to invent ways to save face. The manager demonstrated creativity, but it was put in the service not of job performance but of defensiveness.

Effective managers regularly perform unrecognized creative acts. But to develop this underrated talent in the art of managing, and to harness the talent for useful purposes, is no mean feat. Like any artist, the manager puts in years of practice honing skills to a fine edge, but few managers performing their everyday art get the acclaim accorded artists in other fields.

References

1. L. Sayles (1979) *Leadership*. New York: McGraw-Hill.
2. B. Tuchman (1980) "An Inquiry into the Persistence of Unwisdom in Government." *Esquire*, 93(5), pp. 25–31.
3. R.A. Webber (August 23, 1982) "The Art of Procrastination (Manager's Journal)." *The Wall Street Journal*.
4. W. Bennis (1976) *The Unconscious Conspiracy: Why Leaders Can't Lead*. New York: AMACOM.
5. R.N Ashkenas and R.H. Schaffer (1982) "Managers Can Avoid Wasting Time." *Harvard Business Review* 60(3), pp. 84–104.
6. R.A. Webber (August 23, 1982) *op. cit.*
7. T.J. Peters (Summer, 1980) "A Style For All Seasons." *The Executive*.
8. R.A. Mackenzie (1975) *The Time Trap*. New York: AMACOM.
9. R.M. Kanter (1977) *Men and Women of the Corporation*. New York: Basic Books.
10. G.E. Vaillant (1977) *Adaptation to Life*. Boston: Little, Brown and Company.
11. R. May (1975) *The Courage to Create*. New York: Norton.
12. *Ibid.*, p. 67.
13. J.S. Livingston (1971) "The Myth of the Well-Educated Manager." *Harvard Business Review*, 49(1), pp. 78–89.
14. I.L. Janis (1972) *Victims of Groupthink*. Boston: Houghton-Mifflin.
15. S.E. Asch (1956) "Studies of Independence of Conformity. A Minority of One Against a Unanimous Majority." *Psychological Monographs*, 70(9), Whole Number 416.
16. J.P. Kotter (1982) *The General Managers*. New York: The Free Press.
17. *Ibid.*
18. J.P. Wright (1979) *On A Clear Day You Can See General Motors*. New York: Avon.
19. R. May (1975) *op. cit.*
20. R.E. Kaplan and M.S. Mazique (February, 1983) *Trade Routes: The Manager's Network of Relationships* (Technical Report 22) Greensboro, NC: Center for Creative Leadership.
21. J.P. Kotter (1982) *op. cit.*
22. L. Sayles (1979) *op. cit.*, p. 67.
23. W. Bennis (1976) *op. cit.*, p. 135.
24. J.K. Friend, J.M. Power, and C.J.L. Yewlett (1974) *Public Planning: The Intercorporate Dimension*. London: Tavistock.
25. R.M. Kanter (July-August, 1982) "The Middle Manager As Innovator." *Harvard Business Review*, pp. 95–105.
26. *Ibid.*
27. Lord quoted in R. May (1975) *op. cit.*, p. 9.
28. *Ibid.*, p. 63.
29. J.R. Galbraith (Winter, 1982) "Designing the Innovating Organization." *Organizational Dynamics*, pp. 5–25.

CASES

ROTHMANS ON A SLOW BURN*

Cathryn Motherwell

It was, said one wag, a case of "here today, gone today." The day chairman John Devlin and president Robert Hawkes left Rothmans of Pall Mall Canada Ltd. marked the end of an era for Canada's second-largest cigaret maker. The two top executives embodied the tobacco company's classy image of traditional values and their departures in September 1985 signalled a return of sorts to an earlier Rothmans era, when the brash young company overwhelmed the country with its king-size cigarets.

Senator William Kelly was appointed chairman, and Patrick John Fennell was named president. Known to all as P.J., the 43-year-old Fennell had a scant two months' experience at Rothmans before his promotion to president and chief executive. That staid Rothmans would put its money on an outsider, let alone one who does not smoke cigarets, said a good deal about the trouble the company was in.

In the early days, Rothmans was a Canadian success story. The Rothmans Group, the international tobacco company controlled by South African Anton Rupert's Rembrandt Group, formed a subsidiary to airlift cigarets from Britain, launching a shrewd market assault that shook the Canadian tobacco industry. But when the market began to settle new problems surfaced. Not only did tobacco sales pitch into a decline that shows no signs of reversal, but Rothmans inflicted additional harm on itself by failing to spot an increasing consumer preference for mild and light cigarets. Diversification into brewing was no salvation either, because beer sales went flat. By 1985 the company that "rocked the guts out of everyone in the Canadian cigaret field" was in need of a transfusion. And suddenly Devlin and Hawkes were gone.

To fulfill his mandate of restoring the company's share of the market, improving profitability and developing a long-term strategy, Fennell enjoys a freedom that Rothmans International has not easily granted in the past. "I really think he has a mandate to turn that sucker around," says Michael Palmer, a Toronto securities analyst. Indeed, the new management team has not only cut staff and decided to close a manufacturing plant, but has also ended the Rothmans of Pall Mall era. In October, Rothmans and

---

* From Globe and Mail *Report on Business Magazine*, December 1986, pp. 60–66. Reprinted by permission of the publisher.

Philip Morris Inc. agreed to merge their tobacco subsidiaries to form Rothmans, Benson & Hedges Inc. If Fennell succeeds in the challenge of building the new company into a market leader, he will have achieved a feat as impressive as that of Patrick O'Neil-Dunne, the man who opened up the Canadian market for Rothmans almost 30 years ago.

O'Neil-Dunne's marketing style was blunt and aggressive. "This isn't business," he told employees when the Toronto plant opened in October of 1957. "This is war." In only one year, Rothmans king-size in the flip-top box had 4% of the Canadian market. Within seven years, Rothmans brands grabbed 20% of the market. To company employees, O'Neil-Dunne was a super salesman, a great man and a bulldozer who always got what he wanted.

The name of O'Neil-Dunne remains a symbol of the company's early market successes, and his 1984 visits to Rothmans plants in Toronto and Québec City brought warm recognition from employees eager to be remembered by their former chief. The occasion even prompted O'Neil-Dunne to issue an order. The impending visit of the Pope to Québec City was a marketing coup not to be missed, he told personnel director Louis Boudreau. All that was needed would be a photograph of the Pope in front of the plant. The genial Boudreau replied that security would be tight, and never thought about the matter again.

But O'Neil-Dunne does not let go of an idea. When word reached Boudreau that his former boss was asking for a copy of the photograph, he wondered how to explain that none had ever been taken. Then one day he visited the office of plant manager Jean-Claude Bilodeau and there on his desk was the image of the smiling pontiff, waving to the crowd as he passed the Québec City plant, the Rothmans name clearly visible in the background. Almost speechless at the sight of the photograph, Boudreau learned that it had been taken by a friend of Bilodeau who viewed the papal procession from a vantage point across the road from the plant. Bilodeau had copies of the photograph made and sent one to O'Neil-Dunne, who expected all along that Boudreau would come through.

O'Neil-Dunne's aggressive manner would scare people, but Boudreau believes no one else could have done the job as well. "He would call management in and say 'Here's what we are going to do,'" Boudreau recalls, loudly slapping his hand on a cafeteria table. Asked about his management style in a telephone interview, O'Neil-Dunne, now 77 and living in Hertfordshire, England, replies crisply that he never had one. "I'm just a tobacco man," he says, adding that 80% of his time was spent on marketing, 10% on leaf tobacco and 10% on "finance and stupid directors' meetings."

Fennell's style is more understated. He prefers to describe himself as a team player and considers the fact that he does not smoke cigarets irrelevant to his ability to run the company. Despite lingering doubts about Fennell's sensitivity to industry traditions, the soft-spoken University of Toronto business school graduate is an aggressive player whose strategies emulate those of O'Neil-Dunne. Fennell's experience includes marketing jobs with Simon & Schuster, Harlequin and Pepsico Inc. Some may not think the marketing techniques of romance novels and soft drinks can be successfully transferred to cigarets, but Fennell believes the common thread is a need for creative, innovative programs to get ahead of the competition.

The new president's efforts to rejuvenate Rothmans began even before he joined the staff. Robert Hawkes, who had known Fennell for five years, hired him as a consultant in the spring of 1985 to assess the company's marketing and organizational structure. "I was certainly impressed," says Hawkes, now a corporate lawyer in Toronto. The report said Rothmans suffered from weak brand trademarks, sagging market share, a complacent attitude and too many employees. Its strengths consisted of a quality image, some qualified employees and a sound balance sheet. Fennell proposed a major restructuring. "It was a sleeping giant of a company that could move mountains if it got well positioned," he says. Members of the board of directors did not like what they read, but they did not argue.

Fennell had found a mentor of sorts in Sir Robert Crichton-Brown, the new chairman of Rothmans International and a director of the Canadian company. "He is a very dynamic, extremely hard-working, highly experienced, personable individual," says an admiring Fennell. "An extremely demanding man whom I personally like. And I think the reverse is also true. He's just driven by the opportunity to set companies on the proper course, which is something that motivates me, so we have a tremendous bond." Any praise Sir Robert has for Fennell, however, is kept to himself. "I never talk about personalities," says the genial chairman.

That new relationship, and the contents of Fennell's report, helped spur an exodus of senior Rothmans executives. Officially, they retired or left to pursue new careers, but the timing of their departures was more than coincidence. Concedes Fennell: "This man Crichton-Brown, you either love him or you hate him." That summer Rothmans was restructured to form Rothmans Inc., a holding company that owned 100% of Rothmans of Pall Mall Canada Ltd. and 50.1% of Carling O'Keefe Ltd. Fennell was appointed president of the tobacco operations and Hawkes became president of the holding company. Devlin, who had planned to retire the previous spring, agreed to stay on as chairman of the board for one more year. But by the time the name change became official on Sept. 30, both Devlin and Hawkes had left the company. Within five months, the list of senior Rothmans executives who had departed had grown to include five vice-presidents. "I'm not flattering myself," Fennell says of his own promotion. "I just happened to be the only show in town that day."

For its new chairman, the company looked no further than its board of directors. It selected Kelly, a Harvard-educated engineer, Ontario fundraiser for the Progressive Conservatives, and since 1982 a member of the Senate. "We've been impressed with their abilities," he says of the new executives leading the company. "We like what we see."

But even before the change at the top, Rothmans initiated many of the changes that have since been attributed to Fennell's marketing and management skills. Hawkes had announced diversification plans for several years running, although no companies were acquired. A $40 million program was underway to improve production facilities in Quebec City. And the company had fired the first shot in what became a cigaret price war, by selling its Number 7 brand in packages of 30 cigarets for the same price as packages of 25.

Fennell has kept Rothmans true to that course, and has also taken measures of his own to reduce costs and try to improve the company's market share. The merger of

Rothmans of Pall Mall Canada and Benson & Hedges (Canada) Inc. is a long-awaited move that reduces the number of Canadian tobacco manufacturers from four to three. It was a move analysts believe makes eminent sense because Philip Morris already owns a piece of Rothmans' Canadian subsidiary through a 22.5% stake in Rothmans International. The New York consumer products giant owns 40% of Rothmans, Benson & Hedges, while Rothmans Inc. hold the remaining 60%. The new company, which will have approximately 31% of the Canadian cigaret market, will benefit from lower production costs, as well as from an extensive rationalization program that has cost Rothmans an estimated $10 million this year. Rothmans has already reduced staff by 450 employees, sold the 83 vintage vehicles in the Craven "A" collection (valued at $4 million) and announced that its Toronto manufacturing plant will close by the end of the year, laying off another 170 people. "Some might look back in five years and say this was a pivotal year," says Robert Allan, vice-president of finance and public affairs for Rothmans. But analysts say these are moves any good manager would be expected to make. Whether Fennell's efforts will increase business is another matter.

Closing the Toronto plant is a symbol of Rothmans' new austerity, just as its creation in 1957 was a symbol of the company's commitment to the Canadian market. But a need in the 1980s to cut costs triggered a new assessment of production, and Rothmans concluded it would be more efficient to concentrate manufacturing in Québec City. Proposals to close the Toronto plant were considered before Fennell's arrival, but it was left to the new chief to make the final decision. The move brought more than the usual criticism from workers about to lose their jobs, as employees complained bitterly that demands on them for higher productivity continued even as resources to do the job were shifted to Québec City. (Further bad feelings were aired on news of the Benson & Hedges merger because it brings two plants to the new company, one of which is near Toronto and is expected to remain open, while the other in Montréal could close.)

The Québec City plant, once the home of the Rock City Tobacco Co. Ltd., stands below the ancient city's stone walls in what was a commercial district adjacent to the St. Charles River. Founded in 1899 as a maker of pipe and chewing tobacco, Rock City entered the cigaret business in 1910. Today the sweet smell of tobacco leaves permeates the air inside the five-story building, where cellulose acetate fibre is fed into filter-making machines on the top floor, beginning a process that spews out cartons of finished cigarets into shipping boxes on the ground floor. The flexibility afforded by the plant's top-to-bottom manufacturing process is the primary reason it was selected as Rothmans' only plant. The filters and tobacco (which are processed on the fourth floor) are fed through stainless steel tubes to cigaret-making machines on the second. To change a machine from one brand to another takes as little as seven minutes, resulting in higher efficiency and lower costs. The machines produce 42 million cigarets over two shifts each day, and output will increase by 25% when the Toronto plant closes.

Rothmans of Pall Mall acquired Rock City in a roundabout fashion. Carreras Ltd. of London gained control of Rock City in 1936, and 22 years later the Rothmans Group bought control of Carreras. The London parent combined the sales operations of its two tobacco companies under John Devlin, an acquaintance of O'Neil-Dunne's from pilot training during the Second World War. Devlin became president of the company in late 1959, and over the next four years he integrated the sales and marketing departments of the two companies, offered shares in Rothmans to the public, initiated a sales turnaround of Rock City brands, and put the Canadian company in position to buy the Rock City assets from the Rothmans Group.

While the Rothmans king-size brand took the market by storm, sales of Rock City brands such as Sportsman, Craven "A," and Black Cat were slipping. Rothmans needed those brands to expand its sales base, so it selected them one by one for rejuvenation, developing marketing plans with specific sales and profit targets.

The competition viewed Rothmans as an upstart, a young company (in Canada at least) trying to move too fast. Yet despite the millions of marketing dollars Rothmans spent, it could not shake Imperial Tobacco's hold on the top market position. By 1967 Rothmans wanted to diversify, and in 1968 it purchased 11% of Canadian Breweries Ltd. from E.P. Taylor's Argus Corp. Canadian Breweries (later renamed Carling O'Keefe Ltd.) was the largest brewer in the country, but it was in trouble. Confident it could produce a turnaround, Rothmans made a bid for control, and in late 1969 owned 50.1% of Canadian Breweries at a cost of $145 million. It undertook a major restructuring of the brewery, selling a 5% holding in Bass Carrington (now Bass PLC of London), and diversifying into wine and oil and gas. The wisdom of buying Canadian Breweries was questioned at the time (Devlin agreed the brewery had a history of "massive problems," while others branded it a white elephant) and it has come under even greater scrutiny since. Owning a brewery exposed the tobacco company to the vagaries of yet another cyclical industry, and over the next 15 years the ups and downs of brewing and tobacco would compound internal problems at both Rothmans and Carling O'Keefe.

But first there were good times. So well did brewing recover – helped by the introduction of Miller Lite, bottled under licence from Philip Morris – that Carling O'Keefe undertook a major expansion at three of its breweries to cope with demand. Yet Carling also missed some big chances: It failed to recognize the marketing potential of putting Canadian beer in the distinctive bottles that were winning a market for Miller; and it was late converting to twist-off beer caps.

When Carling O'Keefe surfaced from the high cost of expansion and packaging changes forced on it by the market, it had a capacity problem of another kind. Demand had fallen, and Carling was the smallest of the Big Three Canadian brewers. Its future now rests on the shedding of major assets and concentrating on selling beer. It has sold winery Jordan & Ste.-Michelle Cellars Ltd. and the trademarks for Carling and Black Label in Britain and Europe. Star Oil & Gas Ltd. and the Toronto Argonauts of the Canadian Football League are also rumored to be on the block.

As well as bringing new kinds of trouble, the Carling O'Keefe acquisition hindered Rothmans' performance in the cigaret business. The tobacco operation lost marketing talent to Carling O'Keefe in the early 1970s, at a time when cigaret sales required aggressive marketing skills. Tobacco markets were changing and Rothmans was slow to meet the demands of the growing regular-length part of the market, in which it had only the Craven brand. "I guess we were riding on our success at that time," says vice-president Allan.

In retrospect, employees say the company developed an arrogance toward its workers, its customers and the market. Workers who approached Rothmans management in the mid-1970s about the trend to light cigarets were told to stick to making cigarets. Rothmans did enter the light cigaret market in 1979, but it had given a valuable head start to the competition.

Rothmans' share was sliding, but at least the market was still growing. "There was concern," says Allan, but no one could articulate the source of the problem, even when market research revealed brand identification problems. From a failure to grow, Rothmans spun into an actual sales decline in 1983. Says Allan: "There was a general corporate frustration of 'How come we can't do it in the marketplace?' There was not any finger-pointing or blame or any scapegoats. It was just a general frustration."

Then, says Allan, Rothmans decided to return to basics. But even when it developed a specific marketing scheme in the form of the 30-cigaret package, uncertainty prevailed. "I guess an unspoken but recognized likely result was that there would have to be different people to effect that change," Allan says. Soon after the 30s were launched, Hawkes and Devlin departed.

The 30-pack of Number 7s was a test of smokers' brand loyalty, a traditionally strong allegiance that has been difficult to influence. By offering five more cigarets for the price of a pack of 25, Rothmans showed that even loyalty has its price. But while the 30s boosted brand market share, they also eliminated profit margins. Fennell is banking on a marketing drive strong enough to swing smokers into the Rothmans habit at regular prices, so the Rothmans brand king-size cigarets are now sold in the 30s pack but at a higher price. The merger with Benson & Hedges is expected to bring an end to the discount wars. "Nobody ever becomes financially strong by discounting their product long-term," says Fennell.

Rothmans and Benson & Hedges brands are expected to complement each other, both in product type and in regional market strengths. But a thorough brand assessment at Rochmans could yet yield some change. Market studies indicate a number of brands whose identity for the consumer is weak, and others whose buyers are a demographic blur. The Rothmans king-size brand projected an image of upper-class British tradition, but its purchasers are now a relatively small group of smokers aged 40 or older. It will be promoted as a cigaret for the under-40 set. "It takes time," cautions Fennell. "People don't change their perceptions of things over a short period of time."

Rothmans is also affected by perceptions that clearly have been changing – social attitudes toward smoking. The industry operates in a society where smoking is increasingly unpopular, where tobacco companies are under constant attack, and where some customers have even carried their grievances into court. Cigaret sales, which fell by almost 5% last year in Canada, continue to slide. Fennell sees all that as "a business problem. Since I joined the company there seems to have been an acceleration in terms of criticism of tobacco products. It's probably twice what it was this time last year," he says. "It's up to us to manage it in a way where we are seen to be – which we are – a company that is terribly responsible and believes in moderation." But that is a bigger job than cutting into a booming market as Rothmans did three decades ago. As O'Neil-Dunne observes, "The buccaneer days of mine are over."

Still, Fennell acknowledges a legacy from Rothmans' early success in Canada. Like the company's leaders in the 1950s, "what we are in the process of attempting to do is be creators, innovators and leaders in the market and begin to hopefully steal initiative from our competitors." But in a shrinking tobacco market it has also become a battle for survival, with Fennell, Rothmans and Benson & Hedges fighting every inch of the way. So far they have shown an ability to shake up the market, but have yet to make any gains in market share. "Fennell has done the obvious things that had to be done at Rothmans," says analyst Palmer. "Whether he can ever turn around the market slide is another question."

QUESTIONS

1. Draw up an organization chart for the upper echelon of Rothmans.
2. Describe Patrick O'Neil-Dunne's leadership style.
3. Characterize the managerial style of Patrick John Fennell.
4. What are the main weaknesses of Rothmans?
5. Discover by research how Imasco, through diversification, solved the problem Rothmans faces. How did Rothmans diversify? What went wrong?
6. Use the ideas outlined in the Kaplan article to develop a creative marketing strategy for Rothmans.

LEADERSHIP SUCCESSION BAKER INC.*

A.B. Ibrahim

Markets are changing, competition is becoming more intense and the performance of Baker Inc. has started to slip. It is extremely painful to me to sit and watch Baker Inc.'s profit earning deteriorating. I have put energy, time and more than thirty years into this company. I have asked you to come to this meeting to review the company's situation and to discuss my retirement plan.

So spoke Mr. James D. Parson, President and Chief Executive Officer of Baker Inc. from his executive office on the sixty-second floor of the First Canadian Building. Baker Inc. is a Canadian-owned and managed corporation, manufacturing and selling electrical equipment for industrial and consumer use throughout the world. The

---

* This case was prepared by Dr. A.B. Ibrahim of Concordia University as a basis for class discussion rather than to illustrate either effective or ineffective handling of an administrative situation. Copyright © 1986 by Professor A.B. Ibrahim. Reprinted by permission of the author.

company employs over 3,000 employees and has offices in Italy, England, Egypt, Sweden and the United States.

Baker's historical background would provide any writer with all the ingredients of a corporate drama. Described by a business associate as "a man who felt that he should never quash his instincts with an over-dependency on numbers and facts alone," Mr. James Parson started his business 35 years ago, in 1948, with $10,000 in the bank which he had collected from members of his family, his mother, Eva, his brother, John, now Corporate Vice-President/Human Resources and his brother-in-law, George Brown, now Corporate Vice-President/Organization Development. Company sales were $30,000 in 1948 with operating net profit of $2,500; comparable 1984 fiscal year data were $75,210,150 and $12,642,300.

Mr. Parson's retirement plan was not a surprise to many of his top executives. Many problems were obvious in the past three years. Managers have been complaining of Mr. Parson's interference in their work, specifically his relation with their immediate subordinates. Parson still maintains a good relationship with floor level workers and clerks who started early when Baker was still a small firm. Many times these people had ignored their immediate supervisors and went directly to James Parson with small problems which had offended their superiors.

There have been problems concerning Parson's style of making decisions. As one manager put it, " . . . his entrepreneurial style was okay 30 years ago when Baker was a small business firm." Mr. Parson has recently launched a new product without consulting his top executives and despite the recommendation of his marketing and planning staff that the market is saturated. "Well the company lost 1,000,000 in this project," commented a senior executive.

Executives have been also talking about family vs. non-family, "people in Baker Inc. think, unless you are a member of the family, you will never get to the top," commented a middle level manager. Recently Mr. Parson appointed his son-in-law John McFarland, a recent graduate from a large Canadian school, to the position of Vice-President/Finance (see Exhibit 1).

Executives were also wondering if the time has come for professional management to replace the entrepreneur. Recent figures have revealed that the company is certainly in the stage of maturity.

Attending the meeting in which Parson announced his retirement plan were the following senior executives:

Herbert Johnson, Vice-President/Marketing Herbert joined the company 15 years ago at the age of 26 as a marketing trainee fresh out of college. Instead of being shown to his desk, he was handed a shovel and ordered to help clean out the snow which had collected in the plant during a heavy snow storm. Three years ago, he launched a successful promotion campaign which resulted in a 15 percent increase in sales throughout the world. Mr. Johnson is not a family member and he is one of the few executives that has raised the issue of professional management and family vs. non-family in that meeting, out of loyalty to Mr. Parson and the company. Top executives, including Parson, have always admired his courage and commitment.

Exhibit 1
Baker Inc. Organization Chart

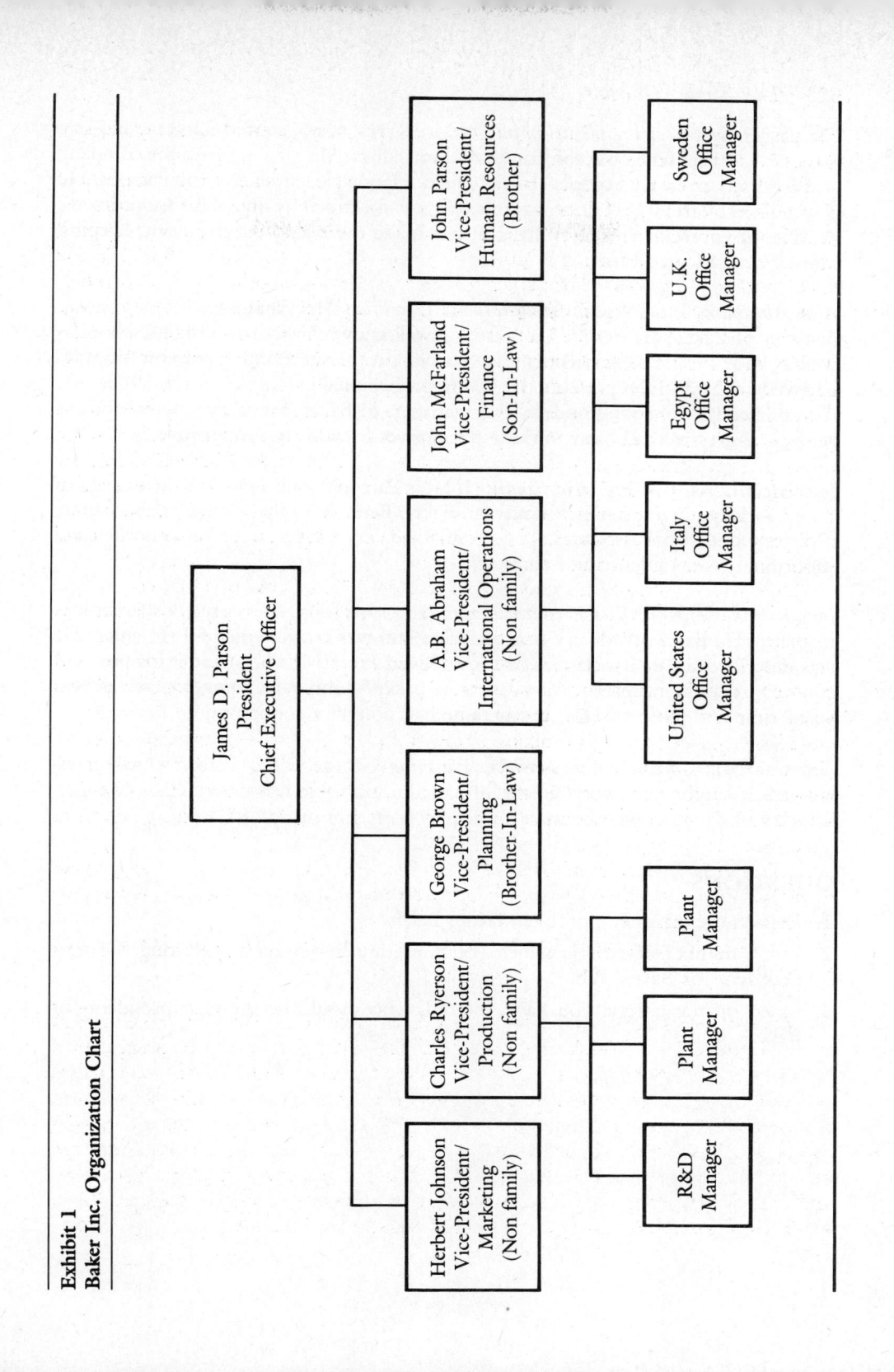

```
                              James D. Parson
                              President
                              Chief Executive Officer
                                      |
   ┌──────────────┬───────────────┬───┴────────────┬────────────────┬──────────────┐
Herbert Johnson  Charles Ryerson  George Brown   A.B. Abraham    John McFarland  John Parson
Vice-President/  Vice-President/  Vice-President/ Vice-President/ Vice-President/ Vice-President/
Marketing        Production       Planning        International   Finance         Human Resources
(Non family)     (Non family)     (Brother-In-Law) Operations     (Son-In-Law)    (Brother)
                                                  (Non family)
                       |                                 |
              ┌────────┼────────┐       ┌────────┬───────┼───────┬────────┐
            R&D      Plant     Plant  United   Italy   Egypt    U.K.    Sweden
          Manager  Manager   Manager  States   Office  Office   Office   Office
                                      Office   Manager Manager  Manager  Manager
                                      Manager
```

Charles Ryerson, Vice-President/Production Mr. Ryerson, 56, started 32 years ago as a foreman in Baker when the company was a small firm. He grew up with the company and acquired extensive experience in the field. He is a close friend to the Parsons. He is well liked by the shop's floor workers. He was described by one of his subordinates as "a do-it-yourself manager who regularly made the rounds of the plant, keeping himself available at all time".

A.B. Abraham, Vice-President/International Operation Mr. Abraham, 34, is a recent member of Baker. He has an MBA from a well-known Canadian business school as well as wide business experiences. He was behind the successful expansion program in Sweden. At 34 he represents the young professional executives of the 1980s. He is well liked by the young middle level managers in Baker. He has been described as "a cool, aggressive and hard working person, yet friendly and supportive."

John McFarland, Vice-President/Finance John is Parson's son-in-law and, at the age of 28, he is the youngest senior executive in Baker. Being a family member is his trouble, explained one of his associates. " . . . he worked very hard to have his associates and subordinates's confidence and respect."

John Parson, Corporate Vice-President/Human Resources John, 64, is a major shareholder in Baker. He has worked very hard in Baker and was certainly helpful to James. He was described by an associate as "a shirt-sleeved executive who made it his personal concern to know intimately every aspect of Baker." John is planning to retire in two years' time and move to Florida where he had bought a condominium last year.

George Brown, Corporate Vice-President/Planning George, 59, is Parson's brother-in-law, a self taught man who had no formal education. He was described as "a quiet, self-centered person who believes a leader is born, not made."

QUESTIONS

1. Discuss the leadership problem facing Baker.
2. List a number of criteria which you think are important in selecting the next president for Baker. Why?
3. Based on the criteria you have selected, who should be the next president for Baker?

EXERCISES

"MY BEST BOSS"

Joe Kelly

The objective of "My Best Boss" is to help you review your experience of being led and to help you to form a clear picture of how you perceived the leadership you were under. Think of a time when you were part of a team in a business organization or in some sort of organized extracurricular activity and answer the following questions.

QUESTIONS

1. Choose the person whom you consider to be the best leader you have served under at any time, anywhere. Write a sketch of that person in about fifty words, making clear the reason that that person impressed you.
2. How did this person's style affect your management style?
3. If the leader had a second-in-command, can you comment on that figure's personality and style?

OPERATING PROBLEMS

Joe Kelly

The purpose of this exercise is to focus on the problems that develop among people at work, particularly among peers and subordinates as they respond to your style of leadership. In formulating these problems, review your experience working in an organization (a business firm, a school club, or an athletics team).

After this exercise is completed, you will have better insight into the problems that inevitably arise when people work together. Moreover, you will be better able to form a judgment about the inevitability of such problems. This exercise should provide a background that will help you to improve your human relations skills.

QUESTIONS

1. What are the three most pressing problems you feel you pose for those who have to work with you? (In trying to answer this question, think back to the experience you have had with people with whom you worked. What were their complaints? Think of actual events and give their actual comments.)
2. Were their comments relevant? In what ways?
3. In the light of their comments, did you change your method of work? Why not?

VIII
CONFLICT MANAGEMENT AND POWER

READINGS

MANAGING CONFLICT*

Leonard Greenhalgh

Managers or change agents spend a substantial proportion of their time and energy dealing with conflict situations. Such efforts are necessary because any type of change in an organization tends to generate conflict. More specifically, conflict arises because change disrupts the existing balance of resources and power, thereby straining relations between the people involved. Since adversarial relations may impede the process of making adaptive changes in the organization, higher-level managers may have to intervene in order to implement important strategies. Their effectiveness in managing the conflict depends on how well they understand the underlying dynamics of the conflict — which may be very different from its expression — and whether they can identify the crucial tactical points for intervention.

CONFLICT MANAGEMENT

Conflict is managed when it does not substantially interfere with the ongoing functional (as opposed to personal) relationships between the parties involved. For instance, two executives may agree to disagree on a number of issues and yet be jointly committed to the course of action they have settled on. There may even be some residual hard feelings — perhaps it is too much to expect to manage feelings in addition to relationships — but as long as any resentment is at a fairly low level and does not substantially interfere with other aspects of their professional relationship, the conflict could be considered to have been managed successfully.

Conflict is not an objective, tangible phenomenon; rather, it exists in the minds of the people who are party to it. Only its manifestations, such as brooding, arguing, or fighting, are objectively real. To manage conflict, therefore, one needs to empathize, that is, to understand the situation as it is seen by the key actors involved. An important element of conflict management is persuasion, which may well involve getting participants to rethink their current views so their perspective on the situation will facilitate reconciliation rather than divisiveness.

Influencing key actors' conceptions of the conflict situation can be a powerful lever in making conflicts manageable. This approach can be used by a third party intervening in the conflict, or even more usefully, by the participants themselves. But using this perceptual lever alone will not always be sufficient. The context in which the conflict occurs, the history of the relationship between the parties, and the time available will have to be taken into account if such an approach is to be tailored to the situation. Furthermore, the conflict may prove to be simply unmanageable: one or both parties may wish to prolong the conflict or they may have reached emotional states that make constructive interaction impossible; or, perhaps the conflict is "the tip of the iceberg" and resolving it would have no significant impact on a deeply rooted antagonistic relationship.

---

* Reprinted from "Managing Conflict" by Leonard Greenhalgh, SLOAN MANAGEMENT REVIEW, Summer 1986, pp. 45–51, by permission of the publisher. Copyright © 1986 by the Sloan Management Review Association. All rights reserved.

Table 1 presents seven perceptual dimensions that form a useful diagnostic model that shows what to look for in a conflict situation and pinpoints the dimensions needing high-priority attention. The model can thus be used to illuminate a way to make the conflict more manageable. The point here is that conflict becomes more negotiable between parties when a minimum number of dimensions are perceived to be at the "difficult-to-resolve" pole and a maximum number to be at the "easy-to-resolve" pole. The objective is to shift a viewpoint from the difficult-to-resolve pole to the easy-to-resolve one. At times, antagonists will deliberately resist "being more reasonable" because they see tactical advantages in taking a hard line. Nevertheless, there are strong benefits for trying to shift perspectives; these benefits should become apparent as we consider each of the dimensions in the model.

Issues in Question

People view issues on a continuum from being a matter of principle to a question of division. For example, one organization needed to change its channel of distribution. The company had sold door-to-door since its founding, but the labor market was drying up and the sales force was becoming increasingly understaffed. Two factions of executive sprung up: the supporters were open to the needed change; the resisters argued that management made a commitment to the remaining sales force and, as a matter of principle, could not violate the current sales representatives' right to be the exclusive channel of distribution.

Raising principles make conflict difficult to resolve because by definition one cannot come to a reasonable compromise; one either upholds a principle or sacrifices one's integrity. For some issues, particularly those involving ethical imperatives, such a dichotomous view may be justified. Often, however, matters of principle are raised for the purpose of solidifying a bargaining stance. Yet, this tactic may work *against* the party using it since it tends to invite an impasse. Once matters of principle are raised, the parties try to argue convincingly that the other's point of view is wrong. At best, this approach wastes time and saps the energy of the parties involved. A useful

Table 1
Conflict Diagnostic Model

Dimension	Viewpoint Continuum	
	Difficult to Resolve	**Easy to Resolve**
Issue in Question	Matter of Principle	Divisible Issue
Size of Stakes	Large	Small
Interdependence of the Parties	Zero Sum	Positive Sum
Continuity of Interaction	Single Transaction	Long-term Relationship
Structure of the Parties	Amorphous or Fractionalized, with Weak Leadership	Cohesive, with Strong Leadership
Involvement of Third Parties	No Neutral Third Party Available	Trusted, Powerful, Prestigious, and Neutral
Perceived Progress of the Conflict	Unbalanced: One Party Feeling the More Harmed	Parties Having Done Equal Harm to Each Other

intervention at this point may be to have the parties acknowledge that they *understand* each other's view but still believe in their own, equally legitimate point of view. This acknowledgement alone often makes the parties more ready to move ahead from arguing to problem solving.

At the other extreme are divisible issues where neither side has to give in completely; the outcome may more or less favor both parties. In the door-to-door selling example, a more constructive discussion would have ensued had the parties been able to focus on the *economic* commitment the company had to its sales force, rather than on the *moral* commitment. As it was, the factions remained deadlocked until the company had suffered irrevocable losses in market share, which served no one's interests. Divisible issues in this case might have involved how much of the product line would be sold through alternative channels of distribution, the extent of exclusive territory, or how much income protection the company was willing to offer its sales force.

Size of Stakes

The greater the perceived value of what may be lost, the harder it is to manage a conflict. This point is illustrated when managers fight against acquisition attempts. If managers think their jobs are in jeopardy, they subjectively perceive the stakes as being high and are likely to fight tooth and nail against the acquisition. Contracts providing for continued economic security, so-called golden parachutes, reduce the size of the stakes for those potentially affected. Putting aside the question of whether such contracts are justifiable when viewed from other perspectives, they do tend to make acquisition conflicts more manageable.

In many cases the perceived size of the stakes can be reduced by persuasion rather than by taking concrete action. People tend to become emotionally involved in conflicts and as a result magnify the importance of what is really at stake. Their "egos" get caught up in the winning/losing aspect of the conflict, and subjective values become inflated.

A good antidote is to postpone the settlement until the parties become less emotional. During this cooling-off period they can reevaluate the issues at stake, thereby restoring some objectivity to their assessments. If time does not permit a cooling off, an attempt to reassess the demands and reduce the other party's expectations may be possible: "There's no way we can give you 100 percent of what you want, so let's be realistic about what you can live with." This approach is really an attempt to induce an attitude change. In effect, the person is being persuaded to entertain the thought, "If I can get by with less than 100 percent of what I was asking for, then what is at stake must not be of paramount importance to me."

A special case of the high-stakes/low-stakes question is the issue of precedents. If a particular settlement sets a precedent, the stakes are seen as being higher because future conflicts will tend to be settled in terms of the current settlement. In other words, giving ground in the immediate situation is seen as giving ground for all time. This problem surfaces in settling grievances. Thus, an effective way to manage such a conflict is to emphasize the uniqueness of the situation to downplay possible precedents that could be set. Similarly, the perceived consequences of organizational changes for individuals can often be softened by explicitly downplaying the future consequences: employees are sometimes assured that the change is being made "on an experimental basis" and will later be reevaluated. The effect is to reduce the perceived risk in accepting the proposed change.

Interdependence of the Parties

The parties to a conflict can view themselves on a continuum from having "zero-sum" to "positive-sum" interdependence. Zero-sum interdependence is the perception that if one party gains in an interaction, it is at the expense of the other party. In the positive-sum case, both parties come out ahead by means of a settlement. A zero-sum relationship makes conflict difficult to resolve because it focuses attention narrowly on personal gain rather than on mutual gain through collaboration or problem solving.

Consider the example of conflict over the allocation of limited budget funds among sales and production when a new product line is introduced. The sales group fights for a large allocation to promote the product in order to build market share. The production group fights for a large allocation to provide the plant and equipment necessary to turn out high volume at high-quality levels. The funds available have a fixed ceiling, so that a gain for sales appears to be a loss for production and vice versa. From a zero-sum perspective, it makes sense to fight for the marginal dollar rather than agree on a compromise.

A positive-sum view of the same situation removes some of the urgency to win a larger share of the spoils at the outset. Attention is more usefully focused on how one party's allocation in fact helps the other. Early promotion allocations to achieve high sales volume, if successful, lead to high production volume. This, in turn, generates revenue that can be invested in the desired improvements to plant and equipment. Similarly, initial allocations to improve plant and equipment can make a high-quality product readily available to the sales group, and the demand for a high-quality product will foster sales.

The potential for mutual benefit is often overlooked in the scramble for scarce resources. However, if both parties can be persuaded to consider how they can both benefit from a situation, they are more likely to approach the conflict over scarce resources with more cooperative predispositions. The focus shifts from whether one party is getting a fair share of the available resources to what is the optimum initial allocation that will jointly serve the mutual long-run interests of both sales and production.

Continuity of Interaction

The continuity-of-interaction dimension concerns the time horizon over which the parties see themselves dealing with each other. If they visualize a long-term interaction – a *continuous* relationship – the present transaction takes on minor significance, and the conflict within that transaction tends to be easy to resolve. If, on the other hand, the transaction is viewed as a one-shot deal – an *episodic* relationship – the parties will have little incentive to accommodate each other, and the conflict will be difficult to resolve.

This difference in perspective is seen by contrasting how lawyers and managers approach a contract dispute. Lawyers are trained to perceive the situation as a single episode: the parties go to court, and the lawyers make the best possible case for their party in an attempt to achieve the best possible outcome. This is a "no-holds-barred" interaction in which the past and future interaction between the parties tends to be viewed as irrelevant. Thus the conflict between the parties is not really resolved; rather, an outcome is imposed by the judge.

In contrast, managers are likely to be more accommodating when the discussion of a contract is viewed as one interaction within a longer-term relationship that has both a history and a future. In such a situation, a manager is unlikely to resort to no-holds-barred tactics because he or she will have to face the other party again regarding future deals. Furthermore, a continuous relationship permits the bankrolling of favors: "We helped you out on that last problem; it's your turn to work with us on this one."

Here, it is easy, and even cordial, to remind the other party that a continuous relationship exists. This tactic works well because episodic situations are rare in real-world business transactions. For instance, people with substantial business experience know that a transaction is usually not completed when a contract is signed. No contract can be comprehensive enough to provide unambiguously for all possible contingencies. Thus trust and goodwill remain important long after the contract is signed. The street-fighting tactics that may seem advantageous in the context of an episodic orientation are likely to be very costly to the person who must later seek accommodation with the bruised and resentful other party.

Structure of the Parties

Conflict is easier to resolve when a party has a strong leader who can unify his or her constituency to accept and implement the agreement. If the leadership is weak, rebellious subgroups who may not feel obliged to go along with the overall agreement that has been reached are likely to rise up, thereby making conflict difficult to resolve.

For example, people who deal with unions know that a strong leadership tends to be better than a weak one, especially when organizational change needs to be accomplished. A strongly led union may drive a hard bargain, but once an agreement is reached the deal is honored by union members. If a weakly led union is involved, the agreement may be undermined by factions within the union who may not like some of the details. The result may well be chronic resistance to change or even wildcat strikes. To bring peace among such factions, management may have to make further concessions that may be costly. To avoid this, managers may find themselves in a paradoxical position of needing to boost the power of union leaders.

Similar actions may be warranted when there is no union. Groups of employees often band together as informal coalitions to protect their interests in times of change. Instead of fighting or alienating a group, managers who wish to bring about change may benefit from considering ways to formalize the coalition, such as by appointing its opinion leader to a task force or steering committee. This tactic may be equivalent to cooptation, yet there is likely to be a net benefit to both the coalition and management. The coalition benefits because it is given a formal channel in which the opinion leader's viewpoint is expressed; management benefits because the spokesperson presents the conflict in a manageable form, which is much better than passive resistance or subtle sabotage.

Involvement of Third Parties

People tend to become emotionally involved in conflicts. Such involvement can have several effects: perceptions may become distorted, nonrational thought processes and arguments may arise, and unreasonable stances, impaired communication, and personal attacks may result. These effects make the conflict difficult to resolve.

The presence of a third party, even if the third party is not actively involved in the dialogue, can constrain such effects. People usually feel obliged to appear reasonable and responsible because they care more about how the neutral party is evaluating them than by how the opponent is. The more prestigious, powerful, trusted, and neutral the third party, the greater is the desire to exercise emotional restraint.

While managers often have to mediate conflicts among lower-level employees, they are rarely seen as being neutral. Therefore, consultants and change agents often end up serving a mediator role, either by design or default. This role can take several forms, ranging from an umpire supervising communication to a messenger between parties for whom face-to-face communication has become too strained. Mediation essentially involves keeping the parties interacting in a reasonable and constructive manner. Typically, however, most managers are reluctant to enlist an outsider who is a professional mediator or arbitrator, for it is very hard for them to admit openly that they are entangled in a serious conflict, much less one they cannot handle themselves.

When managers remain involved in settling disputes, they usually take a stronger role than mediators: they become arbitrators rather than mediators. As arbitrators, they arrive at a conflict-resolving judgment after hearing each party's case. In most business conflicts, mediation is preferable because the parties are helped to come to an agreement in which they have some psychological investment. Arbitration tends to be more of a judicial process in which the parties make the best possible case to support their position: this tends to further polarize rather than reconcile differences.

Managers can benefit from a third-party presence, however, without involving dispute-resolution professionals *per se*. For example, they can introduce a consultant into the situation, with an *explicit* mission that is not conflict intervention. The mere presence of this neutral witness will likely constrain the disputants' use of destructive tactics.

Alternatively, if the managers find that they themselves are party to a conflict, they can make the conflict more public and produce the same constraining effect that a third party would. They also can arrange for the presence of relatively uninvolved individuals during interactions; even having a secretary keep minutes of such interactions encourages rational behavior. If the content of the discussion cannot be disclosed to lower-level employees, a higher-level manager can be invited to sit in on the discussion, thereby discouraging dysfunctional personal attacks and unreasonable stances. To the extent that managers can be trusted to be evenhanded, a third-party approach can facilitate conflict management. Encouraging accommodation usually is preferable to imposing a solution that may only produce resentment of one of the parties.

Progress of the Conflict

It is difficult to manage conflict when the parties are not ready to achieve a reconciliation. Thus it is important to know whether the parties believe that the conflict is escalating. The following example illustrates this point.

During a product strategy meeting, a Marketing Vice-President carelessly implied that the R&D group tended to overdesign products. The remark was intended to be a humorous stereotyping of the R&D function, but it was interpreted by the R&D Vice-President as an attempt to pass on to his group the blame for an uncompetitive product. Later in the meeting, the R&D Vice-President took advantage of an opportunity to point out that the Marketing Vice-President lacked the technical expertise to understand a design limitation. The Marketing Vice-President perceived this rejoinder as ridicule and therefore as an act of hostility. The R&D Vice-President, who believed he had evened the score, was quite surprised to be denounced subsequently by the Marketing Vice-President, who in turn thought he was evening the score for the uncalled-for-barb. These events soon led to a memo war, backbiting, and then to pressure on various employees to take sides.

The important point here is that from the first rejoinder neither party wished to escalate the conflict; each wished merely to even the score. Nonetheless, conflict resolution would have been very difficult to accomplish during this escalation phase because people do not like to disengage when they think they still "owe one" to the other party. Since an even score is subjectively defined, however, the parties need to be convinced that the overall score is approximately equal and that everyone has already suffered enough.

DEVELOPING CONFLICT MANAGEMENT SKILLS

Strategic decision making usually is portrayed as a unilateral process. Decision makers have some vision of where the organization needs to be headed, and they decide on the nature and timing of specific actions to achieve tangible goals. This portrayal, however, does not take into account the conflict inherent in the decision-making process; most strategic decisions are negotiated solutions to conflicts among people whose interests are affected by such decisions. Even in the uncommon case of a unilateral decision, the decision maker has to deal with the conflict that arises when he or she moves to *implement* the decision.

In the presence of conflict at the decision-making or decision-implmenting stage, managers must focus on generating an *agreement* rather than a decision. A decision without agreement makes the strategic direction difficult to implement. By contrast, an agreement on a strategic direction doesn't require an explicit decision. In this context, conflict management is the process of removing cognitive barriers to agreement. Note that agreement does not imply that the conflict has "gone away." The people involved still have interests that are somewhat incompatible. Agreement implies that these people have become committed to a course of action that serves some of their interests.

People make agreements that are less than ideal from the standpoint of serving their interests when they lack the *power* to force others to fully comply with their wishes. On the other hand, if a manager has total power over those whose interests are affected by the outcome of a strategic decision, the manager may not care whether or not others agree, because total power implies total compliance. There are few situations in real life in which managers have influence that even approaches total power, however, and power solutions are at best unstable since most people react negatively to powerlessness *per se*. Thus it makes more sense to seek agreements than to seek power. Furthermore, because conflict management involves weakening or removing barriers to agreements, managers must be able to diagnose successfully such barriers. The model summarized in Table 1 identifies the primary cognitive barriers to agreement.

Competence in understanding the barriers to an agreement can be easily honed by making a pastime of conflict diagnosis. The model helps to focus attention on specific aspects of the situation that may pose obstacles to successful conflict management. This pastime transforms accounts of conflicts — from sources ranging from a spouse's response to "how was your day?" to the evening news — into a challenge in which the objective is to try to pinpoint the obstacles to agreement and to predict the success of proposed interventions.

Focusing on the underlying dynamics of the conflict makes it more likely that conflict management will tend toward resolution rather than the more familiar response of suppression. Although the conflict itself — that is, the source — will remain alive, at best, its expression will be postponed until some later occasion; at worst, it will take a less obvious and usually less manageable form.

Knowledge of and practice in using the model is only a starting point for managers and change agents. Their development as professionals requires that conflict management become an integral part of their use of power. Power is a most basic facet of organizational life, yet inevitably it generates conflict because it constricts the autonomy of those who respond to it. Anticipating precisely how the use of power will create a conflict relationship provides an enormous advantage in the ability to achieve the desired levels of control with minimal dysfunctional side effects.

MAKE CONFLICT WORK FOR YOU*

Joe Kelly

Contrary to conventional wisdom, the most important single thing about conflict is that it is good for you. While this is not a scientific statement of fact, it reflects a basic and unprecedented shift of emphasis — a move away from the old human relations point of view where all conflict was basically seen as bad.

The modern organizational revolution has been characterized by an acceleration of healthy subversive tendencies which gathered force and speed in the 1960s in protest against the brittle iron law of corporate oligarchy; a protest against the presumption that, in organizations, policies and instructions flow down the hierarchy and reports flow up.

It is a protest against the cozy paternalistic world of classical management theory where top

---

* Reprinted by permission of the *Harvard Business Review*. "Make Conflict Work for You" by Joe Kelly (July/August 1970). Copyright © 1970 by the President and Fellows of Harvard College; all rights reserved.

Author's note: This article is adapted from a chapter on conflict which appears in my book, *Organizational Behavior* (Homewood, Illinois, Richard D. Irwin, Inc., 1969).

management carries total responsibility. It is a protest exemplified by the success of *The Peter Principle*[1] which was on the best seller lists for many months. It is increasingly a middle-class protest by executives and professionals, and decreasingly a protest from a diminishing shop floor. It is a protest with its own particular diabolism; some of the games played in executive suites make Edward Albee's "Get the Guests" and "Bring up the Baby," as portrayed in "Who's Afraid of Virginia Woolf?" seem like nursery pastimes.

In brief, in our new frontier environment, conflict is the order of the day.

The new look is so radical that many top managers wonder just how this change came about. Not that most knowing managers have not adopted a different posture to conflict management; most have mastered the new argot that includes such choice phrases as "structure me a meeting," "let's go for confrontation," "they're definitely going to escalate this one," "minimize our maximum losses," "let's introduce a little uncertainty into the situation," and so on. Most experienced executives recognize the script, know they have learned new parts, but are curious to discover how it all came about. But this is not only intellectual curiosity as to what happened in the past; it also conceals a deep and pervasive need to try to guess the practical implications of "conflict nouveau."

In this article, I shall argue that the old concept or human relations view of conflict fails to acknowledge its importance as a creative force in today's society. What is needed, in my judgment, is a new look or realistic reassessment of conflict that, if properly handled, can make conflict work for you in your role as a business manager.

REALISTIC REASSESSMENT

The emerging new view of conflict, as shown in Exhibit I, reverses many of the cozy nostrums of human relations management, which had its intellectual origins in the famous Hawthorne studies of the 1920s. These studies "proved" the then startling proposition that interpersonal relations counted more for productivity than the quality of the physical environment, such as the level of illumination. An entire school of management grew up around the then advanced notion that if people were well treated, they would produce. Conflict, by definition, was harmful and

Exhibit I. Human relations and realistic models of conflict

Old view	New look
Conflict is by definition avoidable.	Conflict is inevitable.
Conflict is caused by troublemakers, boat rockers, and prima donnas.	Conflict is determined by structural factors such as the physical shape of a building, the design of a career structure, or the nature of a class system.
Legalistic forms of authority such as "going through channels" or "sticking to the book" are emphasized.	Conflict is integral to the nature of change.
Scapegoats are accepted as inevitable.	A minimal level of conflict is optimal.

should be avoided. Those who generated conflict were troublemakers and were bad for the organization.

It is easy to take a somewhat superior if not jaundiced view of human relations as a management philosophy, but this is to pluck it out of its historical context. In its time, it was quite apposite, essentially part of the New Deal of the 1930s. It might be appropriate to regard human relations as the infrastructure change in the primary work group to correspond with Roosevelt's, "We have nothing to fear, but fear itself," which helped to get America's depression-ridden economy going again. The philosophy of human relations helped to ease Western society into a post-Marxian era in which the robber barons and the sweatshop capitalists have all but disappeared.

But the old concept of human relations does not fit today's facts. It no longer describes the managerial thinking of those men who run enterprises which are a mixture of public and private investment, and who have learned that while they must strive for private profit, they must defer to public welfare. These epoch-making organizational changes have come so quickly and pervasively that the entrepreneurs who have managed through the actual phases of human change are somewhat bewildered by it all.

In brief, the human relations school fails ultimately because it does not have a proper frame of reference; it fails both to acknowledge the importance of sociological forces and also to recognize the importance of conflict as a creative force in society. In particular, the idea that conflict is always bad warrants closer examination. Perfect organizational health is not freedom from conflict. On the contrary, if properly handled, conflict can lead to more effective and appropriate adjustments.

Optimal anxiety

There is a curious link between conflict management and anxiety. At one time, psychologists believed rather naively that anxiety, in any form or level, must by its nature be bad. But studies of both soldiers in combat and patients after surgery strongly suggest that a moderate level of anxiety may be adaptive and facilitate survival.

Other researchers reinforce this point by arguing that an environment devoid of novelty can be unbearable to human subjects. In other words, there seems to be an optimal level of uncertainty for effective functioning.

Anxiety (in small quantities) facilitates adjustment; people need some uncertainty. Ethologists like Konrad Lorenz are bringing forward persuasive evidence that controlled aggression has survival value; that although dominance ultimately depends on force, it leads to law and order.[2] Lorenz has argued that aggression is a function of normal selection and produces an increased expectation of survival; further aggression brings about a dispersal of individuals. Lorenz, who has observed animals in their natural habitats, believes that fighting may generate a stable "pecking order." Much the same discussion can be repeated about our own society, which is learning to allow dissent but not unlimited dissent.

Aggression, apparently an essential characteristic of executives, makes many managers miserable with guilt. Adopting an "attack ethos" usually stands an executive in good stead, but it is aggression moderated by a need to maintain social acceptability.

Conflict management recognizes that executives have aggressions to expend, can withstand a fair amount of anxiety, and welcome uncertainty as an opportunity to restructure their environment. Hence the way conflict is *managed* — rather than suppressed, ignored, or avoided — contributes significantly to a company's effectiveness.

Dissensus and consensus

In this section, let us turn our attention to the intellectual origins of this new approach to conflict management. Some executives, perhaps jaundiced by the distressing skill that social psychologists have shown in managing and eventually dissipating conflict in laboratory situations, have blamed the behavioral scientists.

But the more mathematically oriented executive might be tempted to think it all began with game theory that refers to a mathematical technique which finds an optimal strategy for a player, taking into consideration all options open to an opponent. Reflection suggests, however, that its mathematical assumptions are too abstruse and abstract to have much organizational relevance.

Nevertheless, many executives have found the language of game theory, such as zero-sum or mini-max strategy, easy to incorporate into their argot. Other executives blame the cold war and quote Thomas C. Schelling, who has pointed out:

> "The precarious strategy of cold war and nuclear stalemate has often been expressed in game-type analogies: two enemies within reach of each other's poison arrows on opposite sides of a canyon, the poison so slow that either could shoot the other before he died; a shepherd who has chased a wolf into a corner where it has no choice but to fight, the shepherd unwilling to turn his back on the beast; a pursuer armed only with a hand grenade who inadvertently gets too close to his victim and dares not use his weapon; two neighbors, each controlling dynamite in the other's basement, trying to find mutual security through some arrangement of electric switches and detonators."[3]

A more fundamental reason has been the demise of human relations as a mangement philosophy and the emergence of the task approach to conflict management where the emphasis has been on developing the optimal organization by considering both the task to be done and the resources available. In the task approach, the exploitation of crisis becomes a major avenue of development. For example:

In the Apollo Project, the capsule fire which took the lives of three astronauts was seized as an opportunity to change relations between NASA officials and executives of contracting companies. Whereas before the fire two parties had met in a negotiating context, after the fire they got together to solve problems. The result was not only increased effectiveness, but the beginning of a change in the role of the liaison executives; their companies began to question to whom they owed their allegiance – NASA or the contractors.

CRISIS: USE AND MISUSE

In the creative use of crisis, the effective executive welcomes uncertainty and plans for its exploitation, if not its creation. An example of this is provided by the experience of a British manufacturing company which reacted to the government's introduction of a payroll tax by grasping the chance to reorganize and rationalize its product lines, so that each factory was charged with the making of one component instead of two.

What is significant about this case is not only that the company subsequently had the tax and a bit more refunded to it, but also that the chief executive grabbed the chance to make dramatic organizational changes which he had been mulling over for some time. In other more tranquil circumstances, such changes would have been subject to considerable and sustained negotiations both in the front office and in the work councils.

Creative tension

In the turbulent environment of contemporary business suffused with ambiguity, the hard-headed executive with strong nerves and a feel for the moment of drama that a crisis affords has the chance to restructure the organizational scene in a way which at once may well meet his needs for self-fulfillment as well as the interests of the institution.

Moreover, the social science "angels" would be on the side of this hardheaded but imaginative executive. Research evidence suggests that tension needs to be reappraised and that the exploitation of healthy tension can (a) stimulate learning, (b) serve to "internalize" the problems of other managers, (c) increase critical vigilance and self-appraisal, and (d) induce decision makers to examine conflicting values more discerningly (including their own) when they are making decisions.[4]

There is also considerable and growing research

evidence from the study of creative tension and scientific performance that research scientists, if they are going to function effectively and achieve excellence, require an intellectual and social environment made up of two sets of apparently inconsistent factors: one set related to stability, confidence, or security; and the other pertained to an optimal level of disruption, intellectual conflict, or "challenge."

To illustrate, the most effective researchers are those who control their product mix of personal interaction in such a way that they get sufficient critical feedback from competitive colleagues; they also have a steady supply of "generally supportive" human backup which they can use as a form of "psychic heavy water" to keep the fissions and fusions of intellectual ferment from becoming critical and detonating.

In brief, at the risk of oversimplification, what the social scientists are saying is that there is an optimal level of anxiety, arousal, and conflict for man to function effectively. Fortunately, this intelligence is coming to business leaders at an appropriate moment because, both at home and abroad, conflict is manifesting itself in ways which challenge conventional wisdom in management theory.

To make this point of theory meaningful, it is necessary to distinguish between structure and process. The structure, in terms of organization shapes, definitions, and roles, we seem to know a lot about; but about the process, in terms of what actually happens within or without the structure, we seem to know very little. The student revolution of the sixties, with its emphasis on confrontation, conflict, and crisis, is but one vivid example of the organizational process bursting the conventional structure of bureaucracy.

Organizational attrition

Conflict is endemic, inevitable, and necessary to organizational life and always involves some testing of the power situation.[5] A typical example of organizational conflict is revealed in this case based on an actual but disguised corporate situation:

Bill Jones, a department manager, was sent to a management course and on his return found that his auxiliary but highly valued position of assistant general manager was apparently up for grabs. Before his departure, his name had appeared on the organization chart set aside for assistant general manager (see Exhibit 2). On his return, he found that a new organization chart had been issued, but that this particular box had been left empty.

Jones was thus faced with a dilemma: Had it been done deliberately? The decision which he had to make at this stage was whether he ought to keep silent and bide his time, or to raise this matter with the general manager, John Fulton, to try to have his name put back in this box.

As it was, he decided to follow a policy of "wait and see." But when he returned from his annual vacation, he discovered that the name of a rival department manager, Ned Carter, was in the assistant general manager's box.

Taken with other signs, Jones realized he was getting the treatment. His boss was using the technique of "nonlosing hazard" which put Jones at a considerable disadvantage, and describes a strategy that can produce a win but not a loss for the general manager. In other words, if Jones had reacted to the first move of "leaving the box empty," then the general manager might have acquiesced but accused him of being paranoiac and generally oversensitive.

In fact, Fulton continued the squeezing process, circumscribing Jones's role by establishing very close standards of performance for his department and leaving him without much organizational slack. Fulton, in his inspection tours freely criticized the department's performance.

Jones experienced a good deal of stress and anxiety, and he had to exercise considerable restraint to ensure that he did not transmit his anxiety to his subordinates, who were already under enough pressure from the more exacting performance standards required by the general manager. In view of this level of conflict, Jones had understandably begun the search for a more secure niche elsewhere in the corporation.

Exhibit 2:
Typical Example of Organizational Attrition

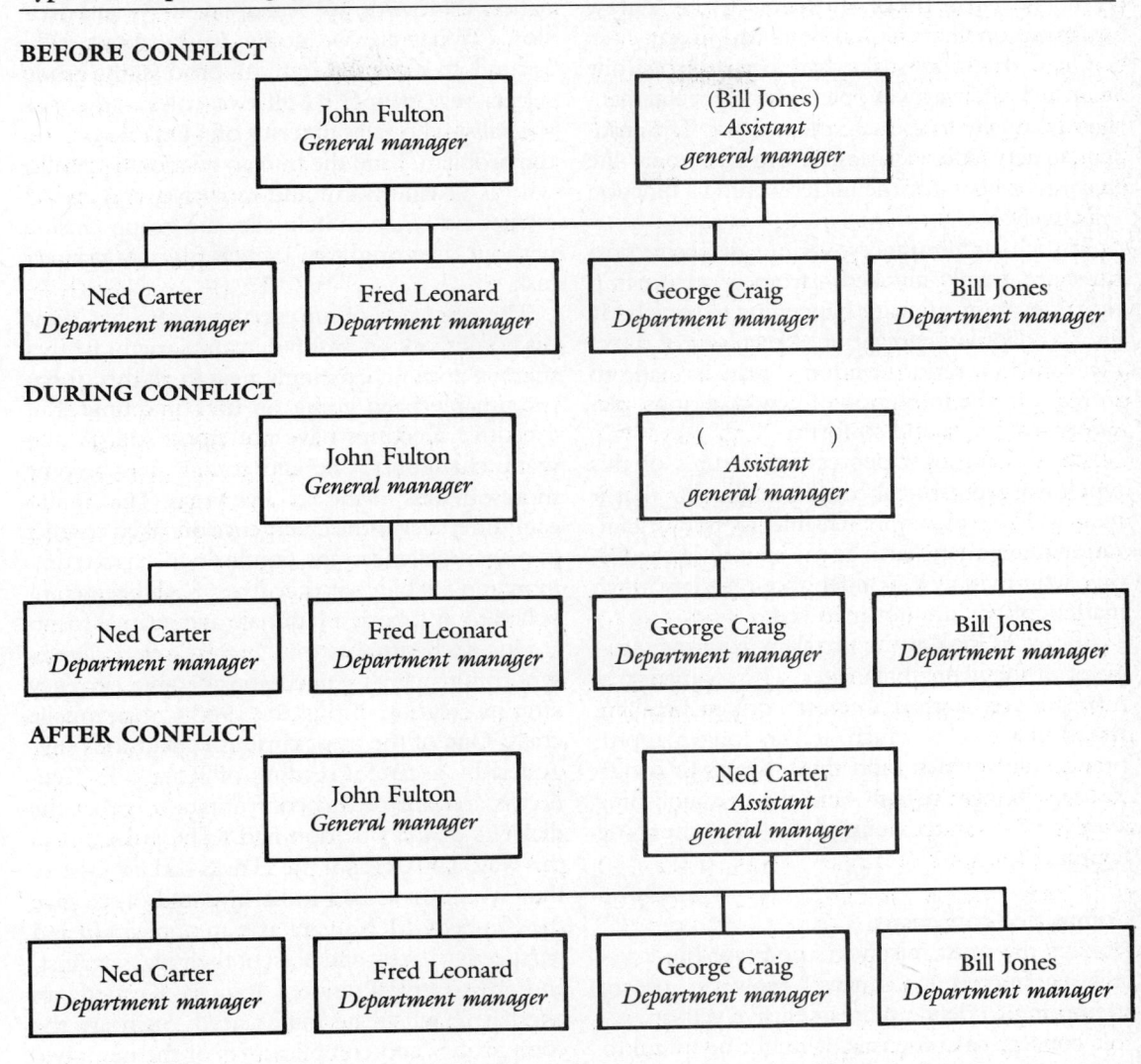

BEFORE CONFLICT

```
            John Fulton                    (Bill Jones)
          General manager               Assistant
                                        general manager

  Ned Carter      Fred Leonard      George Craig      Bill Jones
Department manager  Department manager  Department manager  Department manager
```

DURING CONFLICT

```
            John Fulton                    (            )
          General manager               Assistant
                                        general manager

  Ned Carter      Fred Leonard      George Craig      Bill Jones
Department manager  Department manager  Department manager  Department manager
```

AFTER CONFLICT

```
            John Fulton                    Ned Carter
          General manager               Assistant
                                        general manager

  Ned Carter      Fred Leonard      George Craig      Bill Jones
Department manager  Department manager  Department manager  Department manager
```

Dilemma and defense

The type of organizational conflict we have just seen starts in a very low key. The first move of "omitting the name" faces the department manager with alternate choices — neither of which is particularly attractive — to accept or protest. With the latter strategy, it might be possible to go over the general manager's head to the divisional vice president. Most department managers would likely regard this move as a strategy of last resort. If Jones had protested to the general manager, Fulton might well, with bad grace, have acquiesced and allowed the name to be reinserted; or, alternatively, "suggested" a postponement of decision, say, for three months, when a new organization chart would be issued in any case.

Once this first strike had been successfully launched, the way was open for the general manager gradually to escalate the conflict. The ensuing anxiety and vagaries of organizational life make it difficult for the target victim to function effectively.

In such circumstances, various defensive postures are usually invoked – from depersonalization ("try to imagine it's happening to somebody else"), adaptive segregation ("keep out of direct contact"), or rationalization ("man is made to suffer"), to the formation of new coalitions, placatory behavior, and so forth.

One of the most depressing features of this type of organizational conflict is the fact that it may well be incomprehensible to non-organizational members, such as the spouse of the victim, who may well wonder about anxiety when matters of pay are not involved.

But let us look at the problem from the viewpoint of the general manager. The sophisticated manager has a great interest both in breaking traditional modes which are no longer appropriate – and which bind the business to conditions no longer existent – and also in establishing a new consensus defined by the emerging legitimacy.

Committee consensus

Perhaps the most misunderstood word in executive parlance is "consensus." However, before attempting to define such an elusive yet serviceable concept as consensus, it might be useful to review changes emerging from research on executive meetings.

In my opinion, the most brilliant research on what happens in discussion groups was conducted by R.F. Bales, Professor of Social Relations at Harvard, who made two extremely telling points – one regarding process ("What actually happens at meetings?") and the other about structure ("Who does what in meetings?").[6]

Briefly, on the first point, groups work through three phases: clarification ("What is it?"), evaluation ("How do we feel about it?"), and decision ("What are we going to do about it?"). Second, to work through this process, the group selects two people to fill two roles – the task specialist who talks in terms of, "Let's zero in on the problem," and the human relations specialist who is usually warm and receptive, and acts as a "first-aid" man to help alleviate group tension without diverting it too much from its primary task.

The response of an executive who has done his homework on group dynamics might be that there is nothing excitingly new in all this; it has presumably been going on for some time. But executive meetings have not stood still. A dramatic change in tone and content has become more obvious in the last five years. The significant difference is the emergence of naked conflict in managerial meetings, conflict which is so common and visible that executives have been compelled to find both a rationale and a ritual for it.

One such ritual is the "Hawks versus Doves syndrome" which gained considerable currency after its creation during the 1962 Cuban missile crisis. One of the most curious conclusions suggested by a careful reading of Robert F. Kennedy's account of this confrontation is that the dialectic of the situation had to be polarized in this way. Thus, even if the Hawks had *not* existed, they would have had to be invented (a) to give the Kennedy-McNamara axis an opposition and perspective to test and present their ideas against, and (b) to give President John F. Kennedy an alternative which he might need. Such are the complexities and complications of the new-style executive meetings.

Within the foregoing context, it is possible to define consensus. No longer are chief executives prepared to be guided by simple majorities; nor for that matter are they prepared to wait for unanimity. They shoot for the consensus which implies two conditions – one positive and the other negative.

On the positive side, the presumption is that

the significant authorities endorse, or at least tolerate, the proposed solution. On the negative side, sufficient feedback is available to indicate that a vociferous minority will not emerge which will make the solution inoperable.

Such is the nature of the modern management process; risks are high, stakes are high, and the risks must be syndicated among the executives.

Role interdependence

The principle invoked in this section of the article is one of deadly simplicity, capable of wide application, but difficult to understand and even more difficult to apply. It is the proposition that in an organization executive action must take cognizance of interdependence of roles.

If this statement seems simplistic, invite someone in your peer group to define his role. The answer usually involves a list of functions and decisions emphasizing responsibility to the person's superior. Such a "worm's eye" response reveals an underlying organizational philosophy where the emphasis is on the exclusively vertical dimension of bureaucracy and where a person can be held "totally responsible" for something.

A more intelligent answer, emphasizing the concept of interdependence, would be, "You define your role and then I shall try to define mine." More briefly a role can only be delineated by defining a set of roles. Consider this illustrative scene:

The time is late Friday afternoon and the locus is the general manager's office of a medium-sized engineering firm which makes components for the aerospace industry. The general manager, G.B. Macdonald, is in the process of firing his personnel manager, Bill Murray.

Macdonald: You're all washed up, Murray. You're through.

Murray: I'm sorry, but I didn't quite catch that.

Macdonald: Look, I'm telling you that you've done your last job around here. The way you really botched up that negotiation with the shop stewards on the new contract is unforgivable. Besides, I'm sick of the way you keep coming back to me for policy decisions. If I heard you say, "Could I have your policy input?" once more, I'd go right out of my skull.

The one-sided tirade continues for some minutes with Murray, his back to the wall, silently waiting for his chance. Abruptly and unexpectedly, the general manager begins to fumble for feedback.

Macdonald: Well, Murray, isn't it valid? You keep coming back to me, then botching it?

Murray: Sir, could I ask you to cast your mind back to when you *invited* me to become your personnel manager. Your very words were, "As general manager, I shall retain the executive function, whether it is programming, technical, or personnel. You are merely the personnel extension of my role." I accepted the job on those terms. With all due respect, in firing me, you are really firing yourself.

Macdonald: What are you driving at?

Murray: I'm merely saying that as the "personnel executive," you are unjustifiably blaming me for living up to your own prescribed terms.

Macdonald: Wait a minute, Bill. I'll get the sherry bottle from my liquor cabinet....

What is significant about this incident is the exploitation by Bill Murray, the acting personnel manager, and perhaps more important, the general manager's acceptance of a line of argument that ten years ago would have been unthinkable.

What I am arguing in more general terms is that conflict is always moral conflict. Where there is a dispute, values, norms, roles, and statuses will be involved. What this means for the hard-pressed executive is that he must dig beneath such clichés as, "It's a problem in communication." Searching behind such gadget words for their value orientation makes the latter-day executive a thoughtful man who understands semantics.

NEW PERSPECTIVE

An excellent test of a graduate business administration student's understanding of the new behavioral approach to management would be to ask that he "reconcile the psychologically distant, task-oriented executive of the 1960's with the human relations directed, democratic manager of the 1940's." It would be impossible for him to respond properly without getting involved in a discussion of the new morality.

Traditional morality is dead. It is a victim of the new technology exemplified by the "pill," organ transplants, instant communication, and zero privacy (generated by electronic bugging devices). In addition, it is aided and abetted by a new organization logic which somehow resolves the dilemma of trying to integrate self-fulfillment and loyalty to the traditional institution, whether it be the corporation, the church, or the crack combat unit. The mobicentric manager has considered the permissiveness of Freud, worried with Sartre about the futility of "choosing to act unfree," knows something about game theory, and feels a diminishing loyalty to traditional forms of organization. In his view, "Everything is up for grabs; the next move is yours."

A case example
Now let us turn to a case illustration of how conflict technology can be used as a means of improving corporate effectiveness. This will serve to set up the ground rules for the several roles the executive may have to play in a conflict situation.

In the past, an independent soical science research institution had achieved considerable success and growth by creating a democratic work atmosphere in which some of the best social scientists in North America had done research, mainly for the government but also for large corporations. All major decisions were agreed on by the heads of the various departments, and this executive consensus was then pumped through a corporate research council which met every month.

The director, who was younger than any of his department heads, and who had managed the institution to its present dynamic position by a combination of aggressiveness, political acumen, and administrative know-how rather than research excellence, was dissatisfied with the institution's present performance. He had made up his mind to do something about it, and he planned his moves most carefully.

In the evolution of this research institution, three large departments had evolved, each of which was run by a department head who was distinguished in his own field.

One of the many anomalies in the institutional structure was that the "behavioral science group" handled marketing projects. The rationale for this was never fully explicated. One view was that when the company got into marketing, much of the work had been concerned with exploring consumer attitudes to new products; thus a psychologist had been nominated for this function and located in the behavioral science group.

Starting at a lower level, the director decided he was going to transfer the marketing function to the "computer science group." He began his strategic ploy at a private meeting in his office with the department head of the behavioral science group. After some general discussion of the group's performance, the director began his attack on the specific situation.

Director: I am going to initiate a major change of policy; in fact, a large reorganization of our existing structure. I am going to move marketing from your behavioral science group. I want this out in the open. I am not going behind your back in this. I want the discussion to be all above board.

Department head: I have no strong views on this either way, but I would like to consult with my group.

Director: Marketing is not functioning well at the moment because we can't get the people we need who can do forecasting using mathematical models; that type of person would be more at home in the computer science group.

Ten days after this meeting, at which no decision had been made, the director launched his second strike at the situation at the weekly meeting of the department heads; he invited the head of the behavioral science group to raise the question of the location of marketing in his department. This the department head did. Opinions among his subordinates had varied, he reported, but the majority had agreed that for political purposes they wished to hang on to marketing.

The director made his move. He first asked for the documentation of the decision and then asked for and received permission to attend the next meeting of the department.

At that subsequent meeting, the director presented his plans for how the marketing function would have to be developed, and challenged the department to reveal its plans (if any) for marketing. Considerable uncertainty had been aroused that had focused on how the company got research contracts in the first place and, second, on how they were processed. But still no agreement was reached to release marketing.

The director then decided to change direction. At the next meeting of the department heads, he put forward the proposal that an organizational analyst spend sufficient time with the company to thoroughly assess the entire situation. This was agreed on, and some six weeks later, the analyst came up with this proposition:

"The company is a 'gourmet' organization which specializes in finding interesting problems and then solving them. In such a context, the conventional form of organization is quite inappropriate and an organic rather than mechanistic model is needed.

"In a task-oriented business, R&D can be defined and therefore managed; objectives are specified; programs are produced and policed. Research standards are of necessity less detailed, but both modern behavioral science investigation and executive experience confirm that social scientists are able and willing to work within such constraints.

"The conventional departments should be abolished and the task-force concept used – with interdisciplinary task groups set up to handle the specific problems which arise; further, these groups should be headed by the person most expert in that problem."

A special weekend meeting of the corporate research council was called and over a period of three days the researchers debated their future and presented position papers. The proposal to dissolve the departments and replace them with task forces was regarded as too radical; but it was acceptable that task forces would be created from department members who would still be part of their respective departments for "pay and rations."

What does examination of this case tell us about conflict management? The most significant point to emerge is that it is not always necessary to have a clearly stated set of operational objectives in mind before you initiate change. It is necessary, of course, to have a set of criteria to judge the efficiency of the change (e.g., return on investment, share of the market, and so on).

The director started from a vague but strong hunch that performance could be improved. Instead of issuing an order to move marketing from the behavioral group to the computing group (which he legitimately could have done), he opted for a more general revision which led to a major change in policy – that is, the use of the concept of task forces. This was a concept not imposed by fiat, but one that the whole organization had a chance to look at and debate.

In brief, what the director did was to work systematically through a well-conceived plan for achieving change by initiating conflict. Because he understood the inevitable process of conflict, he was able to maintain a balance between (a) creating uncertainty and maintaining a data base, and (b) getting people to participate and keeping direction.

GROUND RULES...

To this point in the discussion, we have been looking at theories of conflict. Next, let us turn our attention to specific guidelines which may help the hard-pressed executive to apply these theories in such a way that conflict can be meaningfully exploited. The important thing is that the objective must be to achieve, at all times, a creative, acceptable, and realistic resolution of conflict.

One of the most effective means of formulating ground rules for executive conflict is to consider the three roles which an executive might play in a conflict situation. He can be: (a) the initiator, (b) the defendant, or (c) the conciliator. At one time or another, most executives are called on to play each of these roles.

... for the initiator

- Start at a low level and advance on a narrow front on one or two related issues, following a well-documented route.
- Maintain second-strike capability.
- Pick the terrain with care; where and when the case is heard is vital.
- Be prepared to escalate, either to a higher level in the organization or to a meeting of peers.
- Make it objective, private, and routine; above all, keep it formal.
- Search for reaction; remember that you may have to settle for token conformity in the first instance.
- Reinforce success and abandon failure.

... for the defendant

- Do not overract; keep your cool; let the initiator state his case; listen carefully and neutrally.
- Ascertain scale of the strike; try to build a decision tree with "go/no go" decision rules.
- Ask for the name of the game (e.g., Is it a courtroom? If yes, ask for the counsel of the defense).
- Ask not only for an exact definition of the charge, but also for the evidence with, if possible, identification of the sources.
- If it is a "minor crime," be prepared to plead guilty.
- Ascertain the various lines of appeal.
- Consider the option "Waiting Brief" and be prepared to reserve your defense; take notes; above all, let the initiator score somewhere — and then try for informality.

... for the conciliator

- Get the parties of the dispute to realize that conflict is not only universal but a necessary requisite of change.
- Break down the attitudinal consistency of each disputant (belief that his attitudes do not contain contradictory elements).
- After breaking down frozen but antithetical attitudes of the disputants, minimize their individual "loss of face."
- Break the conflict into fractional workable components.
- Consider common enemy, high interaction, shared subordinate goal strategies.
- Remember, nobody loves a go-between.

CONCLUSION

For the contemporary manager, one of the most exciting organizational developments may well be in the efforts of behavioral scientists to approach conflict as a subject whose structure and process can be properly exploited as a means of promoting effective change. Guided by a realistic model that recognizes the importance of conflict as a creative force, scientists are now searching for hypotheses about conflict to test both in the laboratory and in the executive suite.

Even such subjects as ethology (the study of animal behavior) have been relevant. The new attitude toward aggression, while admitting that it may be triggered by environmental stimuli, also recognizes its hereditary basis. Further, it is now recognized that humans, like all other animals, have some kind of pool of aggression that, when properly mobilized, facilitates the emergence of stable social structures.

The works of Konrad Lorenz,[7] of Robert Ardrey,[8] and of Desmond Morris[9] fascinate many managers who recognize the truth of linking conflict and social space and who derive some satisfaction from the proposition that "zoos drive apes psycho." But these same managers appear to forget that "the corporate zoo drives man anomic." When applied in an organizational context, the social space (i.e., "elbow room") and the territorial imperatives of the ethologists refer not only to physical things but, more importantly, also relate to matters of rules, roles, and relations. An organization consists of a network of roles, structured in a particular way to achieve a particular purpose.

What the systems concept of management teaches the contemporary manager is that if one of the interlocking elements in this network is changed, then some or all of the other elements will be affected. Inevitably change will be resisted and conflict generated. The modern theory of conflict emphasizes the importance of structural factors in predetermining how conflict will develop; the structure of an organization is largely determined by how authority and power are distributed.

What causes conflict is the fact that the organization exists in a social environment which may be thought of as a turbulent environment. In a state of turbulence, the rate of change in the environment inevitably outstrips the rate of change in the organization, thus leaving the organization in a maladapted state.

Change is endemic to any organization due to the fact that the less powerful members in it have a vested interest in recognizing that the organization is a phase behind its environment, while the more powerful members have a vested interest in denying this phase lag. This introduces an element of inevitability into organizational conflict and change.

Of course, sometimes the conflict may be the unintended result of poor coordination. In a positive sense, conflict may be deliberately created to compel the organization to define goals, change processes, and reallocate resources. But conflict is only likely to produce constructive change when there is a rough balance of power between the parties of the dispute.

Predictable pattern

Conflict usually follows a particular pattern and is frequently quite predictable. For example, the pattern of wage negotiations is well established, although a change in economic conditions, such as the government's fiscal policy defining its reaction to inflation, can affect the ritual.

Most organizations have evolved procedures that deal with such contingencies, but not all. The university administrators in the late 1960s discovered to their horror that they had no procedures for dealing with conflict, and no properly constituted lines of appeal.

In fact, even a cursory examination of the student revolution emphasizes that the pattern is predictable: (1) *crisis* (the establishment commits a "crime"), (2) *escalation* (occupation of administrative offices), (3) *confrontation* (show-down with officials), and (4) *further crisis* (challenging of the legitimacy of the committee appointed to investigate original charge). And when the immediate fight is over, the organization is left to build not only a new hierarchy of an appeals system, but also a new code of ethics.

None of these processes will work, however, unless executives fully understand the concept of good faith. Good faith demands that in communication one party does not deliberately control the flow of information in such a way as to manipulate the interests of the other party. In the new approach to organizational behavior, which is based on information science concepts, authority is defined in terms of three factors: location, function, and reference. Location refers to a particular node in the matrix of information processes; function describes the requirement the manager has to search, collect, process, and disseminate particular kinds of information; and reference defines the constituency which he represents.

To the information scientist, a measure of the amount of information that a message contains is the degree of surprise it induces, but the breach of good faith also produces a surprise. The offended party invariably presumes that he has the necessary information to participate in the exchange.

Even the way the information is sequenced may well induce this feeling of bad faith. A great number of managers have experienced this sensation, which they usually describe as a manipulation. Knowledge of the management of conflict may give one party in a dispute a significant advantage over his opponent, and his use of such knowledge may in itself be seen as an act of bad faith.

Thus the need for more managers to familiarize themselves with the structures and processes of conflict becomes more pressing. How to make conflict work for you is going to be an increasingly crucial management issue in our rapidly changing industrial society.

References

1. L.J. Peter and R. Hull (1969) *The Peter Principle*. New York: William Morrow and Company, Inc.
2. K. Lorenz (1966) *On Aggression*. New York: Harcourt, Brace and World, Inc.
3. T.C.Schelling (1960) *Strategy of Conflict*. Cambridge, MA: Harvard University Press, p. 120.
4. See, for example, D.W. Ewing (September-October 1964) "Tension Can Be an Asset." *Harvard Business Review*, p. 71.
5. A. Zaleznik (May-June 1960) "Power and Politics in Organizational Life." *Harvard Business Review*, p. 47.
6. R.F. Bales (March-April 1954) "In Conference." *Harvard Business Review*, p. 44.
7. K. Lorenz (1966) *op. cit.*
8. R. Ardrey (1961) *African Genesis*. New York: Atheneum Publishers.
9. D. Morris (1969) *The Naked Ape*. New York: Dell Publishing Company.

CASES

R. BRUCE GATES: THE POW-WOW VICE-PRESIDENT OF CANADIAN INTERNATIONAL COMPUTERS*

Joe Kelly

R. Bruce Gates, a University of Western Ontario MBA, is a highly successful VP of a computer manufacturing company. Gates has an argumentative, polemical, verbally fluent style, is forceful and outspoken, but also hard-headed and demanding. He is also extremely effective. Not too surprisingly, his subordinates, the general managers of the plants, feel they have to respond to him. He enjoys persuasion, cajoling and "seduction" as means of influencing, directing, controlling and possessing his subordinates who regard him as an amiable S.O.B. Gates enjoys part time teaching in a Toronto business school. He believes that the man who makes it to the top in business is usually a Pow-Wow man. The plant manager of the Montréal factory, Gavin Jones, a B. Comm. from Halifax, is for him. Jones is obsessed with getting other men to love him and has a strong need for affiliation. According to Gates, such n Aff (need for Affiliation) men seek opportunities for friendly interactions, and, in his mind, are most attracted to personnel positions, but not line positions.

THE TWO FACES OF POWER

In the world according to Gates, since executives are primarily concerned with influencing and managing others, it seems patently obvious that they should be characterized by a high need for power. At a recent sales training conference, Jones told Gates, "In American society at least, most executives take the hangout road, are proud of having the high n Ach (need for Achievement) but dislike being told they have a high n Pow (need for Power). People are suspicious (and for good reasons) of a man who wants power, even if he claims to do so for sincere and altruistic reasons." Jones has until recently been doing a good job for the company. But his work is beginning to show signs of slippage. Gates answers charges of this by saying, "Managers have to be subtle, sly and careful. You do not want to be in a position in which people think you are seeking power and influence to exploit them."

One thing that is worrying Gates is that according to psychologists at the sales training conference, there are alternative manifestations of the power drive – either heavy drinking or holding office. It was found that the orientations of the power thoughts of these two types of people were quite different. Men whose power thoughts centered on having impact for the sake of others tended to hold office, whereas those whose thoughts centered on personal dominance tended to drink heavily.

IF I WIN: YOU LOSE

One of the psychologists puzzled Gates by telling him, "There are two faces of power. One is turned toward seeking to win out over active adversaries. At the level of action, personal power concern is associated with heavy drinking, gambling, having more aggressive impulses, and collecting "prestige supplies." The other face of the power motive is more socialized and is aroused, for example, by the possibility of winning an election, a war, a contract, or a woman. In terms of activities, people concerned with the more socialized aspect of power not only join more organizations, but also are more apt to become officers in them. They are also more apt to join in organized informal sports, even as adults."

The president of the company, an American named Albert Ringrose, has quite a different leadership style. Ringrose, who is very old fashioned, does not force his VP's to submit and follow him by the sheer overwhelming magic of his personality and persuasive powers. In fact, he achieves influence by strengthening and inspiring their positions. At the conference, Ringrose stated, "The effective VP arouses confidence in his team. The followers feel better able to accomplish whatever goals the VP and they themselves share. But whatever the source of the manager's ideas, he cannot inspire his people unless he expresses vivid goals and aims which, in some sense, they want. His role is to clarify which goals the group should achieve and then create confidence in its members so that they can achieve them."

One strange thing that happened at the training conference related to an encounter between Bruce Gates and Carol Nevis, an MBA from Harvard, who is the Personal Assistant of Gavin Jones. Nevis, who is a computer whiz, seemed to be getting involved, on her own initiative, with Gates in heavy discussions about management styles. Nevis, besides being a self-proclaimed feminist, is divorced. Apparently, Nevis and Gates got into a shouting match at midnight in the bar after a training session.

THURSDAY: SCENE 1

R. Bruce Gates is talking on the telephone to his Personal Assistant, Roger Bennett, who is doing a quality study in the Montréal plant. Gates' reactions to the information Bennett gives him are recorded below.

"Put him on the line."
"What?"
"You've got to be kidding."

Exhibit 1:
Organization Chart for Toronto Office of Canadian International Computers

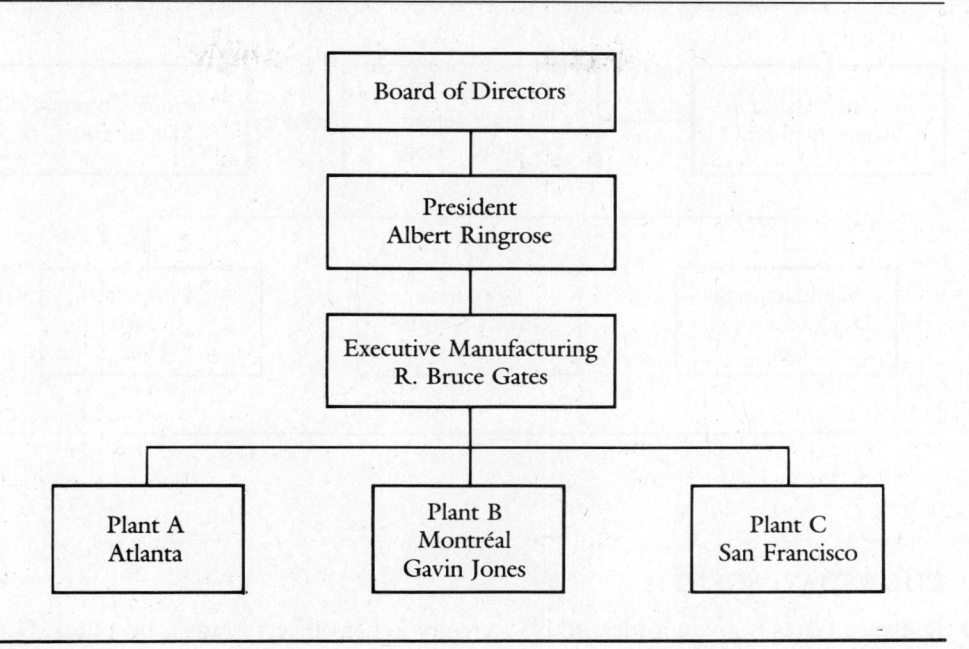

```
                    Board of Directors
                           │
                       President
                    Albert Ringrose
                           │
                 Executive Manufacturing
                      R. Bruce Gates
                           │
         ┌─────────────────┼─────────────────┐
      Plant A           Plant B           Plant C
      Atlanta           Montréal       San Francisco
                      Gavin Jones
```

"Did you fire Jones?"

"Why not? Why not?"

"You're telling me that buffoon Jones, the plant manager, has been crediting computers into the warehouse that haven't been made yet."

"How did he manage that?"

"He entered production for the first three days of February as the last three days of January. January owed December . . . Whaat!"

"You should have . . . he has written orders . . . Stop it. You're hurting me. Don't crack any more of these comic turns until I force down a gulp of this coffee."

"There's more . . . Who needs this?"

" . . . The Dispatch Manager is shipping out empty boxes with no computers."

"Look. Get to work on the Dispatch Guy; make him give you his private records. Get the goods on that ding-a-ling Jones. I'm going to have his head served up on a platter."

"Last shot, meet me at Dorval tomorrow morning. I'll be on the first jet out of here tomorrow morning."

"Oh, I nearly forgot. What's the weather like there?"

"You're too knocked out. Cut the BS. See you, man. Don't sleep in."

Exhibit 2:
R. Bruce Gates' Toronto Office

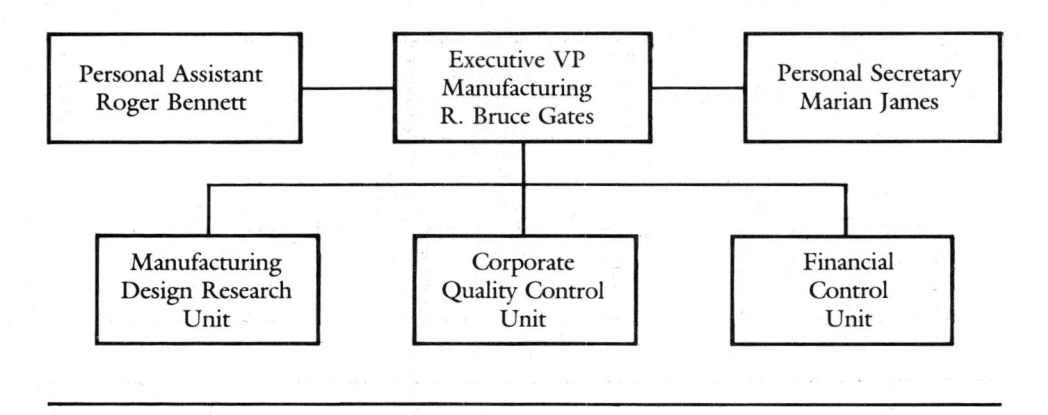

```
┌─────────────────┐     ┌─────────────────┐     ┌─────────────────┐
│ Personal Assistant│────│  Executive VP   │────│Personal Secretary│
│  Roger Bennett  │     │  Manufacturing  │     │  Marian James   │
│                 │     │ R. Bruce Gates  │     │                 │
└─────────────────┘     └────────┬────────┘     └─────────────────┘
                                 │
        ┌────────────────────────┼────────────────────────┐
        │                        │                        │
┌───────────────┐        ┌───────────────┐        ┌───────────────┐
│ Manufacturing │        │   Corporate   │        │   Financial   │
│Design Research│        │Quality Control│        │    Control    │
│     Unit      │        │     Unit      │        │     Unit      │
└───────────────┘        └───────────────┘        └───────────────┘
```

THURSDAY: SCENE 2

R. Bruce Gates is giving orders to his secretary in her office. "Marian, be a dear. Get me on the first plane to Montréal tomorrow morning. Call my old woman, tell her I'm leaving for Montréal this afternoon. Tell her I'll call tonight about midnight. Tell her to look out for the driver calling for my overnight bag. I'm going to do some dictation tonight. Cando? Last thing, get me the President, Albert Ringrose, and book me a five-minute one with the 'old man' for five o'clock. You're wonderful. Let's move."

FRIDAY: SCENE 3

The same time, following day, in a Montréal bar near the plant, R. Bruce Gates is talking to Roger Bennett.

"Two dry martinis. One very dry. Just run the Vermouth cork over the gin."
"You think we should take Jones out."
"You do, Eh, Eh. Come on, you're itchy for blood. I can see your nostrils flaring."
"Yeh. Well we ain't. Jones can do things for me, for us. He's grateful. He needs a let-off. He needs a real vicious KITA which will be transmitted right down the line."
"I've instructed Jones to fire his PA, Carol Nevis, that MBA with the computer for a brain. She's out. And a memo is being printed up tonight, reading the riot act. What the 'old man,' Ringrose, really objects to is not the production nonsense, but the 'fixing of the books.'"
"Here's to bigger and better bonuses. Two more, Miss."

Exhibit 3:
Montréal Plant

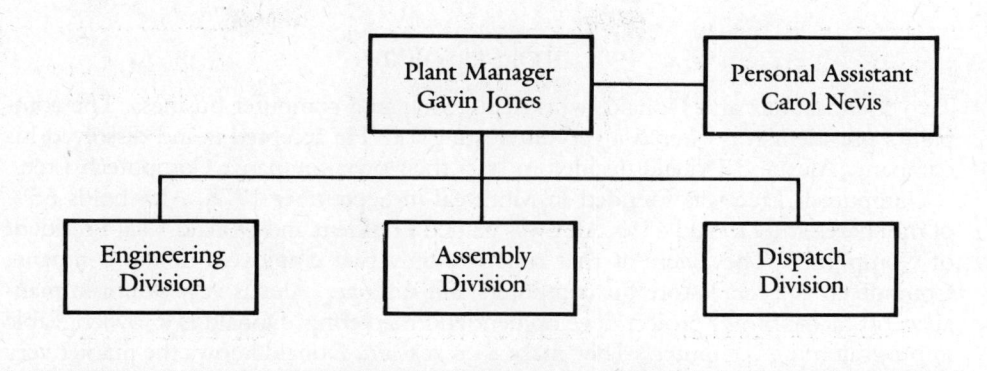

```
                    ┌──────────────┐      ┌──────────────────┐
                    │ Plant Manager│──────│Personal Assistant│
                    │  Gavin Jones │      │   Carol Nevis    │
                    └──────┬───────┘      └──────────────────┘
            ┌──────────────┼──────────────┐
    ┌───────┴──────┐ ┌─────┴──────┐ ┌─────┴──────┐
    │ Engineering  │ │  Assembly  │ │  Dispatch  │
    │   Division   │ │  Division  │ │  Division  │
    └──────────────┘ └────────────┘ └────────────┘
```

MONDAY: SCENE 4

The President, Albert Ringrose, has received a call from the company attorney advising him that Carol Nevis is filing for unfair dismissal and is planning to go on CBC-TV Toronto that night to denounce both Canadian International Computers and its Vice-President for sexism. R. Bruce Gates has been in Atlanta but is flying back and is expected in the President's office in 15 minutes. President Ringrose, who has had the full story from Roger Bennett, Marian James and Gavin Jones, has been invited by CBC to give his side of the story. Albert Ringrose has 15 minutes to decide what to do about R. Bruce Gates. After he deals with Gates, he has to respond to the CBC invitation.

QUESTIONS

1. R. Bruce Gates is an effective executive, but he has a problem. What is his problem?
2. What went wrong between R. Bruce Gates and Carol Nevis at the training conference?
3. What is the problem in the Montréal plant? Was Gates right to order the firing of Nevis?
4. Does Nevis have a case?
5. What should Albert Ringrose do about R. Bruce Gates?
6. What should Ringrose say on TV that night?

ALEX AND DONALD: A POWER STRUGGLE*

Carole Groleau

Two friends, Alex and Donald, worked together in a computer business. The company's president was offered a very interesting job. He accepted it and dissolved his company. Alex and Donald decided to start their own company: Computech Ltée.

Computech Ltée was founded in Montréal in September 1978. Alex holds 55% of the shares and Donald 45%. Alex was named President and Donald Vice-President of Computech. They were at that time the only two employees of the company. Computech is a retail store for computers and software. Alex is very skilful in management, accounting, project development and marketing. Donald is knowledgeable in programming computers. They make a great team. Donald knows the market very well and is apt to choose to sell what is going to be popular. Alex makes most of the decisions but Donald wants to be consulted on the decision-making process.

The store is doing very well in January 1979 and the partners need help to assume all of the workload. They hire new employees, including their friends and family. In a way this divides the employees; some come from Alex's relations and others from Donald's.

Alex develops projects and has a long term vision of his business. Alex proposed to Donald to set up a yearly event to popularize computers, to show what is available on the market and also to have a yearly meeting place for computer specialists. A new company is formed, the Computer Fair, founded by Alex and Donald, to organize that yearly event. The shares of the new company are divided similarly to the ones of Computech. This event will also help the Computech sales and can also utilize the expertise of the new employees by splitting the salaries they earn between the two companies. The Computer Fair takes place for the first time in Montréal in October 1980. During that time the retail store is doing okay. The fair requires a lot of energy from Alex and Donald, but the new challenge gets them very excited. Alex takes care of government subsidies, sponsors, marketing and budgeting while Donald looks after the content of the event: guest speakers, company arrangements to participate . . . .

The Computer Fair is a local success in 1980 and by 1983 the event gets international recognition. People from Europe and Asia come to Montréal to cover the event for the international press.

The retail business is doing well and by 1983 Computech is profitable. The retail store now requires less energy from the associates. The number of employees working for Alex and Donald for both companies went from two in 1978 to 30 permanent employees in 1983. Because of this big volume change, a formal structure was instituted. The staff was organized into a communication department, an accounting

---

* "Alex and Donald: A Power Struggle" is used by permission of the author.

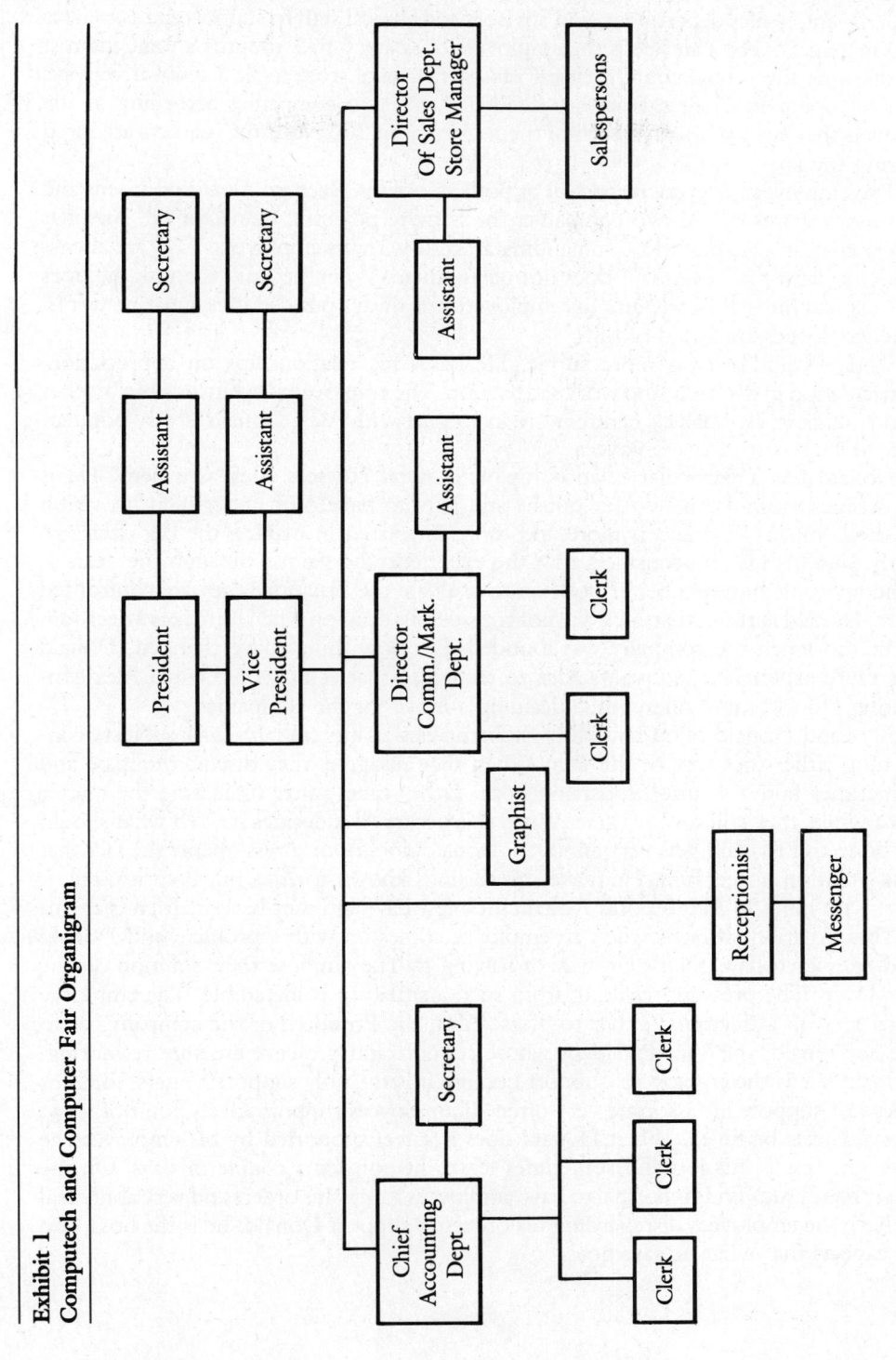

Exhibit 1
Computech and Computer Fair Organigram

```
                President ── Assistant ── Secretary
                    │
                Vice ────── Assistant ── Secretary
                President
                    │
     ┌──────────────┼──────────────┬──────────────┐
     │              │              │              │
Director       Director        Graphist      Chief Accounting
Comm./Mark.    Of Sales Dept.                Dept. ── Secretary
Dept. ──       Store Manager ──                │
Assistant      Assistant                       │
     │              │                          │
  ┌──┴──┐      Salespersons              ┌─────┼─────┐
Clerk Clerk                            Clerk Clerk Clerk

              Receptionist ── Messenger
```

Other employees are hired during the fair but the managers and directors of the department stay the same.

department, a sales department, and advisors and clerical staff to support the associates and managers. The Fair keeps the employees busy for 6 to 7 months a year, the rest of the time they concentrate their efforts on the retail store to find innovative ways of developing it. Their salaries are divided in the two companies according to the months they have worked in each of them. A total of 300 part time workers are hired during the fair.

The employees are very respectful of both associates. Because Alex is president and has more shares of the two companies, he is more powerful than Donald. Alex has a very cold, impersonal and commanding attitude with his employees. They are always agreeing with him, even if it does not please them. When he assigns a task, he does not express himself clearly and his employees are always puzzled over what he wants. The employees are afraid of him.

Donald's authority is more subtle. He bases his relationships on appreciation, participation in decision, and work satisfaction. The employees see him as a big brother and confidant, especially when they are in conflict with Alex. Donald is very popular. He rarely gets mad at employees.

Donald has a particular relationship with Alex. He sees Alex as a hero. He is sometimes intimidated by Alex but he still likes to have Alex understand his vision of the company. Donald is more and more interested in making the big decisions with Alex because he considers that the experience he gained through the years is valid and puts him in a better position to evaluate the situations they are confronted with. Donald is afraid that Alex will not consider his opinion when he makes a decision, as he did when the company was founded. But now things have changed; Donald has more experience and wants Alex to recognize that. This would entail Alex consulting Donald more often while deciding a move for the companies.

Alex and Donald often have very different viewpoints on particular subjects concerning either the store or the Fair. When they disagree, they discuss the issue and sometimes find a solution satisfying both. Other times, after discussing the matter for a while, they still do not agree. When this occurs Alex decides himself what should be done and Donald gets very annoyed. Donald does not express openly the fact that this situation upsets him. He makes his feelings known to Alex but does not talk it over with him. So Alex ignores Donald for a few days and they become friends again.

This situation worsens when an employee comes up with a problem and Donald and Alex each have their own way of solving it. They impose their solution on the employee. The pressure resulting from such a situation is incredible. The employee is faced with a dilemma: either to please Alex, the President of the company, or to please Donald, the Vice-President whose support and presence are very reassuring. Donald needs the employees' support because it is the only support he gets, for Alex does not support his associate very often. If employees support Alex's point of view, Donald feels betrayed. When Donald does not feel supported by his employees he loses interest in his job and sometimes leaves his job for a couple of days. On the other hand, Alex finds it normal to have employees follow his orders and very abnormal to have the employees disregarding his orders to support Donald; he is the boss, and he expects that what he says goes.

Alex and Donald agree on an important matter: when Alex is absent, Donald runs the company by himself and has the full responsibility for it.

The employees have difficulty understanding the power pattern in this company. They want everyone to be happy but they do not know how to behave.

Here are a few situations to illustrate this matter:

SITUATION #1

Once there was a meeting at 4 a.m. in a restaurant. Alex, Donald, Susan (directing the communication dept) and Luke (Susan's assistant) attended. They were looking at the details of a press conference being held the upcoming afternoon.

"The press conference will be a traditional one. I will be sitting at the end of a table with Donald and we will answer the journalists' questions," said Alex. He added, "we will give basic information in our press kits, participation ratio . . . ."

Donald disagreed: "Let's have it in an informal way, having the journalists sit around us in the press room and ask questions. This would not establish a barrier between us and the journalists and would be more casual. The number of journalists would be limited."

Alex kept on explaining his way and so did Donald. At the end of the meeting Alex and Donald still did not agree on how the press conference should be held. Susan and Luke took notes during the whole meeting and tried to solve the disagreement.

Susan and Luke prepared the press conference according to Alex's demands. Donald showed up at the press room and saw the table with chairs around it and microphones at the end of the table. He stayed a few moments and left slamming the door. Susan followed him, knowing why he was mad. She tried to reason with him. He did not want to hear it and left quickly. Alex came in late. The journalists were waiting for him. Susan explained the situation to him. He told her she had done the right thing, and not to worry.

Donald did not talk to Susan or Luke for the following three months. Alex did not talk over the problem with Donald. The only consequence was a suggestion by Donald to have both Susan and Luke fired, and Alex refused. The matter was forgotten in time and was never discussed.

SITUATION #2

Ian (the graphic artist) was preparing an ad to announce the Computer Fair.

"Align the special presentation that way, put the sponsors over here and the ticket explanation on this side," ordered Alex. A few moments later Donald came in:

"About the ad, I thought it would be much more effective if we reversed the special presentation with the hours the fair is open and give more space to the sponsors. Do it that way, it will be clearer."

"But Alex just gave me some other indications," replied Ian.

"Do it my way," concluded Donald while leaving the artist's office.

The ad was due and Ian still could not figure out how to put it all together to satisfy both. During that same day he went back to see Donald to have him change his mind but it did not work out. He tried to talk to Alex, but he was too busy and finally ordered to have it done his way.

"What will I do? I cannot please both," said Ian while talking to himself in front of the ad that was due. He was the only person left there to work that night.

He finally delivered the ad. It was part of Donald's concept and part of Alex's idea. Both would be happy and the mix did not look too bad.

The ad was printed. That morning Ian had two angry visitors.

"What have I told you, this is not what I have asked for, don't you understand what I took an hour to explain to you? Now this ad has been printed in 300,000 copies and it is wrong. Next time do it my way or you will have some serious trouble with me," said Alex. He left without hearing the explanation Ian wanted to give him.

Donald came in an hour later and went to see Ian. "I can't believe what you have done with this ad; it is ridiculous. Aren't you aware of the price we have to pay to have this information printed?"

Ian replied, "Why don't you talk to Alex? I had to do wonders to have everything the way you both wanted it."

"Never mind Alex, he is not always right. When I ask for something, which is not too often, I want to have it done my way. I hope I have made myself clear!"

Ian was puzzled. He tried to sort out the problem but did not succeed. He thought that the following week instead of trying to please both he could just try to please one of them and not get in such a mess.

QUESTIONS

1. What are the causes of the conflict between Alex and Donald?
2. Describe Alex's managerial style. Describe Donald's style.
3. How is this conflict affecting employees?
4. How can this conflict be resolved?

EXERCISES

A CONFLICT DRAMA

When you become an executive a confrontation may blow up between you and a colleague, and you may lose your cool. You will not know what to do or what is really happening. As a management student, you need to be ready to try to understand such a situation and able to respond. You may be faced with the dilemma of whether to act immediately on the problem or stall. Which is the proper solution? As you prepare your analysis of this confrontation in terms of values, attitudes, needs, and expectations of the two parties involved, you will develop a better appreciation of the choices open to both people. Learning the skill to create, cool, or exploit executive confrontations is a major management asset.

The scene is a bedroom of an expensive hotel in Vancouver with the noises of an expense account cocktail party which is going on next door percolating in. The President is standing with his back to the window; he has a large scotch, still untouched, in his hand. Facing him with his back to the door is the Executive, with a nearly empty glass in his hand.

President: I wanted to have a chance to talk to you, John.
Executive: Yes, Sir.
President: You're brilliant, but bored. I'm brilliant and you're fired.
Executive: What do you mean, Sir?
President: I mean you have too much IQ for this assignment and therefore I'm letting you go.
Executive: Just like that?
President: I'm giving you three months' salary in lieu of notice.
Executive: You mean I'm off payroll as of now.
President: In effect, yes. I want you to fly back tomorrow morning to Toronto to clean out your desk. I have already hired your replacement.
Executive: Can't I stay on in Vancouver over the weekend and clean out my desk on Monday morning?

The argument shifts from the focus of firing to cleaning out desks and continues for some time. Eventually . . .

President: OK, Monday's all right by me.
Executive: I appreciate that, Sir.

President: Can I ask you a question? About your feelings?
Executive: Sure, go ahead.
President: What are you planning to do tonight? I suppose once you have called your wife, you might get a few drinks under your belt.
Executive: The thought had crossed my mind.
President: I wonder if you would be offended if I offered you this bottle of Chivas Regal – for old time's sake.
Exeuctive: Okay, I don't mind.
President: I want you to do one last thing for me.
Executive: Such as?
President: Go next door. Say good-bye to your Personal Assistant and the company Treasurer. Bill has an envelope for you with your cheque in it.
Executive: Right now?
President: (nods) Good luck and goodbye.

The president shakes hands with the executive who leaves. No sooner has the executive put down the phone from calling his wife than he receives a call from his personal assistant who offers to spend the evening commiserating with him over the Chivas Regal.

WORK SHEET FOR PRESIDENT VERSUS EXECUTIVE

Briefly define:

	PRESIDENT	EXECUTIVE
Objectives:		
Values:		
Attitudes:		
Needs:		
Expectations:		
Advice for:		

Who is in the right in this case?

Why?

CONFLICT AT MONTRÉAL PUMP & VALVE COMPANY

Luke Novelli
J. Bruce Prince

INTRODUCTION

Conflict is a natural and predictable event which all managers at some point in their career must face. Conflict can either be a creative or destructive force depending on how well it is managed. This exercise provides an opportunity for you to practise your conflict management skills.

THE EXERCISE

Bill Marshall (Comptroller and General Counsel) and Tom Everts (Research and Development) are at loggerheads over the budget issue. West (the Plant Manager) worked out the budget for this year, but he wants to make sure that there is not a repeat performance next year. He has instructed Marshall and Everts to have a meeting, and to come up with a process for establishing future budgets in a timely fashion. As you might imagine, Marshall and Everts have different points of view. Prepare to participate in a role play of the Marshall and Everts meeting by re-reading the In-Basket correspondence items #2, #6, #7 and #9 (in the first section of the book) to refresh your memory about the relationship of these two people. Your instructor will give you further instructions on preparing for this exercise. Do not read any further at this time.

Bill Marshall, Comptroller and General Counsel
Use this information to guide your strategy during the role play.

Ideal Outcome You want Everts to have budgets and supporting documents completed days prior to the submission deadline and to allow time for your department to review the materials.

Timing Your department's busiest time is the first few days of each quarter; consequently, budget work should be scheduled for the second and third week of each quarter.

Resources Even though your staff is large, there is a massive quantity of work to be done, and it is difficult to keep up without an excessive amount of overtime. Late budget submissions undermine your efforts to plan and schedule work so as to avoid needless overtime expenditures.

Planning Budgets are crucial for the effective planning of sources and uses of funds which, in turn, keeps the cost of capital at a minimum – a primary responsibility of the your department.

Tom Everts, Research and Development

Use this information to guide your strategy during the role play.

Ideal Outcome You want to be able to submit lists of contemplated projects along with rough estimates of expenses to Marshall's department and have them complete many of the budget details. After the initial check by Marshall's people, you would then like to make a few adjustments and re-submit it for finalization.

Timing Your department's work runs in spurts. Therefore, budget preparation can best be accomplished during slack periods between projects – whenever they occur.

Resources Your staff is not really trained to complete budgets. It takes them longer and they make more mistakes than people who are trained for this task.

Planning Budgeting a year ahead is not very realistic for departments like Research and Development. It is better to justify and request funds as the need arises. No one can realistically tell ahead of time which projects will pan out, where they will lead, or how much development will cost until the project unfolds.

Role play instructions

Your instructor will assign you to one of the three role play situations presented below.

Role play #1 Everts and Marshall are to approach the meeting from a competitive conflict resolution perspective.

Role play #2 Everts and Marshall are to approach the meeting from a compromise conflict resolution perspective.

Role play #3 Everts and Marshall are to approach the meeting from a collaborative conflict resolution perspective.

PART FOUR
BEHAVIOR OF INDIVIDUALS AND GROUPS IN ORGANIZATIONS

IX
HUMAN RESOURCE MANAGEMENT

READINGS

INCREASING ORGANIZATIONAL EFFECTIVENESS THROUGH BETTER HUMAN RESOURCE PLANNING AND DEVELOPMENT*

Edgar H. Schein

INTRODUCTION

In this article I would like to address two basic questions. First, why is human resource planning and development becoming increasingly important as a determinant of organizational effectiveness? Second, what are the major components of a human resource planning and career development system, and how should these components be linked for maximum organizational effectiveness?

The field of personnel management has for some time addressed issues such as these and much of the technology of planning for and managing human resources has been worked out to a considerable degree.[1] Nevertheless there continues to be in organizations a failure, particularly on the part of line managers and functional managers in areas other than personnel, to recognize the true importance of planning for and managing human resources. This paper is not intended to be a review of what is known but rather a kind of position paper for line managers to bring to their attention some important and all too often neglected issues. These issues are important for organizational *effectiveness,* quite apart from their relevance to the issue of humanizing work or improving the quality of working life.[2]

The observations and analyses made below are based on several kinds of information:

- Formal research on management development, career development, and human development through the adult life cycle conducted in the Sloan School and at other places for the past several decades;[3]
- Analysis of consulting relationships, field observations, and other involvements over the past several decades with all kinds of organizations dealing with the planning for and implementation of human resource development programs and organization development projects.[4]

WHY IS HUMAN RESOURCE PLANNING AND DEVELOPMENT (HRPD) INCREASINGLY IMPORTANT?

The Changing Managerial Job
The first answer to the question is simple, though paradoxical. Organizations are becoming more

---

* Reprinted from "Increasing Organizational Effectiveness through Better Human Resource Planning and Development" by Edgar H. Schein, SLOAN MANAGEMENT REVIEW, Fall 1977, Volume 19, Number 1, pp. 1–20, by permission of the publisher. Copyright © by the Sloan Management Review Association. All rights reserved.

Much of the research on which this paper is based was done under the sponsorship of the Group Psychology branch of the Office of Naval Research. Their generous support has made continuing work in this area possible. I would also like to thank my colleagues Lotte Bailyn and John Van Maanen for many of the ideas expressed in this paper.

dependent upon people because they are increasingly involved in more complex technologies and are attempting to function in more complex economic, political, and sociocultural environments. The more different technical skills there are involved in the design, manufacture, marketing, and sales of a product, the more vulnerable the organization will be to critical shortages of the right kinds of human resources. The more complex the process, the higher the interdependence among the various specialists. The higher the interdependence, the greater the need for effective integration of all the specialities because the entire process is only as strong as its weakest link.

In simpler technologies, managers could often compensate for the technical or communication failures of their subordinates. General managers today are much more dependent upon their technically trained subordinates because they usually do not understand the details of the engineering, marketing, financial, and other decisions which their subordinates are making. Even the general manager who grew up in finance may find that since his day the field of finance has outrun him and his subordinates are using models and methods which he cannot entirely understand.

What all this means for the general manager is that he cannot any longer safely make decisions by himself: he cannot get enough information digested within his own head to be the integrator and decision maker. Instead, he finds himself increasingly having to manage the *process* of decision making, bringing the right people together around the right questions or problems, stimulating open discussion, insuring that all relevant information surfaces and is critically assessed, managing the emotional ups and downs of his *prima donnas*, and insuring that out of all this human and interpersonal process, a good decision will result.

As I have watched processes like these in management groups, I am struck by the fact that the decision emerges out of the interplay. It is hard to pin down who had the idea and who made the decision. The general manager in this setting is *accountable* for the decision, but rarely would I describe the process as one where he or she actually makes the decision, except in the sense of recognizing when the right answer has been achieved, ratifying that answer, announcing it, and following up on its implementation.

If the managerial job is increasingly moving in the direction I have indicated, managers of the future will have to be much more skilled in how to:

1. Select and train their subordinates,
2. Design and run meetings and groups of all sorts,
3. Deal with all kinds of conflict between strong individuals and groups,
4. Influence and negotiate from a low power base, and
5. Integrate the efforts of very diverse technical specialists.

If the above image of what is happening to organizations has any generality, it will force the field of human resource management increasingly to center stage. The more complex organizations become, the more they will be vulnerable to human error. They will not necessarily employ more people, but they will employ more sophisticated highly trained people both in managerial and in individual contributor, staff roles. The price of low motivation, turnover, poor productivity, sabotage and intraorganizational conflict will be higher in such an organization. Therefore it will become a matter of *economic necessity* to improve human resource planning and development systems.

Changing Social Values

A second reason why human resource planning and development will become more central and important is that changing social values regarding the role of work will make it more complicated to manage people. There are several kinds of research findings and observations which illustrate this point.

First, my own longitudinal research of a panel of Sloan School graduates of the 1960s strongly suggests that we have put much too much emphasis on the traditional success syndrome of "climbing the corporate ladder."[5] Some alumni indeed want to rise to high-level general manager positions, but many others want to exercise their particular technical or functional competence and only rise to levels of functional management or senior staff roles with minimal managerial responsibility. Some want security, others are seeking nonorganizational careers as teachers or consultants, while a few are becoming entrepreneurs. I have called these patterns of motivation, talent, and values "career anchors" and believe that they serve to stabilize and constrain the career in predictable ways. The implication is obvious – organizations must develop multiple ladders and multiple reward systems to deal with different types of people.[6]

Second, studies of young people entering organizations in the last several decades suggest that work and career are not as central a life preoccupation as was once the case. Perhaps because of a prolonged period of economic affluence, people see more options for themselves and are increasingly exercising those options. In particular, one sees more concern with a balanced life in which work, family, and self-development play a more equal role.[7]

Third, closely linked to the above trend is the increase in the number of women in organizations, which will have its major impact through the increase of dual career families. As opportunities for women open up, we will see more new life-styles in young couples which will affect the organization's options as to moving people geographically, joint employment, joint career management, family support, etc.[8]

Fourth, research evidence is beginning to accumulate that personal growth and development is a life-long process and that predictable issues and crises come up in every decade of our lives. Organizations will have to be much more aware of what these issues are, how work and family interact, and how to manage people at different ages. The current "hot button" is *midcareer crisis*, but the more research we do the more we find developmental crises at *all* ages and stages.[9]

An excellent summary of what is happening in the world of values, technology, and management is provided in a recent text by Elmer Burack:

> The leading edge of change in the future will include the new technologies of information, production, and management, interlaced with considerable social dislocation and shifts in manpower inputs. These developments are without precedent in our industrial history.
>
> Technological and social changes have created a need for more education, training, and skill at all managerial and support levels. The lowering of barriers to employment based on sex and race introduces new kinds of manpower problems for management officials. Seniority is coming to mean relatively less in relation to the comprehension of problems, processes, and approaches. The newer manpower elements and work technologies have shifted institutional arrangements: the locus of decision making is altered, role relationships among workers and supervisors are changed (often becoming more collegial), and the need to respond to changing routines has become commonplace....
>
> These shifts have been supported by more demanding customer requirements, increasing government surveillance (from product quality to anti-pollution measures), and more widespread use of computers, shifting power bases to the holders of specialized knowledge skills.[10]

In order for HRPD systems to become more responsive and capable of handling such growing complexity they must contain all the necessary components, must be based on correct assumptions, and must be adequately integrated.

COMPONENTS OF A HUMAN RESOURCE PLANNING AND DEVELOPMENT SYSTEM

The major problem with existing HRPD systems is that they are fragmented, incomplete, and sometimes built on faulty assumptions about human or organizational growth.

Human growth takes place through successive encounters with one's environment. As the person ecounters a new situation, he or she is forced to try new responses to deal with that situation. Learning takes place as a function of how those responses work out and the results they achieve. If they are successful in coping with the situation, the person enlarges his repertory of responses; if they are not successful the person must try alternate responses until the situation has been dealt with. If none of the active coping responses work, the person sometimes falls back on retreating from the new situation, or denying that there is a problem to be solved. These responses are defensive and growth limiting.

The implication is that for growth to occur, people basically need two things: *new challenges* that are within the range of their coping responses, and *knowledge of results*, information on how their responses to the challenge have worked out. If the tasks and challenges are too easy or too hard, the person will be demotivated and cease to grow. If the information is not available on how well the person's responses are working, the person cannot grow in a systematic, valid direction but is forced into guessing or trying to infer information from ambiguous signals.

Organizational growth similarly takes place through successful coping with the internal and external environment.[11] But since the organization is a complex system of human, material, financial, and informational resources, one must consider how each of those areas can be properly managed toward organizational effectiveness. In this article I will only deal with the human resources.

In order for the organization to have the capacity to perform effectively over a period of time it must be able to plan for, recruit, manage, develop, measure, dispose of, and replace human resources as warranted by the tasks to be done. The most important of these functions is the *planning* function, since task requirements are likely to change as the complexity and turbulence of the organization's environment increase. In other words, a key assumption underlying organizational growth is that the nature of jobs will change over time, which means that such changes must be continuously monitored in order to insure that the right kinds of human resources can be recruited or developed to do those jobs. Many of the activities such as recruitment, selection, performance appraisal, and so on presume that some planning process has occurred which makes it possible to assess whether or not those activities are meeting *organizational needs*, quite apart from whether they are facilitating the individual's growth.

In an ideal HRPD system one would seek to match the organization's needs for human resources with the individual's needs for personal career growth and development. One can then depict the basic system as involving both individual and organizational planning, and a series of matching activities which are designed to facilitate mutual need satisfaction. If we further assume that both individual and organizational needs change over time, we can depict this process as a developmental one as in Figure 1.

In the right-hand column we show the basic stages of the individual career through the life cycle. While not everyone will go through these stages in the manner depicted, there is growing evidence that for organizational careers in particular, these stages reasonably depict the movement of people through their adult lives.[12]

Given those developmental assumptions, the left-hand side of the diagram shows the organizational planning activities which must occur if human resources are to be managed in an optimal way, and if changing job requirements are to be properly assessed and continuously monitored. The middle column shows the various matching activities which have to occur at various career stages.

The components of an effective HRPD system now can be derived from the diagram. First, there have to be in the organization the overall planning components shown on the left-hand side of Figure 1. Second, there have to be components which insure an adequate process of staffing the organization. Third, there have to be components which plan for and monitor growth and development. Fourth, there have to be components which facilitate the actual process of the growth and development of the people who are

Figure 1
A Developmental Model of Human Resource Planning and Development

Organizational Needs	Matching Processes	Individual Needs
	Primarily initiated and Managed by the Organization	
Planning for Staffing		Career or job choice
Strategic business planning Job/role planning "Manpower" planning and human resource inventorying	Job analysis Recruitment and selection Induction, socialization, initial training Job design and job assignment	
Planning for Growth and Development		Early career issues: locating one's area of contribution, learning how to fit into the organization, becoming productive, seeing a viable future for oneself in the career
Inventorying of development plans Follow-up and evaluation of development activities	Supervising and coaching Performance appraisal and judgment of potential Organizational rewards Promotions and other job changes Training and development opportunities Career counseling, joint career planning, and follow-up	
Planning for Leveling Off and Disengagement		Mid career issues: locating one's career anchor and building one's career around it; specializing vs. generalizing
	Continuing education and retraining Job redesign, job enrichment, and job rotation Alternative patterns of work and rewards Retirement planning and counseling	
Planning for Replacement and Restaffing		Late career issues: becoming a mentor; using one's experience and wisdom; letting go and retiring
	Updating of human resource inventorying Programs of replacement training Information system for job openings Reanalysis of jobs and job/role planning New cycle of recruitment	New human resources from inside or outside the organization

brought into the organization; this growth and development must be organized to meet *both* the needs of the organization and the needs of the individuals within it. Fifth, there have to be components which deal with decreasing effectiveness, leveling off, obsolescence of skills, turnover, retirement, and other phenomena which reflect the need for either a new growth direction or a process of disengagement of the person from his or her job. Finally, there have to be components which insure that as some people move out of jobs, others are available to fill those jobs, and as new jobs arise that people are available with the requisite skills to fill them.

In the remainder of this article I would like to comment on each of these six sets of components and indicate where and how they should be linked to each other.

Overall Planning Components

The function of these components is to insure that the organization has an adequate basis for selecting its human resources and developing them toward the fulfillment of organizational goals.

Strategic Business Planning These activities are designed to determine the organization's goals, priorities, future directions, products, markets growth rate, geographical location, and organization structure or design. This process should lead logically into the next two planning activities but is often disconnected from them because it is located in a different part of the organization or is staffed by people with different orientations and backgrounds.

Job/Role Planning These activities are designed to determine what actually needs to be done at every level of the organization (up through top management) to fulfill the organization's goals and tasks. This activity can be thought of as a dynamic kind of job analysis where a continual review is made of the skills, knowledge, values, etc. which are presently needed in the organization and will be needed in the future. The focus is on the predictable consequences of the strategic planning for managerial roles, specialist roles, and skill mixes which may be needed to get the mission accomplished. If the organization already has a satisfactory system of job descriptions, this activity would concern itself with how those jobs will evolve and change, and what new jobs or roles will evolve in the future.[13]

This component is often missing completely in organizations or is carried out only for lower level jobs. From a planning point of view it is probably most important for the highest level jobs — how the nature of general and functional management will change as the organization faces new technologies, new social values, and new environmental conditions.

Manpower Planning and Human Resource Inventorying These activities draw on the job/role descriptions generated in job/role planning and assess the capabilities of the present human resources against those plans or requirements. These activities may be focused on the numbers of people in given categories and are often designed to insure that under given assumptions of growth there will be an adequate supply of people in those categories. Or the process may focus more on how to insure that certain scarce skills which will be needed will in fact be available, leading to more sophisticated programs of recruitment or human resource development. For example, the inventorying process at high levels may reveal the need for a new type of general manager with broad integrative capacities which may further reveal the need to start a development program that will insure that such managers will be available five to ten years down the road.

These first three component activities are all geared to identifying the *organization's* needs in the human resource area. They are difficult to do and tools are only now beginning to be developed for job/role planning.[14] In most organizations I have dealt with, the three areas, if they exist at all, are not linked to each other organizationally. Strategic planning is likely to exist in the Office of the President. Job/role planning is likely to be an offshoot of some management development activities in Personnel. And human resource inventorying is likely to be a specialized subsection within Personnel. Typically, no one is accountable for bringing these activities together even on an *ad hoc* basis.

This situation reflects an erroneous assumption about growth and development which I want to mention at this time. The assumption is that if the organization develops its present human resources, it will be able to fill whatever job demands may arise in the future. Thus we do find in organizations elaborate human resource planning systems, but they plan for the present people in the organization, not for the organization *per se*. If there are no major changes in job requirements as the organization grows and develops, this system will work. But if jobs themselves change, it is no longer safe to assume that today's human resources, with development plans based on *today's* job requirements, will produce the people needed in some future situation. Therefore, I am asserting that more job/role planning must be done, independent of the present people in the organization.

The subsequent components to be discussed which focus on the matching of individual and organizational needs all assume that some sort of basic planning activities such as those described have been carried out. They may not be very formal, or they may be highly decentralized (e.g. every supervisor who has an open slot might make his own decision of what sort of person to hire based on his private assumptions about strategic business planning and job/role planning). Obviously, the more turbulent the environment, the greater the vulnerability of the organization if it does not centralize and coordinate its various planning activites, and generate its HRPD system from those plans.

Staffing Processes

The function of these processes is to insure that the organization acquires the human resources necessary to fulfill its goals.

Job Analysis If the organizational planning has been done adequately, the next component of the HRPD system is to actually specify what jobs need to be filled and what skills, etc. are needed to do those jobs. Some organizations go through this process very formally, others do it in an informal unprogrammed manner, but in some form it must occur in order to specify what kind of recruitment to do and how to select people from among the recruits.

Recruitment and Selection This activity involves the actual process of going out to find people to fulfill jobs and developing systems for deciding which of those people to hire. These components may be very formal including testing, assessment, and other aids to the selection process. If this component is seen as part of a total HRPD system, it will alert management to the fact that the recruitment selection system communicates to future employees something about the nature of the organization and its approach to people. All too often this component sends incorrect messages or turns off future employees or builds incorrect stereotypes which make subsequent supervision more difficult.[15]

Induction, Socialization, and Initial Training Once the employee has been hired, there ensues a period during which he or she learns the ropes, learns how to get along in the organization, how to work, how to fit in, how to master the particulars of the job, and so on. Once again, it is important that the activities which make up this component are seen as part of a total process with long-range consequences for the attitudes of the employee.[16] The goal of these processes should be to facilitate the employees becoming productive and useful members of the organization both in the short run and in terms of long-range potential.

Job Design and Job Assignment One of the most crucial components of staffing is the actual design of the job which is given to the new employee and the manner in which the assignment is actually made. The issue is how to provide *optimal chal-*

lenge, a set of activities which will be neither too hard nor too easy for the new employee, and which will be neither too meaningless nor too risky from the point of view of the organization. If the job is too easy or too meaningless, the employee may become demotivated; if the job is too hard and/or involves too much responsibility and risk from the point of view of the organization, the employee will become too anxious, frustrated, or angry to perform at an optimal level. Some organizations have set up training programs for supervisors to help them to design optimally challenging work assignments.[17]

These four components are geared to insuring that the work of the organization will be performed. They tend to be processes that have to be performed by line managers and personnel staff specialists together. Line managers have the basic information about jobs and skill requirements: personnel specialists have the interviewing, recruiting, and assessment skills to aid in the selection process. In an optimal system these functions will be closely coordinated, particularly to insure that the recruiting process provides to the employee accurate information about the nature of the organization and the actual work that he or she will be doing in it. Recruiters also need good information on the long-range human resource plans so that these can be taken into account in the selection of new employees.

Development Planning

It is not enough to get good human resources in the door. Some planning activities have to concern themselves with how employees who may be spending thirty to forty years of their total life in a given organization will make a contribution for all of that time, will remain motivated and productive, and will maintain a reasonable level of job satisfaction.

Inventorying of Development Plans Whether or not the process is highly formalized, there is in most organizations some effort to plan for the growth and development of all employees. The planning component that is often missing is some kind of pulling together of this information into a centralized inventory that permits coordination and evaluation of the development activities. Individual supervisors may have clear ideas of what they will do with and for their subordinates, but this information may never be collected, making it impossible to determine whether the individual plans of supervisors are connected in any way. Whether it is done by department, division, or total company, some effort to collect such information and to think through its implications would be of great value to furthering the total development of employees at all levels.

Follow-up and Evaluation of Development Activities
I have observed two symptoms of insufficient planning in this area – one, development plans are made for individual employees, are written down, but are never implemented, and two, if they are implemented they are never evaluated either in relation to the individual's own needs for growth or in relation to the organization's needs for new skills. Some system should exist to insure that plans are implemented and that activities are evaluated against both individual and organizational goals.

Career Development Processes

This label is deliberately broad to cover all of the major processes of managing human resources during their period of growth and peak productivity, a period which may be several decades in length. These processes must match the organization's needs for work with the individual's needs for a productive and satisfying work career. The system must provide for some kind of forward movement for the employee through some succession of jobs, whether these involve promotion, lateral movement to new functions, or simply new assignments within a given area.[18] The system must be based both on the organization's need to fill jobs as they open up and on employees' needs to have some sense of progress in their working lives.

Supervision and Coaching By far the most important component in this area is the actual process of supervising, guiding, coaching, and monitoring. It is in this context that the work assignment and feedback processes which make learning possible occur, and it is the boss who plays the key role in molding the employee to the organization. There is considerable evidence that the first boss is especially crucial in giving new employees a good start in their careers,[19] and that training of supervisors in how to handle new employees is a valuable organizational investment.

Performance Appraisal and Judgment of Potential This component is part of the general process of supervision but stands out as such an important part of that process that it must be treated separately. In most organizations there is some effort to standardize and formalize a process of appraisal above and beyond the normal performance feedback which is expected on a day-to-day basis. Such systems serve a number of functions – to justify salary increases, promotions, and other formal organizational actions with respect to the employee; to provide information for human resource inventories or at least written records of past accomplishments for the employee's personnel folder; and to provide a basis for annual or semiannual formal reviews between boss and subordinate to supplement day-to-day feedback and to facilitate information exchange for career planning and counseling. In some organizations so little day-to-day feedback occurs that the *formal* system bears the burden of providing the employees with knowledge of how they are doing and what they can look forward to. Since knowledge of results, of how one is doing, is a crucial component of any developmental process, it is important for organizations to monitor how well and how frequently feedback is actually given.

One of the major dilemmas in this area is whether to have a single system which provides both feedback for the growth and development of the employee and information for the organization's planning systems. The dilemma arises because the information which the planning system requires (e.g. "how much potential does this employee have to rise in the organization?") may be the kind of information which neither the boss nor the planner wants to share with the employee. The more potent and more accurate the information, the less likely it is to be fed back to the employee in anything other than very vague terms.

On the other hand, the detailed work-oriented, day-to-day feedback which the employee needs for growth and development may be too cumbersome to record as part of a selection-oriented appraisal system. If hundreds of employees are to be compared, there is strong pressure in the system toward more of general kinds of judgments, traits, rankings, numerical estimates of ultimate potential, and the like. One way of resolving this dilemma which some companies have found successful is to develop two separate systems – one oriented toward performance improvement and the growth of the employee, and the other one oriented toward a more global assessment of the employee for future planning purposes involving judgments which may not be shared with the employee except in general terms.

A second dilemma arises around the identification of the employee's "development needs" and how that information is linked to other development activities. If the development needs are stated in relation to the planning system, the employee may never get the feedback of what his needs may have been perceived to be, and, worse, no one may implement any program to deal with those needs if the planning system is not well linked with line management.

Two further problems arise from this potential lack of linkage. One, if the individual does not get good feedback around developmental needs, he or she remains uninvolved in their own development and potentially becomes complacent. We pay lip service to the statement that only the individual can develop himself or herself, but then deprive the individual of the very information that would make sensible self-development possible. Two, the development needs as stated for the various employees in the organization may have nothing to do with the organization's needs for certain kinds of human resources in the future. All too often there is complete lack of linkage between the strategic or business planning function and the human resource development function resulting in potentially willy-nilly individual development based on today's needs and individual managers' stereotypes of what will be needed in the future.

Organizational Rewards – Pay, Benefits, Perquisites, Promotion, and Recognition Entire books have been written about all the problems and subtleties of how to link organizational rewards to the other components of a HRPD system to insure both short-run and long-run human effectiveness. For purposes of this short paper I wish to point out only one major issue – how to insure that organizational rewards are linked *both* to the needs of the individual and to the needs of the organization for effective performance and development of potential. All too often the reward system is neither responsive to the individual employee nor to the organization, being driven more by criteria of elegance, consistency, and what other organizations are doing. If the linkage is to be established, line managers must actively work with compensation experts to develop a joint philosophy and set of goals based on an understanding of both what the organization is trying to reward and what employee needs actually are. As organizational careers become more varied and as social values surrounding work change, reward systems will probably have to become much more flexible both in time (people at different career stages may need different things) and by type of career (functional specialists may need different things than general managers).

Promotions and Other Job Changes There is ample evidence that what keeps human growth and effectiveness going is continuing optimal challenge.[20] Such challenge can be provided for some members of the organization through promotion to higher levels where more responsible jobs are available. For most members of the organization the promotion opportunities are limited, however, because the pyramid narrows at the top. An effective HRPD system will, therefore, concentrate on developing career paths, systems of job rotation, changing assignments, temporary assignments, and other lateral job moves which insure continuing growth of all human resources.

One of the key characteristics of an optimally challenging job is that it both draws on the person's abilities and skills and that it has opportunities for "closure." The employee must be in the job long enough to get involved and to see the results of his or her efforts. Systems of rotation which move the person too rapidly either prevent initial involvement (as in the rotational training program), or prevent closure by transferring the person to a new job before the effects of his or her decisions can be assessed. I have heard many "fast track" executives complain that their self-confidence was low because they never really could see the results of their efforts. Too often we move people too fast in order to "fill slots" and thereby undermine their development.

Organizational planning systems which generate "slots" to be filled must be coordinated with development planning systems which concern themselves with the optimal growth of the human resources. Sometimes it is better for the organization in the long run not to fill an empty slot in order to keep a manager in another job where he or she is just beginning to develop. One way of insuring such linkage is to monitor these processes by means of a "development committee" which is composed of both line managers and personnel specialists. In such a group the needs of the organization and the needs of the people can be balanced against each other in the context of the long-range goals of the organization.

Training and Development Opportunities Most organizations recognize that periods of formal training, sabbaticals, executive development programs outside of the company, and other educational activities are necessary in the total process of human growth and development. The important point about these activities is that they should be carefully linked both to the needs of the individual and to the needs of the organization. The individual should want to go to the program because he or she can see how the educational activity fits into the total career. The organization should send the person because the training fits into some concept of future career development. It should not be undertaken simply as a generalized "good thing," or because other companies are doing it. As much as possible the training and educational activities should be tied to job/role planning. For example, many companies began to use university executive development programs because of an explicit recognition that future managers would require a broader perspective on various problems and that such "broadening" could best be achieved in the university programs.

Career Counseling, Joint Career Planning, Follow-up, and Evaluation Inasmuch as the growth and development which may be desired can only come from within the individual himself or herself, it is important that the organization provide some means for individual employees at all levels to become more proactive about their careers and some mechanisms for joint dialogue, counseling, and career planning.[21] This process should ideally be linked to performance appraisal, because it is in that context that the boss can review with the subordinate the future potential, development needs, strengths, weaknesses, career options, etc. The boss is often not trained in counseling but does possess some of the key information which the employee needs to initiate any kind of career planning. More formal counseling could then be supplied by the personnel development staff or outside the organization altogether.

The important point to recognize is that employees cannot manage their own growth development without information on how their own needs, talents, values, and plans mesh with the opportunity structure of the organization. Even though the organization may only have imperfect, uncertain information about the future, the individual is better off to know that than to make erroneous assumptions about the future based on no information at all. It is true that the organization cannot make commitments, nor should it unless required to by legislation or contract. But the sharing of information if properly done is not the same as making commitments or setting up false expectations.

If the organization can open up the communication channel between employees, their bosses, and whoever is managing the human resource system, the groundwork is laid for realistic individual development planning. Whatever is decided about training, next steps, special assignments, rotation, etc. should be jointly decided by the individual and the appropriate organizational resource (probably the supervisor and someone from personnel specializing in career development). Each step must fit into the employee's life plan and must be tied into *organizational needs*. The organization should be neither a humanistic charity nor an indoctrination center. Instead, it should be a vehicle for meeting both the needs of society and of individuals.

Whatever is decided should not merely be written down but executed. If there are implementation problems, the development plan should be renegotiated. Whatever developmental actions are taken, it is essential that they be followed up and evaluated both by the person and by the organization to determine what, if anything, was achieved. It is shocking to discover how many companies invest in major activities such as university executive development programs and never determine for themselves what was accomplished. In some instances, they make no plans to talk to the individual before or after the program so that it is not even possible to determine what the activity meant to the participant, or what might be an appropriate next assignment for him or her following the program.

I can summarize the above analysis best by emphasizing the two places where I feel there is the most fragmentation and violation of growth assumptions. First, too many of the activities occur without the involvement of the person who is "being developed" and therefore may well end up being self-defeating. This is particularly true of job assignments and performance appraisal where too little involvement and feedback occur. Second, too much of the human resource system functions as a personnel *selection* system unconnected to either the needs of the organization or the needs of the individual. All too often it is only a system for short-run replacement of people in standard type jobs. The key planning functions are not linked in solidly and hence do not influence the system to the degree they should.

Planning for and Managing Disengagement
The planning and management processes which will be briefly reviewed here are counterparts of ones that have already been discussed but are focused on a different problem – the problem of the late career, loss of motivation, obsolescence, and ultimately retirement. Organizations must recognize that there are various options available to deal with this range of problems beyond the obvious ones of either terminating the employee or engaging in elaborate measures to "remotivate" people who may have lost work involvement.[22]

Continuing Education and Retraining These activities have their greatest potential if the employee is motivated and if there is some clear connection between what is to be learned and what the employee's current or future job assignments require in the way of skills. More and more organizations are finding out that it is better to provide challenging work first and only then the training to perform that work once the employee sees the need for it. Obviously for this linkage to work well continuous dialogue is needed between employees and their managers. For those employees who have leveled off, have lost work involvement, but are still doing high quality work other solutions such as those described below are more applicable.

Job Redesign, Job Enrichment, and Job Rotation This section is an extension of the arguments made earlier on job changes in general applied to the particular problems of leveled off employees. In some recent research, it has been suggested that job enrichment and other efforts to redesign work to increase motivation and performance may only work during the first few years on a job.[23] Beyond that the employee becomes "unresponsive" to the job characteristics themselves and pays more attention to surrounding factors such as the nature of supervision, relationships with co-workers, pay, and other extrinsic characteristics. In other words, before organizations attempt to "cure" leveled off employees by remotivating them through job redesign or rotation, they should examine whether those employees are still in a responsive mode or not. On the other hand, one can argue that there is nothing wrong with less motivated, less involved employees so long as the quality of what they are doing meets the organizational standards.[24]

Alternative Patterns of Work and Rewards Because of the changing needs and values of employees in recent decades, more and more organizations have begun to experiment with alternative work patterns such as flexible working hours, part-time work, sabbaticals or other longer periods of time off, several people filling one job, dual employment of spouses with more extensive childcare programs, etc. Along with these experiments have come others on flexible reward systems in which employees can choose between a raise, some time off, special retirement, medical, or insurance benefits, and other efforts to make multiple career ladders a viable reality. These programs apply to employees at all career stages but are especially relevant to people in mid and late career stages where their own perception of their career and life goals may be undergoing important changes.

None of those innovations should be attempted without first clearly establishing a HRPD system which takes care of the organization's needs as well as the needs of employees and links them to each other. There can be little growth and development for employees at any level in an organization which is sick and stagnant. It is in the best interests of both the individual and the organization to have a healthy organization which can provide opportunities for growth.

Retirement Planning and Counseling As part of any effective HRPD system, there must be a clear planning function which forecasts who will retire, and which feeds this information into both the replacement staffing system and the counseling functions so that the employees who will be retiring can be prepared for this often traumatic career stage. Employees need counseling not only with the mechanical and financial aspects of retirement, but also to prepare them psychologically for the time when they will no longer have a clear organizational base or job as part of their identity. For some people it may make sense to spread the period of retirement over a number of years by using part-time work or special assignments to help both the individual and the organization to get benefits from this period.

The counseling function here as in other parts of the career probably involves special skills and must be provided by specialists. However, the line manager continues to play a key role as a provider of job challenge, feedback, and information about what is ahead for any given employee. Seminars for line managers on how to handle the special problems of pre-retirement employees would probably be of great value as part of their managerial training.

Planning for and Managing Replacement and Restaffing

With this step the HRPD cycle closes back upon itself. This function must be concerned with such issues as:

1. Updating the human resource inventory as retirements or terminations occur;
2. Instituting special programs of orientation or training for new incumbents to specific jobs as those jobs open up;
3. Managing the information system on what jobs are available and determining how to match this information to the human resources available in order to determine whether to replace from within the organization or to go outside with a new recruiting program;
4. Continuously reanalyzing jobs to insure that the new incumbent is properly prepared for what the job *now* requires and *will* require in the future.

How these processes are managed links to the other parts of the system through the implicit messages that are sent to employees. For example, a company which decides to publicly post all of its unfilled jobs is clearly sending a message that it expects internal recruitment and supports self-development activities. A company which manages restaffing in a very secret manner may well get across a message that employees might as well be complacent and passive about their careers because they cannot influence them anyway.

SUMMARY AND CONCLUSIONS

I have tried to argue in this article that human resource planning and development is becoming an increasingly important function in organizations, that this function consists of multiple components, and that these components must be managed *both* by line managers and staff specialists. I have tried to show that the various planning activities are closely linked to the actual processes of supervision, job assignment, training, etc. and that those processes must be designed to match the needs of the organization with the needs of the employees throughout their evolving careers, whether or not those careers involve hierarchical promotions. I have also argued that the various components are linked to each other and must be seen as a total system if it is to be effective. The total system must be managed as a system to insure coordination between the planning functions and the implementation functions.

I hope it is clear from what has been said above that an effective human resource planning and development system is integral to the functioning of the organization and must, therefore, be a central concern of line management. Many of the activities require specialist help, but the accountabilities must rest squarely with line supervisors and top management. It is they who control the opportunities and the rewards. It is the job assignment system and the feedback which employees get that is the ultimate raw material for growth and development. Whoever designs and manages the system, it will not help the organization to become more effective unless that system is *owned* by line management.

References

1. P. Pigors and C.A. Myers (1977) *Personnel Administration*, 8th ed., New York: McGraw-Hill. E. Burack (1975) *Organizational Analysis* Hinsdale, IL: Dryden.

2. J.R. Hackman and J.L. Suttle (1977) *Improving Life at Work*. Los Angeles: Goodyear. H. Meltzer and F.R. Wickert (1976) *Humanizing Organizational Behavior*. Springfield, IL: Charles C. Thomas.

3. D. McGregor (1960) *The Human Side of Enterprise*. New York: McGraw-Hill. W.G. Bennis (1966) *Changing Organizations*. New York: McGraw-Hill. P. Pigors and C.A. Meyers (1977) *op. cit.* E.H. Schein (1970) *Organizational Psychology*. Englewood Cliffs, NJ: Prentice-Hall. J. Van Maanen (1976) "Breaking In: Socialization to Work" in *Handbook of Organization and Society*, R. Dubin, ed. Chicago: Rand McNally. L. Bailyn and E.H. Schein (1976) "Life/Career Considerations as Indicators of Quality of Employment," in *Measuring Work Quality for Social Reporting*, A.D. Biderman and T.F. Drury, eds. New York: Sage Publications. R. Katz (1977) "Job Enrichment: Some Career Considerations," in *Organizational Careers: Some New Perspectives*, T. Van Maanen, ed. New York: John Wiley and Sons.

4. R.D. Beckhard (1969) *Organization Development: Strategies and Models*. Reading, MA: Addison-Wesley. W.G. Bennis (1966) *op. cit.* E.H. Schein (1963) *Process Consultation: Its Role in Organization Development*. Reading, MA: Addison-Wesley. J. Galbraith (1973) *Designing Complex Organizations*. Reading, MA: Addison-Wesley. F.G. Lesieer (1958) *The Scanlon Plan*. New York: John Wiley and Sons. T. Alfred (January-February 1967) "Checkers or Choice in Manpower Management." *Harvard Business Review*, pp. 167–169.

5. E.H. Schein (1975) "How 'Career Anchors' Hold Executives to Their Career Paths." *Personnel* 52, Number 3, pp. 11–24.

6. E.H. Schein (forthcoming) *The Individual, the Organization and the Career: Toward Greater Human Effectiveness*. Reading, MA: Addison-Wesley.

7. L. Bailyn and E.H. Schein (1976) *op. cit.* C.A. Meyers (1974) "Management and the Employee," in *Social Responsibility and the Business Predicament*. J.W. McKie, ed. Washington, DC: Brookings. J. Van Maanen, L. Bailyn and E.H. Schein (1977) "The Shape of Things to Come: A New Look at Organizational Careers," in *Perspectives on Behavior in Organizations*, J.R. Hackman, E.E. Lawler and L.W. Porter, eds. New York: McGraw-Hill. R.J. Roeber (1973) *The Organization in a Changing Environment*. Reading, MA: Addison-Wesley.

8. J. Van Maanen and E.H. Schein (1977) "Improving the Quality of Work Life: Career Development," in *Improving Life at Work*, J.R. Hackman and J.L. Suttle, eds. Los Angeles: Goodyear. L. Bailyn (1970) "Career and Family Orientations of Husbands and Wives in Relation to Marital Happiness." *Human Relations*, pp. 97–113. R.M. Kanter (1977) *Work and Family in the United States*. New York: Russell Sage.

9. G. Sheehy (February 1974) "Catch 30 and Other Predictable Crises of Growing Up Adult." *New York Magazine*, pp. 30–44. L.E. Troll (1975) *Early and Middle Adulthood*. Monterey, CA: Brooks-Cole. R.F. Pearse and B.P. Pelzer (1975) *Self-directed Change for the Mid-Career Manager*. New York: AMACOM.

10. E. Burack (1975) *op. cit.*

11. E.H. Schein (1970) *op. cit.*

12. G.W. Dalton and P.H. Thompson (November-December 1976) "Are R&D Organizations Obsolete?" *Harvard Business Review*, pp. 105–116. D.E. Super and M.J. Bohn (1970) *Occupational Psychology*. Belmont, CA: Wadsworth.
13. D.T. Hall (1976) *Careers in Organizations*. Los Angeles: Goodyear. E.H. Schein (forthcoming) *op. cit.*
14. *Ibid.*
15. E.H. Schein (1964) "How to Break in the College Graduate." *Harvard Business Review*, pp. 68–76. E.H. Schein (forthcoming) *op. cit.*
16. E.H. Schein (Winter, 1968) "Organizational Socialization and the Profession of Management." *Industrial Management Review*, pp. 1–16. J. Van Maanen (1976) *op. cit.*
17. E.H. Schein (1964) *op. cit.*
18. E.H. Schein (1971) "The Individual, the Organization and the Career: A Conceptual Scheme." *Journal of Applied Behavioral Science*, 7, pp. 401–426. E.H. Schein (forthcoming) *op. cit.*
19. E.H. Schein (1964) *op. cit.* D.W. Bray, R.J. Campbell and D.E. Grant (1974) *Formative Years in Business*. New York: John Wiley and Sons. D. Berlew and D.T. Hall (1966) "The Socialization of Managers." *Administrative Science Quarterly*, 11, pp. 207–223. D.T. Hall (1976) *op. cit.*
20. G.W. Dalton and P.H. Thompson (November-December 1976) *op. cit.* R. Katz (1977) *op. cit.*
21. R. Heidke (1977) *Career Pro-Activity of Middle Managers*. Master's Thesis. Massachusetts Institute of Technology.
22. L. Baily (1977) "Involvement and Accommodation in Technical Careers," in *Organizational Careers: Some New Perspectives*. J. Van Maanen, ed. New York: John Wiley and Sons.
23. R. Katz (1977) *op. cit.*
24. L. Bailyn (1977) *op. cit.*

AN INTEGRATED MANAGEMENT SYSTEM: LESSONS FROM THE JAPANESE EXPERIENCE*

Nina Hatvany
Vladimir Pucik

Productivity increases in Japan have been two to three times the U.S. rate over the past three decades. Absenteeism in most Japanese companies is low, turnover rates are about half the American figures, and commitment to the firm is high (Cole, 1979).[1] Certainly, the productivity increases result not only from management practices but also from overall economic and sociohistorical conditions specific to Japan. For example, Japan's productivity growth has probably been raised as much by massive capital investments per worker (Denison & Chung, 1976)[2] as by effective labor management. Nevertheless, the fact that many Japanese companies have developed management practices associated with high productivity and low turnover and absenteeism has received a great deal of attention in the popular press as well as in the recent organizational literature (e.g., Marsh & Mannari, 1976; Pascale, 1978).[3]

Past examinations of management in Japan have seldom been related to universal organizational theories. Rather, they have concentrated on confirming or disconfirming the existence of sup-

* From the *Academy of Management Review*, 1981, Volume 6, Number 3, pp. 469–480. Reprinted by permission of the authors and publishers. © 1981 by the Academy of Management 0363—7425.

Acknowledgements: We wish to thank Koya Azumi, Mitsuyo Hanada, Blair McDonald, Bill Newman, Bill Ouchi, Hans Pennings, Tom Roehl, and Michael Tushman for their helpful comments on earlier drafts of this article. We are grateful to Citibank, New York, and the Japan Foundation, Tokyo, for their financial support during the preparation of this article.

posedly unique characteristics of workers and companies in Japan (such as permanent employment and bottom-up decision making), which were analyzed in isolation from the other structural and process variables. In contrast, our model of Japanese management rests on fairly universal elements suitable for a comparative review.

A MODEL OF JAPANESE MANAGEMENT

We believe the essence of management in large Japanese companies is a focus on human resources (Clark, 1979; Tsurumi, 1977),[4] which reflects an explicit preference for the maximum utilization of the firm's human resources as well as an implicit understanding of how an organization ought to be managed.

The focus on human resources is manifested in three interrelated strategies (see Figure 1). First, an internal labor market is created to secure a labor force of the desired quality and to induce the employees to remain in the firm (Pucik, 1979).[5] Second, a company philosophy is articulated that expresses concern for employee needs and emphasizes cooperation and teamwork in a "unique" environment (Ouchi & Jaeger, 1978).[6] Third, close attention is given both to hiring people who will fit well with the values of the particular company and to integrating employees

Figure 1
A Model of Japanese Management

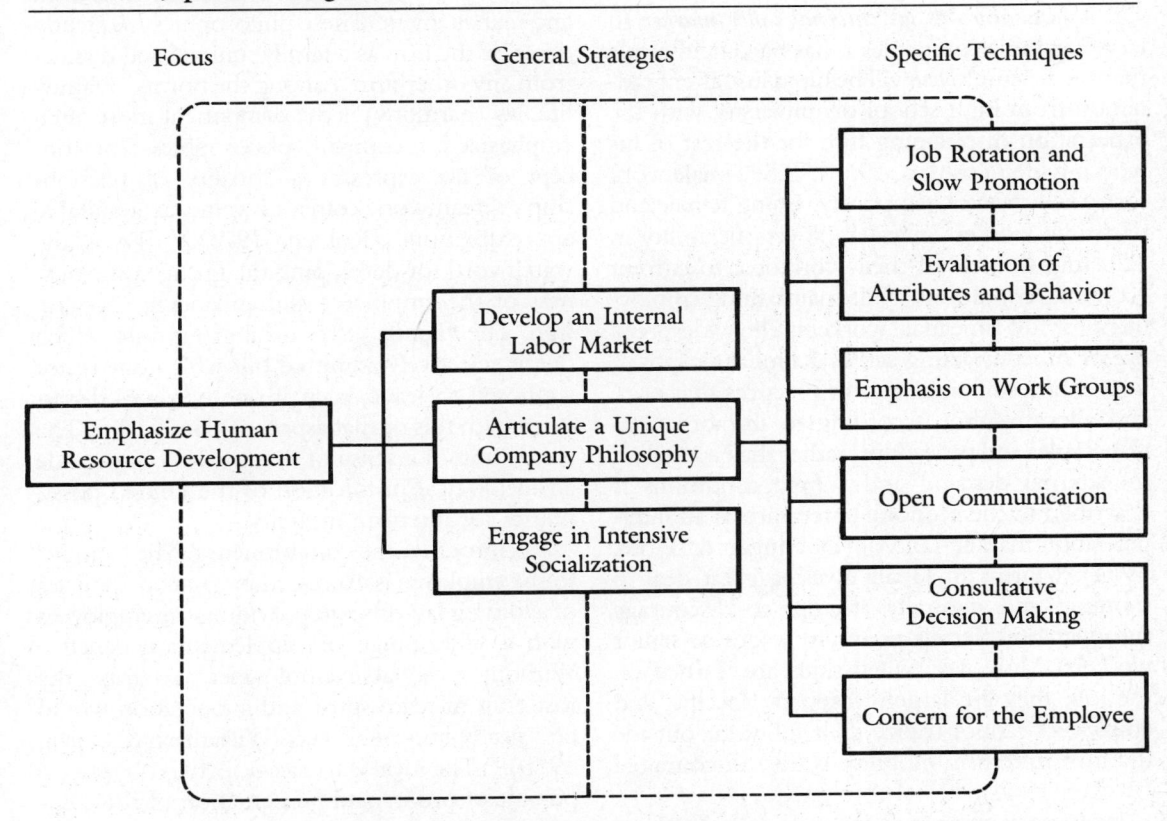

Focus	General Strategies	Specific Techniques
Emphasize Human Resource Development	Develop an Internal Labor Market	Job Rotation and Slow Promotion
		Evaluation of Attributes and Behavior
	Articulate a Unique Company Philosophy	Emphasis on Work Groups
		Open Communication
	Engage in Intensive Socialization	Consultative Decision Making
		Concern for the Employee

into the company at all stages of their working life (Rohlen, 1974).[7]

These general strategies are translated into specific management techniques. Emphasis is placed on continuous development of employee skills; formal promotion is of secondary importance. Employees are evaluated according to a multitude of criteria rather than on just individual bottom-line contribution. Work is structured so that it can be carried out by groups operating with a great deal of autonomy. Open communication is encouraged, supported, and rewarded. Information about pending decisions is circulated widely before the decisions are actually made. Active, observable concern for each and every employee is expressed by supervisory personnel (Clark, 1979; Rohlen, 1974).[8]

Strategies

The organization as an internal labor market In large Japanese companies it has become the rule that a male employee will be hired just after graduation from high school or university with the expectation of retaining him for the rest of his working life (Yoshino, 1968).[9] The female work force, is, however, temporary. Using female and part-time workers gives employers flexibility in adjusting the size of their workforce to current economic conditions while maintaining employment for full-time male workers. The widespread use of subcontracting serves a similar purpose.

Such a set of employment practices that price and allocate labor according to intraorganizational rules and procedures rather than according to external demand and supply conditions is described in the economic literature as an internal labor market (ILM) (Doeringer & Piore, 1971).[10] Firms in Japan invest a great deal in training, and naturally attempt to discourage turnover by offering premium wages to senior workers. Moreover, when skills are learned on the job, they are largely company specific, and employees cannot realize their full value outside the firm; interfirm mobility is thus discouraged (Becker, 1964).[10a]

Japanese workers at early stages of their careers are underpaid relative to what they contribute (Cole, 1971).[11] They are compensated for this at later stages in their tenure with the firm, in that the wages of the most senior class of workers may surpass the pay of new employees by 200–400 percent, depending on the company (Haitani, 1978).[12] However, this kind of wage system does not preclude the existence of additional merit differentials within older age-groups. The seniority benefits and the lack of alternative employment opportunities at comparable wage levels for workers with previous experience, as well as the insufficiency of public welfare, combine to make an employee both unwilling and unable to move (Pucik, 1979).[13]

Articulated and unique company philosophy Many chief executives of major Japanese firms have written books expressing their philosophy of work and management. These philosophies frequently describe the firm as a family, unique and distinct from any other firm. Among the norms of family life, *wa* (harmony) is the component most often emphasized in company philosophies. The concept of *wa* expresses a "quality of relationship...teamwork comes to mind as a suitable approximation" (Rohlen, 1974).[14] *Wa* is the watchword for developing the group consciousness of the employees and enhancing cooperation. The "family" is a social group into which one is selectively admitted but which one is not supposed to leave, even if one becomes dissatisfied with this or that aspect of "family" life. The cultivation of a sense of uniqueness can provide an ideological justification of the limited possibilities for interfirm mobility.

Reciprocally, the commitment of the "family" to the employee is expressed in company policies of avoiding lay-offs and providing the employees with a wide range of supplementary benefits. Without reasonable employment security, the fostering of team spirit and cooperation would be a nearly impossible task (Williamson & Ouchi, 1980).[15] The ideal is to reconcile two objectives: pursuit of profits and perpetuation of the company as a group.

Intensive socialization The development of cohesiveness within the firm is a major objective of Japanese personnel policies throughout the working life of an employee. In the initial screening process, young graduates are not favored solely because of structural features of the internal labor market in the firm. " 'Virgin' work forces are preferred for the reason that they can be readily assimilated into each company's unique environment as a community" (Hazama, 1979).[16] The basic criteria for hiring are moderate views and a harmonious personality. Ability on the job is obviously also a requirement, but applicants may be eliminated during the selection process if they arouse the suspicion that they cannot get along with people, possess radical views, or come from an unfavorable home environment (Rohlen, 1974).[17]

The socialization process begins with an initial training program, which may last up to six months and is geared toward familiarizing new employees with the company. They are expected to assume the identity of a "company man"; their vocational specialization is of secondary importance. The process continues with a "resocialization" experience (Katz, 1980)[18] each time the employee enters a new position, to become acquainted with a new set of people and tasks. Employees are transferred for two main reasons: to learn additional skills, and as part of a long-range experience-building program, through which the organization grooms its future managers (Yoshino, 1968).[19] By rotating semilaterally from job to job, employees become increasingly immersed in the company philosophy and culture.

Techniques

Because the components reinforce each other, our model should not be interpreted as strictly causal. The strategies that reflect management's focus on human resources are closely interrelated, as are all the specific techniques through which the strategies are realized.

Job rotation and slow promotion Under conditions of lifetime employment, rapid promotion is unlikely unless an organization is expanding dramatically. Limited upward mobility encourages lateral job rotation in Japanese organizations, and carefully planned lateral transfers add substantial flexibility to job reward and recognition. Not all jobs at the same hierarchical level are equal in their centrality or importance to the organization's activity (Schein, 1971).[20] By assigning individuals to jobs that are at the same level but vary in centrality, the organization can distinguish among individuals who share the same formal status, salary, and privileges (Rohlen, 1974).[21] This informal recognition system has the effect of providing or withholding opportunities to learn skills required for future formal promotions.

An additional feature adding flexibility to the promotion systems of many Japanese firms is a dual promotion ladder (Haitani, 1978).[22] Promotion in "status" is based on past evaluations and seniority within the firm; promotion in "position" is based on evaluations and the availability of vacancies in the level above. Even if promotion in position is blocked by lack of a vacancy, promotion in "status" will provide an employee with more respect and money.

Job rotation is also encouraged by the need for in-house training in an ILM, which discourages hiring outsiders. Through job rotation, employees become generalists. Lifetime employment and a nonspecialized career path reinforce one another in reducing interfirm mobility.

Evaluation of attributes and behavior Employee evaluations are usually conducted on an annual or semi-annual basis. The evaluation criteria include not only performance measures on the individual and, especially, the team level, but also desirable personality traits and behaviors, such as creativity, emotional maturity, and cooperation with others (Hazama, 1979).[23] In most companies, personality and behavior, rather than output, is the key criterion (Ouchi & Jaeger, 1978),[24] yet the difference is often merely symbolic. Output measures may easily be translated into attributes such as leadership ability, technical competence, relations with others, and judgement. In this way, the employee is not made to feel that effectiveness and efficiency, which may sometimes be beyond his control, are the main criteria in the evaluation. Occasional mistakes, particularly for lower-level employees, are considered part of the learning process (Tsurumi, 1977).[25] Evaluations do, however, clearly discriminate among employees, in that each employee is compared to other members of an appropriate group and ranked accordingly.

Because group performance is also a criterion of evaluations, peer pressure on an individual to contribute sufficiently to the group's performance becomes an important means of performance control. Long tenure, friendship ties, and informal communication networks enable both superiors and peers to have a clear sense of the employee's performance and potential relative to others.

Importance of the work group Many other company policies revolve around groups. Tasks are assigned to groups rather than to individuals (Rohlen, 1974),[26] which, along with job rotation and group-based performance feedback, stimulates group cohesion. Job rotation not only develops each employee's skills but also prevents production losses for the group when workers are absent. The fact that group performance is a criterion of evaluation encourages cooperation for pragmatic reasons. Not surprisingly, these elements of job design are similar to those employed in work-group job enrichment programs in the U.S. (e.g., Hackman, 1977).[27]

Group autonomy is enhanced by not using experts to solve operational problems for specific groups. Autonomy is, however, clearly delimited in that the company carefully coordinates team activities and controls the training and evaluation of members, the size of the group, the amount of job rotation, and sometimes even the speed and amount of production (Cole, 1979).[28] Yet within these limits, the work group constitutes the linchpin of the company.

Open communication Both the emphasis on team spirit in work groups and the network of friendships that employees develop during their long tenure in the organization encourage the extensive face-to-face communication reported in several studies involving Japanese companies (e.g., Pascale, 1978).[29] Open communication is also an inherent part of the Japanese work setting. Work spaces are open and crowded with individuals at different levels in the hierarchy. Subordinates can do little that the supervisor is not aware of and vice versa. Even high-ranking office managers seldom have separate private offices. In factory situations, the formen and even senior plant managers are constantly on the floor discussing problems, helping with pieces of work, talking to outsiders, and instructing the inexperienced (Rohlen, 1974).[30]

Open communication is not limited to the vertical exchanges often emphasized in the literature (e.g., Nakane, 1970).[31] Job rotation stimulates the emergence of extensive informal lateral communication networks. Without these networks, the transfer of much job-related information would be impossible.

Consultative decision making The extensive face-to-face communication observed in Japanese companies is sometimes confused with participative decision making. However, data from Pascale's (1978)[32] study indicate that the extent of face-to-face communication bears no relationship to employees' perceptions of their level of participation in decision making. The usual procedure for management decision making is that a proposal is initiated by a middle manager, most often under the directive of top management (Hattori, 1977).[33] This middle manager will engage in informal discussion and consultation with peers and supervisors. When all are familiar with the proposal, a request for a decision is made formally and, because of the earlier discussions, it is almost inevitably ratified, often in a ceremonial group meeting. This does not indicate unanimous approval, but does imply consent to its implementation. "The manager will not decide until others who will be affected have had sufficient time to offer their views, feel they have been fairly heard, and are willing to support the decision even though they may not feel that it is the best one "(Rohlen, 1974)[34]. This kind of decision making is not "participative" in the American sense of the word, which implies frequent group meetings and negotiation between manager and subordinates. Nor is it bottom-up, as suggested, for example, by Drucker (1975);[35] rather it is a top-down or interactive consultative process, especially when long-term planning and strategy are concerned. Although the locus of responsibility may appear ambiguous to outsiders (Tsuji, 1968; Yoshino, 1968),[36] it is actually quite clear within the organization, especially at the upper levels (Clark, 1979).[37]

Concern for the employee Informal communication not only facilitates decision making but also provides a way to express management concern for the well-being of employees. Managers invest a great deal of time in talking to employees about everyday matters. Indeed, the quality of relationships with subordinates is an important part of their evaluation (Cole, 1971).[38] Managers thus develop a feeling for an employee's personal needs and problems, as well as for his performance. Obviously, long tenure makes it easier to get to know an employee intimately.

Deepening the company's involvement with employees' lives is the sponsoring of various cultural, athletic, and other recreational activities, resulting in a heavy schedule of company social affairs (Rohlen, 1974).[39] The company allocates substantial financial resources to pay for benefits that are given all employees, such as a family allowance and various commuting and housing allowances. Furthermore, there are various welfare systems that "penetrate into every crack of workers' lives" (Hazama, 1979).[40] These range from company scholarships for employees' children to credit extension, savings, and insurance. Thus, employees perceive their own welfare and the financial welfare of the company as being identical (Tsurumi, 1977).[41]

In this sense, the reciprocal relationship between the employee and the organization is especially important. The Japanese management system is based on the understanding that, in return for the employee's contribution toward the company's growth and well-being, the profitable firm will provide him with a stable and secure work environment and protect his welfare even during a period of economic slowdown. However, we believe that there is nothing uniquely Japanese in this exchange.

THE COMPARATIVE PERSPECTIVE

Twenty years ago, when Japan's economic growth first caught the attention of management experts, it was widely believed that the modernization of the Japanese economy would force radical changes in "traditional" management methods in the direction of "modern" American management style (Harbison & Myers, 1959).[42] However, the expected shift to greater interfirm mobility and intrafirm conflict did not occur and Japanese companies continued to exhibit strong productivity gains. The explanation for Japan's success is now often sought in personality traits, either inherently characteristic of Japanese people or induced by their cultural traditions (Tsuda, 1979.)[43] It is asserted that were it not for these unique personality traits, Japanese management practices could not survive. However, as Cyert and March observe: "An organization is unique when we fail to develop a theory which would make it nonunique"(1963).[44] As a first step toward a theory that would integrate findings from studies of Japanese organizations with organizational theories developed outside Japan, we shall highlight the relationship between the Japanese management strategies and techniques just described and positive work outcomes such as commitment to the organization and productivity. Our review is not intended to be exhaustive, but rather to suggest the feasibility of integrating findings from Japan with more general concepts. We therefore focus exclusively on relationships that may be derived from observations of behavior in non-Japanese settings.

CONCERN FOR HUMAN RESOURCES, COMMITMENT, AND PRODUCTIVITY

The internal labor market (ILM) and its relationship to commitment is a convenient starting point for our discussion. The guarantee of job security implicit in an ILM is a marked departure from conventional American managerial assumptions. It is often thought that institutionalized labor security deprives the manager of the ultimate tool of control — the threat of firing. However, more subtle forms of control are still available in an ILM, such as a placement in a dead-end position or one of low centrality. Moreover, job security has advantages for the organization. One is the reduction of employee hostility to the introduction of labor-saving technology or to organizational changes. Employees know that they may be transferred to new jobs, but do not fear losing their jobs altogether. Another, as suggested by Hall (1976)[45] and Salancik (1977)[46], is that long tenure is positively associated with commitment to the organization. High commitment is also elicited by actions expressing the company's concern with the employee's welfare. Data presented by Steers (1977)[47] indicate that an employee's level of commitment is strongly related to, among other things, feelings of personal importance to the organization, which are based on the actions of that organization over a period of time.

The link between commitment and other behavioral outcomes is complex and is complicated by the fact that commitment is a multifaceted variable comprising acceptance of the organization's goals and values, willingness to exert effort on behalf of the organization, and desire to maintain membership in the organization (Steers, 1977).[48] One can assume that all these facets are not always oriented in the same direction. For that reason, high commitment *per se* may have only a limited effect on performance. However, high commitment does reduce turnover, according to Porter, Steers, Mowday, and Boulian (1974).[49] High commitment in conjunction with binding choice also leads to high satisfaction (Salancik & Pfeffer, 1978).[50] The results of four studies connecting labor market structure and commitment (Blauner, 1964; Cole, 1979; Marsh & Mannari, 1977; Ouchi & Jaeger, 1978)[51] support these assertions in general. Analysis by age group, years of tenure, level of education, and position in the hierarchy consistently shows significant differences in the concomitant variance of commitment and turnover among employees who work in an ILM setting and those who do not.

A philosophy that is both articulated and enacted may facilitate a transformation of commitment into productive effort because it presents a clear picture of the organization's goals, norms, and values, thus providing direction for individuals, setting constraints on their behavior, and enhancing their motivation (Scott, 1966).[52] In fact, the strategy of disseminating an articulated company philosophy has been adopted by a number of American companies.

Ouchi and Price (1978)[53] suggest that an organizational philosophy may also be regarded as an elegant informational device for providing a form of control at once all-pervasive and effective, because it offers managers an all-purpose basic theory of how the firm should be managed. The benefits of an articulated company philosophy are lost, however, if it is not properly communicated to employees, or not visibly supported in management's behavior. Therefore, ensuring that employees have understood the philosophy and seen it in action must be one of the primary functions of the company's socialization effort.

As we pointed out earlier, employees in Japanese companies are selected partly on the basis of their perceived ability to fit in with the company values and philosophy. Such congruence increases the motivation of employees both to remain organizational members and to be productive (Lawler, 1973; Ouchi, 1980).[54] In addition, when entry requirements are stringent, employees tend to rationalize the effort they exerted in order to enter the organization by becoming highly committed to the organization and satisfied with their membership in it (Aronson & Mills, 1959; Salancik, 1977).[55]

As employees remain in an organization over an extended period of time, they tend to adopt the positive values, attitudes, and performance levels of their co-workers. This is partly a function of conformity in order to avoid rejection as a deviant organization member (Asch, 1951; Schachter, 1951)[56] and partly a reflection of the behavior modelling that occurs as the young employee develops within the organization (Bandura, 1969).[57] Acknowledging the important influences of co-workers in enforcing norms and affecting the beliefs and values of members (Hackman, 1976),[58] organizations devote far greater attention to structural factors that enhance group motivation and cooperation than to the motivation of individuals.

Individuals who are strongly committed to an organization can be relied on to do their best for it in a variety of situations. Research by Edstrom and Galbraith (1977)[59] shows that an organization may actively use this effect of socialization. They examined a multinational organization in which the sub-unit decision-making environment varies extensively, while some degree of coordination and uniformity is essential. The company makes use of managerial transfers, rotating seasoned managers around the company. A well-socialized manager – one who has held positions in various functions and locations within the company – has a feel both for the needs of the organization and for the appropriate course of action in a variety of cases.

Transfers also increase the chances of employees finding a niche in the organization for which they are especially well suited. A good fit between the ability of the employee and the requirements of the job encourages the expenditure of effort (Nadler & Lawler, 1977).[60] Furthermore, job rotation facilitates the development of informal communication networks that help in coordinating the flow of work across functional areas and in the speedy resolution of problems (Roberts & O'Reilly, 1979; Tushman, 1977).[61] Finally, job rotation "unfreezes [individuals] from being unresponsive to the demands of their jobs"(Katz, 1980).[62]

We have pointed out that job rotation in Japanese firms is closely linked to the promotion system and that it compensates for some of its restrictions on upward mobility. Moreover, although one may argue that deferred promotion may be a source of frustration to highly promising employees, several positive influences ought to be noted as well. First, no particular individual is discriminated against; promotion rules are the same for all relevant others and are thus perceived as equitable (Adams, 1965).[63] Second, deferral may have positive motivational consequences. The public identification of "losers," who are in the majority when compared to "winners" in any hierarchical organization, is deferred. This implies prolonged competition as the losers – still hoping to beat the odds – struggle to do well.

Also, the evaluation system in a Japanese company has several facets that may enhance organizational effectiveness. Because evaluations are based on the observations made by managers during their frequent, regular interactions with subordinates, the cost is relatively low (Williamson, 1975).[64] The evaluation system, in conjunction with the ILM arrangements, has another interesting effect. Employees are not formally separated according to their ability until late in their tenure. Therefore, ambitious workers who seek immediate recognition must engage in activities that will get them noticed. The system encourages easily observable behavior the demonstrates willingness to exert substantial effort on behalf of the organization (Akerlof, 1976; Miyazaki, 1977).[65]

It is often said that the emphasis on long-term objectives in Japanese organizations distinguishes their market strategy from that of their U.S. counterparts (Drucker, 1975; Tsurumi, 1976).[66] A long-term perspective is indeed encouraged by the internal evaluation system. When behavior is the focus of evaluation, means as well as ends may be assessed. This approach may well lead to a better match between employee efforts and company objectives (Levinson,

1976).[67] In addition, fear of risk is minimized and creativity encouraged, both by the assumption of permanent job tenure and by the tolerance of honest mistakes.

Basing performance evaluation and rewards on work-group performance, such that all group members share the consequences of their efforts, tends to increase productivity as well as the level of mutual aid and tutoring (Wodarski, Hamblin, Buckholdt, & Ferritor, 1973).[68] In general, group members can help each other develop job-relevant knowledge and skills in three ways: by direct instruction, by providing feedback about behavior, and by serving as models of appropriate behavior (Hackman, 1976).[69] Also being in close proximity to others increases physiological arousal and enhance performance, particularly on routine tasks (Zajonc, 1965).[70] From another perspective, peers in work groups can make assessments of an individual's performance based on information that only they possess (Kane & Lawler, 1978),[71] and hence can exert powerful control over an individual's career path. In recognition of this, an individual may attempt to be as productive as possible.

The structuring of tasks around groups not only enhances performance but also controls stimuli that are directly satisfying, such as acceptance, esteem, and a sense of identity (McClelland, 1961).[72] Satisfaction with group membership tends to be self-reinforcing, in that expecting to have to interact with other individuals tends to increase one's liking for them (Darley & Berscheid, 1967),[73] as do actual proximity with and increased information about other individuals (Berscheid & Walster, 1969).[74] In sum, membership in a small work group seems to be characterized by higher job satisfaction, lower absence rates, lower turnover rates, and fewer labor disputes (Porter & Lawler, 1964).[75]

Decision making, like so many tasks in Japanese organizations, is structured to involve the whole group rather than only a few individuals. We have already expressed our opinion that the consultative decision making in Japanese firms is not truly participative. Nevertheless, early communication of the proposed changes helps to reduce uncertainty in the organization (Thompson, 1967).[76] In addition, information on upcoming decisions provides employees with an opportunity to rationalize and accept the outcomes (Janis & Mann, 1977).[77]

CONSTRAINTS ON ADOPTING THE JAPANESE MODEL

It is often said that the high productivity in many Japanese companies is largely a result of the unique cultural characteristics of the Japanese people. Certainly, societal norms about work in organizations are an important factor. However, measures designed to tap workers' diligence show similarity in the characteristics of Japanese and American workers (Cole, 1979).[78] It seems that there is more to Japan's high productivity than the psychological traits of the Japanese people, and thus there is no reason not to look seriously at the possibility of borrowing their management model.

It has also been argued that several external factors and the dominance of craft-based unions in the U.S. (verus enterprise-based unions in Japan) preclude the emergence of organizations here using the strategies and techniques found in Japanese corporations. For example, it is sometimes said that a "negotiated environment" or a position of market dominance is essential for resistance to economic fluctuations and the attendant ability to provide stable employment. Furthermore, the opportunities for interfirm mobility are greater in the U.S. and thus probably less conducive to the development of an internal labor market. Also, American employees are less reliant on their companies for welfare, this being the purview of the government.

According to Williamson (1975),[79] market imperfections and transaction costs make an ILM a feasible alternative to other forms of employment contracts even for firms that do not enjoy a position of market dominance. Moreover, the opportunities for interfirm mobility and a government-supported welfare system have not precluded the development of organizations of an ILM nature in the U.S. and Western Europe (Doeringer & Piore, 1971; Mace, 1979).[80] It may be that certain aspects of the ILM are emphasized to a lesser extent in the U.S., but clearly the ILM concept is not an all-or-none proposition.

The argument made with respect to craft-based versus enterprise unions is also countered by the evidence. The management practices we have described can be successfully implemented even in union-organized plants in countries like Britain, known for militant craft-based unionism (Takamiya, 1979).[81] We believe that the existence of enterprise unions is an effect, rather than a cause, of the mutually beneficial relationship between employee and company.

The feasibility of transplanting Japanese management practices is also empirically supported by the relative ease with which these practices have been introduced in Japanese subsidiaries abroad (Johnson & Ouchi, 1974; Takamiya, 1979).[82] Certain practices, such as hiring and promotion on the basis of soft rather than hard criteria, may need to be curtailed in the context of the U.S. regulatory environment, but several recent studies demonstrate the existence in Western companies of organizational practices similar to those of Japan (e.g., Ouchi & Jaeger, 1978; Tsurumi, 1977; Zager, 1978).[83] Several of these companies are among the largest of American corporations, and have excellent records of innovation, growth, and high employee morale. These companies are known for providing long tenure for their employees, as well as articulating a company philosophy and practicing job rotation and consultative decision making (Ouchi & Jaeger, 1978; Ouchi & Johnson, 1978; Wilkins, 1978).[84] However, we know little about communication patterns in these organizations, the role of work groups, and other features that are important in Japanese settings.

It is important to point out that the employment practices we have described pertain to large Japanese companies. Similar practices are found in small companies, but the emphasis on permanent employment is less pronounced, because most of the small companies are vulnerable to drops in economic activity (Cole, 1979).[85] Thus, in Japan, as well as in other countries, the organization's ability to control at least some sources of uncertainty probably influences the feasibility of a given set of management techniques.

CONCLUDING REMARKS

We have proposed a model of the Japanese management system that rests on elements and relationships that are not unique to any one culture. The strategies and techniques we have reviewed constitute a remarkably well-integrated system. The management practices are highly congruent with the way tasks are structured, with the goals of individual members, and with the climate of the organization. Such congruency is expected to result in a high degree of organizational effectiveness or productivity.

It follows from our model that the successful adaptation of Japanese management methods in the United States in feasible. For a *rapid* implementation, certain environmental changes (e.g., changes in tax and antitrust laws) that would make it easier for organizations to focus on long-term utilization of human resources would be desirable. However, the crucial change needed is in management's thinking about the nature of the relationship between the employee and the organization. Without this change, we can expect the United States to fall ever further behind in the race among nations for increased productivity.

References

1. R.E. Cole (1963) *Work, Mobility, and Participation*. Berkeley, CA: University of California Press.
2. E.F. Denison and W.K. Chung (1976) *How Japan's Economy Grew So Fast*. Washington, DC: Brookings Institution.
3. R.M. Marsh and H. Mannari (1976) *Modernization and the Japanese Factory*. Princeton, NJ: Princeton University Press. R.T. Pascale (1978) "Communication and Decision Making Across Cultures: Japanese and

American Comparisons." *Administrative Science Quarterly*, 1, pp. 91–110.
4. R.C. Clark (1979) *The Japanese Company*. New Haven, CT: Yale University Press. Y. Tsurumi (1977) *Multinational Management: Business Strategy and Government Policy*. Cambridge, MA: Ballinger.
5. V. Pucik (1979) "Lifetime Employment in Japan: An alternative to the 'Culture-Structure' Causal Model." *Journal of International Affairs*, 1, pp. 158–161.
6. W.G. Ouchi and A.M. Jaeger (1978) "Type Z Organization: Stability in the Midst of Mobility." *Academy of Management Review*, 2, pp. 305–314.
7. T. Rohlen (1974) *For Harmony and Strength*. Berkeley, CA: University of California Press.
8. R.C. Clark (1979) *op. cit.* T. Rohlen (1974) *op. cit.*
9. M. Yoshino (1968) *Japan's Managerial System*. Cambridge, MA: Massachusetts Institute of Technology Press.
10. P. Doeringer and M. Piore (1971) *Internal Labor Markets and Manpower Analysis*. Boston: D.C. Heath.
10a. G. Becker (1964) *Human Capital*. New York: National Bureau of Economic Research.
11. R.E. Cole (1971) *Japanese Blue Collar: The Changing Tradition*. Berkeley, CA: University of California Press.
12. K. Haitani (1978) "Changing Characteristics of the Japanese Employment System." *Asian Survey*, 10, pp. 1029–1045.
13. V. Pucik (1979) *op. cit.*
14. T. Rohlen (1974) *op. cit.*, p. 74.
15. O.E. Williamson and W.G. Ouchi (Summer 1980) *Efficient Boundaries*. Paper presented at the Conference on the Economics of Organization, Berlin.
16. H. Hazama (1979) "Characteristics of Japanese-Style Management." *Japanese Economic Studies*, 6(3–14), pp. 110–173.
17. T. Rohlen (1974) *op. cit.*
18. R. Katz (1980) "Time and Work: Towards an Integrative Perspective," in B.M. Staw and L.L. Cummings, eds., *Review of Research in Organizational Behavior*. Greenwich, CT: JAI Press.
19. M. Yoshino (1968) *op. cit.*
20. E.H. Schein (1971) "The Individual, the Organization and the Career: A Conceptual Scheme." *Journal of Applied Behavioral Science*, pp. 401–426.
21. T. Rohlen (1974) *op. cit.*
22. K. Haitani (1978) *op. cit.*
23. H. Hazama (1979) *op. cit.*
24. W.G. Ouchi and A.M. Jaeger (1978) *op. cit.*
25. Y. Tsurumi (1977) *op. cit.*
26. R. Rohlen (1974) *op. cit.*
27. J.R. Hackman (1976) "Designing Work for Individuals and For Groups," in J.R. Hackman, E.E. Lawler, and L.W. Porter, eds., *Perspectives on Behavior in Organizations*. New York: McGraw-Hill, pp. 242–256.
28. R.E. Cole (1979) *op cit.*
29. R.T. Pascale (1978) *op. cit.*
30. T. Rohlen (1974) *op. cit.*
31. C. Nakane (1970) *Japanese Society*. Berkeley, CA: University of California Press.
32. R.T. Pascale (1978) *op. cit.*
33. J. Hattori (Autumn, 1977) "A Proposition on Efficient Decision Making in the Japanese Corporation." *Management Japan*, 10, pp. 14–23.
34. T. Rohlen (1974) *op. cit.*, p. 308.
35. P. Drucker (1975) "Economic Realities and Enterprise Strategy," in E.F. Vogel, ed., *Modern Japanese Organization and Decision Making*. Berkeley, CA: University of California Press.
36. K. Tsuji (1968) "Decision Making in the Japanese Government: A Study of Ringisei," in R.E. Ward, ed., *Political Development in Modern Japan*. Princeton, NJ: Princeton University Press. M. Yoshini (1968) *op. cit.*
37. R.C. Clark (1979) *op. cit.*
38. R.E. Cole (1971) *op. cit.*
39. T. Rohlen (1974) *op. cit.*

40. H. Hazama (1979) *op. cit.*, p. 43.
41. Y. Tsurumi (1977) *op. cit.*
42. E. Harbison and C.A. Nyers (1959) *Management in the Industrial World: An International Analysis.* New York: McGraw-Hill.
43. M. Tsuda (1979) "Japanese-Style Management." *Japanese Economic Studies,* 7(4), pp. 3–32.
44. R.M. Cyert and J.G. March (1963) *A Behavioral Theory of the Firm.* Englewood Cliffs, NJ: Prentice-Hall.
45. D.T. Hall (1976) *Careers in Organizations.* Pacific Palisades, CA: Goodyear.
46. G.R. Salancik (1977) "Commitment and the Control of Organizational Behavior and Belief," in B.M. Staw and G.R. Salancik, eds., *New Directions in Organizational Behavior.* Chicago: St. Clair Press.
47. R.M. Steers (1977) "Antecedents and Outcomes of Organizational Commitment." *Administrative Science Quarterly,* 1, pp. 46–56.
48. *Ibid.*
49. L.W. Porter, R.M. Steers, R.T. Mowday, and P.V. Boulian (1974) "Organizational Commitment, Job Satisfaction, and Turnover Among Psychiatric Technicians." *Journal of Applied Psychology,* 17, pp. 135–148.
50. G.R. Salancik and J. Pfeffer (1978) "A Social Information Processing Approach to Job Attitudes and Task Design." *Administrative Science Quarterly,* 2, pp. 224–253.
51. R. Blauner (1964) *Alienation and Freedom: The Factory Worker and His Factory.* Chicago: University of Chicago Press. R.E. Cole (1979) *op. cit.* R.M. Mannari (1976) *op. cit.* W.G. Ouchi and A.M. Jaeger (1978) *op. cit.*
52. W.E. Scott (1966) "Activation Theory and Task Design." *Organizational Behavior and Human Performance,* 1, pp. 3–30.
53. W.G. Ouchi and R.L. Price (1978) "Hierarchies, Clans and Theory Z: A New Perspective on Organizational Development." *Organizational Dynamics,* 7(2), pp. 24–44.
54. E.E. Lawler (1973) *Motivation in Work Organizations.* San Fransico: Brooks/Cole. W.G. Ouchi (1980) "Markets, Bureaucracies and Clans." *Administrative Science Quarterly,* 25, pp. 129–140.
55. E. Aronson and J. Mills (1959) "The Effect of Severity of Initiation on Liking for a Group." *Journal of Abnormal and Social Psychology,* 59, pp. 177–181. G.R. Salancik (1977) *op. cit.*
56. S.E. Asch (1951) "Effects of Group Pressure Upon the Modification and Distortion of Judgment," in H. Guetzkow, ed., *Groups, Leadership, and Men.* New Brunswick, NJ: Rutgers University Press. S. Schacter (1951) "Deviation, Rejection and Communication." *Journal of Abnormal and Social Psychology,* 46, pp. 190–207.
57. A. Bandura (1969) *Principles of Behavior Modification.* New York: Holt, Rhinehart and Winston.
58. J.R. Hackman (1976) "Group Influences on Individuals," in Marvin D. Dunnette, ed., *Handbook of Industrial and Organizational Psychology.* Chicago: Rand McNally, pp. 1455–1515.
59. A. Edstrom and J.R. Galbraith (1977) "Transfer of Managers as a Coordination and Control Strategy in Multinational Organizations." *Administrative Science Quarterly,* 22, pp. 248–263.
60. D.A. Nadler and E.E. Lawler (1977) "Motivation: A Diagnostic Approach," in J.R. Hackman, E.E. Lawler, and L.W. Porter, eds., *Perspectives on Behavior in Organizations.* New York: McGraw-Hill, pp. 85–98.
61. R. Roberts and C. O'Reilly (1979) "Some Correlations of Communication Roles in Organization." *Academy of Management Journal,* 22, pp. 42–57.
62. R. Katz (1980) *op. cit.*
63. J.S. Adams (1965) "Inequity in Social Exchange," in L. Berkowitz, ed., *Advances in Experimental Social Psychology.* New York: Academy Press, pp. 276–299.
64. O.E. Williamson (1975) *Market Hierarchies: Analysis and Antitrust Implications.* New York: The Free Press.
65. G.A. Akerlof (1976) "The Economics of

Caste and of the Ratrace and Other Woeful Tales." *Quarterly Journal of Economics*, 4, pp. 599–617. H. Miyazaki (1977) "The Rat Race and Internal Labor Markets." *Bell Journal of Economics*, 2, pp. 394–418.

66. P. Drucker (1975) *op. cit.* Y. Tsurumi (1976) *The Japanese Are Coming*. Cambridge, MA: Ballinger.
67. H. Levinson (1976) "Appraisal of What Performance?" *Harvard Business Review*, 4, pp. 30–46.
68. J.S. Wodarski, R.L. Hamblin, D.R. Buckholdt, and D.E. Ferritor (1973) "Individual Consequences Versus Different Shared Consequences Contingent on the Performance of Low-Archieving Group Members." *Journal of Applied Psychology*. 3, pp. 276–390.
69. J.R. Hackman (1976) *op. cit.*
70. R.B. Zajonc (1965) "Social Facilitation" *Science*, 149, pp. 269–274.
71. J.S. Kane and E.E. Lawler (1978) "Methods of Peer Assessment." *Psychological Bulletin*, 85, pp. 555–586.
72. D.C. McClelland (1961) *The Achieving Society*. Princeton, NJ: Van Nostrand.
73. J.M. Danley and E. Berscheid (1967) "Increased Liking as a Result of the Anticipation of Personal Contact." *Human Relations*, 20, pp. 29–40.
74. E. Berscheid and E. Walster (1969) *Interpersonal Attraction*. Reading, MA: Addison-Wesley.
75. L.W. Porter and E.E. Lawler (1964) "The Effects of 'Tall' Versus 'Flat' Organization Structures on Managerial Job Satisfaction." *Personnel Psychology*, 17, pp. 135–148.
76. J.D. Thompson (1967) *Organizations in Action*. New York: McGraw-Hill.
77. I.L. Janis and L. Mann (1977) *Decision Making*. New York: The Free Press.
78. R.E. Cole (1979) *op. cit.*
79. O.E. Williamson (1975) *op. cit.*
80. P. Doeringer and M. Piore (1971) *op. cit.* J. Mace (1979) "Internal Labor Markets for Engineers in British Industry." *British Journal of Industrial Relations*, 17, pp. 50–63.
81. M. Takamiya (1979) *Japanese Multinationals in Europe; Internal Operations and Their Public Policy Implications*. Discussion Paper, International Institute of Management, Berlin.
82. R.T. Johnson and W.G. Ouchi (1974) "Made in the U.S. (Under Japanese Management)." *Harvard Business Review*, 52(5), 61–69. M. Takamiya (1979) *op. cit.*
83. W.G. Ouchi and A.M. Jaeger (1978) *op. cit.* Y. Tsurumi (1977) *op. cit.* R. Zager (1978) "Managing Guaranteed Employment." *Harvard Business Review*, 3, pp. 103–115.
84. W.G. Ouchi and A.M. Jaeger (1978) *op. cit.* W.G. Ouchi and J.B. Johnson (1978) *op. cit.* A.L. Wilkins (June, 1978) *Interpreted Organizational History: Myths, Legends and Organizational Solidarity*. Dissertation Proposal, Stanford University.
85. R.E. Cole (1979) *op. cit.*

DO MOONLIGHTERS REALLY HURT THE ORGANIZATION?*

Muhammad Jamal

"Moonlighters" is a term which is normally used to describe people who hold a second, paid job in addition to their full-time primary job. Systematic research on moonlighters is almost nonexistent. To some it may not be a worthwhile area of research because of the limited number of people involved in it. To others it may be difficult, if not impossible, to collect systematic information on moonlighters because of the expense involved in obtaining a sample large enough to provide a sufficient number of moonlighters. To yet others, and consistent with popular belief, moonlighters generally are socially

* Reprinted by permission of the author. © January 1987.

withdrawn and economically deprived, and there is no reason why their perspective on moonlighters should not be taken as valid.

Whatever is available on moonlighters in the literature to date focuses mainly on the issues of understanding the motivation of moonlighters. With few exceptions, these studies have been conducted by the U.S. Department of Labor and are reported in *Monthly Labor Review* (Grossman, 1975; Hayghe & Michelott, 1971; Perrella, 1970; Stinson, 1986; Taylor & Skescenski, 1982).[1] Two major findings of this stream of research can be noted. First, the moonlighting rate in the U.S. has been fairly consistent for the past ten years and is around 4-5% of the nonfarm labor. While the rate of moonlighting among men has been decreasing (from 7% in 1970 to 5.9% in 1985), the rate among women has been increasing steadily (2.2% in 1970 to 4.7% in 1985) (Stinson, 1986).[2] Second, the reasons for moonlighting among the general labor force, in terms of their importance, include: meeting regular expenses (32%); enjoying work on the second job (18%); saving for the future (10%); buying something special (9%); getting experience (6%); paying off debts (6%); helping a friend or relative (5%); and other miscellaneous reasons (13%). Some differences in reasons for moonlighting among men and women might be noticeable. While both men and women cited meeting regular expenses and enjoying their work most often, larger proportions of the women than of the men were holding second jobs to buy something special or to help friends, and a smaller proportion was moonlighting to save for the future (Grossman, 1975).[3]

Notwithstanding the above-mentioned anecdotal studies, only a few studies (Miller & Sniderman, 1974; Mott, 1965; Wilensky, 1962)[4] systematically examined the differences between moonlighters and nonmoonlighters with regard to personal and organizational consequences. In a comprehensive classic study of moonlighters among six professional groups and a cross-section of the "middle mass" in the Detroit area, Wilensky (1963) found that "compared to nonmoonlighters, moonlighters have had chaotic or partially-chaotic work histories – a large proportion of their work lives was spent on jobs which were neither functionally related, nor hierarchically arranged."[5] Additionally, at one time or another, their mobility was blocked and they felt economically deprived. In another study of moonlighters in five plants of two continuous-process industries, Mott (1965) found no significant differences between moonlighters and nonmoonlighters in terms of marital happiness. However, he found that on four of the seven measures of self-esteem, moonlighters scored higher than nonmoonlighters.[6] Mott (1965) also found that on six of the seven measures of participation in voluntary organizations, moonlighters were more active in participation than nonmoonlighters.[7] Finally, Mott's study (1965) also highlighted the differences between moonlighters and nonmoonlighters on several personal traits.[8] Generally speaking, the moonlighters were higher on dominance and were more practical, realistic, emotionally stable, masculine, and independent than were the nonmoonlighters. They also suffered less from anxiety than did the nonmoonlighters. Another study of moonlighters among Wichita public school teachers (Miller & Sniderman, 1974) found no differences in job satisfaction between moonlighters and nonmoonlighters.[9] However, it was found that moonlighters had a stronger work ethic than the nonmoonlighters.

In sum, studies which examined the differences between moonlighters and nonmoonlighters with regard to personal and organizational outcomes lead to two conclusions. First, the rate of moonlighting is much higher than reported in official statistics. The rate of moonlighting found among the above-mentioned studies ranged from two-and-one-half times to three times the official rate of 4-5% of the nonfarm labor force. The higher rate of moonlighting found in these studies seems to be a more accurate reflection of the extent of moonlighting in the labor force due to the recent upsurge of homeworking in North America (Lipsig-Mumme, 1983).[10] Second, significant differences were found between moonlighters and nonmoonlighters on a number of dependent variables. However, the findings of these studies may be open to question on several grounds. Foremost is the lack of attention paid in these studies to organizational outcomes such as job performance, absenteeism, and organizational loyalty which are generally the reasons for management's apprehension about moonlighting (Davey & Brown, 1970; Habbe, 1957; Lasden, 1983; Mullally, 1976; Ryval, 1984).[11] Similarly, both work ethic and job satisfaction were measured by a single item in another study (Miller & Sniderman, 1974).[12] Finally, the atheoretical nature of these studies made the interpretation of their findings simply descriptive and journalistic in nature.

The present research program was undertaken in order to overcome some of the shortcomings of the previous empirical studies of moonlighters. Three separate studies were conducted among rank-and-file workers (clerical and production employees), firefighters, and blue-collar workers. These studies examined the differences between moonlighters and nonmoonlighters on personal outcomes, social outcomes, and organizational outcomes. Personal outcomes studied included physical and mental health, quality of life, social support available, occupational stress, and job satisfaction. Social outcomes included memberships in voluntary organizations, executive positions held in such organizations during the past five years, meetings attended in the last two months, and the number of hours spent in voluntary organization activities in the last four weeks. Organizational outcomes studied included organizational commitment, turnover intention, absenteeism, and job performance. Wherever possible, standardized scales available in the management literature were employed to assess study variables. Information about the measurement of different variables and their psychometric properties (validity and reliability) are reported elsewhere (Jamal, 1986; Jamal & Crawford, 1981 a, b).[13]

Two competing hypotheses were developed which guided the present line of research. The first hypothesis is referred to as the *energic/opportunity* hypothesis and asserts that moonlighters are, generally speaking, a special breed. They have more energy as human beings, and they have higher social and economic expectations in life than the average person. In the pursuit to satisfy their higher expectations, they voluntarily exert a higher level of effort and energy than nonmoonlighters – perhaps the phenomenon of "self-selection" in moonlighting is quite important to this perspective of moonlighters. Those who find moonlighting difficult or taxing may leave it quickly. Those who stay with moonlighting may be able to function as effectively as nonmoonlighters because of their extra energy and effort. Since moonlighters come into contact with people at two job settings, they might be construed as having greater opportunity for social participation. Thus, from the perspective of the first hypothesis, moonlighters might be more active in participation in voluntary organizations than nonmoonlighters. In addition, moonlighters might be able to function at their jobs as effectively as nonmoonlighters and might not be different from the nonmoonlighters with regard to personal consequence.

The second competing hypothesis about moonlighting is called the *deprivation/constraint* hypothesis. This hypothesis asserts that moonlighters are generally economically squeezed and socially deprived. Research on the question of why people moonlight has consistently supported the role of economic factors in moonlighting. Similarly, the perspective on the compatibility of hours of work and leisure (Frost & Jamal, 1979)[14] would predict a poor fit between hours of work and nonwork for moonlighters. This perspective suggests that hours of work which create constraints for activities during nonwork hours (such as shift work) would be perceived unfavorably by employees. Since moonlighters work longer hours than nonmoonlighters, they might be construed as experiencing the poor fit between the hours of work and nonwork. The poor fit between work and nonwork would imply that nonmoonlighters would be better off than moonlighters with regard to personal, social, and organizational outcomes. Thus, the second hypothesis views moonlighters as being taxed for their time and energy, and predicts the negative consequences of moonlighting. Therefore it is predicted that, as compared to nonmoonlighters, moonlighters might be lower on organizational commitment and job performance, and higher on absenteeism and anticipated turnover. In addition, moonlighters might be lower on social participation and might experience more problems of a personal nature than nonmoonlighters.

SAMPLE CHARACTERISTICS

Data were collected with a survey questionnaire from rank-and-file workers, firefighters, and blue-collar workers. The rank-and-file sample was drawn from six organizations which represented the cement product, electrical equipment, woodworking, and advertising industries and ranged in size from 100 to 300 employees. The firefighter sample was drawn from 11 different firefighter departments in a metropolitan city on the east coast. The blue-collar sample was drawn from a large manufacturing organization involved in producing small consumer products. A brief description of the respondents' characteristics in the three samples is presented below.

Rank-and-file sample Approximately 900 questionnaires were distributed among employees in six companies and, with one follow-up, 404 (45%) usable questionnaires were received. Response rates varied from 35% to 68% across companies. A majority of respondents were married (68%); were male (76%); were over age 35 (68%); had a Grade Eleven education or less (79%); belonged to a union (53%); and had been raised in large cities (71%).

Firefighters sample Approximately 600 questionnaires were distributed among firefighters working in various departments of different sizes. With one follow-up, 252 (42%) usable questionnaires were returned. The average age of the respondents was 35 years; average length of service was 12 years; and the average educational achievement was Grade Twelve. The majority of respondents were union members (95%); were married (71%); and were raised in an urban environment (62%). All respondents were male.

Blue-collar sample The organization had over 2,000 full-time, blue-collar workers on the payroll at the time of the survey. Because of budgetary constraints, a sample of 550 employees were selected randomly from the list provided by the organization. The selected employees were given copies of the questionnaire and with one follow-up, 283 (51%) usable questionnaires were returned. The average age of the respondents was 34 years; average length of service was 11 years; and the average educational achievement was Grade Ten. The majority of empoloyees were married (58%); were male (82%); and were unionized (78%).

FINDINGS

The rate of moonlighting found in the three samples was much higher than reported in official statistics, both in the U.S. and in Canada. The proportion of respondents who said that they were moonlighting at the time of the survey was 15% for the rank-and-file workers and 20% for both the firefighters and blue-collar workers. It is probable that the use of verbal probes and the inclusion of irregular moonlighting, investment activity, and barter transactions might have at least doubled that rate.

A one-way analysis of variance (ANOVA), with unequal cell frequencies, was used to examine the differences between moonlighters and nonmoonlighters on personal, social, and organizational outcomes. No significant differences were found between moonlighters and nonmoonlighters in the firefighters sample or the rank-and-file sample on any of the personal outcome variables. That is, in these two samples, moonlighters were not different from nonmoonlighters with regard to mental and physical health, job satisfaction, job stress, and social support. In the blue-collar sample, significant differences were found between moonlighters and nonmoonlighters on job satisfaction. Moonlighters' job satisfaction was higher than nonmoonlighters'. Thus, with regard to personal outcomes, the energic/opportunity hypothesis tends to be supported by the data in this study.

With regard to organizational outcomes, no significant differences were found between moonlighters and nonmoonlighters in the rank-and-file sample or the blue-collar sample on any of the variables, including job performance. That is, in these two samples, moonlighters were not different from nonmoonlighters with regard to organizational commitment, job performance, absenteeism, and turnover intention. In the firefighters sample, significant differences were found between moonlighters and nonmoonlighters on organizational commitment. Moonlighters had lower organizational commitment than did the nonmoonlighters. Thus, with regard to organizational outcomes, data in the present study appeared to be more supportive of the energic/opportunity hypothesis than of the deprivation/constraint hypothesis.

Significant differences were found between moonlighters and nonmoonlighters in the rank-and-file sample on all four indicators of social outcomes. That is, moonlighters held more memberships, attended more meetings, held more executive positions, and spent more hours in voluntary organizations than did nonmoonlighters. In the firefighters sample, significant differences were found between moonlighters and nonmoonlighters on two of the four social outcome variables. Moonlighters attended more meetings and spent more hours in voluntary organizations than did nonmoonlighters. In the blue-collar sample, moonlighters held more memberships, attended more meetings, and spent more hours in voluntary organizations than nonmoonlighters. Thus, the data in this study from three samples appeared to be clearly supportive of the energic/opportunity hypothesis concerning moonlighters' social participation.

An attempt was made to develop a profile of moonlighters. For this purpose, discriminant function analysis, with stepwise procedure for selecting the best discriminating variables (SPSS) between moonlighters and nonmoonlighters, was employed. In the rank-and-file sample, meetings attended and memberships held in voluntary organizations were found to be the best discriminatory variables, respectively. In the firefighters sample, meetings attended in voluntary organizations was found to be the single best discriminant variable between moonlighters and nonmoonlighters. In the blue-collar sample, meetings attended and hours spent in voluntary organizations were found to be the two best discriminatory variables, respectively. Put differently, employees who were more active in social participation in the present study were more likely to moonlight. Strange as it might appear, this conclusion is consistent with the adage that "if you want to be certain a job gets done, ask the busiest person to do it."

DISCUSSION

The findings of the present study from three occupational groups indicated that nonmoonlighters are not better off than moonlighters in terms of emotional and physical health, quality of life, occupational stress, social support, absenteeism, anticipated turnover, and job performance. On the contrary, moonlighters were more active in participation in voluntary organizations than nonmoonlighters. Whereas in the blue-collar sample moonlighters had higher job satisfaction than did nonmoonlighters, in the firefighters sample nonmoonlighters showed higher organizational commitment than moonlighters.

In general the findings of the present study tend to be *more* supportive of the energic/opportunity hypothesis of moonlighters than of the deprivation/constraint hypothesis. At the same time, our findings appeared to be in agreement with the few available studies which systematically examined the differences between moonlighters and nonmoonlighters (Miller & Sniderman, 1974; Mott, 1965; Wilensky, 1963).[15] Since in the present study a variety of personal, social, and organizational outcomes were assessed with standardized scales, the results could be construed as extensions of the previous studies. In addition the potential effects of variables such as age, education, marital status, sex, and income on the study's dependent variables were found to be negligible, which further enhances the confidence in the findings.

Several plausible reasons may account for the support of the energic/opportunity hypothesis in this study. First, the demands of moonlighters may not be as great as anecdotal evidence has suggested. The total work week of moonlighters, in most cases, is less than the normal work week of a generation ago. If those extra hours are taken from the time which others now spend watching TV or in a similar fashion, the entire issue might be moot. Alternatively, employees may adapt more readily to extended schedules than management has suspected. Shift work, for example, places significant strain on family and social life, yet most shift workers adapt satisfactorily unless their shifts are rotating ones (Jamal & Jamal, 1982).[16] A final explanation may lie in selective factors affecting who decides to work extra hours, and who subsequently continues, reduces, or eliminates those schedules. It may very well be that those who find moonlighting difficult may leave it quickly.

One possible reason for the absence of potential effects of sociodemographic variables on moonlighting and its consequences in the present study may be the homogeneous nature of the three occupational groups studied. Empirical studies of moonlighters in the general population have normally found a variation in the rate of moonlighting in various sociodemographic groups (Grossman, 1975; Perrella, 1970; Stinson, 1986; Taylor & Sekscenski, 1982).[17] A fruitful area of future research would be to examine whether the findings of the present study can be replicated in a heterogeneous sample drawn from the larger population or among different occupational groups.

Another caveat which should be kept in mind about the findings of the present study is the fact that the respondents were not asked directly for their probable reasons for moonlighting. Studies of moonlighters in the general population have consistently shown the importance of economic factors in moonlighting. One wonders why, in somewhat economically tough times, the hypothesis of deprivation/constraint was not supported. Probably, the phenomenon of self-selection played a significant role in moonlighting. Those who could not stand moonlighting quickly became history. Perhaps future research should look into the motivational patterns of moonlighters while examining the relationship between moonlighting and outcome variables.

The generalizability of the findings to other types of employees, especially to managers and professionals, should be done with caution. The normal working hours of managers and professionals are often loosely defined, normally do not include work hours at home or on the road – hours which are typically uncompensated. The payoff for those hours may be raises, promotions, or bonuses. A comparison of the actual work hours of managers, professionals, or sales people with the types of employees studied in this paper might give us a more realistic picture about the required working hours of different occupational groups. Similarly, the traditional image of moonlighting might require reconceptualization in the case of managers and professionals. Paid outside activities such as consulting, directorships, teaching, and contract research are actively encouraged for public relation and developmental purposes in many companies. Higher-ranking employees also appear to engage in different kinds of moonlighting activites: instead of working directly for another company, managers and other such employees seem more apt to deal in investments, real estate, small business enterprises, and comparable undertakings. If the time and energy devoted to these activities is considered moonlighting, then the prevalence of such activity may make the nonmoonlighter an exception.

In conclusion, the findings of the present study cast doubt on the value of strict management control of moonlighting. Outright bans or rigid reporting systems appear unnecessary if there are only a few problems to prevent. A more liberal policy, based upon intervening with employees who are clearly in poor emotional and physical health, whose performance and attendance have deteriorated, or who might be disclosing the secrets of the primary employer to competitors would appear more realistic. It is felt that the above suggestions might be instrumental in enhancing the organizational commitment of moonlighters because, as suggested by Becker (1960),[18] increasing sidebets play an important role in building organizational commitment among employees.

References

1. A. Grossman (1975) "Multiple Job Holding in May 1974." *Monthly Labor Review*, 98(2), pp. 60–64. H.V. and K. Michelotti (1971) "Multiple Jobholding in 1970 and 1971." *Monthly Labour Review*, 94 (10), pp. 38–45. V.C. Perrella (1970) "Moonlighters: Their Motivation and Characteristics." *Monthly Labor Review*, 93(8), pp. 57–64. J.F. Stinson (1986) "Moonlighting by Women Jumped to Record Highs." *Monthly Labor Review*, 109(11), pp. 22–25. D.E. Taylor and E.S. Sekscenski (1982) "Workers on Long Schedules, Single, and Multiple Job Holders." *Monthly Labor Review*, 105(5), pp. 47–53.
2. J.F. Stinson (1986) *op. cit.*
3. A. Grossman (1975) *op. cit.*
4. G.W. Miller and M.S. Sniderman (1974) "Multijobholding of Wichita Public School Teachers." *Public Personnel Management*, 3, pp. 378–403. P.W. Mott (1965) "Hours of Work and Moonlighting," in C.E. Dankert, F.C. Mann, H.R. Northrup, eds. *Hours of Work*. Harper and Row Publishers, pp. 76–94. H.L. Wilensky (1963) "The Moonlighter: A product of Relative Deprivation." *Industrial Relations*, 3, pp. 105–124.
5. H.L. Wilensky (1963) *op. cit.* p. 109.
6. P.W. Mott (1965) *op. cit.*
7. *Ibid.*
8. *Ibid.*
9. G.W. Miller and M.S. Sniderman (1974) *op. cit.*
10. C. Lipsig-Mumme (1983) "The Renaissance of Homeworking in Developed Economies." *Industrial Relations* (Laval), 38, pp. 545–567.
11. P.J. Davey and J.K. Brown (1970) "The Corporate Reaction to 'Moonlighting.'" *The Conference Board Record*, 7, pp. 31–35. S. Habbe (1957) "Moonlighting and its Controls." *Management Record: The Conference Board*, 2, pp. 234–237. M Lasden (1983) "Moonlighting: A Double Standard." *Computer Decisions*, 15(3), pp. 83–92. J. Mollally (June 21, 1976) "Moonlighting? Even Managers Do It." *Industry Week*, 188–180, pp. 22–29. M. Ryval (May 1, 1984) "Where Moonlighters Shine: In Every Field, From Truck Driving to Tax Planning." *The Financial Post Magazine*, pp. 36–44.
12. G.W. Miller and M.S. Sniderman (1974) *op. cit.*
13. M. Jamal (1986) "Moonlighting: Personal, Social, and Organizational Consequences." *Human Relations*, 39, pp. 977–990. M. Jamal and R.L. Crawford (1981a) "Moonlighters: A Production of Deprivation or Aspiration?" *Industrial Relations* (Laval) 36, pp. 325–335. M. Jamal and R.L. Crawford (1981b) "Consequences of Extended Work Hours: A Comparison of Moonlighters, Overtimers and Modal Employees." *Human Resource Management*, 20(3), pp. 18–23.
14. P.J. Frost and M. Jamal (1979) "Shift Work, Attitudes and Reported Behaviour: Some Associations Between Individual Characteristics and Hours of Work and Leisure." *Journal of Applied Psychology*, 66, pp. 7–81.
15. G.W. Miller and M.S. Sniderman (1974) *op.*

cit. P.W. Mott (1965) *op.cit.* H.L. Wilensky (1963) *op. cit.*

16. M. Jamal and S.M. Jamal (1982) "Work and Nonwork Experiences of Employees on Fixed and Rotating Shifts: An Empirical Assessment." *Journal of Vocational Behavior*, 20, pp. 282–293.

17. A. Grossman (1975) *op. cit.* V.C. Perrella (1970) *op. cit.* J.F. Stinson (1986) *op. cit.* D.E. Taylor and E.S. Sekscenski (1982) *op. cit.*

18. H.S. Becker (1960) "Notes on the Concept of Commitment." *American Journal of Sociology*, 66, pp. 32–42.

CASES

QUÉBEC NATIONAL BROKERAGE

J. Bruce Prince

Louise Gauthier, the new president of Québec National Brokerage, sat back in her chair and thought about her accomplishments over the last two weeks. Starting up a new subsidiary at the same time she was being introduced to a new organization was every challenge she had imagined and then some. Getting to know the key players in the hierarchy of the parent organization, Québec National Bank, and figuring out their agenda and personal idiosyncracies was a challenge she had faced before. Figuring out these "ropes to know and the ropes to skip" while working out the design and implementation issues of a completely new organization seemed overwhelming at times. It was 9:30 at night and the summer sun had once again gone down before she was able to leave the office.

Her mind wandered momentarily as she thought about how nice things would be once she got this new subsidiary off the ground. The click of a door from the cleaning people down the hall brought her back to the reality of her present situation. It was time to head for home. The single agenda item she had not accomplished once again today was easily her most pressing issue. Once again she was no closer to arriving at a plan for staffing this new organization and creating a human resource management system which would accomplish the goals of innovativeness and efficiency top management expected of "her" new subsidiary.

BACKGROUND

In 1980 Québec National Bank (QNB) was a small, but profitable, regional bank with 12 branches in the Montréal area which catered to middle income and below average wage earners. Over the last ten years the bank had seen many changes. QNB had expanded into the Québec City, Hull and Ottawa regions and had had a sound pattern of growth and profitability. The last ten years had also seen many changes in the legal and social environment all banks in Canada face. An increasing number of laws which had both protected their turf and restricted their activites were being removed. Trust companies were now as much QNB's competitors as the Bank of Montréal branches down the street.

In the late spring of 1990, the board of directors had approved the establishment of a subsidiary which would specialize in discount brokerage services to lower and middle income wage earners. The board believed that they had some unique strategic advantages which would allow them to attract plenty of this booming business. Part of their advantage was that security conscious customers felt safer coming to a full-service bank rather than the non-bank affiliated discount brokerage houses. Market research also indicated that the major banks which were jumping into this market seemed to be ignoring lower to mid-level income clientele on which QNB had historically focused. Also management believed that the discount brokerage industry called for a "lean and mean" organization which they, rather than Bank of Commerce or Royal Bank, could best operate.

Once the market research had been accomplished and the board had approved the establishment of a new subsidiary, top management felt that they must move quickly. A "head hunter" executive recruitment agency had quickly located Louise Gauthier and everyone agreed she seemed to be perfect for the position of president.

THE NEXT DAY...

Louise looked at her daily agenda. Finally, a two-hour block of time was designated in which to outline an approach for staffing her organization. The management had established November 15 as the date when Québec National Brokerage would open for business. It was now mid-July. This left four months to get staff into place and establish policies and procedures for managing them once they were in place. Top management of QNB had concurred that the brokerage subsidiary should have a new look and not be a carbon copy of the bank. This meant that the human resource policies and procedures should be designed to fit the unique situation of the brokerage business. It all sounded good in theory to Louise, but she was at a loss as to where to begin. The intercom buzz interrupted her thoughts. Her secretary explained that due to a scheduling mix up, she would have to spend an hour with a group of Dean's List Scholars from a local university. The group consisted mainly of commerce students who expected to graduate next year. Their visit was both a public relations activity for the bank as well as an opportunity to spot some outstanding talent and attract them to QNB. The students were now waiting outside her office and Louise had no choice but to meet with them.

Louise had her secretary take coffee requests and distribute some reading materials, while she collected her thoughts on what she should say to the students. She decided that the best strategy was to let them play "executive" and have them try to answer the staffing and human resource management questions she was facing. After the usual introductions and presentation of the subsidiary's background information, she challenged the students to act as consultants and answer the following questions.

1. What are her priority staffing decisions, i.e., decisions which must be made before other choices and decisions can be made?
2. Effectively managing the organization's human resources ultimately involves trying to match individual and organizational needs. What are the key components of a human resource planning and development system which must be developed to insure that the right people get into the right jobs at the right time?
3. Creating an effective human resource planning and development system seems much more critical today than it was 20 years ago. Why is that so?

COMMUNICATION PROBLEMS AT DECO FURNITURE CO.*

Dr. A.B. Ibrahim

Described by an economic observer as one of the classic success stories in the home furniture industry, DECO Furniture Co. of Montréal had achieved major corporate success both in terms of financial results as well as technical reputation. Much of this was due to the entrepreneurial skills of its President and Chief Executive Officer, Mr. William Miller. Under his leadership, DECO had raised itself from near-bankruptcy in 1956 and emerged as a major force in the home furniture market both domestically and internationally.

However, Mr. Miller was concerned with the internal problems that had developed in the past two years. Lennart Nilsson, the Divisional Manager in Sweden, had been complaining about communication between his division and the corporate level. "... My people can't find time to do their work, we spend our time answering memos and writing reports to everybody in corporate headquarters, ... we have to report almost everything in our division." John Kingsford, U.K. Divisional Manager and David Ewing, U.S. Divisional Manager echoed Lennart Nilsson's complaint. "... I have a problem with the controller of my division ... he doesn't listen to me anymore because people in the corporate level send him different instructions ... ," added Ewing.

Mr. Miller was also aware of the slight deterioration in net profit of the Swedish division. In fact in the last board meeting, chaired by Miller in Montréal, a board member had voiced his concern that even the U.S. division, which has a large market share and potential for expansion, had been lagging behind competitors for some time. Corporate executives had assured Miller in different meetings that they would tighten the control over divisional performance. Mr. Miller, however, was not satisfied with the corporate response and decided to hold a general meeting attended by both divisional and corporate executives. The agenda of the meeting included the following issues: organization structure, communication between corporate and divsional levels, and divisional performance.

At the meeting all divisional managers argued that the company was no longer a small business operating in Montréal but rather a large divisional firm and therefore organizational structure should change to fit the strategic change. On the other hand, corporate executives voiced their concern that structural change would only satisfy divisional managers' need for power, reduce the corporate authority, and hence the ability to integrate the different divisions under the corporate umbrella (see Exhibit 1).

---

* This case was prepared by Dr. A.B. Ibrahim of Concordia University as a basis for class discussion rather than to illustrate either effective or ineffective handling of an administrative situation. Copyright © 1986 by Professor A.B. Ibrahim. Reprinted by permission of the author.

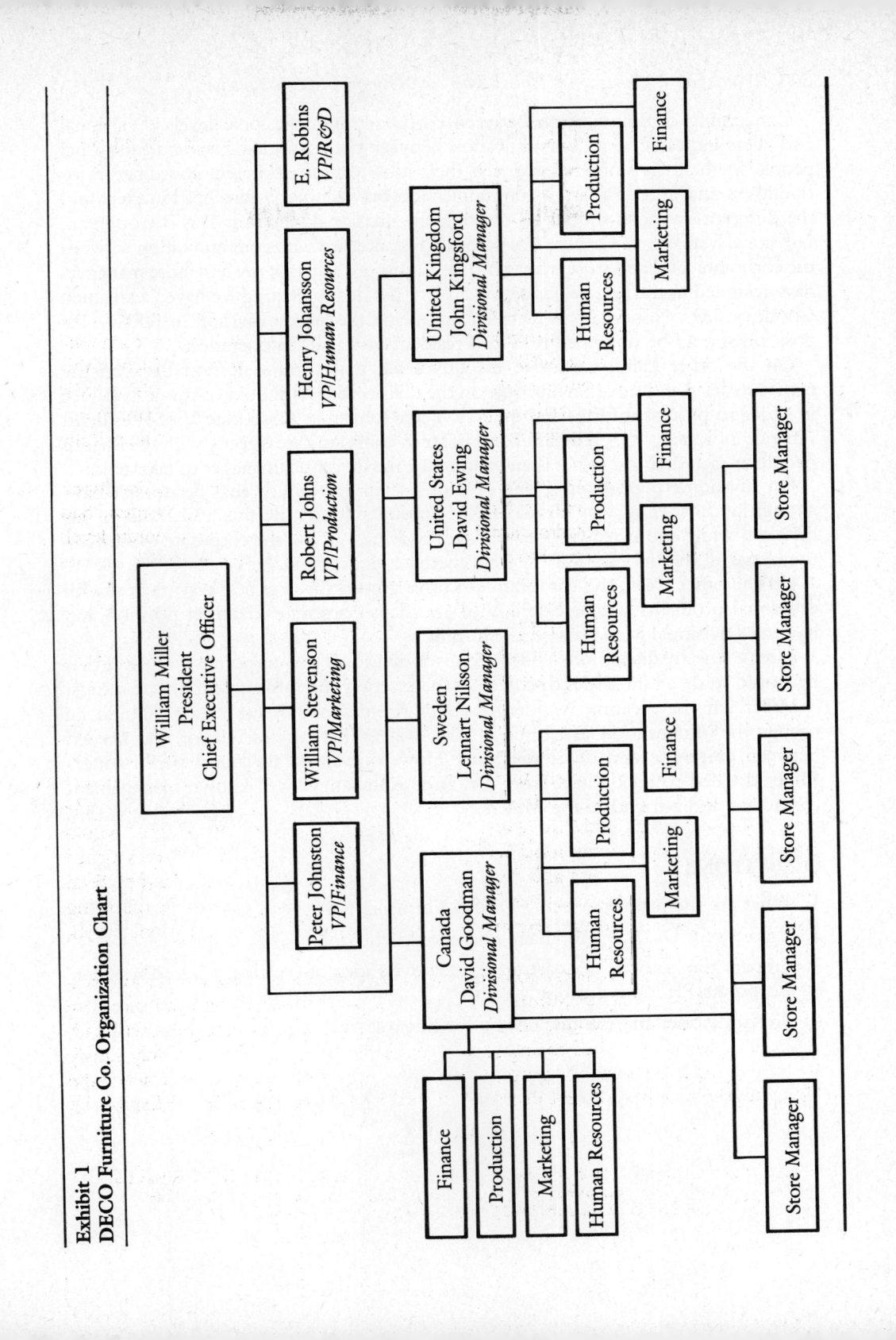

Exhibit 1
DECO Furniture Co. Organization Chart

```
                          William Miller
                            President
                       Chief Executive Officer
        ┌──────────────┬────────────┬──────────┬──────────────┬──────────────┐
   Peter Johnston  William Stevenson  Robert Johns  Henry Johansson   E. Robins
     VP/Finance      VP/Marketing    VP/Production  VP/Human Resources  VP/R&D
        │
        ├───────────────────┬───────────────────┬───────────────────┐
   Canada              Sweden              United States      United Kingdom
  David Goodman     Lennart Nilsson       David Ewing         John Kingsford
 Divisional Manager Divisional Manager  Divisional Manager  Divisional Manager
        │                    │                    │                    │
   ┌────┼────┬────┐      ┌───┼───┬───┐        ┌───┼───┬───┐        ┌───┼───┐
 Finance Prod Mktg HR   HR Prod Fin Mktg     HR Prod Fin Mktg     HR Prod Mktg Fin

        Store Managers (Canada, Sweden, United States, United Kingdom)
```

Concerning communication between corporate and divisional levels, Divisional Managers indicated that communication between the corporate level and functional people in their divisions has reduced their jobs to that of merely coordinators or caretakers and argued that all communication between corporate headquarters and the different divisions should go through the divisional manager. David Goodman, Divisional Manager of Canada, was particularly concerned with communication between the corporate level and store managers (see Figure 1). "Two of my best store managers have resigned in the past two years because of the dual reporting we have," explained Goodman. Mr. Goodman also argued that being the largest division in DECO, his position should be upgraded to Vice-President of Canadian operation.

On the other hand, corporate executives felt that communication between the corporate level and functional people on the divisional level should continue as before in order to process information quicker. Peter Johnston, Corporate Vice-President/Finance indicated, " . . . it is easier and faster to communicate directly with the finance people in each division rather than waiting for the divisional manager to take action."

On divisional performance, one divisional manager argued that he doesn't have enough authority, so why should he be accountable for the financial result of his division, while another divisional manager added, " . . . ask the corporate executives, they have all the information . . . I am merely a figure-head."

On the other hand, the corporate executive argued that the best way to deal with divisional problems is to create a Vice-President/Corporate Planning position and have all Divisional Managers report to him.

After a lengthy discussion, Miller promised divisional and corporate executives that he would study all the issues discussed in the meeting and inform them of the results.

Miller left the meeting wondering about the different issues raised. Should he change the organization structure? In what way? What type of relation was needed between corporate and divisional level? How to evaluate divisional performance? Miller decided to seek advice from Dr. A.B. Abraham, a well known management consultant and a friend to the Millers.

QUESTIONS

1. What are the problems facing DECO Furniture Co.?
2. If you were Dr. A.B. Abraham what would you do?
3. Prepare the case for the corporate executive's idea of creating a Vice-President/Corporate Planning position.
4. Prepare a brief and job description for this role.

CHANGE IN THE BELL SYSTEM*

Zane E. Barnes

I welcome your kind invitation to this Academy of Management symposium because I consider its subject matter so critically important to all business. Southwestern Bell, of course, recently experienced the historic breakup of the Bell System, the dissolution of a century-long relationship with AT&T. That extraordinary experience qualifies us, I suppose, to discuss organizational change — and perhaps some other topics as well.

It's clear that a good deal more than court-ordered divestiture is driving change in today's economy and boardrooms. For example, it is crystal clear that our economy is undergoing a fundamental shift. It is changing rapidly and basically from a production base to an information base. It is equally clear that our economy is no longer national but global in scope. The ramifications of these two trends are vast. And we could spend the rest of this symposium and many more discussing them. My point is simply this — managing organizational change is a topic American business needs to examine and understand, because fundamental change will be the order of the day for the foreseeable future. And, obviously, the company that can adapt its culture to change, quickly and successfully, will have a powerful competitive advantage.

• • •

CULTURE CHANGE AT SOUTHWESTERN BELL

According to a recent *Business Week* cover story, if you reviewed a list of today's most successful companies, the "build on what we know" philosophy would apply to all but a few. And the trend is that corporations are shedding units that don't fit the "build on what we know" idea. A point that I particularly like about our growth strategy is that it involves every corner of our business and every person. It follows that every work group and every individual can take part. And that is our goal, to extend this to tap the ingenuity and expertise of each Southwestern Bell person, and put it to use.

Of course, the question is, do our organizational changes and growth strategy exist merely on paper — or do they actually live in the behaviors of our people? Is our culture really changing from that of a utility monopoly to the entrepreneurial, competitive culture that our dynamic marketplace demands? A definitive answer is difficult. Certainly, in fewer than two years' time, we can't quantify changes. However, there are clear signs from throughout the organization and from all levels that culture change is occurring in the direction we want.

I'll share some of these signs with you. But first, let me outline steps we've taken to bring about necessary culture change. One obvious step toward creating a new culture is creating new activities — entirely new behaviors. That divestiture did *for* us, in spades.

---

* Reprinted from the *Academy of Management Executive*, February 1987, pp. 43–46. Used by permission of the author and publisher.

As I mentioned earlier, we assumed all the functions AT&T had handled for us for decades. The list runs the gamut from purchasing to investor relations to developing new lines of business. For a company of our size, none of these activities is small time. We not only have taken on these new responsibilities but have done so in a highly professional and successful way. Of course we had to, because we couldn't put our customers on hold. The important point is that our people quickly developed new expertise and mastered new responsibilities. Their success inspired confidence not only in the people who succeeded but throughout the organization. And confidence is critical to the ability to grow and develop.

Closely linked to confidence is communications. We have made every effort to communicate the messages that would steer our culture in the way it needs to develop. An excellent example occurred within days after divestiture. We viewed divestiture as a kind of emotional pressure point for people — and our research backed up this view. So right after divestiture, we staged a gigantic get-together that linked 55,000 employees and spouses in 57 locations via satellite. The objective was to provide a positive vent for divestiture-related emotions — an electronic catharsis, if you will. And we did, with visible leadership, hard business information, *and* old-fashioned fun through humor, music, and dance. It was an unprecedented event for us, which helped teach the power of shared emotional experiences and nontraditional media.

In this example and all our communications media, we have directly referred to the need for cultural change. And we have supported this message in a variety of ways. Perhaps the most important is to spotlight those individuals who act on their own initiative to further common goals. Because the behavior we need starts with the individual, we're making a special effort to recognize those special people. Another communications effort is a week-long program we call Corporate Policy Seminar (CPS). The focus of the week is intrapreneurship and how it can be stimulated throughout the corporation. All mid-level and above managers attend CPS, and they're equipped with a take-home package so they can share the program with their work groups.

We believe that participative management is basic to intrapreneurial thinking and behavior. So we have a broad Quality of Work Life (QWL) program with a number of impressive success stories to its credit. One of my favorites comes from Kansas City, Missouri. The QWL team took on the task of developing a new storm restoration plan. Their objective was to improve coordination between work groups so everyone could pull together to repair service when the need arose. In Kansas City, you don't have to wait too long for a service-affecting storm. When it came, the plan worked like the QWL team knew it would. It worked so well, in fact, that we estimate it saved us $480,000. Of course, the payoff went far beyond dollars. The morale of the employees during the service restoration was much better. They felt they were really accomplishing something. The plan also made for a lot of satisfied customers who got their service back in a hurry.

To us, QWL is an extremely simple proposition. If someone is to feel a sense of ownership, each person must feel free to contribute ideas and have the expectation that something will happen when they do. In this connection, I remember Tom Peters discussing his recurring experience of talking to plant employees and hearing all kinds of great ideas. Peters said that, without fail, he always asks why they don't tell someone their ideas. And again, without fail, the sad answer is, "Nobody asked." We hope that our supervisors do ask. We hope that everyone wants to share ideas. QWL is a way to share ideas that gets everyone involved and used to the fulfillment of truly participating.

Earlier I mentioned that we've increased individual managers' responsibility and accountability. To make that work for cultural change, we also gave managers a much-expanded chance to share in organizational success. Senior managers who meet financial and service goals can now be rewarded with bonuses of up to 30% of their base salaries. And below senior management, we reward outstanding performance with lump-sum bonuses that range from 3 to 20% of the midpoint of base salary. All managers participate in this plan, including executive secretaries.

This is an admittedly abbreviated overview of steps we've taken to change Southwestern Bell's culture. And as I said earlier, the story of change is still being written. I can't give you definitive answers today on our progress. But we do have indicators of our performance objective measures and many individual success stories.

One basic objective measure is our quality of service. And at the end of our first year as an independent corporation, Southwestern Bell outranked all other former Bell companies in a variety of categories, including local service provided by our telephone subsidiary. That finding came from the respected industry publication *Communications Week*, which interviewed industry analysts, consultants, regulators, and major customers to arrive at its ratings.

Another objective measure is our performance in customers' eyes. Again, we've made solid progress. Research shows that we've recovered or surpassed the customer goodwill we enjoyed *before* divestiture. Considering the fact that divestiture has made basic service more complex and generally more costly, that is a notable achievement.

And a final objective measure: We've consistently met or exceeded our earnings goal since divestiture.

As for subjective success stories, we have plenty of evidence that Southwestern Bell people not only understand the intrapreneurial mindset, but also are practicing it. Some examples:

A telephone company engineer in Texas invented a faster, cheaper way to restore service to customers with defective lines. We've estimated that his invention could save our company $50 million per year.

A Kansas City work group created a "War Room" planning and presentation center and a proactive marketing approach that has persuaded major customers that we're the company with which they want to do business.

A Mobile Systems engineer had an idea that means we can monitor cellular systems second by second without manning control centers around the clock.

There are many, many more stories of individuals who are leading and creating our new culture. And that leads me to the generalized point I want to make – a point that we all know but, I believe, too often ignore. The point simply is that in the final analysis, cultures are shaped and changed not so much by organizational structures, management process or salary plans, but by people. By people who lead.

Don't mistake my point. There is no question that any organization, and certainly one as large and complex as Southwestern Bell, must have structure, must have process, and must have professional managers. But it is equally clear that all organizations need real leaders – leaders throughout their ranks. I'm talking about individuals who value action over analysis. People who love results and not process. Individuals who motivate through personal commitment and not professional technique. And most importantly, men and women who concern themselves with people over structure.

I suggest to you that American business and American educators have been too enamored of the professional, career manager. Educators produce them and business recruits them, with admirable efficiency. But in the process we, both educators and business, have devalued real leadership. It has simply been easier to find managers rather than leaders.

At Southwestern Bell, we have no magic answers. Nor do we have a secret formula for developing leaders. We have, however, recently introduced a Management Continuity Program to better identiy and develop high-potential individuals.

The extraordinary event of divestiture awakened us to the need to find the many leaders we have, nurture them, and get them out on their way. That is a top priority.

QUESTIONS

1. The executive who wrote this case seems to have brought this organization through a traumatic period of change. What were the key strategies he used to accomplish this transition?
2. Does this executive use a "Japanese" approach to managing human resources? Support your answer with specific examples.

EXERCISES

SALARY NEGOTIATION AT THE MONTRÉAL PUMP AND VALVE COMPANY*

Philip Menard

Executives have to learn how to live and manage within tight constraints which may not be of their making. One major problem which executives face is evaluating and rewarding subordinates — sometimes when the amount of money available for increase is quite limited. This exercise will help business students to practise this skill of evaluation in a compensation context.

The Personnel Department had been in recent months actively engaged in developing a compensation program for all company employees. The new compensation plan would be based on a theme labelled "pay for performance." The salary increase afforded to an employee would be based on such criteria as: present salary, average salary within the industry for the given position, consumer price index, financial standing of the company; with the greatest weight placed on the performance rating of the respective employees.

The ratings were broken down into five categories: marginal, adequate, competent, commendable, and excellent. Unlike in the past, the appraisal process focused on two-way communication between supervisors and subordinates. The setting of objectives was also of prime importance.

Employees were told that this new program would be implemented in the near future. The feeling among the employees was that a better program of financial compensation lay ahead for them. Unfortunately, the company had experienced a year of declining profits and management had decided to postpone the implementation of the new program. Management felt that it would not be able to truly compensate for superior performance.

---

* "Salary Negotiations at the Montréal Pump and Valve Company" was prepared for this book by Philip Menard. It is used by permission of the author.

Instead, management decided that for that year, only a lump sum of money would be provided to departments for salary increases and would be divided within the organization using a complex formula which included among other things: branch profit contributions, existing labor market conditions, future earnings potential, etc.

John Richler, Assistant Manager of the Customer Service Department in Toronto, was called in by the Department Manager Bill Wright and was told that $8,000 had been allocated to his area for salary increases for the ensuing year.

Bill explained to John that this amount included his own salary increase and asked

---

Exhibit 1
Organization Chart of the Customer Service Department (Toronto)

```
                        Manager
                       Bill Wright
                           |
        _____|_____
       |                   |                   |
   Asst. Mgr.         Asst. Mgr.          Asst. Mgr.
   Operations        Client Services     Re-organization
                                          John Richler
                                              |
                                              |————— Systems Analyst
                                              |         Peter Greer
                                              |
                                              |——— Supervisor
                                              |     Richard Groom
                                              |
                                              |——— Admin. Asst.
                                              |     Fred Moore
                                              |
                                              |——— Senior Clerk
                                              |     Alice Murphy
                                              |
                                              |——— Clerk
                                              |     Robert Albert
                                              |
                                              |——— Typist
                                                    Carol Baker
```

Exhibit 2
Average Salary Levels within the Industry — Location: Toronto

Position	Average Salary*	Employee	Present Salary
Assistant Manager	45,000	John Richler	43,000
Systems Analyst	32,000	Peter Greer	28,800
Supervisor	30,000	Richard Groom	31,000
Administrative Assistant	26,000	Fred Moore	24,500
Senior Clerk	22,000	Alice Murray	19,000
Clerk	19,500	Robert Albert	19,650
Typist	18,000	Carol Baker	17,000

* Salary Levels varied by plus or minus 10% depending on years of experience and performance rating.

him to submit his recommendations for salary increases within the week. Bill also explained that the theme of "pay for performance" had filtered through the organization and while not implemented, his decisions should lean towards this philosophy.

The organizational chart attached (see Exhibit 1) indicates the employees reporting to John Richler. To assist John, Bill had given him a study completed by an independent firm indicating average salary levels within the Trust industry for the positions of concern within his area of responsibility (see Exhibit 2). The consumer price index rose by 6% in the past year.

The following is a brief description of each employee:

John Richler (Assistant Manager)
Background: Age 42, 10 years experience, 2 children ages 8 & 11
Duties: Co-ordinating activities of the section, maintaining a high level of service and efficiency
Performance: Above average worker, good delegator, respected by subordinates and management, advancement potential limited

Peter Greer (Systems Analyst)
Background: Age 26, single, B. Sc. – Computer Sciences, first job out of university, 1.5 years in the department
Duties: Streamline processing by developing suitable computer programs aimed at cost reduction and increased efficiency.
Performance: Very productive, bright, innnovative, ambitious, demand for his expertise in the industry is growing, good rapport with co-workers.

Richard Groom (Supervisor)
Background: Age 32, B.Com. – Finance, 4 years experience. He is Bill Wright (manager's) son-in-law, enrolled in MBA program.
Duties: Assist John Richler in co-ordinating the activities in the section. Reconciles all accounts.
Performance: Difficulty dealing with staff, responds quickly to requests from manager only, lazy at times, appears unmotivated, manager has high opinion of him, marginally productive.

Fred Moore (Administrative Assistant)
Background: Age 29, Cegep education, 7 years experience
Duties: Processes large incoming deposits, authorizes issuance of cheques, maintains control totals on each project, etc.
Performance: Hard worker, handles most assignments on an efficient basis, good problem solver, well liked, productive, often works overtime without demanding compensation, taking night courses for degree in business.

Alice Murphy (Senior Clerk)
Background: Age 54, high school education, 24 years experience, recently widowed, has been asked by the company to take early retirement at 55, her pension benefits are derived from the average of her last 3 years income.
Duties: Reviewing increasing deposits, batching, recoding, processing, etc.
Performance: Constant worker, average productivity, conscientious, does not work overtime, spots most clerical errors made thereby reducing potential claims

Robert Albert (Clerk)
Background: Age 22, 1 year of experience, taking night courses for degree in electrical engineering
Duties: Receipt incoming items, distribute outgoing items, answer enquiries, research
Performance: Good worker, insists on being paid overtime, does not intend to stay in industry, productive.

Carol Baker (Typist)
Background: Age 25, 2 years experience, expecting her second child, rumour indicates that she will not return to work, single mother supporting a child of age 3
Duties: Types letters, reports, cheques, mails forms etc.
Performance: Excellent worker, very productive, takes a lot of sick days, willing to work overtime when necessary.

What do you think John Richler's recommendations for salary increases should be for his staff as well as for his own increase?

INSTRUCTIONS

1. This is a seven person game. Each player assumes a role as a member of this department.
2. John Richler calls a meeting of his department to get his group to agree on salary increases.
3. The first step is to prepare a chart with suggested headings.
4. Secure (or impose by vote) an agreement on salary increases.

	Name	Salary	Position	Age	Qualifications	Duties	Performance	Recommended Increase
1.	John Richler							
2.	Peter Greer							
3.	Richard Groom							
4.	Fred Moore							
5.	Alice Murray							
6.	Robert Albert							
7.	Carol Baker							
	Totals							

MANAGING CAREERS: YOU'RE THE CONSULTANT

J. Bruce Prince

This exercise requires you to apply your understanding of career management and career development to some real situations. Read through each situation and take the role of a consultant who has been asked for help. For each situation (1) identify conceptual material which appears to be relevant and additional facts you would need to gather to do a thorough analysis, and (2) be ready to present your preliminary assessment and suggest some specific ways to meet the client's needs.

A. BAD TIMES AT MOBCORP

During your initial contact with Mobcorp the Human Resource Vice-President restated the facts which had emerged from last week's meeting of the top executive group. The basic concern of the executive group is that the turnover of technicians in various engineering categories has continued to grow. A similar labor category in a technically related area of manufacturing is evidencing the same trend. Those leaving seem to be predominantly those who have spent several years in their positions and are in the 35-45 age category. Management is concerned that younger employees are not ready to take over the duties of these senior technicians and that without experienced people to work with them, they may never be ready. A check of the salaries of the people leaving indicated that their wages were comparable to what other employers in the area were paying. Exit interviews have found that many simply wanted to try something new. One person put it this way: "Seven years ago when I started, my job was quite exciting. I faced a new challenge every week. I guess the problem is that I've changed and my job hasn't. Every problem I face, I've seen numerous times before. I hate it when people ask me what's new. I sometimes feel like saying that I'm just getting older — that's all!"

B. CAREER PLANNING AT EDUCORP

Career planning programs certainly seem to be the thing to do these days. A few of your consulting clients have heard about other companies' efforts and have decided that it is time to test out a program. Your contacts say that the main pressure for this sort of program is from younger people who are not satisfied with letting their careers just happen and want the company to help them manage their own careers. One Human Resources executive came to the conclusion that "either we do it and give them more information on what the company has to offer or the best ones will leave." You have come to the conclusion that, with so many clients wanting it, it is time you develop an approach to helping employees plan their career. You have scheduled a lunch appointment with Fred Emery, VP/Human Resources at Educorp for next week. It is now time to come up with a preliminary design of a career planning program to present to Fred. Also, you need to identify several specific areas in which you will need further information in order to complete the design of the program.

C. PROBLEMS AT STUCORP

John Davis, VP/Manufacturing at Stucorp, has offered you a "free" lunch. You know from past experience that these lunches are hardly ever free and that there is usually a pressing problem with which the person wants some help. Lunch with Davis was no exception. In between cocktails and coffee, he told you about Dan, the manager of the component reliability section who had spent over 27 years with the company and had served in a number of capacities over the years. Six years ago, he started his present position and problems are now starting to appear. At the time of the transfer, the previous VP had concluded that Dan's managerial competencies would be a real asset and would outweigh his lack of technical experience in the area. The component reliability section had always been staffed with junior people who were very technically qualified, but had unknown managerial abilities and interests. Over the last couple of years, some top people had left the area with complaints that Dan did not give them adequate autonomy, tried to get too involved in the details of their work, and made some decisions which any good reliability engineer would know were wrong. Behind his back the employees referred to him as "Deadwood Dan" and considered him to be very defensive to the technically competent people in the department. Recently, Human Resources has had a hard time interesting people in transferring into the department. Morale and performance has been falling. Davis took a sip of coffee and said, "This whole problem is probably the company's fault, so I certainly can't fire him. Besides, he has given 27 years of generally good service to the company. But I don't have any openings elsewhere for him." Davis paused for a few seconds, requested a second cup, and then asked, "Do you have any suggestions on how I should handle this?" He is now waiting for your reply.

X
ORGANIZATIONAL CULTURE

READINGS

COMING TO A NEW AWARENESS OF ORGANIZATIONAL CULTURE*

Edgar H. Schein

The purpose of this article is to define the concept of organizational culture in terms of a dynamic model of how culture is learned, passed on, and changed. As many recent efforts argue that organizational culture is the key to organizational excellence, it is critical to define this complex concept in a manner that will provide a common frame of reference for practitioners and researchers. Many definitions simply settle for the notion that culture is a set of shared meanings that make it possible for members of a group to interpret and act upon their environment. I believe we must go beyond this definition: even if we knew an organization well enough to live in it, we would not necessarily know how its culture arose, how it came to be what it is, or how it could be changed if organizational survival were at stake.

The thrust of my argument is that we must understand the dynamic evolutionary forces that govern how culture evolves and changes. My approach to this task will be to lay out a formal definition of what I believe organizational culture is, and to elaborate each element of the definition to make it clear how it works.

ORGANIZATIONAL CULTURE: A FORMAL DEFINITION

Organizational culture is the pattern of basic assumptions that a given group has invented, discovered, or developed in learning to cope with its problems of external adaptation and internal integration, and that have worked well enough to be considered valid and, therefore, to be taught to new members as the correct way to perceive, think, and feel in relation to those problems.

1. PATTERN OF BASIC ASSUMPTIONS

Organizational culture can be analyzed at several different levels, starting with the *visible artifacts* – the constructed environment of the organization, its architecture, technology, office layout, manner of dress, visible or audible behavior patterns, and public documents such as charters, employee orientation materials, stories (see Figure 1). This level of analysis is tricky because the data are easy to obtain but hard to interpret. We can describe "how" a group constructs its environment and "what" behavior patterns are discernible among the members, but we often cannot understand the underlying logic – "why" a group behaves the way it does.

To analyze *why* members behave the way they do, we often look for the *values* that govern behavior, which is the second level in Figure 1. But as values are hard to observe directly, it is often necessary to infer them by interviewing key members of the organization or to content analyze artifacts such as documents and charters.[1]

---

* Reprinted from "Coming to a New Awareness of Organizational Culture," SLOAN MANAGEMENT REVIEW, Winter 1984, pp. 3–16, by permission of the publisher. Copyright © 1984 by the Sloan Management Review Association. All rights reserved.

Figure 1
The Levels of Culture and Their Interaction

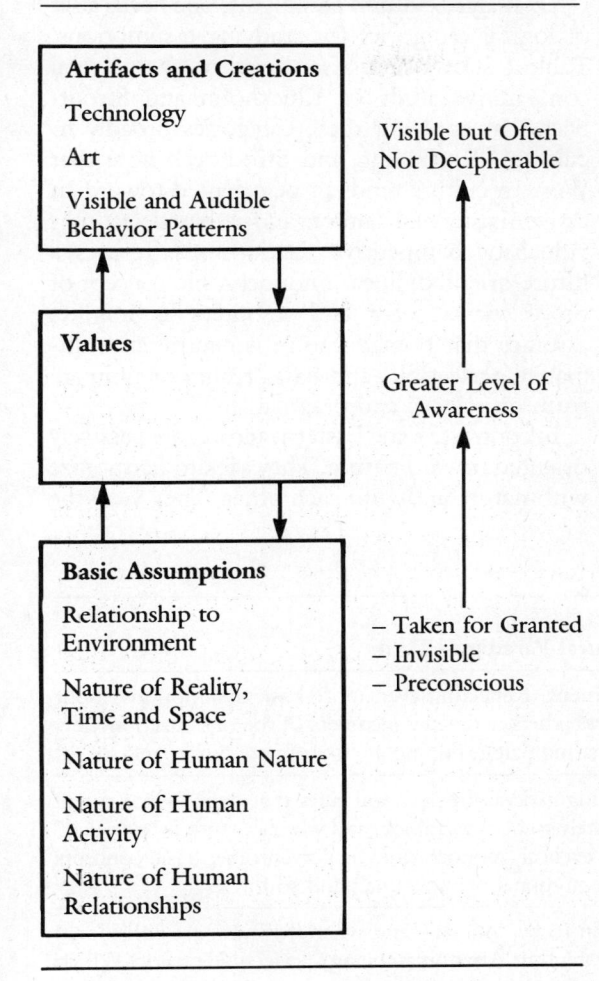

Artifacts and Creations
- Technology
- Art
- Visible and Audible Behavior Patterns

↕ Visible but Often Not Decipherable

Values

↕ Greater Level of Awareness

Basic Assumptions
- Relationship to Environment
- Nature of Reality, Time and Space
- Nature of Human Nature
- Nature of Human Activity
- Nature of Human Relationships

– Taken for Granted
– Invisible
– Preconscious

However, in identifying such values, we usually note that they represent accurately only the manifest or espoused values of a culture. That is, they focus on what people say is the reason for their behavior, what they ideally would like those reasons to be, and what are often their rationalizations for their behavior. Yet, the underlying reasons for their behavior remain concealed or unconscious.[2]

To really *understand* a culture and to ascertain more completely the group's values and overt behavior, it is imperative to delve into the *underlying assumptions*, which are typically unconscious but which actually determine how group members perceive, think, and feel.[3] Such assumptions are themselves learned responses that originated as espoused values. But, as a value leads to a behavior, and as that behavior begins to solve the problem which prompted it in the first place, the value gradually is transformed into an underlying assumption about how things really are. As the assumption is increasingly taken for granted, it drops out of awareness.

Taken-for-granted assumptions are so powerful because they are less debatable and confrontable than espoused values. We know we are dealing with an assumption when we encounter in our informants a refusal to discuss something, or when they consider us "insane" or "ignorant" for bringing something up. For example, the notion that businesses should be profitable, that schools should educate, or that medicine should prolong life are assumptions, even though they are often considered "merely" values.

To put it another way, the domain of values can be divided into (1) ultimate, non-debatable, taken-for-granted values, for which the term "assumptions" is more appropriate; and (2) debatable, overt, espoused values, for which the term "values" is more applicable. In stating that basic assumptions are unconscious, I am not arguing that this is a result of repression. On the contrary, I am arguing that as certain motivational and cognitive processes are repeated and continue to work, they become unconscious. They can be brought back to awareness only through a kind of focused inquiry, similar to that used by anthropologists. What is needed are the efforts of both an insider who makes the unconscious assumptions and an outsider who helps to uncover the assumptions by asking the right kinds of questions.[4]

Cultural Paradigms: A Need for Order and Consistency

Because of the human need for order and consistency, assumptions become patterned into what may be termed cultural "paradigms," which tie together the basic assumptions about humankind, nature, and activities. A cultural paradigm is a set of interrelated assumptions that form a coherent pattern. Not all assumptions are mutually compatible or consistent, however. For example, if a group holds the assumption that all good ideas and products ultimately come from individual effort, it cannot easily assume simultaneously that groups can be held responsible for the results achieved, or that individuals will put a high priority on group loyalty. Or, if a group assumes that the way to survive is to conquer nature and to manipulate its environment aggressively, it cannot at the same time assume that the best kind of relationship among group members is one that emphasizes passivity and harmony. If human beings do indeed have a cognitive need for order and consistency, one can then assume that all groups will eventually evolve sets of assumptions that are compatible and consistent.

To analyze cultural paradigms, one needs a set of logical categories for studying assumptions. Table 1 shows such a set based on the original comparative study of Kluckhohn and Strodtbeck.[5] In applying these categories broadly to cultures, Kluckhohn and Strodtbeck note that Western culture tends to be oriented toward an active mastery of nature, and is based on individualistic competitive relationships. It uses a future-oriented, linear, monochronic concept of time,[6] views space and resources as infinite, assumes that human nature is neutral and ultimately perfectible, and bases reality or ultimate truth on science and pragmatism.

In contrast, some Eastern cultures are passively oriented toward nature. They seek to harmonize with nature and with each other. They view the

---

Table 1
Basic Underlying Assumptions Around Which Cultural Paradigms Form

1. **The Organization's Relationship to Its Environment.** Reflecting even more basic assumptions about the relationship of humanity to nature, one can assess whether the key members of the organization view the relationship as one of dominance, submission, harmonizing, finding an appropriate niche, and so on.

2. **The Nature of Reality and Truth.** Here are the linguistic and behavioral rules that define what is real and what is not, what is a "fact," how truth is ultimately to be determined, and whether truth is "revealed" or "discovered"; basic concepts of time as linear or cyclical, monochronic or polychronic; basic concepts such as space as limited or infinite and property as communal or individual; and so forth.

3. **The Nature of Human Nature.** What does it mean to be "human" and what attributes are considered intrinsic or ultimate? Is human nature good, evil, or neutral? Are human beings perfectible or not? Which is better, Theory X or Theory Y?

4. **The Nature of Human Activity.** What is the "right" thing for human beings to do, on the basis of the above assumptions about reality, the environment, and human nature: to be active, passive, self-developmental, fatalistic, or what? What is work and what is play?

5. **The Nature of Human Relationships.** What is considered to be the "right" way for people to relate to each other, to distribute power and love? Is life cooperative or competitive; individualistic, group collaborative, or communal; based on traditional lineal authority, law, or charisma; or what?

Source: Reprinted, by permission of the publisher, from "The Role of the Founder in Creating Organizational Culture," by Edgar H. Schein, *Organizational Dynamics*, Summer 1983 © 1983 Periodicals Division, American Management Associations. All rights reserved.

group as more important than the individual, are present or past oriented, see time as polychronic and cyclical, view space and resources as very limited, assume that human nature is bad but improvable, and see reality as based more on revealed truth than on empirical experimentation.

In this light, organizational culture paradigms are adapted versions of broader cultural paradigms. For example, Dyer notes that the GEM Corporation operates on the interlocking assumptions that: (1) ideas come ultimately from individuals; (2) people are responsible, motivated, and capable of governing themselves; however, truth can only be pragmatically determined by "fighting" things out and testing in groups; (3) such fighting is possible because the members of the organization view themselves as a family who will take care of each other. Ultimately, this makes it safe to fight and be competitive.[7]

I have observed another organization that operates on the paradigm that (1) truth comes ultimately from older, wiser, better educated, higher status members; (2) people are capable of loyalty and discipline in carrying out directives; (3) relationships are basically lineal and vertical; (4) each person has a niche that is his or her territory that cannot be invaded; and (5) the organization is a "solidary unit" that will take care of its members.

Needless to say, the manifest behaviors in these two organizations are totally different. In the first organization, one observes mostly open office landscapes, few offices with closed doors, a high rate of milling about, intense conversations and arguments, and a general air of informality. In the second organization, there is a hush in the air; everyone is in an office and with closed doors. Nothing is done except by appointment and with a prearranged agenda. When people of different ranks are present, one sees real deference rituals and obedience, and a general air of formality permeates everything.

Nonetheless, these behavioral differences make no sense until one has discovered and deciphered the underlying cultural paradigm. To stay at the level of artifacts or values is to deal with the *manifestations* of culture, but not with the cultural essence.

2. A GIVEN GROUP

There cannot be a culture unless there is a group that "owns" it. Culture is embedded in groups, hence the creating group must always be clearly identified. If we want to define a cultural unit, therefore, we must be able to locate a group that is independently defined as the creator, host, or owner of that culture. We must be careful not to define the group in terms of the existence of a culture however tempting that may be, because we then would be creating a completely circular definition.

A given group is a set of people (1) who have been together long enough to have shared significant problems, (2) who have had opportunities to solve those problems and to observe the effects of their solutions, and (3) who have taken in new members. A group's culture cannot be determined unless there is such a definable set of people with a shared history.

The passing on of solutions to new members is required in the definition of culture because the decision to pass something on is itself a very important test of whether a given solution is shared and perceived as valid. If a group passes on with conviction elements of a way of perceiving, thinking, and feeling, we can assume that that group has had enough stability and has shared enough common experiences to have developed a culture. If, on the other hand, a group has not faced the issue of what to pass on in the process of socialization, it has not had a chance to test its own consensus and commitment to a given belief, value, or assumption.

The Strength of a Culture

The "strength" or "amount" of culture can be defined in terms of (1) the *homogeneity* and *stability* of group membership and (2) the *length* and *intensity* of shared experiences of the group.

If a stable group has had a long, varied, intense history (i.e., if it has had to cope with many difficult survival problems and has succeeded), it will have a strong and highly differentiated culture. By the same token, if a group has had a constantly shifting membership or has been together only for a short time and has not faced any difficult issues, it will, by definition, have a weak culture. Although individuals within that group may have very strong individual assumptions, there will not be enough shared experiences for the group as a whole to have a defined culture.

By this definition, one would probably assess IBM and the Bell System as having strong cultures, whereas, very young companies or ones which have had a high turnover of key executives would be judged as having weak ones. One should also note that once an organization has a strong culture, if the dominant coalition or leadership remains stable, the culture can survive high turnover at lower ranks because new members can be strongly socialized into the organization as, for example, in elite military units.

It is very important to recognize that cultural strength may or may not be correlated with effectiveness. Though some current writers have argued that strength is desirable,[8] it seems clear to me that the relationship is far more complex. The actual content of the culture and the degree to which its solutions fit the problems posed by the environment seem like the critical variables here, not strength. One can hypothesize that young groups strive for culture strength as a way of creating an identity for themselves, but older groups may be more effective with a weak total culture and diverse subcultures to enable them to be responsive to rapid environmental change.

This way of defining culture makes it specific to a given group. If a total corporation consists of stable functional, divisional, geographic, or rank-based subgroups, then that corporation will have multiple cultures within it. It is perfectly possible for those multiple cultures to be in conflict with each other, such that one could not speak of a single corporate culture. On the other hand, if there has been common corporate experience as well, then one could have a strong corporate culture on top of various subcultures that are based in subunits. The deciphering of a given company's culture then becomes an empirical matter of locating where the stable social units are, what cultures each of those stable units have developed, and how those separate cultures blend into a single whole. The total culture could then be very homogeneous or heterogeneous, according to the degree to which subgroup cultures are similar or different.

It has also been pointed out that some of the cultural assumptions in an organization can come from the occupational background of the members of the organization. This makes it possible to have a managerial culture, an engineering culture, a science culture, a labor union culture, etc., all of which coexist in a given organization.[9]

3. INVENTED, DISCOVERED, OR DEVELOPED

Cultural elements are defined as learned solutions to problems. In this section, I will concentrate on the nature of the learning mechanisms that are involved.

Structurally, there are two types of learning situations: (1) positive problem-solving situations that produce positive or negative reinforcement in terms of whether the attempted solution works or not; and (2) anxiety-avoidance situations that produce positive or negative reinforcement in terms of whether the attempted solution does or does not avoid anxiety. In practice, these two types of situations are intertwined, but they are structurally different and, therefore, they must be distinguished.

In the positive problem-solving situation, the group tries out various responses until something works. The group will then continue to use this response until it ceases to work. The information that it no longer works is visible and clear. By contrast, in the anxiety-avoidance situation, once a response is learned because it successfully avoids anxiety, it is likely to be repeated indefinitely. The reason is that the learner will not willingly test the situation to determine whether the cause of the anxiety is still operating. Thus all rituals, patterns of thinking or feeling, and behaviors that may originally have been motivated by a need to avoid a painful, anxiety-provoking situation are going to be repeated, even if the causes of the original pain are no longer acting, because the avoidance of anxiety is, itself, positively reinforcing.[10]

To fully grasp the importance of anxiety reduction in culture formation, we have to consider, first of all, the human need for cognitive order and consistency, which serves as the ultimate motivator for a common language and shared categories of perception and thought.[11] In the absence of such shared "cognitive maps," the human organism experiences a basic existential anxiety that is intolerable — an anxiety observed only in extreme situations of isolation or captivity.[12]

Secondly, human experience the anxiety associated with being exposed to hostile environmental conditions and to the dangers inherent in unstable social relationships, forcing groups to learn ways of coping with such external and internal problems.

A third source of anxiety is associated with occupational roles such as coal mining and nursing. For example, the Tavistock sociotechnical studies have shown clearly that the social structure and ways of operation of such groups can be conceptualized best as a "defense" against the anxiety that would be unleashed if work were done in another manner.[13]

If an organizational culture is composed of both types of elements — those designed to solve problems and those designed to avoid anxiety — it becomes necessary to analyze which is which if one is concerned about changing any of the elements. In the positive-learning situation, one needs innovative sources to find a better solution to the problem; in the anxiety-avoidance situation, one must first find the source of the anxiety and either show the learner that it no longer exists, or provide an alternative source of avoidance. Either of these is difficult to do.

In other words, cultural elements that are based on anxiety reduction will be more stable than those based on positive problem solving because of the nature of the anxiety-reduction mechanism and the fact that human systems need a certain amount of stability to avoid cognitive and social anxiety.

Where do solutions initially come from? Most cultural solutions in new groups and organizations originate from the founders and early leaders of those organizations.[14] Typically, the solution process is an advocacy of certain ways of doing things that are then tried out and either adopted or rejected, depending on how well they work out. Initially, the founders have the most influence, but, as the group ages and acquires its own experiences, its members will find their own solutions. Ultimately, the process of discovering new solutions will be more a result of interactive, shared experiences. But leadership will always play a key role during those times when the group faces a new problem and must develop new responses to the situation. In fact, one of the crucial functions of leadership is to provide guidance at precisely those times when habitual ways of doing things no longer work, or when a dramatic change in the environment requires new responses.

At those times, leadership must not only insure the invention of new and better solutions, but must also provide some security to help the group tolerate the anxiety of giving up old, stable responses, while new ones are learned and tested. In the Lewinian change framework, this means that the "unfreezing stage" must involve both enough disconfirmation to motivate change and enough psychological safety to permit the individual or group to pay attention to the disconfirming data.[15]

4. PROBLEMS OF EXTERNAL ADAPTATION AND INTERNAL INTEGRATION

If culture is a solution to the problems a group faces, what can we say about the nature of those problems? Most group theories agree it is useful to distinguish between two kinds of problems: (1) those that deal with the group's basic survival, which has been labeled the primary task, basic function, or ultimate mission of the group; and (2) those that deal with the group's ability to function as a group. These problems have been labeled socioemotional, group building and maintenance, or integration problems.[16]

Homans further distinguishes between the *external system* and the *internal system* and notes that the two are interdependent.[17] Even though one can distinguish between the external and internal problems, in practice both systems are highly interrelated.

External Adaptation Problems

Problems of external adaptation are those that ultimately determine the group's survival in the environment. While a part of the group's environment is "enacted," in the sense that prior cultural experience predisposes members to perceive the environment in a certain way and even to control that environment to a degree, there will always be elements of the environment (weather, natural circumstances, availability of economic and other resources, political upheavals) that are clearly beyond the control of the group and that will, to a degree, determine the fate of the group.[18] A useful way to categorize the problems of survival is to mirror the stages of the problem-solving cycle as shown in Table 2.[19]

The basic underlying assumptions of the culture from which the founders of the organization come will determine to a large extent the initial formulations of core mission, goals, means, criteria, and remedial strategies, in that those ways

Table 2
Problems of External Adaptation and Survival

Strategy:	Developing consensus on the primary task, core mission, or manifest and latent functions of the group.
Goals:	Developing consensus on goals, such goals being the concrete reflection of the core mission.
Means for Accomplishing Goals:	Developing consensus on the means to be used in accomplishing the goals – for example, division of labor, organization structure, reward system, and so forth.
Measuring Performance:	Developing consensus on the criteria to be used in measuring how well the group is doing against its goals and targets – for example, information and control systems.
Correction:	Developing consensus on remedial or repair strategies as needed when the group is not accomplishing its goals.

Source: Reprinted, by permission of the publisher, from "The Role of the Founder in Creating Organizational Culture," by Edgar H. Schein, *Organizational Dynamics*, Summer 1983 © 1983 Periodicals Division, American Management Associations. All rights reserved.

Table 3
Problems of Internal Integration

Language:	Common language and conceptual categories. If members cannot communicate with and understand each other, a group is impossible by definition.
Boundaries:	Consensus on group boundaries and criteria for inclusion and exclusion. One of the most important areas of culture is the shared consensus on who is in, who is out, and by what criteria one determines membership.
Power and Status	Consensus on criteria for the allocation of power and status. Every organization must work out its pecking order and its rules for how one gets, maintains, and loses power. This area of consensus is crucial in helping members manage their own feelings of aggression.
Intimacy:	Consensus on criteria for intimacy, friendship, and love. Every organization must work out its rules of the game for peer relationships, for relationships between the sexes, and for the manner in which openness and intimacy are to be handled in the context of managing the organization's tasks.
Rewards and Punishments:	Consensus on criteria for allocation of rewards and punishments. Every group must know what its heroic and sinful behaviors are; what gets rewarded with property, status, and power; and what gets punished through the withdrawal of rewards and, ultimately, excommunication.
Ideology:	Consensus on ideology and "religion." Every organization, like every society, faces unexplainable events that must be given meaning so that members can respond to them and avoid the anxiety of dealing with the unexplainable and uncontrollable.

Source: Reprinted, by permission of the publisher, from "The Role of the Founder in Creating Organizational Culture," by Edgar H. Schein, *Organizational Dynamics*, Summer 1983 © 1983 Periodicals Division, American Management Associations. All rights reserved.

of doing things are the only ones with which the group members will be familiar. But as an organization develops its own life experience, it may begin to modify to some extent its original assumptions. For example, a young company may begin by defining its core mission to be to "win in the marketplace over all competition," but may at a later stage find that "owning its own niche in the marketplace," "coexisting with other companies," or even "being a silent partner in an oligopolistic industry" is a more workable solution to survival. Thus for each stage of the problem-solving cycle, there will emerge solutions characteristic of that group's own history, and those solutions or ways of doing things based on learned assumptions will make up a major portion of that group's culture.

Internal Integration Problems

A group or organization cannot survive if it cannot manage itself as a group. External survival and internal integration problems are, therefore, two sides of the same coin. Table 3 outlines the major issues of internal integration around which cultural solutions must be found.

While the nature of the solutions will vary

from one organization to another, by definition, every organization will have to face each of these issues and develop some kind of solution. However, because the nature of that solution will reflect the biases of the founders and current leaders, the prior experiences of group members, and the actual events experienced, it is likely that each organizational culture will be unique, even though the underlying issues around which the culture is formed will be common.[20]

An important issue to study across many organizations is whether an organization's growth and evolution follows an inherent evolutionary *trend* (e.g., developing societies are seen as evolving from that of a community to more of a bureaucratic, impersonal type of system). One should also study whether organizational cultures reflect in a patterned way the nature of the underlying technology, the age of the organization, the size of the organization, and the nature of the parent culture within which the organization evolves.

5. ASSUMPTIONS THAT WORK WELL ENOUGH TO BE CONSIDERED VALID

Culture goes beyond the norms or values of a group in that it is more of an *ultimate* outcome, based on repeated success and a gradual process of taking things for granted. In other words, to me what makes something "cultural" is this "taken-for-granted" quality, which makes the underlying assumptions virtually undiscussable.

Culture is perpetually being formed in the sense that there is constantly some kind of learning going on about how to relate to the environment and to manage internal affairs. But this ongoing evolutionary process does not change those things that are so thoroughly learned that they come to be a stable element of the group's life. Since the basic assumptions that make up an organization's culture serve the secondary function of stabilizing much of the internal and external environment for the group, and since that stability is sought as a defense against the anxiety which comes with uncertainty and confusion, these deeper parts of the culture either do not change or change only very slowly.

6. TAUGHT TO NEW MEMBERS

Because culture serves the function of stabilizing the external and internal environment for an organization, it must be taught to new members. It would not serve its function if every generation of new members could introduce new perceptions, language, thinking patterns, and rules of interaction. For culture to serve its function, it must be perceived as correct and valid, and if it is perceived that way, it automatically follows that it must be taught to newcomers.

It cannot be overlooked that new members do bring new ideas and do produce culture change, especially if they are brought in at high levels of the organization. It remains to be settled empirically whether and how this happens. For example, does a new member have to be socialized first and accepted into a central and powerful position before he or she can begin to affect change? Or does a new member bring from the onset new ways of perceiving, thinking, feeling, and acting, which produce automatic changes through role innovation?[21] Is the manner in which new members are socialized influential in determining what kind of innovation they will produce?[22] Much of the work on innovation in organizations is confusing because often it is not clear whether the elements that are considered "new" are actually new assumptions, or simply new artifacts built on old cultural assumptions.

In sum, if culture provides the group members with a paradigm of how the world "is," it goes without saying that such a paradigm would be passed on without question to new members. It is also the case that the very process of passing on the culture provides an opportunity for testing, ratifying, and reaffirming it. For both of these reasons, the process of socialization (i.e., the passing on of the group's culture) is strategically an important process to study if one wants to decipher what the culture is and how it might change.[23]

7. PERCEIVE, THINK, AND FEEL

The final element in the definition reminds us that culture is pervasive and ubiquitous. The basic assumptions about nature, humanity, relationships, truth, activity, time, and space cover virtually all human functions. This is not to say that a given organization's culture will develop to the point of totally "controlling" all of its members' perceptions, thoughts, and feelings. But the process of learning to manage the external and internal environment does involve all of one's cognitive and emotional elements. As cultural learning progresses, more and more of the person's responses will become involved. Therefore, the longer we live in a given culture, and the older the culture is, the more it will influence our perceptions, thoughts, and feelings.

By focusing on perceptions, thoughts, and feelings, I am also stating the importance of those categories relative to the category of *overt behavior*. Can one speak of a culture in terms of just the overt behavior patterns one observes? Culture is *manifested* in overt behavior, but the idea of culture goes deeper than behavior. Indeed, the very reason for elaborating an abstract notion like "culture" is that it is too difficult to explain what goes on in organizations if we stay at the descriptive behavioral level.

To put it another way, behavior is, to a large extent, a joint function of what the individual brings to the situation and the operating situational forces, which to some degree are unpredictable. To understand the cultural portion of what the individual brings to the situation (as opposed to the idiosyncratic or situational portions), we must examine the individual's pattern of perceptions, thoughts, and feelings. Only after we have reached a consensus at this inner level have we uncovered what is potentially *cultural*.

The Study of Organizational Culture and Its Implications

Organizational culture as defined here is difficult to study. However, it is not as difficult as studying a different society where language and customs are so different that one needs to live in the society to get any feel for it at all. Organizations exist in a parent culture, and much of what we find in them is derivative from the assumptions of the parent culture. But different organizations will sometimes emphasize or amplify different elements of a parent culture. For example, in the two companies previously mentioned, we find in the first an extreme version of the individual freedom ethic, and in the second one, an extreme version of the authority ethic, *both* of which can be derived from U.S. culture.

The problem of deciphering a particular organization's culture, then, is more a matter of surfacing assumptions, which will be recognizable once they have been uncovered. We will not find alien forms of perceiving, thinking, and feeling if the investigator is from the same parent culture as the organization that is being investigated. On the other hand, the particular pattern of assumptions, which we call an organization's cultural paradigm, will not reveal itself easily because it is taken for granted.

How then do we gather data and decipher the paradigm? Basically, there are four approaches that should be used in combination with one another:

1. Analyzing the Process and Content of Socialization of New Members By interviewing "socialization agents," such as the supervisors and older peers of new members, one can identify some of the important areas of the culture. But some elements of the culture will not be discovered by this method becase they are not revealed to newcomers or lower members.

2. Analyzing Responses to Critical Incidents in the Organization's History By constructing a careful "organizational biography" from documents, interviews, and perhaps even surveys of present and past key members, it is possible to identify the major periods of culture formation. For each crisis or incident identified, it is then necessary to determine what was done, why it was done, and what the outcome was. To infer the underlying assumptions of the organization, one would then look for the major themes in the reasons given for the actions taken.

3. Analyzing Beliefs, Values, and Assumptions of "Culture Creators or Carriers" When interviewing founders, current leaders, or culture creators or carriers, one should initially make an open-ended chronology of each person's history in the organization — his or her goals, modes of action, and assessment of outcomes. The list of external and internal issues found in Tables 2 and 3 can be used as a checklist later in the interview to cover areas more systematically.

4. Jointly Exploring and Analyzing with Insiders the Anomalies or Puzzling Features Observed or Uncovered in Interviews It is the *joint inquiry* that will help to disclose basic assumptions and help determine how they may interrelate to form the cultural paradigm.

The insider must be a representative of the culture and must be interested in disclosing his or her *own* basic assumptions to test whether they are in fact cultural prototypes. This process works best if one acts from observations that puzzle the outsider or that seem like anomalies because the insider's assumptions are most easily surfaced if they are contrasted to the assumptions that the outsider initially holds about what is observed.

While the first three methods mentioned above should enhance and complement one another, at least one of them should systematically cover all of the external adaptation and internal integration issues. In order to discover the underlying basic assumptions and eventually to decipher the paradigm, the fourth method is necessary to help the insider surface his or her own cultural assumptions. This is done through the outsider's probing and searching.[24]

If an organization's total culture is not well developed, or if the organization consists of important stable subgroups, which have developed subcultures, one must modify the above methods to study the various subcultures.[25] Furthermore, the organizational biography might reveal that the organization is at a certain point in its life cycle, and one would hypothesize that the functions that a given kind of culture plays vary with the life-cycle stage.[26]

Implications for Culture Management and Change

If we recognize organizational culture — whether at the level of the group or the total corporation — as a deep phenomenon, what does this tell us about when and how to change or manage culture? First of all, the evolutionary perspective draws our attention to the fact that the culture of a group may serve different functions at different times. When a group is forming and growing, the culture is a "glue," a source of identity and strength. In other words, young founder-dominated companies need their cultures as a way of holding together their organizations. The culture changes that do occur in a young organization can best be described as clarification, articulation, and elaboration. If the young company's culture is genuinely maladaptive in relation to the external environment, the company will not survive anyway. But even if one identified needed changes, there is little chance at this stage that one could change the culture.

In organizational midlife, culture can be managed and changed, but not without considering all the sources of stability which have been identified above. The large diversified organization probably contains many functional, geographic, and other groups that have cultures of their own — some of which will conflict with each other. Whether the organization needs to enhance the diversity to remain flexible in the face of environmental turbulence, or to create a more homogeneous "strong" culture (as some advocate) becomes one of the toughest strategy decisions management confronts, especially if senior management is unaware of some of its own cultural assumptions. Some form of outside intervention and "culture consciousness raising" is probably essential at this stage to facilitate better strategic decisions.

Organizations that have reached a stage of

maturity or decline resulting from mature markets and products or from excessive internal stability and comfort that prevents innovation[27] may need to change parts of their culture, provided they can obtain the necessary self-insight. Such managed change will always be a painful process and will elicit strong resistance. Moreover, change may not even be possible without replacing the large numbers of people who wish to hold on to all of the original culture.

No single model of such change exists: managers may successfully orchestrate change through the use of a wide variety of techniques, from outright coercion at one extreme to subtle seduction through the introduction of new technologies at the other extreme.[28]

Summary and Conclusions

I have attempted to construct a formal definition of organizational culture that derives from a dynamic model of learning and group dynamics. The definition highlights that culture: (1) is always in the process of formation and change; (2) tends to cover all aspects of human functioning; (3) is learned around the major issues of external adaptation and internal integration; and (4) is ultimately embodied as an interrelated, patterned set of basic assumptions that deal with ultimate issues, such as the nature of humanity, human relationships, time, space, and the nature of reality and truth itself.

If we are to decipher a given organization's culture, we must use a complex interview, observation, and joint-inquiry approach in which selected members of the group work with the outsider to uncover the unconscious assumptions that are hypothesized to be the essence of the culture. I believe we need to study a large number of organizations using these methods to determine the utility of the concept of organizational culture and to relate cultural variables to other variables, such as strategy, organizational structure, and ultimately, organizational effectiveness.

If such studies show this model of culture to be useful, one of the major implications will be that our theories of organizational change will have to give much more attention to the opportunities and constraints that organizational culture provides. Clearly, if culture is as powerful as I argue in this article, it will be easy to make changes that are congruent with present assumptions, and very difficult to make changes that are not. In sum, the understanding of organizational culture would then become integral to the process of management itself.

References

1. J. Martin and C. Siehl (Autumn 1983) "Organizational Culture and Counterculture: An Uneasy Symbiosis." *Organizational Dynamics*, pp. 52–64.
2. C. Argyris (Autumn 1982) "The Executive Mind and Double-Loop Learning." *Organizational Dynamics*, pp. 5–22.
3. E.H. Schein (Fall 1981) "Does Japanese Management Style Have a Message for American Managers?" *Sloan Management Review*, pp. 55–68.
4. R. Evered and M.R. Louis (1981) "Alternative Perspectives in the Organizational Sciences: 'Inquiry from the Inside' and 'Inquiry from the Outside.'" *Academy of Management Review*, pp. 385–395.
5. F.R. Kluckhohn and F.L. Strodtbeck (1961) *Variations in Value Orientations*. Evanston, IL: Row Peterson. An application of these ideas to the study of organizations across cultures, as contrasted with the culture of organizations can be found in W.M. Evan (1976) *Organization Theory*. New York: John Wiley and Sons, ch. 15.
6. E.T. Hall (1959) *The Silent Language*. New York: Doubleday.
7. W.G. Dyer, Jr. (1982) *Culture in Organizations: A Case Study and Analysis*. Cambridge, MA: Sloan School of Management, MIT, Working Paper #1279-82.
8. T.E. Deal and A.A. Kennedy (1982) *Corporate Culture*. Reading, MA: Addison-Wesley. T.J. Peters and R.H. Waterman, Jr. (1982) *In Search of Excellence*. New York: Harper and Row.

9. J. Van Maanen and S.R. Barley (November 1982) "Occupational Communities: Culture and Control in Organizations." Cambridge, MA: Sloan School of Management.

10. R.L. Solomon and L.C. Wynne (1954) "Traumatic Avoidance Learning: Ten Principles of Anxiety Conservation and Partial Irreversibility." *Psychological Review*, 61, p. 353.

11. D.O. Hebb (1954) "The Social Significance of Animal Studies," in G. Lindzey, ed., *Handbook of Social Psychology*. Reading, MA: Addison-Wesley.

12. E.H. Schein (1961) *Coercive Persuasion*. New York: Norton.

13. E.L. Trist and K.W. Bamforth (1951) "Some Social and Psychological Consequences of the Long-Wall Method of Coal-Getting." *Human Relations*, pp. 1–38. I.E.P. Menzies (1960) "A Case Study in the Functioning of Social Systems as a Defense against Anxiety." *Human Relations*, pp. 95–121.

14. A.M. Pettigrew (1979) "On Studying Organizational Cultures." *Administrative Science Quarterly*, pp. 570–581. E.H. Schein (Summer 1983) *op. cit.*, pp. 13–28.

15. E.H. Schein (1961) *op. cit.* E.H. Schein and W.G. Bennis, *Personal and Organizational Change through Group Methods*. New York: Wiley and Sons.

16. A.K. Rice (1963) *The Enterprise and Its Environment*. London: Tavistock. R.F. Bales (1950) *Interaction Process Analysis*. Chicago, IL: University of Chicago Press. T. Parsons (1951) *The Social System*. Glencoe, IL: The Free Press.

17. G. Homans (1950) *The Human Group*. New York: Harcourt, Brace.

18. K.E. Weick (1979) "Cognitive Processes in Organizations," in B. Staw, ed., *Research in Organizational Behavior*. Greenwich, CT: JAI Press, pp. 41–74. J. Van Maanen (1979) "The Self, the Situation, and the Rules of Interpersonal Relations," in W.G. Bennis, J. Van Maanen, E.H. Schein and F.I. Steele, *Essays in Interpersonal Dynamics*. Homewood, IL: Dorsey Press.

19. E.H. Schein (1969) *Process Consultation*. Reading, MA: Addison-Wesley.

20. When studying different organizations, it is important to determine whether the deeper paradigms that eventually arise in each organizational culture are also unique, or whether they will fit into certain categories such as those that the typological schemes suggest. For example, Handy describes a typology based on Harrison's work that suggests that organizational paradigms will revolve around one of four basic issues: (1) personal connections, power, and politics; (2) role structuring; (3) tasks and efficiency; or (4) existential here and now issues." See: C. Handy (1978) *The Gods of Management*. London: Penguin. R. Harrison (September-October 1972) "How to Describe Your Organization." *Harvard Business Review*.

21. E.H. Schein (October-November 1970) "The Role Innovator and His Education." *Technology Review*, pp. 32–38.

22. J. Van Maanen and E.H. Schein (1979) "Toward a Theory of Organizational Socialization," in B. Staw, ed., *Research in Organizational Behavior*, Vol. 1. Greenwich, CT: JAI Press.

23. *Ibid*.

24. R. Evered and M.R. Louis (1981) *op. cit.*

25. M.R. Louis (1981) "A Cultural Perspective on Organizations." *Human Systems Management*, pp. 246–258.

26. H. Schwarts and S.M. Davis (1981) "Matching Corporate Culture and Business Strategy." *Organizational Dynamics*, pp. 30–48. J.R. Kimberly and R.H. Miles (1981) *The Organizational Life Cycle*. San Fransico: Jossey Bass.

27. R. Katz (1982) "The Effects of Group Longevity on Project Communication and Performance." *Administrative Science Quarterly*, 27, pp. 81–194.

28. A fuller explication of these dynamics can be found in my forthcoming book on organizational culture.

DECISION MAKING IN THE YEAR 2000*

John C. Papageorgiou

Although forecasting techniques in the year 1882 were not as developed as they are today, nevertheless, it would probably have been easier to predict what the world would be like 18 years later than it is today. Of course, changes were taking place in 1882 but they were not so dramatic that they made forecasting almost impossible as they do nowadays. It is the classical situation of an exponential growth curve whose first part rises at a slow rate. If we were to assume that we lived in 1882, we could extrapolate the past pattern, into 1900 and be quite accurate in terms of absolute values at least.

Today we cannot be as precise because we have reached the fast-rising part of the exponential growth pattern. Extrapolating the past pattern into the year 2000 could lead us to forecasts in absolute numbers that could be far from each other. Consequently, we cannot today make similar long-term forecasts of variables with exponential growth patterns in absolute numbers.

However, we can make an approximate extrapolation into the future of some trends from the past and draw an approximate scenario of the world of 2000 within which the manager will operate and make decisions. We are living in the first phases of an Electronic Revolution which is expected to affect society as much as the Industrial Revolution (Abelson, 1982).[1] Without doubt our world will be transformed by this revolution.

THE GROWTH OF ELECTRONICS AND COMPUTERS

In 1955 when the first electronic business computer was delivered to General Electric, they esti-

* Reprinted by permission of John C. Papageorgiou, "Decision Making in the Year 2000," *Interfaces* 13, April 1983. Copyright 1983 The Institute of Management Sciences.

mated that the possible users in the United States of such electronic brains would be around 50. Today, there are more than half a million general purpose computers in the United States, and the available computer power is growing by about 40 percent per year [Blasgen, 1982].[2] Five years ago the personal computer was a hobbyist's toy with a few thousand produced a year. Almost three million of them will be sold this year, and *Newsweek* estimates that by 1985, 50 million will be in use (1982).[3]

At the heart of this phenomenal progress is the microprocessor, a tiny electronic computer engraved on a silicon chip. The number of circuits that can be placed on a silicon chip has been increased exponentially for about 20 years. (Abelson, 1982).[4] Today, it is possible to build over half a million logic circuits at once on a single wafer. An experimental memory chip can store 288,000 bits (binary digits) of information, enough capacity to store four copies of the Declaration of Independence. Sixty-five such chips with a total capacity of 18,720,000 bits have been fabricated simultaneously on a wafer 82 millimeters in diameter (Branscomb, 1982).[5]

This miniaturization has brought about phenomenal computational speeds and great improvements in reliability. Circuits today are 10,000 times more reliable than they were 25 years ago. Miniaturization has also made costs decrease continuously. Since the 1950s, prices for small, general purpose computers of comparable power (expressed in dollars per instruction executed per second), have been dropping at an annual compound rate of about 25 percent per year. For large general purpose computers, the decrease in costs has been about 15 percent per year (Branscomb, 1982).[6]

The use of very large scale integrated (VLSI) circuits has increased the level of intelligence in computers and has made them cheaper and more reliable. At the same time it has made computers friendlier, that is, people not versed in computer science can learn to use them easily. For example, the computer might give a series of simple instructions asking the user to answer and ask for more elementary information where needed, it will also present complex information in color on the screen of a cathode-ray tube (CRT). The person-machine interface will improve further with further improvements in input-output devices. By the mid-1980s, computers are expected to be able to optically scan hand-printed information. It would be ideal if this kind of interface could be achieved for speech. However, although computers today can be made to talk quite well, and they can recognize a limited number of isolated spoken words, continuous, general purpose speech recognition at a reasonable cost remains a distant goal (Branscomb, 1982).[7]

INFORMATION SYSTEMS

The phenomenal growth of electronics and computers has affected information processing and distribution more profoundly than could be imagined a few years ago. During the 1980s, improved computers, satellites, cable television systems, and telephone lines will deliver low-cost videotex information services directly into businesses and homes. In addition, the laser video disk will allow inexpensive access to large libraries of stored information. Each surface of these disks can contain 54,000 color television images, equivalent to 10 billion bits of coded information plus two channels of stereo sound. this means that the equivalent of a 300-page book could be encoded in each square centimeter of its surface (Branscomb, 1982).[8]

The amount of information that can be transferred with an organization and between different locations depends on sending and receiving devices and on the communications links between them. Sending massive amounts of data among different locations of a major company requires very high bit transmission rates. For example, a large nation-wide retail chain store in the United States creates approximately 1 billion bits of sales information per day which must be shared by the headquarters and different locations to control inventory and procurement (Edelson and Cooper, 1982).[9]

In the past, business communications have been carried over analog communication channels, transmitting information as continuously varying electrical currents, through a number of transmission media (telephones, teletypes, etc.). Computer-controlled switches and digital transmission equipment (which transmit information by the presence or absence of electrical pulses), are now being installed and they will permit compatible communication operations of digital computers and office equipment. Starting in the mid-1970s, many nations launched satellites to provide good communications links between countries, between cities and towns, and even between buildings. There are now 22 separate operational satellite systems and 30 more are being built or planned (Edelson and Cooper, 1982).[10] The result is a largely digital, multipurpose, intelligent network which supports a wide variety of communication services today and offers an enormous potential for tomorrow. The United States network includes 22,000 switching centers and over one billion miles of transmission paths; it is able to make any of 6,000 trillion possible connections promptly (Mayo, 1982).[11]

These technological advances and trends will have enormous impact on the processing of business information. In the automated office of tomorrow, the electronic desk is expected to become standard equipment. It will consist of a large display screen, a keyboard, and a convenient pointing device, backed up by a local processor, a local file, a storage unit, and maybe a local printer and it will be linked to the rest of the system. This desk will allow users to review and update personal files, store notes, prepare documents, create diagrams and charts, and do computations. This desk will also have access to the organization's central files. Furthermore, the office can be connected to the outside world to achieve an inter-organizational communication system with access to databases outside the office system (Spinrad, 1982).[12] A multinational corporation now has a network of more than 500 computers in over 100 cities in 18 countries, and this network has been growing at the rate of about one computer per week for the past several years (Branscomb, 1982).[13] Today, there are more than 15,000 database systems in use in the United States (Blasgen, 1982).[14] The result will be that routine intellectual work may be automated as heavy mechanical work was after the Industrial Revolution (Spinrad, 1982).[15]

THE PRODUCTION SYSTEM

We will have to use our imagination to draw a picture of the factory in the year 2000. The increasing power and simplification of computers combined with advances in computerized manufacturing and robotics will change factories significantly in the next two decades. New developments in computer-aided design (CAD) and computer-aided manufacturing (CAM) are expected to create a new industrial revolution.

With CAD the user can describe the shape of a part so that the computer converts it into a mathematical model. This model can then be used to calculate the part's weight, volume, surface area, moment of inertia, and center of gravity. It can be used to determine stresses, deflections, and other structural characteristics; to examine the effects of moving parts; to modify the structure and observe its behavior without building costly physical models and prototypes; and to draft drawings automatically for use in manufacturing.

Computer-aided manufacturing is expected to have significant impact upon the management of plant operations. New tools, machines, and fixtures can be designed and then automatically controlled through prerecorded, numerically-coded information (numerical control tools), or through a minicomputer which stores the machining instructions as software that can easily be modified (computer numerical control). The automation of process and materials planning in CAM systems contributes to the optimum use of production equipment to avoid bottle-necks and to allow minimum investment in inventory. Furthermore, robots can be used to select and position tools for operation under computer numerical control and to operate tools such as drills and welders, and to perform tests and inspections. They can even use sensory perceptions, detect changes in work environments and make on-the-spot manufacturing decisions (Hudson, 1982).[16]

There are more than 80,000 robots in Japan today and they are expected to increase ten-fold by the end of the decade. However, only 2,000 of them are "intelligent" robots, that is, having sensory functions and capable of making decisions, mainly on assembly lines. Although it is possible today to program a single multipurpose robot to pick the tools needed for a wide range of purposes and also to load, unload, weld, and paint, the factory still lacks intelligent robots that can assemble machinery. Because of robots, flexible manufacturing systems can be developed, like that of the Japanese company Yamazaki that permits production to go on with only six workers on duty during the day shift and none at night (*Sunday Boston Globe*, 1982).[17] Intelligent robots could do jobs that present serious health hazards for people, for example, they could detect trouble in a nuclear power plant, and they could pick up flaws on the surface of hot steel sheets while the steel was still 800 or 900 degrees centigrade before the rolling process.

Robots are not used as extensively in the United States as in Japan; there are only about 4,000 in the US. The reasons given for reluctance to use them are their high initial cost, their bulkiness, and the availability of relatively cheap manual labor. The situation is changing, however, as firms adopt innovative technology, as costs of robots decline rapidly and their appearance becomes streamlined, and as labor costs increase. Further development of intelligent robots will fill the expected gap caused by the shortage of skilled labor, as the labor force shifts from production jobs to service jobs. Two thirds of the United States work force and 85 percent of its college graduates are now in service-related jobs (Hudson, 1982).[18]

A great deal of work has yet to be done to integrate the CAD (computer-aided design) system, which makes use of graphics-oriented computer databases, and the CAM (computer-aided manufacturing) system which uses mainly text-oriented information. When this is accomplished, the digital output from the CAD system will be fed directly into the CAM system to reprogram the plant's manufacturing computers. The ultimate goal is totally integrated manufacturing systems like that proposed by the ICAM (integrated computer-aided manufacturing) Air Force program. The objective of this program is to develop mutually compatible subsystems that will computerize and tie together the design, analysis, fabrication, materials handling, inspection, and distribution processes. Once integrated, these subsystems will achieve a comprehensive control and management package (Hudson, 1982).[19]

THE HUMAN ELEMENT

The Electronic Revolution is going to affect people in the workplace and society in general. As routine tasks are automated in factories, offices, warehouses, stores, banks, and insurance companies, and even in doctors' offices and hospitals, the nature of employment for a large fraction of the work force will change. The demand for highly intelligent and educated people will increase and concurrently the demand for less well-endowed and less adequately-trained people will decrease.

At the same time, what high level workers expect from their jobs will change. They will seek more intellectual and psychological fulfillment rather than just financial reward. Job satisfaction will come from greater involvement and increased sophistication, which will be provided by advances in technology. Work that was normally performed by engineers five or ten years ago is today performed by draftsmen who use CAD. As a result, engineers perform more technically sophisticated tasks (Hudson, 1982).[20] Similarly, workers who are displaced by automation can be retrained and assigned more challenging jobs.

In Japan, where robots are used more than anywhere else, concern has been expressed that workers will be forced out of their jobs by robots, but there is little alarm. Labor unions have cooperated with industry to study the possibilities opening up instead of protesting. Kanji Yonemoto, executive director of the Japan Industrial Robot Association, even questions whether there will be enough blue collar workers to fill all the jobs that robots will not be able to perform. The percentage of white collar-workers in the Japanese workshop is currently 30 percent and is expected to increase to 70 percent during the next decade. At the same time, 40 percent of Japanese high school graduates go to college today and it is expected that this percentage will increase to 85 percent in five years (*Sunday Boston Globe*, 1982).[21] If this happens, there will be a shortage of people willing to do blue collar jobs.

The exponentially increasing availability of computers to almost any individual in any environment is going to affect the work environment. Through personal computers, a limitless wealth of knowledge can be accessible to the masses, contributing to more educated and more sophisticated people in the workplace of tomorrow. As computers have been introduced into schools and homes, the current generation of children is taking them for granted and learning to use them easily. This familiarity and comfort with the use of computers will transform the work place to one with different ways of performing tasks and making decisions.

THE BUSINESS ENVIRONMENT

The Electronic Revolution is going to be a dominant factor in shaping the future business environment. In parallel with these technlogical advances a number of other forces will have (or continue to have) an impact on the business environment. I emphasize here that I am not trying to forecast the future on the basis of forecasting techniques but to draw a scenario of what can be expected according to educated guesses. In any case, the future is something that we will create ourselves within the constraints imposed by decisions made and actions taken in the past and the present (Jensen, 1974).[22]

As the world population grows and becomes more industrialized, we can expect that the concern for a cleaner and purer environment will continue to have an impact upon economic decisions about the production, distribution, and use of manufactured goods. Closely associated with environmental problems is the problem of diminishing natural resources, particularly energy. Nuclear energy that could replace other less clean sources of energy like oil and coal, has serious drawbacks, such as the problem of disposing of nuclear wastes and the risk of nuclear accidents. These factors cannot be ignored in making economic decisions.

Advances in communications are expected to make national borders less and less important at least with respect to business activity. The number of companies entering the international arena will increase, and this will cause both increased international cooperation and increased competition. This competition will aim to capture product markets and also to secure leadership in different technological fields.

Expanding competition and diminishing natural resources will cause greater efforts to increase productivity. Automation will increase productivity on the factory floor. It will also increase the productivity of white collar workers. But this will not be enough. Human attitudes and modes of operation must also change. The Japanese experience of achieving increases in productivity through labor commitment to the organization and labor participation in decision making suggests that decision making may have to be moved downward in the corporate structure and that current attitudes towards the organization may have to change.

Business plays a variety of roles in society simultaneously: it is the employer of its work force, the producer of its goods and services, and the financial engine for its funds. At the same time, business is expected to behave according to social objectives. To insure compliance with social objectives, legislative measures have been enacted and regulatory agencies established. In the United States, the 1890 Sherman Antitrust Act was the first of a series of federal regulations controlling acceptable market behavior and rate structures and standards for the purity of foods and efficiency of drugs. In the 1960's even broader social goals were added such as a cleaner environment, safety in the work place, less hazardous consumer products, and the end of discrimination in employment. Public concern over such issues will probably continue to grow, and regulation for social goals will therefore increase. Social forces outside corporations are increasingly important in their decision making, making it necessary to acquire and use social data in the corporation's management information system and decision making process (Zentner, 1981).[23]

Because of technological advances in communication, production and distribution; increased competition, nationally and internationally; the tendency of corporations to become more international; the need for productivity improvements; and increased pressures to maximize social goals; the size of the average corporation will increase. Consequently, the complexity of managerial problems will increase, whether operational, strategic, or design problems. By increased complexity, I do not mean increased largeness. Complex problems are not just collections of simpler problems; they are more messy, fuzzy, ill-structured, and qualitative problems (Zeleny, 1975).[24]

THE ROLE OF MANAGEMENT SCIENCE

Management science and operations research have made significant contributions to solving industrial and other system problems during the last three decades. Like other disciplines, they have gone through an evolutionary process producing a number of changes in both the structure and purpose of managerial problems, and the basic philosophy of modeling managerial processes. In the early years, it was assumed that a model could include all the complexities of a managerial problem, and OR analysts were given the responsibility of finding the optimum solution. However, analysts are not able to experience all the factors affecting the manager; their models are based on narrower representations of reality, and in many cases the optimum solutions they found were to the wrong problems (Emshoff, 1978).[25]

The availability of on-line interactive computer terminals has made it possible to construct interactive decision models that allow managers to insert their own evaluations of key problems, derive results under a variety of conditions, and judge them on a variety of criteria. Even the present level of participation by the decision maker is considered inadequate; most of the critical assumptions are still made by the analyst in designing the basic model. Emshoff (1978)[26] proposes the approach of experience-generalized decisions where the focus of models is based on the personal perspectives of decision makers. "The structure and key assumptions of all decision models will be formulated by the managers who are responsible for the decisions; model-building staff work will consist of formalizing instead of formulating." The increased involvement of managers is needed, and it will be demanded in the years ahead. However, in order for the experience-generalized decisions approach to become the standard approach in the future, operations research has to "become an epidemic" (Jensen, 1974)[27] was widespread as mathematics and physics nowadays.

Even should management science not become an epidemic and decision makers not involve themselves as thoroughly as the experience-generalized decisions approach demands, decision makers will be more familiar with management science and will get more involved in its applications. The complexity of the problems will make necessary an increased synergism between analysts and managers and will press them towards shared roles and responsibilities. Without systematic approaches, it will be impossible to solve the complex and multidimensional problems of the future, and unless full advantage is taken of the manager's experience, the solutions obtained will not be to the right problems.

The combined advances in computer technology and management science will bring increased automation to operational decision making parallel to the increased automation of the production floor. Increasingly, decision systems will be included in computer systems to automatically make decisions on operational problems. This automation will allow valuable managerial time to be devoted to developing new decision systems and to working on strategic planning. Management science has so far not been as successful in strategic planning as it has been in operational planning. To produce successful models for strategic planning, all relevant information must be part of the strategy formulation. To insure this, managers must participate. Releasing managers from operational decisions will allow this participation.

The operations research approach itself is expected to become easier in some phases and more difficult in others. The phases of problem formulation, optimization criteria identification, and model construction will become more complex and difficult. Formulating a messy, fuzzy, ill-structured problem and constructing a model for it that represents the key facets of reality is more difficult than for simpler problems. Furthermore, the optimization criteria will become more numerous, and multi-goal optimization approaches are expected to gain attention. On the other hand, the phases of data collection, model solution, and solution verification will become easier because of advances in computer technology.

CONCLUSION

Forecasting, even for the near future, is so difficult that there are as many forecasts as forecasters. Making predictions for the year 2000 is even more difficult. I have attempted only to draw a scenario of the managerial environment within which decisions will be made.

The Electronic Revolution is going to change managerial and social life as profoundly as did the Industrial Revolution. The computer's exponentially increasing capability and exponentially decreasing cost has made it available even to households and has accomplished automation that we could not have imagined a few years ago. This trend is expected to continue in the future and will have great impact upon the factory, the office, communications, and other aspects of economic and social life. Robots, particularly intelligent robots, combined with advances in computer-aided-design and computer-aided-manufacturing are expected to transform the appearance of the factory. Correspondingly, the composition of the labor force, the pay system for workers, and the nature of problems to be solved will all change.

The Electronic Revolution has also revolutionalized the collection, processing, storage, and distribution of information. The electronic desk and advances in telecommunications will diminish the significance of distances and national borders. The result will be larger and more international systems characterized by higher interdependence but also high competition. Social forces are expected to continue to impose constraints upon corporate behavior and to affect their optimization criteria in decision making.

Solving the future's complex and multidimensional problems will not be possible without decision support systems. By the same token, management science alone will not be able to handle these problems. The manager's role in applying management science will increase and managers will increasingly seek the help of analysts in finding solutions of their complex problems. Simple, operational problems are expected to be handled automatically by computerized decision systems, and this will free the manager's and the analyst's time for dealing with strategic problems.

Let us hope that the ongoing electronic and managerial revolution will bring more benefits to society than problems, just as the industrial revolution did.

References

1. P.H. Abelson (February 12, 1982) "The Revolution in Computers and Electronics." *Science*, 215, no. 4534, pp. 751–753.
2. M.W. Blasgen (February 12, 1982) "Database Systems." *Science*, 215, no. 4534, pp. 869–872.
3. "To Each His Own Computer" (February 22, 1982) *Newsweek*, pp. 50–56.
4. P.H. Abelson (February 12, 1982) *op. cit.*
5. L.M. Branscomb (February 12, 1982) "Electronics and Computers: An Overview." *Science*, 215, no. 4534, pp. 755–765.
6. *Ibid.*
7. *Ibid.*
8. *Ibid.*
9. B.I. Edelson and R.S. Cooper (February 12, 1982) "Business Use of Satellite Communications." *Science*, 215, no. 4534, pp. 837–842.
10. *Ibid.*
11. J.S. Mayo (February 12, 1982) "Evolution of the Intelligent Telecommunications Network." *Science*, 215, no. 4534, pp. 831–837.
12. R.J. Spinrad (February 12, 1982) "Office Automation". *Science*, 215, no. 4534, pp. 808–813.
13. L.M. Branscomb (February 12, 1982) *op. cit.*
14. M.W. Blasgen (February 12, 1982) *op. cit.*
15. R.J. Spinrad (February 12, 1982) *op. cit.*
16. C.A. Hudson (February 12, 1982) "Computers in Manufacturing." *Science*, 215, no. 4534, pp. 818–825.
17. "Japanese Robotics: A Drive for Supremacy" (February 14, 1982) *Sunday Boston Globe*.
18. C.A. Hudson (February 12, 1982) *op. cit.*
19. *Ibid.*
20. *Ibid.*
21. *Sunday Boston Globe* (February 12, 1982) *op. cit.*

22. A. Jensen (August, 1974) "International Aspects of Operations Research and the Future of Our Industrial Society." *Interfaces*, 4, no. 4, pp. 1–5.

23. R.D. Zentner (February, 1981) "2001: Can Management Science Keep Up?" *Interfaces*, 11, no. 1, pp. 56–58.

24. M. Zeleny (August, 1975) "Managers Without Management Science?" *Interfaces*, 5, no. 4, pp. 35–42.

25. J.R. Emshoff (August, 1978) "Experience-generalized Decision Making: The Next Generation of Managerial Models." *Interfaces*, 8, no. 4, pp. 40–48.

26. J.R. Emshoff (August, 1978) *op. cit*.

27. A. Jensen (August, 1974) *op. cit*.

CASES

STEVEN JOBS: AN INNOVATOR WHO FAILED AS A MANAGER*

Nick Brown

Steven Jobs is the 30-year-old computer enthusiast who, together with the like-minded Stephen Wozniak, founded Apple Computer. As computer hobbyists in 1976, Jobs and Wozniak were members of a computer club in Santa Clara, California (the center of "Silicon Valley") and began constructing small computers using the newly available microprocessor chips. When other hobbyists began to take an interest in their designs, Jobs and Wozniak supplied them with kits, consisting of components and printed circuits to mount them on. Jobs began to realize the commercial possibilities, and approached the owner of an electronics hobby shop, offering the right to sell the kits in return for components supplied on credit. Sales proved to be surprisingly strong and the two began assembling the computers in a garage, Wozniak attending to the technical aspects of the operation and Jobs the commercial.

After selling Jobs' Volkswagen bus for seed capital, the two neophyte entrepreneurs persuaded Regis McKenna, a prominent local advertising firm, to promote them and enticed Mike Markkula, marketing manager of Intel Corporation, into joining them. With venture capital provided by Bank of America and Arthur Rock, the company began distributing and selling the assembled Apple I computer in 1977. Sales grew strongly and the Apple I was succeeded by the Apple II and other versions. By 1980, sales had reached $100 million per annum, with correspondingly rapid growth in the organization. At this point, the founders decided to take the company public, becoming one of the most successful high technology offerings ever made (Jobs' shares were valued at $165 million).

In order to meet the threat of competition that was growing with equal rapidity (by this time Commodore, Atari, Radio Shack, and many other companies had entered the fray) Apple designed and introduced the "LISA", a much more technically advanced model that sold for over $8,000 and was aimed at the sophisticated user and small businessman. The model failed in the marketplace (largely because of the high price and lack of software support) and was subsequently withdrawn, but a lower priced "little sister" of the Lisa, the Macintosh, was a success when later introduced.

Apple's extraordinary growth during the late seventies and early eighties resulted

---

* "Steven Jobs: An Innovator Who Failed As A Manager" was prepared by Nick Brown. It is used by permission of the author.

in severe "growing pains" as management struggled to match demand, counter competition, increase distribution and production, and impose the financial discipline required by the SEC of public companies. Noting that the bulk of its buyers had changed from hobbyists to middle class home-owners with less computer experience, Jobs sought to remedy Apple's managerial deficiencies and alter its marketing outlook by hiring John Sculley, formerly President of Pepsi Co, as President of Apple in 1983.

Sculley's role was to bring some much needed professional management and consumer marketing expertise to the company. In 1981, IBM had introduced the PC microcomputer and, by taking advantage of their credibility in the eyes of businessmen and existing channels of distribution, had quickly stolen 42% of the market, leaving Apple with 11%.

At the present time, sales of the Macintosh have begun to falter in spite of Mr. Sculley's management reforms. The Apple II competed with IBM's PC Jr (now withdrawn) in the lower price range of the market and accounted for 70% of Apple's revenues; however, Apple has shifted the focus of its marketing attention to the Macintosh (and its successor the Macintosh II), with the intent of selling to the larger corporate buyer. Software for the Macintosh was slow to arrive and while Apple has captured a large part of the home and educational markets, it is struggling to compete with giant IBM on its own ground. Larger corporations are traditionally more conservative than their smaller brethren and many managers were weaned on IBM computers. In addition, other office product manufacturers (e.g., Digital Equipment Corporation and Wang) report slower sales in office products.

Apple's new strategy has met with disfavor among many of its original managers — particularly Stephen Wozniak who left the company in consequence and disposed of his shares. Other managers have also resigned, with as yet undetermined effect on company morale. As previously recorded, Apple's public share offering dictated stricter controls. This, coupled with the company's swelling payroll and broader market base, necessitated a more formal management structure. The adjustment left Jobs with less control: the LISA project, Apple's principal competitive thrust in the early eighties, was widely expected to be commanded Jobs himself. It wasn't. Jobs was dismayed to discover that the firm's other senior executives opposed his appointment as project manager on the grounds that he lacked experience (he was all of 26).

Jobs disconsolately cast about for another vehicle for his ambitions. He found it in the form of the Macintosh division — a project team put together by Apple to produce a scaled down version of the LISA computer. He saw in the Macintosh group the opportunity to relive the struggles and triumphs that he had lived and breathed while working on the original Apple with Wozniak.

With Apple's chairman at the helm, the Macintosh division was an organization apart; a culture within a culture. The self-styled renegades were housed in a building of their own and Jobs in particular viewed the toilers in Apple's other divisions with what many saw as a mixture of disdain and indifference. There was a pervasive belief in the Macintosh division that theirs was the only true fight; that Jobs was to be the saviour of Apple and they his disciples. Jobs demanded and got the best from his team; realizing that stricter management could hamper innovation, he set out to reproduce the same conditions of creative pressure and informal interaction that he and Wozniak had flourished under years earlier. He succeeded.

Under Jobs' "outlaw" regimen the Macintosh team assembled a computer that was every inch the commercial success that the LISA had failed to be. In addition the Macintosh was technically superior to its rival, the IBM PC, and was far easier for the untrained user to operate.

Unfortunately, Jobs found it impossible to sustain the organizational vision and relentless pace within the division after its price and joy had been introduced to the marketplace. Close on the Macintosh's heels should have come add-on hardware such as printers, hard disk drives and software, yet they were slow to arrive – principally as a result of the group's faltering commitment. Jobs' own cavalier and occasionally abrasive style did little to ameliorate the tensions caused by newer and tighter deadlines. It was soon apparent to all (save Jobs) that what was by then a large division could not be run on the same rules that a small development team lived by. The first seeds of discontent were sown.

Apple's sales during the early months of 1985 were sufficiently low to prompt Sculley to begin pressing Jobs for results. Jobs retaliated by questioning Sculley's competence, and wondered aloud if Sculley knew enough of the "nuts and bolts" of the computer business. An abortive attempt by Jobs to have the board of directors oust Sculley turned the squabble into an open feud. Finally, at a fateful board meeting in mid-1985, a re-organization was decided upon and Jobs dropped from the masthead, in spite of his 11% shareholding.

Why has Apple (until recently at least) been successful? Much of the company's early achievement can be credited to the fact that the company virtually created the market before it, then moved quickly with a product to fill it. Up until that time, computers had been thought of as large machines requiring the resources of a large corporation to own and run them. Much of the appeal of the home computer was that it provided the owner with his own computing power wholly at his beck and call.

The major reason for Apple's success however, is that it has always been able to respond quickly to changes in the marketplace or in available technology. During its rapid growth in the late seventies, the company had little time for the niceties of organizational design and was, by and large, an "adhocracy." Apple's staff were mostly youthful; innovation and creativity flourished in an optimistic environment unfettered by rigid rules. Whether or not this effervescent atmosphere and organizational flexibility will become the casualties of growth is very much a matter of debate among industry critics at present.

QUESTIONS

1. Steven Jobs is an example of the Existential Executive. Describe Job's existential characteristics.
2. Research John Sculley's background.
3. Describe Job's "Outlaw Culture" in the Macintosh division.
4. What was the cause of the conflict between Jobs and Sculley? Was the difference ultimately cultural? In what ways?
5. Why could Jobs not change the culture at Apple ultimately?

BAXTER INDUSTRIES LTD.*

Peter E. Pitsiladis

Baxter Industries Ltd. is a large manufacturer of light- and medium-weight metal products such as metal frames, vestibule intercom panels, assorted metal containers, boxes, and cabinets. As part of a diversified line, it also produces baseboard type heaters for high rise apartments and other multi-unit dwellings. Its primary customers are building contractors and hardware wholesalers. Distribution of its products is effected through an extensive network of manufacturers' representatives and the company's own direct sales personnel. From rather modest beginnings in 1925, the company had steadily expanded with few exceptions, and by 1986 it enjoyed a large volume of sales for the type of industry. In its market, the company has a well established reputation as a highly quality innovative manufacturer and supplier. While a large portion of its sales are made to accounts located in Ontario and Québec recent corporate "successes" took the company heavily into the Northeastern United States and Western Canada. Some of the growth in the late 1970s and early 1980s were achieved through acquisition of smaller firms in these new markets. The company is located in Montréal, Québec, where a total of nearly 400 persons are employed.

THE BAXTER FAMILY AND EMPLOYEE RELATIONS

Over the years the ownership and top management control of the company had remained in the hands of the Baxter family, John Baxter, the majority shareholder and current president, was the grandson of a wealthy Québec financier and industrialist. The money John Baxter inherited from his own father enabled him to underwrite his many business ventures, including his activities in Baxter Industries Ltd. There were several branches of the Baxter family in Montréal and all traced their origins back many generations in Québec. Largely through their support and heavy involvement in civic, cutural, and philanthropic activities, the Baxter families historically had a high social profile and were widely known throughout the Francophone and Anglophone segments of Montréal society and in the community at large. John Baxter continued in this tradition of civic involvement as did most other family members who participated in the company.

The company itself had always enjoyed an excellent reputation for the treatment of its employees. For the type of industry, working conditions were good and wage levels throughout the company were unusually high. Applications for employment had always for exceeded the number of vacancies available, especially in the plant jobs. With the drop in economic activity during the mid-1980's and the increase in the unemployment rate in Montréal—there was, in fact, a corresponding increase in the number of applications for job openings at the company. This was regarded by

---

* Prepared by Professor Peter E. Pitsiladis, Faculty of Commerce and Administration, Concordia University, Montréal, May 1987. The case was prepared as a basis for class discussion rather than to illustrate either effective or ineffective handling of an administrative situation. Reprinted by permission.

one Human Resources Department official in the company as "a consequence of the company's solid reputation as an employer." Although the company had a formal association of employees, several attempts by outside labor unions, including the largest and most militant of them, to further organize the production and maintenance employees of the firm had all failed; the main resistance to integration with unions had apparently come from the employees themselves. The certification votes involved had overwhelmingly rejected the idea of formal union organization or affiliation.

When questioned about the company's philosophy in the area of personnel relations, several senior executives made reference to the company's "progressive" stance in relation to Law 101 which was enacted by the the separatist Parti Québécois Government less than a year after their election in November 1976.[1] John Baxter talked about company policy in this regard:

> One objective of the law was to provide Francophones in Québec with the chance to pursue employment opportunities and career paths in their own language . . . . Given Québec's demographics, we found this to be natural enough and co-operated fully with government agencies to bring about an appropriate level of Francization of all our corporate communications – correspondence, contracts, policies, procedures, and so on. We ensured through personnel recruitment and language training that bilingual personnel were positioned in those jobs throughout the company where contact in French either was required by law or deemed by us to be otherwise important . . . . Our acceptance of Law 101 and the company's related affirmative action programs were very well received by the Francophone employees . . . . Our strategy was to outflank the radical nationalists, keep abreast of the contemporary thinking in Québec, and avoid all unnecessary irritants . . . . In some ways, we approached the problem very differently from other companies which either left Québec for Ontario and other provinces, or damaged their own cause by opposing the law and dragging their feet in its administrative application . . . . Our family history in Quebec and our commitment to this fair province simply dictated that we would make all reasonable accommodations to current political and social realities. We don't regret the outcome . . . .

The members of the Baxter family were primarily oriented to production activities, the majority of them having served an apprenticeship in the production department during the earlier days of the company when production was, in fact, the only formally established and organized function. Apprenticeship in the production department had become a training custom with the family, and it was fully expected that this custom would be maintained in the years ahead by younger members of the family, if and when they joined the company. While the Baxter family members occupied the most senior corporate positions, they continued to display a rather keen interest in the day-to-day activities of the production department. For example, it was common practice for Dick Baxter, Senior Vice-President of the firm, to make periodic visits to the production department to inquire into current problems and to chat informally among the rank-and-file employees. The employees, in turn, seemed proud of the "shirt-sleeve" relations they had with Dick Baxter and other family members.

Over one-half of the company's personnel worked in the production department. A large majority of the jobs in this area were held by Francophones, most of whom were French Canadians, or "Québécois" as they were termed in the current vernacular. A large number of these French Canadians had considerable seniority with the company. Service history records of fifteen and twenty years were quite common. French Canadian employees in the production department seemed especially to cherish the freedom they enjoyed under their supervisors who, for the most part, were also French Canadians. There appeared to be no special work problems between the supervisors and their men. Grievances were infrequent, and it was not unusual for some of the foremen to be seen with their subordinates during lunch hours in one or more of the "greasy spoons" near the plant in east end Montréal and after hours in the local "brasserie" (tavern). Most of the non-supervisory jobs in the production area were unskilled or semi-skilled, necessitating only a couple of weeks on-the-job training for new employees. It was common knowledge, however, that the employees (supervisors and subordinates) in this area were among the highest paid in the company. For example, salaries were a frequent topic of conversation among members of the accounting department, some of whom estimated that the salaries of their counterparts in production were at least a fifth higher than their own.

STUDY OF OPERATIONS

In 1985 Mr. Donald Chapman, General Manager of the Baxter Industries, conducted a review of all the firm's operations. The company had been facing keener price competition since the early 1980s; although sales had continued at higher levels, profits had begun to drop off noticeably because of reduced margins. The President and other senior company officials had become most anxious to improve the profitability of the company, but they were unsure as to how this might be done. Mr. Chapman, who had joined the company some ten years earlier, concluded as a result of the study that cost and procedural controls throughout the organization were lacking. He believed, as well, that the rapid growth of the company in the 1970s and 1980s had created a need for additional specialized staff personnel in accounting, marketing, and related areas. This need, in his opinion, had not been satisfied. Additions to staff had simply not kept pace with company growth. Accordingly, he made it generally known that if the company was to maintain its market position and improve its profits, some of the "organizational vacuums" would have to be filled. This, he thought, would also be necessary for orderly succession in middle management ranks.

ORGANIZATION AND PROCEDURAL CHANGES

In the early part of 1986, Mr. Chapman appointed Jack Sillman as the first Comptroller and Manager of the company's new Administrative Services Department. As a chartered accountant, Sillman had previously served as a senior management officer in the Revenue Department of the Ontario provincial government. According to organizational plans, the Administrative Services Department was to include, as a start, all the existing accounting functions such as accounts payable, accounts receivable, general accounting and data processing. In the months subsequent to the appointment, Sillman and Chapman held private, regular meetings to hammer out a long-term program for the Administrative Services Department. The primary function of the department was to tighten up administrative and accounting controls throughout the company, but more particularly in "those areas where the potential for new economies was greatest."

In addition to the accounting functions, two new sections would eventually be established within the Administrative Services Department. First, a budgeting section would be needed to install and administer a more sophisticated company-wide, computer-based budgeting program. Budgeting, as it had existed up until that time, was informal and for the most part consisted simply of each department manager submitting an annual estimate of expenditures for the coming year to the company Treasurer for approval. Second, a systems section would be needed to conduct a procedures program involving the study and write-up of the more important of the interdepartmental administrative practices and information systems. Chapman regarded this function (of the systems section) as a particularly important means of outlining the responsibilities of various departments and of encouraging uniformity in recurring day-to-day practices. It would also serve to "clean-up" existing information systems before their eventual conversion to computer. The heads of the sections in question would be hired as soon as possible, with additional staff being added gradually as the direction of the work became clearer and as the volume began to increase (see organization chart Exhibit 1).

IMPLEMENTATION OF NEW PROGRAM

By the summer of 1986 both section heads had been appointed. George Finch, the new Supervisor of the budgeting section, was to devote his time to developing the framework and details of the budgetary control program. Charles Bond, formerly a branch manager of a systems service organization, was to begin, as supervisor of the systems section, the study and write-up of interdepartmental procedures. In his discussions with the two men, Jack Sillman outlined the philosophy and the long-term program of the Administrative Services Department, and he continuously emphasized the importance of diplomacy and "go-softly" approach in dealing with other departments. He candidly pointed out that all of them were "green" to the company and that they should make every effort to avoid antagonizing anyone. All of the men were enthusiastic about the nature of their assignment and saw in it as opportunity to make a substantial contribution to the organization.

Although the work of the systems section for the first six months was largely confined to the accounting area, the volume of work was such and the progress sufficient as to warrant the addition of several staff members, all of them graduates of local universities. With the advantage of a larger staff, Bond was advised by Sillman to begin working in the "direction" of the production department. George Finch, in the meantime, had worked out what he thought would be an acceptable budgetary control program. After Sillman had examined and approved the new program Finch suggested that a meeting be arranged with all the department managers affected at which time the new program could be outlined and feedback received.

The meeting that followed was attended by selected staff of the Administrative Services Department and all of the departmental managers involved except "Rollie" Cloutier, Manager of Production. Chapman and other senior management officials had previously declined to attend, indicating they preferred not to "interfere." Sillman was surprised by Cloutier's absence, however, inasmuch as he had been assured by Cloutier that the date and the time of the meeting were perfectly acceptable. Finch described the new budgetary program to those present; no major objections were

Exhibit 1
Baxter Industries Ltd. Partial Organizational Chart, Summer 1986

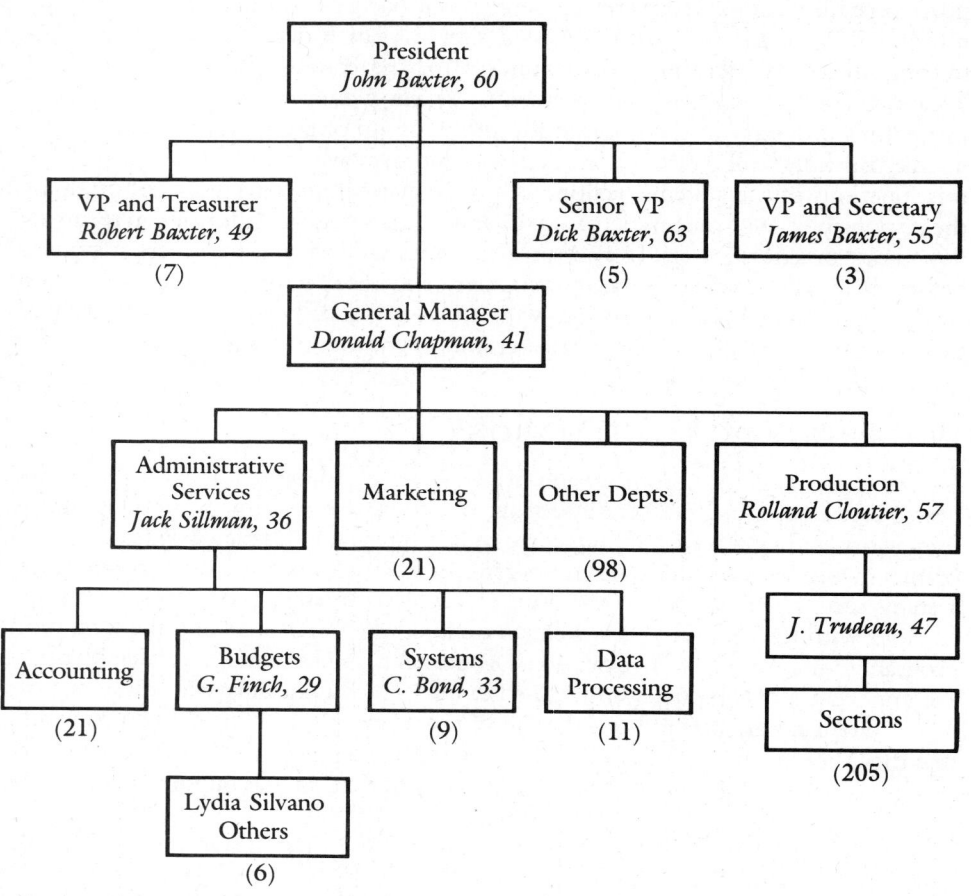

```
                          President
                       John Baxter, 60
         ┌─────────────────┼─────────────────┐
   VP and Treasurer    Senior VP         VP and Secretary
   Robert Baxter, 49   Dick Baxter, 63   James Baxter, 55
         (7)               (5)                (3)
                           │
                     General Manager
                     Donald Chapman, 41
         ┌──────────┬──────────┬──────────┐
   Administrative  Marketing  Other      Production
   Services                   Depts.     Rolland Cloutier, 57
   Jack Sillman, 36 (21)      (98)
                                          │
                                       J. Trudeau, 47
                                          │
                                       Sections
                                         (205)
   ┌──────┬────────┬────────┬──────────┐
Accounting Budgets  Systems  Data
           G. Finch,29 C. Bond,33 Processing
   (21)              (9)        (11)
              │
         Lydia Silvano
         Others
           (6)
```

Ages shown after names are estimates.

Numbers shown in parentheses are totals of employees in each department.

raised and some minor suggestions were made, but overall the reception was hardly more than luke-warm. Nonetheless, the department managers did agree to Sillman's suggestion that a task force be established to assist Finch in implementing the program and working out any of the problems that might arise. The task force was to consist of departmental representatives appointed by each of the managers. Finch had decided some time earlier with Sillman's approval that he would assign Lydia Silvano in whom he had much confidence to be the "point man" and do the "interfacing" with the production people. Lydia, like many of the other members of the Administrative Services Department, was a local university graduate and had transferred into the department from Marketing. She had demonstrated considerable competence and promise in the time she had been with Baxter Industries and had eagerly faced her new assignment.

INTERDEPARTMENTAL DIFFICULTIES

In the months that followed, Sillman kept receiving unfavorable progress reports from both Finch and Bond. Bond complained:

> My guys can't seem to make any headway in their procedure work; the biggest problem is the Production Department; those people never have the time for us. Whenever we do manage to nail them down to a time and a place, they often don't bother to show up anyway. We are generally left standing around sucking our thumbs. To top it all off, we've found that those procedure instructions which we have managed to issue over your signature are being ignored by the production people altogether. I'm fed up with the whole thing. So are my staff. We're are not getting the support of the management and the people we are supposed to be working with won't cooperate.

Finch's complaints to Sillman were of the same nature. He reiterated his support for the idea of the task force arrangement but decried the lack of cooperation:

> Nobody seemed particularly enthusiastic about the idea of the new budgetary program. The decisions made in the task force meetings were not being followed up. Jacques Trudeau was totally indifferent and couldn't be relied upon to look after his end of things. This is the first time I've seen Lydia stumble on any project and I'm damn sure the problem is not hers.

From the reports he received and from his own personal feelings on the matter, Sillman believed that the situation had become acute. However, as a start, he thought that a heart-to-heart talk with Rollie Cloutier might be helpful. Early one morning Sillman called Cloutier and suggested they get together to discuss the situation. "There is no point in it, Jack," Cloutier replied, "I might as well be sincere.[2] [We are busy people here in Production and we do not have a lot of time to play around. Our problems are a hell of a lot more complicated than anything you'll find in bookkeeping. We'll work with you but it will have to be in our spare time".]

Sillman was taken aback by Cloutier's reaction; he pondered the situation for a few hours and then decided to refer the entire matter to Chapman, the General Manager.

References

1. Formal title of the law is *The Charter of the French Language*. The Parti Québécois Government was defeated in the December 1985 provincial election.
2. At this point Cloutier switches into French; text of his comments is a translation.

QUESTIONS

1. Who are the political actors in this case? Who has power and how is this indicated? What are the determinants and consequences of power? How is power used? Are all the conditions for the further use of power present? What are the contingencies that influence power relationships in this situation? What role do the environment and cultural differences play in this case?

2. What are the forms of conflict present in this situation? Why does the conflict arise? What organizational and contextual factors are influencing relationships and resultant conflict? What are the functional and dysfunctional consequences of the conflict?

3. What type of change was initiated in this case? What are the reasons for the apparent indifference or resistance to the new program? Are the elements for effective change present? Why? Why not? Are English - French cultural and linguistic differences at the heart of the problem?

4. What would you have done at the end of the case if you were in Sillman's position. Why? If you were in Chapman's position, how would you respond to Sillman at the end? Why? What consequences would you anticipate? What options are open to Chapman? As a consultant responsible for the implementation of the administrative and budgetary controls, how would you have acted differently? What would you have done the same?

EXERCISE

CHARACTERISTICS OF CORPORATE CULTURE*

Joe Kelly

Corporations differ on many levels: the number of employees, the size of earnings, the hierarchical structure, the technology. They also differ in another respect, one which is not tangible, and that is culture. Corporations develop a culture of their own which incorporates a complex set of attitudes, values, and beliefs as well as traditions, symbols, and language (jargon particular to the company) that are shared by the members of the organization. These elements all interact to determine a certain "way of life" and are a powerful force in determining behavior patterns.

Just as a child must master the culture of the society in which he or she lives, so must members of an organization become acquainted with the cultural norms of the company. Culture is learned and inculcated, that is, passed down from the veterans to the new recruits. While socialization refers to the process of learning the culture in which one is raised, acculturation refers specifically to the learning of another culture different from the one in which the individual is brought up. Within the organization, acculturation refers to the way newcomers are introduced to the means and methods of coping with their environment. To many, the term socialization has a pejorative connotation, in that the process means conformity; however, what must be realized is that corporations work better as a unit if the many parts think as one.

A strong culture which brings about internal consistency seems to be the hallmark of success. Corporate giants, such as IBM and P&G have mastered the socialization process which includes all the following elements. The recruiting process is a gruelling experience for the candidate who is given every opportunity to bow out, if his or her style and values are not congruent with those of the organization. Once hired, the new recruit is handed various assignments designed to make the person more receptive to the company's norms and values by driving home the fact that no matter how accomplished or intelligent the individual is, he or she is still a beginner at the organization. Such experiences take many forms from too much work for one person

---

* This exercise was adapted from "Fitting New Employees into the Company Culture" by Richard Pascale, *Fortune* May 28, 1984, with permission.

to handle to assignments which may be considered an insult to the individual's intelligence. Next, the recruit is sent into the field to try his hand at doing business the company's way. His performance is closely monitored and determines future promotional opportunities. The individual's progress is evaluated through formal appraisal systems which measure performance based on managerial skill as well as quantitative data such as sales, profit, or market share figures. Mechanisms for rewarding (salary increases, recognition, promotions) deserving members as well as punishing (undesirable assignments, promotion delays) individuals who violate organizational norms are used. Furthermore, the company tries to promote employee identification with corporate values that rise above and beyond daily operating concerns – such as helping people to learn and grow – which enables employees to make personal sacrifices for the good of the company. Finally, the company provides role models for younger professionals to emulate. The key is to supply mentors who are consistent in the qualities which spell success.

By incorporating these steps in the socialization process, the company can successfully assimilate newcomers into its culture. While most companies rely heavily on formal systems of control, a strong culture embodies a tablet of unwritten laws which facilitate day-to-day operations by providing consistency. More time and energy is spent getting things done, than wondering how to get them done.

On the other hand, the absence of cultural guidelines removes this sense of continuity and stability. There is no consistent method within the organization for accomplishing tasks. What works well for one boss, may not work well for another. Employees become confused about what to expect in terms of their career: qualities they should explore and master, career paths, promotion opportunities, and rewards. People do not speak the same language, communication lines break down, signals and messages are misinterpreted with potentially harmful results.

One's ability to make decisions and implement change depends on power as much as formal authority. The building blocks of a power base include reputation, track record, skills and expertise, and connections – one's "social currency" – which is accumulated over time. Corporations with a strong cultural background allow employees to build a reserve of social currency by providing a working milieu which is consistent and unambiguous.

PREPARING NOTES TO DEFINE AN ORGANIZATION'S CULTURE

Briefly describe the prevailing values of your organization. Think in terms of:

1. (a) economic values (attitudes to profitability, ROI, long-term versus short-term)
   (b) social values (attitudes to people)
   (c) technological values (innovation, etc.)
2. language
3. symbols
4. (a) socialization (introduction, career development, retirement)
   (b) company parties, get-togethers
5. reward system

6. decision making (autocratic versus democratic)
7. unwritten laws
8. attitude to women
9. attitude to minorities
10. overall description of culture

Is the culture consistent and unambiguous?
Will this organization survive?

XI
MANAGEMENT OF ORGANIZATIONS

READINGS

LEADERSHIP STYLE AT THE POLICY LEVEL*

A.B. Ibrahim
J. Kelly

Our corporate prima donnas, are they in for a lifetime? In other words, can organizations in the 80s afford to have CEOs running the show for fifteen or twenty years – in different seasons? Can our organizations survive with the original values and philosophies of the entrepreneur irrespective of whether the firm is in maturity, decline, or turn-around? Can the typical executives in maturity with their conservative view turn their organizations around? In an attempt to answer these questions let us examine the state of leadership research, and that of corporate strategy as a choice of top management.

It almost goes without saying that there is disagreement in the academic community as to the state of leadership research, principally because there are anomalies which the present paradigm does not address. For Kuhn, anomalies inexplicable by the current paradigm lead to crisis, to a proliferation of competing articulations, explicit discontent, debate over fundamentals, and ultimately that form of scientific revolution we describe as paradigm shift.[1] It is on the verge of this state that research in leadership finds itself today. This research focuses on a required paradigm shift and investigates the relation between executive personality and its values on the one hand, as revealed in videos of actual executive behavior, and the organization's strategy or life cycle stages on the other hand.

GENERALLY ACCEPTED PARADIGM WHICH DOES NOT SEEM TO WORK

Many studies have been undertaken to investigate the personality of the leader. For example, it has been reported that the leader tends to have some of the following characteristics: analytical, intelligent, keen, aggressive, enthusiastic, dominant, extroverted and persuasive.[2]

Other studies analyzed the leader's behavior according to two dimensions: initiating structure and consideration.[3]

Fiedler's empirical works postulate three important dimensions of the total situation which structure the leader's role: leader-member relations, task structure, and position power.[4]

Finally, House and Mitchell in their path-goal theory identified four kinds of leadership behavior: directive, supportive, participative, and achievement oriented.[5]

As scholars, most leadership researchers are thoroughly familiar with the classical scientific research model as stated by Kaplan,[6] and Kuhn.[7] In brief, observation is followed by theory, theory is followed by applied research, modified with a view toward application of valid behavioral science knowledge. By any objective assessment, leadership theories have failed to produce generally accepted, practically useful, and widely applied scientific knowledge.[8] Thus, we are in a

---

* "Leadership Style at the Policy Level" by A.B. Ibrahim and J. Kelly is reprinted from the *Journal of General Management*, Vol. II, No. 3, Spring 1986, pp. 37–46. Used by permission of publisher and authors.

position of having a generally accepted paradigm, which does not seem to work. Why?

The major criticism of leadership theories from executives is that they are essentially academic, and no significant effort has been made to apply the findings to actual management operations as a means of improving corporate performance.

A PARADIGM SHIFT

A different approach to organizational leadership seems to be emerging now in the area of business policy that focuses on the fit and match between the executive on one hand and organizational strategy or life cycle stages on the other hand;[9] Ansoff,[10] Adizes,[11] Wissema et al.[12] Miller, Ket de Vries and Toulouse.[13] This marriage of organization behavior and policy represents a paradigm shift in leadership research. However, it must be noted that little empirical research has been reported.

To understand the link or fit between organization strategy and leadership, let us examine now the research on strategy.

CORPORATE STRATEGY: A CHOICE OF TOP MANAGEMENT

There are many factors which shape the formulation of strategy or influence the decision maker. Environmental factors, including economic trends, industry structure, and competition, are very important in deciding what course of action the organization should pursue. The internal capability of the firm, 'corporate resources,' is another aspect in shaping strategic decision: factors such as the financial position of the firm, the strengths and weaknesses in different functional areas have to be considered. In essence, a situational audit of the internal and external capability of the organization is an essential part of the strategic decision.

However, these factors though important are just ingredients in the decision-making process. Executives in charge of corporate destinies do not look only at these factors; they in most cases are heavily influenced by what they personally want to achieve. In other words, strategic decision is a choice of top management. For example, Chandler[14] defines strategy as the determination of the basic long-term goals of an organization, while Ansoff[15] defines it as a rule for making decisions. Hofer and Schendel[16] define strategy as a pattern of objectives, purposes or goals defining what business we are in or should be. Mintzberg[17] defines strategy as a pattern in streams of organizational decisions or 'actions.'

In effect, strategy is a decision, a clinical decision, a choice made by a leader, and like any decision-making process is filtered by our perception, personality, motivation, and expectations. This relationship could be described by the following proposed model (see Figure 1). Accordingly, one way to study strategy is to study the decision makers, the strategists, their personalities, values and motivation—in other words, their leadership styles.

Strategy–leader fit

The proposed paradigm shift in leadership/strategy research is not without support. Research by Wissema, Vander Pol and Messer,[18] helps to spell out a link between a specific strategy and a certain style or personality of the leader. In fact their typology is based on the idea that certain behavioral characteristics are necessary for different strategic direction. They reported six strategic directions and the type of leader or manager to match each strategy.

For Wissema et al.,[19] if the strategic direction is explosive growth, then the best type of manager to fit such strategy would be a 'pioneer' type of strategist. The 'pioneer' type manager has certain personality characteristics: very flexible, very creative, divergent, very extrovert, hyperactive, restless, dare-devil, intuitive and irrational. These characteristics are completely different under 'contracting' type of strategy. The managerial style here is what the researchers termed 'insistent diplomat': flexible, with fixed objective, considerate, broad, relativistic, many-sided.

Figure 1
A Proposed Strategy Formulation Model

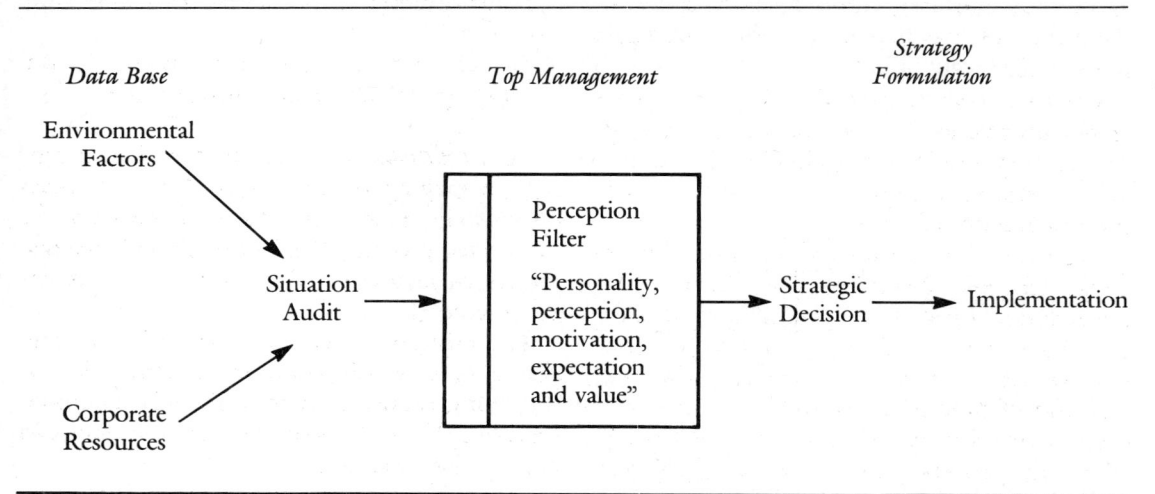

Data Base — Environmental Factors, Corporate Resources → Situation Audit → *Top Management*: Perception Filter "Personality, perception, motivation, expectation and value" → *Strategy Formulation*: Strategic Decision → Implementation

Miller, Kets de Vries, Toulouse[20] studied 33 organizations in the Montréal area and reported similar findings. Entrepreneurial type executives were found to have different distinct personalities (i.e., more innovative and creative).

Khandwalla,[21] based on a study of different Canadian firms reported similar findings to Wissema *et al.*[22] Effectiveness of different managerial styles under different environments were investigated. The researcher reported seven managerial styles each with behavioral dimensions to fit a certain type of environment.

Miles and Snow[23] explored the need for congruence or fit between top management, environment and their four different strategic directions: defender, prospector, analyzer, and reactor.

Ansoff[24] suggested that 'general management capability' should be modified to match different stages in the organization life cycle. Ansoff[25] discussed three different components to achieve management capability: 'culture,' 'competence,' and 'capacity,' and described different attributes and skills required for each component.

Adizes[26] reported that different skills are needed in different stages of the organization life cycle. The authors of this research strongly believe that the organization life cycle greatly influences organization strategic direction. Certainly the infancy stage of the organization life cycle needs a different personality and managerial style from that of the death or declining stage.

RESEARCH METHOD

The present study tracks strategy and leadership succession over a period of 15 years in four large firms in Montréal, Canada. The first organization is a large firm in the food retail and self services department stores; the second firm is a large conglomerate which offers a broad range of services and products in the following categories: financial services, pulp, paper and packaging; the third is a large corporation which directly and through subsidiaries, carries on transportation and related operations, consisting of rail, telecommunication, airlines, and hotels; and the fourth organization is engaged in the motor transport business, real estate and vehicle rental and leasing.

Leadership succession and strategic directions in each organization were carefully identified. Twelve CEOs, presidents, and SBU managers were studied.

The research study is based on interviews, study of documents, as well as videotapes. Dramatic new development in video technology has allowed management researchers the opportunity to study executives more effectively.

The methodology utilized to identify the corporate strategic direction was a form of direct research developed at McGill University and can be summarized as follows: (1) listing key decisions or actions made by each organization over a period of time under study; (2) inference of the strategic direction from the previous listing; (3) finally, periods of change are thoroughly analyzed. In addition to the McGill approach, sixty executives and MBA students were shown the videotapes and other related documents and were asked to answer a questionnaire concerning leadership styles of different CEOs, presidents and SBU managers in the four organizations under study.

STUDY FINDINGS

Although there were obvious dissimilarities in strategy and executive styles adopted by these four organizations, a sufficient number of commonalities and themes appear with reasonable consistency to facilitate development of a model of strategy/leader fit. Four distinct executive styles were identified that match different strategic directions. The following is a description based on the research findings.

1. The Entrepreneur This proposed style fits executives managing organizations that have been described in the strategy literature as 'stars' (Boston Consulting Group); 'explosive growth' and 'expansion';[27] 'prospectors'[28] or under the general term growth strategy, be it expansion, mergers, and/or acquisitions.

The entrepreneur can be described as very innovative, creative, intuitive, flexible, extrovert, optimistic, motivated, excitable, dominant and a risk-taker.

The entrepreneur fits organizations in the developing and aggressive growth stage.

2. The Professional This proposed style fits executives managing organizations that have been described in the strategy literature as 'cash cows'[29]; 'continued growth;[30] 'defenders',[31] and strategic directions such as holding, or harvesting (General Electric).

The professional can be described as a team player, bureaucratic, conformist, systematic, stable, calm, cautious, mature, friendly, and conservative. The professional is slow to change and to meet increases in threat.

The professional fits organizations in the maturity stage of the organizational life cycle with a stable domain.

3. The Caretaker This proposed style fits executives managing organizations that have been described in the strategy literature as 'dogs' (BCG), 'contraction strategy'[32] and generally retrenchment strategy, be it divesting, holding, liquidating or harvesting.[33]

The caretaker can be described as strong, dominant, tolerant, calculative, selfish, specialized, hard nosed, budget efficient, priority oriented, legalistic, introverted, status quo man and dogmatic.

The caretaker fits organizations in the declining stage (retrenchment) where cash flow is the name of the game.

4. The Visionary This proposed style fits executives managing organizations that have been described in the strategy literature as turnaround.[34]

The visionary can be described as a strong, hard nosed leader/manager with flair and an analytical mind. They seek challenges and take calculated risks. They set flexible assignments of resources and short communication channels.

Their main goal is to be a winner. They are people of vision.

The visionary fits organizations that have been able to move from a stagnating decline to growth again.

Table 1 presents a model of strategy – leader fit based on the research findings.

Implication – human resource strategy

As Tichy[35] pointed out, our organizations need to apply more strategically oriented approaches to human resource management to gain competitive edge in the 1980s. The model described in this research achieves such alignment between strategy and human resources. The model could be utilized by many firms, specifically firms that are in a process of changing strategic direction, or entering a different stage in the organization life cycle. Human resource management could play an important role in implementing this model. We suggest the following propositions:

1. The assessment center methods be utilized in managerial selection of key tasks. The method has been used successfully to identify potential executives that fit different organization climates.

2. Human resource management must constantly scan the external and internal environment looking for the right people to achieve effective alignment with corporate strategy. This requires an efficient and possibly computerized data base that provides the organization with profiles and assessments of executives.

3. The promotion pattern should be modified to match the intended strategy.[36] Executive promotion should be based on the values and skills required under different strategic directions. Again, assessment center reports could be helpful here.

4. The reward system should also be modified to match the intended change in strategy.

Table 1
Strategic Fit – A Model of Strategy – Leader Fit

	Strategic Direction	Characteristics of the Style
1. The Entrepreneur	Developing/ Aggressive Growth	Innovative, creative, intuitive, flexible, extrovert, optimistic, motivated, excitable, dominant, risk-taker, and little consultation with employees.
2. The Professional	Maturity/ Stable Domain (Neutral)	Team player, bureaucratic, conformist, systematic, stable, calm, cautious, mature, friendly, conservative, decisions are based on facts and consultation, slow to change and to meet increases in threat, a skilled executive.
3. The Caretaker	Decline/ Retrenchment	Strong, tolerant, calculative, selfish, specialized, budget efficient, hard nosed, priority oriented.
4. The Visionary	Turnaround	Strong, hard nosed, flair, analytical, seeks challenge and takes calculative risk, replaces mediocrity, very demanding, flexible assignment of resources, short communication channels, non conformity, his main goal is to be a winner.

Specifically, the reward system should be able to support both short and long term strategic goals. The key to an effective reward system is to ensure that people under different strategic directions continue to perceive that significant career opportunities are available to them.

5. Training and development. The purpose of this step is to reorient and introduce human resources to the critical thrust of the strategic change and what kind of organization should follow. Skills, attitudes and values are the core of such induction and training.

CONCLUSION

The purpose of this paper is to present some findings for a research project that investigates the relation between executive personality and its values on one hand and the corporate strategic direction on the other hand. Four distinct leadership styles that match different strategic direction have been proposed in this research: the entrepreneur; the professional; the caretaker, and the visionary.

The present research suggests that there is no way to divorce executive values, motivation, expectations, and perception from the strategic decision process. A model of strategy formulation was proposed to account for the above factors. Clearly this paper demonstrates an important issue: the paradox that those things that accounted for early success were among the very things that had to be changed to ensure long run success.

Finally this study suggests that, the most successful organizations in the years ahead will be those that best match top executives with their strategic direction. It is the CEO who sets the tone for the entire organization.

References

1. T.S. Kuhn (1970) *The Structure of Scientific Revolutions*. Chicago: University of Chicago Press.
2. L. Sank (1974) "Effective and Ineffective Managerial Traits Obtained as Naturalistic Descriptions from Executive Members of a Super Corporation." *Personnel Psychology*, 27, pp. 423–434.
3. R.M. Stogdill (1974) *Handbook of Leadership: A Survey of Theory and Research*. New York: The Free Press.
4. F.E. Fiedler (1967) *A Theory of Leadership Effectiveness*. New York: McGraw-Hill.
5. R.J. House and T.R. Mitchell (1974) "A Path-Goal Theory of Leadership." *Journal of Contemporary Business*, 3(4), pp. 81–97.
6. A. Kaplan (1963) *The Conduct of Inquiry: Methodology for Behavioral Science*. New York: Harper and Row Publishers.
7. T.S. Kuhn (1970) *op. cit.*
8. J.C. Hunt and L.L. Larson (1977) "Some Additional Facets of the Cutting Edge: An Epilog," in J.G. Hunt and L.L. Larson, eds., *Leadership: The Cutting Edge*. Carbondale, IL: Southern Illinois University Press.
9. P.N. Khandwalla (1977) "Some Top Management Styles, Their Context and Performance." *Organization and Administrative Sciences*, 7, 4, pp. 21–51.
10. I.H. Ansoff (1965) *Corporate Strategy: An Analytical Approach to Business Policy for Growth and Expansion*. New York:
11. I. Adizes (1979) "Organizational Passages – Diagnosing and Treating Life Cycle Problems of Organizations." *Organizational Dynamics*, 4, pp. 110–116.
12. J.G. Wissema, H.W. Vander Pol, and H.M. Messer (1980) "Strategic Management Archetypes." *Strategic Management Journal*, 1, pp. 237–253.
13. D. Miller, M. Dets de Vries, and J.M. Toulouse (1982) "Top Executive Locus of Control and Its Relationship to Strategy-Making, Structure, and Environment." *Academy of Management Journal*, 25, 2, pp. 237–253.
14. A.D. Chandler (1962) *Strategy and Structure: Chapters in the History of the American Industrial Enterprise*. Cambridge, MA: MIT Press.
15. I.H. Ansoff (1965) *op. cit.*

16. C.W. Hofer and D. Schendel (1978) *Strategy Formulation: Analytical Concepts*. St. Paul, MN: West Publishing.
17. H. Mintzberg and I. Walters (1980) *Tracking Strategy in an Entrepreneurial Firm*. Montreal: McGill University.
18. J.G. Wissema *et al.* (1980) *op. cit.*
19. *Ibid.*
20. D. Miller *et al.* (1982) *op. cit.*
21. P.N. Khandwalla (1977) *op. cit.*
22. J.G. Wissema *et al.* (1980) *op. cit.*
23. R. Miles, C. Snow, A. Meyer, H. Coleman, Jr. (1978) "Organizational Strategy, Structure, and Process," *Academy of Management Review*, 3, 7, pp. 546–562.
24. I.H. Ansoff (1965) *op. cit.*
25. I.H. Ansoff (1978) *Corporate Capability for Managing Change*. SRI International.
26. I. Adizes (1979) *op. cit.*
27. J.G. Wissema *et al.* (1980) *op. cit.*
28. R. Miles *et al.* (1978) *op. cit.*
29. *Ibid.*
30. J.G. Wissema *et al.* (1980) *op. cit.*
31. R. Miles *et al.* (1978) *op. cit.*
32. J.G. Wissema *et al.* (1980) *op. cit.*
33. C.W. Hofer *et al.* (1978) *op. cit.*
34. *Ibid.*
35. N. Tichy (1983) *Managing Strategic Change: Technical, Political, and Cultural Dynamics*. New York: Wiley.
36. N. Tichy, C. Fombrun, and M.A. Devanna (1982) "Strategic Human Resource Management." *Sloan Management Review*, Winter, pp. 47–60.

ORGANIZATION DESIGN: AN INFORMATION PROCESSING VIEW*

Jay R. Galbraith

THE INFORMATION PROCESSING MODEL

A basic proposition is that the greater the uncertainty of the task, the greater the amount of information that has to be processed between decision makers during the execution of the task. If the task is well understood prior to performing it, much of the activity can be preplanned. If it is not understood, then during the actual task execution more knowledge is acquired which leads to changes in resource allocations, schedules, and priorities. All these changes require information processing *during* task performance. Therefore *the greater the task uncertainty, the greater the amount of information that must be processed among decision makers during task execution in order to achieve a given level of performance*. The basic effect of uncertainty is to limit the ability of the organization to preplan or to make decisions about activities in advance of their execution. Therefore it is hypothesized that the observed variations in organizational forms are variations in the strategies or organizations to (1) increase their ability to preplan, (2) increase their flexibility to adapt to their inability to preplan, or (3) to decrease the level of performance required for continued viability. Which strategy is chosen depends on the relative costs of the strategies. The function of the framework is to identify these strategies and their costs.

---

* "Organization Design: An Information Processing View," by J.R. Galbraith was prepared for *Interfaces*, Vol. 4, No. 3, May 1974. Copyright 1974. Reprinted by permission of the author and the publisher.

THE MECHANISTIC MODEL

This framework is best developed by keeping in mind a hypothetical organization. Assume it is large and employs a number of specialist groups and resources in providing the output. After the task has been divided into specialist subtasks, the problem is to integrate the subtasks around the completion of the global task. This is the problem of organization design. The behaviors that occur in one subtask cannot be judged as good or bad *per se*. The behaviors are more effective or ineffective depending upon the behaviors of the other subtask performers. There is a design problem because the executors of the behaviors cannot communicate with all the roles with whom they are interdependent. Therefore, the design problem is to create mechanisms that permit coordinated action across large numbers of interdependent roles. Each of these mechanisms, however, has a limited range over which it is effective at handling the information requirements necessary to coordinate the interdependent roles. As the amount of uncertainty increases, and therefore information processing increases, the organization must adopt integrating mechanisms which increase its information processing capabilities.

Coordination by Rules or Programs

For routine predictable tasks March and Simon have identified the use of rules or programs to coordinate behavior between interdependent subtasks (March and Simon, 1958, Chapter 6).[1] To the extent that job related situations can be predicted in advance, and behaviors specified for these situations, programs allow an interdependent set of activities to be performed without the need for interunit communication. Each role occupant simply executes the behavior which is appropriate for the task related situation with which he is faced.

Hierarchy

As the organization faces greater uncertainty its participants face situations for which they have no rules. At this point the hierarchy is employed on an exception basis. The recurring job situations are programmed with rules while infrequent situations are referred to that level in the hierarchy where a global perspective exists for all affected subunits. However, the hierarchy also has a limited range. As uncertainty increases the number of exceptions increases until the hierarchy becomes overloaded.

Coordination by Targets or Goals

As the uncertainty of the organization's task increases, coordination increasingly takes place by specifying outputs, goals, or targets (March and Simon, 1958, p. 145).[2] Instead of specifying specific behaviors to be enacted, the organization undertakes processes to set goals to be achieved and the employees select the behaviors which lead to goal accomplishment. Planning reduces the amount of information processing in the hierarchy by increasing the amount of discretion exercised at lower levels. Like the use of rules, planning achieves integrated action and also eliminates the need for continuous communication among interdependent subunits as long as task performance stays within the planned task specifications, budget limits and within targeted completion dates. If it does not, the hierarchy is again employed on an exception basis.

The ability of an organization to coordinate interdependent tasks depends on its ability to compute meaningful subgoals to guide subunit action. When uncertainty increases because of introducing new products, entering new markets, or employing new technologies these subgoals are incorrect. The result is more exceptions, more information processing, and an overloaded hierarchy.

DESIGN STRATEGIES

The ability of an organization to successfully utilize coordination by goal setting, hierarchy, and rules depends on the combination of the frequency of exceptions and the capacity of the hierarchy to handle them. As the task uncertainty increases, the organization must again take organization design action. It can proceed in either of two general ways. First, it can act in two ways to reduce the amount of information that is processed. And second, the organization can act in two ways to increase its capacity to handle more information. The two methods for reducing the need for information and the two methods for increasing processing capacity are shown schematically in Figure 1. The effect of all these actions is to reduce the number of exceptional cases referred upward into the organization through hierarchical channels. The assumption is that the critical limiting factor of an organizational form is its ability to handle the nonroutine, consequential events that cannot be anticipated and planned for in advance. The nonprogrammed events place the greatest communication load on the organization.

Creation of Slack Resources

As the number of exceptions begin to overload the hierarchy, one response is to increase the planning targets so that fewer exceptions occur. For example, completion dates can be extended until the number of exceptions that occur are within the existing information processing capacity of the organization. This has been the practice in solving job shop scheduling problems (Pounds, 1963).[3] Job shops quote delivery times that are long enough to keep the scheduling problem within the computational and information processing limits of the organization. Since every job shop has the same problem standard lead times evolve in the industry. Similarly, budget targets could be raised, buffer inventories employed, and so on. The greater the uncertainty, the greater the magnitude of the inventory, lead time or budget needed to reduce an overload.

All of these examples have a similar effect. They represent the use of slack resources to reduce the amount of interdependence between subunits (March and Simon, 1958, Cyert and March, 1963).[4] This keeps the required amount of information within the capacity of the organization to process it. Information processing is reduced because an exception is less likely to occur and

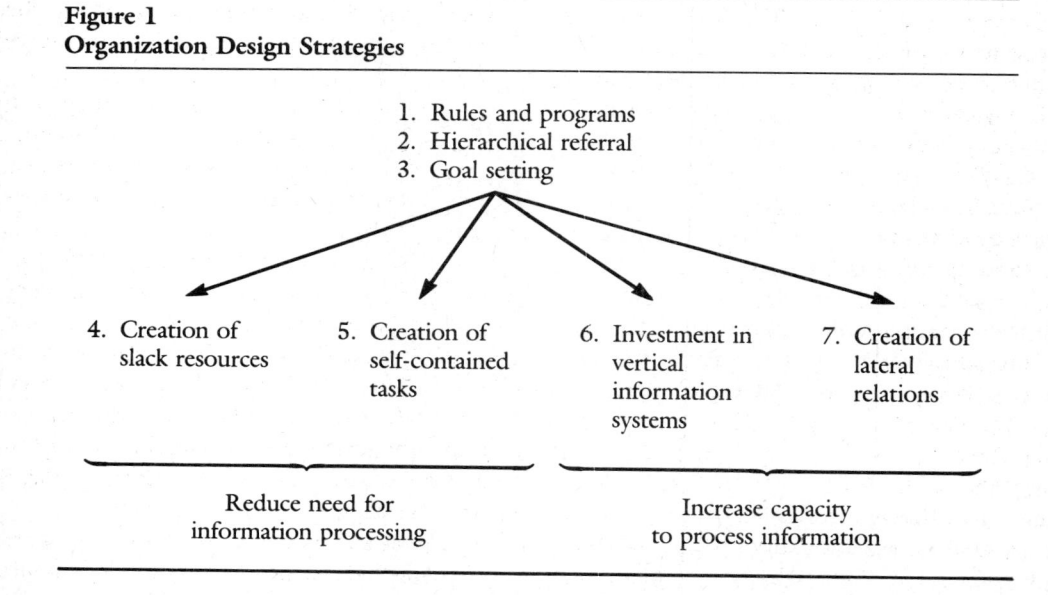

Figure 1
Organization Design Strategies

1. Rules and programs
2. Hierarchical referral
3. Goal setting

4. Creation of slack resources
5. Creation of self-contained tasks
6. Investment in vertical information systems
7. Creation of lateral relations

Reduce need for information processing | Increase capacity to process information

reduced interdependence means that fewer factors need to be considered simultaneously when an exception does occur.

The strategy of using slack resources has its costs. Relaxing budget targets has the obvious cost of requiring more budget. Increasing the time to completion date has the effect of delaying the customer. Inventories require the investment of capital funds which could be used elsewhere. Reduction of design optimization reduces the performance of the article being designed. Whether slack resources are used to reduce information or not depends on the relative cost of the other alternatives.

The design choices are: (1) among which factors to change (lead time, overtime, machine utilization, and the like) to create the slack, and (2) by what amount should the factor be changed. Many operations research models are useful in choosing factors and amounts. The time-cost trade-off problem in project networks is a good example.

Creation of Self-Contained Tasks

The second method of reducing the amount of information processed is to change the subtask groupings from resource (input) based to output based categories and give each group the resources it needs to supply the output. For example, the functional organization could be changed to product groups. Each group would have its own product engineers, process engineers, fabricating and assembly operations, and marketing activities. In other situations, groups can be created around product lines, geographical areas, projects, client groups, markets, and so on, each of which would contain the input resources necessary for creation of the output.

The strategy of self-containment shifts the basis of the authority structure from one based on input, resource skill, or occupational categories to one based on output or geographical categories. The shift reduces the amount of information processing through several mechanisms. First, it reduces the amount of output diversity faced by a single-collection of resources. For example, a professional organization with multiple skill specialties providing service to three different client groups must schedule the use of these specialties across three demands for their services and determine priorities when conflicts occur. But, if the organization changed to three groups, one for each client category, each with its own full complement of specialties, the schedule conflicts across client groups disappear and there is no need to process information to determine priorities.

The second source of information reduction occurs through a reduced division of labor. The functional or resource specialized structure pools the demand for skills across all output categories. In the example above each client generates approximately one third of the demand for each skill. Since the division of labor is limited by the extent of the market, the division of labor must decrease as the demand decreases. In the professional organization, each client group may have generated a need for one third of a computer programmer. The functional organization would have hired one programmer and shared him across the groups. In the self-contained structure there is insufficient demand in each group for a programmer so the professionals must do their own programming. Specialization is reduced but there is no problem of scheduling the programmer's time across the three possible uses for it.

The cost of the self-containment strategy is the loss of resource specialization. In the example, the organization forgoes the benefit of a specialist in computer programming. If there is physical equipment, there is a loss of economies of scale. The professional organization would require three machines in the self-contained form but only a large time-shared machine in the functional form. But those resources which have large economies of scale or for which specialization is necessary may remain centralized. Thus, it is the degree of self-containment that is the variable. The greater the degree of uncertainty, other things equal, the greater the degree of self-containment.

The design choices are the basis for the self-contained structure and the number of resources to be contained in the groups. No groups are completely self-contained or they would not be part of the same organization. But one product divisionalized firm may have 8 of 15 functions in the division while another may have 12 of 15 in the division. Usually accounting, finance, and legal services are centralized and shared. Those functions which have economies of scale, require specialization, or are necessary for control remain centralized and not part of the self-contained group.

The first two strategies reduced the amount of information by lower performance standards and creating small autonomous groups to provide the output. Information is reduced because an exception is less likely to occur and fewer factors need to be considered when an exception does occur. The next two strategies accept the performance standards and division of labor as given and adapt the organization so as to process the new information which is created during task performance.

Investment in Vertical Information Systems

The organization can invest in mechanisms which allow it to process information acquired during task performance without overloading the hierarchical communication channels. The investment occurs according to the following logic. After the organization has created its plan or set of targets for inventories, labor utilization, budgets, and schedules, unanticipated events occur which generate exceptions requiring adjustments to the original plan. At some point when the number of exceptions becomes substantial, it is preferable to generate a new plan rather than make incremental changes with each exception. The issue is then how frequently should plans be revised – yearly, quarterly, or monthly? The greater the frequency of replanning the greater the resources, such as clerks, computer time, input-output devices, and the like, required to process information about relevant factors.

The cost of information-processing resources can be minimized if the language is formalized. Formalization of a decision-making language simply means that more information is transmitted with the same number of symbols. It is assumed that information processing resources are consumed in proportion to the number of symbols transmitted. The accounting system is an example of a formalized language.

Providing more information, more often, may simply overload the decision maker. Investment may be required to increase the capacity of the decision maker by employing computers, various man-machine combinations, assistants-to, and so on. The cost of this strategy is the cost of the information-processing resources consumed in transmitting and processing data.

The design variables of this strategy are the decision frequency, the degree of formalization of language, and the type of decision mechanism which will make the choice. This strategy is usually operationalized by creating redundant information channels which transmit data from the point of origination upward in the hierarchy where the point of decision rests. If data is formalized and quantifiable, this strategy is effective. If the relevant data are qualitative and ambiguous, then it may prove easier to bring the decision down to where the information exists.

Creation of Lateral Relationships

The best strategy is to employ selectively joint decision processes which cut across lines of authority. This strategy moves the level of decision making down in the organization to where the information exists but does so without reorganizing around self-contained groups. There are several types of lateral decision processes. Some processes are usually referred to as the informal organization. However, these informal processes do not always arise spontaneously out of the needs of the task. This is particularly true in multinational organizations in which participants are separated by physical barriers, language differences, and cultural differences. Under these circumstances lateral processes need to be designed. The lateral processes evolve as follows with increases in uncertainty.

Direct contact Between managers who share a problem. If a problem arises on the shop floor, the foreman can simply call the design engineer, and they can jointly agree upon a solution. From an information processing view, the joint decision prevents an upward referral and unloads the hierarchy.

Liaison roles When the volume of contacts between any two departments grows, it becomes economical to set up a specialized role to handle this communication. Liaison men are typical examples of specialized roles designed to facilitate communication between two interdependent departments and to bypass the long lines of communication involved in upward referral, Liaison roles arise at lower and middle levels of management.

Task forces Direct contact and liaison roles, like the integration mechanisms before them, have a limited range of usefulness. They work when two managers or functions are involved. When problems arise involving seven or eight departments, the decision-making capacity of direct contacts is exceeded. Then these problems must be referred upward. For uncertain, interdependent tasks such situations arise frequently. Task forces are a form of horizontal contact which is designed for problems of multiple departments.

The task force is made up of representatives from each of the affected departments. Some are full-time members, others may be part-time. The task force is a temporary group. It exists only as long as the problem remains. When a solution is reached, each participant returns to his normal tasks.

To the extent that they are successful, task forces remove problems from higher levels of the hierarchy. The decisions are made at lower levels in the organization. In order to guarantee integration, a group problem-solving approach is taken. Each affected subunit contributes a member and therefore provides the information necessary to judge the impact on all units.

Teams The next extension is to incorporate the group decision process into the permanent decision processes. That is, as certain decisions consistently arise, the task forces become permanent. These groups are labeled teams. There are many design issues concerned in team decision making such as at what level do they operate, who participates, and so on (Galbraith, 1973, chaps. 6 and 7).[5] One design decision is particularly critical. This is the choice of leadership. Sometimes a problem exists largely in one department so that the department manager is the leader. Sometimes the leadership passes from one manager to another. As a new product moves to the market place, the leader of the new product team is first the technical manager followed by the production and then the marketing manager. The result is that, if the team cannot reach a consensus decision and the leader decides, the goals of the leader are consistent with the goals of the organization for the decision in question. But quite often obvious leaders cannot be found. Another mechanism must be introduced.

Integrating roles The leadership issue is solved by creating a new role – an integrating role (Lawrence and Lorsch, 1967, Chap. 3).[6] These roles carry the labels of product managers, program managers, project managers, unit managers (hospitals), materials managers, and the like. After the role is created, the design problem is to create enough power in the role to influence the decision process. These roles have power even when no one reports directly to them. They have some power because they report to the general manager. But if they are selected so as to be unbiased with respect to the groups they integrate and to have technical competence, they have expert power. They collect information and equalize power differences due to preferential access to knowledge and information. The power equalization increases trust and the quality of the joint decision process. But power equalization occurs only if the integrating role is staffed with someone who can exercise expert power in the form of persuasion and informal influences rather than exert the power of rank or authority.

Managerial linking roles As tasks become more uncertain, it is more difficult to exercise expert power. The role must get more power of the formal authority type in order to be effective at coordinating the joint decisions which occur at lower levels of the organization. This position power changes the nature of the role which for lack of a better name is labeled a managerial linking role. It is not like the integrating role because it possesses formal position power but is different from line managerial roles in that participants do not report to the linking manager. The power is added by the following successive changes:

a. The integrator receives approval power of budgets formulated in the departments to be integrated.
b. The planning and budgeting process starts with the integrator making his initiation in budgeting legitimate.
c. Linking manager receives the budget for the area of responsibility and buys resources from the specialist groups.

These mechanisms permit the manager to exercise influence even though no one works directly for him. The role is concerned with integration but exercises power through the formal power of the position. If this power is insufficient to integrate the subtasks and creation of self-contained groups is not feasible, there is one last step.

Matrix organization The last step is to create the dual authority relationship and the matrix organization (Galbraith, 1971).[7] At some point in the organization some roles have two superiors. The design issue is to select the locus of these roles. The result is a balance of power between the managerial linking roles and the normal line organization roles. Figure 2 depicts the pure matrix design.

The work of Lawrence and Lorsch is highly consistent with the assertions concerning lateral relations (Lawrence and Lorsch, 1967, Lorsch and Lawrence, 1968).[8] They compared the types of lateral relations undertaken by the most successful firm in three different industries. Their data are summarized in Table 1. The plastics firm has the greatest rate of new product introduction (uncertainty) and the greatest utilization of lateral processes. The container firm was also very successful but utilized only standard practices because its information processing task is much less formidable. Thus, the greater the uncertainty the lower the level of decision making and the integration is maintained by lateral relations.

Table 1 points out the cost of using lateral relations. The plastics firm has 22 percent of its managers in integration roles. Thus, the greater

Table 1

	Plastics	Food	Container
Percent new products in last 10 years	35 percent	20 percent	0 percent
Integrating devices	Rules	Rules	Rules
	Hierarchy	Hierarchy	Hierarchy
	Planning	Planning	Planning
	Direct contact	Direct contact	Direct contact
	Teams at 3 levels	Task forces	
	Integrating department	Integrators	
Percent integrators/managers	22 percent	17 percent	0 percent

Source: Adopted from Lawrence and Lorsch, 1967, pp. 86–138 and Lorsch and Lawrence, 1968.

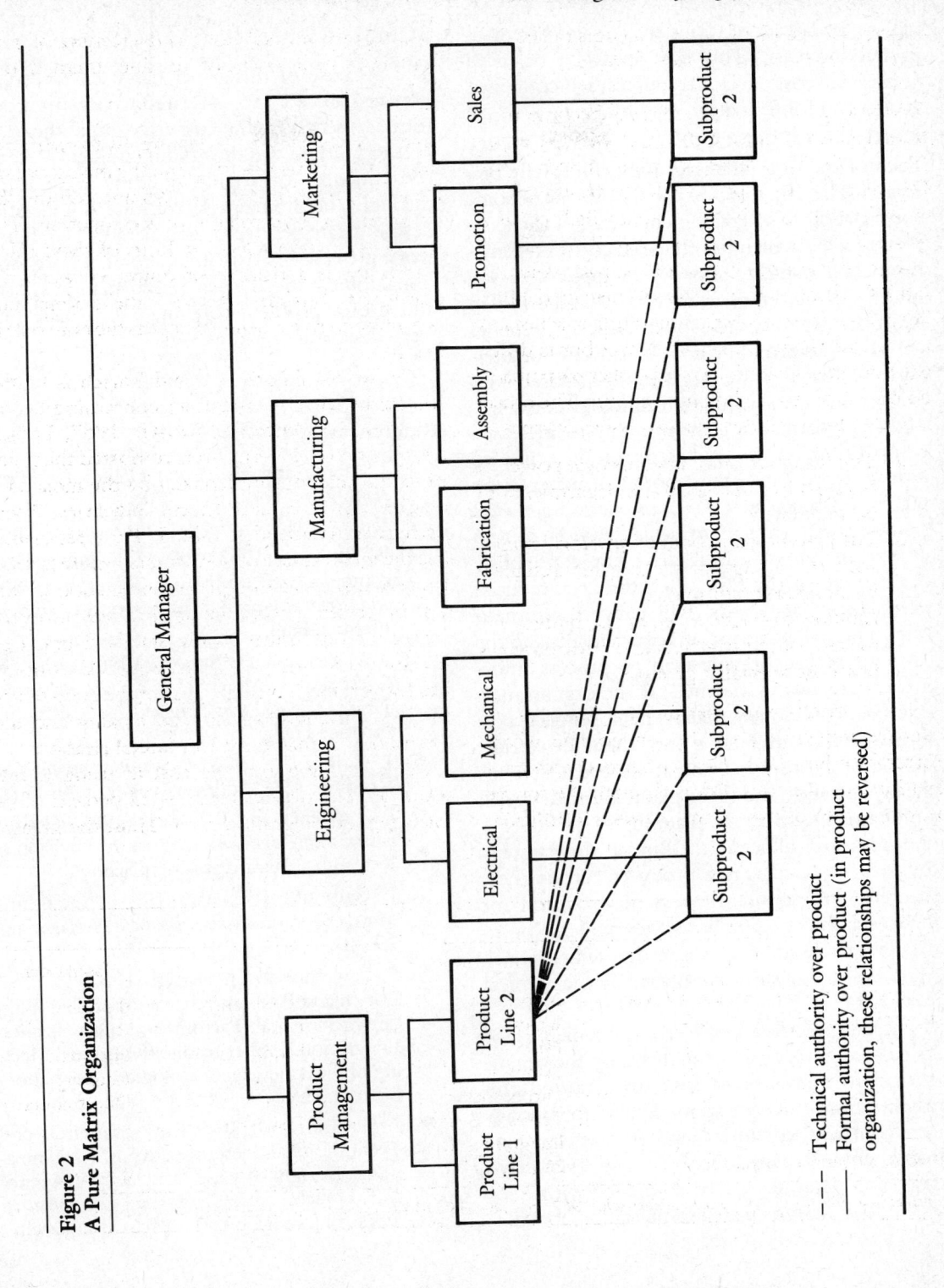

Figure 2
A Pure Matrix Organization

--- Technical authority over product
—— Formal authority over product (in product organization, these relationships may be reversed)

the use of lateral relations the greater the managerial intensity. This cost must be balanced against the cost of slack resources, self-contained groups, and information systems.

CHOICE OF STRATEGY

Each of the four strategies has been briefly presented. The organization can follow one or some combination of several if it chooses. It will choose that strategy which has the least cost in its environmental context. (For an example, see Galbraith, 1970.)[9] However, what may be lost in all of the explanations is that the four strategies are hypothesized to be an exhaustive set of alternatives. That is, if the organization is faced with greater uncertainty due to technological change, higher performance standards due to increased competition, or diversifies its product line to reduce dependence, the amount of information processing is increased. *The organization must adopt at least one of the four strategies when faced with greater uncertainty.* If it does not consciously choose one of the four, then the first, reduced performance standards, will happen automatically. The task information requirements and the capacity of the organization to process information are always matched. If the organization does not consciously match them, reduced performance through budget and schedule overruns will occur in order to bring about equality. Thus the organization should be planned and designed simultaneously with the planning of the strategy and resource allocations. But if the strategy involves introducing new products, entering new markets, and so on, then some provision for increased information must be made. Not to decide is to decide, and it is to decide upon slack resources as the strategy to remove hierarchical overload.

There is probably a fifth strategy which is not articulated here. Instead of changing the organization in response to task uncertainty, the organization, through strategic decisions, long-term contracts, coalitions, and the like, can control its environment. But these maneuvers have costs also. They should be compared with costs of the four design strategies presented above.

SUMMARY

The purpose of this paper has been to explain why task uncertainty is related to organizational form. In so doing the cognitive limits theory of Herbert Simon was the guiding influence. As the consequences of cognitive limits were traced through the framework, various organization design strategies were articulated. The framework provides a basis for integrating organizational interventions, such as information systems and group problem solving, which have been treated separately before.

References

1. J. March and H. Simon (1958) *Organizations*. New York: John Wiley.
2. *Ibid*.
3. W. Pounds (1963) "The Scheduling Environment," in Muth and Thompson, eds., *Industrial Scheduling*. Englewood Cliffs, NJ: Prentice-Hall.
4. J. March and H. Simon (1958) *op. cit*. R. Cyert and J. March (1963) *The Behavioral Theory of the Firm*. Englewood Cliffs, NJ: Prentice-Hall.
5. J. Galbraith (1973) *Organization Design*. Reading, MA: Addison-Wesley Publishing.
6. P. Lawrence and J. Lorsch (1967) *Organization and Environment*. Boston: Division of Research, Harvard Business School.
7. J. Galbraith (February 1971) "Designing Matrix Organizations." *Business Horizons*, pp. 29–40.
8. P. Lawrence and J. Lorsch (1967) *op. cit*. J. Lorsch and Paul Lawrence (August 27, 1967) "Environmental Factors and Organization Integration." Paper read at the Annual Meeting of the American Sociological Association, Boston, MA.
9. J. Galbraith (1970) "Environmental and Technological Determinants of Organizational Design: A Case Study," in Lawrence and Lorsch, eds., *Studies in Organization Design*. Homewood, IL: Richard D. Irwin.

CASES

STRATEGIC PLANNING AT ALFA ELECTRONICS INC.*

A.B. Ibrahim

ALFA Electronics Inc. was founded in Waterloo, Ontario, in 1975 by J.R. Gordon, a computer engineer. Mr. Gordon had developed a successful design for a new type of electronic security alarm system and under his leadership ALFA emerged as a major force in the electronic security alarm market. However, since 1981 the company has been experiencing a decline in profit and market share. The decline was said to have been a result of generally poor economic conditions in Canada and higher overall costs of doing business.

However, Mr. Gordon was concerned with the growth and strategic position of his company in the next decade. In May 1983, Gordon hired John Hunt, a recent MBA graduate from a leading Canadian business school, as a corporate planner and instructed him to prepare a strategic plan for ALFA as soon as possible.

John Hunt, 33, had worked in corporate planning for over 5 years with a leading American electronics firm in New York before taking his MBA, and was well qualified for his new position.

John worked assiduously during July, reading ALFA reports and its Mission Statement. The Mission Statement described the company as "a highly innovative firm in the electronic alarm field . . . ." The statement went on to outline ALFA's goals: "to grow and earn at a rate commensurate with the best in the industry." Throughout the corporation there existed a strong emphasis on growth and return on equity.

John also set out to gather information about the internal capabilities of ALFA in different functional areas such as production, finance and marketing. Functional managers were invited to write a brief report assessing their area's strengths and weaknesses. The following is a summary of their report.

PRODUCTION

ALFA produces electronic security alarm systems and has recently introduced a new

---

* This case was prepared by Dr. A.B. Ibrahim of Concordia University as a basis for class discussion rather than to illustrate either effective or ineffective handling of an administrative situation. Copyright © 1986 by Professor A.B. Ibrahim. Used by permission of the author.

line of fire protection equipment. The electronic security alarm system is of superior quality and technically advanced. However, ALFA has very little experience in fire protection equipment. The company has recently modernized its production facilities, but production lines are working at only 80 percent capacity.

FINANCE

The company has a strong financial position. ALFA has a very high liquidity ratio and its debt ratio is below average in this type of business. However, the inventory turnover for fire protection equipment is very low.

MARKETING

The company employs three energetic sales people who travel extensively to Toronto, Montréal and Vancouver on a salary/commission base. Lately, however, the sales people have been complaining that ALFA's fire protection equipment is not doing well in the market.

ALFA has 64 percent of the Canadian security alarm market, mostly in Québec and Ontario. Its main competitors are small Swedish and Dutch firms. However ALFA is facing stiff competition in the fire protection equipment line, with three large Canadian and American firms competing for 86 percent of the Canadian market and more than 30 small firms competing for the remaining 9 percent.

Demand analysis indicated customers prefer ALFA electronic security alarm systems because of their high quality and advanced technology. Demand analysis also indicates an increase in demand for alarm systems in Québec because of provincial regulations

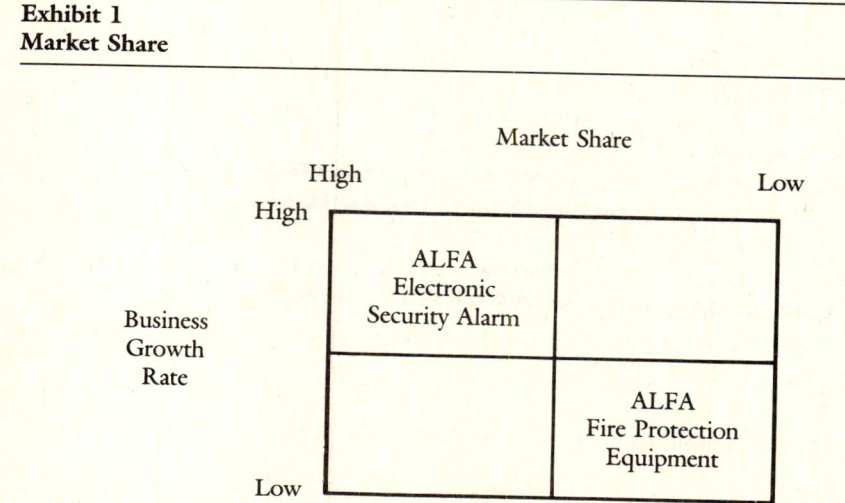

Exhibit 1
Market Share

	Market Share	
Business Growth Rate	High	Low
High	ALFA Electronic Security Alarm	
Low		ALFA Fire Protection Equipment

regarding security in public buildings. However, demand for ALFA's fire protection is expected to decline because of stiff competition (large competitors depend on mass production, low price, high quality and a large dealer network).

External analysis revealed that the Ontario government has started a 5 year tax exemption program for small business in the high technology industry.

Based on the above data John utilized the Boston Consulting Matrix (BCG) to identify the business growth rate and market share for the electronic fire alarm and fire protection equipment that ALFA produces (see Exhibit 1).

John decided that there was a need for selecting alternative strategies of ALFA and making a strategic choice after assessing each alternative. John had come up with two alternatives available to ALFA: (1) to drop the fire protection equipment line and to focus on ALFA Electronic Fire Alarm systems, (2) to pursue an aggressive growth strategy in both fire alarm and fire protection. John had to assess each alternative before reporting his final recommendations.

QUESTIONS

1. Based on the information provided in this case, assess each alternative.
2. Which alternative strategy would you recommend for ALFA? Why?
3. Evaluate John's strategic plan.

CHEMCO INTERNATIONAL INC.*

B.J. Austin

As the New York commuter flight halted at Toronto's International Airport, Alan Richardson, President of Chemco Inc. closed his briefcase and fished his sportsbag containing the week's laundry from under his seat. Chemco's Vice-President, Bill Ross, mechanically repeated the exercise. For the past year Richardson and Ross had shared the company's New York apartment as they put in 15-hour days managing Mundt Inc., an American company acquired by Chemco a year previously. Most weekends the two men caught a Friday evening flight home to Toronto. Over the past year flights to Mundt's European operation in Brussels, as well as to its joint ventures in South America and the Far East, had become routine. Richardson broke the tired silence. "See you tomorrow Bill, among all of us we ought to work out something to get us off this grindstone."

Richardson's wife was waiting in the short-term parking area rehearsing amusing ways to tell him about the latest crises of their three teenage daughters and the current

---

* This case was prepared by Dr. B.J. Austin as a basis for class discussion rather than to illustrate either effective or ineffective handling of an administrative situation.
Copyright © 1987 by Professor B.J. Austin. Used by permission of the author.

list of home repair jobs she had coped with. Richardson could only offer suggestions. He would spend Saturday discussing restructuring alternatives in the executive committee meeting at Chemco's Toronto head office and on Sunday evening catch a flight back to New York. He hoped that this Sunday his wife would prepare a family meal instead of telephoning for takeout food as she had done for the past few months.

Chemco was founded in 1927 as Ontario Chemical Company, an amalgamation of several small firms supplying industrial chemicals to the agricultural, mining, and pulp and paper industries. Originally the firm was highly centralized, with all orders coming down from the President. The Selling Department had sold mostly to wholesalers. In the 1950s the sales department had been enlarged and organized into product divisions.

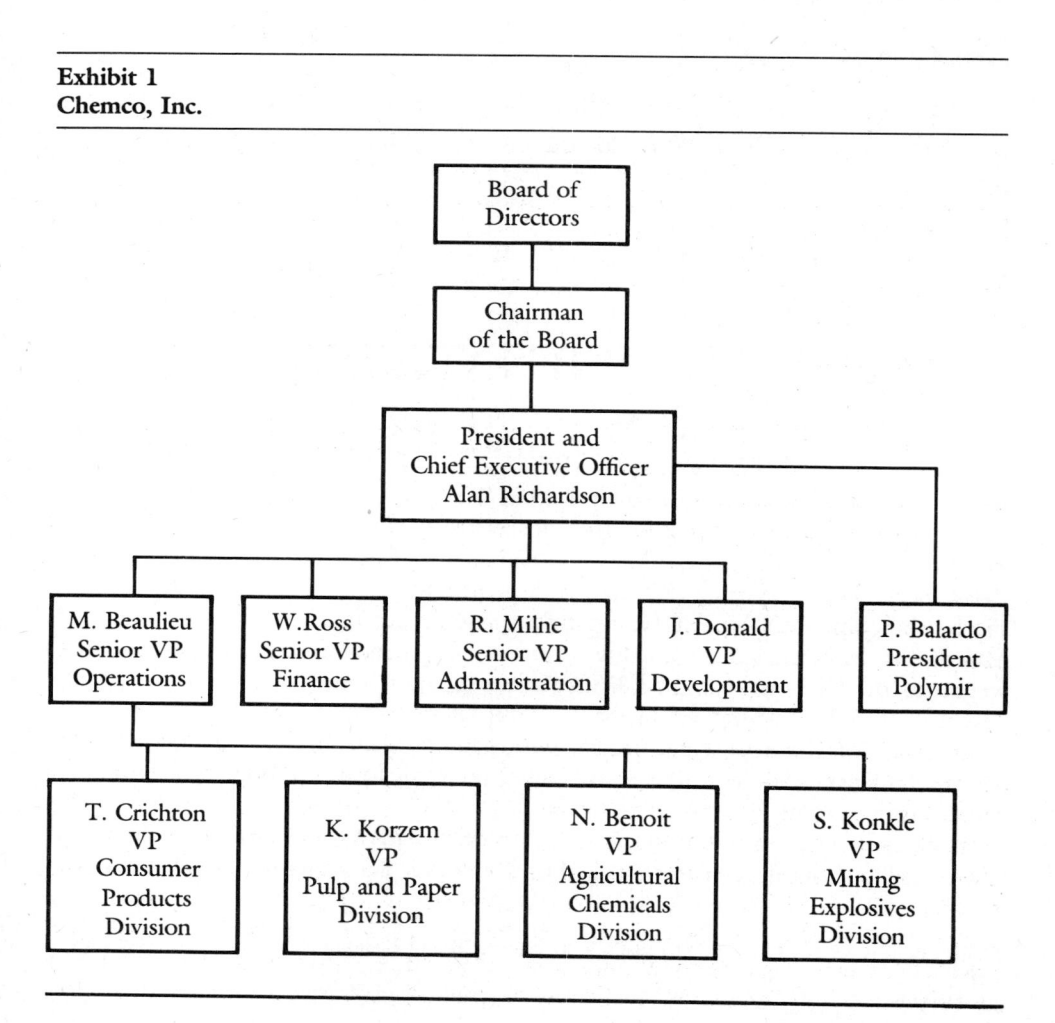

Exhibit 1
Chemco, Inc.

```
                        Board of Directors
                               |
                      Chairman of the Board
                               |
                   President and Chief Executive Officer
                            Alan Richardson
    _____|_____
    |              |              |              |              |
M. Beaulieu     W. Ross       R. Milne      J. Donald     P. Balardo
Senior VP      Senior VP     Senior VP         VP         President
Operations     Finance      Administration  Development    Polymir
    |
    |_____
    |              |              |              |
T. Crichton   K. Korzem      N. Benoit     S. Konkle
    VP           VP             VP             VP
 Consumer    Pulp and Paper  Agricultural     Mining
 Products      Division       Chemicals     Explosives
 Division                     Division       Division
```

Exhibit 2
Mundt Inc.

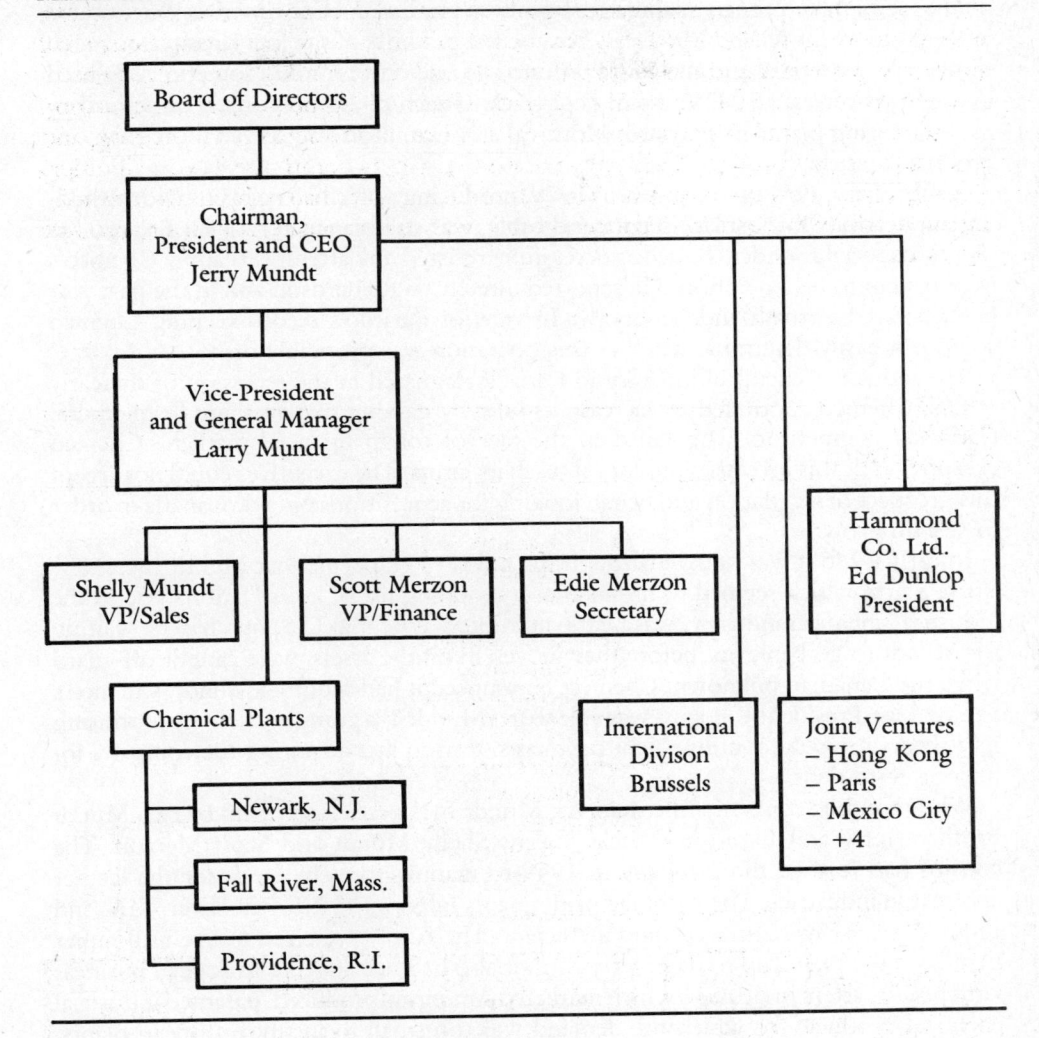

```
                    ┌─────────────────────┐
                    │ Board of Directors  │
                    └──────────┬──────────┘
                               │
                    ┌──────────┴──────────┐
                    │    Chairman,        │
                    │ President and CEO   │──────────────────────┬───────────────┐
                    │   Jerry Mundt       │                      │               │
                    └──────────┬──────────┘                      │               │
                               │                                 │               │
                    ┌──────────┴──────────┐                      │               │
                    │  Vice-President     │                      │               │
                    │ and General Manager │                      │               │
                    │   Larry Mundt       │                      │               │
                    └─────┬────┬────┬─────┘                      │      ┌────────┴────────┐
                          │    │    │                            │      │   Hammond       │
                          │    │    │                            │      │   Co. Ltd.      │
                          │    │    │                            │      │   Ed Dunlop     │
                          │    │    │                            │      │   President     │
          ┌───────────────┤    │    │                            │      └────────┬────────┘
          │               │    │    │                            │               │
  ┌───────┴──────┐  ┌─────┴────┐  ┌─┴──────────┐      ┌──────────┴───────┐  ┌────┴─────────────┐
  │ Shelly Mundt │  │Scott Merzon│ │Edie Merzon │      │ International    │  │ Joint Ventures   │
  │   VP/Sales   │  │ VP/Finance │ │ Secretary  │      │   Division       │  │ – Hong Kong      │
  └───────┬──────┘  └────────────┘ └────────────┘      │   Brussels       │  │ – Paris          │
          │                                            └──────────────────┘  │ – Mexico City    │
  ┌───────┴───────┐                                                          │ – +4             │
  │Chemical Plants│                                                          └──────────────────┘
  └───────┬───────┘
          ├──────────┬─────────────┐
          │          │             │
  ┌───────┴────┐ ┌───┴──────────┐ ┌┴───────────────┐
  │Newark, N.J.│ │Fall River,   │ │Providence, R.I.│
  │            │ │  Mass.       │ │                │
  └────────────┘ └──────────────┘ └────────────────┘
```

In 1972 Chemco gradually began decentralizing management into four product divisions based on its major product lines – pulp and paper chemicals, agricultural products, mining explosives and consumer products, a branded line of chemicals for swimming pools and water purification. At the same time the corporate name was shortened to Chemco Inc. to reflect its sales to industrial and consumer clients across Canada. The divisionalized structure allowed senior executives time to examine long range plans, freeing them from being constantly concerned with day-to-day operating decisions. Each of the divisions was responsible for its own accounting, marketing and human resource functions. All divisions operated out of the company's Toronto headquarters. Until the acquisition of Mundt Inc., the Senior Vice-Presidents had been in day-to-day contact with the divisional Vice-Presidents.

The firm's three primary manufacturing plants producing basic materials were located in Welland, Cornwall and Montréal. Because the products of the four divisions required similar raw materials, and the waste products of one process could sometimes be used in other processes, an MIS system kept track of each division's costs. The secondary manufacturing plants in Toronto, Montréal and Hamilton also served more than one product division.

A subsidiary, Polymir, acquired in 1979, producing polyethelene resins with moulding applications for insulating wire and cable, was still managed by Paul Balardo, its entrepreneurial founder. Balardo successfully resisted any attempt to apply Chemco's MIS system to his operation. He reported directly to Richardson and in the past year had operated virtually independently. In view of Balardo's record-keeping Chemco could not easily determine whether this operation was profitable or not.

The industrial chemical industry in Canada stagnated in the recession of the early 1980s. Chemco continued to increase its sales by gaining market share from several Canadian competitors who failed in the face of tough financial markets. Chemco executives felt this growth would soon reach its limits. The executives could not accept this prospect of stagnation and began looking for acquisitions outside Canada in order to sustain growth.

In early 1986 it was known through the industry grapevine that Mundt Inc., New York, a firm which seemed to fit Chemco's shopping list of a firm half its size in the industrial chemical industry, was near bankruptcy. Potential U.S. purchasers, waiting for Mundt to go bankrupt before they moved in on the assets, were caught off guard when the Canadian unknown, Chemco, announced it had acquired Mundt. Chemco's Senior Vice-President Bill Ross was able to get Mundt as a going concern by promising its debtors it would continue debt payments, thus in fact acquiring the company for its long term debt.

While a public company, the shares of Mundt Inc. were closely held by two Mundt brothers Jerry and Larry, and their cousins Shelly Mundt and Scott Merzon. The cousins had formed the company in 1949 to manufacture chemicals for the leather and textile industries. The manufacturing plants in Newark, NJ, Fall River, MA, and Providence, RI were now old and inefficient. The family preferred to live well rather than keep the plants up to date. Jerry Mundt also had developed a European business with headquarters in Brussels which marketed American-produced, patented industrial chemical products for which the demand was too small to justify European plants. This moderately profitable business was operated as an International Division from New York. Jerry Mundt also set up joint ventures manufacturing leather and textile chemicals, based on friendships made in the industry, with partners in Hong Kong, Mexico City, Rio de Janeiro, Barcelona, Cape Town, Milan and Paris.

In 1982 Mundt Inc. financed, through short term bank loans, the acquisition of Hammond Chemicals Co. Ltd., a company with a modern profitable plant in Syracuse, NY, producing polyethelene resins for insulating cable wire. Ed Dunlop, Hammond's President, reported directly to Jerry Mundt. While Hammond was the most profitable part of Mundt, the debt charges on the bank loans had brought Mundt virtually to bankruptcy before its acquisition.

Executive positions at Mundt Inc. were filled by the family: Jerry Mundt was President; brother Larry, Vice-President; cousin Shelly Mundt, Vice-President/Sales; and cousin Scott Merzon, Vice-President/Finance. Scott's wife Edie, the sister of the Mundt brothers, was company Secretary. Overhead at Head Office was unusually high. Among the employees on staff was the family's golf pro. The Mundt Inc. Lear jet was used to shuttle family members between homes on Long Island and Florida.

Chemco assumed on taking over Mundt that the senior executives would continue to work for them, at least during the transition period, to help them understand the personal arrangements on which much of the company's business was based. Instead, all the family members immediately resigned, along with their golf pro, leaving no one with inside information in the company. All management functions had to be taken over by Canadian executives from the Toronto head office. Fortunately the Canadian firm's divisionalized structure allowed it to send top men down to New York to manage Mundt without seriously damaging the Canadian operations, at least in the short run.

For the first six months the Canadian managers, operating from Mundt's New York offices, managed crisis by crisis keeping the three parts of the company afloat. Now, by the end of the second six months Mundt is no longer in critical condition. Hammond Co. Ltd. under its own president Ed Dunlop continues to perform well. The European marketing business held steady, but the basic business of leather and textile chemicals continues to lose money. Shortly after the acquisition the New Jersey plant was ordered closed by the U.S. government because it exceeded pollution standards. Establishing a working relationship with the seven joint ventures proved difficult because the agreements hinged on personal deals made by Jerry Mundt. The problems in dealing with different national business cultures had strained the adaptability of the Toronto executives.

Now, a year later, the initial shock caused by the acquisition has been overcome. It is time for Chemco to adjust its structure to include the enlarged international operations. Until now Canadian managers have been used as expatriate managers, but the company hopes to develop local managers in the countries where new operations are located.

The Canadian executives are uncertain whether or not to have all operations directed from the Toronto headquarters or locally, and how best to manage the joint ventures. The Canadian executives know that in the U.S. firms with international operations are usually handled by an International Division administered by the U.S. parent at head office. Yet already the international operations comprise 40% of the firm's sales. Hammond Co. Ltd. and the Brussels sales operation are growing faster than the Canadian business. The executives wonder whether they can respond to different national conditions from their Toronto headquarters. The situation cannot remain the way it is much longer because the New York office is taking the full attention of several key Canadian executives whose talents are needed in Toronto. The subsidiary Polymir, under Paul Balardo, needs close attention. The change in capital markets in the mid-1980s means the company can consider building a new plant and perhaps reorganize its manufacturing facilities. Richardson hopes that the meeting of the Senior Vice-Presidents tomorrow will generate possible ways of restructuring Chemco to reflect the international operation it has become.

PROBLEM

Design a structure for Chemco which incorporates Mundt Inc.

QUESTIONS

1. Can the organization design problems be solved immediately, or will it be necessary to make the changes in stages over several years?
2. Is it possible to operate divisions which have operations in two or more countries?
3. Should any part of the business be sold?
4. On which parts of its operations should Chemco International concentrate its efforts?

EXERCISES

SETTING UP A FIRM: A CONSULTANCY PROBLEM

You are a group of people who have decided to set up a joint consultancy firm. You are to consider the main difficulties which the project will have to overcome to get started and, secondly, the services to be offered. You will appoint a chairman to structure the discussion.

INSTRUCTIONS

Step 1 Prepare an agenda. Develop an organization structure.
Step 2. Identify the skills the group has.
Step 3. Define your market.
Step 4. Determine the *per diem* rates.

"AIRSHIPS" THE TOTAL ORGANIZATION EXERCISE*

J.R. Goodwin

PURPOSE

This exercise focuses upon the usefulness, interest, and applicability of organization theory concepts. The purpose of this exercise is to heighten your awareness of these underlying concepts by giving you an experience in the formation of an organization designed to deal with a complex task. As outlined below, you and your fellow students

---

* Reprinted by permission of the author.

464   Part Four   Behavior of Individuals and Groups in Organizations

are to design an organization whose task is to develop successfully a niche in the transportation industry.

PROCEDURE

After having read the material, you and members of your group are to meet for approximately one and one half hours to design an organization to meet the situation outlined below. Your end product is to be a written report (or a verbal presentation) describing that organization. You are to assume that each of you will hold a position in that organization.

THE SITUATION

As a group of entrepreneurs, with your heads in the sky, you wish to go into the transportation business. The vehicle of your affection is the "airship." Attached is the latest information available on the vehicle. This vehicle has been virtually ignored since the "Hindenberg" incident. However, a small group of fanatics have once again produced a superior type airship with a much improved lifting capability. Your group have each invested $10,000 in order to get the organization off the ground. You have also obtained a grant of $250,000 from the Ministry of Transport to assist you in setting up your organization. You are to produce a transportation organization which will serve the interests of Canada. Among the things you should consider are recent environmental factors, organization goals, structure, size of the organization, technology, human resources, and measures of effectiveness.

At the end of approximately one and one half hours, Mr. Richards, President of Venture Risk Inc. will expect a report from each group in the class outlining its organization of the Airship Company. He is interested in finding new companies to invest in. His group consists of high risk takers. It has large sums of money to invest and looks for innovative challenges with a greater than normal expectation of return on investment.

One measure this group is particularly interested in is the organization you would set up so as to get the job done. It is imperative that your report be well presented. It should include an analysis of the environment, organization goals, organization structure, division of labor, measurement of effectiveness, and your control system.

Mr. Richards will decide which design is best and which group his organization will finance. He may decide on more than one group if the presentations warrant it.

AIRSHIPS – GENERAL INFORMATION

Airships – lighter-than-air aircraft having propulsion and steering systems.

- Technology has reduced the weight of airships by 80%. Engines weigh less and are more efficient. Frame is lighter but stronger.
- Airships have the ability to remain airborne with all power units stopped.
- They have very low landing speed.
- They are provided with an emergency deballast capability, such as fuel and water, if a loss of lift occurs.
- Environmental hazards include high winds and icing conditions.

- Shipping costs per ton mile; water $0.23; Rail $0.0432; Airship $0.0445; Truck $0.0514; Airplane $0.1356.
- Lifting gases – Helium – has less lifting capacity than hydrogen
  - 15 times more expensive than hydrogen
  - an inert gas.
  - Hydrogen – highly volatile, explosive gas
    - superior lifting power
    - inexpensive.
- Airships can be moored by mobile mooring masts, mooring vehicles or stationary mooring posts.
- Airship design accommodates containers or passenger gondolas.
- Airships do not need large investments in airstrips, etc.

THE AIRFISH

Designer and Builder – Flugschiffbau Hamburg Company

Design based on the dauphin and the tuna – aquatic animals
Distinctive feature is the high flexible tail section
Present model – capacity 500 passengers and 400 tons of cargo. Freighter model – 2000 tons of cargo
Cruising speed – 150 knots
Cost — $25 million
Power – six turbo-jet engines – can be replaced by hydrogen or nuclear engines
Length – 250 metres
Crew – two pilots, two flight engineers, two crewmen.
Uses mobile mooring mast and engines for stops of short duration.

THE AIRCOPTER

Designer and builder – Goodyear Airship Corp.

Resembles the Goodyear blimp with four helicopters attached, one at each corner
Designed as a skyhook with some potential to carry passengers and cargo
Capable of lifting 400 tons, or 200 tons and 30 passengers
Presently in production for the USAF
Cost – $9-$11 million
Speed – 85 knots
Length – 95 metres
Power – four turbo engines
Crew – 2 pilots, 3 flight engineers, 3 crewmen

THE SKYHOOK

Designer and builder – 1985 design by the National Research Council and Dehaviland Aircraft

Prototype has flown and has tremendous lifting capability — capable of lifting 350 tons straight up, hover, or move to new location

Distinctive features include round balloon, with concentric vanes, attached to three heliocopters
Speed – 30 knots
Size – 125 feet high, 35 feet in base circumference
Crew – two pilots, one engineer, four crewmen
Cost – estimated at $6.5 million
The concentric vanes have dramatically reduced the rapid ascent as the load is released.

INFORMATION EXCERPTS

Dallas Texas – Researchers at Texas A&M University announced the development of an efficient hydrogen generator capable of separating the water molecule and obtaining 15% of the hydrogen available. A generator capable of producing 4% hydrogen was considered to be commercially viable.

Frankfurt Germany – The Zeppelin Corporation announced today a new designed airship called The Airfish. The company claims this radical change in design has resulted in a more stable, faster ship with a greatly increased lifting capacity.

Regina Saskatchewan – The provincial government sent a sharply worded telegram to the Minister of Transport deploring the abandonment of rail trackage in the prairie provinces.

Toronto Ontario – Today Gulf Oil reported a very high rate of oil flowing through the test pipes at their Beaufort Sea exploratory well high in the Arctic. Geologists believe the Arctic reserves are sufficient to make Canada independent of oil imports.

St. John's Newfoundland – Mobil reports extensive oil find in the Hibernia area off the coast of Newfoundland.

Washington D.C. – The government today passed legislation deregulating the transportation industry.

Ottawa Ontario – The railway lobby succeeded in having the government abolish the Crowsnest grain rate.

Regina Saskatchewan – Farmers mourn the loss of the Crow. They claim the increased costs of grain shipments will be carried by the producers. As the grain is sold on the international market and thus subjected to the supply and demand law farmers say they are again being squeezed by the unconcerned government.

Ottawa Ontario – Today the government announced its intention to introduce a bill deregulating the transportation industry.

Ottawa Ontario – Government advises business to become more efficient. The government intends to move towards free trade. The result will be the removal of tariff walls on goods produced in Canada.

Ottawa Ontario – Both the Canadian government and the U.S. government agreed to open talks on a free trade pact.

Ottawa Ontario – The government replaced the Foreign Investment Review Board (FIRA) with Investment Canada. The P.M. indicated to the world that Canada was open for foreign investment.

Toronto Ontario – Concerned bodies questioned the removal of FIRA. They warned this could lead to a take-over of major businesses in Canada which would result in a loss of national identity.

Scientific Journal – A group of German engineers today demonstrated a new hydrogen powered engine. One of its main features is lack of environmental pollution. The exhaust is pure water.

enRoute Magazine – NRC Scientists demonstrated the versatility of their latest prototype of the skycrane airship. The major improvement has been the control of the ascent once the crane releases the load. This new controlling system moves the crane one step closer to acceptance in the business world.

Kabul Afghanistan – Russian troops moved into Afghanistan to back the present government. It has been announced the rebels have been pushed back into the mountains.

Washington D.C. – The President of the United States deplored the action of the USSR in Afghanistan. He asked the western nations to support his stand by placing trade sanctions upon the USSR.

Kansas City Kansas – The federal government today approved a massive grain sale to the USSR.

New York New York – The international teamsters union is on strike at all interstate trucking firms in the United States. They claim it is not over money but job security.

Richmond Virginia – Bands of hoodlums have been vandalizing the independent truckers' using the Interstate Highways. Authorities assume these actions are related to the truckers' strike.

Ottawa Ontario – The Canadian government announced an extension of the petroleum incentive program for exploration in the far north.

London England – The OPEC cartel was not able to agree on oil quotas. Sheik Yamani of Saudi Arabia announced that Saudi Arabia would increase production until some accord can be reached.

Vancouver British Columbia – CP Air lost $38 million for the last fiscal year.

New York New York – The spot price of oil over the last three months has dropped drastically.

Calgary Alberta – Oilmen ask government for tax breaks. With the falling prices of oil they predict massive lay-offs unless the government reintroduces the tax incentives.

Regina Saskatchewan – The Canadian Wheat Board today announced a sale to Mainland China of 25 million tonnes of grain. The grain will be loaded into ships at the west coast terminals.

Montréal Québec – The Québec Department of Tourism indicates a greatly increased number of tourists will visit this summer. This is partially due to the latest territorist action in western Europe.

Rome Italy – Terrorists shot up the passenger area of the Rome International Airport killing 28 and wounding numerous others.

Washington D.C. – The President ordered the Air Force and Navy carrier planes to strike Khadhafy's headquarters in Libya.

Baghdad Iraq – The Iranian army launched a massive attack on Iraqi troops located along the border. Both sides claim victory.

Victoria British Columbia – People were busy today attempting to clean the water fowl caught in the massive oil slick washing up on the beaches. The slick is visible coming from Port Angelese, Washington State Terminal.

Montréal Québec – The government announced the sale of Canadair to Bombardier Corp.

Toronto Ontario – Boeing Aircraft announced the sale of 25 Dash-8 aircraft.

Ottawa Ontario – A small business task force was set up to simplify the amount of paperwork and the tax reporting system for the small business area.

London Ontario – The University Hospital in this city has become the heart transplant capital of Canada. The need for organ donations is much greater than the supply. They urge all citizens to identify themselves as potential doners.

Montréal Québec – Nordair Metro, 35% owned by CP Air, was the successful bidder to purchase Québecair.

Toronto Ontario – The Reichmann brothers are successful in their takeover bid of Gulf Oil Canada Ltd., at a cost of $3.5 billion.

Walkerville Ontario – Walkers Resources Ltd. have introduced gasohol into the Toronto market.

Leisure Time Magazine – The demand for cruises by Canadians is on the increase.

Montréal Québec – The link between Dorval Airport and Mirabel Airport becomes an election issue. One incumbent requests the federal government build the much needed high speed rail line connecting the two terminals. Cost is estimated at $189-million.

Ottawa Ontario – The government has made clear its intentions to privatize as many of the Crown corporations as possible.

Québec City Québec – Bourassa and his government indicated the province will deregulate much of business – commencing with transportation.

Calgary Alberta – Dome Petroleum asks creditors for more time in renegotiating its massive debt.

Mexico City Mexico – The World Bank today loaned the Mexican government $10-billion to be used to pay the interest on its borrowings.

Ottawa Ontario – Inflation rose for the first time in 16 months to 4.3%.

New York New York – U.S. GNP increased in the last quarter by 0.6%.

Sudbury Ontario – Falconbridge closed their Manitoba mine indefinitely. The demand for nickel and copper are at an all time low.

Washington D.C. – The State Department announced grain sales to the USSR. This large order substantially cuts into the normal Canadian grain market.

Kingston Ontario – Dupont introduces a new, static free, exceptionally strong synthetic fibre.

Lakehurst New Jersey – The U.S. Navy retired the last airship after three successful years as an airborne radar station in the North Atlantic.

Montréal Québec – Air Canada lost $16 million in the last quarter.

Toronto Ontario – Sherritt Gordon Mines won the contract for nickel blanks. The blanks will be used for the new dollar coin.

Vancouver British Columbia – The longshoreman's strike is into its third week. 47 ships are waiting to be loaded.

Saskatoon Saskatchewan – CN reports a shortage of grain-handling rail cars.

Toronto Ontario – Gold has moved up sharply in the last month. Gold gurus are predicting a price of $455 per ounce in 1987.

Toronto Ontario – Gulf Oil suspends drilling in the Beaufort Sea area.

Windsor Ontario – The Canadian Labor Congress' Shirley Carr takes a strong stand against the government's proposed free trade pact.

Regina Saskatchewan – The western provinces report bumper crops. With the low level prices, farmers are predicting massive hardships.

Geneva Switzerland – The OPEC oil cartel agreed to reduce the amount of oil produced. Spot prices of oil have increased slightly.

Washington D.C. – The FAA has rescinded the certificate of airworthiness of all DC 10s due to unexplained metal cracks in the wing areas.

Scientific Research – Kevlar, a material much stronger than steel with one tenth of the weight, is now commercially available. It can be used in framing, covering, and as rope or cable replacement.